Résumé

Magic

Third Edition

Trade
Secrets of a
Professional
Résumé
Writer

Susan Britton Whitcomb

JiST Works
America's Career Publisher

Résumé Magic, Third Edition

© 2007 by JIST Publishing, Inc.

Published by JIST Works, an imprint of JIST Publishing, Inc.
8902 Otis Avenue
Indianapolis, IN 46216-1033
Phone: 1-800-648-JIST   Fax: 1-800-JIST-FAX   E-mail: info@jist.com

Visit our Web site at **www.jist.com** for information on JIST, free job search information, book chapters, and ordering information on our many products!

See the back of this book for additional JIST titles and ordering information. Quantity discounts are available for JIST books. Have future editions of JIST books automatically delivered to you on publication through our convenient standing order program. Please call our Sales Department at 1-800-648-5478 for a free catalog and more information.

Trade Product Manager: Lori Cates Hand
Interior Designer: designLab, Seattle
Cover Designer: Aleata Howard
Interior Layout: Marie Kristine Parial-Leonardo
Proofreader: Linda Seifert
Indexer: Kelly D. Henthorne

Printed in the United States of America
11 10 09 08 07 06   9 8 7 6 5 4 3 2 1

Library of Congress Cataloging-in-Publication Data
Whitcomb, Susan Britton, 1957-
  Résumé magic : trade secrets of a professional résumé writer / Susan
Britton Whitcomb. – 3rd ed.
      p. cm.
  Includes index.
  ISBN-13: 978-1-59357-311-9 (alk. paper)
  ISBN-10: 1-59357-311-1 (alk. paper)
  1. Résumés (Employment) I. Title.
  HF5383.W46 2007
  650.14'2–dc22
                                2006018662

ISBN-13: 978-1-59357-311-9

ISBN-10: 1-59357-311-1

Dedication

*To my parents, John and Marlene, whose work ethics are
unparalleled in today's business world…
you have taught me that discipline and integrity are priceless
possessions.*

*To my husband, who is the true reader in the family…
you have taught me to think and to ponder.*

*To Emmeline, who holds the future…
you have taught me the joy of small wonders.*

Acknowledgments

No book is ever the work of one writer, and such is the case with *Résumé Magic*. Between the lines are hundreds of people who have been the inspiration for this book. I am referring to my clients.

In some cases, their career accomplishments have been cause for celebration. Earning regional and national recognition in their professions, I commend them for the commitment and perseverance it takes to truly excel. In other cases, difficult circumstances have been cause to share tears. I'll always be humbled by the quiet courage of the mother who entered my office, eight months pregnant and with two little ones still at home. When I asked why she wanted to update her résumé, I learned that her husband had died in a car accident only two weeks before, leaving her as the sole support for her family. To "L." and others who have faced devastating circumstances, I stand in awe of and am inspired by your resolution to "lean into the wind" and move forward with life. And, there are my "average" clients…the ones who claim, "I haven't done anything special; I just show up and do my job." Right! Forty-plus hours a week, 50-plus weeks a year, decade after decade. The faithfulness and reliability of people like you enable the world to revolve as it does. Two of those people are Jean and Bob Gatewood, and, without them, I wouldn't be half the person I am today.

Behind the pages of this book is a talented publishing team at JIST. The lion's share of the credit goes to Lori Cates Hand, who took the initiative on the second and third editions. Her editorial talent is tremendous, tending to the meticulous details yet simultaneously helping the big picture come into focus. I must say that the work-world would be a nicer place if more people personified her buoyant, "can-do" attitude. And, to my first-edition team, thank you for making it all possible. Marta Justak, then-associate publisher, was instrumental in concept development, copyediting, interior layout, and title development (which has worked like "magic!").

Dr. David Noble, senior editor, was my first contact with the publishing world several years ago when he included a few of my résumé examples in his book *Gallery of Best Resumes* (JIST Publishing). Now in its fourth edition, the book continues to be one of the best collections of professional résumés available and competes only with his subsequent books on résumé writing. On this project, I am indebted to him for sharing his intellect, time, encouragement, and expertise as a writer, editor, and stylist. Thanks also to David's wife, Ginny, a professional editor, who helped with final proofing. Much credit for the first edition goes to JIST editor Susan Pines for helping with development editing and getting *Résumé Magic* into production. A big thank you to Veda Dickerson, Jeanne Clark, and Eric Schroeder for the second edition and Amy Stovall on the first edition for their behind-the-scenes work, and to the capable desktop-publishing and design team of Amy Adams of designLab, Trudy Coler, Aleata Howard, and Kristine Leonardo, who were kind enough to work-in last-minute additions.

Outside of JIST, I must acknowledge the encouragement, support, and collegiality of my résumé-writing colleagues who are scattered from California to New York. Special thanks to Pat Kendall in Oregon and Sally McIntosh in Illinois, both nationally certified résumé writers, who were available as sounding boards on a variety of issues and preproofreaders on a number of résumés for the first edition.

Finally, I am indebted to my husband, Charlie. Without his initial support and encouragement, I would not have started this book (nor its subsequent companion titles *Interview Magic* and *Job Search Magic;* and without his countless extra hours of "dad" duty (and kitchen duty), I would never have finished.

Obtain a Free Résumé Assessment

Thank you for selecting *Résumé Magic* from a shelf full of résumé books. Many résumé books are primarily compilations of sample résumés that you can review and attempt to emulate. But just as viewing masterpieces by Renoir or Picasso may inspire you, the paintings alone won't equip you with the skills to become a great artist. Likewise, combing through résumé samplers may give you good ideas, but the examples alone won't give you the skills to create an outstanding résumé. This book gives you both great samples and solid strategies. The whys, whats, and hows of résumé writing are explained in detail.

For a free résumé review by a Master Résumé Writer (after you've incorporated advice from this book), you may e-mail review@careerwriter.com. To take advantage of the free, Web-based résumé assessment, which provides immediate feedback online, visit www.careerwriter.com/assessment1.html.

The author also welcomes your comments about this book. You can e-mail to let the author know what you found helpful, what you would like more information on, what could be done to make this book stronger, and any other words of wisdom you would like to pass along. Please be sure to mention this book's title in your correspondence.

Susan Britton Whitcomb, CCMC, CCM, NCRW
Whitcomb Career Strategy
Fresno, California 93704
E-mail: susan@careercoachacademy
Web site: www.careercoachacademy.com

About This Book

Successful companies invest a great deal of time and talent in developing persuasive marketing brochures. It often takes a team of business strategists, graphic artists, and copywriters to come up with just the right piece that will capture the essence of the company, its products or services, and the features and benefits it offers…all with the aim of getting the consumer—you—to buy.

Successful job seekers also invest a great deal of time and talent in developing their marketing document, more commonly known as a résumé (pronounced *reh*-suh-may; the word is French for *summary*). A résumé also requires a careful blend of business strategy, artistry, and copywriting to capture the essence of who you are and to communicate the unique selling features that will differentiate you from your competition…all with the aim of getting the consumer—the employer—to "buy."

Despite its French translation, a résumé is much, much more than a summary of whom you worked for and what you did. In my dictionary, I have added these four definitions to describe a résumé:

- An advertisement that reflects your personal brand and appeals to employers' specific needs, such as the need to generate income, save money, or solve a problem.

- A formal business communication that indicates your command of vocabulary, grammar, and punctuation.

- A keyword index that represents your knowledge base, skill set, impressive "name brand" companies or universities, degrees, licensure, software experience, or affiliations.

- A unique art form that combines font-work, layout, and design principles to create definitive visual appeal.

In *Résumé Magic,* I take you step-by-step through the process of crafting this all-important, multidimensional marketing piece.

How This Book Is Organized

Chapter 1 begins with an affirmation that you are capable of carrying out a successful, self-directed job search. The role of the résumé is reviewed, including some common job seeker misconceptions about how hiring managers view résumés. You will also "meet" many individuals, ranging from new graduate to career transitioner to senior executive, whose careers are on track because of the secrets in this book.

The art and science of advertising are applied to résumé writing in chapter 2. Learn how successful copywriters use branding strategies, as well as the AIDA formula to get the **A**ttention of a buyer (the employer), generate **I**nterest in a product (your talents as an employee), and turn **D**esire for that product into **A**ction that will result in a sale (get an interview that will lead to an employment offer).

Chapter 3 introduces you to more than a dozen résumé formats, one of which will help you accentuate the positives and eliminate any negatives from your career. Example résumés for the formats are included, each representing a real candidate who used the résumé to further his or her career.

Chapters 4 and 5 walk you through the steps of outlining and drafting your résumé, including how to incorporate keywords into it. In chapter 6, you learn why accomplishments are the key to transforming an average résumé into an outstanding résumé. More than 200 impact-mining questions will help you identify situations where you might have made unique contributions to employers. These contributions are *key* to differentiating yourself from, and above, your competition.

Chapter 7 offers a quick course in "résumé-speak," a unique style of writing that blends advertising and business formats to give your résumé energy and interest. Learn in chapter 8 what most people overlook when preparing a résumé. This "missing link" will ensure that your boss-to-be has a fabulous first impression of you.

Chapter 9 reviews the latest trends in e-résumés, e-portfolios, and blogs. Learn how applicant-tracking software and employment Web sites factor into your success, as well as the do's and don'ts for various electronic formats.

Finally, chapter 10 addresses the important role that cover letters play in earning an audience with your boss-to-be. Impressive before-and-after examples of cover letters, thank-you letters, references, and résumé addenda will give you inspiration and ideas.

Special icons are scattered throughout the chapters. Magic wands illustrate how advertising principles, writing strategies, or design tools helped a job seeker overcome a special challenge. Tip and Caution boxes emphasize important advice on everything from insider résumé-writing techniques to current job search etiquette. Note boxes highlight other vital information.

Three appendices follow the final chapter. In appendix A you'll find easy-to-use résumé worksheets to help catalog your work history, employer contributions, education, and special skills.

Appendix B presents the statistical results of "What Employers Really Want in a Résumé," an informal survey of human resources professionals from across the country. You can review it to learn employer preferences on questions such as how long should a résumé be, how far back should you go in describing experience that spans several decades, what color paper is preferred, will you be screened out if an ad calls for a degree but you don't have one, what happens if you don't include salary when an ad requests that it be included, and more. Gleaning from the survey responses, I have compiled an enlightening list of 25 pet peeves and common résumé mistakes noted by some of America's top employers.

Of course, no résumé book is complete without a list of action verbs. In appendix C you will find this list categorized by disciplines. Because action verbs are virtually worthless without conveying contributions or value, you will also find an example sentence or accomplishment statement for each of the 600-plus verbs. Each sentence is a fresh idea to help you dress up your writing.

Woven throughout *Résumé Magic* are before-and-after mini-stories of real people who have persevered through the peaks and valleys of career transition. Names have been changed for privacy; virtually all of these people have been clients over the years, and many are now fond friends whom I admire and respect for their can-do attitude, personal accountability, and perseverance in embracing the changes associated with new jobs. Their successes confirm my belief that there is a positive plan for everyone's life. Likewise, I believe that there is an employer out there who needs the unique talents, experience, and value that *you* alone can offer.

As you sit down to write your résumé, draw inspiration from the before-and-after accounts of people who have encountered perhaps the same challenges you face, and be encouraged as you document all that you have accomplished. Most of my résumé clients have this to say after reviewing their newly created résumé: "Wow, I'd hire me." By following the steps in this book, you will feel the same. That sense of worth and self-confidence will be priceless as you walk through the steps of your job search. May it be an enjoyable and swift journey.

Contents

A Résumé Primer

"Every calling is great when greatly pursued."

—Oliver Wendell Holmes

Writing your resume is an opportunity to write your future. This is your preordained appointment to update, advance, and "re-image" who you are. It's a time to ponder your passions, values, and hard-wired skills. It's cause to contemplate your life-work and your distinctive destiny—what is meaningful to you and how you will bring significance and value to your corner of the world.

What circumstances led you here? You may be reeling from the news that *you* are the latest casualty of another corporate cost-cutting, downsizing, or offshoring initiative. Or, perhaps you're reasonably happy with your job but just learned of an unbelievable career opportunity, so you've decided that now is the time to dust off and polish up that outdated résumé. Maybe you've just finished a hard-earned college degree and are ready to bag your first "real" job (preferably one that will pay off your school debts). Perhaps you're one of the millions of Baby Boomers facing retirement, yet you're interested in part-time work for the intellectual challenge or excited to dust off a dream that's been put on the back burner for far too long. For some, philosophical differences with new management or personality conflicts with coworkers are the impetus for your search. Perhaps it's a difficult time of transition—divorce, death of a loved one, children leaving the nest, or changes in your financial status—that has caused your job search. Statistics tell me that a number of you have been out of work for some time and are frustrated with your job search. Perhaps you're researching ways to resurrect a lifeless résumé and jump-start an ailing job campaign. Many of you are simply overworked, undercompensated, or unappreciated, and it is time to move to greener pastures.

Regardless of the circumstances prompting you to write a résumé, be grateful for them. They are the door to a new and important chapter of your life—a chapter that will move you forward and increase your capacity for success.

This book is designed for people like you who are capable of carrying out a successful, self-directed job search. You fall into this "capable" category because you had the sense to get yourself to a bookstore, library, or online bookstore and glean the information and ideas you need. I admire how the literary critic Gilbert Highet captured the wonderment of books:

> *Books are not lumps of lifeless paper, but minds alive on the shelves.*

To open a book is to step into another's mind. To read is to think, to wonder, to be challenged, to find encouragement, and to tap into the energy to try something new. Books equip you with knowledge, and knowledge endows you with power. This book will uniquely equip you with tools that may empower you to land a job that is *better* than the one you have now or just had.

Tools for the Task

Have you ever tried to change a flat tire without a jack? Ever washed soiled clothes without a washing machine? How about cleaning up a yard full of leaves without a rake? These tasks *are* possible without the aid of the right tool, but they will require more time and energy—both precious commodities you'd rather not waste.

Tools are invaluable to life. I'm not just talking about car jacks and rakes. Rather, I refer to any instrument that helps you carry out a task—in this case, growing a career in which you can be radically rewarded and enthusiastically engaged…a career that brings value to others. Think about the cycle that tools set in motion:

⭑ Tools enable you to work.

⭑ Work produces results.

⭑ Results bring about satisfaction.

Satisfaction renders many illusive "possessions" that we crave as members of the human race: happiness, peace of mind, financial security, and a sense of significance. The Greek physiologist and physician Galen recognized this cycle even in the second century with his reflections on work:

Employment is nature's physician, and is essential to human happiness.

One of the first goals in your job search should be to equip yourself with the right tools. You will impede your progress without them; you cannot afford to handicap yourself with out-of-date or inferior tools. Unfortunately, the job search is not like golf, where you're compensated for your lack of skill! You do not want to sabotage your search, and yet many people do by not equipping themselves with the "tools of the trade." (If you need to brush up on job search basics—identifying the right career fit, researching companies, networking, interviewing, salary negotiations—turn to the companion books in this series, *Cover Letter Magic, Interview Magic,* and *Job Search Magic,* all published by JIST Publishing.)

The Résumé Tool: Asset or Liability?

This book focuses on your résumé as one of the tools in the self-directed search process. Is your résumé an asset or a liability? Will it get you noticed or cause you to be passed over? After several decades of helping professionals with the strategy, artistry, and application of their résumés, I've changed my views somewhat about the form and function of résumés. Take the following quiz and see whether you might need to readjust your thinking:

1. *True   False*   Employers and candidates view résumés as having the same purpose.

2. *True   False*   A résumé is most effective when it precedes your interview with the hiring manager.

3. *True   False*   A hiring decision maker will be the one to screen your résumé.

4. *True   False*   Résumés are read thoroughly.

5. *True   False*   You will need a résumé to land a job.

Many people answer True to all of these statements. Read on to find out why I've found them all to be false.

Employers and Candidates Usually View Résumés as Having Different Purposes

Employers use résumés as a screening device to deal with the deluge of responses to job postings. Just as a boat jettisons cargo to stay afloat in a storm, the résumé screener—drowning in dozens if not hundreds or thousands of résumés all vying for one single position—is purposefully looking for reasons to dump you. The slightest "error"—skills missing, disorganized content, a tiny typo—may be cause to disqualify and discard you (your résumé is now a liability). The rules of law and civility do not apply here. You are not presumed innocent or given the benefit of the doubt. The mentality is weed, winnow, and whack to get the pile down to manageable size. A mediocre or even average résumé can knock you out of the running for positions for which you might be wholly qualified.

In contrast, applicants use résumés to introduce themselves to employers, with the hope of getting an audience (interview) with a hiring decision maker. Too often, applicants use résumés incorrectly, making it their primary tool in the job search with the mistaken belief that employers will be thrilled or have the time to read every word about them. That's just not the case in this imperfect world!

A Résumé Is Most Effective When It Follows Face-to-Face or Voice Contact with a Hiring Manager

The employer's initial focus is to find grounds for discarding résumés. Again, your résumé can be more of a liability than an asset. After working with thousands of candidates over the years, I believe a better strategy is to establish rapport with the hiring manager (or others who influence hiring decisions) before submitting a résumé. For most people, an initial face-to-face or voice contact is more engaging than print-on-paper.

In some cases, a direct encounter will be difficult if not impossible because many corporate systems are set up to insulate managers from "interruptions" like you. But with a little sleuthing and perseverance on your part, it can be done (see the hint in the next paragraph). After you've established rapport and the hiring manager knows of your relevant experience in solving problems (you've said so in your rapport building), then you can introduce the résumé to reinforce your initial statements, reveal more about your skills and accomplishments, and remind the hiring manager of how wonderful you are.

Tip When contacting potential employers, don't limit yourself to the company's corporate address. Hiring managers and decision makers also have home addresses, attend professional meetings, participate in community organizations, frequent eating establishments, work out at gyms, have friends you might know, and so on. There are dozens of places where you might "run into" them.

A Support Person or Computer Program Will Probably Be the One to Screen Your Résumé

Unless you're applying to a relatively small organization, it's more likely that a support staff member or computer program, rather than a hiring manager, will be screening your résumé and comparing it to a "walk-on-water wish list" of superhuman endowments, education, and experience. What? Your résumé doesn't include walking on water under the Skills section? Liability. And, if your résumé is being electronically processed, there's an even greater chasm between you and the hiring manager. Depending on the applicant-tracking software the company uses, there's the possibility that your résumé will not be categorized properly or that your terminology will not match the keywords the organization uses to find a strong candidate match. Even executive recruiters hire researchers who spend hours every day combing Internet databases for keywords and key candidates. For these reasons, it's critical that your résumé be as screen-proof as possible. Better yet, use your initiative to get your résumé directly to the decision maker.

Résumés Are Not Read Thoroughly

Not on the first go-around. Feedback from screeners is that an inviting-to-read, "pretty" résumé is more likely to get into the interview pile. Then, if you're lucky enough to get the résumé into the interview pile, you'll eventually get a read-through. However, more than a few candidates report that interviewers admitted not reading their résumés word for word; rather, they liked the look of a résumé and quickly were able to locate key achievements and skills that were important for the position being filled.

You Won't Always Need a Résumé to Land a Job

You will, however, always need an interview. To my continued surprise, I still meet professionals who tell me they got their last job without a résumé. So, as proud as I am of my profession that helps people write their professional "success story," I must humble myself and admit that my services as a résumé writer are not indispensable.

I will report, however, that the number of people who sail into a position *sans* résumé is decreasing. Companies, especially smaller ventures, are finding that formal, well-documented personnel files (complete with résumé) help to comply with labor laws and protect against the litigious attitude so prevalent today.

Some people find themselves in situations where the employer-to-be has obliquely offered a job and requested a résumé as "a formality." Be cautious if this is the case. Remember that you are a slave to your written words and can't easily take them back. A quickly thrown-together résumé reflects the quality of work you will put forth in the future. It may happen that the boss-to-be also has a super-sharp résumé for a candidate competing for your supposed "sure-thing" job.

Then Why Write a Résumé?

With the many negatives associated with résumés, why spend the time, energy, and brain power to write a résumé? After all, you've just read that a résumé can be more of a liability than an asset. Nonetheless, résumés are a necessity in a job search, and they can have value. Here are seven simple reasons why you should write a résumé:

1. **Protocol:** First, although not most important, because convention demands that you have one. If you're in job search mode, virtually everyone will ask to see your résumé. It's integral to the process. Just as books record history, résumés remain a valid tool for cataloging and conveying your professional experiences.

2. **Positioning:** Perhaps most important, an employer-focused résumé that conveys your unique, personal brand can answer the question, "Why should we hire you?" Like a beautifully crafted advertisement, it should magnetically attract the reader, create a picture of high potential, and differentiate you from your competition, including those who may appear *more* qualified than you. After reading your résumé, employers should have the impression that you are an "A-list" player who knows how to deliver results and make an economic impact on the company.

3. **Process:** The adage that the goal is the journey, not the destination, applies. Preparing your résumé is a gestalt-like process that will sharpen your ability to articulate your value while networking, interviewing, and negotiating offers. Furthermore, once you've landed the job,

you'll need to start a career-management file, the contents of which will provide the fodder for updating your résumé. The act of keeping this file up-to-date will keep you focused on making meaningful contributions. You grow professionally, and your employer profits…everybody wins.

4. **Proof:** You'll get an adrenaline boost when you see in print all you've accomplished. Confidence and a strong sense of worth are huge factors in your job search success. If you don't think you've done much, scour the section in chapter 6 on how to unearth impressive accomplishments that prove your worth. I've never met a person who doesn't have some career "gift" that made someone else's life richer.

5. **Plan:** A good résumé can serve as a blueprint for the interview and help keep a "meandering" interviewer focused on your strengths.

6. **Permanent reminder:** Because it is often the only physical, tangible representation of who you are, both before and, just as important, *after* the interview, your résumé needs to look as good as your best interview suit. Keep in mind that your résumé might be used to help justify the hiring decision to others who haven't met you. It should convey not only your professional qualifications, but your personality as well.

7. **Profit:** A dynamite business résumé documents your bottom-line profit orientation. Your ability to make a company healthier or more profitable in turn gives you greater job security and ammunition for commanding a higher salary.

And Why This Book?

Again, I offer seven simple reasons:

1. **Long-standing solutions:** The strategies here work. For more than two decades, they have helped people like you get energized and speed the transition to emotionally satisfying, financially rewarding careers that bring significant value to employers.

2. **Inside scoop:** Exclusive to this book are survey results on résumé protocol from some of the country's top companies to work for. You'll benefit from learning what human resource managers' preferences are in résumés and how to avoid their pet peeves.

3. **Strategy:** You'll learn how proven Madison Avenue advertising formulas can help you out-position your competition in a subtle yet persuasive manner.

4. **System:** There are three major phases to résumé writing. Most people focus only on the first two (targeting a specific employer need or functional area that you are passionate about and developing content that documents your ability to meet that need, including numbers-driven facts that describe your strategic impact on employers). Mastering the third phase (designing your résumé, which is covered in chapter 8), as well as the first and second phases, will give you a definite advantage.

5. **Significance:** Principles of healthy relationships apply to résumé writing. You'll learn how to incorporate them into your writing. For instance, you must identify and address the other person's (employer's) significant concerns and needs based on your potential value, as opposed to focusing only on your wants or demands.

6. **Search savvy:** You'll get a crash course on current technology as it relates to your career-advancement campaign, along with tips on how to format your résumé for readability by scanners and "searchability" for successful database or Internet searches (see chapter 9).

7. **Samples:** Dozens and dozens of sample résumés for jobs with some of the greatest growth potential for the 21st century…and not just the finished version of the résumé but the *Before* version, along with tips on how to take your résumé from average to outstanding.

Some Success Stories

Need more proof? How about the success stories of happily employed people who have used these résumé strategies? Their résumés—camouflaged for confidentiality purposes—are included in this chapter and throughout the book. Here are just a few success stories:

Medical Technologist: Janna, transitioning to college teaching, applied for a community-college teacher internship program and actually received an offer by telephone (without a face-to-face interview!) because of the quality of her résumé. (See Résumés 1.1 and 1.2 at the end of this chapter.)

Management Consultant: Robert applied to the international accounting and consulting firm Ernst & Young. He called with great news: "Shortly after sending in my résumé, I received a call asking me to fly down, meet a few people, and formalize the details. Based on my résumé, they had essentially made the decision to hire me before I even interviewed." (See Résumé 1.3 of Robert Cimino, which was written from scratch.)

Sales Representative: Ron mailed more than 30 résumés to jobs he was qualified for and had "zero response." After his résumé was rewritten to counter potential concerns (his lack of accomplishments reflected the depressed commercial real estate market), he won interviews on 7 of the next 10 résumés he mailed. (See Résumés 1.4 and 1.5 of Ron Calandra.)

Marketing Representative: William tried for months to relocate from Fresno to the Bay Area (three hours away) in order to live under the same roof as his new wife. He reported sending out "nearly 100 résumés" with no response. After redoing his résumé and using the positioning strategies and relocation tips in this book, he had interviews and multiple offers within two weeks. (See Résumés 1.6 and 1.7 of William Burton. The *After* version repositions him from "too many jobs selling cars" to "high-tech sales professional.")

Secretary: Lane is changing industries (from state service with the Department of Motor Vehicles to the private sector) and targeting television stations in a small local market. She reports that, although no positions are presently vacant, "Everyone *loved* the résumé." One station manager said he was keeping it "at the top of the pile" for the next available opening! (See Résumés 1.8 and 1.9 of Lane Easterby. The *Before* version is modified text from her state application form.)

Career Transitioner: Torrey, shifting to the competitive field of pharmaceutical sales, secured dozens of interviews with pharmaceutical companies despite minimal direct sales experience and no formal science background. She was told by one interviewer from a Fortune 500 company that her résumé was the most impressive one they had ever seen. She accepted an offer from another industry leader at twice her former salary. (See Résumés 1.10 and 1.11 of Torrey Wellman. Although the *Before* example was well done, it typecasts her in the child-care industry.)

New College Graduate: Nick had sent out dozens of résumés with "not even a rejection letter." Adding insult to injury, he also hit roadblocks with his attempts to earn a promotion within the company he worked for while attending college. A new résumé was written from scratch (he diagnosed the original résumé as "useless" and wouldn't even let me see it). With the new one, his current employer took a second look and finally considered him for other opportunities.

Nick relates that one short line in the résumé about his mechanical skills and interest in cars really caught the interviewer's attention and helped him land a promotion as an auto-damage appraiser earning three times his prior income. (The company computer rejected several of his new paychecks because it was "unheard of" for someone to move up that quickly or have that large of an increase in pay!) In the meantime, he had the luxury of turning down two other offers. (See Résumé 1.12 of Nick Burns.)

Regional Manager: Maria wrote that she was offered a position based on her reputation in the industry—the résumé was a formality that followed. However, "they were even more impressed with me after they read it." Two other companies to which she submitted the résumé told her directly what a fine résumé it was. (See Résumé 1.13 of Maria Almacci, which was written from scratch. A functional format eliminates a redundant list of responsibilities at each company and camouflages less-impressive accomplishments in the most recent position.)

Employee Advancing Within Company: This California-based employee competed for a corporate slot in North Carolina where his competition had more "relevant experience" and "knew the system." Spencer relates that the résumé format and content were "a notch above everyone else" and helped cinch his promotion to a coveted product-management job in the pharmaceutical industry. (See Résumé 1.14 of Spencer Covington.)

Executive Recruiter's Candidate: Chris Olson, Executive Recruiter, notes, "I tell all my candidates that a well-written, professional résumé is the best investment they can make in their search. It makes a world of difference, and it makes my job of marketing them so much easier." (See Résumés 1.15 and 1.16 of Lawrence Yee, who won a plant-controller position in a competitive, national search.) Chris adds, "It's amazing to see you work your magic!"

Recent Graduate: Shane used his cover letter and résumé (See Cover Letter and Résumé 1.17) to land an $80K position straight out of college. He noted that the cover letter was particularly well received by interviewers. The innovative use of a quote and the bulleted highlights helped to differentiate him from hundreds of other recent graduates.

Electrical Engineering Manager: With downsizing and offshoring, management-level engineers have encountered one of the most challenging job markets ever. This senior candidate noted that the new cover letter and résumé, which adeptly camouflaged his experiences from several decades ago, generated recruiter interest where there had previously been none. (See Résumé 1.18.)

Customer Service Manager: Able worked for a large-scale health-care organization. Although he enjoyed his work, the compensation was neither competitive nor sufficient for his needs. The new résumé gave him the confidence to pursue opportunities outside the health-care field. After he accepted a new position, it enabled him to boost his income from $50,000 to $80,000. (See Résumé 1.19.)

 Note To ensure each candidate's right to privacy, names and other information on sample résumés in this book have been fictionalized. In some instances, information has been omitted or condensed because of space restrictions.

Résumé 1.1. Medical Technologist: Before

JANNA ATHERTON, M.H.A.

2424 South State Street
Chicago, Illinois 60616 jatherton@email.com Residence: (312) 222-4444
Business: (312) 333-5555

* *

OFFERING

Medical Technologist with ten plus years progressive experience in major Regional Blood Bank. Possess excellent team work skills. Calm, confident, proactive attitude. Capable of prioritizing work flow and adjusting to changing work demands. Enjoy new challenges.

SKILLS

Computer: Proficient with Western Star computer system for Blood Banks and hospital HBOC-Clinstar System. Verified Western Star computer upgrades to current version. Authorized computer clearance to review and revise patient and unit results. Instructed personnel in use of these computer systems.

Technical Consultant: Provided technical support to technologists, doctors, and other hospital personnel concerning questions and problem resolutions. Served as Blood Bank liaison with Biotechnical Electronics and sales representatives. Reviewed all antibody panels, problems relating to testing, and reported results.

Technical: Responsible for all aspects of blood banking including: proper specimen processing and component preparation, serological testing, alloantibody and autoantibody identification, neonatal transfusion, transfusion reaction investigation, and alloantibody titration. Processed blood components using IBM cell washer.

Supervisor: Acted as weekend laboratory supervisor. Conducted technologist orientation in departmental and preventative maintenance procedures. Distributed and evaluated technologist proficiency testing. Improved and implemented Blood Bank policies and procedures. Responsible for evaluation and implementation of instruments. Wrote preventative maintenance procedure manuals for instruments. Maintained and reviewed quality assurance and preventative maintenance records. Performed periodic instrument maintenance. Managed inventory control procedures.

Accomplishments: Conducted feasibility study of having autologous donor service, including cost analysis. Member of Continuing Education Committee.

LICENSURE

Illinois State Licensed Medical Technologist #12345
Blood Bank (ASCP) #234
Medical Technologist (ASCP) #567890
Certificate in Alzheimer's Disease—University of Illinois, Chicago
Certificate in Gerontology—University of Illinois, Chicago

Resume of **Janna Atherton** - Con't

EDUCATION

Working on Master of Health Administration Degree (last semester)
University of Chicago

Bachelor of Arts, Microbiology (with High Honors)
University of Illinois, Chicago

Associate of Science Degree
Decatur Community College

HONORS

Member of the National Honor Society of Phi Kappa Phi, Chicago Chapter

Graduate High Honors University of Illinois, Chicago

Member of the Honor Society & Dean's List at Decatur Community College

EXPERIENCE

Medical Technologist II	Saint Paul Medical Center Chicago, Illinois [mo/yr to Present]
Medical Technologist	Illinois Blood Center Springfield, Illinois [mo/yr to mo/yr]
Laboratory Technician, Hematologist & Urinalysis	Mercy Hospital Iowa City, Iowa [mo/yr to mo/yr]
Research Technologist	Lincoln Laboratories Decatur, Illinois [mo/yr to mo/yr]
Laboratory Supervisor	Southern Illinois University Carbondale, Illinois [mo/yr to mo/yr]

Résumé 1.2. Medical Technologist: After

JANNA ATHERTON, M.H.A.

2424 South State Street   Residence: (312) 222–4444
Chicago, Illinois 60616   jatherton@email.com   Business: (312) 333–5555

VALUE OFFERED AS ADJUNCT FACULTY MEMBER

Engaging, interactive classroom instruction ... real–world learning experiences ... contagious passion and advocacy for lifelong learning ... stickler for regulatory compliance ... successful track record in healthcare and administration. Competencies:

- ◆ Medical Technology
- ◆ Health Sciences
- ◆ Assessment
- ◆ Program Development
- ◆ Healthcare Administration
- ◆ Business Administration
- ◆ Multimedia Presentations
- ◆ Coaching–Based Management

Value Translation: Your healthcare/medical students will be intellectually challenged, emotionally inspired, and thoroughly equipped to step into clinical positions ... your institution will solidify its reputation as an organization that produces graduates with practical skills and not just textbook knowledge ... student retention and new enrollment will be positively impacted.

EDUCATION

Master of Health Administration—University of Chicago
Bachelor of Arts, Microbiology (with High Honors)—University of Illinois, Chicago

QUALIFICATIONS

Teaching and Program Development
◆◆◆◆◆◆◆◆◆◆◆◆◆◆◆◆◆◆◆◆◆◆◆◆◆◆◆◆

Assume lead role in program development and technical training for St. Paul Medical Center Transfusion Service. Assess program training needs and develop QA programs for compliance with federal and state regulatory agencies. Present orientation, initial training, and ongoing inservices to laboratory technologists in laboratory protocol, computer applications, and preventative maintenance. As member of continuing education committee, organize accredited seminars and approve curriculum. Career contributions:

- ❖ Wrote department's new quality program for regulatory compliance; presently in implementation stage, program has reduced errors in blood draws from 24 to 4 in first quarter.
- ❖ Created proficiency checklists that resulted in fewer deficiencies on recent inspection.
- ❖ Brought outdated procedural and computer manuals current in limited time constraints for JCAHO inspection.
- ❖ Established linkages with business community, securing vendors to conduct free CE seminars.
- ❖ Developed continuing education seminars for administrators of related entity.
- ❖ Supervised laboratory instruction at the university level.

Administration and Supervision
◆◆◆◆◆◆◆◆◆◆◆◆◆◆◆◆◆◆◆◆◆◆◆◆◆

Administrative experience includes policy and program development, staffing, quality assurance, compliance, interdisciplinary and interdepartmental communications, and daily operations control. Manage department as weekend laboratory supervisor. Supervise staff of 25 (phlebotomists, medical technologists, clerical). Compile utilization data, analyze statistics, and recommend corrective action to improve quality and control costs. Manage inventory control procedures. Career contributions:

- ❖ Designed internal operating systems and staffing model that maintained departmental productivity despite a concurrent 30% workforce reduction.

(continued)

JANNA ATHERTON, M.H.A.

Residence: (312) 222–4444   Page Two   Business: (312) 333–5555

QUALIFICATIONS (continued)

Administration and Supervision

- ❖ Applied theories and concepts gained in Master of Health Administration program to benefit medical center's recent culture shift from "family" philosophy to business focus.
- ❖ Conducted feasibility study on autologous donor service with comprehensive cost analysis.
- ❖ Hold security clearance for management information system.

Technical Consultant

Consultant to technologists, physicians, and allied health professionals for area's highest-volume transfusion service that handles over 50,000 transfusions annually. Excellent generalist skills in hospital and blood bank settings. Liaison with biomedical electronics and technical sales representatives.

- ❖ Resolve complex testing and reporting issues as primary technical representative.
- ❖ Experienced in all areas of laboratory (blood banking, coagulation, serology, microbiology, RIA special chemistry, chemistry, hematology, urinalysis, immunology).

EMPLOYMENT SUMMARY

ST. PAUL MEDICAL CENTER, Chicago, Illinois   [mo/yr–Present]
Medical Technologist II

ILLINOIS BLOOD CENTER, Springfield, Illinois   [mo/yr–mo/yr]
Medical Technologist

MERCY HOSPITAL, Iowa City, Iowa   [mo/yr–mo/yr]
Laboratory Technician, Hematology & Urinalysis

LINCOLN LABORATORIES, Decatur, Illinois   [mo/yr–mo/yr]
Research Technologist

SOUTHERN ILLINOIS UNIVERSITY, Carbondale, Illinois   [mo/yr–mo/yr]
Laboratory Supervisor

LICENSURE

Illinois State Licensed Medical Technologist #12345
Blood Bank (ASCP) #234
Medical Technologist (ASCP) #567890

CERTIFICATION

Certificate in Alzheimer's Disease—University of Illinois, Chicago
Certificate in Gerontology—University of Illinois, Chicago

Résumé 1.3. Management Consultant

ROBERT P. CIMINO, C.P.M.

20 Mallard Pond Court
Milwaukee, Wisconsin 54321
414.359.4321 ~ Mobile: 414.359.1234

Email: rpc@ciminocpm.com
Website: www.ciminocpm.com
Blog: www.ciminocpm.com/blog

■ SENIOR PURCHASING EXECUTIVE

Financial Strategist ... Innovator ... Orchestrator of complex projects who consistently delivered multimillion-dollar savings throughout 20-year career in purchasing/materials management, logistics/traffic, human resource development, and organizational development. Career highlights:

- Director of Materials Management with $50+ million in current annual purchasing responsibility for multisite healthcare network. *Reduced expenditures $3+ million* through implementation of JIT and "stockless" programs.

- Served as key member of corporate purchasing team. Negotiated long-term contracts in excess of $200 million with *10% reductions* that affected all 36 divisions of a Fortune 500 corporation.

- Helped coordinate merger of two manufacturing companies undergoing aggressive growth, centralized procurement and distribution functions to capture *7-figure savings*.

- Implemented in-house trading company for direct sourcing of raw and finished materials from seven countries, resulting in *40-60% savings*.

Credential Highlights: Master of Human Resource and Organization Development; Certified in Purchasing Management (C.P.M.).

■ PROFESSIONAL EXPERIENCE

MAJOR MEDICAL CENTER, Milwaukee, Wisconsin   [mo/yr–Present]

<u>DIRECTOR, MATERIALS MANAGEMENT</u>: Direct Materials Management Group responsible for supply functions for 326-bed acute care hospital, imaging center, rehab hospital, eye institute, and cancer center. Ensure integrated policy implementation for purchasing, receiving, inventory control, and property control. Oversee $54 million in annual purchases of supplies and equipment. Determine budgetary, cost analysis, and cost-containment considerations throughout contract bidding and negotiations.

- □ Provided leadership to newly organized division, encompassing Supply Processing and Distribution (SPD), Linen, Purchasing, Warehouse, Central Reproduction, and Central Mail departments with a total staff of 77.

- □ Introduced and developed innovative JIT/stockless program—program captured hard dollar savings of $2.2 million and reduced excess inventory by $1.1 million.

MADISON MANUFACTURERS, Madison, Wisconsin   [mo/yr–mo/yr]

<u>CORPORATE MANAGER, PURCHASING</u>: Managed purchasing functions and corporate project management responsibilities. As division management team member, involved in short-range and long-range planning for production, purchasing, inventory control, and receiving. Negotiated, administered, and monitored contractual agreements. Managed staff of 16.

- □ Successfully orchestrated the centralization of four purchasing locations, standardized procurement activities, and assembled a new materials team.

- □ Promoted from Purchasing Manager—implemented programs resulting in $1 million cost savings with total purchasing accountability of $50 million annually.

■ continued ■

ROBERT P. CIMINO, C.P.M.

Page Two
Home: 414.359.4321
Mobile: 414.359.1234

Email: rpc@ciminocpm.com
Website: www.ciminocpm.com
Blog: www.ciminocpm.com/blog

■ PROFESSIONAL EXPERIENCE (continued)

WACHUSETTE, INC., Milwaukee, Wisconsin   [mo/yr–mo/yr]

PURCHASING DIRECTOR: Recruited for executive team charged with reengineering of purchasing function. Developed and implemented successful program that enabled company to meet demand immediately and double sales volume within next three years. Restructured department staff and realigned policies with new methodologies. Managed eight-member purchasing department (four buyers, two clerical, two receiving staff). Oversaw warehouse activities.

☐ Reduced finished inventory 30% and work-in-process 45% through JIT programs.

☐ Captured 27% savings in raw materials costs.

GRAND INDUSTRIES, Madison, Wisconsin   [mo/yr–mo/yr]

MANAGER, CORPORATE PURCHASING & TRAFFIC: Managed, planned, and coordinated procurement functions for two manufacturing divisions of a $30 million corporation. Gained international experience in negotiating purchases from seven European and Asian countries.

☐ Reduced shipping costs 25% through development of an inbound/outbound traffic consolidation program.

MINOR MANUFACTURING, INC., Madison, Wisconsin   [mo/yr–mo/yr]

PURCHASING MANAGER [mo/yr–mo/yr]: Planned, directed, and managed material procurement functions for $36 million division of a Fortune 500 corporation. Served on corporate materials team, making purchasing decisions for six U.S. divisions. Managed purchasing staff of seven.

☐ Promoted from Senior Buyer—reduced purchasing costs across-the-board without sacrifice to service or quality.

■ EDUCATION

Master of Human Resource and Organization Development   [year]
University of Wisconsin, Madison

Bachelor of Science, Business Management—Minor in Personnel Management   [year]
University of Wisconsin, Madison

Certified in Purchasing Management (C.P.M. Reg. 12345, current)
National Association of Purchasing Management (NAPM)

■ AFFILIATIONS

National Association of Purchasing Management—Chapter President, Employment Coordinator
American Society for Testing and Materials

■ ■ ■

Résumé 1.4. Sales Representative: Before

RON CALANDRA
1212 N. West
Stockton, CA 95404
(559) 460-4432

EMPLOYMENT BACKGROUND:

[year - year]   THE PROPERTY PROFESSIONALS (formerly FTR, Inc.)
Stockton, California

Office Leasing Specialist. Returned to my prior employment leasing commercial office properties. Focused on the medical market; working primarily with physicians in analyzing various office sites, evaluating/negotiating leasing terms and conditions and working with the construction/contractors in remodeling the office suites to meet the tenant's needs.

[year - year]   MANAGEMENT INVESTMENT PROFESSIONALS
Stockton, California

Real Estate Analyst. Managed the north valley income property portfolio. Consisted of a variety of properties, e.g., retail shopping centers (2), office buildings (3) and self-serve mini storage facilities (2). Overall responsibility for budgets, occupancy levels, on going maintenance and related activities to maintaining the properties. Supervised on-site managers for the two mini-storage facilities and one office building. Directly managed two shopping centers and one office building.

[year - year]   FULLERTON, THIESEN & ROBERTS, INC. (FTR, Inc.)
Commercial Real Estate Brokerage, Stockton, California

Office Leasing Specialist. Worked primarily within the commercial office leasing department with a growing direction into the sales sector. Responsible for the on-going leasing of several professional office complexes ranging in size from 18,000 square feet to 48,600 square feet with a combined market value of approximately $6.5 million. The ownership/leasing agent relationship allowed for a hands-on leasing arrangement whereby I was given substantial latitude in lease negotiations, rental rates, and interior improvements.

[year - year]   ADVERTISING EXECUTIVES
Stockton, California

Sales Agent. Sold broadcast air time for AM and FM radio stations.

EDUCATION:

[year]   Received Bachelor of Arts Degree in History at University of Nevada, Las Vegas

PERSONAL BACKGROUND: Married with three children. Excellent health.

Résumé 1.5. Sales Representative: After

RON CALANDRA
559.460.4432 — 1212 N. West — Stockton, CA 95409 — roncalandra@email.com

---

EXPERIENCE SUMMARY

More than 10 years' commission sales experience in intensely competitive industries and markets. Strengths:

- ☑ Consultative selling
- ☑ Relationship management
- ☑ Qualified lead generation
- ☑ Needs-specific account service
- ☑ Multimedia presentations
- ☑ Negotiation of high-margin sales
- ☑ Transaction financing
- ☑ Development of customer loyalty

> *"Ron is a standout on our sales team ...*
> *He is persistent, proactive, patient, and profit-minded ...*
> *his clients count on him and his colleagues trust him."*
> ~John Mapes, Sales Manager, The Property Professionals

PROFESSIONAL EXPERIENCE

SALES ASSOCIATE — The Property Professionals (formerly FTR, Inc.)   [year]–Present
Fullerton, Thiesen & Roberts, Inc. (FTR), Stockton, CA   and [year–year]

- Managed sales and leasing of commercial office properties . . . specialized in medical office leasing and dominated this niche market in city's northeast sector.

- From "no" client list, built a diverse customer base with cross-market representation from medical, distribution, manufacturing, service, general business, and retail sectors.

- Secured exclusive contracts as owners' representative to lease professional office complexes ranging in size from 18,000 to 48,600 sq.ft., with combined market value of approximately $6.5 million (despite soft economy).

- Consulted with clients to assess needs for commercial office space, interpret lease terms and conditions, and coordinate tenant improvement construction.

LEASING MANAGER — Management Investment Professionals, Stockton, CA   [year–year]

- Managed central California income property portfolio consisting of retail shopping centers, office buildings, and mini-storage facilities; negotiated leases for national, regional, and local tenants; managed budgets, occupancy levels, and facility maintenance; supervised on-site managers.

- Assisted in sale negotiations for multimillion-dollar properties; prepared income and expense pro formas; analyzed financial data; conducted market analyses.

- Focused on increasing occupancy and decreasing operating expenses to improve profitability and marketability for future sale.

SALES AGENT — Advertising Executives, Stockton, CA   [year–year]

- Experienced in difficult sale of intangibles (broadcast advertising); developed new business through cold calling, referrals, telemarketing, and direct sales.

EDUCATION

B.A. DEGREE, History—University of Nevada, Las Vegas   [year]

Résumé 1.6. Marketing Representative: Before

WILLIAM C. BURTON

1255 West Chanute - Madera - CA 93637 - (559) 222-2222 - williamcburton@msn.com

OBJECTIVE: Position utilizing my skills in sales and management of high end products and graduate degree with emphasis in telecommunications in a major telecommunications company in the Bay Area.

EDUCATION: UNIVERSITY OF SAN FRANCISCO, San Francisco, CA
M.B.A., Telecommunications, [year] Courses in Telecommunications Applications & Management, Systems Planning and International Telecommunications.
ST. MARY'S COLLEGE, Moraga, CA
B.S. Business Administration, [year]

EMPLOYMENT HISTORY:

[yr-Present] **Territory Manager** MOTOROLA, DEALER SERVICES, San Jose, CA
Sold hardware, software and factory communication solutions to auto dealerships throughout Central San Joaquin Valley. Achieved 126% of gross sales in first year and President's Club in second year. Recognized at the Motorola National Sales Conference as having "increased territory by 100%."

[yr] **General Sales Manager** BAY RIVER HONDA, Fremont, CA
Responsible for profits of both new and used car divisions. Trained and supervised sales staff of 12. Succeeded in closing deals on sales and leases which were previously considered lost sales, increasing sales beyond established goals.

[yr-yr] **General Sales Manager** BEALLY HONDA, Burlingame, CA
Coordinated the finance and insurance department of Beally Honda. Achieved over $100,000 in finance income with less than 100 cars delivered. Promoted to G.S.M. one month after hire. Recruited, trained and motivated sales staff of 12 emphasizing professional sales approaches. Doubled per car gross income within sixty days. Maintained consistently high closing ratio and achieved store record sales volume during first year. At same time, supervised extensive customer follow-up advancing from 17th to the top 3 in customer satisfaction of all northern California Honda Dealers.

[yr-yr] **Finance & Insurance Coordinator/Sales Manager** Markman Audi/Isuzu, Santa Cruz, CA
Recruited, trained and supervised six business managers at flagship store. Introduced a new computer system organization-wide (six dealerships) and a step sell and package sell concept approaches to Finance and Insurance Department. Raised F & I productivity to 28%. Promoted to sales manager three months ahead of schedule. Consistently produced the top salesperson from my sales crew. Improved faltering sales at new Audi franchise. Increased sales from 7 to 47 units in the first month making it the top Audi dealership in the Western United States in second quarter.

[yr-yr] **Branch Manager** FINANCE AMERICA CORPORATION, a Bank of America company, Newark, CA
Joined growing division of leading financial services corporation to enhance management skills. Responsible for the Western Region Office of the Year with a quarter of a million dollar budget and a staff of five. Conducted sales presentations to clients, bankers and brokers and enlarged dealership portfolio ten-fold. Introduced new financial service products to spur future investments.

EDUCATIONAL RECOGNITION:
International Communications Association (ICA) Telecommunications Scholarship Recipient
Dean's List; Carl Howardson Award for Outstanding Athletic and Scholastic Ability.

ADDITIONAL TRAINING:
Motorola Strategic Sales Training, Hoffman Estates, IL
Audi/Isuzu Sales Training, Los Angeles, CA
Mechanical Insurance Association, Sales Training, Los Angeles
Bank of America, Effective Leadership Program, San Francisco, CA
Dale Carnegie Sales Course, Anaheim, CA

Additional work experience at various auto dealerships in sales, sales management and business operations.

Résumé 1.7. Marketing Representative: After

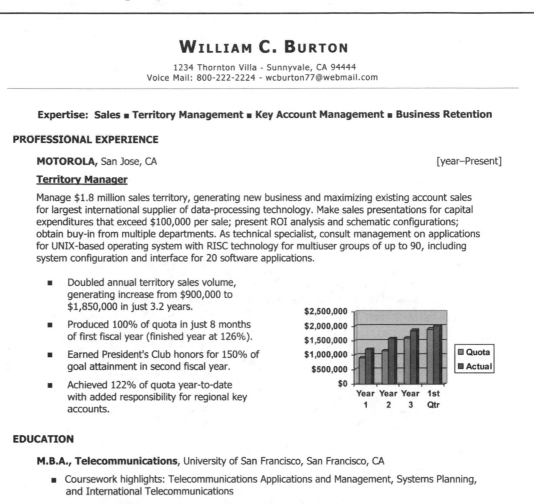

WILLIAM C. BURTON

1234 Thornton Villa - Sunnyvale, CA 94444
Voice Mail: 800-222-2224 - wcburton77@webmail.com

Expertise: Sales ▪ Territory Management ▪ Key Account Management ▪ Business Retention

PROFESSIONAL EXPERIENCE

MOTOROLA, San Jose, CA   [year–Present]

<u>**Territory Manager**</u>

Manage $1.8 million sales territory, generating new business and maximizing existing account sales for largest international supplier of data-processing technology. Make sales presentations for capital expenditures that exceed $100,000 per sale; present ROI analysis and schematic configurations; obtain buy-in from multiple departments. As technical specialist, consult management on applications for UNIX-based operating system with RISC technology for multiuser groups of up to 90, including system configuration and interface for 20 software applications.

- Doubled annual territory sales volume, generating increase from $900,000 to $1,850,000 in just 3.2 years.

- Produced 100% of quota in just 8 months of first fiscal year (finished year at 126%).

- Earned President's Club honors for 150% of goal attainment in second fiscal year.

- Achieved 122% of quota year-to-date with added responsibility for regional key accounts.

EDUCATION

M.B.A., Telecommunications, University of San Francisco, San Francisco, CA

- Coursework highlights: Telecommunications Applications and Management, Systems Planning, and International Telecommunications

- International Communications Association (ICA): Telecommunications Scholarship Recipient

B.S., Business Administration, St. Mary's College, Moraga, CA

SPECIALIZED TRAINING

Motorola Strategic Sales Training, Hoffman Estates, IL
Ford Motor Company, Sales Training, Los Angeles, CA
Mechanical Insurance Association, Sales Training, Los Angeles, CA
Bank of America, Effective Leadership Program, San Francisco, CA
Dale Carnegie Sales Course, Anaheim, CA

PRIOR EXPERIENCE

Personally financed M.B.A. through concurrent full-time employment in sales and management. Prior career highlights:

- Three years in branch management with Finance America Corporation, a Bank of America company— earned Western Region Office of the Year Award for profit performance and growth; and

- Four years in retail sales management—achieved record sales volume, won regional customer satisfaction award, and boosted unit ranking to "Top Producer" status.

Résumé 1.8. Secretary: Before

LANE EASTERBY

2425 California St.
Selma, CA 93632
(559) 222–2222
laneeasterby@email.com

EXPERIENCE:

[year-year]   State of California, Department of Motor Vehicles
Word Processing Center
Selma, CA

Office Automation Assistant
Primary responsibility is typing hearing decisions on Word Perfect, mainly on registration expiration cases, but can be about anything related to DMV programs. These are rough drafts, but are expected to be as close to perfect as possible. Type for hearing officers in region and sometimes others from other regions; each decision writer in each office has their own preferred style and typing must be adapted accordingly. Approximately 90% is by dictaphone, approximately 10% is from handwritten or typed draft.

[year-year]   Kelly Services
Selma, CA

Secretary
Data entry to complete a project against deadline pressure. Data entry to convert a firm from one computer system to another. Phone verification work. Also typed, answered phones, copier work, and receptionist work.

[year-year]   Connection Personnel
Selma, CA

Secretary
Typed, performed data entry, answered phones, receptionist duties.

[year-year]   Summary of previous work performed, both volunteer and paid work, during this period. (Reason for leaving: temporary positions or moved out of state.)

Secretary
Data entry, typed from dictaphone and rough draft, prepared billings, scheduled appointments, answered often busy phones, receptionist, copy machine, and general clerical duties.

Set up a new office within a firm as the secretary to the public relations director. In this position, requested all office supplies needed to set up the office, set-up and updated files, composed and typed letters, kept track of publicity budget, sent out mailings, and performed general clerical duties.

Volunteer--helped plan, organize, and carry out fundraising activities; supervised up to 10 others, depending on the project.

Résumé 1.9. Secretary: After

2425 California Street
Selma, CA 93632
(559) 222-2222
laneeasterby@email.com

LANE EASTERBY

SECRETARY ■ ADMINISTRATIVE ASSISTANT

CAREER SUMMARY

Significant experience in self-directed positions requiring effective secretarial, administrative, and technical/automation skills. Strengths include:

Secretarial
- Compose, edit, and proofread correspondence, reports, proposals, bids, and other business material (good grammar, punctuation, spelling); prepare and review statistical and narrative reports.

Support
- Experience includes calendar management, correspondence, travel arrangements, meeting planning, management team coordination, client interface, management buffer.

Administration
- Office management, supply purchasing, reception, file management, new office start-up, supervision, planning, and orchestration of special events.

Technical
- Computer software (MS Office & WordPerfect), typing (75+ wpm), office equipment (Dictaphones, multiline phone systems, faxes, postage machines), medical terminology.

Education
- General business management and secretarial college-level courses.

EXPERIENCE

Office Assistant
Word Processing Center, State of California, Department of Motor Vehicles   [year-Present]
- *Accountability:* Transcribe reports for 160 regional hearing officers as member of eight-person office team. Assist with email responses, mail distribution, report generation, and payroll input. Helped purge backlog of 1,000 obsolete files.

Secretary
Temporary Agencies (Kelly Services and Connection Personnel)   [year-year]
- *Highlights:* Performed data entry to convert insurance firm to new computer system. Adapted quickly to a variety of business office operations as temp employee.

Secretary
Several Public Relations, Business, and Nonprofit Organizations   [year-year]
- *Highlights:* Assisted Public Relations Director of a think tank and publishing house. Organized new business office—purchased equipment, planned space layout, established filing systems, and developed office procedures. Distributed press kits, prepared mailings, and composed and typed letters.

PROFILE

Comments from supervisors' evaluations: "hardworking . . . always strives to do the best job possible . . . volunteers to help in any area that needs it . . . work is consistently of a very high quality . . . careful and accurate . . . exceptional initiative and resourcefulness in performing work assignments . . . self-motivated . . . an asset to the office."

Résumé 1.10. Career Transitioner: Before

TORREY WELLMAN
234 East Wales
Birmingham, AL 23456
(301) 234-2234 ~ twellman@msn.com

MANAGEMENT/MARKETING PROFESSIONAL

*Exceptional business development background with achievements
in revenue producing, high-growth child care industry.*

SUMMARY OF QUALIFICATIONS

▶ Career encompasses 17+ years of marketing, management, human resource, and budget development experience.

▶ Solid background in program planning and business development for highly successful self-supporting child development programs for school districts with substantial enrollment.

▶ Readily accept new challenges and highly conscientious in the planning, follow-through, and organization of new projects.

▶ Excellent communication skills with substantial public speaking/presentation experience.

▶ Easily establish rapport and interact well with management, staff, and client.

PROFESSIONAL EXPERIENCE

Child Development Resources Specialist
ABC UNIFIED SCHOOL DISTRICT, Birmingham, Alabama   [year-Present]

● Recruited by the school district to establish a self-supporting Child Development Program which included eight elementary schools and two state funded preschools.

● Successfully marketed program which, after only two years, has a budget surplus and services 500-plus children each month.

● Developed and administered the budget, hired and trained personnel, and supervised the program.

● Extensive presentations to parent and faculty groups.

Director of Youth Programs
CENTRAL DISTRICT YMCA, Birmingham, Alabama   [year-year]

● Directed full-time summer programs and part-time programs which were acquired from the ABC Unified School District.

● Developed marketing strategies which included presentations, print materials, public speaking, and fund raising to promote programs for children preschool age through eighth grade.

● Hired, trained, and supervised staff and maintained the budgeting, payroll, purchasing and inventory for multiple locations.

TORREY WELLMAN   Page 2

PROFESSIONAL EXPERIENCE (Continued)

Community Education Specialist
MILLINGS UNIFIED SCHOOL DISTRICT, Millings, Alabama   [year-year]

- Developed the extended day programs for year round schools.
- Coordinated the district-wide Parent Conference, Red Ribbon Week, and Business Partners programs.
- Marketed the day camp and extended child care programs, hired/trained/supervised staff, and maintained budgeting, payroll, purchasing and inventory for multiple locations.

Self-Employed

SUMMER DAY CAMP PROGRAMS, Millings, Alabama   [year-year]

- Developed and implemented a summer day camp program which began with 40 children at one location and ultimately served 300 children per week at two locations.
- This successful program was acquired by the Millings Unified School District.

Previous Experience included:

Marketing Representative, *5 years*
Business Manager, *2 years*

EDUCATION

Regent University, Virginia Beach, Virginia
Bachelor of Arts Degree, Political Science & Education

Federal Executive Institute, Charlottesville, Virginia
Personnel Management Certificate of Completion

National University, Birmingham, Alabama
Masters Program in Education Administration - 33 units completed

Excellent references available upon request.

Résumé 1.11. Career Transitioner: **After**

TORREY WELLMAN

234 East Wales   (301) 234–2234
Birmingham, Alabama 23456   twellman@email.com

PHARMACEUTICAL SALES

Opportunity with an industry leader that will benefit from my proven ability to

Develop New Business ◆ Retain Loyal Accounts ◆ Gain Market Share ◆ Increase Gross Margins

Especially skilled in sales and marketing, demonstrating competency in demanding, customer–focused business development positions. Seventeen years' experience in high–profile roles within the community. Strengths in consultative sales, needs identification, proposal preparation, formal presentations before decision makers, closing, follow–through, and client advocacy.

Value I bring to your organization:

- **Rainmaker:** Consistently exceeded business development goals, generating *more than $1 million in new revenue* throughout career.

- **Program developer/manager:** Developed and launched new program from concept to profitable operation, producing $260,000 in annual revenue with *$32,000 budget surplus*.

- **Marketing strategist:** Envisioned marketing strategies that *built fledgling organization into market leader*, operating at maximum facility and staffing capability and capturing major share of a saturated market.

- **Event/program planner:** Planned well–received educational programs and events (from concept development to completion) with attendance by more than 1,400.

- **Persuasive public speaker:** Made hundreds of presentations to medical, educational, and business leaders.

ENDORSEMENTS

Physician

- "[Torrey Wellman] is a very dynamic and dedicated person . . . whatever task she is involved with, she is always very thorough and follows to completion all of her projects . . . [as] a drug representative, she would be very convincing." *William O. Roberts, M.D.*

Medical Practice Manager

- "Torrey Wellman has tremendous communication skills as well as the ability to accomplish myriad tasks within a very short period of time." *Carol Millingham, Community Family Medical Group*

Pharmaceutical Area Account Executive

- "Torrey Wellman is the type of person I would entrust with my sales territory . . . [she] is self–disciplined . . . a quick learner . . . can guarantee you a successful relationship with your clients and grow your business in today's challenging healthcare environment." *John Shavitz, Abbott Diagnostics Division*

PROFESSIONAL EXPERIENCE

Consulting Projects/Contracted Assignments–Birmingham, Alabama   [year–Present]

- *Highlights:* Sales Consultant for Wholesale Building Supply charged with turnaround of sales and improvement of cash flow–wrote marketing plan, called on key accounts, implemented new operating procedures, and collected outstanding receivables. Women's Health Educator for Community Family Medical Group. Coauthor (with chief executive of County Schools) of Charter School Document for region's first alternative educational program.

TORREY WELLMAN

234 East Wales   (301) 234-2234
Birmingham, Alabama 23456   twellman@email.com

PROFESSIONAL EXPERIENCE (continued)

Program Director–ABC Unified School District, Birmingham, Alabama   [year–Present]
Director of Youth Programs–Central District YMCA, Birmingham, Alabama   [year–year]

- *Highlights:* Recruited to establish enrichment program; successfully marketed program that, after only two years, has a budget surplus (12% net) and services 500+ participants monthly at eight locations.

Community Education Specialist–Millings Unified School District, Millings, Alabama   [year–year]

- *Highlights:* Directly accountable for success of extended care programs including marketing and operations management. Coordinated district-wide events in state's second largest district, including Parent Conferences, Red Ribbon Week, and Business Partners.

Business Principal & Program Director–Summer Day Camp Programs, Millings, Alabama   [year–year]

- *Highlights:* Developed and implemented day program that grew from single site with 40 participants to more than 300 at multiple locations.

EDUCATION

REGENT UNIVERSITY, Virginia Beach, Virginia

- **Bachelor of Arts degree, Political Science & Education**

NATIONAL UNIVERSITY, Birmingham, Alabama

- **Master's Program in Education Administration** (38 units completed)

CONTINUING EDUCATION

- Successfully completed training in the areas of infectious diseases, vaccines, cardiovascular disease, osteoporosis, common respiratory diseases, and managed care.

AFFILIATIONS

Networking and volunteering are integral to my sales philosophy and indicative of my commitment to the community. As such, have been involved in leadership with groups such as:

American Cancer Society (Fund-Raising Chair)
American Heart Association (Fund-Raising Chair)
City Chamber of Commerce (Ambassador)
County Chamber of Commerce (Ambassador)
Birmingham Women's Network (Special Events Cochair)
Junior League of Birmingham (Past President)
Service Guild of Children's Hospital (Committee Chair)

REFERENCES

Strong business, community, and medical references available.

Résumé 1.12. New College Graduate

NICK BURNS

12345 North Palmerton Circle
Sacramento, CA 95845
Business: (916) 999-8888
nickb@nickburnsonline.com
www.nickburnsonline.com/blog

+ **Company-Minded Underwriter**

+ **Expert Researcher**

+ **Technology Enthusiast**

Scrupulous attention to details, deadlines, and the bottom line ... targeting long-term association with an insurance company that will benefit from an industrious, proactive employee with strong academic preparation and innate technology talents.

EDUCATION

UNIVERSITY OF CALIFORNIA, BERKELEY

♦ Bachelor of Arts degree in Social Science, Option in Geography [year]

♦ Representative Coursework: City Management; GIS; MIPS; Remote Sensing; Algebra; Trigonometry; Computer Programming; and Economic & Cultural Studies of Japan, Asia, and South America

PROFESSIONAL EXPERIENCE

MUTUAL INSURANCE COMPANY   [mo/yr–Present]
Sacramento, CA   (full-time in addition to college)

Insurance Underwriter Assistant

Perform underwriting functions for a full range of property, casualty, and inland marine coverage, including RPCs, new business, and cancellations. Rate insurance risks using computer applications. Respond to telephone inquiries for quotes and process new business. Review rating documentation from home office for accuracy. Work closely with underwriters and sales associates. Experience includes property loss reviews.

♦ Trained as agent to conduct online as well as manual system checks.

♦ Experienced with both production and underwriting procedures.

♦ Promoted through two prior grades as insurance rater.

♦ Earned reputation for strong work ethic, honesty, and commitment to giving 100% toward company goals.

ADDITIONAL INFORMATION

♦ **Computer Proficiency**—Views, ACES, IMS, MS Office, WordPerfect, Excel, Turbo CAD, TNT MIPS.

♦ **Other Skills**—Strong mechanical aptitude (rebuilt a car engine; repaired heating/air-conditioning systems and appliances; worked part-time repairing small motors for tractors, lawn mowers, and power equipment).

♦ **Interests**—Avid reader of history, science, and geography.

♦ **Travel**—Accustomed to travel and frequent relocation (father was career military officer).

ACCOMPLISHMENTS

Financed 100% of education through concurrent full-time employment and a small student loan. Maintained grade-point average while carrying up to 15 units per semester, as well as attending to family responsibilities with three young children. This undertaking took strong organizational skills, financial discipline, perseverance, and a timely sense of humor.

◆ ◆ ◆

Résumé 1.13. Regional Manager

MARIA ALMACCI

1324 Realia, Houston, TX 76543   (800) 432-4321   malmacci@email.com

QUALIFICATIONS

Extensive experience in the wholesale ag fertilizer industry with strengths in sales, purchasing, and logistics management. Highlights:

Sales Management, Business Development

❐ Spurred significant growth in large sales territories, managing sales in five Southwestern states with customer base of 400+.

❐ Introduced new applications for established products (feed industry, lawn & garden, industrial), *delivering double-digit gains in organic growth* and consistency in cash flow. Developed successful niche markets for new research products.

❐ Wrote and implemented wholesale marketing plans. Strategies enhanced sales *(revenue jumped by as much as 300%)*, including customer focus meetings, response surveys, in-house sales departments, and top dealer programs.

❐ Mentored individuals new to the business who later received promotions to regional sales, sales management, and international business development positions.

❐ Coordinated joint ventures between foreign investors and Texas dealers and manufacturers.

Procurement, Distribution, Logistics Management

❐ Experienced in procurement, storage, inventory management, order processing, and distribution of agricultural fertilizers.

❐ Negotiated wholesale product pricing and procurement contracts *with savings of up to 30%*; familiar with virtually all major manufacturers and international trading companies.

❐ Formed strategic alliance with international nitrogen company and coordinated set-up and operation of a UAN-32 terminal; knowledgeable in import/export rules and regulations for deep-water ports.

❐ Negotiated rail rates. Coordinated intra- and interstate trucking; managed an anhydrous ammonia rail fleet. Established a U.S. backhaul truck system.

Related Industry Experience

❐ Experienced in product labeling, licensing, and materials registration, including hazardous fertilizer materials; developed numerous contacts within TDFA, with ability to maneuver products through approval process quickly.

❐ Called on to assist with state and national lobbying efforts; served as industry delegate to Washington, D.C., on a number of occasions; assisted with grassroots legislation that favorably affected industry.

❐ Comfortable in public speaking and other high-visibility roles; promote the fertilizer industry through involvement in FFA and other outreach programs; conducted numerous business-related presentations and workshops.

❐ Elected to Board of Directors and appointed to various committees for the Texas Fertilizer Association.

❐ Built relationships with key industry individuals at the wholesale, distributor, and retail levels.

PROFESSIONAL EXPERIENCE

Director of Supply and Distribution—Southwest Chemical Corporation	[year–Pres.]
Western U.S. Regional Manager—Major Chemical Corporation	[year–year]
Western U.S. Regional Manager—Minor Chemical Corporation	[year–year]
Promoted through positions in **Logistics and Sales Management**—Ag-Builders, Inc.	[year–year]

EDUCATION

Continuing Education: Numerous professional development seminars in executive accounting, sales management, negotiations, and TQM, as well as semiannual conferences relating to the agriculture fertilizer industry.
Graduate Studies: Humanities—University of Texas, Austin
Undergraduate Emphasis: Business Law, Criminal Corrections, and English Literature—University of Texas, Houston

▪ ▪ ▪

Résumé 1.14. Employee Advancing Within Company

SPENCER PAUL COVINGTON

2553 Tollhouse Avenue
Piedra, California 95678

Available for Relocation

Mobile: (415) 555-4444
covington@email.com

SALES MANAGEMENT

Pharmaceutical ◆ Biotech Industry

Qualified for management challenges requiring expertise in building market-dominant sales organizations. Excel in team-selling, sales team leadership, and training and development. Equally skilled in financial analysis, new product launches, and change management. Articulate communicator—excellent relationships with physicians and medical office staff. Industry advocate—involved in public policy at local, state, and federal levels.

PROFESSIONAL EXPERIENCE

Senior Sales Representative/Regional Trainer—BIO-PHARMACEUTICAL, INC., San Francisco, CA [mo/yr–Present]

Recruited to manage high-profile territory and gain market share in anti-infective, anti-herpetic, and acid peptic disease markets. Groom new hires to refine skills in sales, territory management, and product knowledge. Plan speaker programs and teleconferences for physicians, gaining support of key medical leaders for endorsement of products.

Sales Performance

➤ Exceeded district and national market-share goals for anti-infective and anti-herpetic markets **(17% vs. 10% nationally and 22% vs. 12% nationally).** Gained top market share in region for oncology product.

➤ Consistently **ranked #1 in district** with eight sales representatives for overall performance (incremental increase over goal, market share, prescriptions sold).

➤ Launched new migraine and asthma products, gaining major market share in less than six months and ranking as **leading territory in region.**

➤ Earned numerous awards; comments from district manager include "I need to know that the best people are out there every day to meet challenges and seize opportunities . . . You are one of those people."

Sales Management Contributions

➤ Presented selling skills seminars for 80 northern California sales representatives, emphasizing solution-based selling, relationship development, reimbursement issues, and patient education.

➤ Trained new representatives with virtually no pharmaceutical sales experience to become solid performers; several were promoted to high-volume territories, sales management, and government affairs positions.

➤ Chosen for two-member training team to facilitate integration of 40+ Pri-PharmaCo representatives.

➤ Earned **highest ROI** for marketing funds ($25K annual budget).

➤ Selected from competitive candidate list for 18-month field management training program.

Licensed Securities Broker—PRUDENTIAL BACHE, Sacramento, California [mo/yr–mo/yr]

➤ Built solid client list of high-net-worth investors. Managed more than $12 million in assets.

Pharmaceutical Sales Representative—PHARMA-COM, INC., Palo Alto, California [mo/yr–mo/yr]

➤ Cultivated relationships with influential Stanford physicians (previously inaccessible), gaining support for new and existing cardiovascular and anti-arthritic products that aggressively affected regional sales.

EDUCATION, PROFESSIONAL DEVELOPMENT

Bachelor of Arts degree, Saint Mary's College, Moraga, California [year]. Ongoing sales and management training.

◆ ◆ ◆

Résumé 1.15. Executive Recruiter's Candidate: Before

RESUME

LAWRENCE YEE
2727 South Venice
Modesto, CA 94567
Residence: 559-460-4321
Cellular: 559-460-1234
Lee.Yee@mail.com

SPECIAL SKILLS

APICS Certified at the CPIM level   LAN/WAN Network Setup & Mgmt
APICS Certified Train-the-Trainer   HP-UX & Novell NetWare 3.x
MRPII Implementation Project Leader   QAD Mfg/Pro & Results
Auditor for Corporate Audit Team   IBM PC, DOS, Lotus & WordPerfect
Excellence Checklist   Microsoft Office

EMPLOYMENT HISTORY

[year-Present]   <u>Controller</u> - MAJOR FOOD PRODUCTS, Modesto, CA. As Controller, I am
                        responsible for managing purchasing, scheduling, and the accounting department.
                        Budgeting, ABC accounting, and managerial accounting fall within the scope of
                        this position. Additionally, I am the MRPII Implementation Project Leader for the
                        Modesto Plant. As Project Leader I am responsible for all in-house APICS and
                        Mfg/Pro education and training. During the past year I have been on the Corporate
                        Audit Team that provides a semi-annual assessment of the checklist scores for our
                        plants in Biloxi, Wilkes-Barre, and Cheyenne. I was the Project Leader for the
                        installation of the LAN/WAN in the plant and am qualified as a network
                        administrator.

[year-year]   <u>Western Division Accounting Manager</u> - FOOD MANUFACTURERS
                        COOPERATIVE, Stockton, CA. Responsible for an accounting staff of 12 people.
                        Specific responsibilities included management of purchasing, scheduling, and
                        inventory control. Budgeting and managerial accounting also feel within the scope
                        of this position. I was responsible for the design and implementation of a MRP
                        system which tied plant production to order entry through the customer service
                        department.

EDUCATION

BSBA, University of California, Berkeley
APICS Certified in Integrated Resource Management (CIRM)
APICS Certified in Production and Inventory Management (CPIM)
APICS Train-the-Trainer
UNIX System Basics, HP-UX System Administrator
Novell NetWare 3.x Administration
RPG Programming, Intro/Advanced/Workstation

Résumé 1.16. Executive Recruiter's Candidate: After

LAWRENCE YEE

2727 South Venice
Modesto, CA 94567

Lee.Yee@mail.com

Residence: 559-460-4321
Cellular: 559-460-1234

QUALIFICATIONS

Career Summary: APICS-certified finance professional with impressive 12-year record of contributing to profit growth, cost containment, and supply chain management in complex manufacturing environments.

Profit Performance: Captured record earnings performance as controller for $65 million division of leading international food manufacturer.

Executive Team: Delivered business-driven solutions in challenging turnaround and growth modes. Expert qualifications in strategic business planning and leadership of integrated accounting, budgeting, cash management, asset management, cost accounting, and credit and collections functions.

Technology Skills: MRPII and QAD MFG/PRO & Results (UNIX-based system); HP-UX & Novell NetWare 6.5 network administrator and LAN/WAN network administrator; fluent in popular PC software.

PROFESSIONAL EXPERIENCE

MAJOR FOOD PRODUCTS, Modesto, CA [year-Present]

CONTROLLER: Charged with enterprise-wide business planning as core management team member for $65 million food manufacturing operation. Plan, manage, and provide leadership for finance and accounting, including budgeting, cost accounting, managerial accounting, financial reporting, financial analysis, banking relationships, capital projects, and purchasing. Supervise accounting staff of six. Implement APICS and MFG/PRO education and training plant-wide. Highlights:

- Met initial challenge of redesigning accounting systems and establishing internal controls to eliminate variances and improve integrity of financial data. Efforts earned first-ever "gold star" on audit package from Big 6 firm.

- Contributed to business process engineering that supported aggressive growth. Sales increased from $39 million to $65 million; concurrently delivered impressive additions to net profit.

- MRPII Implementation Project Leader—Without aid of outside consultants, led team in implementing computer system that significantly affected supply chain functions: slashed inventory 29%; boosted batch yield 1.5%; and maximized order fill rate by a record 3%.

- Ranked as lowest-cost producer among seven comparable U.S. plants, consistently operating at 10% below norm.

FOOD MANUFACTURERS COOPERATIVE, Stockton, CA [year-year]

WESTERN DIVISION ACCOUNTING MANAGER: Managed team of 12 in purchasing, accounts payable, payroll, and inventory control functions. Provided managerial accounting, budgeting, cost accounting, and inventory management. Designed and implemented MRP system linking plant production to order entry via customer service department. Promoted through positions as accounting assistant and accounting department manager.

EDUCATION, CERTIFICATION, AFFILIATIONS

Degree: Bachelor of Science, Business Administration—University of California, Berkeley

Certification: Production and Inventory Management (CPIM)
Integrated Resource Management (CIRM)
Train-the-Trainer

Affiliations: Member, American Production and Inventory Control Society (APICS)
Member, Institute of Management Accountants (IMA)

Résumé 1.17. Recent Graduate's Cover Letter and Résumé

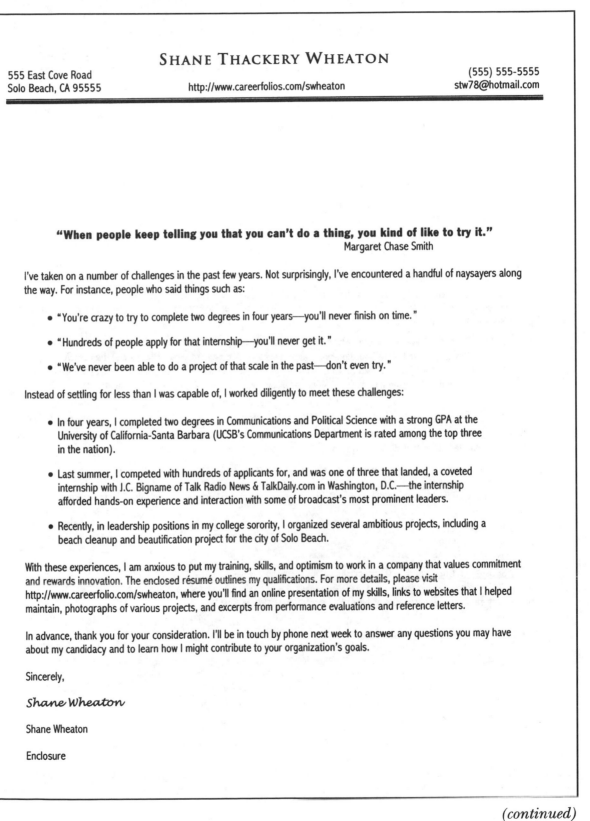

SHANE THACKERY WHEATON

555 East Cove Road
Solo Beach, CA 95555   http://www.careerfolios.com/swheaton   (555) 555-5555
stw78@hotmail.com

"When people keep telling you that you can't do a thing, you kind of like to try it."
Margaret Chase Smith

I've taken on a number of challenges in the past few years. Not surprisingly, I've encountered a handful of naysayers along the way. For instance, people who said things such as:

- *"You're crazy to try to complete two degrees in four years—you'll never finish on time."*

- *"Hundreds of people apply for that internship—you'll never get it."*

- *"We've never been able to do a project of that scale in the past—don't even try."*

Instead of settling for less than I was capable of, I worked diligently to meet these challenges:

- In four years, I completed two degrees in Communications and Political Science with a strong GPA at the University of California-Santa Barbara (UCSB's Communications Department is rated among the top three in the nation).

- Last summer, I competed with hundreds of applicants for, and was one of three that landed, a coveted internship with J.C. Bigname of Talk Radio News & TalkDaily.com in Washington, D.C.—the internship afforded hands-on experience and interaction with some of broadcast's most prominent leaders.

- Recently, in leadership positions in my college sorority, I organized several ambitious projects, including a beach cleanup and beautification project for the city of Solo Beach.

With these experiences, I am anxious to put my training, skills, and optimism to work in a company that values commitment and rewards innovation. The enclosed résumé outlines my qualifications. For more details, please visit http://www.careerfolio.com/swheaton, where you'll find an online presentation of my skills, links to websites that I helped maintain, photographs of various projects, and excerpts from performance evaluations and reference letters.

In advance, thank you for your consideration. I'll be in touch by phone next week to answer any questions you may have about my candidacy and to learn how I might contribute to your organization's goals.

Sincerely,

Shane Wheaton

Shane Wheaton

Enclosure

(continued)

(continued)

SHANE THACKERY WHEATON

555 East Cove Road
Solo Beach, CA 95555
http://www.careerfolios.com/swheaton
(555) 555-5555
stw78@hotmail.com

SYNOPSIS

Dual-degree graduate with D.C. internship experiences, qualified for career opportunities where communications expertise, technology skills, and broadcast background will be of value.

EDUCATION

University of California, Santa Barbara

Bachelor of Arts degree, Communications (Dean's List honors; GPA in major: 3.9)   [date]
Bachelor of Arts degree, Political Science   [date]

INTERNSHIPS

Talk Radio News Service & TalkDaily.com, Washington, D.C.   June-August [date]

Assisted in production of daily radio and Internet broadcasts. Researched Internet sources, national newspapers, and other news sources to assemble show content. Wrote daily news summaries for TalkDaily.com. Assisted with ongoing research on talk-show topics. Highlights:

- Broadcast: Cohosted live, 20-minute daily radio broadcast—an assignment normally reserved for full-time staffers.
- Communications: Covered White House press conferences; posed questions to senior officials and the President. Interviewed guests for *Talkers Magazine*, including hosts of top Boston and D.C.-based talk-radio programs.
- Technology: Updated website with daily highlights of talk personalities, such as Rush Limbaugh and Imus.

U.S. Representative Geraldine Smathers, 22nd District, Washington, D.C.   July-August [date]

Represented congresswoman at hearings and provided written analysis of proposed legislation. Served as office contact for major supporters. Wrote constituent correspondence and franked communications. Highlights:

- Communications: Selected among five interns as media spokesperson for several campaign events. Served as precinct captain on election day.
- Technology: Project managed on-time installation of new communications system at campaign headquarters.

LEADERSHIP SKILLS

Delta Delta Gamma, UC-Santa Barbara Campus

- Social Chair: Organized 15-20 annual events for 100-member organization.
- Philanthropy Chair: Envisioned and managed projects that benefited the campus and city.
- Fund-raising Chair: Introduced activities that generated record revenue.

TECHNICAL SKILLS & INTERESTS

- **Computer Skills:** Dreamweaver website design; MS Office (advanced skills in Word, Excel, PowerPoint); MSIE and Netscape Navigator browsers; email applications (Outlook Express, Eudora); Internet research.
- **Favorite Subjects:** Political communications, lobbying, legal advocacy and argumentation, oral debate, drama.
- **Language:** Basic conversational and business Spanish (completed four years of Spanish course work).
- **Activities:** Tennis, golf, canoeing.

Amplified Résumé and References Online: http://www.careerfolios.com/swheaton

Résumé 1.18. Electrical Engineering Manager Cover Letter and Résumé

FRED G. EWY

555 East Lane
Los Angeles, CA 95555

fgewy@email.com
Phone/Fax (555) 555-5555

In researching executive recruiting firms, I noted that your organization sources senior-level engineering candidates. Perhaps one of your client companies has need of someone with my qualifications.

Roles in which I can deliver immediate value . . .

- **Experienced engineer** who conceived and led cross-functional teams in the design of numerous patented products that *increased annual revenues 50% and 80%* for my past two employers.

- **Capable project manager**, able to create synergy and cooperation across engineering, manufacturing, and marketing disciplines, where there previously had been miscommunications and inefficiencies.

- **Profit-conscious business manager**, driving product and *operating costs down to lowest in the industry* through departmental reorganizations, value-added engineering, and lean manufacturing. Additionally reduced time-to-market through design of rapid product-deployment processes.

- **Long-term focused employee**, with stable, six-year history at most current employer and eight-year tenure with previous employer (both concluding amicably due to mergers/acquisition)—advanced from design engineer to senior-level management team.

Depending on your clients' needs, I am available for full-time or contract assignments. Relocation is an option, given the right opportunity. Past compensation has been in the six-figure range with bonuses for development of proprietary technologies and products.

The enclosed résumé touches briefly on my employer contributions. I look forward to a meeting in which I can further qualify my candidacy, as well as learn about any job orders for which I'd be a good match. The combination of my engineering and management skills would no doubt be of interest to the right client.

Thank you for your consideration.

Sincerely,

Fred G. Ewy

Fred G. Ewy

Enclosure

(continued)

(continued)

FRED G. EWY

555 East Lane   fgewy@email.com
Los Angeles, CA 95555   Phone/Fax (555) 555-5555

SUMMARY OF QUALIFICATIONS

Senior engineering manager with impressive record of patenting new products that transitioned companies from "me-too" status to market-share leaders. Highlights of skill set:

- **Innovative product development:** Directed new product development that bolstered and diversified product lines, *increasing annual revenues 50% and 80% for most recent employers.*

- **Value engineering and lean manufacturing:** Reduced overall product costs 35% while adding product features. Implemented continuous improvement processes that reduced rejected parts 90%. Restructured engineering and manufacturing processes, with *six-figure savings to company.*

- **Process technology development:** Led development of several proprietary abrasion-resistant coating processes for plastic products with high-volume production feasibility.

- **Project management:** Assembled collaborative teams, creating first-time positive dynamics between design, manufacturing, and industrial engineers, as well as collaboration with marketing, sales, and product managers.

- **General management:** Bring a broad-scope view of business (strategic planning, finance, operations, sales, marketing) and manufacturing (QC/QA/CQI, regulatory compliance, ISO 9000, sheet-metal fabrication, tool & die, heating & air conditioning/refrigeration, plastic injection-molding & extrusion processes). Completed graduate courses equivalent to **MBA in business** at UCLA.

PROFESSIONAL EXPERIENCE

Director of R&D and Manufacturing Engineering; Manager of Continuous Improvement
LMNOP Industries (previously XYZ Manufacturing), Fullerton, CA [year-Present]
(Subsidiary of $2 billion heating and cooling manufacturer LMNOP International)

Brought on board to correct quality issues that had impacted sales and market share. Authored and coordinated implementation of product development, value engineering, and lean manufacturing initiatives. Directly supervised 12-member team of engineers (design, manufacturing, industrial), tooling supervisor, and QC technicians. Managed $1.5 million and $1.8 million operating and capital budgets, respectively. Managed projects through full project life-cycle.

- **Product development:** Directed R&D projects that led to four patents, positioning company as industry leader with lowest-cost, highest-feature product on market. *Innovations led to 50% (8-figure) revenue increases.*

- **CPSC testimony:** Represented company before the Consumer Products Safety Commission in Washington, DC, resolving longstanding safety concerns and winning full approval for new designs.

- **Value engineering:** Captured 35% reduction in materials, handling, and overhead costs.

- **Lean manufacturing:** Restructured fabrication and assembly lines for higher efficiency and elimination of nonvalue-added time. Reduced tooling change-over time more than 95% for many parts.

- **Continuous improvement processes:** Improved design and manufacturing processes, decreasing warranty costs more than $750,000 in first year.

- **Program/project management:** Selected to lead special projects to create common design platform, as well as streamline and unify manufacturing processes among plants in California, the Midwest, and Toronto.

(continued)

FRED G. EWY

(555) 555-5555 ~ Page 2 ~ fgewy@email.com

PROFESSIONAL EXPERIENCE (cont.)

Vice President, Engineering and Manufacturing
FGHI Products, City of Industry, CA [year-year]

Recruited to revive product lines of pool heaters and pumps. Managed eight design engineers, electronics engineer, hydraulic engineer, drafting supervisor, and laboratory technicians. Directed development of pump and heating technologies, electronic remote controllers, and equipment for combustion and hydraulic systems.

- **Product development:** Led design team that patented pump and heating systems, propelling company as the instant leader in high-efficiency heater technology. Personally featured in a publication by General Electric for innovative use of plastics.

- **Revenue contributions:** Strength of above products caused company to launch the largest marketing campaign in industry history. Collaborative efforts turned around declining sales and *yielded an approximate 80% increase in annual 8-figure revenue.*

- **Manufacturing engineering:** Initiated ISO 9000 approval process with European agencies.

Highlights as Design Engineer and Engineering and Operations Manager
(International manufacturers of HVAC and energy systems—details available)

- Designed cooling towers, multicircuit air-cooled and evaporative condensers, and freon and ammonia evaporators for freezer tunnels—*products allowed company to capture 50% market share.*

- Developed innovative energy-recovery system for air conditioning and refrigeration systems.

- Established manufacturing operation for waste-heat-recovery systems in New Zealand.

EDUCATION

UNIVERSITY OF CALIFORNIA, LOS ANGELES (UCLA)

- Professional designation in Business Management

- Professional designation in Marketing & Sales Management

FACHTECHNISCHE HOCHSCHULE HANNOVER, GERMANY

- Bachelor of Science degree, Mechanical Engineering (BSME)

AFFILIATIONS

American Society of Mechanical Engineers (ASME)
Society of Manufacturing Engineers (SME)
American Society of Gas Engineers

PATENTS

Nine patents on behalf of employers (details available).

References on Request

Résumé 1.19. Customer Service Manager Résumé

ABLE HERRERA

5555 North Comfort Circle
Phoenix, AZ 55555
Available for Travel & Relocation

AH@yahoo.com
Mobile: (555) 555-5555
Home: (555) 555-5556

CORE BRAND ELEMENTS & CONTRIBUTIONS

Intentional about linking every strategy and activity to socially responsible profitability … skilled at developing customer service initiatives that drive quality and productivity … experienced in creating "customer-centric" cultures and employee loyalty amidst intense change environments. Delivered these core talents and more throughout 10+ years in large-scale organizations, performing responsibilities in the areas of:

- Corporate Administration
- Project Development and Coordination
- Customer Relations Program Management
- Cultural Competency Program Creation

- Staff Recruitment, Supervision and Motivation
- Employee Development and Customer Training
- Creation and Use of Assessment Instruments
- Public Speaking and Multimedia Presentations

Expert communicator with high degree of emotional intelligence … broad knowledge of multicultural business practices as they relate to business development, customer service, and customer retention. **Fully bilingual (Spanish).** Excellent problem-solving, reasoning, decision-making, and creative-thinking skills. Masters degree in social work; advanced studies in leadership management, organizational systems, and business administration.

EXPERIENCE

HEALTH MOUNTAIN, Phoenix, AZ   [year–Present]

(Health Mountain medical centers is a 5,000-member organization that consists of 4 acute care hospitals, 2 freestanding outpatient facilities, and numerous affiliated groups; annual operating budget exceeds $300 million.)

Director, Customer Service and Call-Center Operations

Partner with executive management in the creation, administration, and management of enterprise-wide customer service and cultural service programs aligned with HM's corporate mission and goals. Community liaison for organization and key contact with the Hispanic Chamber of Commerce, UCSF Latino Center, and the local school district (third largest in state). Additionally manage corporate call-center program. Hire, schedule, train, direct, and evaluate a manager, three lead staff, and a 40-member team at three sites. Forecast, administer, and monitor $.75 million budget. Highlights:

- **Selected for projects requiring diplomacy, communication, and change agent skills:**

  o Chaired Customer Service Task Force that defined new corporate customer service mandate. Partnered in development of well-received service initiatives (based on Ritz-Carlton model), as well as creation of "real time" assessment and staff-reporting models that reduced admin costs 8%.

  o Instrumental in creation of new patient satisfaction survey. Evaluate and report data received from Parkside Survey, a national patient satisfaction survey that provides local and national benchmarks. Hospital increased its patient satisfaction ranking to top percentile during my tenure.

  o Served on Staff Integration Committee with Chief Operating Officer and other executives—tasked with blending two distinct workforce cultures resulting from the merger of public and private healthcare organizations and planning staff integration for alignment with new regional medical center.

  o Chaired Task Force for Hispanic and Southeast Asian Cultural Sensitivity Training. Facilitated the creation of multimedia programs featuring video training, classroom instruction, and online components. Implemented program throughout the organization.

> **Strategic Impact:** These projects contributed to the organization's target of boosting patient satisfaction scores several percentage points.
>
> **Feedback from COO:** *"Your initiative and leadership on these projects helped drive progress and meet aggressive goals. As always, thanks for going above and beyond!"*

(continued)

ABLE HERRERA
Page 2

AH@yahoo.com
Mobile: (555) 555-5555

EXPERIENCE (continued)

- o Crafted leading-edge "Cultural Competence Program" applauded by the medical community at-large. Created pre-assessment tools, developed corporate education plan, contracted with training experts, and presented portions of training. Conducted enterprise-wide post-assessment, gaining measurable improvements in cultural competency.

- o Partnered with educational organizations and public agencies (Phoenix Unified School District, Phoenix Adult School, Department of Social Services) to create the Jefferson Anthony Lowell Job Institute, a volunteer back-to-work program for adults.

- **Keynote Speaker:**

  - o Contracted with Regional Care Consortium to teach "Cultural Sensitivity for Health Care Providers" to licensed, certificated healthcare professionals.

  - o Delivered presentations on "Multi-Cultural Issues Affecting End of Life Decisions."

  - o Initiated "Spanish for Health Care Providers" course and presented to physicians and allied medical staff; program content includes direction on how to integrate cultural assessments with initial medical-psychosocial assessment.

  - o Delivered numerous presentations on cultural competency, customer service, stress management, and related topics to licensed professionals, executives, and administrative staff.

- **Delivered solid administrative, budgetary, and supervisory results:**

  - o Consistently met budget targets in all fiscal responsibilities (under budget 7 consecutive years).

  - o Defined core competency levels for call-center staff. Wrote policies that decreased call handle-time 14% yet improved quality of service.

- **Promoted from:**

  - o Clinical Partner—as member of interdisciplinary team, provided individual, family, group, short-term, crisis, and intermittent counseling, as well as discharge planning, rehabilitation case management, and quality and resource case management.

EDUCATION, REGISTRATIONS

ARIZONA STATE UNIVERSITY, TEMPE

- **Master of Social Work** [year]
- **Bachelor of Arts, Psychology** [year]

REGISTRATIONS

- **Registered Hospital Administrator,** Arizona Department of Health Services
- **Registered Contact** for Secret Service, White House Communications, Law Enforcement Agencies, JCAHO

REFERENCES

References and portfolio supplied on request.

Your Most Important Tool

Are these success stories exceptions to the rule? Maybe. Résumés are by no means the professional panacea to unemployment. More typically, before you land your next job, you'll get plenty of practice at the three *N*s—networking, knockin' on doors, and "knockin' 'em dead" in the interview process (okay, so these are just alliterative *N*s, but they do sum up the search process). I don't advocate hanging all your hopes on a great résumé. You could write the most impressive résumé in the world, yet it will be useless if you don't use it properly. Nonetheless, these accounts affirm that, in some cases, a great résumé can be the most important tool in your job search.

Whether you're climbing the corporate ladder, contemplating a new career, considering a lateral move, or determined to come out smelling like a rose after the downsizing/reengineering announcements have been made, this book is filled with relevant, easy-to-apply, insider résumé tips and job search trade secrets. They will put you on the inside track—the most advantageous position in the competition!

Top 10 Tips to Create Résumé Magic

1. **Write your future success story!** This is a prime opportunity to blow the dust off your career dreams and fine-tune your professional image and personal brand. Take time to contemplate your life-work and how you contribute significance and value to your corner of the world. Your résumé should be an authentic representation of who you are and what sets you apart from other candidates. Target positions that excite you! When there is passion in your work, there will be energy, creativity, and drive, the combination of which spells success.

2. **Build a brand that is in market demand.** This is the all-important link between your passions and the employer's productivity and profitability. A "branded" résumé should convey a value proposition and demonstrate a fit with not only the skills required for the position but the company's organizational culture as well. It tells recruiters or hiring managers that you are a "fast match" instead of a "Jack of all trades." It establishes an immediate connection with employers and answers the eternally critical question: "Why hire you instead of someone else with similar skills?"

3. **Think green—emphasize results.** Write from the employers' perspective. They want to know whether you can make a positive economic impact on the company—how you're going to help them generate money or save money. You can tell them by emphasizing benefits and not just features. Features correspond to skills and tasks (such as programming, sales, and customer service). Benefits represent results, accomplishments, and bottom-line profit (such as a 12 percent increase in efficiency, a 24 percent increase in sales, or a 17 percent increase in customer retention). Emphasize benefits throughout the résumé to appear business savvy and underscore your understanding of the bottom line. A clear value proposition is essential.

4. **Lead with a sizzling summary to capture interest and control impressions.** A meaty introductory qualifications section can help employers zero in on the three to five greatest strengths that communicate your brand. Be sure to include tangible, "green" accomplishments (see tip 3) to help substantiate each of your strengths and whet the reader's appetite.

5. **Mirror job postings with relevant content.** Before writing, select several job postings that epitomize your job target. Highlight key responsibilities and results from these postings. Then, diligently weave each of these items into your résumé. (Yes, this means that you must write a focused résumé for each job, not a one-size-fits-all résumé.) If you lack certain qualifications from the postings, strategize about how your experience is close to or parallels the requirements. When writing job descriptions, filter every sentence to ensure that it is relevant to your target. Keep job descriptions to three to seven lines at most (any more than this will make the paragraph look "thick" and uninviting to read).

6. **Separate responsibilities from accomplishments.** Recall from tip 3 that accomplishments are critical. Don't bury them in the same paragraph as responsibilities. Use bullets to set off accomplishments and draw the readers' eye toward the results you have delivered. Remember, when it comes to job search, it's all about them, not you. Show how you can solve problems or serve needs.

(continued)

(continued)

7. **Weave keywords throughout.** Comb Internet postings, company newsletters, and current articles, as well as talk to people in your target industry, for terms that will help your résumé be unearthed after it is dumped into a résumé database. Emphasize critical keywords by leading off a bullet or paragraph with the keyword. For example, if "public speaking" is important to your candidacy, instead of writing "Made presentations to medical, educational, and business leaders," write "**Public Speaking:** Made presentations to medical, educational, and business leaders—regularly earned 'exceeds expectations' on evaluations."

8. **Substantiate personality traits.** Prove that you have any traits you claim. The phrase "**Customer-focused:** selected as primary contact for key account" adds more credibility than simply saying, "customer-focused," or worse yet, "good people skills."

9. **Prune and proofread!** Traditional print résumés should be no more than two pages (exceptions to the two-page rule apply for senior executives, academicians, and licensed medical professionals). Ask yourself, "does this information support or detract from my candidacy?" Omit information if it does not support. Also, weed out personal pronouns (instead of "I managed," just say "managed"), helping verbs, and unnecessary prepositional phrases. After editing, enlist the support of a competent proofreader, preferably one well acquainted with the rules of grammar.

10. **Go for the "wow" factor—make it gorgeous!** First impressions do count. Your résumé should have the look and feel of a polished ad, with a design that is crisp, clean, and eye-catching. Consider tasteful use of graphic elements, color enhancements, or small, relevant logos. Match the résumé design to your industry—if you're in a traditional field, lean toward a more conservative design; if you're in a creative field, a more artistic or imaginative design might be just the thing. Add as much white space as possible to enhance readability—greater readability means you'll get your point across faster. Consistent use of fonts, styles, spacing, and grammar throughout the résumé will also give the résumé a more attractive appearance. And, of course, proof it at least twice; typos will detract from an otherwise perfect résumé.

Bonus Tip:

Use the right delivery method. Résumés are useless if they can't be read! Determine how the employer wants the résumé delivered. Some employers prefer to receive résumés by e-mail with the document attached as a Word or PDF file; others want a text document pasted into an e-mail message or online form; still others want the old-fashioned snail-mail method. If your brand is about technology, an e-portfolio and blog should be part of your suite of career marketing documents. And, be sure to include a brief cover letter regardless of your delivery method—employers don't have time to guess what type of position you want. Even for those employers who make a habit of skipping directly to the résumé, a cover letter remains standard job search protocol. Finally, remember that job search is marketing! You are the product, and the employer is the consumer—find those who need what you love to do!

How to Use Branding and Advertising Strategies to Get an Interview

"Advertising isn't a science. It's persuasion. And persuasion is an art."

—William Bernbach
Founder, Doyle Dane Bernbach Advertising Agency

Strangers have made their way into your home. But you don't know it.

You've put in a long workday. It may have included dealing with a cranky boss, picky customers, colicky coworkers, and a crowded commute. You arrive home, only to find that salespeople have finagled their way into your abode. You know who I'm talking about. They're there every day as you plow through the snail mail. The outside of the envelope is typically stamped with, "You've earned a platinum credit card with no annual fee."

Studies show that direct-mail advertising letters have about five seconds to gain your attention. Résumés get about 10 to 20 seconds, at most. Résumés are, of course, a different medium than direct-mail advertising. At the same time, there are a number of similarities. The most obvious—you have precious, fleeting moments to get your reader's attention and make a great first impression. It's crucial, as these often-overlooked truths reveal:

⁕　A great impression makes an immediate connection and compels your reader to go on reading…right now.

⁕　An average impression may win a read-through…later…maybe.

⁕　A bad impression will halt the process; your résumé (and your aspirations) could be destined for the same place you toss your junk mail.

Using Brand and Ad Agency Strategies to Win an Interview

Every year, American companies spend in excess of $52 billion (that's nine zeros!) on direct-mail advertising, $46 billion on newspaper advertising, and $16 billion on ads in consumer magazine and business publications. Another $88 billion is spent on annual television and radio advertising, with Internet advertising at nearly $7 billion, but fast increasing with double-digit annual growth (Source: *2006 Fact Pack: 4th Annual Guide to Advertising Marketing,* Crain Communications). Like it or not, the advertising gurus are pretty persuasive at getting us to spend part of our hard-earned paychecks.

Because they are so good at their craft, it makes sense to capitalize on some of their "trade secrets." In this chapter, we'll touch on personal branding, as well as explain how adopting and adapting bits and pieces of successful "advertising formulas" to the résumé-writing process has brought great success to people from all walks of life, from entry level to executive.

Personal or career branding is all about image (what you want to be known for) and connection or attraction (what kind of employer you want to connect with or attract). A compelling career brand can

⁕　Make you more attractive to employers, even when there are no formal job openings

⁕　Control what networking contacts and interviewers remember most about you

⁕　Lower the barriers to hiring by creating trust and conveying value

⁕　Elevate you from the status of commonplace commodity to one-of-a-kind service

⁕　Differentiate you from the competition

⁕　Guide you in your decisions about which interviews to pursue

⁕　Create employer desire to buy (hire)

Many of the same dynamics behind why a consumer chooses Crest over Colgate also apply in hiring. That's why it's important to have a clear brand and communicate it consistently. Creating your brand is *not* a five-minute exercise, but there are some key points that will fast-forward the process.

Elements of Your Career Brand

For your brand to accomplish its purpose, it must knit together these three *A*'s:

- Authentic Image
- Advantages
- Awareness

Authentic Image

Your Authentic Image is the genuine you—not costumed to play the part of someone else, but cast in the right role—a role that allows you to be radically rewarded and enthusiastically engaged in work that adds value to others. This requires some careful analysis and soul-searching. The Magic F.I.T.™ is a model that will help you zero in on your authentic image. The acronym stands for ingredients that are critical to career success:

- **F**—**F**unction and **F**ulfillment
- **I**—**I**ndustry/**I**nterests and **I**dentity
- **T**—**T**hings That Matter, and **T**ype

Table 2.1 briefly describes each element.

Table 2.1: Elements of the Magic F.I.T.™

	F	**I**	**T**
External Variables	**F**unction Function represents job titles and tasks; for example, titles such as accountant, copywriter, or customer service representative or tasks such as analyzing, planning, or writing. Although you're capable of doing a number of different functional jobs or tasks, you'll want to concentrate on your innate talents and skills, and favorite experiences.	**I**ndustry/Interests Industry refers to *where* you will apply your functional skills. Frequently, your functional interests can be used within a number of industries. For example, a customer service representative (Function) with a passion for organic products might target call centers (Industry) or retailers (Industry) that specialize. in natural products (Interests).	**T**hings That Matter Wouldn't it be wonderful if you could open the medicine cabinet each morning and pop a pill that would motivate you to go to work? That pill *does* exist! It takes the shape of having your values and needs met. Your "Things That Matter" category might include an impressive title, solid relationships with your boss or peers, a high level of authority, salary range or perks, cultural diversity, independence, travel, or a host of other elements that will take your job from good to great!
Internal Variables	**F**ulfillment Fulfillment is synonymous with purpose. Career purpose can be defined as being "radically rewarded and enthusiastically engaged in work that adds value to others." Your definition should capture the essence of how you will bring value to your employer, as well as how you will fulfill yourself. It's something you can intentionally look forward to on a Monday morning and say, "this is what I am committed to," as well as look back on Friday afternoon and say, "I have accomplished my purpose."	**I**dentity Identity refers to how you see yourself—your internal self-image. Who are you and who are you becoming? What distinguishing characteristics do you want others to perceive in you? What do you *believe* you are capable of accomplishing? How do you want others to perceive you? Those who experience the greatest meaning and fulfillment in life and work periodically redefine themselves and move beyond their previously accepted limitations.	**T**ype Type refers to your personality. You came wired-at-birth with four main personality preferences: where you focus your energy (your outer world or inner world); how you take in information (concretely or intuitively); how you make decisions (based on logic or feelings); and how you approach the world (in a planned or spontaneous manner).

If you're thinking that it will be a challenge to target a position that ideally suits all six elements—your functional skills, ideal industry/interests, personality type, fulfilling purpose, evolving identity, and things that matter—don't be discouraged. It *is* possible; however, recognize that it is a process of fine-tuning your career over time. Start by making sure you're clear about the first-level elements—Function, Industry/Interests, and Things That Matter—as you target new positions. Then, weave in your second-level elements—Fulfillment, Identity, and Type—to take your career to the next level. Complete the Magic F.I.T.™ form in Figure 2.1 to help you home in on positions that will be a good fit for you.

Advantages

The second *A* in your personal brand, Advantages, is synonymous with benefits and value. These are the advantages that you bring to employers. They should be linked to the employer's "buying motivators," such as the ability to help generate income or save costs for the company. You'll learn more about these in this chapter and in chapter 6 on accomplishments.

Awareness

The final *A,* Awareness, refers to communicating your brand in a manner that makes people attentive and responsive to it. You can do that both in print and in person during your job search. Your résumé and career marketing documents (cover letters, follow-up letters, reference sheets, project lists, online portfolio, and so on) can all convey your brand in print. Your choice of font, tasteful use of color in traditional paper résumés, use of visuals and color in online résumés, insertion of industry icons or logos, and so on will add to brand identity. And, of course, getting your résumé in front of decision makers is an important aspect of brand awareness. I'll cover résumé delivery and distribution in chapter 10.

In person, you'll communicate your brand through networking, interviewing, and, in general, interacting with people in your professional realm. Your demeanor, confidence, and character impact your brand. The clothes you wear, the way you conduct yourself, the pen you use, and the briefcase you carry all contribute to brand image. (For more on finding the right fit and in-person branding, see *Job Search Magic,* also published by JIST.)

Figure 2.1: Elements of the Magic F.I.T™

Career "Magic F.I.T.™"	
External "F.I.T." (the easily observable F.I.T.)	**Internal "F.I.T."** (the less observable, but equally important F.I.T.)
Function (<u>What</u> you *want and like* to do! What strengths/talents/skills/passions have you excelled at in the past? What would you like to learn to do? What job titles are associated with these functions? Conversely, what do you want to avoid? If there were one task you couldn't give up in your current career, what would it be? Job titles will often be associated with the <u>F</u>unction.)	**Fulfillment** (<u>Why</u> do you work? What is your purpose/cause/destiny? What difference do you want to make? How would you describe your living legacy? Why will this be rewarding?)
Industry (<u>Where</u> do you want to use your "function" skills? Where do your interests, knowledge, or experiences lie? What industries/companies/products do these interests represent? Conversely, what situations do you want to avoid?)	**Identity** (<u>Who</u> are you? Who are you becoming? What adjectives best describe your present and future you? How do you want others to perceive you? Who are your role models?)
Things That Matter (<u>Which</u> values and priorities—financial, work/lifestyle, environmental, intellectual, emotional, spiritual—must be present for you to be your best in your work?)	**Type** (<u>How</u> do you prefer to re-energize, take in information, make decisions, and orient your environment? For instance, are you more energized by people and things or ideas and concepts? Do you primarily trust information that is tangible and concrete or abstract and conceptual? Do you prefer to make decisions based on logic or how it will affect people? Do you prefer an environment that is more controlled and predictable or unstructured and variable? How do you learn best?)

Best Career/Job Search Targets Based on Above Answers: _____

_____

_____

A Quick Way to Generate Your Brand

A quick method to think about your brand is to use the grammatical framework of nouns, adjectives, and verb phrases. For example, if you were in education

- **Nouns** that describe your brand might include *teacher, reading specialist,* or *literacy trainer.*

- **Adjectives** might include *passionate, committed, caring, interactive, innovative,* or *tech-savvy.*

- **Verb phrases** might be empowering students through knowledge, touching lives with transformational change, enlightening others through awareness, or challenging others in critical thinking.

The Proven Ad Agency Formula

Advertising agency copywriters leverage brand elements when writing ads. Robert Bly, author of the timeless *The Copywriter's Handbook* (Owl Books, 2006), tells us what an ad must do to convince you to buy. It's a four-step process known as the AIDA formula—advertising copywriters continue to use it today in both print and online format. AIDA stands for the following:

1. Get **A**ttention.

2. Capture **I**nterest.

3. Create **D**esire.

4. Call to **A**ction.

Using these advertising principles has helped thousands of people in their job search—some of whom were up against formidable odds. These principles can help you promote yourself as well and give you the ammunition and confidence to target higher-paying jobs.

In the rest of this chapter, here's what you'll do:

- Learn how the four-step AIDA formula works.

- Understand how each step relates to the résumé process.

- See before-and-after examples of real people who used brand and ad strategies to their advantage.

Later in the book, you'll learn specific strategies for formatting (chapters 3 and 4) and writing (chapters 5 and 6).

Step 1: How to Grab Your Reader's Attention

To get your attention, copywriters focus on the single strongest benefit the product offers—*first*. You don't have to "skip to the end of the book," so to speak, to find out what the benefit is. Next time you flip through a magazine or turn on the radio, pay close attention to the ads. You'll begin to see a pattern. More often than not, you'll see the strongest benefit up front. Here are some examples:

Type of Ad	Where First Impression Is Made or Strongest Benefit Is Presented
Magazine or newspaper ad	Headline and picture
Brochure	Cover
Direct mail	Copy on outside of envelope or first couple of sentences in the letter
Radio or television ad	First few seconds of commercial
Web site	First screen

The principles used in magazine or newspaper ads also hold true for your self-marketing documents:

Type of Ad	Where First Impression Is Made or Strongest Benefit Is Presented
Résumé	Headline and visual appeal/overall look and feel of résumé
Cover letter	First couple of sentences in the letter or bulleted items that highlight accomplishments

Advertising combines visuals and headlines to get attention. Résumés use good copy and eye appeal to get attention. By the way, the word copy, short for *copywriting*, is the term ad agencies use for the headlines, paragraphs, sentences, and slogans that accompany the visuals (pictures). I'll be using the term *copy* to refer to your résumé content—the headlines, descriptions, tag lines, and other features that will wow and woo your boss-to-be. For the résumé, a good first impression requires persuasive copy and good visual appeal. Let's look at copy first.

Headlines and Hard-Hitting Leads

David Ogilvy, the messiah of Madison Avenue and author of *Confessions of an Advertising Man,* says that headlines are "the most important element in most advertisements…five times as many people read the headline as read the body copy." Here are a few headlines that got my attention:

**You're born, you go to school,
then one day things begin to get interesting.**

*(Photo in ad: young sailor aboard a gleaming ship, overlooking a beautiful
Mediterranean port city. Ad recruiting for U.S. Navy.)*

Oh, baby, where have you been all my life?

*(Caption below photo is "half the fat, really cheesy."
Photo in ad: happy couple eating Kraft Deluxe Macaroni & Cheese Dinner.)*

**Doctors are too busy to wait minutes for the correct temperature.
Guess what, mothers are busier.**

*(Photo in ad: close-up of a mother holding a sick baby. The ad is for an ear ther-
mometer that takes baby's temperature in one second.)*

A good lead will do two things:

- Get your attention.
- Draw you into reading the whole ad.

You're probably shaking your head, wondering if I'm going to ask you to write a catchy headline for your résumé or cover letter—maybe even put it to music! Something along the lines of the following:

You can double your sales in the next six months. Your competition has.

(Salesperson touting past sales performance.)

"Boutique" customer service wins over "wholesale" pricing…hands-down!

(Retail customer-service manager emphasizing service to support premium pricing.)

You're too busy to worry about the "everyday details." Let me help.

(Secretary targeting an executive support position.)

The preceding examples are intentionally bold, but they get attention because they offer a benefit to the target audience. The first example offers increased sales; the second, loyal customers (who will generate repeat and referral business); and the third, a saving of time for the boss.

If you'd like a subtler introduction, here are a few conservative headlines:

Profit-Driven Manager with Strong Customer Focus

Law Enforcement Professional with Vision…Courage…Leadership

Experienced Educator—Devoted 20+ Years to the Study of Sociology and Its Cultural, Economic, Political, and Spiritual Impacts on Our Local and Global Community

What headline would appeal to your boss-to-be? Some careful study of advertising strategy and human behavior can get your creative juices flowing. Chapter 5 will help you develop your own headlines. Use them to do the following:

⁕ Focus on your key selling points.

⁕ Communicate those selling points to your audience.

You can use your "headlines" as a theme throughout your job search. Make them a common thread in your networking, cover letters, résumés, and interviewing. Table 2.2 lists four "headlines" an advertising copywriter might use in networking, cover letters, the résumé, or the interview process.

Table 2.2: Where You Can Use Your Headlines

Situation	Headline
Networking	"I'm Sheridan McKenzie and I write for a living. I specialize in success stories." *(Use of intrigue in response to the age-old inquiry, "So what do you do for a living?")*
Cover letter	Creating attention-getting, hard-selling television ads has generated millions for my clients. *(Example of a hard-hitting introductory sentence.)*
Résumé	CLIO award–winning writer featured in *Advertising Age* and *AdWeek*. *(Qualifications summary.)*
Interview	"As a top-notch agency writer, I have delivered copy and concepts that exceeded clients' marketing objectives. I can do the same for you." *(In response to the interview statement, "Tell me, in 25 words or less, why I should hire you.")*

A real benefit to preparing your résumé is that none of your prep work will go to waste. Every minute you put into it can be used throughout the networking, job search, and interview process. More important, the process will add to your sense of accomplishment and, best of all, your confidence! You'll need every ounce you can muster as you launch your job search.

Visual Appeal

Most of us think of visuals as pictures. For the purposes of designing your résumé, I'll use the word *visual* to refer to overall *eye appeal*. It takes just three to four seconds to decide whether the "look" of a résumé has eye appeal. The key to eye appeal is using classic design elements—with consistency! Inconsistency in design (also referred to as formatting) makes for an ugly-duckling résumé, and ugly-duckling résumés are often passed over for those with swan status.

Consistency Worked for Javier

Magic

Can you find 10 or more design inconsistencies in the following example? Some are more obvious than others.

Tip To spot inconsistencies, look for use of bold, underlining, bullets, tab sets/indentations, full versus left justification of text, and so on.

Inconsistent Formatting	Consistent Formatting

ADMINISTRATION: Directed the production and control of administrative and personnel programs. Managed $256K operating budget. Trained and supervised staff of 45.
• Reduced error processing rate from 75% to 1.2%.
• Negotiated discounts to achieve 64% savings (valued at $1,685,000) in travel expenses.
 	
• Obtained highest possible ratings on internal audit, reversing 3-year history of failure to pass.
PERSONNEL: Managed generalist functions including staffing, training, benefits and compensation, records management, and employee assistance programs.
  ·   Turned around personnel support operations from last to #1-ranking division among 26.
 	
  ·   Resolved staffing issues which reduced delays in filling vacancies from 2 weeks to 2 days.
  ·   Raised manning levels from 63% to 89.9% (above standard).
 	
CUSTOMER SERVICE:
•   Selected to revitalize a foundering Reserve Personnel Support Desk.
•   Implemented programs which transformed "a mediocre operation into a source of pride" for the division.
 	
  ·   *Slashed time to complete relocation process from 45 to 2 working days (standard is 5).*
	ADMINISTRATION: Directed the production and control of administrative and personnel programs. Managed $256K operating budget. Trained and supervised staff of 45.
	
	• Reduced error processing rate from 75% to 1.2%.
	• Negotiated discounts to achieve 64% savings (valued at $1.6 million) in travel expenses.
	• Obtained highest possible ratings on internal audit, reversing 3-year history of failure to pass.
	
	PERSONNEL: Managed generalist functions including staffing, training, benefits and compensation, records management, and employee assistance programs.
	
	• Turned around personnel support operations from last to #1-ranking division among 26.
	• Resolved staffing issues which reduced delays in filling vacancies from 2 weeks to 2 days.
	• Raised manning levels from 63% to 89.9% (above standard).
	
	CUSTOMER SERVICE: Selected to revitalize a foundering Reserve Personnel Support Desk.
	
	• Implemented programs which transformed "a mediocre operation into a source of pride" for the division.
	• Slashed time to complete relocation process from 45 to 2 working days (standard is 5).

Consistent formatting for Javier's résumé not only improved its eye-appeal, but also sped up his transition from the military to the private sector.

In some résumés, you can also draw in your reader by using an image they can relate to, such as a small graphic that represents your industry or profession.

Using a Graphic Worked for Jennifer

Jennifer, a recent graduate, used the graphic of a mortar and pestle for her pharmaceutical sales search. The graphic gives the impression of industry identification despite the fact that Jennifer had no experience in pharmaceutical sales. The goal statement was developed from researching Web pages of pharmaceutical companies. (The full text of Jennifer's résumé is in chapter 3 as an illustration of a three-column newsletter format.)

> *Goal: Pharmaceutical sales position with a research-driven organization committed to manufacturing and marketing products that preserve and improve the quality of human life.*

Visual appeal is a *huge* factor in successful résumé design. Consistent formatting and use of a tasteful graphic can help accomplish the first step in the employer's "buying" process: Get your reader's attention! Chapter 8 equips you with the complete "how-to's" on design, layout, and tweaking of format for maximum visual appeal. Don't miss this chapter. But now, on to Step 2 in the buying process: capturing the reader's interest.

Step 2: How to Capture Your Reader's Interest

In real estate, it's *location, location, location.* The value of a property is based on where it's located. My husband and I own a 1940s home with what some people consider loads of charm—arched doorways, shiny hardwood floors, ice-cube brick accents, panel doors, and a picture window overlooking the garden. It's located in a nice and relatively safe neighborhood (but I guess no place would qualify as *absolutely* safe these days). The neighborhood just a half mile north of us boasts "preferred" schools, upscale shopping within walking distance, and lower crime rates. The result: Homes of quality and character equal to ours sell for double or more. Location, location, location.

> *Tip* Positioning information is *the* critical element in capturing the reader's interest. If you don't deliver the goods at the visual center of the page, you've lost the reader.

In résumé writing, it's *position, position, position.* Unless your key information is seen, regardless of its merit, it won't have value. You may be the indisputable, undeniable, hands-down best candidate for the position, but if the evidence to prove it requires your reader to have the investigative skills of Sherlock Holmes, or (my favorite) Hercule Poirot, forget it.

> *Tip* It is your job—not the reader's—to prove that you fit the position to a *T.* Organize your material in such a way that the reader cannot miss your key selling points.

Later in the book, we'll walk through the steps of *what* you should write. First, however, let's focus on *where* you should position your strongest information—your heavy artillery, if you will.

Selling Points—Front and Center

Art directors at advertising agencies pay careful attention to designing ad layouts, and you should too. Remember what the preceding primer on advertising taught you? The headline's job is to do this:

GET ATTENTION

To get attention, the headline should focus on your product's single strongest benefit. A common mistake people make in résumé writing is waiting too late to list their most impressive accomplishments. Suppose that your best accomplishment is buried in your reference to an employer from several years ago. The reader might need to wade through 7½ inches of text before seeing that accomplishment. Will it be seen before the 10-second screening is up? Without hitting hard at the beginning, you're gambling that the reader will read far enough to see your best point. A better strategy is to place your strongest selling points at the visual center of the page.

Where's the Center of the Page?

It may seem obvious. Nonetheless, take a break from reading and try this quick exercise. It will show you where the "visual center" of the page really is. You'll need two pieces of paper, a ruler, and your thumbnail.

1. Take two pieces of paper, standard size, 8½ by 11 inches.

2. Fold one sheet in half (top to bottom).

3. Fold the other in thirds (a trifold), as you would for a regular business-size envelope.

4. Give both of the papers good creases, using your thumbnail.

5. Now unfold the papers.

The first paper, with just the one fold, will show you where the vertical center of the page is. The second paper, the trifold, will give you the visual center of the page. It's where the upper fold was made. For résumé-design purposes, you're interested in the visual center of the page. This is where the reader's eye will typically stop *first*. This is where you should pack your punch!

Obviously, it will be difficult to fit much on the exact line where your thumbnail made the uppermost crease. So, take out your ruler. Measure approximately 1 inch above the crease and draw a horizontal line across from left to right. Now measure 1 inch below the crease. Draw a second horizontal line from left to right. This will provide you with a 2-inch-high band. Another way to find this band is to measure 2⅝ inches down from the top of the page (mark it off) and then add another 2 inches from that point. The following example is what your paper should look like:

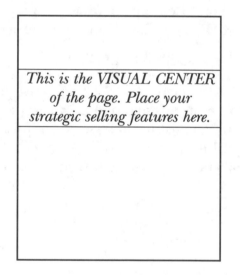

This is the VISUAL CENTER of the page. Place your strategic selling features here.

This formula is not a magic measurement, but it will give you an idea of where you should place strategic information.

A Visual-Center Strategy Worked for Sean

The following example illustrates how the visual-center technique helped an applicant earn an interview with an employer that had previously screened him out. Sean, a construction-management professional, was with a company that was headed south, and not in the geographic sense.

Despite Sean's accomplishments, market factors beyond his control led corporate execs to close the Boston office. Sean was working with a headhunter who presented Sean's résumé for a business-development position. The company said it wasn't interested.

Sean faxed me the résumé he had been using. He knew that his "better" material was buried toward the bottom third of his résumé, but he wasn't sure how to overcome this. I suggested a number of changes, including a qualifications section (called Key Accomplishments/Values Offered) with subheadings such as Strategic Planning and Profit Performance. The *Before* (résumé 2.1) and *After* (résumé 2.2) versions are shown next.

Sean tried again with the employer that had turned him down. He got the interview, and he also got several others, which eventually presented even better opportunities.

Résumé 2.1: Before

SEAN L. ROBERTS
24 Cortolla Drive
Cape Anne, MA 01456
(508) 456-6543 sroberts@email.com

BREADTH OF EXPERIENCE:

- Project Development
- Lead Generation Proposals
- Private/Public Sector & Developers
- Preconstruction & Construction Management
- Project Management
- Negotiations

CAREER DEVELOPMENT:

[year-present] NATIONAL CONTRACTORS - *Business Development Manager.* Directed business development and pre-construction estimating in New England states; worked on projects for major universities; worked on pre-construction for Boston Memorial Hospital; was responsible for marketing budget and profit.

[year-year] BIOTECH BUILDING INCORPORATED - *General Manager.* Responsibility is to capture new business for the New England region. Involved in the overview for construction operation Biotech had under contract. Over 200 million dollars of correction work under contract. Had responsibility for design/build project as well as conventional bid award. Had total responsibility for profit and loss.

[year-year] NATIONAL BUILDING CORPORATION - *Business Development Manager.* Responsibilities included business development and management of projects from inception to completion. From ground zero; secured 128 million dollars in new contracts in region.

[year-year] INTERNATIONAL CONSTRUCTORS - *Business Development Manager.* Directed all marketing efforts within northern portion of state. Marketing and Sales effort included 80 million dollar Major Medical Office Building and Ambulatory Care Center and stadium project at Major University.

[year-year] WALLEN CONSTRUCTION - *Business Development Manager.* Was responsible for marketing, airports and airlines, consisted of new terminal at Logan International Airport; projects at Dallas/Ft. Worth, St. Louis Terminal, and Seattle's Delta Terminal. Was involved in design/build project along with mechanical estimating and preconstruction services.

EDUCATION

Executive M.B.A., Finance / Marketing -- University of Southern California (USC)
B.S.M.E. -- University of California, Los Angeles (UCLA)

AFFILIATIONS

A.I.A., Health Care Forum
S.M.P.S. (Past President)
I.S.P.E.
I.F.M.A.

Résumé 2.2: After

SEAN L. ROBERTS

(508) 456-6543 — sroberts@email.com

GENERAL MANAGER / VICE PRESIDENT

Heavy Commercial Construction — Airports, Hospitals, R&D, Education

KEY ACCOMPLISHMENTS . . . VALUE OFFERED

Strategic Planning:	Envisioned business initiatives to <u>earn record profits, capturing returns of 30%</u> or better for companies with historically stagnant performance. Led process to craft short and long-range strategic plans; comprehensive experience in marketing, finance, operations, estimating, engineering, bonding, etc.
Profit Performance:	Delivered approximately <u>$10 million in additional profit through value-added engineering</u>. Focused on developing alternative, like-type systems and cost-effective construction methods without compromising design intentions.
Start-up Operations:	Opened several new branches in competitive markets and <u>met targets for break-even and profit performance as much as 12 months ahead of schedule</u>. Industry contacts attracted and retained "known" talent in the disciplines of estimating, construction technology, and field operations.
New Market Development:	Targeted, courted, and sustained private- and public-sector relationships, which led to <u>more than $1 billion in new business</u> over career. Laid groundwork for new players in New England market to gain status as qualified bidder and land negotiated projects.
Negotiations / Troubleshooting:	Maintained <u>litigation-free record</u> for claims throughout career. Paired business savvy with technical expertise to avoid costly disputes. Corporate troubleshooter for turnaround of problem projects (e.g., averted $500,000 loss on environmentally sensitive project).

EXPERIENCE SUMMARY

Business Development Manager   [year-Present]
National Contractors, Boston

Built sales from $30 million to $50 million in less than 2 years. Negotiated $750,000 in additional revenue on sports complex through value-added engineering. Led turnaround of complex biotech project.

General Manager   [year-year]
Biotech Building Incorporated, Hartford

Recruited to lead BBI's entry into New England's negotiated market with direct accountability for operations, planning, finance, marketing, and general management decisions. Delivered revenue growth above target and recouped start-up costs ahead of schedule amid volatile market conditions.

Business Development Manager   [year-year]
National Building Corporation; International Constructors; Wallen Construction, New York

Key in taking companies to record sales and profits. Delivered 130% increase ($114 million) in revenue and 30% increase in profit at NBC; brought in $125+ million in new business for Int'l Constructors (from no client list); quadrupled sales from approx. $50 million to $200 million at Wallen. (Details and prior career history available.)

EDUCATION, AFFILIATIONS

Executive M.B.A., Finance / Marketing — University of Southern California (USC)
B.S.M.E. — University of California, Los Angeles (UCLA)
Affiliations — A.I.A., Health Care Forum, S.M.P.S. (Past President), I.S.P.E., I.F.M.A.

■ 24 Cortolla Drive ■ Cape Anne, MA 01456 ■

Place Supporting Information Below the Visual Center

Use the area immediately below the visual center of the page for supporting or secondary information. If you still have your ruler out, this measurement is the four-inch horizontal band of space from approximately 4⅝ to 8⅝ inches down the page.

Don't be misled by the words *supporting information*. I am not saying that you should relegate filler material to this area of the résumé. To the contrary, you can and should include accomplishments and contributions here. You've already caught your readers' attention by packing great copy at the visual center of the page. They have a vested interest in reading on and learning what makes you uniquely able to meet their needs. Reward them in their quest.

Magic

Using Supporting Material Worked for Veronica

Veronica wrote the following paragraph. Look closely for the 11-word phrase that indicates her accomplishments as regional manager.

Regional Manager:

Responsible for operation of Dallas and Fort Worth facilities; broker of auto salvage for major insurance companies. Develop and monitor operational budgets; surpassed company goals in sales and service while decreasing operational costs. Develop and organize biweekly auction sales. Client development and ongoing services. Recruit, train, evaluate, and supervise staffs in Dallas and Fort Worth offices. Report directly to company vice president.

Did you find it? Good job. Now, write the accomplishment on the blank line below the job description:

Regional Manager:

Responsible for operation of Dallas and Fort Worth facilities; broker of auto salvage for major insurance companies. Develop and monitor operational budgets. Develop and organize biweekly auction sales. Client development and ongoing services. Recruit, train, evaluate, and supervise staffs in Dallas and Fort Worth offices. Report directly to company vice-president.

Accomplishments:

_____

It's amazing how repositioning information can improve your résumé. Veronica's accomplishment now stands out simply by separating it from her daily responsibilities and introducing it with the brief heading "Accomplishments." It gives it a fresh look, sort of like rearranging the furniture in your living room.

Skimmable Material Goes at the Bottom of the Page

Your readers will rarely take the time to read a block of thick, paragraph-formatted information at the very bottom of the résumé—at least not on the first read. So make it easy on them. Reserve your final 1 to 1½ inches of the page for list-driven material—that is, information that lends itself to a listing of items rather than full-sentence descriptions. Categories such as Education, Training, Affiliations, Travel, and Computer Skills are good candidates for lists.

Magic

A List Worked for Carmen

The following *Before* text was reformatted for easier reading:

Before

COMMUNITY INVOLVEMENT
The Volunteer League is an international nonprofit, community service and leadership training organization. Member of the Board of Directors for eight years. Served as president twice, with the ultimate responsibility for operations, achievements and morale of the membership. Served as Vice-President and Projects Board Chairman, Nominating Chairman, Membership Chairman, Chairman of Volunteer of the Year Award Community Luncheon, Fashion Show Chairman, and Chairman of Annual Sponsor Dinner. Attended training and leadership conferences the past six consecutive years. Alumni Advisor to the Board of Directors.

After

COMMUNITY INVOLVEMENT (partial list)

The Volunteer League (international service organization; local chapter is 400 members strong):

Board of Directors	Nominating Chairman
Alumni Board Advisor	Membership Chairman
President (2 terms)	Volunteer-of-the-Year Chairman
Vice-President	Tri-County Fashion Show Chairman

National training and leadership conferences in:

Atlanta	Dallas	San Diego
Chicago	Philadelphia	San Francisco

Step 3: How to Create Desire for Your Product—You!

You've passed the first and second benchmarks in the advertising sequence: You've got your reader's attention and you've generated an interest in you. Your next move is to create desire.

Desire is created when you

- Show why the employer needs you.
- Show how *you* can satisfy the need.
- Prove *your* superiority in fulfilling the need.

When your effort to create desire is persuasive, the buyer (your boss-to-be) will want to "own" the product (your services).

Why You Buy

Your decision to buy a product is driven by different needs and wants, such as the following:

- Prestige
- Security
- Convenience
- Comfort
- Fun
- Health
- Greed
- Guilt
- Vanity

Here's a list of things I've spent my discretionary income on recently and why.

Item Purchased	Motivation to Buy
Black corduroy jumper	Fun (plus the sale price) Vanity (My husband tells me I look "young" in it!)
Haircut	Vanity (and comfort—it drives me crazy when my bangs get in my eyes.)
Espresso/cappuccino maker	Prestige, convenience, and a little greed (Now I don't have to pay four bucks for a quad-shot espresso at Starbucks. Only 20 more and the thing'll be paid for!)

It's interesting to stop and really think about what motivates us to spend. Take out your checkbook and look over your recent purchases. In the chart that follows, list in the left column a few items that you have bought in the past month or so. Review the preceding list of buying motivators (prestige, security, convenience, and so on) and identify what prompted you to buy. You might have buying motivators that aren't on the list. And, just as I found, you might have more than one buying motivator per purchase.

Item Purchased	Your Motivation to Buy

Why Employers Buy

Employers also have motivations to "buy." Among them are the following:

- Make money.
- Save money.
- Save time.
- Make work easier.
- Solve a specific problem.
- Be more competitive.
- Build relationships/an image.
- Expand business.
- Attract new customers.
- Retain existing customers.

Finding your boss-to-be's "buying motivators" might take some digging. Research the Internet, industry publications, company newsletters, and annual reports. Call friends in the industry. Network online. Interview company employees, customers, or competitors. In short, develop a list of specific needs and interests the company has; then address those needs in your résumé or cover letter. When researching, categorize your findings according to these TOP issues:

- **T**rends—the company's five-year financial trends, strategic direction, and industry trends
- **O**pportunities—new ideas on the drawing board and company priorities
- **P**roblems/**P**rojects—competition or challenges that are keeping the organization from being as productive or profitable as possible— projects the company needs help implementing.

This information will be critical in your networking and interviewing.

> *Tip* Don't overlook chemistry when it comes to buying motivators. Hiring managers (or their computer systems) may screen initially on competencies, but final decisions will factor heavily on chemistry. Include character traits or other personal branding elements that hint of positive chemistry and a good organizational cultural fit.

Use the next chart to begin thinking of the specific needs employers have that you can meet. Jot these down in the left column. In the right column, select a corresponding buying motivator from the preceding list. This exercise can help you get into an employer-focused mindset.

Employer's TOP Issues	Motivation to Buy

Both sides win when you address *buying motivators* in your résumé. Your boss-to-be will get the company's needs met: problems solved and profits realized. And you'll get your needs met: You'll be employed, appreciated, and paid more!

Addressing Buying Motivators Worked for Mario

Magic

Mario heard that DataSafe Company was growing by leaps and bounds. The company specialized in data security and disaster recovery. He'd read about the company in the Business section of the newspaper. (This is a great source of job leads. If you're on the prowl for a new job and haven't been reading the *Wall Street Journal* or local business paper, get to the library today and check out back issues.) A star salesman, Mario wanted to be part of the action with this local company that had made *Fortune's* list of fastest-growing companies.

Mario made three calls: one to an employee in the company, one to a customer, and one to a competitor of the company. Asking a few pointed questions, he found out what the hot buttons were for DataSafe: territory expansion and product launches. Although he had extensive experience in both areas, his résumé didn't show it. The following section shows how rewriting just a few of his accomplishments homed in on his boss-to-be's needs.

Before

> ➤ Managed geographic region from Stockton to Bakersfield.

> ➤ Negotiated contracts where TelTech served as exclusive supplier.

> ➤ Managed campaigns for three new products.

After

☑ **Customer Conversion:** Persuaded 15 major accounts to sign exclusivity contracts that generated more than $700,000 in annual sales.

☑ **Product Launch:** Orchestrated introductory campaigns for three new products, gaining market share ratings as high as 70% and shattering competitor's control of market.

☑ **Territory Expansion:** Recruited to open new 300-square-mile central California territory; met 12-month sales goals in less than nine months.

Notice how Mario introduces his accomplishments with words that specifically address his target company's needs. He also uses check boxes instead of more traditional bullets. They give the reader the subconscious impression that "yes, this candidate has everything I need."

Prove Your Superiority

Remember that every candidate must answer the employer's question of "Why hire you over someone else?" You must prove your superiority! This is most easily done through the use of comparison—with others on your team, with other regions or districts in your company, with your company's competitors, or with the industry standard.

Caution When comparing yourself with others on your team or within your company, be careful! You don't want to sound like a narcissistic Lone Ranger in a climate that worships the consummate team player. Use phrases like "contributed to company successes in revenue growth, profit enhancement" or "member of team that delivered threefold growth in sales."

Asserting Superiority Without Put-Downs

Magic Liz had interviewed for a sales position in the DME (durable medical equipment) industry. During the battery of interview questions from the interviewer, she was asked, "Where do you rank among your sales team?"

Liz's response was, "Well, I don't have a ranking, since I'm the company's only full-time sales associate."

After the interview, Liz reviewed her handwritten notes. She realized her response to the "where do you rank" question could have been stronger. So, in her thank-you-for-the-interview, follow-up letter, she redeemed this weak response by writing the following:

> During our conversation, you inquired about my sales ranking. As I mentioned, the present structure at Dantron does not lend itself to ranking since I am the branch's only full-time sales associate. However, I did some research and found a few numbers that will confirm my performance as a top producer.
>
> The average sales production for the two sales associates who preceded me was $27,000 per month. As of January, my monthly average was $39,000—<u>a 44% increase in sales activity and a record for the branch.</u>
>
> Branch performance is, of course, a team effort. At the same time, it is driven by individual sales. Again, because I was the branch's sole full-time sales associate, my contributions were critical in improving performance scores across the board last year. For instance
>
> - Irvine tied for first place in the gross profit percentage category.
>
> - The branch generated 100% of sales to budget in a year when the figures for promotions and other expense categories more than tripled.
>
> - Most important, we finished first among eight offices for pretax income to budget.

Notice how Liz demonstrates her superiority through comparison with former sales associates and with other branches without stepping on anyone's toes. She dispels any unvoiced thoughts of the Lone Ranger syndrome by weaving in the sentence, "Branch performance is, of course, a team effort." She also addresses another of the interviewer's buying motivators. The interviewer told Liz her DME company was "driven by sales." Liz had taken good notes in the interview, so she "fed" this point back to the interviewer with the sentence "At the same time, it is driven by sales."

> *Tip* If you're like most of us, you'll walk out of the interview wishing you had phrased something differently. Or, two hours later, you'll remember a great example that would have perfectly illustrated your skills. The follow-up letter is a great place to polish responses that might have been rough or lacking during the interview.

Step 4: Call to Action

You've caught attention, captured interest, and created desire. You're at the last step in the sales process—*ask for the order.* Obviously, at this juncture it's pretty hard to ask for the job. What you'll want to accomplish, however, is to get your reader to *take action*—any step that will bring you more face-to-face time to create trust so that you can eventually "ask for the sale."

Magic

Getting the Reader to Act Worked for William

Many job hunters close their cover letters with something along the lines of this:

> Thank you for the opportunity to be considered for the Product Engineer position.

Much more effective is the technique that William, a production engineer, used. Here's the closing paragraph on his cover letter:

> Your schedule permitting, I'd like just a few minutes to show you some prototypes. The technology I developed was successful in solving issues similar to what ABC Company faces. I'll be in the area next week and will call on Monday, the 21st, to see what time might work best with your schedule.

William persuasively, yet politely, wrangled himself an audience with the plant manager who, by the way, cleared a 2 p.m. slot to look at William's prototypes.

Magic

Adding a Pager with an 800 Number

Make it easy for your reader to take action. Make sure your telephone number is easy to see. If you're relocating for your next job, consider getting a pager or telephone with an 800 number to overcome any employer concern about an area code that seems like it's from a strange and distant land. Or use a friend's telephone as a message number to give the impression you're serious about relocating.

Ross had recently married. His wife, Zena, lived in San Francisco. He lived and worked in Fresno. A seven-hour, round-trip commute is not terribly conducive to a healthy marriage. Ross was looking for a new job in the Bay Area. Simply revising his *Before* résumé heading helped to generate callbacks on three of the next five résumés he sent:

Before

ROSS SIMOLIAN

1442 East Sunnyside
Fresno, CA 93727
(559) 222-7474

After

ROSS SIMOLIAN

1437 12th Avenue #1
San Francisco, CA 94122
(415) 222-7474 ~ Pager: (800) 222-7474
ross@abcde.com

The address and telephone were his wife's apartment in the city, and the pager made it easy for employers to reach him. Your accessibility may mean the difference between getting an interview or not.

The quote that introduces this chapter asserts that advertising is not a science but an art. I believe that the art of persuading can be likened to science. Just as in chemistry, where mixing certain compounds produces specific results, incorporating time-tested advertising formulas into your résumé can get employers' attention, capture their interest, and create desire in your candidacy. When used thoughtfully and tastefully, advertising formulas can produce the desired outcome—an interview with your boss-to-be.

The following checklist will help ensure you're following the "AIDA" (Attention, Interest, Desire, Action) advertising formula in your résumé and cover letter.

What-2-Do Checklist

☐ **Catch Attention**
Create a lead or headline that creates chemistry and is in sync with the employer's most pressing needs.

Ensure visual appeal.

- Use classic design elements with consistency.
- Experiment with a tasteful industry-related graphic.

☐ **Capture Interest**
Position selling points (especially numbers-driven accomplishments and your core brand elements) at the visual center of the page.

Position supporting material in the middle to lower range of the page.

Position skimmable list material at the bottom of the page.

☐ **Create Desire**

Show or address some need.

Satisfy the need.

Prove your superiority in fulfilling the need.

☐ **Call for Action**

Offer some enticement for the employer to meet you (work samples, ideas, and so on).

Ask for the interview; politely suggest a time frame if your work schedule takes you out of town frequently.

Make it easy for your reader to contact you.

Top 10 Résumé Strategy Tips

1. Write like an advertising copywriter, not an autobiographer.

2. Connect with the employer by targeting positions that capture elements of your Magic F.I.T.™ (see appendix A). These positions should be consistent with your career brand. Who you are should align closely with what you want to do.

3. Zero in on what the employer needs by reviewing position postings, networking (in person or online), or conducting research or informational interviews. These needs can be categorized as TOP issues: Trends, Opportunities, Problems/Projects.

4. Substantiate your ability to do the job and meet the needs by including numbers-driven results. Make an economic case for hiring you!

5. Omit extraneous information—employers looking for a sales professional will rarely care that your degree is in Home Economics (list the Bachelor's degree but not the subject area).

6. Create multiple résumés for multiple targets—one résumé will suffice for the targets of sales and business development; two résumés are appropriate for unrelated targets, such as sales and procurement.

(continued)

(continued)

7. <u>Position critical information</u> (such as keywords and accomplishments) <u>in the first third of the page.</u> Briefly summarize or omit dated information.

8. <u>Prioritize the sentences</u> that comprise your job descriptions—place the most relevant information first and less relevant information last.

9. <u>Spin information to be as transferable as possible.</u> If an employer needs someone who can make electronic widgets and your background involves only mechanical widgets, refer to your experience with "widgets" rather than "mechanical widgets."

10. Use your résumé wisely—it plays a supporting role and is not the star of your job search show. Too often, job seekers hide behind résumés, thinking that if they just mail or e-mail enough résumés, a job will materialize. Yes, it's appropriate to e-mail résumés or post them on your target companies' Web sites. But you must <u>combine these activities with extreme networking.</u> Humans make hiring decisions—get face-to-face with employers and show them you can meet their needs. This will give you an edge over your competition!

Chapter 3

How to Choose the Most Flattering Format

"The only place where success comes before work is in the dictionary.

—Vidal Sassoon
American Hairstylist

W hat do astronauts and Goldilocks have in common? Most of us know the predicament Goldilocks faced. Foods were either too hot, too cold; beds were either too hard, too soft. The gal had a tough time finding what was "just right" for her. Mir, the Russian space station that partnered with NASA, was fraught with problems, from mechanical failures to ill-fitting space suits. One of the U.S. astronauts faced the "Goldilocks dilemma" as well. Of the two suits he had, one was too tight. He couldn't even squeeze into it to make do. The other suit was too large. The sleeves, which were several inches too long, would prevent him from handling the ship's controls with any degree of precision (sort of an important skill in his profession; the ramifications could mean never coming home again).

Moral of the story: When your clothes don't fit, you can't perform. And if your résumé format doesn't fit, it won't perform for you either. Armed with the information in this chapter, you'll solve a potential Goldilocks dilemma and be able to perform. You'll learn what formats are available— the tried-and-true ones, along with a few new twists. You'll learn each format's points and pitfalls, as well as which works best for certain career challenges, why they work, and how to choose one that fits you to a T.

Two Tried-and-True Winning Formats: Chronological and Functional

Ninety-nine percent of business résumés fall into two distinct genres: chronological and functional. I'll lump the other one percent into a "creative" category, reserved for those artistic gurus who have been bestowed with extra right-brain gray matter.

If you're in a hurry (your résumé has to be in a hiring manager's hands by 8 a.m. tomorrow), take the quick quiz that follows. It will give you an idea of which of the two main formats (chronological or functional) to use. *If the indicator in the first column is true for you, place a check mark in the shaded box. If it is not true for you, place a check mark in the unshaded box.* Although your situation might not be clear-cut, limit your responses to one check mark per row.

One-Minute Quick Quiz

Indicator	Chronological	Functional
Strong career progression over past five-plus years, seeking position similar to current or most recent position	■	☐
Impressive employers (large, strong name recognition; favorable reputation; Fortune 500 companies)	■	☐
Executive or management candidate	■	☐
Working through executive recruiter for your job search	■	☐
International job search	■	☐
Conservative field or industry (law, accounting, government)	■	☐
Reentering the workforce (same career) after a several-year hiatus	■	☐
Reentering the workforce (different career) after a several-year hiatus	☐	■
Changing careers (new function, say, from secretarial to sales)	☐	■
Changing fields (same function, new industry)	■	■

(continued)

(continued)

Indicator	Chronological	Functional
Leaving the military, performing similar job function	■	☐
Leaving the military, pursuing different job function	☐	■
Lots of volunteer experience related to your chosen field	☐	■
New graduate with experience related to chosen field	■	☐
New graduate with experience *unrelated* to chosen field	☐	■
Performed very similar responsibilities repeatedly for past employers and looking for similar position	☐	■
Unstable work history (changed jobs too often, lots of gaps in employment timeline, spouse relocated frequently, and so on)	☐	■
"Overqualified" and looking for less responsibility	☐	■
"Seasoned citizen" with extensive work history looking for less responsibility	☐	■
Totals		

Now add the check marks for both the Chronological and Functional columns and place the total for each column in the Totals row. If the number of "chronologicals" outweighs the "functionals," you should probably use a chronological format. If the reverse is true, and you have more "functional" responses, consider presenting your skills in a functional format.

> *Tip* Weigh the pros and cons of each format when determining which to use. If you're a candidate who might go either way, write both versions; then "test market" the résumé with friends or colleagues who have human resources backgrounds or hiring experience. Honest feedback from colleagues can be invaluable in determining the best presentation for your résumé.

Remember, this quiz is a simplified formula to use when you want to crank out a résumé in about an hour. For those of you with inquiring minds who want to know the strategy behind *why* you're using a particular format (remember, knowledge is power), you'll benefit from reading the rest of the chapter. In it, you'll learn that, beyond the chronological and functional formats, you can choose from many other format variations, one of which will suit your unique mix of career experiences. You'll also be encouraged when you see how these different formats solved a variety of professional problems for some average people and some not-so-average people.

One Page or Two?

Résumé length should be determined by several factors, including the number of years of experience you possess, your position level, and your industry (for instance, résumés for educators are typically longer than résumés for sales professionals). Use this general rule of thumb for deciding on length:

- One page for new graduates or people with 5 to 10 years of experience.

- Two pages for management-level candidates and those with more than 10 years of experience.

- Two to three pages for "C"-level executives (such as chief executive officer, chief operating officer, or chief financial officer).

The Chronological Format

Just as its name implies, the chronological format offers a chronology—a historical timeline—of your work experience. The distinguishing characteristic is that descriptions of what you did and how well you did it are grouped together with the employer information.

The bulk of the résumé is devoted to this Experience section, also known as your Employment History. In most cases, your most recent employer is listed first, and your least recent employer is listed last. Other sections, such as Education and Affiliations, generally follow the Experience section.

The chronological format wins "The People's Choice Award." Why? Plain and simple. Employers prefer it! In economic parlance, the buyer (your prospective employer)—who usually holds the upper hand in the supply-demand model—can better evaluate what the seller (you, the candidate) has to offer. Most hiring managers have an innate curiosity about what you've done and where you've done it. A logical, straightforward chronological format answers their questions.

Magic

A Chronological Format Worked for David

Because the chronological is the most common format, you're probably familiar with its look. Nonetheless, check out David Dillingham's résumé for a *Before* and *After* of a standard chronological format (see Résumés 3.1 and 3.2). Compare how bullets are used in the *Before* and *After* résumés. This sales tool worked for David, landing him a job with a leading textbook publisher.

Points

Many! The chronological format is easily digested and won't raise suspicions that you are attempting to hide vocational skeletons, such as a former conviction as a serial job hopper. A chronological format's most obvious advantages are these:

- Showcases a progression of increasingly responsible positions, especially preferred by executive recruiters and decision-making boards for management and top-tier executive slots.

- Demonstrates that you are qualified to take the next step in your career.

- Highlights impressive employers who will add weight to your credentials because of their name recognition, comprehensive training programs, or strong market position.

- Answers the employer's question of whether your work history has been stable.

Pitfall

The chronological format really puts you under the microscope and can make you feel a bit naked. I liken it to wearing skimpy spandex to the gym: If you're not in great shape, it will show every roll and dimple.

Résumé 3.1: Before

David D. Dillingham
4321 South Johnstone Boulevard
Laguna Niguel, CA. 92321
(714) 455–4431

PUBLISHING WORK EXPERIENCE:

International Publishing - Los Angeles, CA
Careers Division, Marketing Manager 10/00 to Present
Children's Division, Field Sales Representative 8/99 to 9/00

- Responsible for Marketing Twenty-five Million Dollar Careers List
- Maintain Correspondence between Authors, Editors and Sales Force
- Hire, Train and Manage Marketing Assistants
- Developed Marketing Materials, Sales Tools and Advertisements for Sales Force and Consumers
- Service Universities, State Colleges, Community Colleges, Proprietary Schools, Post Secondary Vocational Technical Schools and Bookstores
- Demonstrate Product through Personal Visits, Book Fairs and Trade Shows
- Plan Travel Itineraries, Yearly Budgets and Forecasting of Sales Goals
- Develop, Maintain, and Service Accounts
- Annually Obtained and Increased Sales Goals

Eastern Publishing Company- New York, NY
Field Sales Representative 6/96 to 7/99

- Represented Mathematics List to Universities, State Colleges and Retail Bookstores
- Set Appointments, Processed Orders, and Provided Customer Service
- Responsible for Administrative Tasks, Filing, and Documentation of all Data
- Prepared Mailings, Handled all Correspondence

Harcourt Publishing Company- San Francisco, CA
Inside Sales Representative 1/91 to 5/96

- Sold Computer Science, Physics, Mathematics, Science and Nursing Textbooks
- Contacted Accounts via Telemarketing
- Uncovered Potential Reviewers and Authors
- Increased Territory 30%

EDUCATION:

B.S. Degree in Political Science, University of California- Berkeley, 1991
A.A. Degree, The Community College, El Cajon, California

APPLICABLE SKILLS:

PowerPoint, Word, Access, Excel, WordPerfect, Lotus Notes, Internet Explorer, Employee Appraiser, Professional Selling Skills Training (PSS), Los Angeles County Aids Project Volunteer

Résumé 3.2: After

DAVID D. DILLINGHAM

4321 Johnstone Boulevard   (714) 555-5555
Laguna Niguel, CA 92321   ddd234@excite.com

SALES & MARKETING
Publishing Industry

SALES & MARKETING EXPERIENCE

MARKETING MANAGER—International Publishing, Los Angeles, CA   2000–Present

Manage marketing for $25 million careers list. Develop product strategies, marketing materials, sales tools, and advertisements for international sales force of 500. Hire, train, and manage marketing assistants. Forecast and manage operating budgets and sales goals. Personally sell to and service universities and retail booksellers. Promote product at trade shows and book fairs.

- Delivered 27% sales growth through development of innovative international marketing strategies.
- Doubled individual sales volume from $149,000 to $312,000, an unprecedented increase for territory.
- Led region of 10 reps in sales volume, achieving 22% above goal (well above company average of 8%).
- Initially challenged with turnaround of product line that had not been serviced in over a year; successfully converted key clients from primary competitor and captured new nationwide sales.

FIELD SALES REPRESENTATIVE—Eastern Publishing Company, New York, NY   1996–2000

Generated sales for Mathematics Division in seven western states and three Canadian provinces.

- Gained access to prestigious clients, such as Stanford University and UC Berkeley (previously "no see" accounts).
- Increased sales in territory that had a several-year history of stagnant sales.

INSIDE SALES REPRESENTATIVE—Harcourt Publishing Company, San Francisco, CA   1991–1996

Promoted 100+ item catalogue of computer science, physics, mathematics, science, and nursing textbooks to college bookstore market in California, Nevada, and Oregon.

- Increased territory sales 30% to rank #1 in division (with no prior industry knowledge).
- Researched and uncovered potential reviewers and new authors.

EDUCATION & TRAINING

Bachelor of Science, Political Science—University of California, Berkeley   1991
Professional Selling Skills Training (PSS)

COMPUTER SKILLS

MS Office (PowerPoint, Word, Excel, Access), WordPerfect, Lotus Notes, MSIE, Employee Appraiser

◆ ◆ ◆

The Functional Format

A functional résumé relies on categorical, skills-based sections to demonstrate your qualifications for a particular job. Company names, employment dates, and position titles are either deemphasized or intentionally omitted.

I'm convinced the functional format was invented for my husband. In the course of a decade or so, he had lived and worked in seven different states, with as many different jobs, including cross-country ski instructor, heating and air-conditioning mechanic, interdenominational minister in two national parks, grocery bagger, camp manager, and environmental impact analyst. His tangential career path (prior to settling down with the girl of his dreams!) definitely didn't lend itself to a chronological presentation. (He has since parlayed all those experiences into an academic career track and now uses a chronological format to catalog high school and university teaching experience.)

If your professional pilgrimage hasn't been "politically correct" either, give serious consideration to a functional format.

A Functional Format Helped Grace Get a New Life

Magic

Grace needed a change. The survivor of a messy divorce, she opted to explore other career options to give her a change of pace. After a long tenure as a classroom teacher, she wanted to pursue customer-service work in the private sector. Her new résumé is a strong example of a functional format and landed her a "fun and upbeat" job in the tourism industry. Here are Grace's *Before* and *After* résumés (see Résumés 3.3 and 3.4).

Résumé 3.3: Before

GRACE COLTERMAN

One Riverplace Parkway
Selton, Alabama 42315
(423) 413-9887

OBJECTIVE	Teacher: Elementary Education (K–8)
EDUCATION	UNIVERSITY OF ALABAMA Degree: Bachelor of Arts, Public Relations / Journalism – 1987 Honors: Dean's List; Greek Leadership Award; Outstanding College Students of America
CREDENTIAL	Multiple Subject Clear Credential – 1989

EXPERIENCE

Teaching Experience

Alton Unified School District, Alton, Alabama   9/92–Pres.
1st Grade Teacher
Plan and implement integrated curriculum in all subject areas. Utilize Project READ, a multisensory approach to reading with emphasis on phonology strategies. Applied Rebecca Sitton's Integrated Spelling & Writing program, focusing on daily writing across the curriculum. Taught core literature books using whole language approach and incorporating McCracken Reading ideas.

Mifflin Union High School, Mifflin, Alabama
3rd Grade Teacher   9/91–6/92
Applied current teaching techniques, including AIMS projects, manipulatives, writing process, and cooperative learning. Implemented the Total Reading Program, a multi-sensory phonetic reading program that emphasizes development of reading, language, and spelling skills. Developed and taught units on reptiles, Indians, and Mifflin County; integrated all curricula areas and culminated in group experiences with the entire 3rd grade. Taught segments of a Physical Education course in a pilot cooperative teaching program.

Kindergarten Teacher   9/89–6/91
Utilizing a thematic approach, created and taught lessons incorporating programs such as Math Their Way, Project AIMS, Come With Me Science, and Sunshine/Story Box with big book illustrations emphasizing whole language. Administered the Brigance testing format; gathered parent input to determine children's classroom readiness prior to new school year.

Student Teaching

Atherton School District, Atherton, Alabama
2nd Grade Teacher — Sterling Elementary School   3/89–5/89
4th Grade Teacher — McKinley Elementary School   1/89–3/89

RELATED ACTIVITIES

Alton Unified School District, Alton, Alabama
- Served on School Site Council.
- Coordinated school-wide Speech Festival and Peach Blossom Oral Interpretation and Speech Festival.
- Participated in Learning Club, a monthly group for 1st graders and their parents; program focuses on introducing math and reading activities to parents that can then be reinforced with students at home.

INTERESTS   Coaching (Cross-Country) • Public Speaking • Yearbook Publications

Résumé 3.4: After

GRACE COLTERMAN

One Riverplace Parkway
Selton, Alabama 42315

gracec@juno.com
(423) 413-9887

GOAL

Customer support position where my strengths in communications, sales, and administration will be of value.

PROFESSIONAL EXPERIENCE

COMMUNICATIONS: *Public Relations, Advertising, Training, Staff Development*

♦ *Degree in Public Relations/Journalism:* Completed comprehensive training in public relations, including advanced course work in mass communications, newswriting, editing, advertising, media, and graphic arts.

♦ *Writing/Verbal Skills:* Excellent communication skills for effective customer communications, proposals, correspondence, flyers, newsletters, internal communications, and public speaking.

♦ *Staff Development:* Successfully coordinated and implemented monthly training programs—assessed learning needs, created curriculum, presented instruction, and secured nationally recognized guest speakers.

♦ *Background as Educator:* Able to provide client-centered interactive training sessions, emphasizing practical applications for customer education and/or staff development.

SALES: *Presentations, Negotiations, Customer Relations, Event Planning, Fund-Raising*

♦ *Persuasive Communicator:* Made formal presentations to boards and decision makers; sold new program ideas and secured approval for funding. Demonstrated ability to sell varied products as "floater" for upscale retailer; generated daily sales equal to that of experienced sales associates.

♦ *Customer Relations:* Selected by management as liaison and troubleshooter to resolve concerns with coworkers, external customers, and vendors.

♦ *Event Planning:* Organized well-received special events in work and community volunteer capacities. Planned events for up to 400. Initiated fund-raising projects to offset a $250,000 reduction in state funding.

ADMINISTRATION: *Program Management, Planning, Development, Budgeting, Supervision*

♦ *Management:* Held direct accountability for planning, staffing, facilities management, and coordination of educational program with 250 enrollees and 15 instructors. Hired, placed, and evaluated certificated instructors.

♦ *Program Development:* Created successful programs (business-school partnerships, volunteerism, community outreach), from concept development through implementation at multiple sites.

♦ *Planning:* Served on cross-functional team that conducted strategic planning, developed budgets in excess of $345,000, determined programming, and ensured compliance for school site serving 650+ students.

EMPLOYMENT HISTORY

Prior experience in education as a teacher and site administrator. Excellent record with former employers, Alton Unified School District (1992–Present) and Mifflin Union School District (1989–1992).

EDUCATION

DEGREE: *Bachelor of Arts in Public Relations/Journalism—University of Alabama (1987)*

References on Request

A "Wonder Mom" Goes Back to Work

Functional résumés are often the best choice for parents entering the workforce with minimal or no paid experience. Marlene, a career mom who did an admirable job of raising three children (I speak from personal experience) used a functional format to sum up several decades of volunteer work. Her only paid experience was two years of secretarial work several decades ago.

With skills in planning, administration, and business-office operations, she now manages business affairs for a production agriculture company. My "wonder mom" was kind enough to let me present her reentry résumé (see Résumé 3.5) as an example of how to convert countless hours of volunteer service to an attractive, business-oriented presentation for employers.

Marching to New Orders

James Delano's résumé (see Résumé 3.6) displays how a career military officer can facilitate a transition to the business world. Note the emphasis on quantifiable results and supervisor quotes—both of which were gleaned from past military performance evaluations—to help fill in the full picture of James's capabilities and professionalism. All military-speak (acronyms, project names, numbered forms, and so forth) was translated to business terms.

Résumé 3.5

Marlene Britton

(555) 555-5555

target

Business Office Administration and Support

qualifications

Accounting . . . Business Office . . . Clerical

- Performed full-charge bookkeeping functions for family partnership—accounts payable, accounts receivable, payroll, payroll tax returns, and working papers for CPA preparation of federal and state returns (volunteer bookkeeper, 5 years).

- Provided secretarial support for Burroughs Corporation sales office—typed correspondence and reports, transcribed dictation, maintained files (secretary, 2 years).

- Developed and maintained a system to track invitations (1,000+), reservations, ticket sales, and deposits for annual fund-raising event (reservations chair, 5 years).

Leadership . . . Community Service

- Elected president of nonprofit guild benefiting a regional children's hospital. Directed 30-member organization in planning dinner-dance attended by 600-1,000 each year. Asked to return and serve another term as president to help revitalize organization when on the verge of disbanding—membership grew and participation increased by year's end.

- Served as adult advisor to nonprofit girls' organization. Supported girls, ages 13 to 18, in conducting monthly meetings, developing public speaking skills, and planning community service projects. Recruited and worked with adult advisory board.

- Regularly supported junior high and high school bands in practice sessions and state-wide competitions. Helped arrange fund-raisers that generated finances to send 100-member marching band to Europe for two-week tour.

- Counted on as a reliable committee member and volunteer for numerous church, school, and community service projects. Assist wherever needed (program planning, record keeping, letter writing, needlepoint and sewing projects, baking, and more).

education, computer skills

- Recent workshops in Internet navigation and research, Microsoft applications, and specialized agricultural accounting and production software. Keyboard skills: 65 w.p.m.

- College courses in accounting, business office operations, and secretarial science at Fresno State College, Fresno, California.

résumé

111 North Washoe Avenue ▪ Great Little Town, CA 91111

Résumé 3.6

JAMES P. DELANO

1344 Tippendale
Lakeside, CA 93222

(319) 234-4405
jamesd@msn.com

OBJECTIVE

QUALIFIED for mid-management administrative assignments requiring proven ability to enhance operational efficiency, affect team productivity, and maximize operating funds.

PROFESSIONAL EXPERIENCE

Twenty-year military career highlighted by promotion through increasingly responsible decision-making capacities, including Asst. Officer-in-Charge, Officer-in-Charge, and Administrator. Experience includes:

ADMINISTRATION: Directed the production and control of administrative and personnel programs. Managed $256K operating budget. Trained personnel on internal operating systems and documentation procedures. Supervised staff of up to 45. Prepared written reports and delivered oral presentations. Created and directed task force teams for special projects. Compiled and analyzed workload statistics. Computer-literate.

- Implemented revised procedures to reduce error processing rate from 75% to 1.2%.
- Negotiated discounts to achieve a 64% savings (valued at $1,685,000) in travel expenses.
- Prepared organization for annual Quality Assurance inspections; reviewer comments included "200% improvement," reversing 3-year history of failure to pass to highest attainable rate.
- Supervisor comments: "Unparalleled performance resulted in the flawless processing of all required reports, travel arrangements, 100+ enlisted evaluations, 300 personal awards, and 1,000 pay entries."

PERSONNEL/HUMAN RESOURCES: Experience includes staffing, training, discipline, records management, travel arrangements, and benefits administration. Directly responsible for staffing of three aircraft carriers (typically handled by three separate individuals) with a total of 16,500 individuals matched to 64 different position descriptions. Managed personnel support functions for 2,600-member organization.

- Turned around personnel support operations from last to #1 ranking division among 26.
- Resolved staffing issues that resulted in accurate accounting of personnel assets and reduced delays in filling vacancies.
- Successfully raised manning levels from 63% to 89.9% (above standard) in limited time constraints.

CUSTOMER SERVICE: Selected to revitalize a foundering Reserve Personnel Support Desk.

- Implemented corrective measures that transformed "a mediocre operation into a source of pride" for the division and left 95% fewer service record maintenance errors and a 65% reduction in customer traffic.
- Created innovative programs, such as a "Customer Command Quality Assurance Checklist" that reduced travel liquidation time-frames from 45 days to 1 working day (standard is 5 days).

PROFESSIONAL PROFILE: Offer well-rounded and versatile background with experience as Administrative Officer, Legal Officer, Personnel Officer, Educational Services Officer, Ship's Secretary, and Work Center Supervisor.

- In virtually every assignment, exceeded performance criteria and assumed added responsibilities.
- Comments from supervisors: "Unmatched in personal initiative"; "unlimited potential"; "his wisdom and energy inspire trust and confidence"; "the consummate professional who gets results."

▸ Continued ◂

(continued)

(continued)

JAMES P. DELANO

Page Two

CAREER HISTORY

UNITED STATES NAVY   1983–Present

Highlights include:

‣ Administrator	5/99 – Present
‣ Assistant Officer in Charge/Officer in Charge	6/95 – 5/95
‣ Personnel Officer/Educational Services Officer	10/93 – 6/95
‣ Division Officer	5/93 – 9/93
‣ Staffing Manager	9/91 – 5/93
‣ Branch Head	12/90 – 9/91
‣ Director, Administrative Services Division	12/88 – 11/90
‣ Administrative Office Supervisor	12/88 – 11/89
‣ Various Admin Personnel Positions	1983 – 1988

GLASS MANUFACTURER CO., Bath, Maine   1981–1983

‣ Sales Associate & Notary Public

EDUCATION

Coursework and seminars included: TQL/TQM . . . Management Fundamentals . . . AA/EEO . . . miscellaneous industry-related training.

HONORS (Partial List)

Navy Commendation Medal for meritorious service as Administrative Dept. Leading Chief Petty Officer; three Navy Achievement Medals; Combat Action Ribbon; five Good Conduct Awards; Air Force Outstanding Unit Award and Air Force Organizational Excellence Award; Humanitarian Service Medal; Management Excellence Award

TRAVEL

Guam
Hong Kong
Iceland
Japan
Philippines
Singapore
Thailand
Various U.S. regions

‣ **References Available** ‣

Points

Although not a cure-all for every career inadequacy, the functional format can camouflage the appearance of an unstable, unorthodox, or interrupted career caused by

- Gaps between jobs
- Job hopping
- Spouse relocation
- Typecasting
- Limited paid experience
- Returning to a career after time off for family or personal reasons
- Recent graduation with limited experience

Also a valid vehicle for conventional careers, the functional format shouldn't be associated only with "fixing" employment problems. If you belong to any of the following categories, the functional might be your best fit:

- Career specialization (performed the same responsibilities at multiple employers)
- Overqualified
- Senior citizen
- Military conversion

If your vocational hurdle is included above (from job hopping to military conversion), the skills section in chapter 5 will show you how the functional format can get you back in the race.

Pitfall

The functional format's greatest plus is also its primary pitfall. Employers know that a functional format will camouflage career glitches, thus raising the question, "What is the candidate trying to hide?" Again, refer to chapter 5 for strategies on countering this objection.

Genetic Variants of the Two Main Résumé Types

Both chronological and functional résumés have spawned a number of variations in format, some earning their own titles, such as the accomplishments format, the targeted format, the linear format, and the keyword format. Whether these warrant distinction into separate genus, phylum, and species is debatable. Is it science or semantics? Here's my take on the issue:

Alterations to the genetic makeup of a chronological or functional résumé don't necessarily make a new résumé breed.

In the final analysis, it's not critical what you call the format or how you categorize it. If it works, it's right. However, for clarification, I'll give some detail on each format variation (presented alphabetically), followed by examples. Whenever possible, *Before* examples are included to show how the candidate's résumé looked initially.

The Accomplishments Format

I like this name. It sounds so positive! However, don't think that by using this format, your *content* will be drastically different. It will simply be arranged differently. Remember what you learned just a few paragraphs ago? Play *Wheel of Fortune* with me for a minute and finish the following sentence. (I've bought you a few vowels to get you started.)

***Every* business résumé should include**

A __ __ __ __ __ __ I __ __ __ E __ __ __

Hard-driving copy that shows your track record with past employers will transform your résumé from a ho-hum job description to an impressive marketing piece. When your "trophies" are placed together under a separate Accomplishments heading (instead of grouping accomplishments with the associated employer), the accomplishments format materializes. Typically, the Accomplishments section follows your Objective or Qualifications Summary. Following the Accomplishments section is an employment summary, with little or no description of your responsibilities, and dates sometimes omitted.

An Accomplishments Format Worked for McKenzie

Magic

McKenzie, a buyer for a New York–based retail chain, had a great list of accomplishments, backed by verifiable factoids. By grouping the accomplishments together and placing them at the visual center of the page, she looked unbeatable on paper. See McKenzie's résumé (3.7) on the next page.

Résumé 3.7

McKenzie Johnstone

4789 Minarets Avenue
Fishkill, New York 01242

Business: 914.422.2341
Residence: 914.424.3312
Email: mckenziej@yahoo.com

Objective

Senior Buyer (Shoes/Accessories) with a regional retailer that will benefit from an impressive 18-year history of contributions to gross margin improvement, comparable store sales, and product development.

Representative Accomplishments

◆ Drove gross margins from 41.7% to 45.6% to capture record $860,000 net profit.

◆ Exceeded comparable store sales increases with 13% departmental improvement (storewide average, 1.4%).

◆ Set up and launched shoe departments for six new stores; generated comparable business increase of 15.4%.

◆ Reversed history of shoe losses, delivering overall increase of $935,000 in profit (from negative 5-figure loss).

◆ Built department volume from $6.9 million to more than $10.0 million with a 3.9% increase in gross margins.

◆ Contributed an average of 48% net profit to store's total net income.

◆ Introduced and promoted several items that earned "key item" status, a first for the department.

◆ Served on EDI Implementation Committee and Fast-Track Warehousing Committee (reduced merchandise flow through warehouse from 5 days to 48 hours).

◆ Appointed to national Buying Office Steering Committee, with extensive domestic and foreign travel for private label programs for member stores (projected sales of $80 million for shoes).

Professional History

Senior Shoe Buyer: Recruited to turn around underperforming department for $450 million retailer with 42 stores in the New England area. Exceeded all performance benchmarks as detailed above.
Clothing, Etc., New York, New York, 3/94–Present

Senior Buyer: Slated for fast-track promotion as Management Trainee, Assistant Buyer, Associate Buyer, Buyer and Senior Buyer. Instrumental in increasing sales from $2.5 million to $8.5 million during buying tenure.
Regional Retailers, Amherst, Massachusetts, 5/80–3/94

Strengths

Expertise in private label programs, multistore buying, new store launch and domestic/import buying. Accomplished in all aspects of sales promotions (ROP, direct mail, newspaper standard advertising catalog vehicles), inventory tracking, EDI reordering, vendor negotiations, and competitive pricing. Hands-on manager with skills in supervising and coaching buying staff.

Education

University of Texas: Concentration in Engineering with strong preparation in Business Finance and Marketing

Available for Relocation

Points

✳ Positions your strongest selling points front-and-center.

✳ Unearths buried accomplishments from long ago.

Pitfalls

✳ Limits the space you might use to flesh out details of your past responsibilities.

✳ Won't work as well if you're short on accomplishments or in a profession that's difficult to quantify.

The Combination Format

The most common variant of the chronological résumé is the combination résumé (sometimes referred to as a hybrid résumé). It takes this name because it combines elements of both a chronological and functional résumé.

Typically a Summary section leads off the résumé. The Summary might be quite brief, as short as two to three lines. Or it might be an introductory sentence followed by a bulleted list, as in the résumé of Helen Wolchek (see Résumé 3.8). The Summary can also be quite extensive, such as an Executive Summary that consumes nearly three-quarters of a page in a two-page résumé.

Résumé 3.8

HELEN E. WOLCHEK

3999 West Cherry Lane • Fresno, CA 93792 • (209) 406-3210

QUALIFICATIONS SUMMARY

Management professional with 20-year career distinguished by promotion to challenging multibranch assignments. Strengths:

- ❑ Staff Development & Training
- ❑ Customer Service & Client Retention
- ❑ Sales & Business Development
- ❑ Branch/District Operations Management
- ❑ Process & Controls, Cost Containment
- ❑ Information Systems

FINANCIAL EXPERIENCE

Promoted through positions with leading financial institution, National Bank:

Assistant Vice President	2002 – Pres.
Customer Service Manager	1994 – 2002
Assistant Operations Manager	1987 – 1994
Customer Service Representative	1983 – 1987

Currently accountable for central California district containing 26 sites with total staff of 635 FTEs. Provide operational support to division, district, branch, and customer service managers in the areas of production management, quality control, policy development, risk management, staffing, and customer service. Highlights of responsibilities and career accomplishments include the following:

General Management — Business Development, Customer Service, Cost Controls, Productivity

- ▪ **Increased district ranking from #8 to #1** for service and production management.
- ▪ **Minimized total operating losses to 40% under plan**, with 85% of sites under plan for risk management.
- ▪ Initiated new policy for currency handling with resultant **savings to company of $1.5 million.**
- ▪ Played an integral role in organizing a new central California division comprising 250 branches.
- ▪ Designed an improved system (subsequently **implemented statewide in some 500 sites**) for out-of-balance conditions and cash shortages.
- ▪ Directed the integration of two newly acquired branches into corporate system with minimal downtime; success acknowledged by Senior Vice President with written commendation.
- ▪ Earned excellent biannual corporate audit ratings for cash control, security, and policy compliance.

Training / Development

- ▪ Certified Instructor for National Bank's Retail University: **wrote and taught corporate courses** for executive training program (topics included production management, ethics, understanding branch reports).
- ▪ Assisted in writing job descriptions for operations staff utilized systemwide (520 locations).
- ▪ **Cross-trained operations staff well beyond scope of normal job profiles;** efforts resulted in increased productivity, reduced loss liability, and improved customer service response time.

Human Resources Management

- ▪ Administered corporate human resource policies.
- ▪ Recruited and interviewed candidates for midmanagement positions.
- ▪ Conducted monthly officer meetings, addressing policy changes, training, and problem-solving needs.

Special Honors

- ▪ District Service Specialist of the Year (statewide award; selected among 45 candidates).
- ▪ Customer Service Manager of the Year (for effective management of high-volume $145 million branch).

References on Request

Magic

Condensing 30 Years of Experience

Finance and management executive Jonathan had an extensive background that spanned 30 years. His résumé detailed all of it—four pages worth—without zeroing in on the highlights. I've included just two pages of the *Before* picture (see Résumé 3.9), followed by the *After* picture (see Résumé 3.10). Note how effectively the Executive Summary takes older but impressive accomplishments and positions them front and center.

Résumé 3.9: Before

JONATHAN L. BURLE
53 Del Oro Drive
Davis, CA 95722
(916) 432-2315
jlb1212@aol.com

EXECUTIVE **SUMMARY**	Over 15 years of experience in hospital administration and finance Designed, developed and directed marketing effort for finance and medical records software Conducted feasibility studies and test marketed computer software products Proven communicator, motivator and team builder Consulted extensively in health care finance, systems, reimbursement and managed care areas Creative, resourceful and energetic manager Able to solve major business problems and manage large and complex projects Experienced in business acquisitions, facility expansion, construction, bond financings Knowledgeable in modern management techniques. Trained as TQM facilitator Proficient in FoxPro, dBase and Access database programming environments Heavy systems background - RFP development, system selection and implementation
CAREER **PROGRESSION**	MBA (UC Berkeley) CPA in public practice Chief Financial Officer and member of the Board of Directors Acting CEO for multi-state retailer Management consultant in health care industry Designed, developed and marketed health care software Instructor at graduate schools for three universities Active in teaching and public speaking
[month, year] to present	**Christians' Business Men's Committee** Administrator, Christian Business Men's Committee of US, Northern California Area. CBMC is an international organization of Christian Businessmen Position - Executive Administrator Serve as acting director in absence of permanent Director on medical leave. Reports to a Board of Directors composed of prominent area business leaders. • Conducts operations for Northern California area, serving approximately 400 members. • Serves as the primary public relations contact person with businesses and the community. • Does extensive public speaking to elicit support and to educate, motivate, and inspire members. • Directs media relations and publicity. • Arranges and directs executive luncheons, programs and seminars for businessmen.

[month, year]
to [month, year]
	National Distribution, Inc., Sacramento, California
	Position - Member of the Board and Chief Financial Officer
	
	Reported to president and served as a key member of the Board of Directors. Responsible for
	financial management, long range planning and information technology.
	
	• Trained, organized and facilitated executive team meetings using TQM approach.
	• Played major role in determining overall company priorities, major focus and objectives.
	• Developed marketing plans, sales forecasts and budgets for operations in five states.
	• Upgraded warehouse management and financial accounting systems from System 36 to Unix
	  system/Windows NT system.
	• Implemented Electronic Data Interchange (EDI) and Radio Frequency communications
	• Designed and developed a Web page on the Internet.
	• Upgraded accounting and warehouse management systems from System 36 to nationally state-
	  of-the art systems.
	• Revised, amended and qualified company's ESOP and retirement profit sharing plan with the
	  IRS (company 75 percent owned by ESOP)
	• Implemented Company's *open book financial reporting system*.

(continued)

(continued)

Jonathan L. Burle, page 2

[month, year] to [month, year]	<u>Consulting Network</u>, Sacramento, California Position - President and CEO. Lead Consultant.

- Determined major marketing strategies and directed marketing campaigns
- Developed and marketed software, systems, and consulting services in 50 states.
- Managed and directed major trade show presentations throughout the US.
- Conducted hospital cost and reimbursement studies resulting in savings of over $10 million.
- Developed strategic relationships with business partners, consultants, analysts and medical associations.
- Marketed and installed medical information systems and ICD-9-CM encoding software for medical records departments in hospitals nationally.
- Designed, developed and marketed leading physician office software product.
- Conducted feasibility analyses, sold and installed managed care software and systems for HMO's and hospitals.
- Consulted extensively with health care institutions and physicians in budgeting, reimbursement, rate setting and major bond financings.
- Directed and coordinated implementation of Transition Systems, Inc., world-renowned decision support system, at Stanford University.
- Provided contracted support for Novell, NT, IBM, and DEC systems.
- Assisted hospitals extensively in connection with reimbursement negotiations and capitation arrangements.

[month, year] to [month, year]	<u>YRC Technology Consulting</u>, Davis, California Position - Vice President

Provided consulting services directed toward increasing Medicare and Medicaid reimbursement. Also conducted large engagements in rate setting, revenue maximization and managed care negotiations.

- Marketed and performed consulting services to hospitals nationally.
- Helped develop industry's first computerized Medicare reimbursement reporting system
- Conducted rate and system's review resulting in savings of $3 million during first year alone.

[month, year] to [month, year]	<u>Saint John's Medical Center</u>, Big City, California Position - Chief Financial Officer

As chief financial officer, responsible for financial management and controls, budgeting, general accounting, business office, admissions, and utilization review. Responsible for budget in excess of $100 million.

- Delivered oral financial presentations to Board of Directors monthly.
- Developed and implemented Medical Center's first budgeting and cost containment system.
- Co-authored Certificate of Need filing for $20 million construction project involving critical units, dialysis center and air ambulatory services landing field.
- Handled financial aspects of several hospital mergers and acquisitions.

EDUCATION	Bachelor of Science degree in Business Administration form University of California, Berkeley MBA degree from University of California, Berkeley
PROFESSIONAL CREDENTIALS	Certified Public Accountant, State of California (Certificate 55555)

(Other sections follow—Teaching, Personal Development, Other Experience, Military Experience — 4 pages total)

Résumé 3.10: After

JONATHAN L. BURLE

53 Del Oro Drive
Davis, CA 95722

(Available for Relocation)

(916) 432-2315
jlb1212@aol.com

EXECUTIVE SUMMARY

Astute business executive with strong combination of cross-functional experience in diverse industries and markets (hospital administration, managed care, emerging technologies, distribution, nonprofit). Strengths:

FINANCE / ACCOUNTING

→ Captured $10 million in "lost" revenue for hospitals nationwide; advised on rate structures, revenue maximization, Medicare/Medicaid reimbursement issues, and capitation negotiations.

→ Key player in increasing stockholder returns from $100,000 to $450,000 in just one year; introduced financial system that was major factor in earning public honors as one of the "Top 5 Businesses in Northern California."

→ As CFO, led $100 million medical center through complex merger and acquisitions.

MARKETING / SALES

→ Built start-up company to experience phenomenal revenue growth—in excess of 150% each year.

→ Envisioned and led successful strategic marketing initiative for national launch of managed care software product.

→ Gained access to key players in managed care (Blue Cross, Columbia HCA), landing contracts which collectively managed in excess of 5 million lives.

MIS / TECHNOLOGY

→ Eliminated $750,000 in technical consulting fees based on IS skills. Initiated programs that merged disparate technologies and supported technology advances (designed Web page for company's first Internet presence).

→ Unprecedented track record in development and delivery of systems that increased productivity and efficiency.

→ Pioneered concept for managed care software that became international standard for the industry.

MANAGEMENT / OPERATIONS

→ Strong leader with ability to initiate change, obtain buy-in from divergent interests, and implement reengineering/quality improvement processes while maintaining positive environment.

→ Experienced with start-up, turnaround, aggressive growth environments, mergers and acquisitions, bond financing, and major construction projects.

→ Advanced TQM concepts companywide (formal training as TQM facilitator); team leader for ISO 9000 certification.

PROFESSIONAL EXPERIENCE

EXECUTIVE ADMINISTRATOR—CBMC, Northern California Area   (interim position) [date]-Present

Provide hands-on leadership to 400-member nonprofit organization.

♦ Working with mayor and business leaders, was instrumental in pitching area as site for "Promise Keepers" conference (first nonmetropolitan city to secure group; attendance was largest convention in city's history).

♦ Introduced business-driven orientation to nonprofit group that improved organization's financial stability, focus, and vision.

(continued)

(continued)

(continued)

JONATHAN L. BURLE
Page Two

PROFESSIONAL EXPERIENCE

CHIEF FINANCIAL OFFICER—National Distribution, Inc., Sacramento, CA   [date–date]

Executive team member and Board Member accountable for strategic planning, marketing strategy, financial management, and information technology for national logistics, warehousing, and transportation company operating in five western states.

- Surpassed all records for profitability (350% increase) in company's history.
- Led initiative to implement world-class accounting and warehouse management systems to drive strategic plan.
- Escaped several hundred thousand dollars in potential tax liability by bringing ESOP plan into IRS compliance.
- Introduced emerging technologies (Electronic Data Interchange and Radio Frequency communications).

PRESIDENT / CHIEF EXECUTIVE OFFICER—Consulting Network, Sacramento, CA   [date–date]

Led national healthcare consulting and software development company through critical start-up, growth, and operations cycles. Planned and managed marketing, sales, publicity, client education, and account management functions. Conducted feasibility analyses, sold, and coordinated installation of managed care software and systems for hospitals.

- Pioneered development of managed care/ICD-9-CM interface for hospital medical records and finance departments; technology continues to be model for industry standard.
- Cemented business relationships with managed care executives and hospital administrators. Garnered support from key industry associations (AHIMA, CHIA, HIMS).
- Directed implementation of Transition Systems, Inc., world-renowned decision support system, at UC Davis Medical Center.

VICE PRESIDENT—YRC Technology Consulting, Davis, CA   [date–date]

Piloted consulting engagements for hospitals nationwide, addressing issues relating to pricing, revenue maximization, and managed care negotiations. Hands-on involvement in marketing, business development, and client retention.

- Helped develop industry's first computerized Medicare reimbursement reporting system.
- Saved more than $3 million during first year alone through rate and systems review.

CHIEF FINANCIAL OFFICER—Saint John's Medical Center, Big City, CA   [date–date]

Planned and directed finance and accounting for leading regional healthcare system. Accountable for budget in excess of $100 million, as well as general accounting, business office, admissions, and utilization review. Primary interface with Board of Directors on all finance matters.

- Delivered an additional $1 million to bottom line profit through introduction of center's first cost containment system.
- Coauthor of Certificate of Need filing for $20 million construction project.

EDUCATION, LICENSURE

MBA / Marketing Emphasis—University of California, Berkeley
Bachelor of Science, Business Administration—University of California, Berkeley
CPA — State of California

Points

⭐ Capitalizes on the strengths of both the chronological and functional formats.

⭐ Preps the reader (through use of the introductory Summary section) to focus on what you deem most important.

Pitfalls

⭐ None of any consequence!

⭐ Well, maybe one. If your career is relatively young, this format might be overkill: You'll likely find yourself repeating information in the functional section and the experience section.

The Creative Format

Creative résumés defy strict definition because their form follows the originality and imagination of the creator (the writer). They're dicey, but they can work. Sometimes.

A Creative Format Worked for a TV News Anchor

Magic

Steve Horstman, an on-camera newsman who is not afraid to stand out, used a three-column newsletter format to differentiate himself from his competition. This creative résumé helped him secure a main anchor slot in one of the top 30 U.S. markets (a strong jump from a mid-50s market). Compare his *Before* and *After* résumés (see Résumés 3.11 and 3.12).

You can also design a "theme" résumé to complement a particular company's interests. For instance, a marketing representative applying to an amusement water park might use a long and narrow paper (card-stock weight) that folds into thirds. When opened, it displays a shadow of a waterfall (using a word-processing watermark function) on a light jade-green background. Alternative category headings can replace traditional ones: Make a Splash instead of Accomplishments, Water Chemistry instead of Experience, Pooled Resources instead of References, and so on.

Résumé 3.11: Before

STEVE HORSTMAN

1234 Windsor
Oak Heights, OK 78212
Pager: 800-523-2323

EXPERIENCE

KWWW-TV Oklahoma City, Oklahoma (26th ADI) **Main Anchor**	Present
KWRH TV San Diego, California (53rd ADI) **Main Anchor**	1991-1996
KJAC TV (NBC Affiliate) Lubbock, Texas (119th ADI) **Main Anchor**	1990-1991
KOLO TV (ABC Affiliate) Reno, Nevada (124th ADI) **Reporter**	1989-1990
KTTF Reno, Nevada **Reporter**	1988
KCBT (CBS Affiliate) Tucson, Arizona **Reporter**	1985-1987

EDUCATION

University of California at Los Angeles (UCLA) Bachelor of Arts Degree in Broadcast Journalism	1983
University of Southern California (USC) Management and Finance Courses	

Résumé 3.12: After

STEVE HORSTMAN
"TV ANCHOR WITH AN ATTITUDE"

Nontraditional anchor delivers news

New approach to the news

Steve Horstman, proclaimed by news critics as the "anchor with an attitude," doesn't fit the norm when it comes to the traditional television news anchor.

How many news anchors do you know whose background includes:

- **3 years as a Cop**

- **2 years as a Marine**

- **3 years as a Pro Ballplayer?**

His hard-hitting news delivery stems from his time in the "real world" in touch with real people.

Broad-based training

Horstman is a 1983 graduate of University of California at Los Angeles (UCLA), holding a Bachelor of Arts degree in Broadcast Journalism.

Expanding his knowledge of the world of business and finance, he completed graduate studies in management and finance at the University of Southern California (USC) before pursuing a career in broadcast.

Fast-track promotion

Horstman has enjoyed a rapid rise in popularity in the news business. He is currently the Main Anchor at KWWW-TV in Oklahoma City (26th ADI), where he has provided extensive coverage of the **Jonbenet Ramsey Murder Case** and the **Timothy McVeigh / Oklahoma City Bombing Trial**, including numerous national television show appearances.

In his previous Main Anchor slot (1991-1996) for KWRH TV (53rd ADI) in San Diego, California, Horstman earned the distinction of being the **youngest anchor in the station's history.** His anchoring of the nightly news broadcast led to consistent ratings growth.

Earlier assignments included Main Anchor for NBC Affiliate KJAC TV (119th ADI) in Lubbock, Texas, from 1990 to 1991 and Reporter for ABC Affiliate KOLO TV in Reno, Nevada (124th ADI), from 1989 to 1990.

In 1988 he joined KTTF, where he worked on a riveting documentary that chronicled the life of an 8-year-old gang member. The piece won **national acclaim and was awarded an Emmy.**

Horstman began his broadcast career in 1985 as a Reporter with CBS Affiliate KCBT in Tucson, Arizona.

A glimpse into his private life

The son of a West German businessman, Horstman was the oldest of eight children growing up in Nuremberg, Bavaria.

His initial interest in broadcast journalism stems from close family ties to the business. His sister cohosts a popular late night news magazine. Her advice to big brother: "Get people's attention."

He's done just that. Once, when between jobs, he attended an annual convention of news directors. On his name tag he wrote: "Steve Horstman: Looking for a job." It landed him a Main Anchor slot.

Beyond his extended workday, Horstman also makes time for mentoring at-risk youth and fund-raising for nonprofit organizations.

A demanding schedule? Yes. Yet Horstman manages it with the same composure and energy he brings to his nightly newscast.

Get in touch

Horstman can be reached via E-mail at anchor@aol.com or his residence at 1234 Windsor Circle, Oak Heights, OK 78212. For immediate access, contact his digital pager at 800-523-2323.

Magic

Using Specialty Paper

Specialty paper is another tool you can use to display your creativity. The next four examples use unusual paper stock to complement each job seeker's profession or industry.

Randy Bez's *Before* résumé (see Résumé 3.13) is a list-driven, "just the facts" presentation. The *After* version (see Résumé 3.14) reflects his talents in the classroom and offers an inspiring "blackboard" quote, perfect for a teacher in the early elementary grades.

Sandi Stroop, an elementary educator specializing in early literacy development, uses an "ABC" paper and a font that looks like a child's handwriting (see Résumé 3.15). Tiny book images are used as bullets to set off key qualifications.

Finally, Sasha Berenton chose a jungle-theme paper to apply for a marketing position with a regional zoo (see Résumé 3.17). Note the complete revision of content as well, which was needed because her *Before* version (see Résumé 3.16) was intended for use in education.

Résumé 3.13: Before

RANDY BEZ

123 E. Kids Circle
Fresno, CA 93711
(209) 234-2342

OBJECTIVE: To secure a teaching position with Metro Unified School District, Grades 2-5

CREDENTIAL Multiple Subject Credential
Language Development Specialist Certificate

EDUCATION **California State University, Fresno**
Bachelor of Science degree, Education

University of Texas, Austin
Elementary Education Major

TEACHING EXPERIENCE

Teacher - Grades 3 and 3-4 Combination [date-Present]
HIGH ELEMENTARY SCHOOL - Fresno Unified School District

Literacy Summery School Teacher [date]
STARS SCHOOL

Certificated Math Tutor [date-date]
ARIANA ELEMENTARY

Summer School Teacher [date]
MIDDLETON SCHOOL

PROFESSIONAL ACCOMPLISHMENT and QUALIFICATIONS

- Mentor Teacher 19xx - 19xx
- Master Teacher, California State University, Fresno - Option IV
- Experience working with culturally and linguistically diverse student populations
- Classroom management and assertive discipline
- Whole group, small group and individual instruction
- Use of SDAIE
- Identification and referral of students for special services
- Computer literate: Experience and training with Macintosh Apple

Received training in and implemented the following:

- Multi-Sensory Teaching Approach
- C-Sin (CA Science Implementation Network)
- Lee Canter's Assertive Discipline
- Lee Canter's Beyond Assertive Discipline
- Discipline Based Art Education
- Santillana
- Peer Coaching
- Tribes - Self Esteem, Conflict Resolution
- True Colors
- Math Camp - FUSD, [date]
- Grade 3 Mathematics Replacement Project
- Conducting staff and parent In-services
- Cooperative Learning
- Portfolio Assessment

EXTRACURRICULAR ACTIVITIES

- Ariana Elementary Writing Team
- Program Quality Review Team
- Math Adoption Committee
- Science Adoption Committee

REFERENCES FURNISHED UPON REQUEST

Résumé 3.14: After

RANDY BEZ

123 E. Kids Circle
Fresno, CA 93711
randyb@msn.com
(559) 234-2342

> *One hundred years from now it will not matter what my bank account was, the sort of house I lived in, or the kind of car I drove but the world may be different because I was important in the life of a child.*
>
> —*Anonymous*

PROFESSION

Elementary Educator, Grades 2-5—highlights of 16-year career with Fresno Unified include the following:

♦ Three years' experience as Mentor Teacher.

♦ Experience as Master Teacher for CSUF Option IV Program.

♦ Strengths in science and math; effective classroom management skills; excellent rapport with multicultural, LEP, special needs, and at-risk students.

EDUCATION, CREDENTIAL

Language Development Specialist Certificate
Multiple Subject Credential—California State University, Fresno
B.A., Education/Biology Minor—University of Texas, Austin

PROFESSIONAL EXPERIENCE

FRESNO UNIFIED SCHOOL DISTRICT   [date]–Present

Teacher, 3/4 Combination—High Elementary (date-Present)
Literacy Summer School Teacher—Stars School (date)
Certificated Math Tutor—Ariana Elementary (date–date)
Summer School Teacher—Middleton School (date)

♦ Create an engaging, positive learning environment featuring integrated curriculum, hands-on lessons, computer applications, and use of portfolios to document students' growth and talents.

♦ Structure whole group, small group, and individual instruction to accommodate different academic levels and learning styles.

♦ Apply cooperative learning and cross-age tutoring to increase learning, self-esteem, and cross-cultural understanding.

♦ Employ C-SIN and AIMS in science and math to develop critical thinking skills and improve overall comprehension.

♦ Utilize SDAIE, Natural Approach, Language Experience Approach, and TPR to overcome language barriers.

♦ Selected by principal to develop special programs, such as Margaret Smith's MTA, TRIBES conflict resolution, and DBAE.

♦ Wrote and received community partnership minigrant "Walk Through California."

CONTINUING EDUCATION—Received training in and implemented the following:

Multi-Sensory Teaching Approach	Tribes
C-SIN (CA Science Implementation Network)	True Colors
Lee Canter's Assertive Discipline	FUSD Math Camp
Lee Canter's Beyond Assertive Discipline	Santillana
DBAE (Discipline-Based Art Education)	Cooperative Learning
Portfolio Assessment	Peer Coaching
Conducting Staff In-services	SDAIE
Parent Partnerships	Early Literacy

Résumé 3.15

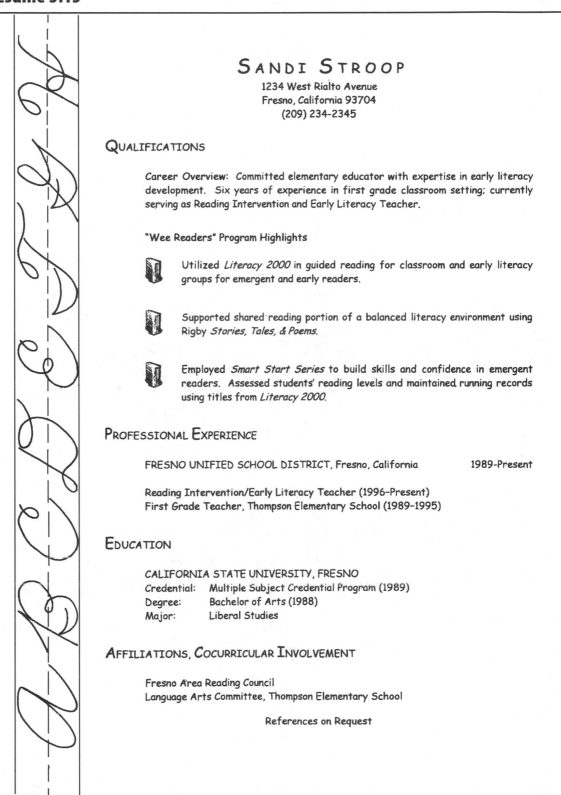

SANDI STROOP
1234 West Rialto Avenue
Fresno, California 93704
(209) 234-2345

QUALIFICATIONS

Career Overview: Committed elementary educator with expertise in early literacy development. Six years of experience in first grade classroom setting; currently serving as Reading Intervention and Early Literacy Teacher.

"Wee Readers" Program Highlights

- Utilized *Literacy 2000* in guided reading for classroom and early literacy groups for emergent and early readers.

- Supported shared reading portion of a balanced literacy environment using Rigby *Stories, Tales, & Poems.*

- Employed *Smart Start Series* to build skills and confidence in emergent readers. Assessed students' reading levels and maintained running records using titles from *Literacy 2000.*

PROFESSIONAL EXPERIENCE

FRESNO UNIFIED SCHOOL DISTRICT, Fresno, California   1989-Present

Reading Intervention/Early Literacy Teacher (1996–Present)
First Grade Teacher, Thompson Elementary School (1989–1995)

EDUCATION

CALIFORNIA STATE UNIVERSITY, FRESNO
Credential: Multiple Subject Credential Program (1989)
Degree: Bachelor of Arts (1988)
Major: Liberal Studies

AFFILIATIONS, COCURRICULAR INVOLVEMENT

Fresno Area Reading Council
Language Arts Committee, Thompson Elementary School

References on Request

Résumé 3.16: Before

SASHA BERENTON

1420 East Rainwater
Great City, GA 23456
(313) 212-1212

OBJECTIVE

To obtain a position that will enable me to utilize my strong organizational skills, educational background, and ability to work well with people in a career that is fast-paced and rewarding.

EXPERIENCE

| 1988–1996 | Teacher | Great City School District |

- 1994–1996, Washington School
- 1992–1994, Jefferson School
- 1988–1992, Adams School

| 1996–1999 | | Southeast (Georgia, Florida) |

Consultant/Presenter/Marketing

- Gave presentations to community and School Board members regarding new science textbooks. Included information regarding new science standards, state goals and objectives and how text incorporated new mathematical curriculum.

- Gave training sessions to staff in implementation of effective use of new materials in alignment with new standards.

EDUCATION

| 1986 | University of Georgia | Athens |

- B.A., Liberal Studies
- Professional Clear Multiple Subject Credential, Supplemental Authorization in Science
- Professional Growth classes and Teaching Strategies classes have been an ongoing commitment since xxxx with over 230 hours of classes, seminars, conferences and workshops in the last 8 years.

Résumé 3.17: After

SASHA BERENTON

1420 East Rainwater • Great City, GA 23456
(313) 212-1212

OBJECTIVE

Professional alignment with the City Zoological Society in a position that will benefit from my:

Marketing Skills • Community & Educational Contacts • Commitment to Wildlife Conservation & Education

RELATED EXPERIENCE

Marketing Representative with XYZ Publishing, science textbook division of Major Publisher (1996–1999)

- Marketed textbooks and influenced purchasing decisions among school districts throughout the Southeast.
- Crafted client-specific marketing strategies for school boards, administrators, and textbook committees. Closed sales in majority of accounts.
- Designed and implemented training seminars for staff on implementation and effective use of materials in alignment with new State standards.

Volunteer with City Zoological Society

- Chaired registration of 900+ volunteers for the City Zoological Society's past four special events.
- Volunteered at seven City Zoological Society special events over the past three years.
- As Environmental Club Advisor for City Intermediate School, guided students in raising money for "Adopt-an-Animal" project and "Pau Pau" panda fund. Coordinated students' planting of trees and flowers on two occasions at the zoo.

PROFESSIONAL HISTORY

Eight years' experience as Educator with Great City Unified School District (1988–1996). Recruited by Major Publisher to market science textbooks (1996–1999). Presently employed with ABC Co.—perform computerized materials management with accountability for $500,000+ in capital equipment.

EDUCATION and CREDENTIALS

Bachelor of Arts Degree, Liberal Studies
University of Georgia, Athens

Professional Clear Multiple Subject Credential; Supplemental Authorization in Science
More than 230 hours of continuing education seminars in business and education.

Point

This is a great forum to showcase talents in a profession that calls for inventiveness—art, design, special events, promotions, and the like.

Pitfalls

↗ Creative résumés are difficult to pull off and should not be attempted by the imaginatively challenged (for example, novice writers and inexperienced graphic designers). Your intention is to be remembered, not embarrassed.

↗ Even if you are a creative genius, a traditional business format for the résumé is often preferred. Word has it from most advertising agencies that you should save the creative material for your "book" (your portfolio).

↗ Although the possibilities for creative résumés are endless, the professions for which they work are not.

The Curriculum Vitae (CV)

If you're a member of the cerebrally elite "SAM's" Club, you'll need a CV, which is an abbreviation for *curriculum vitae* (pronounced *ka-rick-ya-lem vee-tie*). SAM is my acronym for the scientific, academic, and medical communities that typically use CVs. Environments that demand doctoral degrees typically require a CV. Although CVs typically follow a chronological layout, I am describing CVs separately because they possess some distinct characteristics.

If you took Latin (and remember what you studied), you'll know that curriculum vitae means "the course of one's life." A CV relies on the use of complete lists rather than a narrative or sentence/paragraph presentation of material. Education and a doctoral dissertation usually lead off the CV, followed by medical or academic posts, research, publications, presentations, awards, appointments, committees, and other professional activities. CVs are credentials-driven rather than accomplishments-oriented, to the point of self-effacement.

Thorough and typically tedious, these documents can run into double-digit page length, complete with addenda. One CV for a physician—who had a 30-year career as a researcher, writer, and practitioner—yielded 24 pages. If this is your case, for the sake of your reader's ophthalmologist bills, try culling some of the older, less-important committees or professional activities (but never drop journal articles or publications). Even veteran academicians and physicians should keep it to 10 or so pages. For the sake of space, I've shortened the entries under each category to abbreviate the sample CV of Eloise Stanlake-Waxman to just two pages (see Résumé 3.18). But it gives you an idea of which categories a CV normally includes.

Résumé 3.18

ELOISE STANLAKE-WAXMAN, M.D., Ph.D.

Business:	*Curriculum Vitae*	Residence:
St. John's Medical Center 4403 Broadway Boulevard Houston, TX 72115 (713) 987-9876		2727 Northpark Drive The Woodlands, TX 72004 (713) 987-9876 Fax (713) 987-7890

EDUCATION

Medical	University Southern California, Los Angeles M.D.	1975
Graduate	University of California, Los Angeles Ph.D., Biochemical Pharmacology	1973
Undergraduate	Massachusetts Institute of Technology (MIT) B.S., Chemistry	1969

MEDICAL TRAINING

Residency	Walter Reed Army Medical Center Radiation Oncology	1979-1982
Fellowship	Los Angeles Memorial Medical Center Medical Oncology	1978-1979
Residency	San Francisco General Hospital Internal Medicine	1976-1978
Internship	San Francisco General Hospital Internal Medicine	1975-1976

LICENSURE AND CERTIFICATION

M.D.	California License Number S44552 Texas License Number G54321	1976 1983
Diplomate	American Board of Radiology American Board of Internal Medicine National Board of Medical Examiners	1982 1978 1976
Clinical Investigator	Texas Clinical Oncology Program (TCOP)	1983

TEACHING APPOINTMENTS

Associate Professor Radiation Oncology	University of Texas, Medical School Houston, Texas	1983-Present
Clinical Instructor Radiation Oncology	University of California, San Diego (UCSD) Medical Center San Diego, California	1982
Clinical Instructor Internal Medicine	University of Southern California (USC) Medical School Los Angeles, California	1980

(continued)

(continued)

ELOISE STANLAKE-WAXMAN, M.D., Ph.D.

C.V., Page Two

PROFESSIONAL EXPERIENCE

Chief of Staff	St. John's Medical Center Houston, Texas	1987-Present
Chief of Oncology	St. John's Medical Center Houston, Texas	1983-1987
Oncologist / President	Oncology Medical Group, Inc. The Woodlands, Texas	1983-Present
Associate Oncologist	Memorial Medical Center San Diego, California	1981-1983
Staff Oncologist	Children's Medical Center Los Angeles, California	1979-1981
Staff Oncologist	St. Francis Medical Center San Francisco, California	1977-1979

PUBLICATIONS

Author or coauthor of 36 articles. See addenda for detailed bibliography.

COMMITTEES

American Cancer Society, Southwest Division Board

- Executive Committee
- Cancer Control Group
- Chair, Community Access to Resources
- Early Detection and Treatment Committee
- Research Committee
- Cancer Center Medical Directors' Task Force

American Cancer Society, Houston Unit Board

- Executive Committee
- Chair, Professional Education
- Division Board Representative

AFFILIATIONS

American College of Radiology
American Society of Therapeutic Radiology and Oncology
American Society of Clinical Oncology
Radiological Society of North America
American Medical Association
Texas Medical Association
Houston Metro Medical Society

A hybrid of the typical business résumé and the CV has evolved for those scientists, academicians, and physicians who have combined management degrees and executive responsibilities with their primary discipline. For instance, a radiologist with an MBA degree seeking a physician executive position could use an executive CV format. Beyond mere lists, the document should give credit for business outcomes resulting from your management savvy.

Just as Dr. Stravilovich did in his sample executive CV (see Résumé 3.19), detail any of your accomplishments that reflect profit, productivity, or quality improvements.

Résumé 3.19

SAMUEL B. STRAVILOVICH, M.D.

1255 West Shore Avenue
Lunenburg, MA 01246
Available for Relocation

Residence: (508) 582-0123
Facsimile: (508) 583-4321
Email: sbs@harvard.edu

QUALIFICATIONS

PHYSICIAN EXECUTIVE qualified for senior-level management opportunities where strengths in strategic planning, development, and visionary leadership will promote high-growth business ventures. Highlights:

♦ **Market-Driven Executive**–Initiated business re-engineering in a 38-physician practice to address the emerging commercialization of medicine; cut operating costs through innovative cost-containment programs; brought consensus among divergent interests during transition to market-focused paradigm.

♦ **Academic Qualifications**–Harvard Executive MBA program graduate with management and financial skills backed by clinical competence of 15+ years of practice as a board-certified internist and anesthesiologist. Substantial experience in emergency services, aeromedical evacuation, and special operations.

♦ **International Orientation**–Advanced the accessibility of health care in third world nations through commitment to international healthcare organizations (eight trips to Honduras, Mexico, and Vietnam as team chief and service as program director for an overseas teaching hospital).

♦ **White House Fellowship**–Regional finalist among highly competitive candidate list of 800+; seeking to address global health care issues (special project: research for development of counter-strategies for medical terrorism).

PROFESSIONAL EXPERIENCE

HEALTHCARE MANAGEMENT–Partner, Medical Consultants, Boston, MA   1/93–Present
Partner, Medical Group, Boston, MA   1/90–12/93

Provide executive leadership as managing partner in a 38-physician group generating $18 million in annual revenue. Lead through hands-on involvement in financial affairs, professional/support staff administration, service planning, patient care, quality improvement, peer review, and credentialing. Well-versed in managed-care operations and negotiation of managed care/capitation contracts. Provide comprehensive anesthesia services and internal medicine consultations for Boston Memorial and other locations. **Accomplishments:**

▸ Led practice through successful transition to thrive in a managed-care environment utilizing new market-driven, community-oriented patient care model.
▸ Delivered significant savings through development of operational enhancements and strategic alliances.
▸ Researched and implemented computerized digital technology for cellular, paging, and voice mail services.
▸ Consultant for critical start-up of innovative home pain management therapy service.
▸ Resolved sensitive physician relations issues as member of Medical Staff Quality Council for 300-bed hospital.
▸ Mentored new physicians, helping to grow practice by 30%.

OPERATIONS MANAGEMENT–Chief, Aerospace Medicine, Virginia Air National Guard   1989–Present

Plan and direct medical services to ensure health and combat readiness of 72 aircrew and over 1,500 ground personnel. Liaison between flying squadron and medical services. Participate regularly in flying missions including active duty deployments and mission qualification in RF4-C, a supersonic fighter aircraft. Directly supervise 25 officers and enlisted personnel. Additionally accountable for public health and safety, bio-environmental engineering, and occupational health issues.

♦ continued ♦

SAMUEL B. STRAVILOVICH, M.D.   Page 2

Accomplishments:

- Selected for fast-track promotion to rank of Major and Lt. Colonel.
- Designed and implemented innovative flying safety and emergency medical training programs.
- Recipient of two Air Force Achievement Medals, Air Force Outstanding Unit Award, Armed Forces Reserve Medal, and National Defense Service Medal.
- Wrote 100-page guide to human factors and physiological stress in flying advanced tactical fighter aircraft, providing flight surgeon support for the zero mishap record during the ANG transition to F-16 aircraft.
- Formerly served as Chief, Clinical Services (1989-1992); Commander, Squadron Medical Element (1984-1989); and General Medical Officer (1982-1984).

Prior Experience:

- Clinical Faculty, Department of Internal Medicine, Boston Medical Center   1980-1982
- Attending Physician, Emergency Dept., New Bedford County Medical Center   1979-1980
- Medical Director, Medical Clinic   1978-1979

EDUCATION

M.B.A., Management–Harvard University, School of Business, Cambridge, MA   1994-1996
Residency in Anesthesiology–Boston Medical Center, Theilen, MA   1983-1986
Residency in Internal Medicine–Boston Medical Center, Theilen, MA   1979-1981
M.D.–San Francisco State University School of Medicine, San Francisco, CA   1978
B.S., Biology (cum laude)–Arizona State University, Tempe   1973

CERTIFICATION, LICENSURE

Diplomate–National Board of Medical Examiners
Diplomate–American Board of Internal Medicine
Diplomate–American Board of Anesthesiology
Flight Surgeon–USAF School of Aerospace Medicine
Medical Licensure–Massachusetts, Arizona, New York

AFFILIATIONS

American College of Physician Executives
Aerospace Medical Association
American Society of Pathologists
Massachusetts Society of Pathologists
Undersea and Hyperbaric Medical Society
American Medical Association

PROFESSIONAL APPOINTMENTS

Utilization Review Committee–Boston Medical Center
Medical Staff Quality Council–Boston Medical Center
Chair, Department of Pathology–Children's Hospital
District Director and Board of Directors–Massachusetts Society of Pathologists

ADDITIONAL DATA

Commercial Pilot
Concert Violinist
Conversant in Spanish, French, and Italian

◆ ◆ ◆

The Dateless Chronological Format

A dateless chronological format might seem like a contradiction in terms. However, there are occasions when it might behoove you to follow the traditional chronological layout but simply omit dates. You may be a new graduate who has racked up lots of related volunteer or internship experiences, possibly during short-term assignments or overlapping time periods. These short stints or concurrent dates might appear confusing and diminish the impact of the experience.

This format is also a great answer if you're returning to your prior career after a hiatus as "my kid's mom" (or dad!).

A Dateless Chronological Format Helped Anne

Anne, a career mom, had a solid work history before leaving the workforce (that is, the paid and tangibly rewarded workforce). Once her wee ones were in school, she wanted to return to work. A chronological format (see Résumé 3.20) without dates was just the thing to downplay a seven-year hiatus. It worked especially well for her because of her positions with prestigious name-brand employers like Procter & Gamble and Hershey Foods.

Points

✦ Perfect for individuals who have been out of the job market for a time but whose prior career path has been otherwise flawless.

✦ Eliminates confusion about overlapping or concurrent work assignments.

✦ Allows the reader to focus on the substance of your experience rather than the length of your employment.

Pitfall

May give rise to suspicions that you don't have much experience. Counter this by including a statement in the Objective or in your cover letter that gives an idea of how long you've been working (for instance, "Sales position in telecommunications where my 12 years of industry experience will be of benefit").

Résumé 3.20

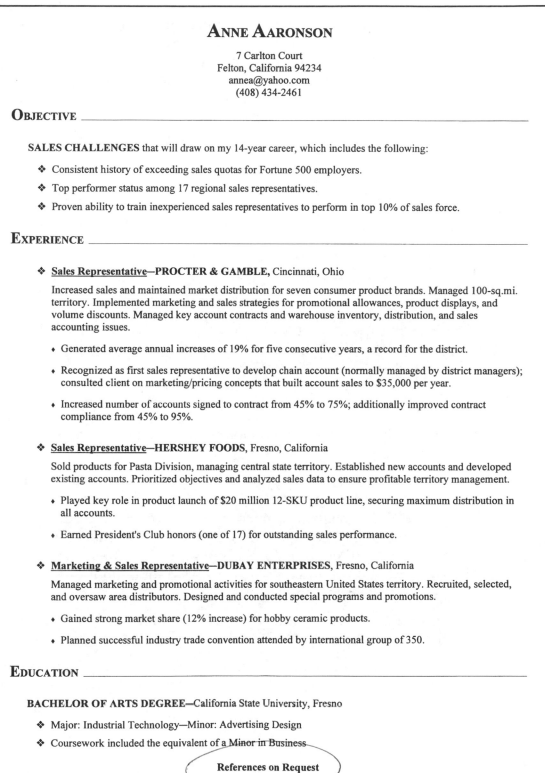

ANNE AARONSON

7 Carlton Court
Felton, California 94234
annea@yahoo.com
(408) 434-2461

OBJECTIVE

SALES CHALLENGES that will draw on my 14-year career, which includes the following:

❖ Consistent history of exceeding sales quotas for Fortune 500 employers.

❖ Top performer status among 17 regional sales representatives.

❖ Proven ability to train inexperienced sales representatives to perform in top 10% of sales force.

EXPERIENCE

❖ <u>Sales Representative</u>—**PROCTER & GAMBLE,** Cincinnati, Ohio

Increased sales and maintained market distribution for seven consumer product brands. Managed 100-sq.mi. territory. Implemented marketing and sales strategies for promotional allowances, product displays, and volume discounts. Managed key account contracts and warehouse inventory, distribution, and sales accounting issues.

♦ Generated average annual increases of 19% for five consecutive years, a record for the district.

♦ Recognized as first sales representative to develop chain account (normally managed by district managers); consulted client on marketing/pricing concepts that built account sales to $35,000 per year.

♦ Increased number of accounts signed to contract from 45% to 75%; additionally improved contract compliance from 45% to 95%.

❖ <u>Sales Representative</u>—**HERSHEY FOODS,** Fresno, California

Sold products for Pasta Division, managing central state territory. Established new accounts and developed existing accounts. Prioritized objectives and analyzed sales data to ensure profitable territory management.

♦ Played key role in product launch of $20 million 12-SKU product line, securing maximum distribution in all accounts.

♦ Earned President's Club honors (one of 17) for outstanding sales performance.

❖ <u>Marketing & Sales Representative</u>—**DUBAY ENTERPRISES,** Fresno, California

Managed marketing and promotional activities for southeastern United States territory. Recruited, selected, and oversaw area distributors. Designed and conducted special programs and promotions.

♦ Gained strong market share (12% increase) for hobby ceramic products.

♦ Planned successful industry trade convention attended by international group of 350.

EDUCATION

BACHELOR OF ARTS DEGREE—California State University, Fresno

❖ Major: Industrial Technology—Minor: Advertising Design

❖ Coursework included the equivalent of a Minor in Business

References on Request

The International Résumé

You'll also hear this format referred to as an international CV. My colleagues seem to agree that the terms "international résumé" and "international CV" are interchangeable. If you're applying for positions in international circles, international CV expert Miriam-Rose Kohn of JEDA Enterprises (www.jedaenterprises.com) recommends following the suggestions for the traditional chronological format. Next, she suggests fleshing out the details—more is better. Then add an "illegal" section—as in answers to questions that employers are barred from asking when you apply in the United States. Here are a few examples of this type of information:

- Marital status: Single

- Date of birth: November 14, 1957

- Place of birth: Nice, France

- Dual citizenship: U.S.A. and France

- Passport: U.S.A. and French (both currently valid)

- Health: Excellent

- Availability: Immediate; open to travel or relocation worldwide for the right opportunity

- Languages: French, Italian, English (fluent), German (business fluency)

Other notables:

- **Currency:** Specify monetary denominations, such as U.S. dollars, by writing "US$1 billion."

- **Telephone:** Because you may not know what country your potential employer is calling from, do not include an international access code because it differs slightly from country to country. Instead, when residing in the United States, list only the country code (1), your area code, and telephone number. For instance, if you were targeting jobs in Europe while living state-side, your telephone number would appear as +1-707-222-3333.

- **Country:** Remember to add "U.S." to your address if you're using an address in the States.

- **Education:** Different countries have different protocol on detailing education. If you're looking for jobs in Asia, employers prefer details on education as far back as grammar school.

Points

⭑ Shows your international business savvy by using the appropriate format.

⭑ Allows you to take advantage of the "tell more, sell more" theory. You can offer readers a lengthy, blow-by-blow narration of your track record.

Pitfalls

⭑ Reveals personal information you might not want employers to know.

⭑ Sets you up for discriminatory hiring practices (if you're not of the "right" age, ethnicity, marital status, or other persuasion).

The Linear Format

The distinguishing characteristic of a linear format is its visual orientation. Drawing its name from the linear style of art, where forms and shapes are precisely defined by line, the linear résumé limits its information to a one-sentence-at-a-time presentation.

Each sentence is bulleted and is often limited to one line, two at the most. The writing style is punchy. Forget the frills and fluff—just highlight experience and accomplishments.

Magic

A Linear Format Worked for Richard

Richard earned an audience with several companies by dressing up his résumé. The *Before* and *After* versions follow (see Résumés 3.21 and 3.22). Documenting specific accomplishments was key to an offer he received for a promotion and salary increase.

Points

⭑ Delivers a hard-hitting sales presentation of your skills.

⭑ Is quickly scanned by people or computers.

⭑ Great for professions that have easily measured performance criteria, such as sales or production.

Pitfall

Same as for the accomplishments format. It hogs the space you might use to describe details with past employers.

Résumé 3.21: Before

RESUME

RICHARD STOVAN, CPIM
4312 Canandaigua Way
Salinas, California 92342
(408) 423-4321

CAREER PROFILE

mo/yr–Present Design Works, Inc., Salinas, CA
[date]–Present Inventory Control Manager
Direct supervision of 12 Material Handlers with responsibilities of receiving, stocking, supply of manufacturing, coordination of all outside processing of parts, and non-conforming material control. Immediate goal/requirement of achieving 98% inventory record accuracy (from 80%) by June, date. Restarted investigative cycle counting to find and resolve inventory problems. Actively involved in consolidating inventory and manufacturing systems for all north American manufacturing divisions (6) into a single database and software systems. Also organizing the relocation of two product lines from other divisions into the Salinas operation.

[date]–[date] Manufacturing Coordinator
Direct supervision of fabrication teams. Responsible for the development of the teams and team members, quality, production efficiency, and safety. Primary objective is to improve the effectiveness of all the fabrication units in providing the product required to meet the on time delivery dates of all widget production lines and service parts orders. Current widget lead times are 2 days, possibly more depending on the model, and 24 hours on service parts orders.

[date]–[date] Senior Demand Flow Technology Specialist
Project assignment to work with the xyz assembly line to improve the use of Kanban, implement a computer-based shortage tracking system, implement broadcasting of sub-assembly requirements to support flow line assembly, debug computer-generated option placement to provide correct user defined specifications, process and procedure improvements to achieve cost efficiency goals in labor and material. Continues support of the inventory and production improvements in the Mississippi facility.

mo/yr–mo/yr Major Manufacturing Company
[date]–[date] Inventory Manager
Converted the existing manual inventory system to IBM xx system. Installed computerized production and inventory control systems to meet government contract requirements.

[date]–[date] Expediter
Planned and expedited raw materials to production floor. Implemented computer system for production and purchasing.

[date]–[date] Master Production Scheduler
Scheduled production for three shifts operating six days per week.

[date]–[date] Manufacturing Analyst
Generated daily production figures and analyzed line productivity, output, downtime, etc.

EDUCATION PROFILE / AFFILIATIONS

California State University, Chico - B.S., Industrial Technology, [date]
Red Bluff College - A.A., General Education, [date]
- Member, American Production and Inventory Control Society (CPIM).
- Member, Association for Manufacturing Excellence.

PERSONAL

Family: Married, [xx] years, four children (20, 18, 15, 12), excellent health.
Interests: Wood-working, hiking, exploring, motor cycle touring, martial arts.

Résumé 3.22: After

RICHARD STOVAN, CPIM

4312 Canandaigua Way   Work: (408) 223-4213
Salinas, California 92342   Extension 2341
(408) 423-4321   Pager: (800) 234-4231
                                                        richards@msn.com

QUALIFICATIONS SUMMARY

- 20 years' experience in inventory/production management in high-tech, ISO 9000 manufacturing environments.
- Strong record of contributing to quality outcomes, productivity improvements, and profit performance.
- Well-versed in computerized Kanban DFT production control systems, IBM AS 400 BPCS, and MRPII.
- CPIM, American Production & Inventory Control Society (APICS); Member, Association for Manufacturing Excellence.

PROFESSIONAL EXPERIENCE

DESIGN WORKS, INC., Salinas, California, [date]–Present

INVENTORY CONTROL MANAGER (date–Present)

- Challenged initially with turnaround of inventory record accuracy (IRA), improving performance from 80% to 93%.
- Consolidated six North American manufacturing divisions into single software system; met all project benchmarks.
- Led cross-functional team in relocation of two production lines to single warehouse and assembly arena.
- Promoted from . . .

MANUFACTURING COORDINATOR (date–date)

- Change agent, successfully gaining buy-in from fabricators to adhere to Kanban production control system.
- Transitioned production from "batch-oriented" to "cell groups," slashing internal lead time from 20 days to 2.
- Promoted from . . .

SENIOR DEMAND FLOW TECHNOLOGY SPECIALIST (date–date)

- Reduced "non-buildable combinations" from approximately 40 to fewer than 5 items per week.
- Virtually eliminated downtime and "turnarounds" through implementation of computer-based shortage tracking system.
- Implemented process and procedure improvements that achieved record cost efficiencies in labor and materials.

MAJOR MANUFACTURING COMPANY, Bakersfield, California, [date–date]

INVENTORY MANAGER (date–date)

- Converted existing manual inventory system to state-of-the-art IBM system.
- Installed computerized production and inventory control systems to meet government contract requirements.
- Promoted through prior positions as Expediter, Master Production Scheduler, and Manufacturing Analyst.

The Newsletter Format

Also called a vertical or columnar format, the newsletter format follows a two- or three-column layout (four columns generally look too busy). Visual distinction is the hallmark of a newsletter format. Accordingly, it is most appropriate for professions that appeal to the senses (television, advertising, graphic design). It can also be used for disciplines such as sales and customer service. Be cautious about using this format if you're in a very conservative field or pursuing management positions.

The content can be written in either traditional business style or newspaper style. Résumé 3.12 earlier in this chapter illustrates the newspaper style. Layout is a matter of mastering the column function on your word-processing program.

Some Newsletter Formats That Worked

Magic

Just a moment ago I cautioned you against using a newsletter format for management positions. Nonetheless, the following example (see Résumé 3.23) of a two-column newsletter format worked well for this loss-prevention manager because it "buried" his current employment (in an industry unrelated to his career goal) at the bottom left of the page and accented his strongest selling points at the visual center of the page (his position as vice president of safety management).

The résumé (see Résumé 3.24) of Jennifer, a new graduate, illustrates a three-column format. Note the dotted line under category headings to help set off new sections.

Maude Marvalla's résumé (see Résumé 3.25) uses the double-column layout to showcase some impressive excerpts from letters of appreciation.

Point

Visually appealing. Reflects a creative mindset. Distinguishes you from the dozens/hundreds of other candidates applying for the same job.

Pitfalls

- Not well received in traditionally conservative settings (such as government, public accounting, or legal).

- Until résumé-scanning software masters the recognition of columns, this format is akin to dropping paragraphs into a food processor. Your keyword phrases may come out as alphabet soup.

Résumé 3.23

JOHN B. BRADFORD

440 E. Princeton ♦ Palo Alto, CA 95555
johnbb@juno.com
(510) 555-5555

LOSS PREVENTION MANAGER

Safety ♦ Loss Control ♦ Workers' Compensation
Hazmat ♦ Environmental ♦ Fire Suppression

QUALIFICATIONS SUMMARY

LOSS PREVENTION MANAGER with impressive 14-year career highlighted by contributions in the areas of:

♦ **Risk Management:** Developed safety, loss control, workers' compensation, hazmat, environmental, and fire suppression programs for commercial and industrial accounts that resulted in a 60-80% reduction in losses.

♦ **Operations Management:** Turned around departmental operations with poor performance history to rank first in the nation. Developed and implemented TQM programs that reduced losses by approximately 33%.

♦ **Marketing:** Instrumental in developing new business valued in excess of $57 million.

EDUCATION, CREDENTIALS

B.S. degree, Microbiology
University of California, Los Angeles

Registered Environmental Assessor
California Environmental Protection Agency

Certified Health & Safety Technologist
American Board of Industrial Hygiene

PRESENT EMPLOYMENT

EXECUTIVE OFFICER

Sierra Medical, Richmond, CA—2/01–Present

Manage medical clinic with $26 million budget including supervision of 54 professional and technical staff.

PROFESSIONAL EXPERIENCE

V.P., SAFETY MANAGEMENT

American Insurance, Los Angeles, CA—1989–2001
($900 million workers' compensation & liability carrier)

Managed loss control department providing customized service for approximately 60 accounts totaling $125 million in premium. Surveyed accounts for workers' compensation, general liability, products, completed operations, and auto/fleet coverage. Prepared and administered $350,000 departmental budget.

♦ Reversed department's poor internal audit ratings from #13 (lowest division in the nation) to #1; awarded "Department of the Year" for seven consecutive years.

♦ Active member of business development team; increased revenue from $18 to $125 million in a 4-year period and met premium renewal goal of 100% renewals for four consecutive years.

♦ Recommended risk management programs for high-tech, construction, agriculture, food processing, distribution, and manufacturing accounts that yielded a 60-80% reduction in losses within the policies' first year.

LOSS CONTROL REPRESENTATIVE

World Insurance, Los Angeles, CA—1985–1989
($200 billion property & casualty carrier)

Surveyed and recommended loss control programs for national accounts throughout the United States and Asia. Investigated and analyzed loss trends.

PROFESSIONAL AFFILIATIONS

American Industrial Hygiene Association
American Society of Safety Engineers
National Fire Protection Association

Résumé 3.24

Jennifer Marsden

residence: (813) 894-4324

message: (813) 831-3442

PROFESSIONAL GOAL

Pharmaceutical sales position with a research-driven organization committed to manufacturing and marketing products that preserve and improve the quality of human life.

CONTACT DATA

School:

3676 N.W. 22nd Street
Apartment 152
Miami, Florida 22143
(813) 894-4324

Permanent Address:

4123 Seashell Drive
Boca Raton, Florida 21234
(813) 831-3442

EDUCATION

UNIVERSITY OF MIAMI
Coral Gables, Florida

Degree

Bachelor of Science
Kinesiology
May [date]

Representative Coursework

Organic Chemistry
General Biochemistry
Advanced Nutrition
Biophysical Aspects of Aging
Kinesiology
Physiology of Exercise
Human Anatomy
Trigonometry
Statistics & Probability

MEDICAL & HEALTH CARE EXPERIENCE

CARDIOLOGY ASSOCIATES
Coral Gables, Florida
[date]–Present

Medical Assistant – Back Office Functions

Interview patients, measure vital signs, and record data in patients' charts. Assist physician with examinations and procedures. Operate electrocardiograph (EKG) and other equipment for diagnostic tests. Perform laboratory tests. Administer treatments. Process requests for medication refills.

Medical Assistant – Front Office Functions

Serve as initial contact with patients, pharmaceutical representatives, and vendors. Schedule patient appointments, complete insurance forms (Medicare, HMO, private insurance, etc.), maintain billing records, and purchase medical supplies inventory.

CORAL GABLES ACADEMY
Coral Gables, Florida
[date]–[date]

Athletic Trainer's Assistant

Promoted prevention and rehabilitation of sports injuries. Under direction of Certified Trainer, taped injuries and administered modalities such as intermittent compression and pulsed ultrasound.

SALES & CUSTOMER SERVICE EXPERIENCE

ELAN GIFTS
Boca Raton, Florida
[date]–[date]

Sales Associate

Assisted clientele of upscale boutique located in the city's premier shopping gallery. Generated consistent growth in sales, averaging 20% increases annually. Began a customer database, cataloguing birthdays and special interests to capture greater repeat business. Created visually distinctive displays.

GALÁN COUTURE,
Miami, Florida
Summers [date]–[date]

Assistant to V.P. of European Couture

Assisted fashion executive in the selection, buying, and merchandising of haute couture. Traveled to New York, France, Italy, and Spain on buying trips.

REFERENCES

Maria DeSoto, M.D., FACP
Endocrinologist
(813) 432-3421

Jon Cale, Certified Athletic Trainer, Univ. of Miami
(813) 444-2312

Theo Miller, V.P. Corporate Affairs, Union Finance
(800) 423-2234

Résumé 3.25

MAUDE MARVALLA

55 West Pico, #206
New York, NY 55555

(555) 555-5555
maudemarv@hilite.com

Trainer & Coach

Specialist in Delivery of Live & Online Communication & Presentation Skills Development

"Maude Marvalla's training program far exceeded our expectations. Participant feedback included:

'A superb, skillful class with great application'

'Maude is a highly effective presenter who uses humor, vitality, and skill to enthrall her students ... a very effective teaching style.'

'Full of tools and tips ... one of the most enjoyable training experiences I've had in a long time!'

'Great mix of play and reality training.'

'Informative, interesting, confidence building, and a lot of fun. I'm normally quite a skeptic about this type of thing, so please take my comments as unusual compliments!'

"As you can see, everyone found sessions enlightening, entertaining, and empowering."

~ Bette Maller, Director of Client Services, Big Consulting Group

STRENGTHS

- **Trainer and Coach** – High-energy trainer with polished "business theater" and presentation delivery skills. Performance-focused, intuitive coach. Published writer. Well networked with innovators in the training/development and e-learning world. International orientation—extensive travel; lived abroad (Israel, Netherlands, UK). Broad cross-industry experience in ...

Broadcasting	Hi-Tech
Career Management	Pharmaceuticals
Education	Publishing
Financial Services	Trade Associations

- **Online Learning Expert** – Created innovative Web-based model for delivery of e-coaching. Helped design prototype for one of the nation's first distance-education advanced degree programs. Credentialed college educator (computer science instructor). Worked extensively with hi-tech companies on retooling platform presenters for online presentations, including ...

Webinars	Audio Conferencing
Teleclasses	Voice Messaging

- **Veteran Presenter** – More than a decade of experience delivering T&D to Fortune 1000 leaders, colleges, training companies, and professional associations. Excellent platform and delivery skills for both executive and employee audiences, equipping them to communicate with greater clarity, confidence, and persuasion in face-to-face, telephone, and electronic communication situations. Partial list of corporate clients ...

Bank of Japan Excite.com	Johnson & Johnson
Doubleday	M.D. Anderson
Hallmark Greetings	Tenspeed Press
Hewlett-Packard	Yahoo!

- **Professional Performer** – Engaged audiences as a humorist, corporate entertainer, and film, television, and radio performer. Voiceover talent for radio commercials and industrials. Professional voice and theatre training from the Rubin Conservatory (Jerusalem), City Literary Institute (London), and Royal Academy of Dramatic Arts (London).

continued

(continued)

(continued)

MAUDE MARVALLA

(555) 555-5555   maudemarv@hilite.com

EXPERIENCE

TRAINING WORLD, New York, NY   1992–Present

Manage boutique presentation skills training/coaching company and professional speakers' bureau (leadership training, customer service, sales training, negotiations, cross-cultural communications). As founder and principal, design and deliver professional development programs aligned with corporate initiatives. Determine instructional strategies including online/webinar solutions, simulations, role-plays, student workbooks, leader guides, and support materials for a variety of media.

Selected Highlights:

- Custom designed innovative training and coaching for senior banking executives of Silicon Valley Bank. Selected as exclusive "Alliance Partner" (communications training category) for bank's e-Source (global portal initiative). Coached bank's entrepreneurial companies on funding presentations to venture capitalists, analysts, and investors—100% of clients obtained some level of funding.

- Designed virtual university concept for EATA – (East Asia Travel Association) to leverage instructor reach and minimize training expenses using customizable, scalable webinar and teleclass formats.

- Earned coveted "Alliance Partner" status with ABC Consulting Group. Designed training to complement company's existing career management services. Trained hundreds of senior executives from various industries (hi-tech, healthcare, retail, financial services, banking).

- Authored articles on training/presentations published in *New York CEO, The Business Times, The Professional Consultant, National Law Firm Marketing Association* publication, *Career Chronicles,* and others.

- Strengthened company's market position through media interviews (Momentum, The Organization Doctor, *The Village Chronicle*) and trade show appearances.

Prior experience highlights: Instructor, City College of New York & Kings College. **Regional Registrar,** Amherst College.

EDUCATION & PROFESSIONAL DEVELOPMENT

- **BA, Communications**—State University of New York, Amherst
- **Graduate Work (MBA Program)**—National University
- **Credential**—Lifetime Community College Instructor Credential
- **Affiliation**—ASTD (American Society for Training & Development)
- **Continuing Education**—Educational Technology, Vocational Education, Seminar Production, Coaching, Public Speaking, Sales Training, Teleclass Leadership, Online Training Facilitation

---

"I absolutely could not have had my recent successful speaking opportunities without Maude's expert coaching of both content and technique. Maude's coaching turned it around."

~ Suchi Tenchai
Winners on Wheels

"Your entertaining style was a refreshing change. We all enjoyed your commentary and the interactive game which truly proved the point you were trying to make ..."

Lawson E. Bart,
President
National Human
Resources Association

"Your presentation was rated a 10 out of a possible 10 by our members ... One of the best WIB meetings I have attended to date ... energizing ... engaging ... entertaining!"

Laney King, VP Programs
Women in Business–New York City

The Reordered Chronological Format

Here's another twist on the chronological format. It lists job experience in chronological "groupings" rather than in a strict, reverse-chronological list. Use this format when you don't want to list your most recent experience first.

Magic

A Reordered Chronological Format Helped John

In analyzing John Freeman's format, you will note that he had 10 years of experience in retail, followed by 10 years in real estate. To help with his transition back to retail, his résumé lists this older experience first under the heading "Retail Sales and Management" and the more recent experience second under the heading "Additional Sales Experience." Compare the *Before* (see Résumé 3.26) and *After* (see Résumé 3.27) examples.

Here's how to create a reordered chronological format. Look back over your work history, bracket common jobs, and assign an industry or professional label (such as retail, real estate, or sales) to each of those clusters. Now arrange those categorical labels with the most relevant experience first, regardless of the dates.

Points

- A great tool for individuals with solid work histories who want to pursue opportunities that relate to older, more dated experience.

- Positions your buried treasure at the focal center of the page.

Pitfalls

- Think carefully before using this format. There must be some semblance of order and logic to it, or you'll confuse the reader.

- If your employment history doesn't nicely fit into two or three groupings with a solid number of years of experience for each, you will probably be better off with a functional format.

Resumé 3.26: Before

JOHN CARLTON FREEMAN

432 East Millerton
Palo Alto, California 94340
(630) 442-3413

PROFESSIONAL OBJECTIVE

Management position with an organization that will benefit from my ability to build sales, control costs, and service customers. Excellent leadership skills, "people" skills, and motivation.

EXPERIENCE

Broker Associate - Gunther Mather Real Estate
Palo Alto, California   1990-Present
Sell residential real estate in highly competitive market. Set sales goals, formulate marketing strategies, advertise product, generate leads, and manage timely closing. Excellent service and follow-up skills. Well-versed in financing, investment strategies, and structuring of complex transactions and exchanges.
  • Earned top industry honors seven consecutive years as member of Million Dollar Plus Club.
  • Built substantial repeat and referral business based on knowledge and dependable service.

Sales Associate - Coldwell Banker Real Estate
Palo Alto, California   1988-1990
Sold residential real estate concentrating in the northwest sector of the city.
  • Generated sales volume comparable to experienced sales professionals very early in career.

Sales Associate / Store Manager - Fashion Threads
Palo Alto, California   1985-1988
Initially worked as Sales Associate and promoted to Store Manager in one year. Trained, scheduled, and supervised 65 employees. Responsible for merchandising the floor, displays, ads, credit, stock management, and accounting.
  • Trained and developed inexperienced sales staff to perform among top 10% of sales producers.
  • Initiated a telephone "thank you" campaign that increased repeat customer purchases by 25%.

Assistant Manager - Miller's Outpost
Sacramento, California   1980-1985
Assisted in managing high-volume mall location staffed with 60 employees. Primarily responsible for daily reporting functions, including daily sales, productivity, inventory, and stock control.

Sales Associate / Management Trainee - The May Company
Los Angeles, California   1978-1980
Selected for management training program.

EDUCATION

Bachelor of Arts Degree, Political Science
University of California, Berkeley

References provided upon request

Résumé 3.27: After

JOHN CARLTON FREEMAN

432 East Millerton
Palo Alto, California 94340
johnc@att.net
(630) 442-3413

EXPERTISE

RETAIL MANAGEMENT: Qualified for career opportunities where ability to enhance retail operations, control labor/shrinkage, and affect net margins will be of value. Ten-year history with leading retailers includes multidisciplinary experience in:

- Staff Recruitment/Supervision
- Sales/Management Development
- Merchandising/Display
- Advertising/Promotions

- Trend Analysis/Forecasting
- Receiving/Pricing
- Inventory Management
- Security/Loss Prevention

Articulate communicator with ability to motivate others through leadership modeling and consensus building. Noted by customers, management, and staff as ethical, intelligent, and hardworking.

RETAIL SALES AND MANAGEMENT

Sales Associate/Store Manager—Fashion Threads, Palo Alto, California	1985–1988
Assistant Manager—Miller's Outpost, Sacramento, California	1980–1985
Sales Associate/Management Trainee—The May Company, Los Angeles, California	1978–1980

Highlights: Accountable for profit performance of high-volume store located in regional mall. Supervised sales team of up to 65. Scope of responsibility extended to staffing, merchandising/display, advertising copywriting, credit approval, buyer input, stock transfers, receiving, and corporate accounting. Reporting functions included daily sales, productivity, inventory, and stock control. Experienced in men's suits, men's trend, and shoes.

- ❑ Trained and developed inexperienced sales staff to perform among top 10% of sales producers.

- ❑ Initiated a telephone "thank you" campaign that increased repeat customer purchases by 25%.

- ❑ Promoted to management position based on record-setting sales performance; continued to maintain personal sales production while handling full store management responsibilities.

ADDITIONAL SALES EXPERIENCE

Broker Associate—Gunther Mather Real Estate, Palo Alto, California	1990–Present
Sales Associate—Coldwell Banker Real Estate, Palo Alto, California	1988–1990

Highlights: Veteran skills as commissioned sales associate in highly competitive real estate market. Set sales goals, formulated marketing strategies, advertised product, generated leads, presented features and benefits, overcame buyer objections, and closed sales. Excellent service and follow-up skills. Well-versed in financing, investment strategies, and structuring of complex transactions and exchanges.

- ❑ Earned top industry honors seven consecutive years as member of Million Dollar Plus Club.

- ❑ Built substantial repeat and referral business based on knowledge and dependable service.

- ❑ Very early in career, generated sales volume comparable to experienced sales professionals.

EDUCATION

Bachelor of Arts degree, Political Science—University of California, Berkeley

• • •

The Targeted Format

A targeted résumé addresses the employer's need for a specific skill or skills. To consider this format, you must first know what skill(s) the company needs, which necessitates some research on your part. When your sleuthing is done, you then focus the résumé content to include experience and accomplishments that are relevant to the targeted skill or skills.

Magic

A Targeted Format Helped Jillian

Jillian, a talented project manager in the telecommunications industry, effectively used a targeted format to catalog her project-management skills (see Résumé 3.28). She also avoided the major pitfall of this format: appearing single-dimensional. She did it by listing a broad range of projects she had managed (database design, application development, computer operations). If you use this format, look for angles in your experience that will give the reader clues to broader skills. Then be prepared to elaborate on them in an interview.

Point

Quickly demonstrates to the employer that you are a perfect match for the position you have targeted.

Pitfalls

★ Beware the snare of appearing single-dimensional. Many companies appreciate generalist skills (as opposed to specialist skills), especially small- to medium-sized companies where you're often expected to wear many hats.

★ By eliminating broad-based, value-added skills, you may appear less qualified in comparison with other candidates.

Résumé 3.30

JILLIAN DENAY MICHAELS

Pager: (800) 932-2399 • Email: jdm777@aol.com
23424 West Lemont • Dallas, Texas 75024

PROJECT MANAGER
Information & Telecommunications Technology

Results-focused manager with 15 years in database design and data systems applications. Extensive qualifications in all facets of the project life cycle, from initial feasibility analysis and conceptual design through documentation, programming, implementation, training, and system enhancement. Characterized by executives, colleagues, and customers as having:

Well-rounded analytical, technical, communication, and leadership skills.
Hands-on management style . . . readily roll up sleeves and work with programmers.
Expertise with IBM and DEC mainframes, MVS COBOL/DB2, IDMS, VSAM, TSO, and STROBE.

PROJECT MANAGEMENT HIGHLIGHTS

DATABASE DESIGN

- Directed design, development, and implementation of AT&T's reengineered customer database application. Significantly reduced keystroke requirements, supporting companywide minimal entry order process. Delivered project 10 weeks ahead of schedule.

- Led team of 15 in design, development, and implementation of TelComm's $3.7 million Marketing Information System. Replaced 10 disparate systems with common database; satisfied regulatory and internal reporting requirements; supported 60+ users companywide; provided company with commercialization potential (product sold for $500,000).

- Earned CEO's accolades: "Other companies have tried, but none have been able to pull this off!" . . . From VP: "In all my experience, I've not seen anyone who truly listened to people instead of making assumptions; it's been key to delivering what users wanted."

APPLICATION DEVELOPMENT

- Challenged with development and maintenance of core business customer ordering, pricing, account maintenance, and billing software applications. Incorporated new product offerings, regulatory, and user requirements into customer billing design.

- Orchestrated error-free migration of 12 million customer record applications from 2nd to 3rd generation technological environments. Consolidated nine satellite offices into two centralized computer centers.

- Comments from manager: "Your ability to get past the techno babble and bring simple solutions to complex issues is unparalleled."

COMPUTER OPERATIONS

- Directed start-up and brought computer center on-line for new "Baby Bell" company. Recruited management and technical talent.

- Designed disaster and off-site recovery procedures; led recovery project that saved an estimated $7 million in potential lost revenue.

EMPLOYMENT HISTORY

AT&T — Fast-track promotion through positions as Application Programmer (1978–1979), Technical Supervisor (1979–1981), Operations Manager (1981–1983), Senior Application Analyst (1983–1985), and Technical Manager (1985–1988).

TELCOMM, INC. — Advanced as Information Systems Manager (1988–1990), Application Systems Director (1990–1991), Computer Center Manager (1991–1993), and Special Projects Director (1994–Present).

EDUCATION

Bachelor of Science, Engineering Administration (4.0 GPA)—Southern Methodist University, Dallas, Texas

◻ ◻ ◻

If It Works, It's Right

Don't feel limited by the formats I've described in this chapter. You might find one that's a perfect fit. You might need to massage one to make it suit you. Or you might get a flash of inspiration and create something completely new and different. Whatever you choose, put your own unique signature on it. Again, it doesn't matter what you label it. If it works, it's right.

The table that follows summarizes the different résumé formats, along with their points and pitfalls.

Summary of Format Strengths and Weaknesses

Format	Strengths	Weaknesses
Accomplishments	Positions your strongest selling points front and center. Unearths buried accomplishments from long ago.	Limits space to flesh out details about your experience and skills. Doesn't work well if you're short on accomplishments or in a profession where accomplishments are difficult to quantify.
Combination	Capitalizes on strengths of both the chronological and functional formats. Preps the reader (through use of an introductory summary) to focus on your best and brightest qualifications.	Not well suited for young or entry-level candidates with limited experience.
Chronological	Showcases a strong career history. Preferred by employers and recruiters.	Spotlights any glitches in your work history.

Format	Strengths	Weaknesses
	Demonstrates your qualifications to take the next step up the career ladder. Highlights impressive employers.	
Creative	Showcases talents in professions that demand creativity—art, design, event planning, promotions, and so on.	Difficult to pull off. Not to be attempted by those with right-brain deficiencies.
Curriculum Vitae (CV)	Appropriate for scientific, academic, and medical communities where doctoral degrees, research, publications, and presentations are important. Executive CV (hybrid of a typical business résumé and a CV with a focus toward management).	Long and thorough. Can make for a tedious read. Appropriate for scientific, academic, and medical professionals who have slanted their career.
Dateless Chronological	Perfect for people who've not been working for a year or more, but whose career path has been otherwise flawless. Great for return-to-career moms/dads or others who have taken a career hiatus for personal reasons. Eliminates confusion about overlapping or concurrent work assignments.	May raise questions about how many years of experience you do have.

(continued)

(continued)

Format	Strengths	Weaknesses
	Allows the reader to focus on the substance—rather than the length—of your experience.	
Functional	Camouflages the appearance of an unstable, unorthodox, or interrupted career.	Raises employer suspicions that you may be hiding something.
	Counters job gaps, job hopping, and industry typecasting.	
	Smoothes a career transition—especially military to civilian.	
	Helpful for return-to-career moms/dads, recent grads with limited experience, and others with limited paid experience.	
	Great for career specialization; avoids repeating job descriptions from employer to employer.	
	Helps camouflage "overqualified" and "age" issues in nonexecutive searches.	
International	Demonstrates your international business acumen.	Reveals personal information (age, marital status, citizenship, health, religion, and so on).
	Allows you to "tell more and sell more" with a complete narrative of your track record.	Makes you vulnerable to discriminatory hiring practices outside U.S. boundaries.

Format	Strengths	Weaknesses
Linear	Delivers a hard-hitting sales presentation of your skills. Quickly scanned by people and computers or in a profession where accomplishments are difficult to quantify. Great for professionals who have easily measured performance criteria (sales, production, and so on).	Limits space to flesh out details about your experience and skills. Doesn't work well if you're short on accomplishments.
Newsletter	Visually distinctive and distinguishes you from dozens/hundreds of other candidates. Reflects a creative mindset.	Not well received in traditional, conservative settings such as government or public accounting.
Reordered Chronological	Great tool for those who want to switch to a profession that relates to an earlier career track. Unearths older, more dated experience and places it at the visual center of the résumé.	Requires some semblance of order and logic to your career history, such as seven consecutive years in one profession and five consecutive years in the next profession.
Targeted	Screams to the employer that you're a perfect fit for a specific job.	May give a false impression that your qualifications are limited or single-dimensional.

Top 10 Résumé Formatting Tips

1. Choose a format that will best highlight your strengths, yet minimize any shortcomings in your candidacy.

2. Apply white space liberally—learn how to add line space between paragraphs using the Format, Paragraph, Spacing command in MS Word.

3. Limit the number of tab stops on the page—more than three will cause the résumé to look too busy. Create a visual pattern—be consistent in your use of tab sets, fonts, and line spacing from section to section.

4. Use no more than two fonts on the page—one for your name and perhaps the category headings, and another for body text.

5. Use the same font and point size for every heading; use the same font and point size for all body text.

6. Use bullets that complement the body-text font—make sure the size of the bullet doesn't overpower or detract from the text.

7. Divide long paragraphs (more than six or seven lines) into two. Lead off each of the smaller paragraphs with a logical category title.

8. Avoid the "Leaning Tower of Pisa" effect of placing employment dates in the left margin surrounded by too much white space. Dates placed on the right margin allow you to shift body text toward the left and gain room for important content and keywords.

9. Balance the text between top and bottom margins so that there isn't excessive white space at the bottom of the page.

10. Print the résumé, tack it on a wall, and step back five or six feet. Make sure it has some semblance of form and design.

Chapter 4

The Blueprint for a Blockbuster Résumé

"Planning must be a deliberate prelude to writing."

—E. B. White, Author

E. B. White is the coauthor of *The Elements of Style*, a "bible" for anyone who writes for a living or, for that matter, anyone who writes at all. White proposes that the first principle of composition is to "determine the shape of what is to come and pursue that shape." Just as an architect prepares blueprints before a contractor can build, you need an outline before you can write. A lack of planning at this stage will cost you time, energy, and momentum, so resist the temptation to jump in and start composing (you'll get to that in chapter 5).

In this chapter, you'll review the categories, or building blocks, that make up a blockbuster résumé. In chapter 3, you selected the format, or structure, for your résumé. Now it will begin to take shape as you decide on a heading style and choose categories that will best showcase your experience. Many people base their résumés on the three most obvious categories—Objective, Experience, and Education—while overlooking other categories that can help catapult their résumés to the top of the "must interview" list. You'll take a look at each of these categories and decide which are most appropriate for your situation. You'll also receive a refresher course on what not to include—such as information that is illegal, passé, superfluous, or grounds for potential discrimination. At the end of this chapter, you'll have an opportunity to fine-tune your outline for structural integrity and visual appeal.

In creating your résumé outline, you will look at the following categories:

- Data Bits, or Contact Info
- Objective, or Focus Statement
- Key Features, or Qualifications Summary
- Professional Experience
- Skills
- Education, Credentials, and Licenses
- Affiliations
- Publications, Presentations, or Patents
- Awards and Honors
- Bio Bites
- Endorsements

Data Bits, or Contact Info

Info, info, everywhere,
Download oodles of free software!

Cell phones with e-mail help keep us in touch,
Can you chat for a text-messaging power lunch?

With Internet access and new URLs,
Customers go global to buy and sell,

Zillions of facts at the touch of a mouse,
Just plug in at airports, your work, or your house.

First PCs, then laptops, now PDAs a must,
Forgo them and risk being left in the dust.

This info-dense world can cause quite a strain,
So why can't they make a fast chip for my brain?

Info-dense! That's what technology has made our lives. Next time you pick up someone's business card, count how many bits of data are included. It's not unusual to find a cell phone number, a toll-free 800 number, a fax number, an e-mail address, a Web site listing, and a blog, and that's just on the front of the card! Businesses provide these numbers and links to make it easy for customers to gain access to their products.

Now that *you* are the product, take a lesson from business. Make yourself easily accessible to your "customers." Technology makes it possible for employers and recruiters to reach you immediately, and if they can't, they'll find someone else. An employment agency owner tells the story of a sales manager who lost an opportunity because she was out-of-pocket too long. The candidate hadn't promptly checked messages on her home answering machine and missed the window of time for an important first round of interviews. The candidate who ultimately landed the job was less qualified, but he was more accessible.

The following list includes 10 pieces of contact data, or "data bits," that you might use on your résumé to make sure employers can reach you easily. Put a check mark in the box next to each of the data bits you will use in your résumé header. (Your name is a given!) Keep in mind that, on a paper résumé, your name, phone number, and e-mail address are the most important elements. If you allotted one line for every piece of information, you could take up as many as 11 lines on the résumé. Obviously, I don't recommend using this many because it will detract from the visual appeal, make the résumé look cluttered, and steal the limited space available for the text portion of your résumé. So later I'll show you how to combine these data bits to take up less space but still give ample contact information.

Data Bits Worksheet

❑ Name

❑ Street address

❑ City, state, ZIP code

❑ Residence telephone number

❑ Business telephone number

❑ Mobile telephone number

❑ Pager number

❑ Fax number

❑ E-mail address (your personal e-mail, not your company's)

❑ Web page URL (your own, not your company's)

❑ Blog

❑ Availability for relocation

On this line, indicate the number of data bits you'll include in your résumé heading. _____

To List or Not to List Your Business Telephone Number

This is a tricky question. It can be a dilemma for confidential job seekers. If you don't include some sort of daytime contact number, the delay the employer experiences in contacting you might just cost you your dream job. The following suggestions might help you decide whether to list your present work number:

- Definitely include your work telephone number on the résumé if your search is not confidential and your employer has no policy forbidding the acceptance of personal telephone calls.

- Do include your work number if you have a private voice-mail system that guarantees that your messages won't be accessed by others.

- Don't include your work number if your search is confidential and calls will be screened before they get to you.

These suggestions seem like simple advice. However, I've run into many people who didn't think through the consequences of going public with their job search, only to find that a nonconfidential call to the office tipped off a coworker or boss about their search and caused work relationships to be strained (and, in some cases, terminated). If you want employers or recruiters to contact you at work and you don't have confidential voice mail, consider providing your work telephone number in the text of the cover letter but not on the résumé. You can include it in the closing or next-to-last paragraph with words to this effect.

> If you wish to contact me during business hours, please do so with a measure of discretion (any premature speculation about my departure could be advantageous to the company's competitors). My work number is 888-8888.

The preceding sentence is effective because it lets the reader see your professionalism and respect for your current employer. It also implies that you will extend this same courtesy and professionalism to your new employer.

Other Solutions for Daytime Contacts

Human resource professionals, hiring managers, and recruiters prefer not to bring extra work home with them after putting in a long day at the office. Be thoughtful and provide a daytime contact number to make it easy to reach you. If listing your current work number on your résumé is out of the question, consider these ideas:

- For greatest accessibility, put your mobile number on your résumé and carry this phone with you regularly.

If you don't have a mobile phone, a less-expensive alternative is a traditional digital pager. Your caller needs only a push-button telephone to leave you a digital message, meaning a telephone number only. Nationwide or statewide pagers are available. The cost for a pager is nominal.

If your boss or coworker questions the new contraption strapped to your belt or purse, be prepared with some innocuous comment, such as, "I just want to be more accessible to the important people in my life."

Sample Résumé Headers

Review the following sample résumé headers for ideas on how to combine information. Pay special attention to the suggestions that include the same number of data bits as you plan to use in your heading.

Your name should be one of the focal points on your résumé. In paper résumés, your name traditionally appears above any other information. You'll see tips on arranging as many as eight data bits while concurrently keeping the visual focus on your name and squeezing out as much white space as possible.

Three Data Bits

With e-mail addresses as commonplace as telephone numbers, it will be unusual for you to have only three bits of contact info. For those without an e-mail address (I recommend that you get one), the following example is a classic, traditional heading style.

ROBERT ORLANE

1442 W. Netherly Avenue
Fontana, California 93745
(213) 222-6666

Note that you don't need to include the word *residence* or *home* in front of the telephone number. It's assumed that this is a residential number when you list it below a street address. While I'm on the subject of telephone numbers, be certain to avoid the easy-to-make mistake of forgetting to include your telephone number. It wasn't until 30 unanswered cover letters went by that a friend discovered she had accidentally omitted the telephone number from her résumé.

It is important to always include a ruling line under your contact information (also called a graphic line, border line, or rule) because it pulls the reader's focus to the text at the visual center of the page. Recall from chapter 2 that this is where you'll pack the punch for maximum AIDA impact. You'll see what I mean if, after you complete your résumé, you print one version with a ruling line and one without. The one with the line is discernibly more organized, orderly, and focused. You can experiment with the Borders and Shading feature in Word or the Graphic/Custom Line keys in WordPerfect for variations on ruling lines. (You'll read more on this in chapter 8, "Visual Artistry.")

Four Data Bits

If you have an equal number of pieces of information that make up your contact data, consider "splitting" this information on the left and right margins. The following is an example.

ROBERT ORLANE

1442 W. Netherly	boborlane@aol.com
Fontana, CA 93745	(213) 222-6666

In this header, the equal number of data bits is four:

1. Street address

2. City and state

3. E-mail address

4. Home telephone

By arranging this information on just two lines, you gain another line or two of precious space in the body of the résumé. Another benefit is that your name clearly stands out because of the extra white space you've created.

The ruling line style in the next example is also popular; it's simple, yet striking.

ROBERT ORLANE

1442 W. Netherly Avenue
Fontana, CA 93745
(213) 222-6666
boborlane@aol.com

Here's a header example with a bit more personality. The vertical line extends the length of the page on the actual résumé.

1442 West Netherly Fontana, CA 93745 Cell: 213.222.6666 boborlane@aol.com	**ROBERT ORLANE**
OBJECTIVE	Qualified for high-visibility roles with a company that will benefit from my strengths in: **SALES** — business development, account growth, customer advocacy, account retention **MARKETING** — strategy planning, demographic analysis, product positioning and launch **COMMUNICATIONS** — presentations, negotiations, public speaking, user training [etc.]

Note in the following example how the size of Robert's name is increased because of its positioning on the left margin. This was done because the name will be difficult to see if his résumé is in a stack of papers held together by a paper clip at the top-left corner. If your name is short—say, it totals only a few letters, like Lee Wu or Sue Ross—avoid this heading style. Instead, position your name in the center; otherwise you run the risk of being "invisible" when the interviewer flips through a pile of résumés.

The following example uses a text box for the candidate's monogram: The dressier heading suited his career in broadcast sales.

 ## ROBERT LOUIS ORLANE

1442 West Netherly Avenue ▪ Fontana, CA 93745 ▪ Mobile (213) 997-2224 ▪ boborlane@aol.com

The next example is a bold, four-bit version with ruling lines above and below.

1442 West Netherly
Fontana, CA 93745
Cell: (213) 222-6666
boborlane@aol.com

ROBERT ORLANE

Five Data Bits

If you want to add a fifth piece of information, such as an online portfolio, center it between the city-state and home telephone number, as in the following header. It is not always necessary to include the word *e-mail* (or *email*) in front of your electronic address. In cases where this word appears, it was done to add visual balance to the header.

ROBERT ORLANE

1442 W. Netherly		boborlane@aol.com
Fontana, CA 93745	career folios.com/boborlane	(213) 222-6666

> *Tip* When using multiple phone numbers, make it clear where each number rings. For a cellular phone, use the word "Mobile" or "Cell." If you're listing a business and residence number, pair the words *business* and *residence,* rather than *business* and *home.* In the same manner, pair the words *work* and *home,* instead of *work* and *residence. Business* and *residence* correspond in style and length, as do *work* and *home.*

Six Data Bits

The following example lists six pieces of contact data. The placement of the information on the left and right margins was determined from a design perspective rather than a content perspective. Note how each line of information on the left margin is relatively balanced by its counterpart on the right margin. There is a pyramid effect, with Robert's name forming the peak. Some pieces of information could have been swapped—for instance, the home phone number with the e-mail address or Web site URL. Again, I chose this arrangement because it creates a good visual design.

ROBERT ORLANE

1442 W. Netherly	boborlane@aol.com	W: (213) 222-7474
Fontana, CA 93745	careerfolios.com/boborlane	H: (213) 222-6666

> *Tip* Try different arrangements of your "data bits." Your goals in doing this are to keep the visual focus on your name, create an eye-appealing design, and maximize white space.

Seven Data Bits

Of the seven pieces of contact data in the following header, your eye is probably drawn to the URL for the candidate's Web résumé because it has more white space around it.

ROBERT ORLANE

1442 W. Netherly Fontana, CA 93745 (213) 222-6666	careerfolios.com/boborlane	Business: (213) 222-7474 Cellular: (213) 997-1224 boborlane@aol.com

Eight Data Bits

This is the greatest amount of contact information you should consider putting on your résumé. It pushes the limits. Anything more will detract from your name.

ROBERT ORLANE

1442 W. Netherly Fontana, CA 93745 (213) 222-6666	boborlane@aol.com careerfolios.com/boborlane	Business: (213) 222-7474 Cellular: (213) 997-1224 Fax: (213) 222-6667

If relocation is not part of your plan, skip ahead a few pages to the section titled "Objective, or Focus Statement."

Dealing with Relocation on Your Résumé

People relocate for a number of reasons. Career opportunities, quality-of-life issues, family obligations, and health requirements are some of the major ones. Whatever the catalyst for your move, there will be some barriers to overcome. They include the following:

- Accessing job opportunities as quickly as the "local" competition
- Arranging time off from your current employer for interviews
- Keeping travel expenses associated with your interview jaunts to a minimum

Your employer-to-be will have some barriers to overcome as well. In the employer's case, they are more mental than physical. For instance, employers sometimes react to long-distance candidates in the following ways:

* They are wary about an out-of-town candidate's commitment to moving to a new area.

* They perceive local candidates as more settled or better connected in the community.

* They sense that out-of-the-area candidates are difficult to contact and require extra work to schedule for interviews.

* They associate additional expenses with relocation.

Here are a few résumé strategies to help overcome the mental hurdles employers might have with your long-distance candidacy. These strategies will also help level the playing field in competing against local candidates.

* An 800 number is an effective and inexpensive tool for candidates who want to relocate. It removes some of the mental barriers an employer senses because of geographic distance. Place your name, a toll-free 800 number (or, as 800 numbers run out, an 888 or 877 number), and the words *available for relocation* at the top of the page. The 800 number will serve you well if you've gone past the "move date" and résumés are still floating about on employers' desks. You can place the rest of your data bits—address, fax, e-mail, and so on—at the bottom of the page. If you're headed to a specific geographic area, say so. Also include a projected move date because it will make you look more serious about your plans. Here's an example of how your header might look.

ROBERT ORLANE

(800) 222-7474

Relocating to Dallas in January

___

Then, at the bottom of the résumé, provide your current address. This is a psychological strategy that gives the employer an opportunity to be impressed first by your qualifications before seeing how far your cross-country trek might be. Here's what the footer would look like.

___

1442 W. Netherly   Fontana, California 93745   boborlane@aol.com

The following header example illustrates another technique for de-emphasizing a long-distance address. The vertical treatment of the data requires the reader to turn the page sideways to find the address. However, the candidate's name and 800 number stand out, which is part of your design goal.

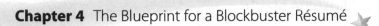

ROBERT ORLANE

(800) 222-7474

■ Email: rorlane@aol.com ■ 1442 West Netherly Avenue ■ Fontana, CA 93745 ■ Residence: (213) 222-6666 ■ Cellullar: (213) 997-1224 ■

Another strategy is to use a header that provides your name, telephone number, and e-mail address and then omit the rest of your address entirely from the résumé. The employer might wonder whether you live in the next county or nine states away. However, by doing this, you might earn a preliminary telephone interview instead of being peremptorily dismissed because of distance.

ROBERT ORLANE

800-222-7474

Email: rorlane@aol.com

Use two addresses—your current address and a "message" address. The message address can be the address of a friend, fiancé, or family member in the area you will be moving to. If you don't have a contact in the new area, hire a service to do the job, such as Postal Annex or Mailboxes Etc. Try to avoid a post office box number—you'd be surprised how many people suspiciously associate them with instability or mail-fraud scams! It's unlikely that employers will contact you via snail mail for an interview. Unfortunately, this mode of communication is typically reserved for letters that say, "Thanks for your interest. We'll be keeping your résumé on file." Nonetheless, use an address in your target area. It will give employers the impression that you're serious about your relocation effort and that you have some immediate connections within the community.

In the next example, note the words *current address* and *relocating mo/yr (use the actual dates)* to explain both addresses.

ROBERT ORLANE

Current address:	*Relocating mo/yr to:*
1442 W. Netherly Avenue	124 North Main Street
Fontana, California 93745	Denton, Texas 75122
(213) 222-6666	(714) 777-2443

If you don't use an 800 number, *do* include a telephone number that gives employers the option of making a local call to leave you a message.

The message number can be the telephone of a friend or family member in your target area—just make sure that anyone in the household who might answer the phone knows that you are also "in residence" there. It will negate your efforts if an employer calls for you and hears, "There's no one here by that name. You've got the wrong number." Also, make sure you have some system for messages to be immediately relayed to you. The goal is to promote, rather than prevent, accessibility.

Now that you've got your contact information formatted, it's time to move on to the next step in your résumé outline.

Objective, or Focus Statement

You're probably familiar with the term *Objective* as it relates to résumé writing. For 50 or more years, objectives enjoyed preeminent positioning in résumés as a one-sentence statement encapsulating the age-old question of "what do you want to be when you grow up?" More often than not, objectives tended to be *de rigueur* statements that were vague, trite, canned, and self-focused. When written in this manner, they were a waste of space, hogging that high-profile "center of the page" you learned about in chapter 2.

I'll confess that when I drafted my first résumé out of college (a mere decade or two ago), I, too, was guilty of such compositional sins. How many of you can relate to the following objective?

OBJECTIVE

Challenging position with a dynamic, growth-oriented company that will lead to advancement opportunities.

Cringe! This ancient objective would definitely flunk the AIDA test today! (Recall the advertising formula from chapter 2: Attention, Interest, Desire, and call to Action.) There's nothing in the preceding objective statement that will grab the reader's <u>A</u>ttention and capture the reader's <u>I</u>nterest. It offers nothing to create <u>D</u>esire in the reader, nor will it cause any <u>A</u>ction by the reader (except perhaps a yawn).

Today, regardless of what job you're going for, your focus should be the employer's needs. Answering those needs will create desire and interest in you. Yes, you can still define what sort of position you want. Yes, you can still convey your qualifications. And, yes, you can still use the term *Objective* if you prefer. The difference is in the perspective—don't write from what *you* want out of the employment relationship. Rather, direct your writing toward what *your employer* wants and how you can give it to them. I can't emphasize this enough:

Focus on the employer's needs!

This explains the use of the word *Focus* in place of *Objective.* Rhetorically, I prefer to use *Focus* because it conveys more energy and concentration. Arguably, it's a matter of semantics. You can use a number of terms, as long as you weave the employer's needs into your statement. Here's an alphabetical list of some alternative headings you can use for this section:

Competency	Mission	Specialist
Concentration	Objective	Specialization
Direction	Plan	Strengths
Expertise	Proficiency	Talents
Focus	Proposal	Target
Forte	Purpose	Value Proposition
Goal	Qualifications	Vocation
Intent	Skills	

Many of these terms can be mixed and matched, such as *Focus & Qualifications* or *Specialization & Qualifications.* Or you can add terms such as *Career, Professional,* or *Vocational* in front of several words in the list. For instance, *Career Target, Professional Plan,* and *Vocational Trade* can each work as a heading. You'll also note some nontraditional words, such as *forte,* which I've included to expand your thinking. These words are best used when woven into a cover letter to describe your strengths or vocational goals. Use such words only if they fit your style of speech.

Your Focus statement will be brief—one or two sentences at most. It can stand alone or be used in combination with a Qualifications Summary (the next section covers that). You are a good candidate for a stand-alone Focus statement if your situation is aligned with any of these four scenarios:

⟡ You specialize in a particular position and want to have that same position in your next job. Note that *Expertise* implies a number of years of experience at your craft. Don't use this term if you're just starting out. Study this example.

EXPERTISE

Licensed Clinical Social Worker with 12-year record of creating award-winning social service programs, accessing "hidden" funding and grant money, and delivering services to medically underserved populations.

You're a recent graduate with limited paid experience.

FOCUS

Management Training Program—BBA graduate with 4.0 GPA from one of the nation's top business schools. Well grounded in simulated corporate scenarios that required solutions to complex manufacturing, distribution, and marketing issues.

You're applying for entry-level, line, or support positions.

INTENT

To support management in a secretarial role where my technical skills, initiative, and understanding of client-driven organizations will be of value.

You're transitioning from one career to another.

GOAL

To parlay 15 years of legal experience as a top-notch business litigator into a career as a consultant, motivational speaker, and business coach.

❑ Check this box if you'll use some form of a Focus statement in your résumé. Select a word from the list on page 146 that best suits your needs and write it on the following line: _____

Key Features, or Qualifications Summary

In recent years, the Qualifications Summary has emerged as a tool to both define the type of job you want *and* to summarize why you're qualified for the job. Because the Qualifications Summary serves both purposes, it is understandably longer than an Objective or Focus statement. If you use a Qualifications Summary, you won't need a Focus statement. The following ingredients typically make up a Qualifications Summary:

- Functional specialty or title (for example, accountant, regional manager, materials manager, or production planner)

- Number of years of industry experience (for example, insurance, finance, manufacturing, or agriculture)

- Expertise, strengths, or specialization (for example, delivered more than $10 million in cost reductions through introduction of just-in-time, stockless, and future-state inventory programs)

- Certification, graduate degree, or licensure (for example, APICS-certified or MBA with strong finance and marketing skills)

★ Language skills or international business skills (for example, fluent in Spanish or familiar with Asian business protocol)

You'll find that this introductory summary section can also be called any of the following:

Accomplishments	Key Features	Representative Experiences
Background	Keyword Summary	Skills Summary
Career Summary		
Chronology	Professional Profile	Strengths
Features and Benefits	Professional Qualifications	Summary of Qualifications
Highlights	Qualifications	Title [your job title used as the heading]

Who should use a Qualifications Summary? Individuals with at least five, and preferably more, years of experience at their craft are better candidates for a Qualifications Summary. The five-year benchmark is not a hard-and-fast rule. It's just that after about five years in your field, you will have accumulated enough experience and accomplishments to warrant a synopsis of your career. You should also consider using a Qualifications Summary if the following are true:

★ You're qualified for the management or executive echelon. The sheer breadth of your experience demands a summary, just as a 200-page thesis calls for an introductory abstract.

★ You're a professional or have broad experiences in your field. A Qualifications Summary will pull broad-based generalist skills into one easy-to-digest paragraph.

★ Your most impressive accomplishments won't be seen until the latter part of the résumé. In this case, a Qualifications Summary will position the heart of your experience at the heart of the résumé.

★ You are targeting a position that calls on experience found only in the early stages of your career. Mentioning earlier experiences in a Qualifications Summary will breathe new life into dated employment.

Your résumé will have to pass the rigors of computer scanning software or Internet search engines.

❑ Check this box if you'll use some form of a Qualifications Summary in your résumé. Select a term from the list on page 148 that best suits your needs; then write your selection on the following line: _____

Professional Experience

Professional Experience, or any of its synonyms, is the mainstay of a chronological format. You will need a "Professional Experience" category if you plan to use any of the following formats:

Accomplishments

Combination

Chronological variants

CV

International

Linear

Targeted market

(If you aren't sure which format to use, refer to the summary at the end of chapter 3.) Although "Professional Experience" implies remuneration for your services, this category can also include nonpaid internships or significant, full-time volunteer positions related to your career goal. If this is the case, title the section something like "Experience" or "Career Highlights" rather than any of the terms in the following list that begin with the word *Employment*. For those retiring from a military career and whose experience best lends itself to a chronological presentation, title your service "Professional Experience" rather than "Military Experience" to make it more palatable for business and industry.

If you've chosen to write a functional, or skills-based, résumé, you can still include a skeleton of your professional experience to lend credibility to your work history. This condensed listing needs to include only your position title, the employer, and dates of employment. You can omit the dates if they reflect employment gaps or instability, but be prepared to explain them in an interview. Here is an example.

Customer Service Associate—Titan Truss Co., Veoria, CA (2006–Present)

Reservations Assistant—Sequoia Tours, Tourtown, CA (2001–2006)

Customer Care Representative—Travel World, Tustin, CA (1998–2001)

Data Entry Processor—Crayton Industries, Marysville, CA (1995–1998)

If you will use a professional experience category, you can choose a title from this menu:

Career Experience	Employment Highlights	Professional History
Career Highlights		
	Employment History	Professional Record
Career History		
Career Record	Employment Record	Record of Experience
Contract Assignments	Experience	Relevant Experience
Employment	Experience Highlights	Work Experience
Employment Background	Professional Experience	Work History
Employment Experience	Professional Highlights	Work Record

❑ Check this box if you'll include in your résumé a traditional time-line of your work experience. Select a term from the preceding list that best suits your needs; then write your selection on the follow-ing line: _____

Skills

This category offers employers a skills-based menu of your talents, rather than a chronological list of employment. Don't confuse the Skills section with an introductory qualifications paragraph or a bulleted summary of your talents. In this case, I refer to a skills section for candidates who can best benefit from a functional résumé format. You'll remember from chapter 3 that these include people in career transition; those with unrelated industry experience, limited paid experience, or no recent work history; those who are unstable, too old, or "overqualified"; and individuals with "career specialization" issues. (In the latter case, a Skills section avoids redundant job descriptions from employer to employer.)

Some alternative headings for a Skills section appear in the following list. Keep in mind that such a heading is only a section head; you can use subheadings under this heading to outline up to a half dozen skill areas that reflect your talents and strengths (I'll discuss this later):

Abilities	Key Qualifications	Strengths
Core Competencies	Knowledge, Skills, and Abilities	Summary of Qualifications
Expertise	Proficiency	Talents

❑ Check this box if you will use a skills-based presentation of your qualifications. Fill in the blank below with the heading you have selected: _____

Education, Credentials, and Licenses

These sections are self-explanatory. If you have trade school or college training, say so—that is, most of the time. The exceptions to this rule pertain to a degree that was "almost" completed, the "wrong" degree, or a degree in progress. I reveal my strategy for dealing with these sticky wickets in chapter 5. If you have only a high school diploma, do not list it or the name of the high school. The exception is if you are a recent high school graduate looking for work. You should include credentials, certificates, and licenses that required course work, internships, or a testing process, provided that the credential or license is still relevant to your field.

Recent grads can go heavy on this section. In other words, if education is your biggest selling point, don't be afraid to let it take up "prime shelf space"—that visual center of the page discussed in chapter 2. In the following example, Stephen leveraged his lack of paid experience by positioning an impressive Education category at the center of the page. He then stretched it to more than three inches of vertical space by using a variety of subheadings (Dual Major, Coursework Highlights, and so on).

EDUCATION

UNIVERSITY OF THE PACIFIC

Dual Major:	Bachelor of Science, Business Administration—Option in Finance Bachelor of Arts, French
Coursework Highlights:	Entrepreneurial Finance; Portfolio Management and Theory; International Finance; Business and Real Estate Economics; Monetary Policy and the Banking System
Honors:	Melvin Peters Scholarship Recipient (based on academic performance) Dean's List (seven consecutive semesters) President's Honors (among top graduating seniors in School of Business)
GPA:	3.9 GPA (4.0 scale)
Cocurricular Activities:	Financial Management Association (President, VP Fundraising—set record for fundraising); Alpha Kappa Psi, Professional Business Fraternity (VP Fundraising); Le Cercle Français French Club (President, Treasurer); International Business Association (various committees)
Language Studies:	French (fluent in language and business protocol) Burmese (fully fluent) Japanese (conversational skills)

Consider any of the following alternative headings for your Education section. You can combine several words if you have degrees and licenses that don't warrant two separate category headings:

Academic Credentials	Credentials	Professional Certification
Academic Preparation	Degrees	Professional Training
	Education	
Certificates	Industry Training	
Continuing Education	Licenses	

❑ Check this box if you have education, credentials, and licenses that will help sell your experience. Select a term or terms from the preceding list that best suit your needs; then write your selection on the following lines: _____

_____

Affiliations

Affiliations can be boiled down to two basic flavors: career and civic. The first has to do with organizations dedicated to a profession, industry, or functional specialty. The second category covers community, nonprofit, and for-fun groups. Volunteerism can fall under either category, depending on whether you are a mentor to business professionals or a role model for youth. Volunteerism is enjoying a renaissance in America, as in America's Promise with powerhouse Colin Powell at the helm and, here in my home state, the California Mentoring Initiative for at-risk youth. Employers will regard this kind of service favorably: It not only benefits your chosen charitable cause, but also is great for business public relations. (Don't, though, let this be your primary motivation for volunteering. The saying "Do something nice for someone today and don't get caught" implies that volunteering has its own rewards!)

If numerous affiliations elevate you to "overachiever" status, consider splitting them into a career-related category and a community-related category for greater readability and impact. If you have only one organization to include, make sure it carries weight, or don't include it. (See the upcoming tip on single-item lists.)

Choose one of following terms if you'll be using an Affiliations category:

Activities	Community Service	Professional Memberships
Affiliations		
	Industry Affiliations	Public Service
Associations		
	Leadership	Trade Organizations
Charitable Commitments		
	Memberships	Volunteerism
Civic Involvement		
	Mentorship	
Community Activities		
	Organizations	
Community Involvement	Professional Affiliations	
Community Organizations	Professional Associations	

> *Tip* If you have a category with just one item in it (such as an affilia-tion, award, or interest), avoid listing it under a separate category. A single item can look "lonely" on its own, diminishing its impact. It also wastes two additional lines of space on the résumé (the heading line and the line space between the heading and the item). Extra space, called white space, also draws the reader's eye to the item. If the single item is fabulously impressive, fine—list it by itself. If it isn't, you have probably succeeded in drawing attention *away* from some other feature on your résumé that should have earned more recognition. This doesn't mean you need to exclude one-liner items from your résumé. If including the item will support your candidacy, look for another category to weave it into, such as a Qualifications Summary or Accomplishments section.

❑ Check this box if you're involved in industry organizations that will add to your marketability. Select a term from the list on page 153 that best fits your needs; then write your selection on the fol-lowing line: _____

Publications, Presentations, or Patents

This category is not limited to the CVs of researchers or academicians. Virtually any professional who has excelled in his or her field, as evidenced by the output of professional writings or public-speaking prowess, will war-rant a Publications and Presentations category.

Publications include books written or contributed to and articles published in newsletters, newspapers, trade journals, magazines, or the Internet. You can list a master's or doctoral thesis here; however, if this is the sum of your publications, combine it with your Education category. Self-published booklets, pamphlets, and guides can be included. You can also weave other writings into this section, such as a script for training videos, copy for advertisements or brochures, or ghost writing for speeches. When this is the case, title your heading "Professional Writing" rather than "Publications."

Presentations should include events where you were the primary presenter or co-presenter. Include presentations made at professional conferences, business symposia, college classes, and company meetings of a district, regional, national, or international scale. Do not include presentations on par with proposing or pitching your services to a customer for a sale. If making presentations is critical to your skill set and you want to emphasize this to the reader, group this experience with other experience in a

Qualifications Summary, Professional Experience section, or Special Skills section.

Patents, pending or otherwise, should be included if research, product development, or design skills are required in your field.

If you have a generous amount of material for the Publications and Presentations section, you might find that using separate headings for each category provides a cleaner presentation of your information.

❑ Check this box if you have articles, books, or presentations to be included in your résumé or CV. Write the heading you plan to use for this category on the following lines: _____

_____

Awards and Honors

This section can include awards relating to your career accomplishments, community volunteerism, contributions to service organizations, or academic accolades. The following is an example.

COMMUNITY & ACADEMIC HONORS

Big Brothers/Big Sisters, Volunteer of the Year

Business & Professional Woman of the Year, Central California Nominee

Tri-County Regional Occupation Program, Outstanding Service Award

State University, Outstanding Senior Graduate, Social Science Department

State University, voted by professors as Commencement Speaker

❑ Check this box if you've earned special awards or recognition by employers, customers, the community, or academia for your skills and contributions. Decide on a category heading (Community Honors, Academic Awards, Awards & Honors, and so on) and write it on the following lines: _____

_____

Bio Bites

Sound bites—snippets of videotape or conversation that capture the essence of a situation—are popular in news and entertainment reporting. "Bio bites"—bits of information that reveal interesting layers of your life—add impact to your résumé and are especially effective when used as a closing tool.

Bio (as in autobiography) bites can include details on where you grew up, travel experiences, language skills, athletic abilities, and other interests. Use caution in divulging telltale information that portrays your age, religion, ethnicity, political persuasion, or a stance on controversial issues that might be used to discriminate against you. If you know your audience's preferences, however, you might want to include some of this information. *The rule of thumb is that it should support your candidacy;* otherwise, don't include it.

The following are other possible names for the Bio section:

Interests	Bio Highlights	Personal Portrait
Other	Miscellaneous	Characteristics
Of Interest	Background	Personal Data
Bio Data	Profile	

You can use bio bites to fill in "missing" elements from your background. Beau, an experienced sales representative, was targeting a sales position with Upjohn's Animal Health Division where he would be selling veterinary medical supplies to cattle feedlot operators, veterinarians, and animal-feed stores. He had the sales background but lacked a degree and the formal animal-science training required for the position. We wrote this Bio data to strengthen his candidacy.

BIO DATA

Raised on fifth-generation cattle ranch (stocker operation), with involvement in all aspects of livestock management. Frequently called on to doctor cattle in remote areas, using knowledge gleaned from self-study of veterinary-medicine textbooks. Competed five years on the amateur rodeo circuit.

Mike, a district manager in his 50s, drew a picture of his health and stamina by including this information at the close of his résumé.

INTERESTS

Runner—Participate in Bay to Breakers Race

Golfer

Downhill Skier

Reader

Mike reported that the Bay to Breakers Race (a famous, fun, but rather grueling runner's event held annually in San Francisco) was one of the first things interviewers commented on when meeting him. In his 50s, he competed in a "youthful" industry (wireless communications). This tie helped to set him apart and underscore his energy, stamina, and physical fitness. He landed a district manager position with a preeminent communications provider and was given the coveted task of launching the first wireless PCS market in the nation.

❑ Check this box if you will include relevant background data, travel, language skills, security clearance, interests, or athletic or avocational pursuits that distinguish you from other candidates. Select a term from the list on page 156 that best describes your information; then write your selection on the following line:

_____

Endorsements

Endorsements are a new spin on an old process: letters of reference (or recommendation). Letters of reference have long been part of the hiring system; in most if not all cases, you will be asked to provide them. This request usually comes after you have submitted your résumé (typically during or after the interview) and signals that an employer is interested in you as a viable candidate. A letter of reference gives hiring managers another person's opinion of you so that they don't have to rely solely on the claims you make in the résumé or interview. These third-party recommendations add weight and credibility to your candidacy.

Endorsements are snippets, or sound bites, of letters of recommendation; performance evaluations; letters of appreciation from customers or vendors; or verbal comments from clients, coworkers, or supervisors. If you want to use verbal comments, get your source to put them in writing for maximum credibility.

This technique works especially well for people who want to transition from one field or profession to another. For instance, Jane, a stay-at-home mother who is reentering the workforce and targeting a position in sales, could use these endorsements to emphasize her selling skills.

"Jane solicited more than $10,000 in donations from business owners, making our fund-raising event the most successful in the school's history." (Sean Lemming, Chief Administrator, Loma Linda High School)

"She is an articulate and persuasive public speaker, delivering arguments at City Council Meetings that persuaded us to vote in favor of her position on a controversial issue." (Jacob Schmidt, City Councilperson)

"A born leader, Jane joined our 200-member service club five years ago and has chaired four key committees in that time. Most recently, she was unanimously elected to the office of President-Elect." (June Wong, President, Junior League of Loma Linda)

You'll also find an excellent use of endorsements in one of the success stories showcased in chapter 1. Torrey, an educator and child-care program manager transitioning to pharmaceutical sales, strategically selected endorsements from a physician, a pharmaceutical sales representative, and a medical office business manager to allay concerns over her lack of industry experience.

Choose any of these names for a header for an endorsements section:

Character References	Customer Testimonials	Industry Endorsements
Complimentary Quotes	Endorsements	Recommendations
Customer Comments	Excerpts from Letters of Support	Testimonials
		Vouchers

You might want to use endorsements without placing them in a separate category. I recently worked with a candidate (Jean) who had some of the most glowing, sincerely written recommendation letters I have ever read—they were full of admiration and verbal applause for her abilities, accomplishments, and outstanding attitude (she lived up to every word). She could easily have been hired based solely on these letters of recommendation. Yet she didn't want to provide prospective employers with six pages of reference information on the first contact (a smart move on her part). In Jean's case, I included each endorsement as a bulleted item under each of her employers.

Advertising Sales Manager—Computer Trends, Houston, TX, 1997–Present

♦ Recruited to boost flat advertising sales for computer publication serving the Houston area. Delivered a 64% increase in sales without additions to the sales force. Personally doubled ad sales in peripherals category.

♦ *"Jean's performance has been extraordinary . . . leads by example . . . energetic support for individuals she supervises . . . consistently made contributions outside the purview of her department . . . very visible ambassador of goodwill."* (Editor/General Manager)

Account Executive—Info Business Systems, Houston, TX, 1995–1997

♦ Ranked #1 in sales of records management systems, despite no prior industry knowledge. Promoted to key account sales (multisite government and education customers, traditionally managed by owner/general manager).

♦ *"Jean brought high energy, infectious enthusiasm and professional integrity . . . had a keen understanding of the organization's goals . . . was dependable and reliable to the nth degree."* (V.P., Sales)

Sales Manager/Sales Associate—The Finance Group, Dallas, TX, 1989–1995

♦ Within 3 months of hire, ranked in top 5% of producers among 2,000 sales associates. Promoted to manage 40-member sales team—reversed stagnant sales performance from #59 to #7 among 75 offices.

♦ *"Clear analytical skills . . . scrupulously honest . . . manifests drive and enthusiasm that is contagious."* (C.E.O.)

❑ Check this box if you have performance evaluations, recommendation letters, or other material that you can use as endorsements on your résumé. Select a heading from the preceding list that best fits your needs; then write your selection on the following line:

_____

What Not to Include

There are a few sound bites that will place you in contention for discreet discrimination. Resist the temptation to include these items:

✧ **Date of birth.** Some companies automatically return résumés to candidates who have referenced their date of birth or age.

✧ **Marital status/children.**

✧ **Personal data.** Height, weight, health status, ethnicity, and so on.

- **Photograph.** Don't do it, even if your physiognomy is suitable for the cover of *GQ* or *Cosmopolitan*—which brings me to the exception to this rule. Actors and models do use a photo, typically an 8-by-10 head shot, on the back of which is the résumé—a listing of performances or shoots/products featured.

- **Letters of recommendation.** Save them for a timely follow-up contact.

- **Salary history/requirements.** If at all possible, save this hot potato for the interview process. You might want to mention a salary range in the cover letter if the employer has specifically asked for it. Check out chapter 10 on cover letters for tips on dealing with this important issue.

- **"Date-stamping" the résumé.** Don't place the date you prepared the résumé in the lower-right corner (or anywhere else); also avoid listing when you are available to begin work unless you're applying, for instance, to a school district that has a school-year calendar or year-round track to staff.

- **Reference list.** Save this one, too, for the interview or a follow-up contact. You might, however, conclude your résumé by centering the words, "References on request." Don't sacrifice additional line spaces by using a separate category heading. Yes, I know—as do the majority of professional résumé writers, employers, and the general public—that you don't need to include these words. However, it is still a common practice to do so, and I'll give you two reasons why:

  - It informs readers that the end of the résumé has come—this is especially helpful if the last category they've read is about your experience rather than a more typical closing category, such as Education or Activities.

  - It brings balance and visual closure to the page. Centering the reference line at the bottom of the page helps to balance your name and contact information, which might be centered at the top of the page.

Putting It All Together

Congratulations! Phase I of construction is almost complete. Skim back over this chapter and note which style you've chosen for your contact data, as well as the category boxes you've checked and the headings you've chosen for them. Fill this information into the following form. If you're more comfortable at a computer, input your outline on a blank screen in your word-processing program.

Your Résumé Outline

Contact Information Header Style:

_____

_____

_____

_____

_____

Chosen Category Headings:

_____　　　_____

_____　　　_____

_____　　　_____

_____　　　_____

_____　　　_____

If you filled in all 10 category blanks and plan to write a one-page résumé, you'll need to combine some of the categories; otherwise, your résumé would be too busy-looking.

Frank Lloyd Wright, the most influential architect of the 20th century, was the first to propose the concept of spacious living spaces rather than the traditional small rooms of typical New England homes, fashioned with quilt-like construction. With missionary zeal, Wright applied this message in all of his architectural projects:

> **[a building] should contain as few rooms as will meet the conditions which give it rise.**

Mr. Wright's maxim on design has application to your résumé as well. For a clean, concise presentation, three to five categories per page works best. With the "as few rooms as possible" principle, consider combining an Objective and Qualifications sections or combining short categories (headings that will have only a few items under them) with the Qualifications section or Professional Experience section.

Now that the skeletal outline of your résumé is finished, it's time to add some heart and soul by learning to write great copy in chapter 5.

Top 10 Résumé Blueprint Tips

1. Plan well! Choose categories that will best showcase your experience.

2. When listing your contact information in the heading, offer employers several options for contacting you, including <u>mobile</u> or daytime <u>phone and e-mail.</u>

3. Do not list your business telephone if you want to keep your search confidential and do not have a secure voice-mail system.

4. <u>Format your heading wisely</u> if you're short on space. Instead of listing street address, city/state/ZIP, telephone, and e-mail on separate lines, place your address and city/state/ZIP on the left margin, and telephone number and e-mail on the right margin to save space.

5. Use an Objective or <u>Qualifications Summary</u> that captures your brand and zeros in on the employer's needs.

6. Always include a Professional Experience category—the mainstay of a chronological format. In a functional format, you can also include a Summary of Professional Experience to lend credibility to the skills cited.

7. An Education category (or related categories such as Credentials and Licenses) should be included <u>if you possess degrees</u> or training relevant to the target position. If you're a recent graduate, expand your education category to highlight honors, course highlights, co-curricular activities, or other items of interest.

8. In addition to other categories such as Affiliations, Publications, and Awards, <u>consider including an Endorsements</u> or Customer Comments category. These third-party comments add weight and credibility to your candidacy.

9. Do not include personal information (your date of birth, marital status, number of children, height and weight, health status, and so on).

10. Limit the total number of categories for optimum visual appeal. Three to five categories per page works best. Consider combining sections, such as Objective and Qualifications, if you have more than five categories per page.

Chapter 5

How to Write Great Copy

"Writing is easy. All you do is sit staring at a blank sheet of paper until the drops of blood form on your forehead."

— Gene Fowler, American Writer

Don't let this humorous analysis cause you dismay. Even experienced writers can feel some fear and trepidation when facing the start of a new project. You already have a good outline from which to work (chapter 4), which puts you beyond the "blank sheet of paper" stage. Using your outline, you'll learn how to flesh out details that will add weight to your candidacy. By the end of the chapter, you will have a healthy rough draft of your résumé. Don't be concerned about polishing and perfecting copy at this point because chapter 7 is a primer on editing and tightening text.

To write a strong résumé, you must know your audience. Advertisers have a target audience in mind when they start the creative process. Authors have a typical reader in mind when they begin to write. Businesses have an average consumer defined before they market their products. By now, you know that *you* are the product (with a clear brand and a target); and, as a product, you must know who your potential buyers are. You may not know them by name, but you should know them by need. What skills and competencies are they looking for? What knowledge do they require? What trends are they capitalizing on? What opportunities are they interested in tapping? What problems do they need fixed? What projects can you help them move forward?

I'll assume that you know the answers to these questions already. If you don't know them, I'll digress for a moment and give you two tools you should quickly master. First, read and research. Consume the Business section of your daily paper (set your alarm clock 15 minutes earlier weekday mornings if need be!), read newsletters and journals relevant to your industry, scan magazines such as *Newsweek* and *Time*, and research the Internet for relevant industry activity.

Second, network and stay on the radar screen of people who have authority or influence in the hiring decision. Don't limit yourself to sources in your industry or the employment/recruitment business. Network with commercial real estate sales associates, professionals in the sign business, contractors who specialize in tenant improvements, reporters, and economic development directors—these people often know of new opportunities before the masses. One of the best ways to expedite your job search is to conduct a targeted campaign in which you identify companies that would be a great fit with your skills, brand, and value, and then network to identify opportunities within those companies. (For more information on this and other search strategies, check out chapter 11 of *Job Search Magic*, published by JIST Works.)

Now, back to the task of writing. First, I'll review keywords and how important they are to the copywriting equation. After that, you'll begin to draft the various categories of your résumé.

Keywords

Every résumé, whether in electronic or paper format, should contain keywords that signal employers you have the skills, talents, and experience to match their job requirements. Because keywords are so critical to résumés—especially résumés that are stored in databases that will eventually be searched for keywords—it's important to discuss what keywords are, where to find them, how and where to use them, and what to do to improve your "hit" ratio.

What Are Keywords?

Keywords refer to those words that describe your title, knowledge base, skill set, impressive "name-brand" companies or Fortune 500 employers, prestigious universities attended, degrees, licensure, software experience, or affiliations, to name a few. They are typically nouns or noun phrases—their substantive nature has caused them to supersede many of the "action verbs" of the 1980s and 1990s. The next *Before* and *After* résumé excerpts illustrate the conversion from action verbs to noun-based keywords.

Before

Troubleshot, repaired, maintained, and monitored computers to component level.

Administered networks, wrote scripts, and conducted diagnostic tests.

After

Extensive component-level troubleshooting, repair, maintenance, and monitoring of advanced supercomputers, massively parallel processing computers, mainframes, PCs, Macs, Sun workstations, and UNIX-based workstations for National Energy Research Supercomputer Center (NERSC).

Advanced skills in UNIX and network system administration support, scriptwriting, electronic testing equipment, diagnostic testing, videoconference services, SMTP-based e-mail, TCP/IP protocol, LAN/WAN, and browser usage.

Compare the first *Before* sentence with the first *After* sentence and note the additional details with respect to the types of computers worked on and where the work was done. The emphasis on keywords necessitates elaboration. Don't be afraid to go into more detail. The constraints of copyfitting your résumé to exactly one page don't apply in e-résumés because page breaks will vary depending on the receiver's software and default settings. This allows you to fudge a bit on length. At the same time, do not turn it into a full-length, unedited autobiography. Remember, even though an e-résumé lacks the luster of pretty fonts and fancy formatting, it is still a marketing piece—the AIDA formula from chapter 2 still applies to the content of the résumé.

> *Tip* The most common type of keyword that employers search for is a position title. To improve your "hit" ratio, use your industry or discipline's keywords along with logical synonyms. For instance, the keywords "materials manager" might be referred to as "supply chain manager," "logistics manager," or "purchasing manager" in another company. To cover your bases, consider leading off your résumé summary (or objective) with a list of synonyms.

Where to Find Keywords

Wouldn't it be nice if you could turn to a book and find all the keywords to ensure that your résumé turns up on the top of the candidate list? This aspect of keyword loading can give rise to anxiety in some job seekers. "Do I have the right keywords? How can I know what keywords to use? Does someone have a magical list of keywords which will ensure that I make the short list?"

Later in this chapter, I cover how to find information for your job description. These same resources are your library for keywords. For simplicity, I'll outline those resources here and then review some helpful online resources for keywords.

Off-Line Resources for Keywords

- Your professional association—read its newsletter (there may also be an online version), attend meetings and conferences regularly, and network outside those meetings with colleagues and mentors.

- Informational interviews or research with other industry contacts.

- Your company's formal job description of your position.

- Job descriptions from your targeted companies (gaining access to them can be tricky).

- Classified advertisements (a.k.a. "help wanted" ads) in newspapers, periodicals, and Web sites.

- Recruiter job orders.

- Current "how to" résumé books with sample résumés from your profession.

- The most current edition of the *O*NET Dictionary of Occupational Titles* (JIST Works, or available online—see the next section).

Without question, involvement in your industry's professional association is the number-one method to stay up-to-date on keywords. There is just no substitute. In the words of Gerry Crispin (coauthor of *CareerXroads*), workers who refrain from involvement in professional associations "are *obsolete* from the day they don't connect." (*Obsolete*—now there's a word that would never find its way into a keyword search.)

Online Resources for Keywords

With access to the Internet, you can find an exhaustive collection of keywords to help your résumé surface from the sea of e-résumés. Here's where to look:

- www.onetcenter.org/overview.html: O*NET, the Occupational Information Network, is part of the Department of Labor's Employment and Training Administration site. Although this database is packed with career keywords, you'll also want to check out resources that provide the latest buzzwords on trends or current vernacular that your target companies are using.

✳ Visit one of the major career Web sites listed in chapter 9 (see page 439, "How to Post an ASCII Résumé to a Web Site"):

- Monster.com

- CareerBuilder.com

- Yahoo! HotJobs.com

- Dice.com

✳ Tour your target company's Web site and click its link to jobs (it will most likely say *careers, jobs, employment,* or *opportunities*). Note the keywords used in postings relevant to your search. Also skim through pages such as About Us or Press Releases, or the annual financial reports for keywords and terms that can help you master the company's unique "corporate-speak." If the company has a blog, be sure to familiarize yourself with hot topics—you can then incorporate those keywords into your résumé and networking.

✳ Don't confine your sleuthing to targeted companies. You can access a list of 60,000+ small and large companies in 200+ categories at sites such as BizWeb (www.bizweb.com).

✳ Bring up a *search engine*. Most of them have a "careers" section that you can explore. Or, at the search engine's home page, you can search for "career Web sites" or other keywords pertaining to your discipline, such as **"civil engineering" + jobs**. If you get an avalanche of sites (they sometimes number in the hundreds of thousands), be prepared to refine your search by city or a subdiscipline. The most popular search engines are Google (www.google.com) and Yahoo! (www.yahoo.com).

How to Position Keywords

Software and search engines will quickly find keywords regardless of where you place them on your résumé. Even if you were to bury keywords at the bottom of a résumé, the computer would still find them. Of the recruiters and HR professionals interviewed, all indicate that the placement of keywords does not matter in the data-mining process. Nonetheless, it stands to reason that if keywords are the golden lure to gain employer interest, they should be displayed prominently. Eventually, human eyes will be sifting through your material, and they—unlike a computer—will appreciate the positioning and presentation of key material.

For paper résumés, recall the strategic placement on the "visual center of the page" discussed in chapter 2 (the 2-inch band that falls approximately

$2\frac{5}{8}$ inches from the top of the page). On e-résumés, the center of the page, in terms of visual impact, falls within the first screen that the viewer sees. With that in mind, be sure to place keywords within the first 20 to 24 lines that appear on a computer screen (before it is necessary to scroll down to view additional information).

Keywords that appear under the first employment entry will also spark employer interest. Several Internet researchers commented that this is an indicator of a "fast match," meaning the candidate has recent, relevant experience and can be placed quickly. If this is the case, you may want to forgo a summary section or use a light hand on it. The result is that your first employment entry will rise into that all-important first screen.

How to Improve Your "Hit" Ratio

To give you an idea of the enormity of cataloging keywords, Resumix (an applicant-tracking system) has poured 30+ person-years of linguistic knowledge and software engineering into its program, which contains more than 10 million skill terms and 140,000 extraction rules. Obviously, you will opt for a minuscule fraction of that number. As few as a dozen keywords may be all that some employers will use to search you out, whereas others might elect to do more elaborate searches. Employers can search by position, function, skill set, date received, name, degree, major, and so on.

Recruiting researchers often conduct several preliminary searches for each position, using different combinations of the keywords listed. In other words, not all of the keywords are used at the same time, enabling the researchers to find as many candidates as possible on the first round of résumé mining. Once a candidate is spotted, he or she can be tracked for placement and notified of subsequent opportunities in the days, months, and years to come.

The following table shows keywords extracted from advertised job descriptions by DSA, a Florida-based executive recruiting firm.

Position: National Account Executive

Advertised description:	Fantastic opportunity for a National Account Executive with Fortune 200 company selling computer solutions for the retail marketplace. Responsibilities will include managing and selling new and existing accounts and building strong relationships in the industry. Qualified candidates will possess a bachelor's degree or equivalent experience selling computer solutions or other capital products to the retail industry, as well as a proven track record of successful selling to the director level, taking a consultative sales approach. Unlimited earning potential with a benefits package second to none. Respond quickly! Position available in San Francisco, CA. Compensation: $80,000–$100,000.
Keywords used in search:	Sales, account executive, bachelor's, computer solution sales, hardware or software sales

Position: Information Technology Professional

Advertised description:	Seeking qualified professional in the Information Technology industry with experience utilizing UNIX, Windows, PowerBuilder, and/or Oracle for a full-time career opportunity. Great opportunity to work with cutting-edge technology and multiple environments. Position available in Philadelphia, PA. Compensation: $40,000–$80,000.
Keywords used in search:	UNIX, Windows, PowerBuilder, Oracle

Position: Technical Architect/Project Manager

Advertised description:	Fantastic opportunity with one of the premier organizations in the world. Presently looking for strong technical people who have a firm grasp on the architecture of an Enterprise Solution. Candidates must possess strong experience in the design, implementation, and execution of architecture for large-scale distributed systems. Experience in design and programming in C, C++, Java, Visual Basic, PowerBuilder, Windows NT, and UNIX (a combination of some is acceptable). In addition, an ability to travel. If you feel you are qualified and you have a desire to have unlimited earning potential with one of the elite organizations in the world, act now!
Keywords used in search:	C, C++, Java, Visual Basic, PowerBuilder, Windows NT, UNIX

(continued)

(continued)

Position: Intellectual Property Attorney

Advertised description:	High-profile multioffice boutique law firm looking for Intellectual Property Attorney for Litigation Group. Ideal candidate should have actual litigation experience with depositions. Trial experience a plus. Four to 7 years' experience with solid credentials (Min 3.0/4.0 GPA). Undergraduate in EE or Mechanical preferred. Position available in Chicago, IL. Compensation: OPEN.
Keywords used in search:	Attorney, JD, depositions, litigation, intellectual property

Position: IP Partner

Advertised description:	Prominent international law firm seeks a 2- to 7-year Associate with an antitrust practice for the Washington, DC, office. Experience within the Antitrust discipline can be in any business or health care area. Solid credentials a must.
Keywords used in search:	Attorney, JD, antitrust, partner

Position: Senior Estimator

Advertised description:	Industry-leading, commercial contractor/construction corporation seeks Senior Estimator for a Jacksonville, FL-based position. Qualified candidate: Considerable experience in construction industry construction-estimation, preferably with multiunit, apartment, condo, or multifamily background. Compensation: Highly competitive salary/bonus…. Attractive benefits package…. Relocation reimbursement for right candidate.
Keywords used in search:	Contractor, construction, estimator, construction-estimation

Position: Junior Project Architect

Advertised description:	Industry-leading construction, engineering, and design firm seeks qualified Architects for Jacksonville, FL-based positions…. Qualified candidates: Commercial/Industrial architectural experience (at least 5 years)…. Requisite degree, certificates, licenses, and/or registrations that are applicable…. Excellent career opportunity with a progressive industry leader…. Highly competitive salary/bonus…. Attractive benefits plan.
Keywords used in search:	Construction, engineering, architect, commercial, industrial

Position: Japanese Translator

Advertised description:	Large manufacturer is looking for a Technical Japanese Translator/Interpreter for a long-term contract-to-permanent position. You will be in charge of translating engineering documents and correspondence from Japanese to English and vice versa. You will also be in charge of interpreting for Japanese management and taking calls from Japan. Must be able to read and write a minimum of 2000 Kanji. Must be very fluent in both Japanese and English. Must have at least one year of translating experience, preferably with technical translation.
Keywords used in search:	Translator, interpreter, Kanji, technical

Position: Consultant

Advertised description:	Exceptional opportunity with one of the most successful global organizations. Qualified candidates must possess 3 years'-plus experience in one or more of the following: instructional design, multimedia, organizational design/restructure organizational behavior, business process reengineering, or human resources. In addition, candidates must be self-motivated with exceptional organizational, written, and oral skills. Realize your potential: apply today!
Keywords used in search:	Instructional design, multimedia, organizational design/restructure, organizational behavior, reengineering, human resources

These examples should help allay any fears about coming up with a magic potion of keywords. Yes, you need to give careful thought to the word ingredients you use; however, virtually all of the preceding keywords were simple, straightforward extractions from position announcements. You can take some comfort in understanding that human resources professionals want to fill open positions and will often perform multiple searches with different combinations of keywords to compile a strong candidate pool.

> *Tip* You might wonder whether double-barrel loading of keywords is helpful. Product managers from Resumix indicate that listing a particular keyword more than once could boost you to a higher position on the candidate match list, yet caution that an electronic exaggeration or manipulation of your skills could work against you once the element of human interaction enters the picture.
>
> Forgo the temptation to trick the software by, for instance, planting the keyword "project manager" nine times throughout the résumé when you might have minimal experience as a project manager. For example, if you were to write "Although my experience as a *project manager* is limited, I performed functions similar to a *project manager* while an intern with XYZ Company. My related *project manager* responsibilities included…." This disingenuous presentation will make you *candidata non grata* in the eyes of recruiters.

Be specific! You can't be all things to all people, and neither can your résumé. Management searches often require a tight industry fit, so junior- and senior-level executives should be specific about their industry experience (provided that you plan to conduct your search in the same field).

Now that you've unlocked the keyword mystery, let's look further at the categories of your résumé that will contain these keywords. As you continue to work through this chapter, keep your outline from chapter 4 in front of you, because you will write copy for *only* the categories in your outline. Just skip over any categories you won't be using—with one possible exception. Please write an Objective, or Focus statement, even if you don't plan to use it as part of your résumé format! The effort won't go unrewarded: Your Focus statement will help you convey your goals in informal networking and formal interviewing situations. The more articulate your communication, the more impressive your presentation.

Top 10 Résumé Keyword Tips

1. Find at least three online postings that contain a full-blown description of your target position. Analyze these postings and highlight common keywords. Consider other sources for keyword research, such as your target company's Web site or blog, publications from your professional association, and networking contacts.

2. Weave the highlighted keywords into your résumé—add common synonyms to augment the keywords.

3. Consider hard skills (such as areas of expertise), soft skills (such as communication, interpersonal skills, attitude), general information (such as affiliations, telephone area codes), and academic qualifications (such as degrees and certifications) as keywords.

4. Fortify keywords by following them with an accomplishment. For instance, you can reinforce the keywords "customer service" in this way: customer service—boosted customer satisfaction scores from 82% to 94%.

5. In your résumé objective or summary, include your position target as well as variations of the keywords. For instance, augment "Customer Service" with terms such as "Client Services," "Account Management," "Customer Relationship Management," or "Sales Support."

6. Don't overlook geographic keywords. If a recruiter is searching for someone in California's Silicon Valley and your home is in "Campbell" rather than "San Jose," add the appropriate terms. For instance, "Campbell, CA 95432—Silicon Valley/San Jose area."

7. If space allows at the bottom of a printed résumé, include a Morse Code-type keyword section (keywords punctuated by commas or bullets).

8. For résumés pasted into e-mail messages or e-forms where space is not an issue, include a separate keyword section.

9. Avoid the temptation of "planting" keywords that are not part of your experience just so that your résumé will be found in an electronic search. Some sneaky job seekers have tried coloring keywords with white text so that the terms are found in computer searches but are not visible to the human eye.

10. If you're submitting an MS Word document to employers, include keywords in the File, Properties, Summary, Keywords area to reinforce your keywords.

The Objective or Focus Statement

"I don't care what I do, I just want a job." You might not care, but you can bet the employer does. Recall that part of your task is to make the job of the hiring manager easier. Don't give that person the investigative assignment of determining your strengths and where you'd best fit into the company. The employer résumé preference survey (see appendix B) turned up a number of pet peeves, two of which apply to the Objective:

⤳ "Not defining the type of position you want."

⤳ "Not researching the company to know what jobs are available."

So if you don't know what positions are available, find out! Call on your networking sources or contact someone within the organization, whether a human resources manager or department representative. Following are three alternatives for presenting your Focus statement, the first of which is a cover letter technique.

Cover Letter Focus Statement

If you opt for no Objective in the résumé for space-saving reasons, you still must clue the reader in to what type of position you want. You can accomplish this in the cover letter by using a "regarding," or subject, line. Add boldfacing to the information—in this case "openings in customer service," to help the reader immediately know your job interests.

[date]

Jane Doe, Director of Staffing
Best Company, Inc.
1234 Sunnyside St.
Dallas, TX 75214

Re: Openings in Customer Service

Dear Ms. Doe:

> *Note* The Gregg Reference Manual, a respected reference guide chock full of more than 1,700 rules for writing and punctuation, places the subject line below the salutation (Dear Ms. Doe:). Many of my colleagues and I take liberty with this rule and place it above the salutation with the rationale that this location gives greater visibility to the subject.

If your target company is large and has a number of opportunities in customer service, elaborate on your subject line in the body of the cover letter and use specific titles the company uses.

> I believe my skills would be best suited to your Customer Service Department—for instance, in positions such as International Account Specialist, Key Accounts Specialist, or Customer Care Coordinator.

Title Statement

You can quickly convey your job focus with a short noun phrase, known as a title statement, centered below the header of your résumé. This technique is clean, gets across your point, and saves you one or two lines of space by eliminating the Objective category heading.

ROBERT ORLANE

1442 W. Netherly		Mobile: (213) 222-7777
Fontana, CA 93745	rorlane@yahoo.com	Home: (213) 222-6666

CUSTOMER SERVICE / SALES SUPPORT PROFESSIONAL

PROFESSIONAL EXPERIENCE

Customer Service Coordinator—PC Manufacturers, Inc., Fontana, CA

[etc.]

Traditional Objective

Recall that you selected a title for your objective category in the preceding chapter. To write the copy for this brief category, break it down into three key pieces of information:

1. The position you want

2. The key skills that qualify you

3. The benefit(s) or value to an employer

Table 5.1 gives examples of these three points. The majority of the examples in Table 5.1 begin with a noun (typically the title of the position desired), shown in Column 1. Reading across the table, Column 1A illustrates wording that will connect your target position with your key skills. Many of the examples in this column are interchangeable and might work well for your particular situation. Columns 2 and 3, key skills and benefit(s)/value to the employer, can be combined, as in the examples for the retail buyer and social services position.

Table 5.1: Components of the Objective Statement

Column 1 Target Position	Column 1A Connective Tissue to Pull the Sentence	Column 2 Key Skills That Qualify You for the Position	Column 3 Benefit(s) or Value to the Employer
Marketing research position →	that will use my strengths in →	demographic research and analysis →	to target, develop, and maintain a dominant market share for your company.
Opportunity	in which my	sales support, customer service, problem-solving, and human relations skills	will grow and retain your customer base.
Retail buyer	with impressive record of		contributing to gross margin improvement, comparable store sales, and product development.
Computer programmer of adventure/ arcade games	with proficiency in	C/C++ and Java	Noted for producing clean, readable, and imaginative code to speed the release of products.
Plant management position	in which	production planning and materials-management skills can be used to	capture cost savings and maximize plant productivity.

Column 1 Target Position	Column 1A Connective Tissue to Pull the Sentence	Column 2 Key Skills That Qualify You for the Position	Column 3 Benefit(s) or Value to the Employer
Elementary teacher	with commitment to		creating a rich, multimedia learning environment through student-centered activities and integrated lessons with meaning-ful "real-world" applications.
Social services position	that will benefit from my		12-year record of creating award-winning social service programs, accessing grant money and "hidden" funding, and delivering es-sential services to medically under-served populations.

Now it's your turn. The following exercise defines the elements that make up an easy-to-assemble Focus statement.

Exercise for Assembling a Focus Statement

1. **Position you are targeting.** (If you are targeting two types of positions in your search, write Focus statements for both.)

   a. _____

   b. _____

2. **Key skills that qualify you.** Identify three key skills, even though you might not use all of them in the Focus statement.

   a. _____

   b. _____

   c. _____

3. **Benefit(s) or value to the employer.** Again, identify three, even though you might not use all of them. In the next chapter on writing accomplishments, you'll find a complete list of employer "buying motivators" on pages 230–238; you might find it helpful to sneak a peek at that list before answering this question.

   a. _____

   b. _____

   c. _____

Now, transfer your answers into the résumé text below.

FOCUS

Career opportunity as (1.a.) _____ that will benefit from my (2.a.)_____, (2.b.)_____, and (2.c.)_____.

or

OBJECTIVE

(1.a.) _____ that will use my strengths in (2.a./b./c.—use one or more of your answers) _____ to (3.a./b./c.— use one or more of your answers) _____.

You can also write an Objective/Focus statement by starting with an infinitive. However, avoid cliché, "me-focused" wordings such as the following.

OBJECTIVE

To obtain a position as a _____ with opportunity for growth and career advancement.

It's understood that you want to expand your skills or advance your career (the alternative is to be stagnant and bored), so drop this idea. Further, the infinitive "to obtain" is candidate-focused; instead, when beginning an Objective with an infinitive verb, use one that is employer-focused, such as the examples in Table 5.2.

Table 5.2: Employer-Focused Infinitives to Start an Objective Statement

Sample Profession	Infinitive at Beginning	Qualifying Skills/ Benefit to Employer
Secretary	To support	management in a secretarial role where my technical skills, initiative, and understanding of client-driven organizations will be of value.
Engineer	To provide	professional engineering skills in the design of large-scale public-works projects.
Motivational Trainer	To parlay	legal experience as a top-notch litigator into a career as a business coach and motivational speaker.
Caseworker	To link	individuals in need of financial, medical, and mental-health services as a social-service caseworker.
Marketer	To assist	your marketing team in identifying, reaching, and persuading customers toward brand loyalty.
Sales Rep	To grow	your customer base through aggressive cold calling, telemarketing, and networking.
Teacher	To develop	inquisitive, lifelong learners as an educator of young children.
Counselor	To influence	at-risk youth through guidance as a reality-based counselor and tutor.
Draftsman	To combine	award-winning CAD skills and business focus with an architectural firm specializing in hospital design.

After the addition of some graphic lines and formatting, this is how the first example from the preceding table might look.

Secretary/Administrative Assistant

Goal:　To support management in a role where my technical skills, initiative, and
understanding of client-driven organizations will be of value.

To develop this type of Focus statement, you can use some of your material
from the exercise. The preceding example is basically a rearrangement
of information from the answers to questions 2 and 3 in the exercise.
(Question 2, key skills, equals "technical skills, initiative, understanding of
client-driven organizations"; question 3, benefit or value to employer,
equals "support management.") You'll also need to select an introductory
infinitive that complements your goal, just as "to influence" works well for
a counselor and "to grow" works well for a sales rep. Here are a few
suggestions:

- To add
- To assist
- To augment
- To combine
- To contribute
- To create
- To deliver

- To develop
- To expedite
- To grow
- To increase
- To influence
- To lead
- To link

- To manage
- To maximize
- To meet the needs
- To minimize
- To parlay
- To provide
- To support

When in doubt, "to contribute" and "to provide" work for a number of professions. In the following space, write your job title under the heading
"position"; then fill in the center column with the infinitive you selected.
The third column—Qualifying Skills/Benefit to Employer—will be your
answer to either question #2 or question #3 (or a combination of both)
from the exercise.

Position	Infinitive at Beginning	Qualifying Skills/ Benefit to Employer
_____	To _____	_____

This might take some tweaking to smooth out. Review the examples from sample professions in the preceding table for different ideas on how to connect the infinitive and skills/benefits.

The Qualifications Summary

Many résumé professionals write their client's Qualifications section last because it is easier and faster to write after the résumé has been composed. I agree that doing it in this order is easier and faster; however, if you're an inexperienced writer who gets to practice your résumé-writing skills only once every few years, it might not yield the results you intended. I call this kind of résumé a "tail that wags the dog."

Here's why. Using a traditional chronological résumé format as an example, if you were to write the Employment Experience section first, you would have a tendency to cover many areas, unrestrained and unfocused. Then, when it comes time to write the Qualifications section, you'll find that your Experience section dictates the contents of your Qualifications Summary. Now let's approach the task in reverse order. Writing your Qualifications Summary first forces you to focus on your brand and the key points you plan to emphasize in your résumé. The Qualifications section becomes a mini-outline for you to follow in creating the remainder of the résumé; everything you write below the Qualifications will support what you've said in the summary. This order mandates that you stay focused and not meander. Recall the messages of E. B. White at the beginning of the preceding chapter: "Planning must be a deliberate prelude to writing." You must "determine the shape of what is to come and pursue that shape."

In crafting your Qualifications Summary, consider these 12 ingredients:

1. Title/functional area

2. Subcategories of functional area or core competencies

3. Industry

4. Number of years of experience

5. Expertise, strengths, specialization

6. "Combination" accomplishment or highlights of accomplishments

7. Advanced degree, certification, licenses

8. Language skills, international business skills

9. Technical/computer skills

10. Personal profile/management style

11. Affiliations

12. Employers or colleges with name recognition

Following are five example summaries, each of which is formatted differently but consists of common elements. The superscript numbers in the summaries correspond to the 12 items in the preceding list and demonstrate how these ingredients can be rearranged.

[1]SUPPLY CHAIN / LOGISTICS MANAGEMENT

[2]Purchasing, Materials, Inventory, Production, Distribution

[7]APICS-certified with [4]20+ years' experience in [3]ISO 9000 manufacturing and industrial food processing environments. [6]Delivered $17 million cost savings through [5]expertise in operational analysis, master production planning, quality/continual improvement processes, and integrated technology. [10]Commitment to partnering with cross-functional teams, support staff, customers, and international suppliers has contributed significantly to successes.

In order of appearance, the ingredients used are as follows: 1) title/functional area; 2) subcategories of functional area or core competencies; 7) advanced degree, certification, licensure; 4) number of years' experience; 3) industry; 6) "combination" accomplishment; 5) expertise, strengths, specialization; and 10) personal profile/management style.

[1]SALES MANAGER

Emphasis in [3]Business Publishing / [2]Advertising / [2]Marketing

- ◆ Fast-track [4]17-year sales and management career in competitive industries and markets ([3]publishing, computers, commercial real estate--California, Florida).

- ◆ [6]Earned distinction as #1 sales producer with each of my three career employers.

- ◆ [5]Especially adept at assembling, coaching, and motivating market-dominant sales teams.

- ◆ [8]International orientation: lived and worked five years in Tokyo; multilingual skills include fluent Spanish and conversational Japanese.

Ingredients and order used: 1) title/functional area; 3) industry; 2) subcategories of functional area or core competencies; 4) number of years of experience; 3) industry; 6) "combination" accomplishment or highlights of accomplishments; 5) expertise, strengths, specialization; and 8) language skills, international business skills.

[1]EXECUTIVE DIRECTOR / PROGRAM MANAGER

[2]Marketing, Public Relations, Event Management, Volunteerism

Qualified for leadership positions where [5]business savvy, public relations talent, and development vision will be of value. [4]15-year career in nonprofit sector reflects an ability to [5]stretch limited operating funds, earn the loyalty of a tireless volunteer corps, and [6]strengthen donations when national averages depict a marked decline in giving.

Career Highlights:

♦ [6]Planned and managed the systems that enabled a long-term infusion of $5.6 million in fund development for one of the nation's leading pediatric hospitals.

♦ [6]Tripled in-house volunteers to 250 through improved recruitment, training, and recognition programs.

♦ [6]Instrumental in focusing the energy of a volunteer corps numbering 1,400+ from 15 support guilds.

♦ [10]Committed to advancing community and business interests as reflected by honors/involvement as:

[6]Professional Woman of the Year; Featured Speaker on Volunteerism, Regional Women's Conference; [11]Past President of Volunteer Network; Board Member for five charitable organizations.

Ingredients: 1) title/functional area; 2) subcategories of functional area or core competencies; 5) expertise, strengths, specialization; 4) number of years of experience; 5) expertise, strengths, specialization; 6) accomplishment; 10) personal profile/management style; 6) accomplishment; and 11) affiliations.

OBJECTIVE & QUALIFICATIONS

[1]SALES CHALLENGE that will draw upon my [4]14-year career, which includes:

☑ [6]Consistent history of exceeding sales quotas for [12]Fortune 500 employers;

☑ [6]Top performer status among 17 regional sales representatives; and

☑ Proven ability to [10/5]train inexperienced sales representatives to [6]perform in top 10% of sales force.

Order of ingredients: 1) title/functional area; 4) number of years of experience; 6) "combination" accomplishment; 12) impressive employers and schools with name recognition; 6) highlights of accomplishments; 10) personal profile/management style and 5) expertise, strengths, specialization; and 6) highlights of accomplishments.

[12]IBM-trained [1]Customer Engineer

with impressive [4]17-year career in technical/customer support

[2]**Technical Skills:** Expertise in [5/9]coaxial and twin axial environments including installation, testing, repair, maintenance, modifications, and upgrades.

[10]**Profit-Oriented:** Suggested operational business enhancements which [6]saved corporation thousands in expenses and drew national recognition from IBM.

[2]**Training & Development:** [6]Selected from team of 14 as district trainer. [6]Wrote script for video training tape for use at six Internal Revenue Service locations throughout the US

Order of ingredients: 12) impressive employer with name recognition; 1) title/functional area; 4) number of years of experience; 2) subcategories of functional area or core competencies; 5) expertise, strengths, specialization, and 9) technical/computer skills; 10) personal profile/management style; 6) "combination" accomplishment; 2) subcategories of functional area or core competencies; 6) accomplishment.

Many writers will attest that the hardest part of writing is organizing material and getting those first few words on the page. After that, ideas and words begin to flow. Table 5.3 parses the first sentence from Qualifications Summary examples and helps you organize and write the first few words in your Qualifications Summary.

Table 5.3: Breakdown of Lead Sentence for Qualifications Summary

Descriptive Word	Job Title or Profession	Level of Experience	Key Feature of Your Career
Seasoned	manager	with 20 years of experience	delivering impressive contributions to productivity and profit.
Experienced	engineer	with significant background in	design and construction of large-scale public-works projects.
Generalist	human resources professional	with 14-year history of	building competent and cohesive work teams.

Descriptive Word	Job Title or Profession	Level of Experience	Key Feature of Your Career
Top-producing	sales representative	with consistent history of	exceeding sales quotas with Fortune 500 employers.
Award-winning	architect		specializing in the design of multispecialty medical centers.
Profit-oriented	executive	with 20-year history of	leading organizations through start-up, turnaround, and aggressive growth campaigns.
Competent	administrator	with 15 years of experience	managing multisite business office operations.
Fast-track career in	retail management		delivering strong increases to volume growth, gross margin, and merchandise turnover.
Impressive 25-year career in	information systems management	with regional accountability	for systems supporting 39 locations and more than 600 users.
Dynamic career in	sales management;	led 6-state region to	1st-place ranking in all perfomance goals.

(continued)

(continued)

Descriptive Word	Job Title or Profession	Level of Experience	Key Feature of Your Career
Dedicated	educator	with 10-year career	helping second-language learners acquire English literacy.
Reality-based	counselor	with lifelong commitment to	helping individuals with disabilities.
Corporate	secretary	with 20 years of experience	supporting senior-level executives.
Licensed	medical technologist	with 10 years of experience in	laboratory, blood banking, and reference laboratory settings.
Patient-focused	nurse	with expertise in	treating home health patients with dual diagnoses and complex medical needs.
Board-certified	ophthalmologist	with 15 years of experience in teaching hospitals and private practice;	clinical expertise in no-stitch phaco, trabeculectomy, scleral buckle, pars plana virectomy, and perfluoro-carbon liquids.
Certified	safety engineer	with history of	reducing lost-time accidents to record low on behalf of all employers.

Descriptive Word	Job Title or Profession	Level of Experience	Key Feature of Your Career
Annenberg	communications graduate	with	internship experiences at CBS/*60 Minutes* and CNN Headline News.
UCLA	graduate	well-grounded in	simulated corporate scenarios that required solutions to complex manufacturing, distribution, and marketing issues.

Many of the adjectives in column 1 are interchangeable and might work to help describe your own profession. As an alternative, you could choose to eliminate an adjective and start your Qualifications Summary with your title (column 2). Column 3 lists the number of years of experience or some other indicator of your level of experience. If you have several decades of experience and age discrimination is a possibility, substitute words such as "significant experience" or "consistent history" for "35-year career." Column 4 contains the key selling feature—it may or may not include a specific accomplishment.

> *Note* You'll see only brief references to accomplishments in this chapter. Because accomplishments are the linchpin of a great résumé, the entire next chapter is devoted to identifying, communicating, and positioning your accomplishments.

To help develop your Qualifications Summary, I have repeated the 12-item ingredient list presented earlier in the chapter, this time with room for you to fill in information applicable to your background. Don't be concerned if you don't come up with information for each category. And even if you do have material for each element, you might not use it all—remember that the title of this category ends with the word *summary*.

Table 5.4: Ingredients of the Qualifications Summary with Room for Your Information

Ingredients for Qualifications Summary	Example (Dana)	Your Information
1. Title/functional area	International sales support	
2. Subcategories of functional area or core competencies	Export documentation, government relations	
3. Industry	Manufacturer of surveillance technology	
4. Number of years of experience	Seven	
5. Expertise, strengths, specialization	Internal communications with credit, production, engineering, manufacturing, and shipping to improve on-time shipment of orders	
6. "Combination" accomplishment or highlights of accomplishments	Led preliminary market research and coordinated opening of international sales office in Mexico City. Supported sales growth of 35%.	
7. Advanced degree, certification, licenses	N/A	
8. Language skills, international business skills	Fluent in Spanish; serviced Central and South American customer base.	
9. Technical/computer skills	MS Office; WordPerfect; Access	
10. Personal profile/ management style	Dedicated and loyal; five-year record of perfect attendance.	
11. Affiliations	N/A	
12. Impressive employers and schools with name recognition	N/A	

Based on the information Dana provided in Table 5.4, I developed this Qualifications Summary.

> **Customer service professional** with seven years of experience servicing international accounts in the United States and Latin America. Worked in tandem with marketing team to support a 35% increase in sales. Improved on-time shipment of orders through collaboration with credit, production, engineering, manufacturing, and shipping matrix. Well-versed in export documentation, international transport, and government export regulations. Fluent in Spanish language, culture, and business protocol.

After completing the preceding table, take a clean sheet of paper or sit down at your computer and begin trying different combinations of your information. Review the suggestions in Table 5.3 for ideas on how to put together your lead sentence. The length of the summary will be determined by your material. Note that some of the example Qualifications Summaries on the preceding pages contained as few as three sentences, whereas others warranted a full paragraph plus bulleted statements. You might find it helpful to focus your statement into a three-point theme:

1. **Experience:** Number of years spent in your target industry, impressive employers, job titles relevant to your goal.

2. **Skills:** Specific job functions, specialty areas of knowledge, advanced training, licensure, certification, language abilities.

3. **Proof of your ability to deliver:** Preferably verifiable facts; consider combining career accomplishments (for example, the total dollar volume of new business you have developed over a seven-year career in sales).

If you find the task of formulating a Qualifications Summary more difficult than you anticipated, take heart:

What is written without effort is in general read without pleasure.

—Samuel Johnson, English lexicographer, 1709–1784

The Qualifications Summary is the hardest part of the writing process. In fact, I'll admit that, when writing for clients, developing the summary (and I've written thousands) always taxes my gray matter. It's much like developing an abstract for a 200-page dissertation, which is not an easy task. However, once you have completed it, your concise synopsis tells employers who you are and what you have to offer. Memorize your summary, because it will come in handy in networking and interviewing situations. (You'll want to adapt it from the telegraphic style of résumé writing into complete sentences with personal pronouns to make it sound smooth and natural.) You can also print an abbreviated summary on business cards for use in informal networking situations.

Professional Experience

To catalog your employment history, use the worksheet guides in appendix A. Your word-processing program might have a résumé template that you prefer; if so, outline your employment history at your computer. This is the basic information you'll use:

- Company name
- City and state (without ZIP code) where you were employed (not the company's corporate headquarters)
- Month and year you began employment
- Month and year you left the company (use the word "Present" if you are still employed)
- Position title

If you held more than one position at a company, list each title followed by the dates (years only) for each position. It isn't necessary to include the company's post office box, street address, ZIP code, or your supervisor's name and phone number on the résumé. The following example shows the past 15 or so years and illustrates one method for listing multiple job titles at one employer.

PROFESSIONAL EXPERIENCE

MAJOR MANUFACTURERS, INC., Sunnyvale, California		1997–Present
V.P., Supply Chain Management	(2002–Present)	
Director, Materials Management	(2000–2002)	
Director, Production Planning	(1998–2000)	
Logistics Coordinator	(1997–1998)	
LEADING OEM COMPANY, INC., San Jose, California		1989–1997
Production Planner	(1992–1996)	
Line Supervisor	(1990–1992)	
Assembler	(1989–1990)	

The next step is deciding how to distribute the weight among the positions, or how much copy you will write for each position. This step will save you time and help you avoid writing full descriptions for every position.

Don't give each position equal treatment in terms of length—your résumé is not a socialist project! Instead, determine where your most relevant experience is and leverage the greatest weight on that position. Later in this chapter, I'll give some tips on what to do when your most recent position is not as impressive or as relevant as prior positions (see the section "Solutions for Downplaying Less-Relevant Positions").

How Far Back?

The jury isn't unanimous on this question. In the résumé preference survey, more human resources managers (63 percent) indicated that a candidate with 15 to 30 years of experience should *not* limit the experience listed on a résumé to just the past 10 to 15 years. Several who voted for "full-term" résumés, however, commented that a short statement to summarize dated experience would suffice. On the other hand, you are still left with 37 percent of human resources managers who feel a listing of 10 to 15 years is sufficient. To satisfy both camps, do detail the most recent 10 to 15 years in a traditional presentation (company name, dates of employment, title, position description, and accomplishments). The further back in the most recent 15 years, the less you need to say. Even if early information is eminently impressive, it will not carry as much weight, simply because it happened more than a decade ago. For experience that is more than 15 years ago, use one of these summary techniques.

> Eight years' prior background in production environments, gaining hands-on experience as Expediter, Cardex Clerk, Production Scheduler, and Manufacturing Analyst.

or

> Prior background in production environments, gaining hands-on experience as Expediter, Cardex Clerk, Production Scheduler, and Manufacturing Analyst.

Enumerate dates only when the dates don't go back too far, with too far being defined as approximately 25 years of total experience. Dates that take you back more than three decades might just as well be emergency flares—they'll attract as much attention.

The next example of earlier experience doesn't date the candidate too much; however, if his dates had extended back any further, I would have used one of the examples immediately above to catalog his earliest history.

PRIOR EXPERIENCE

Manufacturing Analyst—ABC Company	1987–1989
Production Scheduler—Seering Unlimited	1985–1987
Inventory Analyst—Gables Manufacturing	1983–1985
Expediter—Fedco Manufacturing	1981–1983

Where to Find Material for Your Job Descriptions

Consider one or more of these sources to help develop copy for your job descriptions:

- Your company's formal job description of your position (use this as a starting point only—most company job descriptions are lengthier than you'll need for your résumé and many are outdated).

- Job descriptions of positions similar to your own from your targeted companies (gaining access to them can be tricky).

- Internet postings or detailed classified ads in newspapers, periodicals, and Web sites (comb ads for positions similar to your position and note the key qualifications required).

- Recruiter job orders (if you are working with a recruiting firm or personnel agency).

- Informational interviews with industry contacts (find out from managers with hiring authority what they believe the most important functions and keywords are for jobs similar to yours).

- Your professional association's newsletter (almost every association has a newsletter, from which you can glean the latest in industry trends, technology, processes, and keywords).

- "How to" résumé books with sample résumés from your profession (make sure that the books have been published recently—technology advances can cause keywords to change rapidly).

- The Department of Labor's *Occupational Outlook Handbook* online at www.bls.gov/oco/home.htm.

In each of the following three tables, you'll see an example of how information from some of the preceding sources was spun into text for résumé job descriptions. The first table contains a lengthy, detailed company job description that was carved into concise résumé copy. Note how redundant statements are summarized and presented with an emphasis on transferable skills.

Because this candidate, Sean, was interested in both human resources and safety-management positions, the job description was separated into two paragraphs. By doing so, readers interested in human resource experience can easily spot this experience, whereas readers interested in safety-management experience can quickly find relevant safety experience. I have underlined important concepts from the job description; these keywords were then woven into the job description (a few details not found in the original job description were gleaned from the résumé interview).

Table 5.5: A Job Description and the Résumé Written for It

Company Job Description	Actual Résumé Copy
GENERAL ACCOUNTABILITY: The <u>Administrative Human Resources Manager</u> is accountable to the Vice President for the successful development and implementation of XYZ Company human resources practices, procedures, and safety programs concerning employees of the Construction Division. NATURE AND SCOPE: The incumbent is responsible for the <u>develop</u>ment and implementation of the company human resources <u>policy</u> and procedures, both salaried and hourly, as well as the <u>develop</u>ment and dissemination of the <u>safety program</u> and the development and dissemination of EEOC requirements and practices. <u>Accident prevention</u> and the <u>avoidance of conflict with EEOC requirements</u> are paramount in his job responsibilities. The Administrative Human Resources Manager is responsible for maintaining all required <u>files</u> for human resources, safety, and EEO, as well as the <u>investigation</u> and <u>reporting</u> of all thefts and accidents. He is responsible for attending all safety meetings, EEO meetings, and seminars; participating in apprenticeship programs; and performing the necessary <u>recruitment</u> for such apprenticeship programs.	ADMINISTRATIVE HUMAN RESOURCES MANAGER **Human Resources Management:** Managed human resources functions for 130 employees at nine sites throughout the Southeast. Generalist experience includes HR policy design and administration, records management, recruitment, orientation, training, evaluations, employee relations, benefits enrollment, Workers' Compensation administration, labor contract negotiations, and EEOC compliance. Report to and work closely with vice president. • [bulleted list of contributions] **Safety Management:** Created, implemented, and managed division safety program to minimize accidents and injuries. Trained supervisors and communicated safety policies and progress to employees. Conducted investigations and wrote reports. Worked closely with Department of Industrial Safety; OSHA; and Mine, Safety, and Health Administration officials to ensure compliance with environmental and safety regulations. •[bulleted list of contributions]

(continued)

(continued)

Company Job Description	Actual Résumé Copy
The incumbent must <u>work closely with</u> the <u>Vice President</u> of XYZ Company to maintain an open line of communication with other Division safety and employee-relations departments. He must maintain a close working relationship with the <u>Department of Industrial Safety; State OSHA; Federal OSHA; and Mine Safety and Health Administration officials</u>. He should actively participate in safety and EEO committee work. SPECIFIC ACCOUNTABILITIES: Responsible for <u>oversee</u>ing all salaried and hourly personnel activities, including <u>hiring, discharging, training, and performance evaluation</u>. Responsible for the <u>planning</u>, organizing, and implementation of the division's <u>safety program</u>. Also responsible for the <u>train</u>ing of other <u>supervisors</u> to ensure that the safety program is religiously followed. Responsible for the <u>coordination</u> and follow-up of outside agency <u>safety inspections</u>. Responsible for special assignments by the Vice President as they may occur. Responsible for the coordination of all salaried employee functions, including payroll actions (e.g., hires, terminations, salary changes, disabilities), as well as the implementation and enforcement of personnel procedures comprising, but not limited to, new employee <u>orientation</u>, personnel and <u>benefits</u> communications, local <u>compensation</u>	

Company Job Description	Actual Résumé Copy
analyses, employee statistics, and <u>personnel records,</u> including the preparation of all requests for approval and position descriptions.	
Provide pre-employment screening, on-the-job training, and administration of company safety program to ensure production staff work in a safe and efficient manner.	
Perform administrative tasks such as <u>accident/incident reports</u> and MSHA quarterly reports.	
Provide support to operations personnel to ensure that all environmental and safety standards are met.	

Table 5.6: Translating O*NET Data to Résumé Text

O*NET Dictionary of Occupational Titles	Résumé Text
LICENSED PRACTICAL AND LICENSED VOCATIONAL NURSE	LICENSED PRACTICAL & VOCATIONAL NURSE
Observe patients, charting and reporting changes in patients' conditions, such as adverse reactions to medication or treatment, and taking any necessary action. Administer prescribed medications or start intravenous fluids, and note times and amounts on patients' charts. Answer patients' calls and determine how to assist them. Measure and record patients' vital signs, such as height, weight, temperature, blood pressure, pulse and respiration. Provide basic patient care and treatments, such as taking temperatures and blood pressure, dressing wounds, treating bedsores, giving enemas,	Provide high-tech nursing services for home health and hospice patients. Collaborate as member of health care team to assess patient needs, plan and modify care, and implement interventions. Administer prescribed treatments; clinical expertise includes infusion therapy (hydration, antibiotics, chemotherapy, TPN, enteral, amphotericin, gamma-immune, and experimental treatments). Equally experienced in wound management, upper airway and tracheostomy care, hyperalimentation care, Groshong care, and care of drainage tubes. Document patients' response to treatment and medication, as well as fluid/food intake and output. Educate patients and family

(continued)

(continued)

O*NET Dictionary of Occupational Titles	Résumé Text
douches, alcohol rubs, and massages, or performing catheterizations. Help patients with bathing, dressing, personal hygiene, moving in bed, and standing and walking. Supervise nurses' aides and assistants. Work as part of a health care team to assess patient needs, plan and modify care and implement interventions. Record food and fluid intake and output. Evaluate nursing intervention outcomes, conferring with other health-care team members as necessary.	members in wound management, diet, and exercise to promote health.

> *Caution* When responding to classified ads, be cautious not to plagiarize material. There's a fine line to walk in addressing the specific requirements of an ad without copying the information word for word. With the latter, you will be perceived as lacking intelligence, creativity, and initiative.

This classified ad was used to write a tailored qualifications summary.

Table 5.7: Using a Classified Ad to Write a Qualifications Summary

Classified Ad	Actual Résumé/Cover Letter Copy
SALES REPRESENTATIVE—Immediate opening for Sales Rep. Qualified to sell roofing and building materials in northern-state territory. Prefer college degree w/ 5+ yrs proven sales exp. to suppliers, contractors, distributors, applicators, and architects. Position offers salary, comm., bonus, expenses, co. car, liberal benefits, and career growth. Send résumé.	QUALIFICATIONS SUMMARY SALES/TERRITORY MANAGEMENT **Building Materials/Construction Industries** More than 10 years of experience in building materials supply in positions as sales representative, branch manager, and principal/manager for local and regional companies. Delivered sales growth of $8 million over a 7-year period. Strong network of contacts with northern-state suppliers, contractors, distributors, and architects. Thorough knowledge of the trades.

Classified Ad	Actual Résumé/Cover Letter Copy
	Excerpt from cover letter: Beyond the experience found on my résumé, I'd like to add that I virtually grew up in the roofing business. My father owned [name of well-known roofing and building materials supply company], so I had an early exposure to the industry and the people associated with it. I continue to maintain a number of those relationships—many of whom would be potential clients for your company.

How Long Is Too Long?

Think like an advertising copywriter: Be concise, but give enough data to create interest and a desire to meet you. Try to keep your job descriptions to around five lines. More will begin to look too dense and you should either prune it or break it into two paragraphs.

One of the best strategies to improve readability of a too-thick paragraph is to "divide and conquer." Go a step beyond simply splitting the paragraph in two. Instead, group common ideas together, and then introduce them with boldfaced subheadings. This will aid the reader in identifying your skills and give you an opportunity to emphasize important keywords. Using this technique, Dana's *After* job description is notably more readable than her *Before* description.

Before

As accounting manager for start-up organization, designed and implemented formal accounting procedures to support revenue growth from $2 million to $13 million. Hired and supervised customer service, warehouse, and data systems managers. Organized a full complement of training programs for support, administrative, and executive staff. Developed accounting systems for capital expenditures, product costing, and labor reporting. Designed procedures to generate management information in the areas of sales analysis, fixed asset, and inventory accounting. Significantly improved communications among production, accounting, and marketing departments through TQM principles and "brown bag" luncheon series.

After

Accounting: As accounting manager for start-up organization, designed and implemented formal accounting procedures to support revenue growth from $2 million to $13 million. Developed accounting systems for capital expenditures, product costing, and labor reporting. Designed procedures to generate management information in the areas of sales analysis, fixed asset, and inventory accounting.

Human Resources: Management responsibilities were expanded to include hiring and supervision of customer service, warehouse, and data systems managers. Organized a full complement of training programs for support, administrative, and executive staff. Significantly improved communications among production, accounting, and marketing departments through TQM principles and "brown bag" luncheon series.

Solutions for Downplaying Less-Relevant Positions

You might be dealing with a special circumstance that requires some proactive copywriting. For instance, your most recent position may be a demotion because of corporate downsizing, or you might have a nontraditional title that may cause readers to be confused about the level of responsibility you hold. Here are a few solutions to these issues.

Magic

Recently Demoted

Many companies have experienced merger mania or a major reorganization, the result of which has been the elimination of middle management and other positions. If you have been a casualty of company cutbacks or branch closures, you'll want to avoid the appearance of being demoted for reasons of poor performance. This was the case with John, a branch manager who took a cut in title and responsibility (from Branch Manager to Account Manager) rather than relocate with the reorganization of his company. An excerpt from his *Before* résumé follows.

Before

PROFESSIONAL EXPERIENCE
_____

Z-BEST CORPORATION, San Francisco, California   1996–Present

Sales Executive (2003-Present): Responsible for sales to government and commercial accounts in the northern California region.

Branch Manager (1996-2003): Managed strategic planning, sales forecasting, budgeting, expense controls, operational strategies, purchasing and inventory management, sales training and development, marketing, and sales/business development.

- *#1 Ranking:* Reversed branch's historically poor performance from ranking of #33 out of 35 units to #1 in the nation for sales, with added honors as Top Service Branch.

- *50% Increase:* Recruited, trained, and motivated customer-driven sales force that achieved a nationally unprecedented 50% increase for product placed in field.

- *50% Expense Reduction:* Reduced expenses from more than 150% of target to goal attainment in all four major expense categories.

The solution to John's "demotion" is to eliminate dates and present the information in a narrative format. Note in the following revision how I began with his Branch Manager position (an older position), mentioned the number of years of experience in management, and de-emphasized his present position as Account Manager by placing it at the end of the job description.

After

PROFESSIONAL EXPERIENCE

Z-BEST CORPORATION, San Francisco, California   1996–Present

Recruited as Branch Manager, serving seven years in this capacity with full P&L accountability for branch sales performance. Managed strategic planning, sales forecasting, budgeting, expense controls, operational strategies, purchasing and inventory management, sales training and development, marketing, and sales/business development. Presently responsible for sales to large government and commercial accounts.

Accomplishments as Branch Manager:

- *#1 Ranking:* Reversed branch's historically poor performance from ranking of #33 out of 35 units to #1 in the nation for sales, with added honors as Top Service Branch.

- *50% Increase:* Recruited, trained, and motivated customer-driven sales force that achieved a nationally unprecedented 50% increase for product placed in field.

- *50% Expense Reduction:* Reduced expenses from more than 150% of target to goal attainment in all four major expense categories.

To eliminate any possible perception that John was demoted, he used this closing paragraph in his cover letter.

Z-Best has been extremely pleased with my performance—I have managed the number-one branch in the nation for the past several years. With the reorganization of districts, my responsibilities have been moved to Los Angeles. Rather than relocate, I have requested a direct sales position to stay in the area (my wife and I are long-time residents of San Francisco). Given my management track record, I am taking this opportunity to explore sales-management opportunities such as the one with your firm.

Demoted Several Months Ago

Magic

Perhaps the preceding scenario is like your situation (you have lesser or different responsibilities than you had in your older position, and you want to return to a position similar to the older one), with the added variable that you have now spent some time in the new position (say, six months or more). The following *Before* example is an excerpt from a résumé Philip had been using—without success. Philip, a regional manager who was demoted because of the acquisition of his company, wanted to position himself for a regional management position like the one he had worked in for four years. His move to a promotional coordinator from a region manager will likely raise questions or suspicions in a hiring manager's or recruiter's mind. Moreover, placing the coordinator position above the region manager position dilutes the management image that Philip needed to project.

Before

PROFESSIONAL EXPERIENCE

PRIMO CORPORATION / SYNERJEX, INC.

<u>PROMOTIONAL COORDINATOR</u> (Present)

Re-assigned to consolidate promotional purchases into central purchasing district. Analyze sales movement by SKU and provide recommendations for promotional budget.

<u>REGIONAL MANAGER</u> (3 years)

Managed region generating $97 million in annual revenue. Planned and executed sales programs for 7 Western Region states. Hired, trained, and communicated sales directives to 11 district managers; indirectly responsible for sales force of 92.

Achievements:

- Led sales team to attain overall increase from $54 million to $97 million in sales.

- Exceeded 1st year goal with a 20% increase, 2nd year goal with 42% increase, and 3rd year goal with 19% increase.

The solution for Philip was similar to the preceding example for John: Title the narrative paragraph as "Management Experience," launch the description for the position with a litany of prior promotions, elaborate on relevant duties while Regional Manager, and de-emphasize the present position as Promotional Coordinator by placing it at the end of the job description. In addition, since Philip had spent several months in the more recent position, accomplishments were added to demonstrate his consistent history as a top performer. To help his readers follow what was accomplished in each position, I listed the word "Achievements" followed by the name of the company (Primo Corp. or Synerjex, Inc.). Dates in the second achievement statement are dropped in this version to draw attention away from the time elapsed since accomplishing them. The résumé entry now reads as follows.

After

PROFESSIONAL EXPERIENCE

PRIMO CORPORATION / SYNERJEX, INC.

Management Experience:

Promoted through territory manager, training manager, key accounts manager, and region manager with Primo Corp. As region manager (3 years), managed 7-state area generating $97 million in revenue. Planned and executed sales programs. Hired, trained, and communicated sales directives to 11 district managers; indirectly responsible for sales force of 92. As promotional coordinator with the acquisition by Synerjex earlier in the year, challenged with consolidation of promotional purchases into central purchasing district.

Achievements – PRIMO CORPORATION:

- *81% Sales Increase:* Led sales team to attain overall increase from $54 million to $97 million in sales.

- *27% Average Annual Increase:* Exceeded 1st year goal with a 20% increase, 2nd year goal with 42% increase, and 3rd year goal with 19% increase.

Achievements – SYNERJEX, INC.:

- *4-5% ROI Increase:* Analyzed fiscal year promotional spending to identify ad vehicle generating highest ROI; data enabled company to increase ROI from 2-3% to 6-8%.

- *41% Savings:* Captured 41% savings in manufacture and distribution of point-of-sale fixtures through overseas vendor sourcing and renegotiation of freight contracts.

Most Recent Position Title Sounds Like a Demotion, but Isn't

Magic

I have also worked with individuals who have held several positions with one company, each one a promotion to greater responsibility, and yet the title for the most recent position sounded more as if the individual were demoted rather than promoted. Here's a *Before* picture for such a candidate.

Before

PROFESSIONAL EXPERIENCE

MEDICUS CORP., New Haven, Connecticut   1995—Present

Senior Sales Consultant (2002-Present). Perform sales and marketing for specific account list in two states.

- Achieved a 21% rate of sales growth in a static market for most recent fiscal year.

- Delivered a 27% gain in prior fiscal year.

District Manager (1997-2002). Directed 14-member sales team generating $16 million in annual sales.

- Increased overall sales from $4 to $16 million – $7.9 million of which was achieved during challenging economic period for industry.

- Exceeded annual goals by 18.9%, 10.4%, 18.4%, 10.0%, and 11.0% for years ending 1997-2001.

- Consistently earned recognition as #1 or #2 district among 15 in the western United States.

To deal with any misperceptions, summarize your promotional history and begin your description with the words "promoted," "advanced," or, as in the following example, "fast-track promotion."

After

PROFESSIONAL EXPERIENCE

MEDICUS CORP., New Haven, Connecticut   1995—Present

Fast-track promotion through a series of increasingly responsible positions, including sales representative (1995-1996), sales specialist (1996-1997), district manager (1997-2001), and key account sales consultant (current). Highlights:

SALES CONSULTANT—accountable for marketing and sales development among key producers and suppliers in California and Hawaii. Manage $1 million marketing budget.

- Achieved a 21% rate of sales growth in a static market for most recent fiscal year.

- Delivered a 27% gain in prior fiscal year.

DISTRICT MANAGER—directed 14-member sales team generating $16 million in annual sales.

- Increased overall sales from $4 to $16 million – $7.9 million of which was achieved during challenging economic period for industry.

- Exceeded annual goals by 18.9%, 10.4%, 18.4%, 10.0%, and 11.0% for years ending 1997-2001.

- Consistently earned recognition as #1 or #2 district among 15 in the western United States.

Leading off with "fast-track promotion through a series of increasingly responsible positions" reinforces that the ultimate position of Sales Consultant is, indeed, a promotion, even if the company's vernacular is misleading (in many people's minds, a District Manager would have greater responsibility than a Sales Consultant).

Obscure Titles

Titles can be confusing, especially to people outside your professional circle. If you claim ownership to an obscure title that does not convey the level of your responsibility, add a parenthetical statement that gives the reader a better frame of reference. For instance, the nebulous titles of Service Leader and Service Integrator for an executive employed in a large health care system could be translated in a couple of ways. The first example lists actual titles followed by parenthetical descriptions for clarity.

Service Leader, Performance Improvement
(equivalent to Vice President of Operations; report directly to CEO)

Service Integrator, Medical Education
(equivalent to Director of Medical Education and Physician Credentialing)

The second example lists more traditional titles first, followed by actual titles in parentheses.

Vice President, Performance Improvement (Service Leader)

Director, Performance Improvement (Service Integrator)

Both of these translations will improve the candidate's chances of being found in keyword searches of résumé databases.

Skills

If you have chosen a functional format to present your experience, present the bulk of your talents and experience in this section. If you're using a chronological format or one of its cousins, skip this section. The development of a skills-based résumé could warrant an entire chapter, if not an entire book. I will present the basics in a three-step plan and let you work out the details for your unique situation:

1. **Focus on three to five skill areas—these will become your subheadings under the Skills category.** Choose disciplines or occupational areas for your subheadings rather than personal skills. Note the difference between occupational skills and personal skills in the following table. Occupational headings carry more weight with employers—remember that most employers dislike functional résumés to begin with; to pull this format off, you'll need to make sure it's meaty.

Occupational Skills	Personal Skills
Event planning, fund-raising, customer service, marketing, sales, engineering, case management, project coordination, training, office management, inventory management, and so on.	Analytical skills, communication skills, problem-solving skills, organizational talents, attentiveness to detail, and so on.

2. **The selection of your subheadings will be driven by the types of positions you are targeting.** Choose for your subheadings words that can be broadly interpreted, compared to specific job titles. For instance, "Customer Service" as a subheading would be more widely understood by the general public and preferred over a company-specific title such as "Client Account Specialist."

3. **After you have selected your subheadings, develop two to five sentences that encapsulate your experience for each subheading.** To develop copy for your experience, refer back to the ideas under "Where to Find Material for Your Job Descriptions." You will add specific accomplishments later (see chapter 6). Whenever possible, pair experience statements with evidence of where you gained the experience.

It's very, very important to include clues that will help the reader understand when and where you've done things, sort of like a trail of breadcrumbs! There will be a natural curiosity to know the "whens" and "wheres"; not saying so is one of the major irritants of a functional format. If you claim to have sales experience, employers will want to know whether it was recent experience with a reputable employer, compared to running a lemonade stand in your youth. Answering these unvoiced questions will lessen suspicions about an unstable work history.

For instance, compare these *Before* and *After* versions.

Before

Sales: Demonstrated an aptitude for sales; regularly met sales quotas.

After

Sales: Readily transferable sales skills. Demonstrated ability to sell any number of products as "floater" for upscale retailer (Macy's); as a "rookie," generated average daily sales volume equal to or above that of experienced sales associates.

The *After* version tells the reader where you worked, that you can sell a variety of products, and how well you measure up to other salespeople.

Magic

Focusing on Skills Worked for Jan

Jan, a high school teacher, wanted to pursue an opportunity in human resources with an emphasis on training. Rather than use the wording from her public-school teaching résumé, she focused on her overall skills.

Before

Taught biology, chemistry, and computer science to 11th-grade students. Emphasized hands-on, participative lessons directed toward equipping students with "real-world" job and life skills.

After

Six-year background as educator in secondary settings. Able to provide client-centered interactive training sessions, emphasizing practical applications for customer education and/or staff development.

Created and implemented instructional programs in the areas of technology and science. Developed tools to measure retention of subject matter. Success of programs resulted in invitations to speak at regional and national professional conferences.

Refer to chapter 3 for full-page examples of skills-based résumés for a professional in career transition, a "career mother" entering the workforce for the first time, and a military officer "retiring" to a civilian career.

Education, Credentials, Licensure

Place the Education section near the top of the résumé if it is one of your strongest selling points. This applies to recent high school or college graduates. If you've graduated within the past few years and have a degree related to your profession, place it near the top of the résumé as well. Curricula vitae (CVs), regardless of how long ago your degrees were received, also lead off with education.

Recent High School Graduate

If you're in the age bracket of 17 to 19 and fresh out of high school, you'll want to mention your graduation. Include a section on coursework relevant to your job goal, just as Quinn did when looking for a clerical position.

EDUCATION

GRADUATE OF ROOSEVELT HIGH SCHOOL

Business Coursework:	Principles of Accounting; Business Office Protocol; Business English (emphasis on grammar, spelling, punctuation, letter format); Statistical & Business Reporting
Computer Applications:	Excel, Word, Access, Powerpoint, WordPerfect
Co-curricular Activities:	Varsity Volleyball, Marching Band
Leadership:	Elected by classmates as Student Body Secretary/Treasurer. Represented Senior Class before School Board meetings.

Recent College Graduate

Recent grads can go heavy on this section. In other words, if education is your biggest selling point, don't be afraid to let it take up "prime shelf space"—that visual center of the page discussed in chapter 2. Stephen leveraged his lack of paid experience by positioning an impressive Education category at the center of the page; he then stretched it to more than three inches of vertical space by using a variety of subheadings (Dual Major, Course Work Highlights, and so on).

EDUCATION

UNIVERSITY OF THE PACIFIC

Dual Major: Bachelor of Science Degree, Business Administration—Option in Finance [year]
Bachelor of Arts Degree, French [year]

Course Work Entrepreneurial Finance; Portfolio Management & Theory; International
Highlights: Finance; Business and Real Estate Economics; Monetary Policy and the
Banking System

Honors: John Bradford Scholarship Recipient (based on academic performance)

Degree Obtained a Number of Years Ago

There is a three-year rule of thumb (although not a rule set in stone) for determining where to position your education. Place education near the top of the résumé if you received a degree within the past three years and the degree is related to your profession. If you graduated more than three years ago and gained relevant experience in the meantime, consider placing your education toward the bottom of the résumé, below your experience. When decades have passed since you walked the halls of ivy, definitely place education at the bottom of the résumé and eliminate dates of graduation.

EDUCATION

UNIVERSITY OF THE PACIFIC

Bachelor of Science Degree, Business Administration—Option in Finance

Degree in a Field Different from Your Major

Many of you obtained college degrees in an area entirely different from your present profession. When your degree does not support your job target and you are competing against individuals with industry-supporting degrees, consider listing just the degree and eliminating the major. Place both the degree and the college on one line to "thicken" the line and camouflage the fact that you haven't listed the major. Elaine held a 10-year-old degree in music and was applying for a Director of Food and Beverage position, while many of her competitors held degrees in hotel management. She used this approach.

EDUCATION

Bachelor of Arts Degree—University of the Pacific, Stockton, California

Kris, a liberal arts/education major and now an insurance claims examiner, had taken a number of courses in business. She, too, eliminated her major but included the emphasis, along with relevant industry training. Note how she also added certification to her category heading.

EDUCATION, CERTIFICATION

Bachelor of Arts Degree, Business Emphasis—University of California, Santa Barbara

Certification: IEA Certificate; Advanced coursework in Labor Code & Current Case Law and Advanced Issues in Workers' Compensation

This strategy of dropping the major isn't a hard-and-fast rule. In some cases, a major apart from your profession can be a point of interest, especially if you have pursued training in your new profession since graduating from college. Sharon, a secretary applying for similar positions in law firms, held a degree in fine arts. Since many of her competitors had not completed a baccalaureate program, she listed her degree along with additional courses pertinent to her job target. She reported receiving a number of favorable comments about her degree in fine arts from employers with whom she interviewed. In this case, her degree, although not related, helped distinguish her from other candidates.

EDUCATION

Legal Secretarial Program, Sacramento Community College
Coursework included Criminal Justice System, Civil Litigation, Family Law, Criminal Law, Legal Records Management, Trial Preparation, Legal Research, English I & II, and WordPerfect—Advanced Functions

Bachelor of Fine Arts (BFA), University of Kansas, Lawrence

Degree Not Completed

Many people have sincere intentions and plans to finish college, but "life" sometimes gets in the way. For those who completed most of a degree but didn't take home a sheepskin, consider one of the following alternatives. This first presentation uses bold, capital letters for the words "degree program," allowing you to work in the word "degree" despite not having one.

EDUCATION

DEGREE PROGRAM: BUSINESS ADMINISTRATION, Fremont City College

The next example suggests that you almost completed a degree, as well as offers a hint about why you didn't finish it.

EDUCATION

UNIVERSITY OF MINNESOTA

Business Administration Major—completed 3½ years of degree program before accepting management training opportunity with Betsom Engineering Company.

The use of a parenthetical statement about your grade-level status also implies that you have completed most of the requirements for a degree. I don't recommend using this treatment if you've been out of college for a number of years; if this is the case, use the preceding idea. However, if you decide to pick up the reins again and go back to complete your degree, add the words "anticipated completion, June 20__" after the words "Senior Status" (assuming you are less than a year or so away from completion).

EDUCATION

UNIVERSITY OF MINNESOTA

Bachelor of Business Administration Program (senior status)

or

EDUCATION

UNIVERSITY OF MINNESOTA

B.B.A. Degree Program—Senior status, anticipated completion June [date]

Two-Year Degree

Those with a two-year degree (associate of arts, associate of science) who are competing with four-year-degree graduates can add psychological weight to their degrees by printing the word "degree" in capital letters and then abbreviating the associate's degree to A.S. or A.A. On first glance, the reader's focus is on the word "DEGREE" rather than the type of degree.

EDUCATION

DEGREE: A.S., Business Administration / Marketing Emphasis
State Center Community College District

Degree Equivalent

Did you complete your degree in another country? If so, it's often hard for U.S. employers, especially smaller companies, to understand the U.S. equivalent of your degree or take it as seriously as they might a degree conferred by a U.S. institution. For instance, many people would be at a loss to figure out what the phrases "Ordinary Level Certificate" or "High National Diploma" mean. In England, these are similar to a high school diploma and a baccalaureate degree, respectively. When readers could be confused about your degree, offer a parenthetical statement to clarify.

> High National Diploma, Economics and Finance
> (equivalent to Bachelor of Science degree in Economics)

No Degree

No Education section is often better than a weak Education section. If you attended college a short time or took courses of no professional significance, you'll draw more attention to the lack of a degree by including an Education section than if you were to omit it entirely.

To further camouflage any lack of education, make sure you use more than two major category headings in the rest of your résumé (such as Objective and Professional Experience categories). Three categories look more balanced on a one-page résumé, so consider adding a third category, such as a Skills, Affiliations, or Endorsements section.

Including Credentials, Licenses, and Certificates

When you have several elements to list under Education, such as credentials, licenses, and certificates, try giving each listing a subheading. This looks especially clean if each series of items that follows the subheadings fits on one line. Note also that each list after the subheadings begins at a common tab setting.

> ACADEMIC QUALIFICATIONS
>
> Degree: Bachelor of Arts, Liberal Studies, University of Kansas, Lawrence
> Credentials: Single Subject Teaching Credential—English
> Certificates: Language Acquisition Specialist; Early Literacy Certification

Affiliations

In most cases, a simple inventory of your affiliations, presented in order of importance, will suffice. When your involvement included election to an office or other leadership position, mention the title either before or after the organization (be consistent with the placement of the titles). When you held an office but are no longer in that office, preface the title with "past."

AFFILIATIONS

> Association of Supervision & Curriculum Development
> American Association of School Administrators
> Association of California School Administrators
> California Reading Association
> California Math Council—Curriculum Development Committee
> Central Valley Language Arts Council—Past President
> Twin Cities Rotary Club

It is not necessary to include the date you joined each organization. The following example is a traditional one-item-per-line list format.

As a space saver, you can present the information in paragraph form with each organization separated by a semicolon. This presentation will buy you an extra two lines, three if you eliminate the subcommittees and leadership positions and abbreviate the word "association" throughout.

Abbreviations can be risky, however, when your résumé will be scanned. This school administrator was applying to small districts where paper-screening would be conducted by "man" and not machine.

AFFILIATIONS

> Assoc. of Supervision & Curriculum Development; American Assoc. of School Administrators; Assoc. of California School Administrators; California Reading Assoc.; California Math Council; Central Valley Language Arts Council; Twin Cities Rotary Club

If you are no longer a member of some organizations but want to include them for impact, add the words "Past and Present" after the Affiliations category heading; then place the more dated affiliations at the bottom of the list. Yes, doing so makes it unclear which Affiliations are current and which are past (let the interviewer ask which is which), but many candidates have used this strategy to weave in older affiliations that supported their candidacy. This technique allowed Linda to include her former involvement in the arts (the last two listings) that was relevant to her target position as Executive Director of an arts foundation.

AFFILIATIONS (Past and Present)

> Association of Supervision & Curriculum Development
> American Association of School Administrators
> Association of California School Administrators
> California Math Council—Curriculum Development Committee
> Central Valley Language Arts Council—Past President
> Twin Cities Rotary Club
> Twin Cities Art Educators' Network—Founding Member, Past President
> Arts for At-Risk Youth—Founding Member, Past Director

The past-and-present technique illustrated in the preceding example is helpful also when you've moved from one city to another and were very involved in local organizations in your former city but haven't had time to get as involved in your new area.

When you need to present an extensive listing of professional and civic involvement, give each category a subheading and present the items in either a list format or, if you're short on space, a paragraph format. Refer back to the suggestions for subheadings under the "Affiliations" section in chapter 4 if you need ideas on how to break up your information. Note how the following paragraph format saves four (without subheadings) to six line spaces (with subheadings) over a list format. To help set off the subheadings, I used a hanging indent (text after the first line is indented 0.3 inches). This word-processing function is found under the Format, Paragraph command in Microsoft Word (see chapter 8 on visual artistry for more formatting tips).

AFFILIATIONS

> **Professional:** Assoc. of Supervision & Curriculum Development; American Assoc. of School Administrators; Assoc. of California School Administrators; California Reading Assoc.; California Math Council; Central Valley Language Arts Council

> **Community:** Twin Cities Art Educators' Network—Founding Member, Past President; Arts for At-Risk Youth—Founding Member, Past Director; Volunteer League of Milpitas; Twin Cities Women's Network; Twin Cities Rotary Club

This same information presented in list format is cleaner and easier to read; however, I don't recommend taking up this much vertical space for affiliations on a one-page résumé. Go with this format only if your résumé is two pages.

AFFILIATIONS

Professional Associations
Association of Supervision & Curriculum Development
American Association of School Administrators
Association of California School Administrators
California Reading Association
California Math Council
Central Valley Language Arts Council

Community Involvement
Twin Cities Art Educators' Network—Founding Member, Past President
Arts for At-Risk Youth—Founding Member, Past Director
Volunteer League of Milpitas
Twin Cities Women's Network
Twin Cities Rotary Club

Publications, Presentations, and Patents

Publications, presentations, and patents are typically impressive and should be included in your résumé.

Publications

For academic and medical CVs, present journal articles in reverse-chronological order. You can find style guides that advocate an alphabetical listing; however, consistency with the reverse-chronological listings of Education and Professional Experience sections within the CV make it logical to present publications in the same manner. For individuals with careers spanning multiple decades, the query of "how far back?" is often raised.

Donald Asher, in *Asher's Bible of Executive Résumés & How to Write Them,* offers this advice: "Traditionally, in academic circles, one never culls early listings from bibliographies; one simply adds to the list, putting new material at the top in reverse-chronological order." If you want to offer a truncated version of your CV (for instance, when the CV will be used to introduce you as a guest speaker at a business or community meeting), consider using the summary sentence at the end of the following publications list. Present journal publications in the format accepted by the journal (note that the publication *J. Neuropath. & Exp. Neurol.* is written in its accepted abbreviated format). Typically, journal format includes the following items:

- Name of author(s) (last name, plus first and middle initials; or last name, first name, and middle initial) followed by a period

- Title of article in double quotation marks followed by a period (before the closing quotation mark)

- Name of journal in italic followed by a comma

- Volume number (Arabic numeral) underlined and followed by a colon

- Page numbers followed by a comma

- Year published followed by a period

PUBLICATIONS

Schokovitz, D. W. and C. B. Noble. "The muscle biopsy: why? how? and when?" *Neurology*, <u>12</u>:97-118, 1999.

Johns, B. W., C. B. Noble, and F. L. Gaff. "Structure and function of mitochondria from human skeletal muscle in health and disease." International Congress of Neuro-Genetics and Neuro-Ophthalmology. *J. Neuropath. & Exp. Neurol.*, <u>12</u>:174-196, 1997.

Gerald, W. G., C. B. Noble, and B. J. Krikorian. "Electron microscopic localization of phosphatase activities within striated muscle fibers." *Hospital Medicine*, <u>19</u>:332-349, 1996.

Fidden, S. W., C. S. Lanturn, W. G. Gerald, and C. B. Noble. "Mitochondrial myopathy." *J. Neuropath. & Exp. Neurol.*, <u>13</u>:212-229, 1994.

Noble, C. B., W. G. Gerald, W. T. James, and W. M. Realton. "Myopathy with atypical mitochondria in type I skeletal muscle fibers: A histochemical and ultrastructural study." *Neurology*, <u>15</u>:325-347, 1992.

Co-authored more than 30 other journal articles—full bibliography available upon request.

For books, include the following:

- Name of author(s) (last name, first and middle initials; or last name, first name, and middle initial) followed by a period. When a second listing by the same author(s) falls immediately below, replace the names of the author with an underline followed by a period (see the following example).

- Title of book in italic followed by a period.

- City and state of publisher followed by a colon.

- Name of publisher followed by a comma.

- Year published followed by a period.

- If you're including page numbers, place the information before the final period (add a comma after the year published). Use p. or pp. for "page" and "pages," respectively (see the following example).

PUBLICATIONS

> Noble, C. B. and B. W. Johns, "Chapter 29: Serum Enzyme Alterations in Skeletal Muscle Disease of Childhood." *Clinical Pathology of Childhood*. New York: Springer-Verlag Publishing Company, 1998, pp. 321-462.
>
> _____. *Squamous Odontogenic Tumors*. Monterey, California: International Thomson Publishing, 1998.
>
> Nixon, J. B. and C. B. Noble, *Mitochondrial Myopathy*. Monterey, California: International Thomson Publishing, 1995.

Miscellaneous writing, such as self-published booklets, pamphlets, and guides, can be listed in a less formal manner. If you are the sole author of all items listed, forgo the repetition of listing your name for each entry.

PROFESSIONAL WRITING

> "Coaching Candidates to Become PEOs (Profit Enhancement Officers)," career management guide prepared for executive recruitment firms, 2003.
>
> "Managing Your Career: How to Create Value for Your Employer and Job Security for Yourself," study guide for Career Development course, California State University–Fresno, 2002.
>
> "Common Career-Killer Mistakes Women Make," self-published job search pamphlet, 2000.
>
> "Three Things You Must Accomplish to Ace the Interview," self-published job search booklet, 1998.
>
> "Policy & Procedure Manual," a comprehensive 128-page document prepared for the Human Resources Department of Delaney Manufacturing, Inc., 1995.

Presentations

Include the following information when listing presentations:

- Title of presentation in quotations
- What organization it was given to (professional conference, group, meeting)
- Location (city, state)
- Date given (month and year, or year alone is sufficient)
- Summary of presentation (optional)

Ann, a school counselor and enthusiastic advocate for children, had an extensive list of presentations that were listed in a one-page addendum to her résumé. The *Before* and *After* versions are shown next; note how the *Before* picture presents a full page of text with no visual cues to organize content.

Before

PRESENTATIONS

Workshop presentation entitled "Counselor, Heal Thyself!" at the National Elementary/Middle School Guidance Conference, University of South Carolina, 2003.

Workshop presentation entitled "And Still I Rise" at the Endowment For Youth: Rising Force Workshop, Indianapolis, Indiana, 2001.

Workshop presentation entitled "Empower Yourself! Start Your Own Elementary Counseling Program" at the Indiana Association for Counseling and Development State Convention, 2000.

Workshop presentation entitled "Helping At-Risk Students Succeed by Meeting Personal-Social-Affective Needs" at the Indiana Symposium for Student Success, 1998.

Workshop presentation entitled "Making the Mark" at the African-American Student Recruitment Conference, University of Indiana, 1997.

Workshop presentation entitled "Behavioral/Affective/Academic Programs for the 'Total-School': The Ounce of Prevention for a Pound of Cure" at the National Elementary/Middle School Guidance Conference, Purdue University, 1997.

Round Table Discussion entitled "Meeting the Affective Needs of Inner-City Children: Models of Kindergarten-8th Grade Counseling" at the Indiana School Counselor Association State Conference, 1996.

Workshop presentation entitled "The `Right Stuff' for Positive Self-Esteem in the Elementary School" at the Indiana Association for Counseling and Development State Convention, 1995.

Workshop presentation entitled "Total-School Programs for the Elementary Level" at the Indiana School Counselor Association State Conference, 1994.

Workshop presentation entitled "Successful Adoption: A Look at Program Development and Maintenance in the Elementary School" at the National Elementary/Middle School Guidance Conference, Purdue University, 1994.

Presented faculty inservices on "Elementary Counseling," "Self-Esteem," and "Magic Circle/Innerchange Programs," McKinley School, Terre Haute, Indiana, 1993-1996.

Developed total-school programs and presented faculty inservices on "Rights" Program, "Goalie" Program, and "Sylvester the Snail" Program; conducted Systematic Training for Effective Parenting Group for McKinley School, Terre Haute, Indiana, 1992-1994.

The *After* version is organized into national, state, local, and school-site presentations, giving the reader bite-size pieces to digest. This presentation also allows Ann to place the most impressive presentations—her national appearances—at the top of her list. Items begin with the title of the presentation rather than the noun phrase "workshop presentation" for maximum readability.

After

PRESENTATIONS

National:

- "Counselor, Heal Thyself!" National Elementary/Middle School Guidance Conference, University of South Carolina, 2003.

- "Behavioral/Affective/Academic Programs for the 'Total-School:' The Ounce of Prevention for a Pound of Cure," National Elementary/Middle School Guidance Conference, Purdue University, 1997.

- "Successful Adoption: A Look at Program Development and Maintenance in the Elementary School," National Elementary/Middle School Guidance Conference, Purdue University, 1994.

State:

- "Empower Yourself! Start Your Own Elementary Counseling Program," Indiana Association for Counseling and Development State Convention, 2000.

- "Meeting the Affective Needs of Inner-City Children: Models of Kindergarten-8th Grade Counseling," Indiana School Counselor Association State Conference, 1996.

- "The 'Right Stuff' for Positive Self-Esteem in the Elementary School," Indiana Association for Counseling and Development State Convention, 1995.

- "Total-School Programs for the Elementary Level," Indiana School Counselor Association State Conference, 1994.

Local (partial list):

- "And Still I Rise," Endowment For Youth: Rising Force Workshop, Indianapolis, Indiana, 2001.

- "Helping At-Risk Students Succeed by Meeting Personal-Social-Affective Needs," Indiana Symposium for Student Success, 1998.

- "Making the Mark," African-American Student Recruitment Conference, University of Indiana, 1997.

School-Site Faculty Inservices (partial list):

- "Say! Brother!" a Portfolio Program developed for African-American males at Lincoln Middle School, Indianapolis, Indiana, 1998-1999.

- "Elementary Counseling," "Self-Esteem," and "Magic Circle/Innerchange Programs," McKinley School, Terre Haute, Indiana, 1993-1996.

- "Rights" Program, "Goalie" Program, and "Sylvester the Snail" Program--total-school programs developed; and "Systematic Training for Effective Parenting," McKinley School, Terre Haute, Indiana, 1992-1994.

Patents

Patents, both pending and granted, can be presented with the names of the patent holders, the name of the patent, and the patent number.

PATENTS

Lwin, S., and S. Pfeif, Automatic Actuated Surface Irrigation Valve, U.S. Patent #4,733,689

If you are the sole holder of the patent in every case, state the name of the patent and patent number without your name—it will be assumed they belong to you. When a complete listing would be cumbersome to include on your résumé, summarize the patents by describing how many you hold and in what field or discipline. Do, however, be prepared to answer inquiries with an addendum that provides details.

PATENTS

Holder of 20 patents in the area of irrigation technology—details on request.

Awards and Honors

Weigh the impact of an Awards and Honors section before deciding where to position it on your résumé. If content will be limited to community awards or academic honors from outdated college days, position the section toward the bottom of the résumé. On the other hand, if you were the number one sales representative in the nation or received a prestigious, well-recognized professional honor, bump the category into prime shelf space near the top of the page. Recall the single-item list rule—if your award suffers from only-child syndrome, weave it into a Qualifications Summary, the Experience section (under accomplishments with a specific employer), or an Education section if the award is education-related.

This example of an Awards section was relegated to the bottom of the résumé because the candidate was two years past graduating from college and had more impressive business experiences and accomplishments under his belt.

AWARDS & HONORS

Finalist in Division Speech Contests, Toastmasters International
Most Valuable Player, UCLA Water Polo
Outstanding Young Rotarian, Rotary International, Van Nuys Chapter
Academic Scholarship Recipient, National Bank, Promising Professionals Program

This Awards section was well deserving of its position at the visual center of the page.

AWARDS & HONORS

2007	National Salesman of the Year, Syntac Communications, Inc.
2006	Western Region Salesman of the Year, Syntac Communications, Inc.
2005	Rookie Salesman of the Year, Syntac Communications, Inc.
2004	#2 Salesman in California, Pacific Bell Yellow Pages
2003	#3 Salesman in Northern California, Pacific Bell Yellow Pages

> *Caution* A word of caution about listing dates with awards: Make sure your most recent accomplishments are as impressive as or more impressive than previous awards. If it's been several years since you've pulled off a real coup, the gap in dates will give rise to suspicions about your recent performance.

Here's a trick for presenting the same accomplishments as in the preceding list when there has been a gap of several years since winning any special award.

AWARDS & HONORS

Impressive 5-year record of regional and national sales honors, including:

- ☑ National Salesman of the Year, Syntac Communications, Inc.
- ☑ Western Region Salesman of the Year, Syntac Communications, Inc.
- ☑ Rookie Salesman of the Year, Syntac Communications, Inc.
- ☑ #2 Salesman in California, Pacific Bell Yellow Pages
- ☑ #3 Salesman in Northern California, Pacific Bell Yellow Pages

Prefacing the awards with a statement about a "5-year record" eliminates the need to list the actual dates. Savvy interviewers, however, will ask questions about when these awards were attained and what you've accomplished in the meantime. Be ready with a positive response!

Bio Bites

Let your personality, profile, or philosophy shine through in this section. Employers hire people, not robots. Beyond specific skills and experience, employers want to know who you really are, whether you'll fit in with their corporate culture, and what makes you tick. This is a place you can put your signature on the résumé—figuratively speaking. In Table 5.8, consider the elements listed in the left column, review the example candidate's (Paulo's) answers, and then write your own information in the right column. Later, you'll see how Paulo assembles these building blocks into his résumé.

Table 5.8: Example Bio Bites

Element	Example Candidate (Paulo)	Your Own Information
Where you grew up	Brazil, Philippines	
Travel experiences	North, Central, and Pacific Rim South America; Australia	
Language skills	English, Spanish, Tagalog	
Athletic abilities	Soccer	
Involvement in team sports	Team captain, Most valuable player	
Musical/theatrical/ performance abilities	Brass player; performed on several CDs; coordinated music for church productions	
Favorite reading material	Apologetics, biographies, and science fiction	
Unusual experiences	Snorkeled off the Great Barrier Reef; led youth teams through uninhabited rain forest	
Special interests	Genealogy, astronomy, raising my twin boys	
Parents' profession	Missionaries	
Any fact relevant to your job target that isn't already listed on the résumé	NA	
Philosophy	"Always do what's right, even when no one is looking"	

You don't need to use every piece of information from this list. After filling in your own information in the preceding table, circle the items that would be of greatest interest to an employer. Then rank them in order of importance. Next, on a separate sheet of paper, draft two or three alternative paragraphs that combine the information you selected.

Paulo, the candidate profiled in the preceding table, was applying for a management-training program with a Christian bookseller. It was, therefore, appropriate to mention his parents' profession, along with his religious background and knowledge of products that would be sold in the store.

BIO DATA

> Traveled extensively as the son of career missionaries in South America and the Philippines. Work well with diverse staff; speak three languages fluently. Avid reader of apologetics and biographies of religious leaders. Also familiar with contemporary Christian music genre; played on several CDs recorded under the Dove label. Possess a strong work ethic, acquired early in life through competing in team sports and working my way through college.

Typically, riding your parents' coattails is not cool, so use caution in including this information on the résumé. Often you can weave this information more easily into your cover letter. For instance, if you're fresh out of school and applying for a medical sales position, you might say this.

> Growing up, I was surrounded by doctors—my mother, father, and grandfather are all physicians. Roughly 80% of the area's cardiologists, pediatricians, and neurologists know me on a first-name basis—all are potential customers for BioGen Corp. From extensive reading, I know what clinical and managed-care issues they face and can discuss their practice needs as well as many experienced reps.

If you use an Interest category, make sure it is, indeed, of interest. If it reads like the one below, rework or eliminate it.

INTERESTS

> Member of the Irving Lanes Bowling Team
> Play clarinet
> Enjoy gardening, canning, and crocheting
> Scrapbooking

Employers typically don't care that you bowl, play the clarinet, or take scrapbooking classes. What they are more interested in are activities that reveal insights into your character. Executive recruiters tell me that a candidate's past or present involvement in team sports is sometimes a big selling factor, especially for sales and management candidates. The implication is that you are a competitor; understand the importance of teamwork; and know the diligence, sacrifice, and commitment it takes to win. Likewise, if the activities you are involved in will also be a venue for conducting business, such as membership in a country club or tennis club, include them.

Keep in mind that information from the Affiliations category and this category may overlap, so be careful that you don't list anything twice.

ACTIVITIES AND INTERESTS

Member, Mountain Crest Country Club
Member, Twin Lakes Swim & Racquet Club
Avid golfer, tournament tennis player, and black diamond skier
Hold a brown belt in karate

This section is skim material, so make it as readable as possible by keeping each item or thought to one line or presenting the items in paragraph form with ellipses to separate the items.

ACTIVITIES AND INTERESTS

Mountain Crest Country Club . . . Twin Lakes Swim & Racquet Club . . . avid golfer, tournament tennis player, and black-diamond skier . . . hold a brown belt in karate.

Endorsements

"I want to talk to this candidate. Look at these endorsements on his résumé." These are the words of a sales manager who picked my client Tim's résumé out of a stack of 10 résumés. Eight of the 10 candidates had specific industry experience—Tim was the only candidate with no industry experience to be selected for an interview. The use of endorsements is a tremendously effective tool to beef up your candidacy, especially when you are lacking certain qualifications or competing against more experienced candidates. Tim snatched an interview for a pharmaceutical sales position with these endorsements, despite his lack of industry experience.

ENDORSEMENTS

Pharmaceutical Sales Representative: *"I have complete faith in Tim's ability as a sales professional. . .he's highly organized, a good communicator, and able to work independently without supervision. Tim would be ideal for pharmaceutical sales."*

Alex Panach, District Sales Manager, Pfizer

Medical Office Manager: *"I frequently deal with sales representatives in my position and am confident that Tim measures up to the best reps I know. His confidence, assertiveness, and attention to detail are impressive. He'd be an asset to any company in pharmaceutical or medical sales."*

Jon Deming, Medical Office Manager for Dr. Arvin Maxwell

Select your endorsers carefully. Depending on space availability and the length of the testimonials, you can use between two and five—I prefer three. If you're trying to break into a new field or profession, think of people who are well-respected industry leaders, preferably in a management capacity. Potential customers are another good source for endorsements. When you're staying in a similar industry, consider a trio consisting of your supervisor, a customer, and a vendor or colleague. Substitute a former supervisor for your current supervisor when your search is confidential. Pearl used a good mix of individuals who attested to her expertise in her job target (business management and operations). In this case, the type of endorser (consultant, client, vendor) was listed rather than the actual name. If you choose to omit the endorsers' names, be sure to have available the letters from which the quotes were taken.

ENDORSEMENTS

Excellent record with supervisors, clients, and staff. Excerpts from testimonials include:

Consultant: "Pearl has the gift for running a business and making money . . . a great troubleshooter . . . absolutely ethical, honest, trustworthy, energetic, and loyal."

Client: "Give [the project] to Pearl—you won't have to think about it anymore."

Vendor: "The most accurate, organized, efficient person I've ever met . . . hands down."

Occasionally, it will be necessary to smooth out a direct quote to make it more clear. In the actual letter of recommendation, the second quote above specifically reads, "Give it to Pearl, you won't have to think about it anymore." Worded this way, it's confusing what "it" refers to. To clarify, I used brackets around "the project" in place of "it." The brackets signify that original text was changed. Be fastidious in the accuracy of your excerpts and use brackets around words not found in the original letter—chances are employers will ask to see those letters, so you'll want them to be an exact match for maximum credibility.

You've made it through the bulk of the composition process. Congratulations! Your text is "raw" at this point, but that's okay—you'll take care of tweaking later (in chapter 7). Now it's time to add the real buying motivators for hiring managers—those elements that will set you apart from—and above—your competition.

sample posting

Top 10 Tips for Writing Great Copy

1. Know your audience before you begin to write. What skills and competencies are they looking for? What knowledge do they require? What trends are they capitalizing on? What opportunities are they interested in tapping? What problems do they need fixed? What projects can you help them move forward?

2. Pack your resume with keywords—those words that describe your title, knowledge base, skill set, impressive "name-brand" companies or Fortune 500 employers, prestigious universities attended, degrees, licensure, software experience, affiliations, and so on.

3. Find keywords by reviewing relevant job postings online or detailed classified ads in newspapers, reading job descriptions or content at your target companies' Web sites, reading your association's newsletter or trade journals, attending association meetings and talking with thought leaders, conducting informational interviews with industry contacts, and so on.

4. Position critical information at the "visual center" of the page. Weave keywords throughout your Qualifications Summary and Professional Experience, as well as in your cover letter.

5. Resist the temptation to outsmart applicant screening software by, for instance, planting the keyword "project manager" nine times throughout the résumé when you might have minimal experience as a project manager.

6. When writing job descriptions, try to keep your paragraph to around five lines. Summarize any redundant statements and present the material with an emphasis on transferable skills. Always include accomplishments (you'll learn more about accomplishments in chapter 6).

support with examples

7. If you're writing a functional or skills-based resume, focus on three to five skill areas and lean toward occupational skills (such as event planning, marketing, or project coordination) instead of personal skills (such as analytical skills, problem-solving skills, or organizational talents) for category subheadings. After you have selected your subheadings, develop two to five sentences, along with specific accomplishments that encapsulate your range of experience for each subheading.

(continued)

(continued)

8. New graduates with limited professional experience will normally place their Education section near the top of the resume, after the Objective/Focus or Qualifications Summary.

9. For categories such as affiliations, publications, presentations, or awards and honors, consider presenting information in a bulleted list or two-column format to save space and add visual appeal.

10. Think like an advertising copywriter: Be concise, but give enough data to create interest and a desire to meet you.

Accomplishments: The Linchpin of a Great Résumé

"It is most expedient for the wise…to be the trumpet of his own virtues."

—Shakespeare, *Much Ado About Nothing*

P ut 25 hiring managers, résumé writers, or job seekers in a room and ask them what information should be included in a résumé, and you'll get 25 different answers. Why such diversity of opinions, and zealously argued ones at that? I have a couple of theories. First, résumés involve the subjective disciplines of writing and design. Both are subject to personal preferences, interpretation, and experience. What makes one person love the fluid, polysyllabic prose of William F. Buckley, while another prefers the choppy, nickel-word style of Ernest Hemingway? Why do some swoon over the etherealism of Monet and react nonchalantly to the abstract spatters of Jackson Pollock? It's a matter of individual interest and taste.

The second and more visceral reason for disagreement on résumé development is that résumés—or, more appropriately, the impetus for preparing a résumé—can threaten one's sense of security and significance. For many, the mere mention of a résumé conjures up fearful images of unemployment and the financial insecurities that accompany it.

Job search is a task replete with opportunities for roadblocks, rejection, and self-doubt. Because many feel their job hopes hinge on the perfect résumé, they are concerned about it—with good reason. The uncertainty of change is uncomfortable, so people want to lessen that discomfort by taking control: "If I follow the right résumé-writing rules or prescribed formulas, I'll get a job, and everything will be okay." Unfortunately, the rules of résumé writing are a bit like mercury: They're slippery, they're hard to get a handle on, and they quickly change the minute you try to pass them along to someone else.

Validating the mercury theory are responses from the employer preference survey, the complete results of which are detailed in appendix B. We asked a number of comprehensive questions about résumés, and not one received a unanimous response—disappointing news for fellow left-brain types who like to "find the rules and follow them." Take heart, however, because there was *one* survey item that generated nearly universal agreement among human resources executives surveyed:

Verifiable accomplishments should always be included.

Further emphasizing the importance of accomplishments in résumés, several human resources executives indicated that accomplishments are one of the key elements they look for when screening applicants. So why are accomplishments so important? The following section explores the answers to this question.

Tip If you're anxious to start developing your accomplishments, jump ahead to "Strategies for Presenting Accomplishments" on page 239 or the "Impact-Mining" section on page 250.

What's in It for Me?

Most buyers are tuned to radio station WIFM, or "what's in it for me?" Before opening your wallet, you make a decision, consciously or subconsciously, about how you will benefit from making a purchase. The same holds true for companies before they "buy" an employee. In chapter 2, I discussed why employers make the decision to invest their financial, material, and human resources in you as a new employee. As with a capital investment, they expect a return on investment (ROI) on their human capital.

How that return will be defined depends on the type of organization. If it's a sales organization, the powers-that-be might be focused on your ability to bring in new business, maximize sales within existing accounts, and create demand for high-profit products. A service organization would be interested in how you can improve service delivery, expand the menu of services offered, and enhance relationships with key customers. Manufacturers are concerned with issues such as productivity, quality assurance, and on-time shipment of orders. You'll learn later in this chapter what different industries are specifically interested in.

Yet whatever the industry, all employers are ultimately interested in making sure that the company is around tomorrow. To do so, the company must be healthy; to be healthy, it must be profitable. Accordingly, the employer's primary purpose for existence is not to give you a job; rather, corporations exist to make money. If they didn't make money, there would be no funds to offer you a job. Even nonprofit organizations, taxpayer-funded school systems, and government agencies need to be conscious of the need for revenue inflow to exceed outflow. Without a certain level of liquidity, they would suffer much like your household would if, month after month, there wasn't enough money to pay the mortgage.

One human resources manager in the employer preference survey put it well when pinpointing a common faux pas among applicants: It's an "entitlement mentality: I have my degree; I'm sharp; what can you do for me?" Those with this mentality find themselves at the bottom of the pile when it comes to projecting a professional, company-minded attitude. Top companies have a sea of applicants to choose from, many with degrees and many conspicuously sharp. Those who temper their confidence with a measure of humility and a focus on contributing to the bottom line, however, quickly distinguish themselves from the rest of the candidate pool.

Still to many, profit is an ugly word that elicits images of ruthless corporate executives raking in colossal salaries while anonymous workers toil at minimum wages. I won't argue that corporate greed does not exist—the infamous corporate scandals of Enron and WorldCom in the early 2000s attest to its too-prevalent presence. Unfortunately, there is no way that avarice will be abolished in this lifetime! At the same time, you can't broadly paint all companies green with greed or reduce the employer-employee relationship to a callous contract of indentured servitude. A great number of companies are led by principled people who blend profit with purpose and altruistic vision. Wise managers view profits as a natural by-product of efficiency, quality, and service; they then use a portion of those profits to reinvest in their employees and reward them for their contributions to the organization's success. In companies like these, everybody wins.

Armed with a refresher in rudimentary economics, you now understand why accomplishments are the linchpin of a great résumé. With them, you

- Appear business-savvy.
- Indicate your understanding of the bottom line.
- Demonstrate a track record for contributing to it.

Candidates who include accomplishments position themselves above the competition for jobs. To illustrate this point, picture yourself on the other side of the interviewer's desk for a moment. As the corporate recruiter for BBB Medical Equipment, Inc., you must find an experienced sales representative to manage a critical territory. With a query to the company's résumé database, you look for résumés that contain keywords such as "sales representative," "five years' experience," "medical disposables," and so on.

Now in your hands are the résumé printouts for the 10 candidates who surfaced at the top of your keyword "hit list." Each represents a real person who, like most of us, labors to maintain a home and family and hopes for a better job and a better future. With only print and paper as their voices, they now attempt to tell their story and persuade you of their superior ability to do the job. How do you decide who will earn a personal interview and who will get pitched into the wastebasket? You might be measuring candidates against a job order and looking for a specific skill set, a definite number of years of industry experience, or "soft skills" that indicate a particular personality profile. No doubt all of your top candidates meet the job order criteria based on the parameters of your computer search.

Your top two prospects, Candidates A and B, have similar backgrounds in terms of companies worked for and length of experience. The database research ranks these two candidates equally, but it's your task to make a judgment call on who appears most qualified. As you read each candidate's most recent position description, what tips the scales in your mind to make Candidate A or Candidate B stand out as the odds-on favorite?

Candidate A

DEF MEDICAL PRODUCTS CO., Cincinnati, Ohio

Sales Representative: Responsible for four million dollars of sales in medical disposable products to major hospitals, home health agencies, clinics, and retail DMEs in the tri-state area. Duties included conducting CME-accredited workshops for nursing staff and physicians, assisting retailers with inventory management, and training nursing and retail staff on current wound care techniques. 2005 Winner of Award of Excellence (top ten representatives in the company) for achieving sales above quota.

Candidate B

GHI MEDICAL PRODUCTS CO., Dayton, Ohio

Sales Representative: Manage $4 million tri-state sales territory, generating sales of wound care products to major hospitals, home health agencies, long-term care facilities, clinics, and DME retailers. Plan and conduct interactive and informative CME-accredited classes for physicians and nursing staff. Advise retailers on sales and inventory strategies. Exceeded performance expectations every year with company:

Year 1:	Turned around stagnant sales with 18% increase; ranked #1 in division, #2 among 200 in nation.
Year 2:	Generated 14% increase in sales. Won "Award of Excellence," an annual award reserved for the top 10 reps nationwide.
Year 3:	Rolled out two new products, capturing #1 sales in district for both products.
Year 4:	Ranked #1 in region—met challenge of facilitating critical transition period associated with merger/acquisition.
Year 5:	Converted eight of ten largest hospitals in territory to new product—including several "non contract" accounts—for a 27% increase in sales.

Who do you think has a better track record? Most likely, Candidate B. Now, forgive me as I admit that Candidates A and B are actually the same person. The position description for Candidate A was a first draft written by the job seeker. The final version (Candidate B) was written as a result of asking a series of targeted, sequenced questions. (You'll learn more about my interrogation process later in this chapter.) It's obvious who appears most qualified in a hiring manager's mind, and it's this favorable first impression that will give Candidate B an edge over his competitors as he walks on the interview stage.

Tip Some hiring managers admit they often have a definite favorite prior to the interview phase based solely on the candidate's résumé and cover letter. Sometimes unconsciously so, hiring managers want their "first pick" to interview best, thus proving their intuitions correct and making the hiring decision a snap. Other hiring managers say that if two top candidates have similar experience and skills and interview equally well, the résumé can be the factor that decides the deadlock. As one human resources manager put it, the most important element looked for is "that a résumé is the person's best work." It is the one tangible piece of evidence that remains long after your interview impression wears off. Use it to set yourself apart from—and above—the competition by driving home the message that you can make a measurable difference.

Words to Woo Employers

Recall from chapter 2 that the third step in the AIDA advertising formula is to create desire. The stimulus to help trigger desire is your list of accomplishments, also known as results, impact statements, outcomes, contributions, advantages, achievements, or any other equivalent term. I prefer to use "impact statements" or "contributions" because they are employer-oriented terms, whereas "accomplishments" and its synonyms tend to sound more candidate-focused.

Contributions set the stage for showing why the employer needs you and how you can satisfy the need. Your goal is to write impact statements that will cause the employer to stop and think, "This candidate has really made a difference for past employers; we need someone like this who can do the same for our company." Impact statements take you a step beyond the experience and education of your competition; because it is difficult to compare two candidates' contributions, they might keep you in the running longer than a candidate who might have accomplished more than you but didn't communicate it as well on the résumé.

Words that woo employers are words that address the employer's question of "Why buy?" Outlined in chapter 2 are ten of the reasons employers buy. To illustrate how impact statements can address these buying motivators, I've listed each of the 10 reasons again in the following sections, along with possible impact statements for each reason. Later in the chapter, you'll find hundreds of ideas for impact statements for specific professions and industries, many of which are charted for strong growth into the 21st century.

A critical analysis of buying motivators 1 through 10 reveals that some categories are nearly synonymous (such as saving time and saving money, and making work easier and saving time), and a number of impact statements could have fit just as well under another category. Nonetheless, my motivation for supplying this detail is twofold:

- To give you a broad springboard for ideas on how to write your own impact statements.

- To point out how virtually any contribution you make can affect the bottom line.

Buying Motivator #1: Make Money

- Captured a 12% gain in net profit, a record for the company's 60-year history.

- Reengineered operations enterprise-wide to net over $1 million in additional profits.

- Built sales for start-up company from zero to $6.5 million over a four-year period.

- Earned company $350,000 in incentive bonuses through on-time completion of commercial construction projects.

- Countered a $45,000 annual increase in rent (relocated to high-profile location) with a $260,000 increase in sales.

- Introduced new products to boost sales 14%.

- Reversed branch's historically poor performance from ranking #33 out of 35 units to #1 in country for sales, with added honors as Top Service Branch.

- Achieved a nationally unprecedented 50% increase for product placed in field.

- Prepared and presented proposals to secure more than $5 million in venture-capital financing.

- Doubled sales volume for three consecutive years (from 1.2 to 4.9 million units).

Buying Motivator #2: Save Money

- Cut purchasing costs 24% through vendor partnership program.

- Sourced new overseas vendors, providing equivalent quality in raw materials at half the cost.

- Reduced expenses from 150% of target to goal attainment in all major expense categories.

- Initiated cost controls that reduced labor expenses by more than $50,000 (7%).

- Designed purchasing strategy to upgrade communications equipment to digital system at no cost to company.

- Identified obsolete inventory on contractual service agreements to cut equipment maintenance costs 28%.

- Captured a 20% savings for primary expense category via consolidation of services.

- Trimmed more than $20,000 (15%) from upcoming fiscal year budget through business process reengineering.

- Cut the cost-to-hire by 40% through improvements in recruiting policies.

Buying Motivator #3: Save Time

- Retooled job descriptions to eliminate monthly overtime costs of $6,000.

- Performed the work previously required of two full-time employees.

- Reduced time requirements for month-end close of books from seven to two days.

- Introduced technology that took data transfer from two-day process to "real time" mode; idea was subsequently adopted by company's three satellite offices.

- Pared hiring time on "hard to fill" positions from 90 to 30 days through electronic search vehicles.

- Transitioned production from "batch oriented" to "cell groups," slashing internal lead time through fabrication from 20 days to less than 1 day.

- Introduced secretarial staff to timesaving concepts from the classic *One-Minute Manager* and other personal reading; team now has time for special projects that had been "on hold" for more than six months.

- As change agent, analyzed administrative processes and introduced new protocol that reduced weekly report generation time by 75%.

- Created new "find it fast" system for file checkout; idea has eliminated frequent two-hour searches for missing files.

- Redesigned office layout, pairing support units with assigned managers for faster access and communication.

Buying Motivator #4: Make Work Easier

- Consolidated business forms to reduce paperwork and eliminate duplication of information.

- Merged four fragmented service centers into centralized unit to improve order-processing time 40%.

- Anticipated HR issues associated with company's growing pains and put "expandable" systems in place that accommodated a 25% annual growth in staffing.

- Analyzed warehouse receiving process and implemented system that reduced unnecessary and time-consuming steps in stocking.

- Introduced inventory-management software that eliminated costly physical inventory counts.

- Initiated employee town-hall meetings and brown-bag lunches to gather input from all levels of organization; ideas generated from employees collectively boosted productivity 20%.

- Created safety-awareness program that reduced occurrence of back injuries from 20 per year to 1.

- Secured vendor involvement in trade shows to reduce staffing requirements 20%.

- Served as impenetrable gatekeeper for executives, freeing them to focus on leadership responsibilities.

- Created internship program that boosted capability of engineering team while providing mentorship services and an opportunity to screen and recruit some of the university's brightest graduates.

Buying Motivator #5: Solve a Specific Problem

- Troubleshot recurring computer crashes for key customer; traced problem to vendor software, facilitated corrections, and maintained account valued at $70,000 in annual income.

- Appointed to lead team that replaced antiquated computer system for telecommunications leader; produced application that satisfied regulatory and internal requirements, while providing added commercialization potential worth millions.

- Suggested tie-line communication system that enabled employees to call Xerox locations nationwide from customer sites without long-distance charges; idea generated $8,000 savings in branch for first year alone.

- Challenged with providing uninterrupted services to club members during six-month, $4.7 million construction project; accommodated all events without inconvenience, including three-day regional invitational tournament culminating in dinner for 1,000.

- Resolved approximately 25% of calls for service with telephone troubleshooting skills (company average for problem resolution by telephone is only 10%).

★ Addressed recurring quality issue that had been largely ignored by predecessors; resolution resulted in key customer increasing product orders 60%.

★ Assembled cross-functional team representing engineering, production, logistics, and warehousing to tackle complex production problem; initiative led to a 20% cost reduction and a 30% increase in productivity.

★ Virtually eliminated assembly-line "holds" and downtime through implementation of computer-based shortage-tracking system.

★ Suggested voice-mail solution to handle fluctuating volume of customer inquiries; technology saved expense of additional FTEs while making it easier for customers to access needed information.

★ Transferred paper records to magnetic media, simultaneously addressing storage space and ease-of-access issues.

Buying Motivator #6: Be More Competitive

★ Led strategy task force that captured across-the-board, 10-point increase in national regulatory audit (scores indicate quality performance above national average, highest in organization's history).

★ Initiated company-sponsored training and certification programs for technical team; investment positioned XYZ as local market leader and enabled company to earn first-time contracts with Fortune 500 clients.

★ Managed post-acquisition strategy for divestiture of nonperforming assets and reinvestment in high-performance assets, in some cases generating as much as an eightfold increase in annual returns.

★ Accessed influential community resources representing business, education, government, and civic leaders to promote city's bid as site for a new University of California campus.

★ Translated marketing materials into Spanish and Hmong, gaining dominant presence in markets left virtually ignored by competitors.

★ Recruited top talent to expand division 25%; negotiated pay-for-performance contracts that kept labor costs at 10% below national average.

★ Selected for branch troubleshooting assignment to reverse eroding market share with advent of new competitor; inherited dissipating loan portfolio and rebuilt client relationships and deposit/loan portfolios to record levels.

Facilitated transition of company from price-sensitive competitor to a quality-driven service organization; new philosophy attracted niche market customers that boosted earnings 9%.

Challenged with liquidation of difficult-to-sell commercial properties to favorably position bank during aggressive growth (closed several sales in as little as 30 days, with one property selling at $60,000 above book value)—successes helped position branch as most desirable for acquisition.

Offered health benefits and accrued vacation time to temporary workers of a human resources staffing company; initiative increased client orders as a result of attracting better-skilled temps.

Buying Motivator #7: Build Relationships/Image with Internal/External Customers, Vendors, and the Public

Negotiated exclusive referral relationship with prestigious industry resource; alliance created image of a full-service organization for sole proprietor firm, without the need for additional capital infusion.

Debuted quarterly newsletter and grew it to a 20-page publication packed with valuable communiqués on legal concerns, legislative issues, educational updates, and technology advancements.

Spearheaded concept for educational/public relations video and brochures that document the mining industry's success in reclamation of mined areas into viable wetlands, agricultural lands, and commercial uses.

Transformed association from fragmented factions into a cohesive, member-driven alliance proactively representing home education issues throughout the state.

Counseled executives on response to media inquiries and management of critical and potentially volatile issues; proactive stance promoted a favorable understanding of issues by citizens and employees and resulted in positive newspaper editorial and broadcast coverage.

Introduced Supplier Certification/Partnering, achieving company-vendor alliance goals for quality, cost reductions, and expansion.

Initiated proactive telephone campaign to students' parents to address concerns about changes from traditional to year-round school schedule.

➤ Designed and produced series of high-profile communications to create company's first fully integrated corporate communications campaign (annual reports, marketing materials, publications, Web site, print ads, collateral materials, etc.).

➤ Forged with print and broadcast media relationships that have elevated the organization's image as a hub for family-values issues and yielded a tenfold increase in media coverage; introduced sophisticated electronic methods for rapid dissemination of press releases.

➤ Coordinated full-day staff-development event designed to promote departmental communications with internal customers—event was attended by 175+ staff members, physicians, and corporate executives; designed, scheduled, and coordinated interactive, entertaining seminars, such as a well-received spin-off of the game show *Jeopardy*.

Buying Motivator #8: Expand Business

➤ Introduced "service bundling," a concept new to the industry that captured an average 18% increase in 22 branches.

➤ Supported R&D in achieving 50% increase in new products brought to market.

➤ Launched first market in the nation for major Internet service provider; exceeded goals for all key performance indicators.

➤ Collaborated on new product development, pricing, and roll-out—all new products met or exceeded first-year distribution goals.

➤ Acquired undercapitalized competitor to capture dominant market share (up from approximately 25 to 40%).

➤ Created marketing strategies to address fluctuating market conditions—during critical economic period, led company in campaign increases of as much as 153%.

➤ Polled customers to identify preferences for additional services; introduced add-ons that increased average ticket sale by 7%.

➤ Added training component to repair business; demand grew staff from one to four full-time certified instructors, adding $175,000 in revenue.

➤ Launched new products and line extension (R&D, EPA approval, pricing, market planning, and sales presentations), capturing leading market share in less than six months.

⭐ Obtained additional industry certifications, enabling organization to offer exclusive services and capture lucrative add-on sales.

Buying Motivator #9: Attract New Customers

⭐ Cultivated relationships with influential Stanford physicians (previously inaccessible), gaining support for antiarthritic products to drive up regional sales 19%.

⭐ Sourced new customers through electronic research, generating a 12% increase in active accounts.

⭐ Attracted top sales performers from competitors with established client lists, expanding active customer database by more than 200%.

⭐ Offered existing customers referral incentives; program achieved a 10:1 return on investment for marketing funds.

⭐ Gained access to previously "no see" accounts through intensive networking and volunteerism efforts; recently completed contract negotiations with several of these accounts that will double personal sales production.

⭐ Analyzed promotional spending to identify ad vehicle generating largest new-customer response; data will enable company to increase future ROI 5% (from 3 to 8%).

⭐ Directed Chamber of Commerce membership drive that yielded a record 125 new members in a 24-hour period.

⭐ Led company's first foray into television advertising; campaign labeled a "huge success" by Board of Directors and contributed to fourfold sales growth.

⭐ Launched company's first Web page to capture technology-savvy, high-net-worth customers; electronic sales have grown from zero to $30,000 in first six months.

⭐ Secured new business with national accounts such as Wal-Mart (eight states), Home Depot, and Orchard Supply Hardware—national presence supported sales growth from $100,000 to $2 million in five-year period.

Buying Motivator #10: Retain Existing Customers

⭐ Increased customer-retention figures from 70 to 96%.

⭐ Implemented direct-mail follow-up program for new customers; data reflects a 55% increase in repeat customers.

- Boosted policy renewals from below average to top 5% in the country.

- Improved customer satisfaction ranking from #10 to #1 among 12 branches.

- Offered creative, low-cost incentive program for repeat purchases; program was adopted on national scale and contributed to strongest sales growth in company's 77-year history.

- Initiated direct-mail campaign for retail boutique that increased average number of purchases from two to four per year.

- Acquired mailing lists that tapped target audience; tracking of customer purchases showed a 30% greater response than prior direct-mail sources.

- Established company's first customer database, equipping young organization with tools to plan, implement, and carefully monitor success of marketing campaigns.

- Member of customer service team that supported a customer-retention rate of 85%—among the highest in the company.

- Recruited to turn around sales territory with three-year record of declining sales and reputation for poor customer service; within 12 months, rebuilt relationships and obtained orders from key accounts to show a 47% increase in sales.

These sample impact statements should trigger the salivary glands of any profit-conscious manager. Important to note is that the 100 examples cut across professional boundaries. Buying motivators are "seamless" when it comes to your profession—virtually all employers want someone who can help make money, save money, save time, solve problems, and so on. Regardless of your title, there are few limitations on which buying motivator category you can contribute. Some professions will be more closely aligned with certain categories, such as sales professionals with making money and managers with saving money. At the same time, however, secretaries can just as well contribute to the "make money" category, sales representatives can contribute to the "save time" category, and engineers can contribute to the "retain customers" category. Adopting this common-goal mentality makes for a positive corporate culture, adds to your camaraderie with colleagues, and contributes to career satisfaction.

Strategies for Presenting Accomplishments

To help you communicate your commitment to the employer's bottom line, consider one or more of these résumé-writing trade secrets.

Numbers: The Universal Language

The sci-fi film *Contact,* based on Carl Sagan's novel, features an astrophysicist (Jodie Foster) who obsessively devotes her life to radio telescopes, hoping to make contact with other life forms in the universe. The solar system Vega comes through for her, and she, along with a cadre of the most brilliant scientists on the planet, are subsequently challenged with decrypting the mathematical code sent from an advanced source of life some 26 light-years away. At one point, a CIA agent steps in and wisecracks, "If this source is so sophisticated, why don't they just speak English?" Foster replies, "Seventy percent of the planet speaks other languages. Mathematics is the only truly universal language." Moral of the story: Numbers can clarify where words can confuse.

Numbers, unlike words, are universal, no matter what the reader's business idiom or corporate culture is. Note how the lack of numbers in this maintenance director's impact statement creates confusion about whether the statement is even an accomplishment.

Before

Implemented preventative maintenance program that improved downtime.

Thought-provoking! Did the maintenance program increase the amount of downtime? I doubt that this is what the candidate intended to convey, but it could be interpreted in this manner. Specifying the production increase and the before and after numbers on downtime clears up any questions about "improving downtime."

After

Improved production 19% and reduced assembly-line downtime from 7 to .5 hours per week through implementation of preventive-maintenance program.

Here's another impact statement that, although it contains numbers, doesn't convey the full impact of the accomplishment.

Before

Cut production lead time to 4–7 days, depending on model.

Compare this with the *After* version, which contains specific percentages for each model.

After

Cut lead time by more than 50% on model "A" and 40% on model "B"—improvements enabled company to boast fastest order-fulfillment schedule among all major competitors.

In addition to the insertion of specific percentage reductions for each model, I added a comparison to help clarify the impact of the reductions in lead time. Comparison is another technique that talented résumé writers use to convey an individual's value to prospective employers, and I discuss it next.

Comparison—A Powerful Form of Communication

You've heard the phrase, "it's apples to oranges—you just can't compare the two." In communicating, we often use comparisons to help make our point. Careful use of comparisons can help convey that you can run faster, jump higher, and leap tall buildings in a single bound better than the next candidate. For instance, this impact statement tells only half the story.

Before

Improved branch ranking for sales volume to #1.

A comparison with some elaboration tells much more.

After

As branch's sole account executive, improved sales production 42% and increased branch ranking from #12 to #1 in a 15-branch region.

In this case, the addition of the words "As branch's sole account executive" gives the reader a much clearer picture of your role in this accomplishment. And, by telling your reader there are 15 branches total, the increase from #12 becomes much more impressive because it shows that you turned around sales in a branch that was ranking near the bottom of the barrel.

Other comparisons you might make include the following.

Comparisons between competitors

Improved sales production 42% and increased company's market share from #2 to #1.

Comparisons with the industry average

Improved sales production 42%, well above national average of 8%.

Comparisons with the company average

Improved sales production 42%, the largest annual sales increase in the company's 12-year history.

Comparisons with your predecessor in the position

Improved sales production 42% in a territory that had experienced declining sales and negligent account service.

Proceed with caution when you compare yourself with a team member or predecessor, respected or otherwise. Such comparisons can be offensive, so it is best in these cases to stick with a comparison to industry averages, other branches, or competitors.

You'll also want to avoid sounding like the Lone Ranger in a business climate that venerates the consummate team player. At the same time, don't be afraid to list contributions that were accomplished as a team. When it comes to developing impact statements, I commonly see candidates, especially female candidates, make the mistake of entirely omitting an accomplishment if they weren't 100 percent responsible for it. If you are concerned about taking credit for something that was a team effort, there's a simple answer to your dilemma. Simply begin your impact statement with phrasing such as the following:

Contributed to…

Aided in…

Helped to…

Member of 7-person task force that…

Collaborated with department managers to…

Participated on ABC Committee that…

Supported a…

Company-wide efforts led to…

Departmental efforts led to…

Selected for national team that…

Douglas, a vice president for a manufacturing concern, used the following statement as part of his Qualifications Summary to share the applause for his collective accomplishments:

Core management team member who contributed to organization-wide successes in unprecedented revenue growth, profit enhancement, and market positioning.

The noun phrase "core management team member" gives credit where credit is due, and the adjective "unprecedented" provides a comparison with the company average without going into details (specific accomplishments were covered later in the résumé under each of the past employers).

When you get right down to it, an argument can be made that any accomplishment is really a team accomplishment. Sales professionals don't achieve increases in orders without products developed by R&D, literature from marketing, orders processed by customer service, and parcels correctly assembled and delivered by warehousing and shipping. The rule of thumb is to give credit to the team if it was a joint effort, but don't hesitate to claim ownership if you were the one to envision, initiate, or take the leadership role in the effort. If it's the latter and it would be politically savvy of you to give credit to the team you headed up (especially when applying for in-house promotions), try one of these suggestions:

Led task force in…

Assembled 7-person task force that…

Chaired ABC Committee that…

Co-led sales campaign that…

Department team leader who…

Orchestrated cross-functional teams in accomplishing…

Directed collaborative efforts that realized…

Headed up national team that…

In résumé writing, there's a fine line to walk between self-adulation and self-effacement. Too much of the former, and you'll look like a narcissist. Too much of the latter, and you'll look like a Milquetoast. If you're unsure, err on the side of self-effacement, because reference checks that reveal your résumé to be inflated will be grounds for discontinuing your candidacy. You can always elaborate on your contributions in an interview, and you will probably score even more points when your explanations reveal that you did more than the marquee information contained in the résumé. Err too far in understating your contributions, however, and you won't get to the interview. If you're unsure, have a business-savvy friend review your impact statements and get his or her read on whether you're giving yourself enough credit.

ROI—How Quickly Can You Deliver?

ROI is another effective tool to quantify your value to employers. The acronym stands for *return on investment* and is a term companies use to determine how quickly their investment in new equipment or advertising or an expansion will pay for itself. With your new perspective as a PEO, you can concentrate on generating a return on your employer's investment in salary, benefits, training, office space, business cards, and all of the other hidden costs associated with hiring you. Some professions can more easily show a return than others, specifically those that directly affect revenue generation or expense controls. For instance, a top sales performer can show that a $125,000 salary will be justified by her ability to bring in half a million dollars in sales. Here are more examples that demonstrate ROI on a résumé.

- New Business Growth: Brought in more than $300,000 in new business during first six months in territory.
- Existing Account Growth: Added more than $200,000 in sales volume among existing accounts.

A purchasing manager can imply that his past record of negotiating impressive vendor concessions will validate his salary requirements, which happen to be 20 percent more than what the company paid its last purchasing manager! The following impact statements might guarantee his standing as the number-one candidate, despite his higher salary demands.

- Negotiated more than $300,000 in vendor concessions.
- Reduced transportation costs 20%, or $95,000 per year.

ROIs aren't limited to sales representatives or department managers. Support-staff members can also help to offset their salaries by paying attention to bottom-line contributions. Here's how one executive assistant to a management consultant showed her ROI.

- Initiated action on numerous matters, freeing consultant to maximize client time and increase monthly billable hours 27%.

Because the consulting firm was privately held, only the percentage increase in billable hours was listed, rather than the dollar amount it represented, which happens to be nearly $8,000 in new revenue each month. (See chapter 7, page 314, for more information on how to convey data from privately held companies in a confidential manner.) By tracking this information, the executive secretary provides herself with excellent leverage in negotiating future raises with her existing employer or salary increases with a new employer.

You can see how keeping track of contributions can pay off for you. Delivering a healthy ROI is not requisite to substantiating your job, but it is very helpful in promoting job security.

The Company's Mission Statement—Make It Your Mission

Mission-linking, or tying your value to the company's mission statement, is a unique technique for connecting with a prospective employer. To do so, you'll need to know what the company's mission statement is. Corporate public relations departments can provide this information, as can the company's Web site. After you have researched the company's mission statement, begin thinking about how your experience or professional aspirations apply to the company's goals, purposes, or values. You can work mission-linking into your focus statement at the top of the résumé or weave it into the introductory paragraphs of a cover letter.

The CAR Technique—Challenge, Action, and Result

CAR is a vehicle (pardon the pun) you use to highlight a specific **C**hallenge you encountered, the **A**ction taken, and the measurable **R**esult from your action. This technique works especially well if you are transitioning from one industry to another, because it focuses the reader's attention on your skills rather than on the industry in which you performed the skills. Alex had a varied background in nonprofit association management and restaurant management and wanted to take those skills into the corporate sector. A separate Accomplishments section was allotted for his sales and management CARs, helping impress the reader first with his record of contributions rather than where he made the contributions.

REPRESENTATIVE ACCOMPLISHMENTS

SALES/BUSINESS DEVELOPMENT

Challenge:	Build sales in service-driven business catering to corporate clientele.
Action:	Created and implemented targeted marketing, advertising, and promotional strategies.
Result:	Delivered $78,000 increase in higher-profit segment of operation. Achieved 91% rating (above average) from independent review service.

Challenge:	Recruited to turn around operation with stagnant sales ($750K) and declining patronage.
Action:	Brought business-driven initiatives to non-profit setting for operation typically viewed as a "loss leader."
Result:	Increased sales by 46% and 24% in major revenue categories.

MANAGEMENT/OPERATIONS/BUSINESS ADMINISTRATION

Challenge:	Maintain uninterrupted member services during 5-month, $3.2 million construction project.
Action:	Set up temporary business office, maintained access to key materials, designed alternative operating procedures.
Result:	Accommodated all events without inconvenience, including 3-day tournament culminating in dinner for 400.

Challenge:	Inherited operation performing below par for service and quality.
Action:	Recruited new talent, retrained service staff, designed new quality/cost controls.
Result:	Lowered operating costs, increased facility usage by an overall 23%, and earned favorable scores on recent member-survey.

You can also use the CAR technique in place of the job description and accomplishments under your professional experience. When doing so, make sure you are consistent in using the identical CAR format for each of your past employers. This creates a consistent, balanced visual impact and gives the appearance of a strong, long-term history for taking on challenges and delivering results. Keep in mind that the CAR presentation technique is not a space-saver (note that in the Employer Survey, appendix B, 67% of hiring managers preferred that résumés be kept to one to two pages).

If you're trying to keep your résumé to one page, try a more traditional presentation of your job descriptions and accomplishments. Note how the word "solution" was substituted for "action" in the following illustration. You can also substitute synonyms for "results," such as accomplishments, outcomes, contributions, or impacts. Brad's example on the following page is the Professional Experience portion of his two-page résumé.

> *Note* Hanging indents were applied to each paragraph to help the headings stand out. Also different in this example is the use of present-tense verbs rather than past tense in the Solution paragraphs. This helps Brad to connect with the hiring manager and gives the sense that Brad is shoulder-to-shoulder with the reader, advising on solutions to possible challenges the company might be facing. More important, the Results paragraphs are strong with baseline and subsequent data that position Brad as *the solution* to the company's present challenges.

PROFESSIONAL EXPERIENCE

Zelner Unlimited, Salt Lake City, Utah   2002-Present

Sales Manager

Challenge: Recruited to revitalize stagnant sales and reverse declining profit performance in Rocky Mountain states.

Solution: Design an intensive staff training campaign linking marketing, sales, customer service, and operations; capitalize on use of team leaders to empower and motivate sales team of 27; negotiate partnerships with add-on service providers to counter company's major disadvantage as a standalone facility.

Results: Drove gross sales up from 60% of quota to 121% of quota; quadrupled several sales members' production to in excess of $5 million; contributed 8% to bottom-line profits.

Parkland Properties, Inc., Denver, Colorado   1998-2002

Sales Manager

Challenge: Tasked with rebuilding field sales team with 3-year history of declining sales.

Solution: Utilize industry contacts to recruit experienced sales performers; groom existing sales team through exposure to top performers, product incentives, and individual coaching in presentation and closing techniques.

Results: In just four weeks, improved sales production 250% beyond prior year figures; rebuilt sales team from 3 to 10 who generated collective revenues of $4.6 million, a record for the company.

Hall Enterprises, Denver, Colorado   1989-1998

Territory Manager

Challenge: Rectify account relations in territory suffering from history of poor service.

Solution: Implement company-sponsored speaker series for accounts featuring topics of interest, improve visibility in territory through consistent call schedule and direct mail campaign, target and convert key accounts to exclusive contracts.

Results: Built sales from $440,000 to $1.2 million in two years; ultimately grew territory to $4.1 million in sales despite an 80% reduction in geographic area.

Virtual Memories, Denver, Colorado   1985-1989

General Manager

Challenge: Tasked with start-up operations including site selection, capital equipment purchases, and corporate office development.

Solution: Recruit and train sales and management team of 12; design integrated marketing, sales, and operations strategies.

Results: Built company from zero sales to more than $2 million in first year; grew sales to high of $10 million during tenure.

Where to Find Material for Your Accomplishments

For many people, developing impact statements is the hardest part of writing a résumé. Developing the responsibility portion of the résumé is generally easier because there are more sources from which to choose (refer to chapter 5 for source ideas, such as company job descriptions, job announcements, and so on). On the other hand, sources for accomplishments or impact statements are as rare as hen's teeth.

Performance Appraisals

One of the better places for unearthing accomplishments is from the files of your company's human resources department. Performance appraisals can provide a wealth of material; however, I meet many job seekers who haven't kept copies of performance appraisals and many more who haven't even received written evaluations. For those who do have access to performance appraisals, look for instances where you met or exceeded specific goals set by your supervisor. The following table shows just a portion of a performance appraisal for a job seeker who is a loan officer at a regional bank.

Key Objectives and Measurement Criteria	Results
Meet established funding goals of $750,000 per month.	Elizabeth funded 132 loans for $15,924,820 ($1,327,068 monthly average) on originations of 174 loans for $22,756,636 ($1,896,386 monthly average).
By December 31, pipeline to consist of 75% purchase transactions.	Purchase transactions amounted to 82% of all loans funded.

Appraiser comments:

Elizabeth's ability to follow an aggressive and consistent marketing plan has been consistent. Her selling techniques are consistently used to achieve sales and marketing goals. She is a strong supporter of management in helping to carry out bank policies. Moreover, she is a very professional representative of the bank.

We used this year-end appraisal information to write the following impact statements. Note how we used excerpts from the appraiser's comments section of the performance evaluation.

Impacts:

- Generated $15.9 million in annual loan activity, exceeding annual goal by 76%.

- Ranked #1 in "purchase transaction" loans, which yield higher returns to the bank—year-end totals reflect 82% of all loans funded (above goal of 75%).

- Comments from manager include the "ability to follow an aggressive and consistent marketing plan...a strong supporter of management [and] a very professional representative of the bank."

Your Career Management File

By far the best place to find information for impact statements is your own *career management file* (CMF). Every professional should have a growing CMF, so if you can't lay claim to one now, grab the nearest manila file folder or 9-by-12 envelope and label it "How I've Made a Difference." (You can also create a folder in your My Documents folder on your computer.) Your mission as profit-oriented contributor is to solve problems and help affect the bottom line. Just as a CEO needs meaningful data to measure progress, you, too, must gather data to document your contributions. Whether you're beginning a new position or remaining with your present employer, begin today to assemble data and track your progress on performance standards. Consider tossing the following items into your CMF:

- Notes from meetings with supervisors that state what is expected of you or how your performance will be measured.

- Notes (handwritten is okay) which substantiate that you met or exceeded what was expected of you.

- Notes (with detailed names, facts, figures, and so on) of what you consider to be your greatest contributions.

- Company printouts of information relevant to your profession (quarterly sales, productivity, expense controls, and so on). Remember to keep proprietary information extremely confidential.

- Job descriptions.

- Performance evaluations.

- Examples of work you've produced (such as a company brochure or new business form).

- Attaboys (or "attagirls") from the boss.

- Memos documenting your contribution to a team effort.

- Nice notes from customers.

From this raw material, you will compose powerful, substantiated, and impressive impact statements that will give you entrée to better jobs, outfit you with ammunition to win at the salary negotiation table, and document the fact that you *are* making a difference in the health of the company and in other peoples' lives. Next time you have a bad day at the office, take out your career management file and take note of what you have accomplished!

When your CMF begins to overflow, make separate file folders for each employer. To reconstruct data for past employers, you might need to call on former supervisors or contacts within the company. You might ask questions such as these:

- What were sales (or profits, production, cost issues, and so on) when I began with the company and what were they when I left the company?

- Did I (or teams on which I worked) make specific contributions that affected sales (profits, production, cost issues, and so on)?

- What do you think is my greatest contribution to the company?"

- What kinds of problems did I inherit?

- What were the challenges I was hired to meet?

- What numbers were in place when I started the job?

Obviously, the longer you've been away from a company, the harder it will be to find measurable data. That's why it's so important to maintain your CMF as you go. Much like preparing your tax return every April 15, the job is much easier if you've kept detailed records along the way.

As you add to your CMF, you'll begin to see how critical this file is to the all-important task of developing accomplishments for your résumé or for interviewing. It is difficult, if not impossible, to write powerful impact statements without a key ingredient that your CMF will now put at your fingertips: *baseline data.*

With baseline data, you can provide the impressive comparisons that I spoke of earlier in this chapter. Comparison of baseline and subsequent data, or before-and-after facts, will help you draw a much clearer picture of your success, because it will provide the reader a frame of reference. Without a frame of reference or starting point, your results might not sound as impressive. For instance, the following impact statements sound fairly strong.

Before

- Built sales to $270,000 per annum.

- Increased account list to 200.

However, a skeptical reader (most résumé screeners are!) might wonder whether sales were already $250,000 when you started or you inherited an account list of 175. Note the addition of baseline data in these *After* impact statements.

After

- Built sales from zero-base to $270,000 per annum (typical sales order for fastener products averages $75).

- From "no account list," formed relationships with 200 active accounts.

Giving a comparative frame of reference adds considerable weight to the sentences. Your reader now knows that

- ✦ Sales began at $0.

- ✦ You sell inexpensive fasteners where the average sales order is just $75 (it takes thousands of orders to get to the $250,000 mark).

- ✦ Your 200 accounts sprang from a nonexistent account list.

Very impressive!

Impact-Mining: Probing Questions to Unearth Hidden Treasures

Impact-mining is my term for the interrogative process I use to draw out a job seeker's accomplishments. The questions vary somewhat depending on the profession, industry, and job seeker's goals. In the following tables, you'll see more than a dozen industries or professions, from accounting and education to technology and warehousing. The left column of the tables provides suggested questions to measure baseline data and ferret out your effects on the company. The right column provides a corresponding accomplishment or impact statement that might result from tracking your progress against baseline data. There are more than 250 suggested impact statements in these tables. Reading between the lines, you'll see a consistent thread throughout that addresses employer buying motivators and uses techniques discussed earlier, such as numbers (the universal language), comparisons, mission-linking, and inferences to the employer's return on investment for hiring you.

I encourage you to read through tables that are outside your profession because you'll see that in many cases impact-mining is seamless, crossing professional boundaries and industry lines. For instance, one of the questions within the table for construction asks, "Did you win any bonus money for the company by finishing projects ahead of schedule?" This question could just as easily apply to technology-related professionals who might have won a contract bonus for developing a software application ahead of schedule.

If you find it difficult to answer any of the questions related to your profession or industry, it might be because you don't have the hard data to answer the questions. If this is the case, begin today to work on your career management file (explained in the preceding section) and start tracking relevant information. The mere act will help you take your career more seriously and boost your confidence as you see the differences materialize in your before and after data.

As you review these impact-mining questions and suggested Accomplishment statements, jot down or mark any that relate to your situation, for both your present employer and each of your past employers. When you're finished, you will have amassed a treasure chest of impact statements to choose from, the highlights of which you'll want to include in your résumé. You can weave others into your cover letter, follow-up letters, networking situations, and interview scenarios.

Accounting
Private Sector

Impact-Mining Questions	Example Accomplishment/Impact Statements for Résumé
Were there problems with the integrity of financial data when you started with the company?	Redesigned accounting systems and established internal controls to eliminate variances… earned "gold star" on audit package from Big 6 firm.
Was there a prior history of qualified audit opinions?	Reversed several-year history of qualified opinions.
Did you negotiate loan terms to the benefit of the company?	Improved loan terms, saving company $2\frac{1}{2}\%$ through renegotiation of annual interest rates.
Did you have a strong record of controlling costs in comparison with other branches or plants?	Ranked as lowest-cost producer among four comparable U.S. plants, consistently operating at 10% below norm.

(continued)

(continued)

Impact-Mining Questions	Example Accomplishment/Impact Statements for Résumé
Did you improve a past history of write-offs?	Corrected balance sheet deficiencies, virtually eliminating several-year history of 7-figure write-offs.
Did you design or implement policies that reduced the company's debt?	Implemented fiscal policies that enabled corporation to operate without debt for first time since its inception in 1975.
Was the company in a mergers and acquisitions mode?	Recruited to speed privately held company's aggressive growth mode, providing financial savvy and tax expertise to position company for profitable M&A activity.
Were you involved in stock offerings?	Strengthened corporation's financial and secondary stock offerings, including positioning through involvement in initial filing of 10-Ks, 10-Qs, S-3s, and S-4s.
Was the company in a growth mode?	Established and managed financial and operational infrastructure that supported a doubling in revenue from $27 to $56 million.
Were you responsible for treasury functions?	Invested reserve funds to perform above industry average, representing an additional 4% in net profit.
Did you rectify an antiquated cost accounting system?	Introduced Activity-Based Costing (ABC)—system provided first-time detailed costing and enabled general manager to identify and eliminate unprofitable items.
Did you reduce tax liabilities?	Saved $30,000 in tax liens through partnership dissolution and re-creation of corporate entity. Negotiated a $35,000 reduction in IRS taxes for improperly filed fuel tax (returns submitted prior to my arrival).
Did you reduce CPA fees?	Brought previously outsourced accounting functions in-house, saving some $25,000 in annual CPA fees.

Impact-Mining Questions	Example Accomplishment/Impact Statements for Résumé
Did you improve management of a 401(k) plan?	As trustee for 401(k), increased employee participation 20% and access to funds without jeopardizing financial stability of plan.
Did you reduce the time to complete end-of-month closing of books?	Reduced month-end closing time by two days, year-end by five days.
If you managed accounts payable, did you save money in some way?	Identified and eliminated more than $40,000 in double billings through new payables-review process.
If you managed accounts receivable, did you improve collections and, if so, by how much?	Improved 30-day collections from 82% to 95% through improvements in medical billing process.
Did you convert a system from manual to computer or make improvements in use of computer software?	Catalogued 10-year income and expense history to create company's first comprehensive financial report.
	Built sophisticated Excel spreadsheets to capture timely financial data, a first for the company.
	Researched, recommended, and directed installation of $100,000 technology upgrade.

Accounting
CPA/Public Accounting

Impact-Mining Questions	Example Accomplishment/Impact Statements for Résumé
Did your rainmaking skills boost the client list or client billing?	Brought established client base of 250 to firm and added 50 new clients representing large financial, manufacturing, and construction accounts.
How do your billable hours compare with others in the firm?	Generated highest billable production in a seven-member firm.
Did you add products or services that generated increased revenue?	Introduced business-advisory services that expanded gross billings 25%.

(continued)

(continued)

Impact-Mining Questions	Example Accomplishment/Impact Statements for Résumé
What did you accomplish for your clients?	Negotiated favorable client settlements with IRS and lending institutions. Sample cases: • Negotiated loan reduction of 25% for client, saving 2,400 acres of prime farmland. • Presented IRS Offer in Compromise that eliminated 95% of client's federal tax liability. • Represented client with potential accumulated earnings tax of $600,000, reducing tax liability to zero. • For publicly traded corp. and nine subsidiaries, provided in-depth analysis of financial/ADP records, resulting in substantial reduction in tax deficiencies. • Negotiated multimillion-dollar lease settlement with RTC for S&L client.
Were you selected for any significant projects?	Selected over senior staff to manage audit functions for firm's largest California client; reported directly to Chairman of Deloitte & Touche.

Accounting
Credit and Collections Manager

Impact-Mining Questions	Example Accomplishment/Impact Statements for Résumé
Did you turn around outstanding receivables?	Turned around 60+ day outstanding receivables from 18% to an average of 3.8% (and as low as .8%) for DFW and OKC Divisions.
Did you pursue past-due accounts that others had given up on?	Researched and collected on accounts as many as 5 years in arrears, collecting $500,000 in funds deemed "uncollectible."

Impact-Mining Questions	Example Accomplishment/Impact Statements for Résumé
Did you revise policy to improve the company's financial standing?	Redefined credit policy to reduce exposure; authorized credit lines of up to $100,000.
Was your percentage of charge-offs less than industry or company average?	Held write-offs to less than .5% on loan portfolio of $26 million, ranking #1 in state for minimizing charge-offs.
Did you counter the trend of borrowers filing chapter 7?	Used negotiation skills to persuade dozens of bankruptcy customers to reaffirm entire debt (collectively valued at more than $2 million).
Did you reduce days sales outstanding?	Reduced DSO from 68+ days to under 30 (below company directive of 35 days).
Did you eliminate a collections backlog?	Eliminated collections backlog of more than $275,000.

Administration
Administrative or Executive Assistant, Office Technician

Impact-Mining Questions	Example Accomplishment/Impact Statements for Résumé
Was there an inconsistency in systems or were there procedures that you corrected?	Coauthored 100-page Personnel Manual that brought congruity to administrative procedures in seven departments.
Did you manage the same or a greater amount of work while also dealing with cuts in staffing?	Created procedures and documentation systems to accommodate increase in workload despite a 30% cutback in staffing.
Did you improve file management?	Eliminated filing backlog; created new filing systems and procedures that ensured critical material was easily accessible at all times.
Were you hired when the company first opened or did you help launch a start-up operation or new branch office?	Established plans and procedures that supported growth from 30 to 600 employees over 4-year period, with international offices in Canada and the United States.

(continued)

(continued)

Impact-Mining Questions	Example Accomplishment/Impact Statements for Résumé
Did you develop any procedures to speed repetitive tasks?	Wrote and catalogued standardized word-processing clauses to expedite document processing and project completion.
Did you handle an increase in work demand without the need for part-time or temporary help?	Accommodated significant increase in production (from 450 to as many as 720 radio spots per day) without need for additional support staff.
Did you field problems that enabled your supervisor to be more productive or relieve your supervisor of specific duties?	Took on cash-management responsibilities normally handled by supervisor; initiative enabled supervisor to concentrate on special projects that had been "on hold" for more than a year.
Are you more efficient than most? For instance, do you do the job it used to take 1.5 or 2 FTEs (full-time equivalents) to do?	Maintained attorney/support staff ratio below industry norm. Perform volume of work previously handled by 1.5 FTEs.
Did you save the company money?	Restructured use of maintenance contracts for business office equipment, saving department $6,000 per year; procedure was subsequently implemented companywide.
Did you develop forms/systems that improved office efficiency?	Reorganized a supply room that hadn't been given attention since 1980; sorted and moved old files to storage, freeing space for previously inaccessible supplies. Identified and consolidated more than two dozen forms that were outdated or duplicative.
Are you often the first one in and last one out of the office?	Earned reputation as being the first in and last to leave, especially when facing critical project deadlines.

Impact-Mining Questions	Example Accomplishment/Impact Statements for Résumé
Did you rate above average on performance evaluations?	Consistently earned above-average marks on performance evaluations. Comments from supervisor include "Susan is the consummate administrative assistant… outstanding technical skills, polished presentation skills, always anticipating needs… she makes me—and our company—look good."
Did you extend your knowledge beyond your normal responsibilities?	Requested cross-training in order-desk and data-processing functions; initiative spared company from hiring temporary help during short-term absences of staff.
Did you take part in computer conversions or software upgrades?	Aided in major software upgrade, accomplishing task without disruption to work output.

Construction
Estimators, Project Superintendents, Managers

Impact-Mining Questions	Example Accomplishment/Impact Statements for Résumé
Did your value-added engineering skills bring greater profit to the company?	Delivered approximately $10 million in additional profit through value-added engineering.
Did you help bring in new business?	Secured in excess of $1 billion in new business over career; led entry into more lucrative markets.
Did you improve the percentage of bids awarded on estimates?	Improved company's hit ratio by 27%, securing more than $513 million in contracts over a 3-year period.
Do you have a good history of avoiding disputes/claims/litigation?	Maintained litigation-free record for claims throughout 17-year career; paired business savvy with technical expertise to avoid costly disputes/claims.

(continued)

(continued)

Impact-Mining Questions	Example Accomplishment/Impact Statements for Résumé
Do you have a strong record for on-time completion of projects?	Consistently met project deadlines—completed recent $60 million CalTrans project in 60% of time, earning 100% of additional $400,000 incentive bonus for company.
Did you improve customer relations?	Received positive feedback from numerous clients (for example, County of Los Angeles, CalTrans, etc.). Typical client comment: "It's the best-looking job we've seen."

Education
Superintendents

Impact-Mining Questions	Example Accomplishment/Impact Statements for Résumé
How have you demonstrated your leadership skills?	Commissioned with leading district through rapid yet positive and productive change—implemented site-based management that now involves staff and community in identifying curricular needs. Completed strategic planning process that produced district's first mission statement and multiyear district-wide objectives.
What fiscal impacts have you had on the district?	Balanced district's budget, correcting a 5-year deficit-spending pattern and regaining fiscal control from county/state auspices; district continues to maintain a prudent 5% reserve.
	Dealt with severe budget reductions during the state-wide recession to maintain district solvency.
How have you dealt with enrollment increases?	Developed and implemented successful model for a year-round program to accommodate annual 13% student growth factor.

Impact-Mining Questions	Example Accomplishment/Impact Statements for Résumé
Do you have experience with facility-expansion projects?	Addressed a steady and growing annual student enrollment of 15% with an aggressive district-wide facilities plan; built a new 7th–8th-grade junior high school and instituted multiyear modernization program for 12 elementary schools.
Were there divisive issues/groups that you brought to consensus?	Developed a yearly management-by-objective model wherein all district administrators have the opportunity to identify instructional and operational objectives; the program has provided a more unified district direction.
Did you solicit input from leading educational consultants?	Teamed with prestigious Berkeley think tank to shore up strategic plan and reorganize district that services more than 75,000 students.
Were there long-range planning initiatives developed?	Guided strategic planning process built on meaningful involvement of staff, parents, and community—collectively developed a district mission and vision statement incorporated within a five-year plan with corresponding strategic goals through 2007.
How have you affected curriculum development and alignment?	Restructured district's curricular offerings through the vehicle of a District-Wide Task Force—established district's first set of grade-level expectancies through the secondary level.
	Introduced technology initiative and identified appropriate software that supported grade-level competencies ranging from minimum to extended curricular objectives.

(continued)

(continued)

Impact-Mining Questions	Example Accomplishment/Impact Statements for Résumé
How did you draw on or increase support from community groups or the business sector?	Sought input and meaningful involvement from educational stakeholders through district-wide superintendent roundtables, business-education partnerships, law enforcement alliances, and superintendent-parent forums.

Education
Principals/Administrators

Impact-Mining Questions	Example Accomplishment/Impact Statements for Résumé
Did you develop partnerships with community or volunteer resources?	Formed major partnerships with community and religious organizations, including Rotary, Kiwanis, World Impact, and Youth for Christ; results were lauded by city officials and law enforcement for contributing to significant drop in youth crimes near school.
Did you receive any district or regional awards?	Recognized with "Leadership/Management Award" from County Office of Education and "Administrator of the Year Award" from King Unified School District.
Did you involve students in the community?	Involved students and inner-city volunteers in various community clean-up, blight removal, and beautification projects.
Did you acquire grant money?	Recipient of $600,000 Family Preservation Grant.
	One of three schools to receive and share $450,000 for Homeless Program.

Impact-Mining Questions	Example Accomplishment/Impact Statements for Résumé
Was your school nominated for, or did it receive, any awards or honors?	Nominated for Distinguished School Award.
	Selected by National Science Foundation for Case Study of Effective School Leadership.
	Wrote project proposal and was successful in obtaining California Partnership School designation for Washington Junior High School.
Were there situations where you were the first or only one to do something of special note?	First in the district to facilitate the planning of Washington Junior High School's Middle School Reform Programs (Advisories, Exploratory and Elective Programs, Math Renaissance, Vocational Technology Lab).
Did your work extend beyond the school site to work at the district level?	"In-serviced" district social-science teachers on the new California State Social Science Framework and implementation strategies for K–12.
Did your work extend beyond the school site to involvement on a regional level?	Served as Region Coordinator for 10 middle schools in 5 counties in California Partnership Schools' Network.
Did you improve teacher rapport?	Architect for program "Teachers Give Hope," designed to encourage, motivate, and reward teachers for continued professional growth and commitment to students. Program became model for neighboring districts because of its success.

Education
Teachers

Impact-Mining Questions	Example Accomplishment/Impact Statements for Résumé
How does your philosophy of teaching affect your classroom?	Uncompromising advocate of the view that "all children can learn" and facilitator of learning through a positive environment that encourages student exploration and promotes self-esteem.

(continued)

(continued)

Impact-Mining Questions	Example Accomplishment/Impact Statements for Résumé
Were standardized test scores increased?	Selected to teach pilot program focusing on content-specific, standards-based curriculum; program directly yielded an increase in standardized test scores of as many as four grade levels.
Are you often assigned the more challenging students?	Typically assigned the more "diff-cult" students, those suffering from dysfunctional families and lack of English-language literacy. Experienced above-average success in boosting students' confidence and bringing them up to grade level in all core subjects.
Did you work with manipulatives for elementary grades?	Enhanced student comprehension through use of math and science manipulatives such as Mathland, Foss, and AIMS.
Did you emphasize multiculturalism?	Introduced a number of multicultural lessons (cooking, dress/costumes, traditions, artifacts, holidays). Look for and embrace the uniqueness and talent of every child.
Do you have personal resources that you bring to the classroom?	Augment lessons with extensive personal library, realia, and teaching resources collected during travels to 17 countries and 48 states. Principal commented, "Your resources are the most extensive and interesting collection seen in my 25 years in education."
Have you brought students performing at below grade level up to or above grade level?	Brought students from below grade level to two grades above grade level in language arts with strategies such as Interactive Writing, Shared Reading, Story Webs and Comparisons, Reading the Room, Dramatization, ZooPhonics, Proficiency in English, multisensory teaching approach, and various whole-language and phonics-based programs.

Impact-Mining Questions	Example Accomplishment/Impact Statements for Résumé
Did you improve classroom management?	Noted by principal for effective classroom-management skills and selected to "in-service" other teachers in Applied Assertive Discipline, TRIBES, and True Colors programs to enhance the learning environment.
Did you present in-services or teacher development workshops?	Developed and presented in-services as Lead Teacher for California-School Implementation Network (C-SIN).
Did you train new teachers?	Served as Master Teacher for three years and Mentor Teacher, four years.

Appointed by principal as Lead Teacher for new teachers on staff. |
Have you improved parent volunteerism or involvement in the classroom?	Developed excellent relationships with all my students' parents and have enjoyed above-average parent involvement despite language and cultural barriers. Regularly invite parents from various cultures to speak to the children on dress, customs, cooking, etc.
Were you honored by your peers or principal?	Voted by faculty and administration as Jefferson High School Teacher of the Year.
Did you prepare students to compete in regional or state competitions?	Prepared students who earned first-place awards in several categories at California State History Day competitions and a third-place award at the national level.
Did you bring in interesting guest speakers?	Sought respected leaders as guest speakers to present career opportunities in law enforcement, medicine, engineering, architecture, manufacturing, graphic arts, and other disciplines.
What, if any, challenges did you face/overcome because of having second language learners in your classroom?	Simultaneously implemented two Language Arts curricula to address the needs of both English-only and bilingual students.

(continued)

(continued)

Impact-Mining Questions	Example Accomplishment/Impact Statements for Résumé
Did you introduce new classes?	Expanded Agriculture Department offerings, elevated course content, and increased student participation in programs (involvement in inter-curricular activities increased from 5 to approximately 35 students).
Did you help students get involved in any entrepreneurial activities?	Initiated student-run "certified organic program" that raised more than $10,000 in funds, enabling students to participate in regional/state FFA activities and attend national conferences.
Did you help with musicals or special performances?	Produced and directed the school's first musical production, with standing-room-only attendance at all seven performances.
Did you serve on a number of committees?	Serve on numerous district and site-level committees, including School Site Council, Curriculum Advisory Committee (Social Science, Math, Science), Drug Awareness Council, and Talent Show Committee (list of past committees available).
Did you help alternative-education students with work-experience needs?	Developed partnerships with business and community organizations to promote a Teen Job Program in collaboration with Boys and Girls Clubs. Designed programs to enhance academic offerings and comply with State-mandated Voc Tech training (computer programs such as Microsoft Office, Microsoft Project, CAD, etc.).
What do colleagues, parents, or your supervisors/principal say about you?	Comments from: • Principal: "Among top 1% of teachers I have worked with in my 20-year career."

Impact-Mining Questions	Example Accomplishment/Impact Statements for Résumé
	• Fellow Teacher: "A consummate team member. I can always count on Cheryl to help with a special-needs student."
	• Parent: "Her love of students does not stop at the end of the school day."
How would you describe your mission as a teacher?	Promote students' physical, mental, and academic development, emphasizing trust, mutual respect, and high instructor expectations.
Have you attended more continuing-education workshops than those required to maintain your credential?	Dedicated to continually expanding my professional knowledge; annually attend an average of 10 workshops on a range of content-specific topics and instructional strategies.
What training has been most interesting or inspirational to you?	Shifted teacher focus to role as "teacher leader," a concept based on principles from Stephen Covey training.
Did you help support school-reform initiatives?	Supported school-wide educational reform in mathematics and science, with technology and literacy strategies embedded in both curricular areas.

Engineering

Impact-Mining Questions	Example Accomplishment/Impact Statements for Résumé
Did a project you worked on increase productivity or efficiency?	Boosted plant yields 17% through implementation of computer-aided manufacturing software.
Did you assume leadership responsibilities even though your title might not have indicated so?	Appointed from seven-member engineering team as "system owner" for Procter & Gamble's plant-wide power and control systems.

(continued)

(continued)

Impact-Mining Questions	Example Accomplishment/Impact Statements for Résumé
Did any of the projects you worked on save the company time or money?	Called in as troubleshooter to resolve oil and gas field-exploration projects in jeopardy of being terminated; field-engineering skills resulted in saving projects valued at more than $325,000 in revenue to company.
Did any of the projects you were associated with produce a patent? If so, what impact did it have?	Assisted in design and field testing of patented device that gave company an edge over competition. Directional equipment device measures gravitational and magnetic fields and addresses recurring hydraulic and electronic problems.
Did you lead or serve on cross-functional teams whose work had company-wide effects?	Led cross-functional engineering team that conducted time studies, developed process documentation, and converted facility to "work cells," increasing production in one department alone by 37% (represents $1.4 million per year in product sales).
Were you used as a corporate trouble-shooter?	Averted downtime losses of thousands of dollars per hour through technical troubleshooting skills relating to caustic fluids, hydrostatic pressures, etc. Traveled throughout the United States and Europe as troubleshooter.
Did any of the projects you were associated with save money?	Installed advanced water-treatment system that reduced hazardous waste costs by $80,000 annually.
Did you supervise contract engineering consultants?	Served as Project Manager for more than a dozen public-works construction projects for the City of San Leandro; directed managing consultants and contractors in timely completion of projects valued at more than $240 million.

Impact-Mining Questions	Example Accomplishment/Impact Statements for Résumé
Did you reduce dependence on outside engineering consultants?	Reduced dependence on outside consultants, cutting expenses $290,000 over prior fiscal year; leveraged systems and internal resources to resolve complex electrical issues.
Did you work on large-scale or difficult projects that were completed on time; and, if so, were incentive bonuses associated with them?	Won more than $250,000 in incentive bonuses for international communications company through on-time construction of antenna systems (from prototype to customer acceptance).
Did you help create new products; and, if so, what were those new products worth in terms of first-year or total sales to the company?	Directed design and producibility for five new product lines that were introduced to fabrication; combined sales of lines represent 62% of company's total sales volume.
Did you hold secret security clearance or travel extensively?	Top Secret Security Clearance; extensive international travel (Thailand, Morocco, Guam, England, Germany).
Were you selected to direct a large or key project?	Selected to head up the design and construction of underground conduit for 27.4 km of fiber cable with manholes and pull boxes.
Did you contract with a company for a special project; and, if so, what were the impacts to the company?	Selected for 12-member software-engineering team that designed and implemented a $3.7 million product profitability and marketing information system. Team results: • Replaced/consolidated 10 disparate systems with a common database. • Satisfied regulatory, product-management, marketing, service cost, sales analysis, and ad hoc informational requirements. • Supported 60+ users company-wide in multiple disciplines. • Provided company with commercialization potential of $500,000 per sale.

(continued)

(continued)

Impact-Mining Questions	Example Accomplishment/Impact Statements for Résumé
Did you deal with difficult time constraints?	Civil engineering project manager for installation of wastewater land application effluent pipeline for City of Springfield; met tight 6-week schedule, allowing a building and sewer hookup moratorium to be lifted.
Did you work for a consulting firm; and, if so, what were some of the benefits to the firm's clients?	Designed HVAC systems for engineering firm specializing in thermal energy storage; designs reduced energy costs by $79,000 for regional medical center, $62,000 for school district, and $124,000 for food processor.
Did any of your projects have national or international impact?	Led engineering teams to produce industrial engineering solutions for Levi Strauss' Continental Europe Division that increased productivity 4.5% ($1.7 million), raised material utilization 1.5% ($700,000), and shortened product-development cycle (approximately 15%).

Graduates
College Graduates, Management Trainee Programs

Impact-Mining Questions	Example Accomplishment/Impact Statements for Résumé
Did you work while completing your degree?	Managed full-time employment in customer service while carrying 15–18 units per semester.
	Self-financed 90% of college expenses through concurrent employment.
	Completed degree while working 2–3 concurrent part-time positions.
Did you complete your program in less time than normal?	Completed program in 3½ years while maintaining above-average grades.

Impact-Mining Questions	Example Accomplishment/Impact Statements for Résumé
Is your GPA worth writing home about? *Note: This number can be easily compared to other candidates' GPAs, so be careful not to sabotage yourself by listing a GPA that might not be as impressive as you think. My rule of thumb for mentioning GPA is 3.5 or higher for liberal arts and business-related majors and 3.2 or higher for engineering and science-related majors.*	Earned a 3.7 GPA with President's Honors six consecutive semesters.
Did you complete a dual degree?	Completed two baccalaureate degrees in just four years.
Did you take tough electives?	Focused on graduate series courses for electives, including Quantitative Analysis III, Statistical Analysis III, Integrating Databases, Operations Research, and Artificial Intelligence & Expert Systems.
	Challenged myself with graduate-level finance electives that would provide a strong foundation in banking systems, security markets, and international business.
Did you hold leadership responsibilities in cocurricular activities?	Elected by peers to hold leadership roles (President, Vice President, Treasurer) in college organizations and business fraternity.
Were you involved in career-related cocurricular activities?	Involved in cocurricular activities that complemented finance studies and expanded interaction with international students.
Did you organize field trips or travel related to your career interests?	Initiated and organized trips to the Pacific Stock Exchange and Charles Schwab in San Francisco, the corporate offices of Wells Fargo in Los Angeles, and the Port of Seattle in Washington.
Did you study abroad?	Gained fluency in French language and culture during semester abroad at University of France, Aix-en-Provence (in connection with California State University International Exchange Program).

(continued)

(continued)

Impact-Mining Questions	Example Accomplishment/Impact Statements for Résumé
Did you attend a military academy (high school or college)?	Attended Wentworth Military Academy in Lexington, Missouri, a well-respected institution with a 120-year reputation for equipping young men with stringent scholastic and military training.

Health Care
Hospital, HMO, Medical Facility Management

Impact-Mining Questions	Example Accomplishment/Impact Statements for Résumé
Did you improve the financial viability of the organization?	Delivered threefold improvement in hospital's operating margin, from $4.2 million to $16.9 million over a 4-year period.
Did you introduce new programs/profit centers?	Envisioned and managed new profit center, a successful multisite occupational medicine program that grew from start-up phase to generate $1.5 million in annual revenue.
	Challenged with creation and launch of new Medicare-certified home health program—accomplished staffing and obtained certification in only 10 weeks. Program now commands dominant share of home health market with gross revenues in excess of $2 million (24,000 visits per year).
Did you improve the facility's performance on regulatory surveys?	Positioned facilities with several-year history of unfavorable JCAHO survey to capture passing scores.
	Prepared hospital for JCAHO survey, securing 98% survey results with accommodation.

Impact-Mining Questions	Example Accomplishment/Impact Statements for Résumé
Did you start any new programs?	Catalyst behind development of a clinically sound, financially solvent general dentistry residency program at Veteran's Administration Hospital.
Did you introduce new technology?	Instrumental in selection and installation of multisite health system's $100,000 technology upgrade that replaced disparate programs with state-of-the-art technology, integrating critical patient and management data across all functional areas and locations.
Did you undergo any major changes in organizational structure?	Member of transition team that crafted comprehensive plan for merger of 425-bed, county-operated hospital with privately owned health-care system. Sought input from multiple disciplines to ensure sound transitional strategies and uninterrupted provision of services.
Did you have fluctuations in patient care demands?	Devised contractual system to manage fluctuating home health care patient caseload.
Were you in charge of physician credentialing?	Introduced concept for across-the-system physician credentialing used as model for other health systems.
Were there any noncompliance issues that you dealt with?	Brought physician recruitment practices into compliance with Stark II and Fraud & Abuse laws.
Did you foresee problems and devise solutions to avert possible litigation against the facility?	Identified safety issues and risk trends and presented solutions that averted significant exposure/litigation for hospital.
Did you introduce any new systems?	Developed bundling system for physician hospital privileging.
Were you involved in any process reengineering?	Led process reengineering teams that captured a 50% reduction in corporate medical transcription costs.

(continued)

(continued)

Impact-Mining Questions	Example Accomplishment/Impact Statements for Résumé
Did you direct or implement any consolidation or centralization of services?	Consolidated main laboratory facility with six stat labs, reducing operating expenses by approximately 45%. Orchestrated consolidation of management functions relating to three hospitals, yielding a $1.6 million expense reduction.
Did you expand service delivery?	Expanded hospital-based ambulance program from 18 to 26 vehicles, adding $300,000 to profit-center revenues.
Did you prepare your facility or department for accreditation?	Prepared laboratory for successful CAP accreditation process in just seven weeks.
Did you negotiate contracts favorable to the facility?	Negotiated vendor agreements, obtaining reagents at discounted costs normally offered only to labs with three times the volume.
Did you take a money-losing venture and turn it around?	Turned underperforming unit into a viable operation while competing in aggressive managed-care environment.
Were there increased demands on your staff that you accommodated without having to add new employees?	Accommodated 30% increase in volume using existing staff, without compromising quality standards.
Did you establish or help establish a new health-maintenance organization?	Sourced and established competitive provider network (780+ physicians) requisite to HCFA certification in a nine-county service area—accomplished task in just six weeks.
Did you turn around or help turn around an existing health-maintenance organization?	Architect for organizational restructuring that resulted in a 40% growth in revenue, doubling of HMO lives covered, 7% reduction in administrative expenses, and 50% improvement in claims turnaround.
Are you experienced in managed-care contracting?	Formulated contracting strategy for rehabilitation hospital, resulting in three new contracts flowing to organization.

Impact-Mining Questions	Example Accomplishment/Impact Statements for Résumé
Did quality of care improve?	Boosted quality-assurance ratings from 82% to 94% through design and implementation of an enterprise-wide compliance program.
Did patient satisfaction improve?	Improved surgery center's patient satisfaction scores from 92% to 98%, the result of CQI teams and employee-recognition campaign.
Did you save money without compromising care?	Led revision of case-management program; trimmed some $800,000 from upcoming budget in related DRGs.
Have you helped the facility stay at the forefront of industry trends?	Advanced CQI philosophy in late 1980s and early 1990s and defined pathway team functions.
	Initiated formation of Inpatient Care Model, inviting physician collaboration throughout process.
Have you helped your facility or department become more competitive?	Developed business-driven policies for Emergency Department that controlled staffing costs, improved quality of care, and reduced patient wait time to within national average.

Health Care
Director of Nurses, Department Management, Employee Supervision

Impact-Mining Questions	Example Accomplishment/Impact Statements for Résumé
Has your department's budget been cut; and, if so, how have you met that directive?	Met corporate directives for budget cuts, eliminating overtime, and outsourced contracts to achieve savings of $750,000+. Maintained a 100% record for budget compliance throughout tenure as Medical/Surgical Nurse Manager.

(continued)

(continued)

Impact-Mining Questions	Example Accomplishment/Impact Statements for Résumé
Was there a particular problem—for instance, from lax documentation—that you corrected?	Brought past-due evaluations of nursing staff into compliance for 90-day, 120-day, and annual performance reviews; maintained strong record for documentation of disciplinary action (with no legal repercussions).
Did you conduct staff training?	Introduced staff-development program "Seldom-Used but Vital Equipment"; program improved competency on critical emergency department instrumentation and ensured rapid response in emergency situations.
Did you restructure staffing or job descriptions?	Initiated use of nonlicensed assistive personnel to assume nonnursing functions, freeing licensed staff to focus on trauma care.
Did you revise outdated policies?	Revised outdated department policies (last updated circa 1980) for compliance with federal and state mandates.
Were there morale issues you were able to address?	Accepted challenge of supervising medical unit clerks with history of chronic absenteeism; increased their accountability, improved productivity, and negotiated changes in scheduling despite union opposition.
Has your department undergone major changes; if so, how have you managed these changes?	Aided in conversion of Labor & Delivery Unit from traditional model to Labor Delivery Recovery setting; designed staffing and communications systems to accommodate change. Survey feedback from new mothers indicates 96% would return to hospital for their next birth.

Health Care
Hospital, Clinic, Home Health Nursing

Impact-Mining Questions	Example Accomplishment/Impact Statements for Résumé
Did your hospital work include special or more difficult assignments?	Performed all facets of circulating nurse responsibilities in an open-heart setting, including significant medical/pharmacological preparation and intervention.
Did you work in a teaching hospital or regional trauma center?	Provided full-time staff nurse-anesthetist functions in 350-bed regional trauma center/teaching hospital.
Did you serve as a Team Leader or informal resource?	Functioned as Team Leader on Acute Ortho-Neuro Floor serving Level III and IV post-trauma (MVA, GSW) neurovascular injuries.
	Served as resource and clinical expert for nursing staff in Post-Anesthesia and Burn/Pediatric Trauma units.
Is your scope of experience broader than others?	Extensive experience in post-anesthesia recovery, burn care, wound therapy, neurological care, hyperbaric oxygenation, and cardiac care.
Did you work in a rural setting where you typically see a higher level of acuity?	Responded to rural health-clinic patients presenting with a high level of acuity, multisymptom disease, and complex emergent care needs.
	Utilize functional literacy in Spanish to communicate with a primarily Spanish-speaking, migrant farm-worker patient population.
Did your home health nursing include exposure to multisystem disease processes?	Provided high-tech nursing services for home health patients with multisystem disease processes.
Did your home health nursing skills lower return-to-hospital rates?	Reduced return-to-hospital rates to record low through strengths in assessment, problem solving, and clinical intervention.

(continued)

(continued)

Impact-Mining Questions	Example Accomplishment/Impact Statements for Résumé
Did you write nursing protocols?	Designed nursing protocols that assisted physicians in expediting patient care.
How would others describe you?	Proactive patient advocate with in-depth knowledge of Patients' Rights.
	Characterized by supervisors, patients, and their family members as a competent clinician with the ability to bring a reassuring presence to crises.
	"Ms. Benayan consistently handles difficult situations in a calm and efficient manner—making extra efforts beyond the explicit requirements of her position to ensure a well-integrated treatment outcome." Dr. John L. Manton, Director of Medical/Surgical Services, St. Joseph's Hospital.

General Management

Impact-Mining Questions	Example Accomplishment/Impact Statements for Résumé
What improvements did you make to net profit, and were those improvements a record for the company?	Delivered a 7% increase to net profits, a record high for the company.
Were you faced with stagnant/declining revenues?	Recruited as change agent to retool organization and reverse downward revenue spiral; within 12 months, delivered profits representing a 19% improvement.
Did you correct excessive inventory levels?	Rectified half-million-dollar losses resulting from inventory mismanagement.
What was the biggest cost-saving device you implemented?	Slashed key expense item by 62% through improved purchasing and inventory controls.

Impact-Mining Questions	Example Accomplishment/Impact Statements for Résumé
What kind of measurement tracked customer service levels? Did it improve?	Earned 99% CSI ratings, the highest in the district and a first for the branch.
Did you improve morale or productivity, or did you reduce turnover in your workforce?	Reduced turnover from 55% to less than 7% and transitioned unskilled labor force into a culturally diverse staff trained in current technology.
Were there problems with the integrity or accuracy of financial data?	Recruited CFO from Big 6 firm to establish accounting processes and internal controls; collaborated on 5-year financial strategic plan and implementation of world-class accounting system.
Did you correct excessive costs?	Brought aberrant operating expenses in line with national average, significantly reducing annual costs by more than $6 million.
Were you recruited to resolve a major problem?	Reorganized existing business to eliminate company's multimillion-dollar debt within first year.
Did you expand with import or export operations?	Envisioned and brought to fruition a foreign import operation that generated a 40% return.
Were there challenging labor issues?	Led management effort to decertify union, prevent property damage, and protect 800 nonunion workers.
	Rectified long-standing history of management-labor tensions; offered concessions on behalf of company that influenced morale and, ultimately, a 17% increase in plant productivity (without sacrifice to company earnings).
Did you direct any facility expansions or new construction projects?	Proposed, designed, and supervised construction of 180,000-sq.ft. processing and cold-storage facility; $7 million facility captured ROI in less than five years and remains state-of-the-art some 10 years later.

Nonprofit

Impact-Mining Questions	Example Accomplishment/Impact Statements for Résumé
Did you bring new ideas or vision to the organization?	Introduced business-driven orientation and management principles to non-profit organization that contributed to a doubling in general fund reserves.
Did you recruit new volunteers or expand the volunteer base significantly?	Recruited, trained, and motivated a tireless volunteer corps of more than 300, a sixfold increase.
What types of community outreach did you do?	Reached more than 100,000 people annually through wellness programs, health fairs, promotional events, and network meetings.
Did you introduce new ideas to motivate volunteers?	Created "Volunteer Luncheon" as a successful vehicle to inform and increase volunteer participation.
Did you create business partnerships/linkages?	Launched "Automatic External Defibrillator Project," resulting in placement of 20 AEDs in local businesses and a commitment from Community Health System to sponsor this $60,000 project.
Were fund-raising costs reduced or below average?	Cut fund-raising costs to 12% (below national average of 16%).
Were any of your ideas used as a model by other agencies or beyond your area?	Envisioned and planned successful event subsequently used by organization nationwide.
Did you strengthen your Board of Directors?	Revitalized Board of Directors with influential, affluent, and diverse members of the community.

Plant Management

Impact-Mining Questions	Example Accomplishment/Impact Statements for Résumé
Did you increase output?	Boosted productivity 19% through implementation of plant-wide BPE initiatives.

Impact-Mining Questions	Example Accomplishment/Impact Statements for Résumé
Did you improve efficiency?	Cut lead time by more than 50% on primary product line; slashed internal lead time through fabrication from 20 days to less than 1 through cell group concept.
Did you improve inventory record accuracy (IRA)?	Turned around negligent IRA levels, improving performance from 65% to 93%.
Did you reduce packing-line changeover times?	Reduced packing-line changeover times by 40%, resulting in a $125,000 annual savings.
Did you reduce excessive scrap?	Upgraded milling processes that yielded a $300,000 scrap reduction.
Did you decrease labor or material costs?	Decreased expenses 12% through reengineering of procurement and production functions.
Did you acquire certification?	Guided plant through successful ISO 9002 certification.
Did you undergo a major change in technology?	MRPII Implementation Project Leader for facility. Without aid of external consultants, led team in implementing system that significantly affected supply-chain functions: slashed inventory 29%, boosted batch yield 1.5%, and maximized order-fill rate by a record 3%.

Purchasing

Impact-Mining Questions	Example Accomplishment/Impact Statements for Résumé
Did you save the company money?	Delivered savings of $1.2 million during first two years, without sacrifice to raw material quality or service.
How did you save money?	Achieved across-the-board savings of 15–45% through redesign, substitutions, and overseas vendor sourcing.

(continued)

(continued)

Impact-Mining Questions	Example Accomplishment/Impact Statements for Résumé
Did your negotiation skills save money?	Renegotiated freight contracts for savings of $45,000 in annual transportation costs.
Did you reduce the time required to process requisitions?	Introduced "Procurement Card," saving approximately $100 per requisition and reducing turnaround time for purchase orders by as much as four weeks.
Did you improve technology or the use of technology by others?	Conducted user training classes for automated requisitioning and ordering, increasing company-wide use of computer system from 36% to 93%.
Did you reduce the number of SKUs needed?	Slashed SKUs from 1,500 to under 200 (surveyed managers, identified critical forms, and consolidated duplicate items).
Did you tighten up your supplier list?	Reduced vendor base by 90%, leveraging negotiating power with three primary suppliers.
Were any services outsourced at a savings to company?	Outsourced and negotiated contract for primary forms, with a projected first-year savings of $62,000.
Did you form special relationships or arrangements with your suppliers?	Introduced Supplier Certification/ Partnering, achieving alliance goals for quality, cost reductions, and expansion.

Retail
Store Manager, Buyer, Divisional Merchandise Manager

Impact-Mining Questions	Example Accomplishment/Impact Statements for Résumé
Did you increase sales?	Virtually doubled sales from $1.0 million to $1.9 million for Tower Records' downtown store, traditionally a difficult sales location.

Impact-Mining Questions	Example Accomplishment/Impact Statements for Résumé
Did you improve gross margins or turnover?	Improved Better Sportswear gross margin by 18% and turnover by 30%.
Did you implement new ideas that affected sales?	Captured 48% sales increase through negotiation and implementation of three key vendor coordinator/selling specialist programs.
Were your sales increases greater than other stores in the chain?	Exceeded comparable store sales increases with 9% departmental improvement (storewide average is 1.2%).
Did you increase credit conversions?	Increased credit conversions by 3,531, or 47.4 per FTE.
Did you open new stores?	Successfully opened 12 new stores; achieved company record for new store sales volume on opening day and opening week.
Did you take on any remodeling or tenant improvement projects?	Opened 15 new stores, directed 12 major remodels, and supervised 22 tenant improvement projects in an 8-year period, with a 100% record for meeting critical deadlines.
	Created cohesive image for retailer, knitting together discordant color/design motifs into a cohesive theme for company's full-service stores and two specialty divisions.
Did you identify and capitalize on particular sales trends?	Developed sales analysis program that resulted in 10% improvement in regular price sales with corresponding gross margin increase in Bridge/Designer Sportswear.
Did you train any staff members who were promoted?	Coached inexperienced staff who went on to hold Assistant Store Manager and Store Manager positions.
	Transformed a young staff (who had essentially alienated customers) into a dynamic, customer-driven sales force.

(continued)

(continued)

Impact-Mining Questions	Example Accomplishment/Impact Statements for Résumé
Did you rectify specific procedural problems, for instance, with cash-drawer errors, deposit errors, etc.?	Implemented operating controls to virtually eliminate cash-drawer errors (a 60% decrease) and deposit errors (a 75% decrease).
Did you reduce expenses?	Reduced salary expenditures by 1% (a 5-figure savings) through "peak-flow" scheduling strategy.
Were there any difficult transitions to manage?	Maintained morale throughout culture shift associated with ACB's acquisition of XZY Company; accomplished through "town hall" meetings, secret-shopper service incentives, and paid time off for employee suggestions.
Were you promoted over employees who were more experienced than you?	Selected for store-management assignment over more experienced staff because of professionalism and performance record.
Did your computer skills come into play?	Guided a seamless computer system conversion that integrated the store's entire operational infrastructure.
Did you have significant competition to deal with?	Met surge of competition from national "big box" retailers with successful customer-service campaign; conducted surveys to identify niche-market products, designed promotional and pricing strategies, and boosted staff-customer ratio to maintain service levels. Efforts resulted in a 15% increase in average ticket sale.
Were inventory levels too high?	Reduced excess warehouse stock by approximately 20% while avoiding out-of-stocks.
Did you reduce mark-down losses?	Reduced mark-down losses by as much as 50% through improved departmental inventory flow.
Did the department you buy for contribute to a greater portion of net store profit?	Contributed an average of 48% net profit to store's total net income.

Impact-Mining Questions	Example Accomplishment/Impact Statements for Résumé
Was inventory shrinkage below the average of other stores?	Controlled inventory shrinkage at 1.2% (below company average of 2.5%).
Did you introduce any ideas or programs new to your industry?	Recognized as first specialty retailer to introduce "shop concepts," reversing one company's 10-year loss history to profits of $1.5 million in just two years.

Sales and Marketing

Impact-Mining Questions	Example Accomplishment/Impact Statements for Résumé
What was the existing sales volume or prior history of sales when you began?	Reversed 5-year history of declining sales, delivering a 227% sales increase over prior fiscal year.
What was the 5-year history for goal attainment prior to your beginning?	Turned around territory's 5-year history of no goal attainment with 127% of goal by year end.
How many accounts were in place when you began?	Increased account base from 72 to 345.
Did you expand into any new customer markets?	Tapped new market, expanding reach into emerging-technology sector projected for 25% annual growth.
What was your personal ranking among the branch, district, region, or nation?	Improved branch ranking from #33 among 35 to #2 in the nation.
	Improved Fresno branch's sales ranking from 7th to 2nd among 15 in the state, in competition with more densely populated areas such as Los Angeles and San Francisco.
	Ranked #1 or #2 in sales among 17-member sales force throughout 7-year history with company.
Did you make headway against your competition?	Created sales strategies to counter pricing objections and maintain market share despite aggressive competition from "discount wholesalers."

(continued)

(continued)

Impact-Mining Questions	Example Accomplishment/Impact Statements for Résumé
Did you improve the percentage of market share?	Captured dominant market share, catapulting under-capitalized, start-up company into major contender in the competitive managed-care market.
Was the territory improperly serviced, or did you inherit poor account relations?	Rebuilt relationships with customers, persuading a key account that represented 26% of total sales to commit to new exclusive contract.
Did you generate a sales increase despite having your territory size reduced?	Built territory from $400,000 to $2.7 million in sales despite a 60% reduction in geographic area.
	Generated fivefold growth in sales, warranting division of original territory into three separate territories.
Did you sell high-dollar items?	Delivered impressive first-year sales performance of $800,000 in sales of high-dollar items valued up to $60,000 each.
Did you set any records for sales?	Set record sales for region during first two months as Sales Representative, an increase of 61% over prior year.
Did you restore inactive accounts?	Resurrected inactive accounts through consistent sales calls; restored business relationships with a key insurance account and large law firm that had suffered from inconsistent service in the past.
Did you introduce new products?	Launched two new antibiotic products in a saturated market, attaining 100% of goal for both.
Did you help open a new territory?	Launched new central-coast territory, emphasizing value-added service in a market dominated by well-capitalized competitors.
	Recruited to open territory entrenched with established competitors; converted 10 major food manufacturers in first year to capture $750,000 in sales.

Impact-Mining Questions	Example Accomplishment/Impact Statements for Résumé
Did you deliver sales increases every year (even if you didn't meet quota every year)?	Delivered consistent annual growth in sales volume, averaging 17% per year.
If you didn't secure an increase in sales each consecutive year, consider listing the overall territory growth.	Delivered a 37% increase in customer accounts (from 200 to 275) and an overall sales increase of $788,000.
Did you generate a greater percentage of sales than your team members?	Generated 60% of sales volume among sales team of four.
Did you overcome premium-pricing objections?	Persuaded customers to buy based on personalized service and quality, overcoming premium-pricing issues.
Did you achieve your quota quickly?	Met annual business-development goal in less than six months.
Did you win any awards?	Honored with President's Award, reserved for the top 5% of sales representatives among 750 in the nation.

Social Services
Rehabilitation Counselor, Program Manager

Impact-Mining Questions	Example Accomplishment/Impact Statements for Résumé
Was your caseload large or difficult to manage?	Initially challenged with managing a significant backlog of generalist cases; recognized by supervisor for quickly bringing caseload up-to-date and aggressively seeking new clientele. Subsequently incorporated caseload of another Rehabilitation Counselor into existing caseload while producing 102% of quota for job placements.
What are you most proud of?	Created "Jobs for Life" program that was subsequently endorsed by the state and marketed to other Jobs for Life branches, generating $300,000+ in new revenue for local branch.

(continued)

(continued)

Impact-Mining Questions	Example Accomplishment/Impact Statements for Résumé
Did you start any new programs?	Developed, implemented, and managed social service and training programs servicing as many as 300 participants.
Did you put innovative programs in place?	Championed welfare-to-work programs well before the concept was popularly adopted and envisioned; implemented and managed programs that were duplicated by other counties because of their success.
How would colleagues describe you?	Earned a reputation as a goal-oriented, reality-based counselor with a lifelong commitment to helping individuals with disabilities.
	Noted by supervisors and coworkers for sensitivity, rapport, and professionalism in relating to clients of varying ethnic and socioeconomic backgrounds.
Did you create alliances with other agencies that benefited your organization?	Collaborated on writing contract that combined the services of regional mental health, state department of rehabilitation, and local hospitals; outcome provided increased access to services at a reduced cost to the agency.
Did you write grants to access new funding?	Successful grant-writing experience: wrote grants for more than 20 programs; funding received represents more than $750,000 for program services.
Did you find new or different funding sources?	Researched and accessed grants from lesser-known private funding sources, representing more than 40% of the agency's operating budget.
Did you increase traditional funding?	Increased federal funding by 25% for Tri-County Commission on Youth.
Do you have a strong track record for regulatory compliance?	Received flawless state audit, improving prior administration's history of unfavorable survey scores.

Impact-Mining Questions	Example Accomplishment/Impact Statements for Résumé
Did you improve clients' access to services?	Increased clients' access to state services as a result of thorough assessments and intricate knowledge of eligibility requirements.
Did you increase clients' access to services?	Located additional sources of medical and psychosocial services for geriatric population.
Did you work with volunteers?	Revitalized convalescent home's struggling junior-senior volunteer program into a productive operation; coordinate the service of more than 30 volunteers weekly.
Were you able to change/improve the behavior of your clients through various therapeutic interventions?	Introduced innovative music-therapy programs successful in reducing negative behaviors in developmentally disabled adolescents.
Were you selected to present techniques, programs, or findings at a professional meeting?	Invited to present findings on successful program at NAMT's Western Regional Conference.
Have you taught at the college level?	Designed and presented instruction for undergraduate and graduate psychology course work; focused on movement and dance therapy as an adjunct to clinical therapy.
Are you actively involved in professional organizations?	Actively involved in professional organizations; elected President of Sierra Mental Health Advisory Board and President of local chapters of American Psychological Association and Society of Pediatric Psychology.
Are you the office "guru" on any particular subject?	Utilized as a resource by 20-member staff for in-depth knowledge of federal and state assistance programs; committed to memory complex government regulations for five different public-aid programs.

Technology

Impact-Mining Questions	Example Accomplishment/Impact Statements for Résumé
Did you inherit or replace fragmented technology?	Merged disparate technologies into world-class ERP system (BaaN).
	Rehosted system with state-of-the-art Silicon Graphics technology and Encore server.
What were challenges or problems associated with existing system?	Improved error-free ratings from 70% to 95%.
	Increased online service levels to 95% or better—well above industry standards.
Did you show an impressive return on investment for a new system?	Installed state-of-the-art corporate data center capable of supporting company's aggressive growth mode; $400,000 capital outlay will see ROI in 18 months.
Did you reduce time required for specific functions?	Reduced month-end accounting close time from 5 to 1.5 days.
Did any of your improvements affect customer issues?	Quickened customer online response rate to less than ½ second, a 75% improvement.
Did you manage technology upgrades?	Salvaged mismanaged IS conversion (a $300,000 capital investment); researched and directed installation project for world-class computer system to support 24-hour, 7-day operation.
Did you eliminate IS consulting fees by managing issues in-house?	Eliminated $250,000 in technical consulting fees based on IS skills.

Warehouse/Distribution Management

Impact-Mining Questions	Example Accomplishment/Impact Statements for Résumé
Did you improve service to your internal customers?	Improved shipping goals from unacceptable levels to 98% accuracy as part of service commitment to 43 branches.

Impact-Mining Questions	Example Accomplishment/Impact Statements for Résumé
Did you make any changes that improved inventory levels or warehousing?	Disposed of $800,000 in excess inventories and negotiated supplier warehousing of raw materials at no cost to company.
Did you participate in special task forces?	Led Purchasing Task Team for implementation of MRPII program.
Did you generate new money-saving ideas?	Set company record for highest number of successful cost-saving proposals.
Did you set up any new facilities?	Launched successful start-up of three distribution facilities, including site selection, lease negotiations, capital equipment acquisition, personnel recruitment, inventory stocking, and operations policy development.
Did you outsource any operations at a savings to the company?	Coauthored concept for use of third-party contractors, slashing $5.2 million in annual operating costs for warehousing, transportation, and labor; program was subsequently adopted nationwide.
Did you expedite shipments by any measurable amount?	Conceived "drop ship" program that captured $8.2 million savings; engineered production to package and distribute 80,000 units in 5 days for program launch (project of this size typically required one month's lead time).
Did you reduce demands on warehouse operations by any measurable amounts?	Implemented closed-loop MRP in BPCS 6.0; system reduced finished goods inventory 14%, increased turns 30%, reduced raw material packaging inventory 14% ($500K), and increased order-fulfillment levels by 150,000 cases annually.
Were inventory accuracy measurements in place?	Improved inventory accuracy from 78% to 99% through use of structured processes and procedures (cycle counting, input/output controls, etc.).

Sifting Through the Accomplishments You've Gathered

Now that you've completed your impact-mining, you should have several potential impact statements for each employer. If you came up short, review the 10 buying motivators under "Words to Woo Employers" earlier in this chapter and search for parallels to your experience. (If you still come up short, call me! I love helping people see how they've made a difference, and I've never met a candidate who didn't make a contribution in some form or fashion.)

Now take your impact statements and rank them separately for every employer, indicating the most impressive as number one. The number of statements you will use for each employer depends on the length of your résumé, the length of your career history, and the length of employment with each employer. The following guidelines might be of help in determining how many impact statements to use and where to position them:

- **The bulk of your experience is with your most recent employer:** If you've worked for your present or most recent employer for a number of years or for the bulk of your career (and this experience is relevant to what you want to do next), you'll want to give the most weight, and the most impact statements, to this employer. Seven to 10 impact statements might well be in order if this is the case.

- **Your employment history is evenly distributed among employers:** If your employment history has been fairly consistent in length of time spent with employers, use a similar number of impact statements for each employer, perhaps two or three for each. Give slightly more weight to the most recent employer, perhaps three or four impact statements total or one or two more than you allot to the remainder of your employers.

- **You have been employed with your most recent company for a short period of time:** If it's too soon to have made a measurable difference at your current employer, refrain from an impact statement because a weak statement is less impressive than no statement at all. Likewise, be brief with your job description for this employer and begin with wording which implies that you are currently tackling some new challenge. Use, for instance, "Currently charged with…" or "Challenged with…" or "Recruited to…." For the remainder of your work history, follow the preceding guidelines for the scenario most closely aligned with your needs.

There is no *ex cathedra* pronouncement about the "right" number of impact statements to use. In general, the further back in your career the job was, the fewer impact statements you'll use. When space is a consideration, eliminate impact statements from the earliest experience (you'll see this frequently in many of the samples throughout this book). Don't feel that because you included impact statements under the most recent employers, you must include them also under the most dated employers. You have a great deal of flexibility in what information you include.

> *Note* There is one caveat to heed with respect to accomplishments, and that is how you present them. In the employer preference survey (appendix B), human resources executives repeatedly noted disdain for accomplishments that are separated from work history, making it unclear what was done where. In other words, if you are placing accomplishments in a separate Accomplishments section or Qualifications Summary, as I did in the following example, link the impact statements to the company where you were employed at the time.

Focusing on Accomplishments Worked for Patrick

A quick review of Patrick's *Before* résumé (see Résumé 6.1) shows that his most impressive accomplishments are buried with earlier employers. This scenario warranted a revision of his résumé to a blend between a combination format and a functional format. Note in Patrick's *After* résumé (see Résumé 6.2) the statement about being a "top-producing account executive for national manufacturer GHI." Pairing the name of the company with the impact statement allows readers to skim down and see when Patrick worked for GHI Co. Under the sales management bullet, Patrick mentions that he managed the Seattle Division of JKL Company. (The name of the company, which is a very recognizable and reputable national company, is fictionalized for this book.) Again, the reader can refer to the Professional Summary section and see the employment dates for this company.

Résumé 6.1: Before

Patrick Lensmith

One Marketplace Lane
Fremont, California 94444
(510) 555–5555
plensmith@netexec.com

OBJECTIVE: Management or Sales Representative position with a marketing focus. 25+ years sales, training, marketing, operations, and management experience.

PROFESSIONAL HISTORY:

[year - Present]   **ABC Engineering,** Fremont, California
Account Executive

Premium-grade lighting product sales. 100+ new accounts established, anticipated sales $100K per year.

[mo/yr - mo/yr]   **Medical Appliance Industries,** San Francisco, California
Account Executive

Soft medical goods sales to hospitals, medical centers, pharmacies and physicians. Extensive travel - Western US Territory.

[year – year]   **EF Center,** Seattle, Washington
Sales Representative

Boat and boating equipment sales. Utilized extensive customer service program. First year sales $800K.

[year – year]   **GHI Corporation,** Seattle, Washington
Account Executive

Office product paper sales to wholesalers, dealers and college bookstores.
Imprinted merchandise sales to colleges, dealers, and wholesalers.
Increased account base from $90,000 in 19xxo $3 million in 19xx.
Opened 100+ new accounts.
Created custom marketing packages for client advertising.
Organized client sales meetings.
Trained client sales staff for maximum sales of product line.
Western US territory including Washington, Oregon, Montana, Northern Idaho and Alaska.

[year – year]   **JKL Company**, Seattle, Washington
Marketing and Sales Manager

Developed annual marketing and sales plan for Seattle Division.
Created JKL's catalog of 25,000+ products.
Created custom marketing packages for client advertising.
Organized and gave product information meetings for client sales staff.
Responsible for a 26-member staff and training all sales interns.
Averaged 28% growth each year.
Annual sales revenue $15 million.

Patrick Lensmith
Page 2

PROFESSIONAL ACHIEVEMENTS:

Top 20% of sales personnel for 10 years.
Salesman of the Year, 1st Place 19xx
Salesman of the Year, 3rd Place 19xx
Salesman of the Year, 2nd Place 19xx
Graduate of FGI training Program
Exceeded sales and marketing plans set forth by employers.
Developed a large territory of customers throughout the Northwest Region of the United States.

REFERENCES: Available upon request.

Résumé 6.2: After

PATRICK LENSMITH

One Marketplace Lane
Fremont, California 94444
(510) 555-5555
plensmith@netexec.com

CAREER HIGHLIGHTS

Impressive 15+ year career in sales, marketing, and management with respected industry leaders. Strengths and career highlights include the following:

- **Direct Sales:** Top-producing account executive for national manufacturer GHI Co., including Salesman of the Year among national sales team of 50. Consistently exceeded goals in all performance areas: sales ranking (top 10-20% for 10 consecutive years); territory growth (from $90,000 to $3,000,000); new accounts opened (100+); and new product introductions (#1 in the country).

- **Marketing:** Developed strategy for, implemented, and managed marketing plans for JKL Company's 5-state northwest territory. Determined promotional products and equipped accounts with sales tools that in many cases doubled specialty sales. Created custom marketing packages for client advertising. Envisioned concept for and developed JKL's 1st catalog featuring 25,000+ products.

- **Sales Management:** Managed Seattle Division of JKL Company, including recruiting, training, and motivating sales team of 6 and support staff of 20. Built revenues from $4 million to $15 million over a 4-year period, without increasing size of sales force.

- **Customer Advocate:** Sourced, secured, and maintained sales relationships with broad customer-base, including hospitals, commercial businesses, manufacturers, retailers, food processors, wholesalers, dealers, and major universities. Make a conscientious commitment to partnering with accounts to build and sustain long-term business relationships.

PROFESSIONAL SUMMARY

Account Executive – ABC Engineering, Fremont, California   [year–Present]
- *Contributions:* From no account list, cold-called and sold premium-priced industrial lighting to 130+ accounts in California sales territory.

Sales Representative – DEF Center, Seattle, Washington (relocated to California)   [year–year]
- *Contributions:* Delivered impressive 1st year sales performance of $800,000 (sold high-dollar items valued up to $60,000 each).

Account Executive – GHI Corporation, Seattle, Washington (reduction in sales force)   [year–year]
- *Contributions:* Delivered 6-fold sales growth, ranking in top 3 among national team of 50.

Marketing & Sales Manager – JKL Company, Seattle, Washington (recruited by FGI)   [year–year]
- *Contributions:* Achieved 25% annual sales growth for Seattle Division. Graduated from intensive sales management training program with honors. Promoted through direct sales and product promotion positions.

Available for Relocation

The *After* format de-emphasizes the fact that his two most recent employment experiences were not nearly the success that his first two employers were, nor did the more recent companies have the name recognition that the previous employers did. Rather than use a traditional, chronological format, which would emphasize less-impressive positions that might turn off readers before they got to the bottom of the page, we developed a heavy Career Highlights summary, which dominates the visual center of the page and makes the reader see immediately the applicant's most impressive, albeit older, experience. This creativity in formatting not only landed Patrick several interviews in short order, but also boosted his confidence to navigate the choppy waters associated with recent career disappointments.

Use Impact Statements to Portray Yourself as the Right Fit

You, too, can have a great deal of flexibility in forming and fashioning your résumé. In all likelihood, you could make a difference in a variety of positions and companies. To portray yourself as the right fit, carefully select and strategically position information that is relevant to the position or company. Remember that this is *your* marketing piece, unique to *your* dreams and goals, *your* value proposition, and *your* brand. Just as your gene pool is unique to humankind, your work history and accomplishments are unique to you. Although your background may be similar to other candidates, your résumé shouldn't cause readers to wonder whether you have an identical twin. As I mentioned earlier, by far the best way to distinguish yourself from the crowd of candidates is through the use of definitive impact statements (accomplishments) that spell value and emphasize your personal brand. As you finish developing your impact statements using the tools and tips in this chapter, the construction of your career story is nearing completion.

Take pleasure in your progress thus far: The framework is up (format selected), the space planning done (categories selected), the interior constructed (job descriptions written), and furnishings decided on (accomplishments identified). Next, it's time for the "punch list." In construction parlance, this means to go back through and take care of "touch-ups." In résumé parlance, it's time for a quick primer in editing, power-writing, and résumé-speak.

Top 10 Tips for Writing Accomplishments

1. Tune in to the employer's WIFM mantra, meaning "what's in it for me?" by including verifiable accomplishments.

2. Include accomplishments to convey your business savvy, indicate your understanding of the employer's bottom line, and demonstrate a track record for contributing to it.

3. When writing accomplishments, remember employers' key buying motivators, such as making money, saving money, saving time, making work easier, solving a specific problem, and so on.

4. Use numbers, the universal language, to bring your accomplishments to life. For instance, instead of "Improved production and reduced assembly-line downtime," write "Improved production 19% and reduced assembly-line downtime from 7 to .5 hours per week." Be specific!

5. Offer comparisons to help convey that you can run faster, jump higher, and leap tall buildings in a single bound. Examples might include comparisons with competitors, industry averages, company averages, or predecessors in the position. Be cautious about comparing yourself with team members, as you don't want to sound like you're on an ego trip.

6. Provide evidence of a strong ROI (return on investment) for the employer whenever possible; for instance, "Brought in more than $300,000 in new business during first six months in territory."

7. Use the "CAR" Technique—Challenge encountered, Action taken, and measurable Result achieved—to show your problem-solving skills and commitment to delivering results.

8. Find material for your accomplishments in performance appraisals and your personal career management file. Some of these questions will also help you unearth accomplishments: How am I evaluated, and did I go above and beyond this evaluation criteria? What were sales (or profits, production, cost issues, and so on) when I began with the company and what were they when I left the company? Did I (or teams on which I worked) make specific contributions that affected sales (or profits, production, costs, and so on)? What was my greatest

contribution to the company? What kinds of problems did I inherit and resolve? What would have happened had I not done my job?

9. Create five or more accomplishments for each and every position you've held over the years. Rank these separately for every position, indicating the most impressive as number one. Determine which accomplishments you'll include on your resume and which ones you'll deliver verbally in networking or interviewing situations.

10. Include accomplishments throughout your marketing documents, including the Qualifications Summary, Experience section, and Education section (if appropriate) of the resume, as well as the cover letter and any other career marketing documents.

Editing: Résumé-Speak 101

"Words, like eyeglasses, blur everything that they do not make clear."

—Joseph Joubert

How do you make an average résumé outstanding? Edit, edit, edit. Conversely, when you disregard the details of style and punctuation, you can make an average résumé mediocre—certainly not the impression you want to give prospective employers.

Copyediting on résumés presents some special challenges. With too many words, your résumé will look crowded and uninviting to read. With too few, it will look anemic next to its competitors. If you err on the side of too much detail, you might drone on with detailed job descriptions that leave readers offended by your presumption that they are interested in, or have time to read, such minutiae. If you lean too far in the opposite direction you might submit a skeletal, overly generic presentation that leaves readers wondering whether you were purposely vague in an attempt to hide something. The anemic version also presents another risk with the advent of online and employer résumé databases: Your résumé might float aimlessly because search engines cannot find any relevant keywords in it.

To find the right balance, you must "hook-n-hold" your reader—much as an advertisement hooks your attention with sales appeals that address "what's in it for *me*," or as a mystery novel casts clues that hold you captive and make you want to read more.

In this chapter, you'll learn how to write in the language of résumé-speak. This material is divided into two sections:

- Development editing, which covers how to write compelling copy.

- Technical editing (or copyediting), which answers an array of questions on grammar, usage, and style.

Beyond that, you'll review the importance of pruning and proofing your résumé before you send it out.

> *Tip* If you're in a hurry, check the index for the topic on which you need help most and review the top-ten list for writing persuasive copy in the next section.

Development Editing: A Primer in Power Writing

Perfecting your hook-n-hold technique requires fluency in what I call *résumé-speak*, a unique style of writing that is part advertisement and part business communication. You'll get a quick course, "résumé-speak 101," a little later in this chapter. But first, take a look at the top ten tenets of developing your résumé.

Top 10 Tenets of Developing Your Résumé

1. **Address your audience.** Every sentence should pass these test questions: "Is my reader interested in this?" and "Does this information explain <u>why the employer should hire me over my competitors?</u>"

2. **Be accurate.** Check and double-check all details, especially numbers.

3. **Be brief.** Delete information that is repetitive or irrelevant.

4. **Be clear.** Ask two or three people to read your resume. Is anything confusing?

5. **Avoid jargon that is too specific to your current company** (specific names of reports, company-specific acronyms, and so on).

6. **Deliver the goods up front.** Start accomplishment statements with the results and then describe the method for achieving the results.

7. **Start sentences with action verbs** (*directed, led, performed, collaborated with*) or sometimes noun phrases (*operations executive, team member, team leader, sales professional*) instead of passive statements like *Responsible for* or *Duties included.*

8. **Sidestep any potential negatives.** It's easier to address issues in person.

9. **Avoid baseless personality attributes.** Use personality pairing to combine your soft skills with tangible documentation of the skills.

10. **Proof the resume.** Proof it again. Have someone else proof it, as well. read

Examples of Résumé-Speak

Résumé-speak converts a quiet, conversational writing style into a punchy, quasi-advertising writing style, as these examples show.

Before

I had the largest share of sales on staff for over eleven years running. There were nine people on our team.

After

Ranked #1 in sales production among team of 9 for 11 consecutive years.

Before

I am responsible for drawing blood for various types of tests, including microbiology, bacteriology, chemistry, hematology, serology, and special chemistry. I also process these tests.

After

Performed blood draws and processed tests for microbiology, bacteriology, chemistry, hematology, serology, and special chemistry.

Before

I had to handle a lot of extra work recently because our company was going through some difficult times and the department had its staff cut by 30%.

After

Good time-manager—handled notable increase in workload during recent 30% reduction in staffing.

Résumé-speak adheres to accepted grammatical form yet refrains from a rigid, "one-size-fits-all" set of rules. For instance, in formal business communications, you would usually spell out numbers from one through nine.

In résumé-speak, you can present these same numbers as Arabic numerals, which attract the reader's attention and help them pick up the pace of reading, as the first *After* example does.

Résumé-speak is telegraphic yet informative. Note how the second *Before* example uses 25 words to describe a laboratory technician's responsibilities, whereas the *After* example requires only 15.

Résumé-speak is fluid yet forceful. The third *Before* example is written in a style that "explains." The *After* version is written in a style that "sells" the candidate by including keywords (such as *time manager*) and turning the negative statement about the company's trials into an impact statement about the candidate's time-management skills.

Above all, résumé-speak is compelling and leaves the reader with the feeling of "Wow, I'm impressed. I must know more."

The Keys to Writing Compelling Copy

There are three keys to developing clean, compelling copy:

- First, you must address the needs of your audience (your employer-to-be).

- Second, you must be succinct and sum up years of experience within the confines of one or two pages.

- Third, you must focus on your transferable skills so that the reader can relate your experience to his or her frame of reference.

Address the Needs of Your Audience

This advice sounds obvious, but job seekers repeatedly overlook it. I have emphasized this concept since chapter 1 and will continue to hammer it home throughout the book because of its importance. For example, when you edit your résumé, one of the first questions to ask yourself is "Does this information explain why the employer should hire me over my competitors?" The answer to this question will give you clues about how much information to include, what keywords to use (see chapter 9), and what buying motivators to address (see chapters 2 and 6).

Another important question to consider is what salary you anticipate receiving. Employers who are ready to commit to an investment of a healthy salary expect a certain level of intelligence, as manifested by your vocabulary and written communication skills. A phrase misused, a word misspelled, or a comma misplaced could spell disaster for your search. Even if you plan on a modest hourly wage, don't plan on skimming the rest of this chapter. Employers still expect you to have the ability to communicate clearly, regardless of your level of responsibility or ranking. People do judge you by how well you communicate.

Summarize by Using the ABC Method

What does the FBI have in common with résumés? Aside from conducting more thorough background checks than most organizations, not much…with the exception of its formula for report writing. More than a decade ago, the bureau devised the "ABC" method to teach agents effective report-writing skills. Named for the elements of Accuracy, Brevity, and Clarity, you can easily apply this three-step primer to résumé editing:

- **Accuracy:** Check and double-check all your details; make sure that numbers are accurate, especially percentages and dollar figures in your Accomplishment statements.

- **Brevity:** Consolidate years of information onto one or two pages. Look for any information that is repetitive or irrelevant and carve it out. Revisit the advice on addressing your audience and ask yourself, "Is this information so critical that, if left out, it would jeopardize my candidacy?"

- **Clarity:** Ask two or three people who are unfamiliar with your present or past employers to read your job descriptions and point out any confusing or obscure terminology. They should be able to understand what you've done *and* be piqued to know more.

The before-and-after examples in the following table demonstrate how to put the ABC formula to work.

Element	Before	After
Accuracy	Service accounts in large area.	Service more than 50 government, institutional, and manufacturing accounts in a 12,000-square-mile area.
Brevity	Calculate monthly waste loads from the sewage-treatment plants on the watershed and present these loadings along with nutrient concentrations on the graphs to illustrate the effects of pollutants on the watershed.	Calculate and graph pollutant effect on watershed from sewage-treatment plant waste loads.
Clarity	Proven results in maximizing sales by a minimum of $2.3 million dollars per year and building profits with a minimum of 2%.	Proven sales skills—boosted annual sales volume more than $2.3 million, adding an extra 2% to bottom-line profits.

Remember, you are writing an advertisement of your job skills, not a technical manual on how to do your job. If, after reading your résumé, the reader could step into your position and perform the job blindfolded, you've gone too far with details.

Focus on Transferable Skills

Some jobs require you to be bilingual, although not necessarily in a foreign language. I'm referring here to the dialect of a particular company or an industry where, to the ears of an outsider, office-speak is similar to a foreign language—for example, all acronyms and code (the computer industry and medical-insurance billing are two industries that immediately come to mind). You should use caution in loading your résumé with lingo that only coworkers will understand. Also avoid detailed job descriptions that include the names of specific reports, tasks, or processes, especially when looking for work outside your industry. In the example that follows, note how this medical-practice bookkeeper's job description was pared down and translated into transferable skills, enabling her to transfer her bookkeeping skills to a real-estate company.

Here is the job description:

- Review Superbills daily.
- Prepare and process DRGs.
- Prepare Monthly Total Production Report.
- Prepare Total Monthly Accounts Receivable Report.
- Prepare Total Monthly Collected for Month Report.
- Prepare Total Monthly Adjustments Report.
- Prepare Total Monthly New Patients Report.
- Prepare Total Monthly Amounts of Surgery Report.
- Report breakdown for office expenses as to secretarial salaries and office rent. This is to be distributed to other doctors involved in local office and ensure money is collected from them.
- Prepare payroll summary sheet monthly.
- Copy all check stubs and balanced checkbook and send to CPA.
- Prepare expense report for all doctors monthly.
- Make bank deposits and keep current balance in checkbook up-to-date.
- Break down tax percentages for employer on each employee.

- Be responsible for coordinating referral system.
- Perform billing for Dr. S.
- Maintain Dr. S. log of surgeries, payments, and appointments.
- Check on Dr. S. accounts receivable, insurance billing, and payments.
- Balance checkbook monthly.
- Order/procure all office supplics as needed.
- Maintain copy machine supplies and ensure that machine is in proper working order.
- Maintain files on a current and orderly basis. The following are basic files to be maintained: patient charts, payroll, paid bills, insurance, miscellaneous.
- Write checks for payroll and bills.
- Arrange for weekly office meeting (or as indicated).
- Check cash boxes to make sure proper change is present.
- Organize and prioritize office-related duties.
- Assist in answering incoming calls by referring/directing calls and taking messages when necessary.
- Serve as a back-up receptionist to greet people coming into the office.
- Give special attention to new patients.
- Communicate with other offices in your area.
- Monthly calendar scheduling of receptionist's and records clerk's hours.
- Examine and double-check outgoing mail for insurance and billing.
- Ensure that all financial information is logged in and information is transferred to accountant.

The preceding long job description was distilled into the following resume copy:

> Provide accounting and office-management services for five-physician multispecialty practice. Perform bookkeeping functions, including accounts receivable, accounts payable, payroll, monthly tax deposits, quarterly reports, journal entries, and general ledger reconciliation. Experience in complex medical billing processes. Schedule and supervise office staff charged with reception, scheduling, records management, and customer service.

As you move through the primer in résumé-speak in the next section, think back to these principles of addressing your audience, summarizing material, and focusing on transferable skills. They should undergird all of your job search communications.

Résumé-Speak 101

If you were to write a recipe for résumé-speak, it might read like this:

> *Combine:*
>
> *2 parts advertisement*
>
> *1 part business communication*
>
> *Add dash of creative writing*
>
> *Marinate in professionalism*

The nature of advertisements calls for creativity and liberal application and arrangement of words. The nature of business correspondence calls for convention and respectful observation of accepted rules of grammar and letter style. With the greater portion of the résumé recipe allotted to an advertisement, you have some freedom in development and editing. Be cautious, nonetheless, of entirely abandoning good grammatical form. In general, the résumé allows you a bit more latitude to bend (but not break) the rules of conventional style and usage. However, play it safe in the cover letter by adhering to standards for grammar; usage; and, to a lesser degree, layout (see chapter 10 for sample cover letter layouts).

Here's one of the first rules of résumé-speak you'll want to adopt: Deliver the goods up front.

Deliver the Goods Up Front

When readers are doing a quick scan of your résumé, they might read just the first few words of each sentence. To cover your bases, start impact statements with the results and then describe the method for achieving the results. Here are a couple examples of how to write more aggressively.

Before

Represented landowners and made presentations to county appeals board to secure a reduction in property-tax assessments in 100% of cases.

After

Achieved 100% success in negotiating reductions in property-tax assessments as representative for landowners.

Before

Introduced consultative sales approach, resulting in 17% increase in sales.

After

Increased sales 17% through introduction of consultative sales approach.

To write in this manner, analyze your sentence and locate the result—it will often include a number. Place this important information at the beginning of the sentence; you'll find that the rest of the sentence will easily fall into place.

Start Sentences with Action Verbs or Noun Phrases

Twenty years ago, virtually all job descriptions on résumés started with *Responsible for* or *Duties included* (a sure way to add unnecessary words, lengthen copy, and bore your reader). Résumés from this era could easily be mistaken for a collection of phrases taken straight out of a job-description manual. Today, job descriptions begin with action verbs *(directed, led, performed, challenged with)* or sometimes noun phrases *(operations executive, multidisciplinary team member, core member, sales professional)*. There are some situations in which you'll want to use the term *responsibilities,* but this will be as a heading for visual formatting purposes (see "Give Outdated Experience a Feeling of Real Time" later in this chapter).

The next examples show how to convert lifeless introductions into clean, compelling copy. The Solutions section after each pair of examples details specific how-to's.

Before

Responsible for managing the administrative services for a health care system with six clinic sites in Fresno, Selma, Hanford, Kingsburg, Kerman, and Firebaugh.

After

Managed administrative services for multisite health-care system with clinics in Fresno and five surrounding cities.

Solutions

Drop "responsible for" and change the next verb from present progressive (managing) to present tense (manage) if you are still employed with the company, or to past tense (managed) if you are no longer at the company.

Prune the rest of the sentence: eliminate articles *(a, an);* exchange *six clinic sites* for *multisite;* and shorten the list of cities to *five surrounding cities.*

Before

Duties included medical billing, collections, medical-records management, and physician and staff scheduling.

After

Supervised medical billing, collections, medical-records management, and physician and staff scheduling.

Solutions

Substitute the verb *supervised* for *duties included.* (Because this sentence followed the sentence in the preceding example, I opted for the verb *supervised* instead of beginning two consecutive sentences with the verb *managed.*) Other easy substitutions for *duties included* are verbs such as *performed, provided, coordinated, assisted with,* and *charged with.*

In cases where sentences start with *duties included* followed by a verb (for instance, *duties included assembling*), drop *duties included* and change the verb tense to present or past tense *(assemble* or *assembled).*

Sidestep Potential Negatives

Offering to explain a negative can be tempting ill fate. It's not unusual in business to encounter problems and challenges; however, in committing them to paper, you might be laying a minefield for yourself. Give considerable thought before describing a negative circumstance or flaw in your background. In some cases, it might be worth the gamble; in most cases, it is not.

Note how the following *Before* and *After* statements sidestep potential landmines that the reader might construe negatively.

Situation

Sales representative lost major account because of company headquarters moving out of his territory.

Before

Met quota despite loss of major account.

After

Landed 12 new accounts that added $155,000 in new business; figure represents 45% of total annual sales volume.

Situation

Company merged, resulting in demotion from Operations Manager to Operations Supervisor.

Before
Statement positioned as entirely new position entry under company description:

> Returned to supervisory role after merger, overseeing 40 staff in production, distribution, and customer service.

After
Statement positioned as last bulleted item in accomplishments list under the more impressive position title of operations manager:

> Accepted new challenge with merger—instrumental in designing and implementing architecture that merged disparate production, distribution, and customer-service cultures.

Someone once said that you are a slave to your written word and a servant to your spoken word. In questionable cases, it's best to play it safe on paper; then be ready to put a positive spin on issues in an interview.

Give Outdated Experience a Feeling of Real Time
The present progressive and past progressive tenses (*I am managing* or *I was managing*) equip you with a tool for blurring the dates of your experience…yet another trade secret for your résumé arsenal. Because résumé-speak calls for dropping pronouns (*I*) and helping verbs (*am* or *was*) before the verb, you then start the sentence with the main action (*managing*), which makes it possible to give older experience a feeling of real time.

Warren, a self-employed insurance agent for the past dozen years who decided to return to retailing, used the progressive tense to resurrect his old skills in sales and management of a menswear store.

Before
> Directed display, merchandising, promotions, advertising, and in-store sales strategies. Managed receiving, pricing, mark-downs, inventory, and stock transfers. Used consultative and suggestive-sales techniques to maximize add-on sales.
>
> **Results**
> - Created promotional vehicles to generate sales increases of 20% annually.
> - Maintained lowest inventory costs among company's four stores.
> - Earned Top Salesman honors among sales team of 30+.

After
> **Responsibilities**
> - Directing display, merchandising, promotions, advertising, and in-store sales strategies.
> - Managing receiving, pricing, mark-downs, inventory, and stock transfers.
> - Using consultative and suggestive-selling techniques to maximize add-on sales.

Results

- Creating promotional vehicles to generate sales increases of 20% annually.

- Maintaining lowest inventory costs among company's four stores.

- Earning Top Salesman honors among sales team of 30+.

The real-time technique comes across best when you present each sentence with a separate, bulleted line. The alternative course is to group the sentences into a paragraph, which presents a series of sentences starting with the progressive tense (-ing). The drawback to this paragraph presentation is that it can be a bumpy read, especially if you present a full page or two of text. In the preceding example, the word *Responsibilities,* which prefaces the list of experience, is used more for résumé design than reader direction. I used it in this case as a visual marker for the reader; moreover, I like the alliteration of *Responsibilities* and *Results* (you can substitute the terms *Accountability* and *Accomplishments* if you prefer).

Tip Should past experience and accomplishments always be written in past tense? From a timeline perspective, this is a logical argument. Yet, because there are very few hard-and-fast rules in résumé development (other than to include some method for readers to contact you, to provide some measure of your candidacy, and to be honest), it is "legal" to use the progressive tenses if you need to make outdated experience sound fresh and contemporary. The only caveat is that you must be consistent in your usage throughout the résumé.

Avoid an Employer Pet Peeve: Baseless Personality Attributes

Including personality attributes was a common résumé-writing technique begun circa 1980. Typically, a section labeled "Profile" or "Traits" was included toward the bottom (and occasionally near the top) of the résumé. The purpose was to convey those all-important "soft skills" that employers esteem, such as communication, interpersonal, and teamwork skills. Myriad job seekers, knowing that employers valued these skills, began including them on their résumés. The common and overused phrases such as "good oral and written communication skills" and "people-oriented" created silent skepticism among employers, accompanied by the thought "right, what else is new?"

Employers cannot discount soft skills when considering whom to hire. Unfortunately, it is quite easy for every Tom, Dick, and Henrietta to include a list of glowing personal skills on their résumés when, indeed, they might have no such skills. It's analogous to tricking a scanner into selecting your résumé based on keywords, such as "some exposure to electrical engineering; interested in opportunities to learn about Banyan networks, VINES, and TCP/IP," when you have little or no experience whatsoever in those areas. So how do you include soft skills, critically important to the hiring decision, when employers are hardened to commonplace references such as "good communication skills and team player"?

Enter personality pairing, a technique used to counter the complaint of baseless personality skills (see appendix B, employer pet peeve #6). Personality pairing, or simply pairing, combines soft skills with tangible documentation of the skill. In effect, you substantiate ownership of important soft skills and impress your reader by backing them up with cold, hard facts—just another secret to set you apart from, and above, the competition.

Consider the following *Before* example. Although it uses good keywords, only the last item *(advanced quickly throughout career)* adds any tangible documentation to the stated skills.

Before

Profile

Cost-conscious, customer-oriented, problem solver, team player, analytical skills, advanced quickly throughout career.

This next *After* example demonstrates how Karen, an administrative manager, used pairing to emphasize the soft skills listed in the preceding example.

After

Contributions to company

- ***Cost Conscious:*** Slashed administrative purchasing costs 35% through introduction of supplier partnerships, renegotiation of vendor contracts, and implementation of integrated software. Trimmed additional 9% from upcoming FY budget.

- ***Customer-Driven Problem Solver:*** Redesigned company's response to customer problems and introduced new vision of service; assembled materials that responded to issues and simultaneously promoted new products or future buys.

- ***Team Builder:*** Contributed to 12% increase in productivity by participating in quality-improvement activities enterprise wide. Helped bring 10 new products to market while interfacing effectively with executive team, engineers, chemists, production and shipping managers, artists, and support staff.

- ***Analytical Thinker:*** Analyzed systems and retooled department, shifting focus from "processing" to "customer support"; redefined position descriptions and wrote 70-page operations manual—involved staff and obtained buy-in throughout process.

- ***Company Minded:*** Initial 9-month assignment in Safety & Environmental Health Dept. Aided in creation of new safety and haz-mat program.

You can use pairing to preface impact statements in your Experience section (as the preceding administrative manager did) or material in the Qualifications section. Cover letters can also be the vehicle to deliver a rundown of soft skills.

A common mistake candidates make is succumbing to the temptation of parroting the soft-skill requirements listed in employment ads. For instance, note how a novice writer composed a letter using verbatim terminology from an employment ad, which called for these skills: "Credit & Collections Specialist with strong technical skills, effective communication skills, mediation background; must be a team player, PC skills, admin. skills."

Before

Re: Your need for a Credit & Collections Specialist

Dear Ms. Jacquelian:

I am writing regarding your ad for a Credit & Collections Specialist. Enclosed is my résumé that presents my 17 years of experience in credit unions and banks.

As your ad requires, I offer strong technical skills, good oral and written communication skills, mediation skills, and PC skills (Excel). I am also a consummate team player. I am confident I could quickly step into the position and be an asset to your organization.

Thank you for your time. I look forward to hearing from you.

Sincerely,

Compare the preceding cover letter with this next *After* version. In both cases, the candidate states the required skills for the position. The former, however, does not add an explanation of how she gained those skills. The latter uses concrete examples that lend credibility to her claim of strong technical, communication, mediation, and related skills.

After

Re: Your need for a Credit & Collections Specialist

Dear Ms. Jacquelian:

With more than 17 years of experience in credit union and banking environments, I am exploring positions with Bay Area credit unions that need someone with a record of contributing to financial stability, business operations, and portfolio performance. Your opening appears to be an excellent match for my background. Specifically, qualifications I can bring to your members and management are these:

- **Technical Skills:** My knowledge of credit and collections reduced write-offs on a $22 million loan portfolio to a record .7% and decreased delinquency ratios to a low of .5%. Supporting this record are more than 20 seminars in collections and bankruptcy law, including four masters-level bankruptcy courses from McGeorge School of Law.

- **Communication Skills:** My verbal and written skills are demonstrated daily as I counsel members on credit matters, discuss legal strategy with in-house counsel, prepare member correspondence, and draft legal documents. What's more, the credit union saved thousands of dollars in attorneys' fees through my representation in small-claims actions.

- **Team Orientation:** Both management and coworkers characterize me as the consummate team player. I believe in proactively communicating with all levels of the organization, cross-training to understand other employees' roles, and stepping forward to help when an area is temporarily short-staffed.

- **Mediation Skills:** My mission is to identify, mediate, and resolve members' collections issues *before* they escalate to legal action. In more than 75% of cases where members filed bankruptcy papers, I persuaded them to reaffirm their entire debt owed the credit union (a feat unheard of in the company's history).

- **Computer Skills:** I am PC literate, use Excel software daily, and enjoy navigating the Internet. I am excited about advancements in technology and believe they will speed the research required in asset searches, skip traces, and other collections functions.

Given my made-to-order qualifications, I am confident I could easily step into the position and become an asset to Baytech Credit Union. Should your schedule permit, I will call next Tuesday to make certain you received my materials and answer any questions regarding my candidacy. If you would like to speak to me earlier, don't hesitate to contact me at either of the above numbers. I look forward to touching base with you.

Best regards,

One might argue that the *After* version is more for the résumé screener to read, which is true. On the other hand, it distinctly separates the candidate from her competition:

- She took the time (arguably life's most precious commodity) to specifically address the employer's needs.

- She created rapport with the reader through the conversational style of the letter.

- She dangled the proverbial "carrot"—achieving record low write-offs and delinquency, saving attorneys' fees, and persuading bankruptcy customers to pay back their debt—to create reader interest and desire (see chapter 2, steps 2 and 3 in the AIDA formula).

Further, if the résumé is electronically scanned, the detailed information increases her opportunity to rank above other candidates based on a keyword search.

Convey Confidential Information Without Giving Away Proprietary/Trade Secrets

If you haven't already given notice to your present employer, you might find yourself escorted out the door sooner than you wanted if you make the mistake of disclosing confidential or proprietary information on your résumé (especially if you are applying to work for direct competitors). In your quest for offering tangible impact statements, you must be careful to reveal financial information only for corporations that are publicly traded on the stock exchanges, such as the New York Stock Exchange (NYSE), the American Stock Exchange (ASE), and the Chicago Stock Exchange (CSE). These publicly held corporations must file quarterly reports detailing their financial position with both their respective state agency and the Securities and Exchange Commission (SEC). These reports make their financial information fair game for anyone with basic research skills.

> *Tip* If you are interviewing with a publicly traded company, you can do some quick research about it by looking up the EDGAR database on the SEC's Web site, www.sec.gov (click on Search), as well as other financial-services companies such as Hoovers (www.hoovers.com). Google Alerts is another great way to gather intelligence on your target companies. Just enter your search terms at www.google.com/alerts, such as the target company's name and product, and Google will e-mail you relevant news or Web-based information when it is posted online.

The financial data from other organizations—privately held corporations, closely held corporations, family-owned corporations, partnerships, and sole proprietorships—is off-limits for John Q. Public (even if your employer has entrusted you with access to it). This means that if you work for a "mom-and-pop" business, a partnership, or a privately held corporation, you'll need to be a bit obscure in conveying your results. To protect the interests of private employers, translate confidential information into percentage increases or other veiled references. The following table has a number of suggestions for communicating increases for net profit, sales, production, and other confidential information without giving away "family" secrets.

Translating Confidential or Proprietary Information

"Illegal" Wording for Private Companies	"Veiled" References to Convey Data in a Confidential Manner
Increased net profit from 12.2% to 15.7%.	Added 3.5% to bottom-line profits. *or* Delivered healthy 6-figure profit, a record for the company's 25-year history.

"Illegal" Wording for Private Companies	"Veiled" References to Convey Data in a Confidential Manner
Decreased operating expenses from $290,000 to $235,000.	Decreased operating expenses approximately 23%. *or* Reduced operating expenses to record low.
Increased production from 1.9M to 2.4M units per year.	Increased annual production 26%. *or* Increased production to maximum output.
Manage $780,000 sales territory.	Manage sales territory generating healthy six-figure revenue. *or* Manage high-profile territory that generates highest sales among 12 west-coast territories.
Boosted national market share to 7%, ranking 9th in the nation for sales.	Increased market share to place among nation's Top 10 industry competitors (only privately held company to rank among Fortune 500 and multinational corporations).
Built sales from $60,000 in first year to $100,200; $225,450; $290,830; and $325,700 in subsequent four years.	Achieved annual revenue growth of 67%, 125%, 29%, and 12%.* *or* Delivered more than a fourfold increase in sales.**

Calculate the percentage increases by dividing second-year sales of $100,200 by first-year sales of $60,000 (1.67) and then subtracting 1.0 to obtain .67, or 67%. Calculate the next year's sales increase by dividing third-year sales of $225,450 by $100,200 to obtain 2.25 and then subtracting 1.0 to obtain 1.25 or 125%. Repeat the formula for years three and four.

**A 400% increase is considered a fourfold increase.*

Technical Editing/Copyediting: The Mechanics of Résumé-Speak

Proper punctuation and word usage are akin to good grooming: If you discount the importance of them, you'll probably make quite a poor impression on your employer-to-be. Mistakes that might seem small, perhaps just a comma missing or a letter omitted, can actually have far-reaching ramifications. For example, if you drop the *e* from *morale*, you'll have quite a different meaning. Or you might have an even larger faux pas, such as the misuse of a word, as in *whose* for *who's, inane* for *innate*—and your computer's spell-checker won't catch an error like that. Regardless of your "mechanical offenses," intelligent readers will spot them and think less of you for not knowing better.

There are several fine books devoted to the nuts and bolts of business writing. To settle more technical issues than what is presented here, turn to one of these references:

- **William A. Sabin's** *The Gregg Reference Manual* (10th ed., McGraw-Hill/Irwin). *The Gregg Reference Manual* has an exceptional index, giving you quick access to more than 1,800 rules for grammar, usage, and style. Sabin's spiral-bound bible ought to sit on the desk of anyone who has to communicate with others for a living.

- *The Chicago Manual of Style:* **The Essential Guide for Writers, Editors, and Publishers** (15th ed., University of Chicago Press). *The Chicago Manual of Style,* considered the authoritative voice of book publishing, is a reference for the serious writer or editor.

- **Strunk and White's** *The Elements of Style* (Macmillan Publishing Co.). *The Elements of Style,* numbering fewer than 100 pages, is a classic for learning the art of vigorous writing.

Reference books aside, I present the mechanics of résumé-speak in the following sections. For easy reference, topics are arranged in alphabetical order, from Abbreviations and Acronyms to Verbs and Writing in the First Person. As with most rules, there might be exceptions, so think critically about how advice presented here might be interpreted for your particular situation. In all your writing, I challenge you to adopt Sabin's advice, found in his essays in *The Gregg Reference Manual* (McGraw-Hill/Irwin):

> *It is the impoverished person who meets every situation with the same set of clothes. By the same token, it is an impoverished writer who meets all situations with a rigid set of rules.*

Abbreviations

An abbreviation is a shortened form of a word or phrase used primarily to save space. Most familiar to the average user are state abbreviations. The sheer length of some states' names (especially my home state, California) is reason to abbreviate them on a résumé. Scanning technology is another argument for use of state abbreviations because geographic searches are typically conducted by the state's two-letter abbreviation. (Never use periods after a two-letter state abbreviation.)

The National Résumé Writers' Association advocates consistency through-out your résumé. In other words, if you use the two-letter state abbreviation in your header, use the abbreviated form in all later references to states in the Experience and Education sections of the résumé. If you spell out the state in your header, spell out the state in all sections of your résumé.

Other abbreviations you might use in your résumé or cover letters are the following.

Word Mistakes	Correct Abbreviation	Common
continued	cont.	not *contd.* or *cont'd*
department	dept.	not *dep't*
approximately	approx.	not *approx'ly*
Enclosures	Encl.	not *Encls.*
Company	Co.	not *Comp.*

Note that some of the preceding abbreviations require a period. Opinions differ on using periods to abbreviate educational degrees and geographic names. *The Gregg Reference Manual* advises use of periods for academic credentials.

Abbreviation	Meaning	Common Mistakes
A.A.	Associate of Arts (or associate's degree)	Not *Associate in Arts* or *Associate's of Arts*
B.S.	Bachelor of Science (or bachelor's degree)	Not *Bachelor in Science* or *Bachelor's of Science*
M.A.	Master of Arts (or master's degree)	Not *Master in Arts* or *Master's of Arts*
Ph.D.	Doctor of Philosophy	Not *Doctor in Philosophy*
J.D.	Juris Doctorate or Doctor of Juris Prudence	

Some writers prefer to omit the periods after degrees; others religiously spell out degrees to ensure that the reader doesn't associate a coarse or less charitable meaning to the abbreviation! It is unlikely that your choice to use or omit periods or spell out the degree in its entirety will be a deal breaker. Just be consistent from one degree to the next.

In general, be frugal in your use of abbreviations throughout the résumé. With too many, your readers will feel like they're reading a stock market ticker, whch. mks. 4 dfclt. & chpy. rdng.

Acronyms

Can you describe the difference between an abbreviation and an acronym? An acronym is a shortened form of a phrase, like an abbreviation, with the distinction that it can be pronounced as a word. Thus, the IRS (Internal Revenue Service) is an abbreviation, whereas HUD (Department of Housing and Urban Development) is an acronym. Acronyms are coined by taking the first letter or some letter(s) of the words they represent to assemble a pronounceable word. They typically appear in all capitals:

LAN	**l**ocal **a**rea **n**etwork
CD-ROM	**c**ompact **d**isc, **r**ead-**o**nly **m**emory
WYSIWYG	**w**hat **y**ou **s**ee **i**s **w**hat **y**ou **g**et (pronounced wizzy-wig)

In a few cases, the acronym is spelled with lowercase letters (hats off to the thoughtful author of this first example):

laser	**l**ight **a**mplification by **s**timulated **e**mission of **r**adiation
bit	**bi**nary digi**t**
op ed (page)	**op**posite the **ed**itorial page
modem	**mo**dulator and **dem**odulator

When using acronyms, be certain that your readers understand them. If the acronym will be unfamiliar to your readers but is something you need to refer to repeatedly, spell out the meaning after the first reference to it and then use the acronym in future references, as in this cover letter excerpt:

While at Synovex, Unlimited, I created and implemented a program known as STEPS (Support Training Equals Promotion for Success). Many of the company's dramatic improvements can be traced to STEPS. The following are just a few.

Active Voice

Active voice, or use of active verbs, means that the subject of the verb is the doer of the act. Contrasting this is passive voice, where the subject is acted on (for more information, see "Passive Voice" and "Verbs" in this chapter). In the following active example, the subject (*I*) does the action of negotiating. In the passive voice example, the subject (*the contracts*) is receiving the action.

Active voice

The legal department negotiated seven new contracts.

Passive voice

Seven new contracts were negotiated by the legal department.

In virtually all cases of résumé and cover letter writing, employers and grammarians prefer active voice over passive voice. Converting from passive to active voice often makes the subject of the sentence a person (typically you) as opposed to an object.

Articles (in Absentia)

Résumé-speak calls for frugal use, and sometimes a complete absence, of articles. There are just three articles in the English language: *a, an,* and *the.* In grammar, articles are considered adjectives, acting both to modify a noun and subtly signal the reader that a noun is coming. By using articles to signal your readers, you allow them to get comfortable and can lull them into a state of relaxation. This is not the goal of your résumé! Conversely, the absence of articles can startle your readers and keep them on their toes. You want them awake, alert, and anticipatory. Most résumé writers limit the use of articles; some have declared a complete moratorium on them. Advocates for the absolute absence of articles contend that it gives résumé copy an aggressive and powerful presentation. Those who prefer limited use contend that the writing has a more relaxed, conversational tone, whereas total elimination of articles sounds too abrupt and jerky. My preference is to sprinkle sparingly—just enough to smooth out any rough spots.

Read aloud these variations on a professional goal.

No use of articles

Professional Goal: Staff Accountant with public accounting firm where my graduate studies in taxation, experience as IRS revenue agent, and expert knowledge of Tax Reform Act, TEFRA regulations, and other tax legislation will be of value.

Limited use of articles

Professional Goal: Staff Accountant with <u>a</u> public accounting firm where my graduate studies in taxation, experience as IRS revenue agent, and expert knowledge of <u>the</u> Tax Reform Act, TEFRA regulations, and other tax legislation will be of value.

Full use of articles

Professional Goal: <u>A</u> Staff Accountant with <u>a</u> public accounting firm where my graduate studies in taxation, experience as <u>an</u> IRS revenue agent, and expert knowledge of <u>the</u> Tax Reform Act, <u>the</u> TEFRA regulations, and other tax legislation will be of value.

Hearing the words spoken confirms that an intermittent use of articles is better for a smooth read than no use of articles. Without them entirely, you falter, especially when approaching the words "Tax Reform Act." Conversely, using articles before every noun slows the reader and prevents the feeling of forward movement that is accomplished with intermittent use.

Auxiliary or Helping Verbs

Auxiliary verbs are used to help form another verb, thus their alternative designation as "helping" verbs. The auxiliary verbs are the following:

> be, am, is, are, was, were, been, can, could, do, does, did, has, have, had, may, might, must, shall, should, ought, will, would, keep, keeps

Résumé-speak calls for no or limited use of helping verbs because they weaken and elongate your writing. Eliminate helping verbs from your résumé and limit their use in cover letters. To spot helping verbs, look for two or three verbs together. In cases where there is just one helping verb, simply eliminate it.

> The company *has merged* with Motorola.

> The company *merged* with Motorola.

When you have two helping verbs, drop the helping verbs and check to see whether a revision to your verb suffix is in order. In the next case, the suffix *-ing* becomes *-ed*.

> I *have been editing* my résumé.

> I *edited* my résumé.

Capitalization

The use of capital letters gives importance, emphasis, and distinction to a word. There are, of course, the more common rules to follow with respect to capitalization: Capitalize the first word in a sentence (but usually not the first word following a colon or semicolon, unless it starts a full sentence) and capitalize proper nouns (Charlie, July, Massachusetts). Rules on capitalization become foggy when the term in question has importance to you personally but is not a *bona fide* proper noun.

What many writers generally don't know is that it is appropriate to capitalize a given term in some contexts but not necessarily in all contexts. Exceptions to the capitalize-only-proper-nouns rule stem from the writer's or reader's vantage point of what is important. For instance, when writing to a company about a position with one of its departments, you might choose to capitalize the department to indicate that you consider it important.

Acceptable

> The word-processing position in your *Administrative Department* sounds like a great fit.

When writing to mom and dad about the same job, you would not capitalize *administrative department.*

Acceptable

> Great news! You'll be pleased to know I've applied for a job in an *administrative department,* so I should soon be off your "payroll."

If a networking contact sits on a company's board of directors (not considered a proper noun), in writing to her you might want to capitalize *Board of Directors* out of courtesy; references outside the company would be *board of directors.* Likewise, if you are employed by the government, you might consistently capitalize the term *Federal Government* out of respect for the organization that employs you; those in the private sector would refer to it as the *federal government.*

As with most things, it is possible to go overboard with capitalization to indicate importance. In an attempt to point out special skills through the use of capitalization, this writer succeeds only in irritating the reader.

Incorrect

> My Operations-Management strengths in Manufacturing include Materials Management, Warehousing, and Shipping and Receiving.

Correct

My operations-management strengths in manufacturing include materials management, warehousing, and shipping and receiving.

Titles typically give rise to capitalization questions. Other than the President of the United States, titles are not considered proper nouns. Accordingly, do not capitalize a title unless it fits the courtesy-and-respect exception noted above.

Incorrect

The Company's Vice President of Product Development is taking a Sabbatical; a Screening Committee will be looking for an Interim Replacement this Summer.

Correct

The company's vice president of product development is taking a sabbatical; a screening committee will be looking for an interim replacement this summer.

Correct

Tyler Sterling, the company's vice president of product development, is taking a sabbatical; a screening committee will be looking for an interim replacement this summer.

Think twice about using all capital letters for a word or words. All CAPS are big; they stand out conspicuously from the surrounding tissue of words. There are few instances where they are called for; more often than not, they are distracting and difficult to read. If it is necessary to use all CAPS for a series of acronyms or abbreviations, consider reducing the size of your font by one point. Notice the difference it makes between the first and second examples.

I am familiar with MS-DOS, BASIC, FORTRAN, DDE, BIOS, DBMS, PIM, FTP, and OLE.

I am familiar with MS-DOS, BASIC, FORTRAN, DDE, BIOS, DBMS, PIM, FTP, and OLE.

The reduction from 12 points to 11 points keeps the uppercase words from screaming at the reader and might save one line of type.

Colons and Semicolons

Use a colon between two independent clauses when the second clause explains the first.

Your opportunity sounds like a perfect fit: It requires skills in electronic research and technical writing, and the possibility of a long-term contract is very appealing.

A colon is not necessary after the word *of* when it precedes a list.

Incorrect

My challenges consisted of: designing an uninterruptible power supply, upgrading the existing WAN, and developing new disaster-recovery procedures.

Correct

My challenges consisted of designing an uninterruptible power supply, upgrading the existing WAN, and developing new disaster-recovery procedures.

Correct

My job consisted of these challenges: designing an uninterruptible power supply, upgrading the existing WAN, and developing new disaster-recovery procedures.

A very common mistake is to place a colon after a verb, such as *are* or *include*.

Incorrect

Performed warehousing duties, including: receiving freight, preparing manifests, scheduling deliveries, expediting receipt of raw materials.

Correct

Performed the following warehousing duties: receiving freight, preparing manifests, scheduling deliveries, expediting receipt of raw materials.

To help your reader keep information straight, use a semicolon in a series of items that contain commas.

Incorrect

My colleagues on the project were Jane Dillingham, director of marketing, Juan Delgado, director of public affairs, Julio Juegetta, director of special events, and Jackson Pecini, special events coordinator.

Correct

My colleagues on the project were Jane Dillingham, director of marketing; Juan Delgado, director of public affairs; Julio Juegetta, director of special events; and Jackson Pecini, special events coordinator.

Correct

My colleagues on the project were the following people: Jane Dillingham, director of marketing; Juan Delgado, director of public affairs; Julio Juegetta, director of special events; and Jackson Pecini, special events coordinator.

Use a semicolon to separate independent clauses where the conjunction *(and, but, or)* is omitted and the second clause does not explain the first.

Incorrect

Last year I spent a semester in the exchange program at Universidad de Mexico City, this summer I plan to complete an intensive Spanish immersion program in Madrid.

Correct

Last year I spent a semester in the exchange program at Universidad de Mexico City; this summer I plan to complete an intensive Spanish immersion program in Madrid.

Use a semicolon between independent clauses that are separated by transitional expressions (*however, furthermore, consequently, therefore, nevertheless, accordingly*).

Incorrect

After nine months of stagnant sales, our numbers are on the upswing, furthermore, morale among the workforce has improved and productivity is up 12%.

Correct

After nine months of stagnant sales, our numbers are on the upswing; furthermore, morale among the workforce has improved and productivity is up 12%.

Commas

To insert or not to insert—that is the question. This tiny mark is endowed with terrific powers. Used properly, it can clarify and guide readers to the crux of your point; used improperly, it can utterly confuse or amuse.

Incorrect

The chair of the committee, who is out to lunch, until 2:00 will be running the meeting.

Correct

The chair of the committee, who is out to lunch until 2:00, will be running the meeting.

The first sentence raises the question: Will someone more astute be running the meeting after 2:00?

There are dozens of rules regulating commas. Despite one style book's 60-plus pages devoted to instruction on commas, they have but two basic functions: to separate and to set off.

Commas That Separate

Use commas to separate these items:

⋆ **Compound sentences joined by *and, but, or, nor, for, yet,* or *so.***

He came highly recommended by the agency's copywriter, but we decided against him after seeing the punctuation errors on his résumé.

Compound sentences will be a rarity in your résumé but can frequently appear in cover letters. To test whether a sentence is a compound, look for a subject before the verb in the second clause of the sentence. In the preceding example, the pronoun *we* before the verb *decided* signals the start of a second independent clause and calls for a comma before the conjunction *but*.

- **Three or more items in a series** (refer to a later discussion on using or not using a comma before the final *and* in a series).

    Her résumé, cover letter, and personal mission statement are impeccable.

- **Two or more adjectives where the word *and* has been omitted.**

    He is an impressive, well-spoken candidate.

In résumé-speak, you can also use a comma to signal that a word other than *and* has been omitted. The comma in the following example indicates that the verb *rose* has been left out (it is understood through the reference to *rose* in the first clause). This is another technique that will add punch to your writing.

Sales rose an unprecedented 279%; profits, 22%.

Commas That Set Off

Use commas:

- **To set off words, phrases, or clauses that provide additional but nonessential information.** Nonessential means that if you were to remove the words between the commas, the meaning of the sentence would remain the same.

Nonessential phrase

Barry and Eleanor, *who are cofounders of the company*, will meet you at 9:00 a.m. for a formal interview.

Essential phrase

Please talk to the manager who has in-depth knowledge of my performance record.

- **To indicate unusual word order.** Juggling the order of your words, within the confines of common sense, is an easy way to spice up your résumé.

Before

I am applying for the early shift because I don't mind getting up at the crack of dawn.

I gained six years of experience in technical bench work and four years in supervision during my time with Xerox.

After

Because I don't mind getting up at the crack of dawn, I am applying for the early shift.

During my time with Xerox, I gained six years of experience in technical bench work and four years in supervision.

Comma Trauma

Different style books advocate different rules for using commas. The greatest difference among style books centers on the *serial comma*. Listed next is a discussion of the serial comma, followed by highlights of the more common problems associated with the use of commas.

★ **Comma before the final *and* in a series (the serial comma).** Writers differ on use of the serial comma, which refers to the use (or omission) of a comma before the *and* in a series of three or more items. I prefer *The Gregg Reference Manual* (McGraw-Hill/Irwin) ruling on this matter, which recommends a comma before the final *and. The Chicago Manual of Style,* which book editors use, agrees with this recommendation.

Strengths I can bring to the position stem from my 10-year background in appraisal of commercial, industrial, agricultural, and income-producing properties.

The serial comma is especially helpful when you have a series of items (in this case, three departments) where each item is a pair.

My sales in luggage and purses, boys' and girls' casual wear, and jewelry and accessories were the highest among 25 store sales associates.

Some résumé writers adopt newspaper and magazine writing style, which calls for no comma after the penultimate item in a list.

Built relationships among divergent interests including government officials, civil-service workers, private-sector representatives, intra- and inter-county employees and the community at large.

The lack of a comma can be confusing if either the penultimate or last item is a pair: The reader anticipates that the sentence will end after seeing the first *and,* but then is thrown off because a second *and* appears. Whichever style you choose, be religiously consistent in your usage throughout the résumé and cover letter. Don't use a comma in one situation where you want to clarify a confusing last-item pair and then switch to no commas for text that contains a list of items without a last-item pair.

★ **Comma before an ampersand.** Do not use a comma before an ampersand (*&*) in a company name unless you know that a particular company prefers to do so.

My paralegal experience with Dietrich, Paganini & Johnson allowed me to research and draft pleadings for the guilt and penalty phases of a high-profile death-penalty case.

✦ **Comma after the word *that*.** Do not use a comma after the word *that* unless it is followed by a nonessential clause.

Incorrect

BCD Corporation believes that, it has the corner on the market.

Correct, essential clause

BCD Corporation believes that it has the corner on the market.

Correct, nonessential clause

BCD Corporation believes that, because of its new R&D scientists and MBA sales team, it has the corner on the market.

✦ **Comma in an introductory participial phrase.** Using introductory participial phrases is another trade secret to avoid starting too many cover-letter sentences with the word *I* or *my*. Be careful that you punctuate it properly by finishing the participial phrase with a comma.

Incorrect

Having spent the last four years as assistant manager in a high-volume store I am ready for the challenges of managing this new location.

Correct

Having spent the last four years as assistant manager in a high-volume store, I am ready for the challenges of managing this new location.

✦ **Comma splice.** A comma splice results when you use a comma to connect two sentences that should have been treated with some other form of punctuation (such as a semicolon, a dash, or a period).

Incorrect, comma splice

SLM has impressive integrated search capabilities, consequently, it has earned an excellent reputation for sourcing qualified executives.

Correct

SLM has impressive integrated search capabilities; consequently, it has earned an excellent reputation for sourcing qualified executives.

Correct

SLM has impressive integrated search capabilities—it has earned an excellent reputation for sourcing qualified executives.

Correct

SLM has impressive integrated search capabilities. The company has earned an excellent reputation for sourcing qualified executives.

Contractions

A contraction is a shortened form of two words where an apostrophe is used to indicate the missing words or letters; for example, *can't* is the contraction for *cannot*, and *I'd* is the contraction for *I would*. Using contractions gives your writing an informal sound. Weigh the situation before deciding whether to use contractions. If you are on a first-name basis with the recipient of your letter, contractions might be in order to prevent your writing from sounding too lofty. If it is a first-time contact to a prospective employer, lean toward the more respectful, formal tone and spell out all words.

Informal

I'd be happy to meet you at your office anytime, so please don't hesitate to call.

Formal

I would be happy to meet you at your office anytime, so please do not hesitate to call.

A common mistake is confusing *it's* for *its*. *It's* means *it is*. *Its* means the possessive form of the pronoun *it*. Despite this classification as a possessive, *its* does not require an apostrophe.

Contraction

It's a pleasure for me to accept your employment offer.

Possessive

Its major drawback is a lack of health coverage.

In the preceding possessive example, *its* refers to the employment offer.

Who's and *whose* also give some writers problems. *Who's* is a contraction meaning *who is* or *who has*. *Whose* is the possessive form of *who*. To test which to use, substitute the words *who is* or *who has*. If either is correct, use the contraction *who's*.

Contraction

Jean Jocele, who's been a longtime friend and fellow Rotarian in the Downtown Club, suggested I contact you about my employment search. [who has]

Possessive

You mention that the company is looking for the person whose experience is best suited for the position.

Dashes

A dash is a versatile punctuation mark that can add interest, emphasis, and white space to your writing. Dashes come in several lengths: en dashes, em dashes (the most common), and 2-em or 3-em dashes (used to indicate missing letters or words).

Em dashes, also called long dashes or mutt-rules, are relatively new to everyone but those in the publishing industry. The 7th edition of *The Gregg Reference Manual* (McGraw Hill/Irwin), published in 1992, makes no mention of em dashes; the 8th edition, published in 1996, does. An em dash, the most common of the dashes, can be used as a substitute for other punctuation marks, such as the comma, semicolon, colon, or parentheses (use dashes for emphasis and parentheses for subordination). You can also use a dash to set off a single word.

En dashes, which are half the length of an em dash but longer than a hyphen, are used between number ranges:

2006–Present	Dinty Moore & Company
1999–2006	Barington, Chase & Conners

In cases where you are separating numbers that are not inclusive, such as your telephone number, use a hyphen.

209-776-9494

To create an em dash, you no longer have to type two hyphens, as was the case with typewriters. Most word-processing programs contain em and en dashes. Microsoft Word offers them if you choose Insert, Symbol, and then select the dash from the box of special characters. With WordPerfect, you insert an en or em dash by clicking Insert, Character, Typographic Symbols, and then scrolling down and selecting either character 4,33 (en dash) or 4,34 (em dash).

Here are some examples of em dash use.

Em dash in place of comma (résumé copy)

Grew annualized revenues from $6 million to $17 million—delivered impressive 38% profit margin.

Em dash in place of semicolon (résumé copy)

Influenced shift in sales culture from transaction-oriented to planning-based business using a broad array of products and services—efforts maximized high-return accounts and minimized high-maintenance accounts.

Em dash in place of colon (résumé copy)

Reduced a primary expense category (telecom)—aggressively monitored New Jersey home office allocations, yielding a return of $97,000 in income to Denver and Colorado Springs branches in 12-month period.

Em dash in place of parentheses (résumé copy)

Achieved manager status in three years, officer status in another two years—typical management track takes 10+ years.

Em dash to emphasize single words (cover letter copy)

There is one element that has contributed more than any other to my success—commitment.

Do not capitalize the word immediately following the dash, and avoid starting a dash on a new line of type. Do not add a space—before, between, or after—the typewritten dash. Some writers, including me, take liberties with dashes by adding a space on either side. This is commonly seen in advertisements and allows you to add white space for emphasis of certain words or phrases. Adding a space on each side of the dash also prevents characters that precede and follow from touching, which can cause words to be distorted if they are faxed (see chapter 9).

Ellipsis Marks

An ellipsis is a series of three periods which indicates that material from a quotation has been omitted. *Gregg* (McGraw-Hill/Irwin) recommends one space before and after each of the periods. *Collier's Rules for Desktop Design and Typography* (Addison-Wesley Publishing Co.) suggests no spaces between the periods. You may opt for the latter ruling when you need to compress text to "make things fit."

In business communications, ellipses (the plural of ellipsis) are used in the traditional manner (to indicate an omission). In résumé-speak, they are used (sometimes too liberally) to imply that a candidate's skills go beyond what is included on the résumé. Avoid the temptation of using ellipsis marks as a substitute for thoughtfully organizing, meticulously punctuating, and carefully editing your material. Those who use ellipsis marks as an easy way out end up with copy that resembles the debris of a tornado.

Before

Qualification Summary of Skills

....formal education....experienced in customer relations and service....assessing customer needs....inventory control....computerized systems....data entry....typing....software....excellent telecommunication skills....organized record keeping....public relations expert....departmental liaison....reports....budget marketing....pricing....retail sales. . ..purchasing....order entry....warehouse and stockroom management....shipping receiving....staff supervision and training....working with vendors....creative problem solving....quality performance and achievements....ability to work well with all levels of management and personnel....reliable....professional with pride.

The preceding example should be scrapped or logically organized into a Keyword Summary for computer scanning with just one period after each entry rather than the ellipsis marks (which, by the way, are incorrectly punctuated with four periods and no spaces between the periods). Here's the tornado litter from above, edited, reorganized, and focused toward the candidate's goal:

After

Qualifications

Keyword Summary: Inventory control. Purchasing. Warehouse and stockroom management. Shipping and receiving. Records management. Order entry/fulfillment. Vendor and customer relations. Staff supervision, training. Budgeting. Reporting. Pricing.

Profile: Problem solver. Department liaison, team-oriented. Customer-focused. Reliable, on-time, perfect attendance record. Formal training, inventory and warehouse systems. Computer literate.

Use ellipses to reduce a quotation from a letter of recommendation or other source.

Original letter of recommendation

"Mrs. S. has clear analytical skills, is scrupulously honest in her dealings with employees and clients, and manifests drive and enthusiasm that is contagious."

Quotation excerpt for résumé

"Clear analytical skills . . . scrupulously honest . . . manifests drive and enthusiasm that is contagious."

When a whole sentence or more is omitted, the omission is preceded by a period, which brings the total number of periods in the ellipses to four.

Original

"Never before have I met such a devoted teacher as Mr. Whitcomb. He is the first on the school grounds in the morning and often the last to leave at night. He has been diligent in making monthly home visits to meet with each child's parents. His lessons are well planned and innovative; they tap into sequencing processes and critical thinking skills. I wish I had 50 more like him on my staff."

Quotation excerpt

"Never before have I met such a devoted teacher . . . first on the school grounds in the morning . . . last to leave . . . diligent . . . . I wish I had 50 more like him on my staff."

Microsoft Word has a built-in ellipsis character that you can insert with the same keystrokes for inserting a dash (Insert, Symbol, and then select it from the box of special characters). To confuse matters, Word's ellipsis character is treated as just one character with no spaces between the periods; the size of the periods within the ellipsis character is smaller than text on either side of it, causing it to not come across clearly in a fax transmission. For this reason, avoid ellipsis marks (Microsoft Word's version or any other presentation that eliminates the spaces between the periods) when your résumé will be faxed or scanned. Also avoid splitting the periods of an ellipsis between two lines of type.

Elliptical Sentences

An elliptical sentence, not to be mistaken for a sentence fragment (explained later), contains a word or phrase with key words omitted, yet is treated as a complete sentence. Even though the subject or verb might not be expressed, it is still understood, as in "Terrific presentation" (That was a terrific presentation) or "Enough said" (You have said enough). The use of elliptical sentences is another trade secret that résumé writers employ frequently because they save space, appear as a statement of fact, and add momentum to your writing. Note the elliptical sentences at the end of these two examples.

Created concept for cross-promotion with IKEA® and Media Entertainment for *Extreme Home Makeover* special event (including on-air broadcast). *Promotion well received.*

Headed up major project to convert product codes from newly acquired Hartford-based company. Condensed and merged 50,000 codes into existing Western Service inventory system. *Completed in just three weeks.*

Gender Equity

Terms such as *mankind, layman,* and *man-hours* are offensive to many women and men who contend that the terms are gender-specific (and therefore gender-biased) or exclusionary. To avoid stepping on toes (and possible legal repercussions in the workplace), rewrite your sentence or substitute alternative words.

Gender-Specific Term	Generic Term
businessmen	business executives, business owners, business people
foremen	supervisors
mankind	the human race, people
manpower	staffing, workforce, human resources
salesmen	sales team, sales force, sales staff, salespersons, sales representatives
workmen	workers
workmen's compensation insurance	workers' compensation insurance (or workers' comp)

Hyphenation

Knowing when and when not to hyphenate words such as *start up, break down, tie in,* and *change over* can be a challenge. In general, when you use the term as a verb, it does not require hyphenation. When intended as an adjective or noun, it often calls for hyphenation but sometimes is written as one word without a hyphen.

Verb

I *started up* the new office with just a yellow notepad and $50 in a checking account.

Adjective

Our *start-up* program exceeded everyone's expectations.

Verb

Please *break down* the numbers on that report.

Noun

Not once did we experience a *breakdown* in our system.

Verb

Our telecommunications technician *tied in* the purchasing component.

Noun

The promotional *tie-in* with marketing went well.

Verb

Administration *changed over* to the new system yesterday.

Noun

> Our department's *changeover* was a huge success.

Of course, there are always exceptions. The computer industry spells *start-up* as one word with no hyphens when used as an adjective or noun. For an exhaustive presentation on hyphenation of words beginning or ending with *up, down, in, out, on, off, over, back, away, about, around, by, between, through,* and *together,* check *Merriam-Webster's Collegiate Dictionary,* Tenth Edition (Merriam-Webster).

Hyphenation is also in order when one person performs two functions:

> Actor-Director

> Owner-Manager

Here's an exception to the rule. If your title involves compound words, use an en dash instead of a hyphen:

> Director of Materials–Production Manager

If you used a slash (/), which translates as *or,* between the words *actor* and *director,* you would be indicating that the person was either an actor or director and not both, which is not the case.

Hyphens can be a great space saver in résumé-speak. (Make sure that you use the hyphen key on your keyboard and not an en dash or em dash.) By using hyphenated compound adjectives, you can condense your writing and save precious white space. A compound adjective simply means that you have joined by hyphenation two or more words that express one thought. The following examples show how to turn adjective phrases or clauses into compound adjectives.

Space-Saving Compound Adjective	Original Phrase
My *fast-track* career has been punctuated by national awards for sales performance.	a career that has been on a fast track
Our *well-known* program has been adopted as a model for agencies across the country.	a program that is well known
I function well in *a high-pressure* environment.	an environment where employees work under pressure
In-depth experience—gained over more than 15 years in medical claims processing—is what I offer your firm.	experience that has depth in scope

Space-Saving Compound Adjective	Original Phrase
Our team was responsible for *high-level* negotiations.	negotiations that involved individuals at a high level
My *$80,000-a-year* compensation package was based on reaching aggressive sales quotas, which I consistently achieved.	a compensation package of $80,000 a year
Part of my responsibilities involved *short- and long-range* planning.	plans charted over a short time as well as a long time
While selling *high-tech* equipment, I called on OEMs throughout the Silicon Valley and Bay Area.	equipment that contains a high level of technology
Throughout college, I worked two *part-time* jobs.	jobs that required work part of the time

> *Tip* Never hyphenate a compound adjective that starts with a word that ends in -ly, such as "highly skilled executive."

You should turn off the automatic hyphenation feature of word-processing programs to avoid excessive hyphenation of words in your résumé or cover letter. If you must hyphenate a word to avoid an extremely ragged right margin or rivers of white space with fully justified margins, do not do so on the first line or the last line of a paragraph. Divide words at the point of least confusion, always between syllables. Never hyphenate one-syllable words.

Numbers

There are several camps to align with when it comes to presenting numbers in writing. One style manual suggests spelling out numbers up to 100, as well as all round numbers above 100 that require no more than two words (such as *forty-four thousand,* where *forty-four* is counted as one word)— a method that's guaranteed to stretch your one-page résumé to two pages. If you choose to spell out numbers, spell only those from one through nine; then start with the Arabic version for 10, 11, and so on.

Still other writers prefer to use the Arabic form for all numbers. Their rationale is that the résumé is more of an advertising piece, which allows for liberal interpretation of formal grammar rules. Arabic numerals also attract the reader's attention more quickly than do numbers that are spelled out.

I sit on both sides of the fence on the numbers issue. When writing for senior executives, my tendency is to spell out numbers one through nine as a means of demonstrating the candidate's knowledge of business communications. When writing for disciplines such as sales or production, I believe the use of all Arabic numbers (1 through 9 included) picks up the pace for the reader and delivers an extra boost of energy to the résumé.

Parallel Sentence Structure

Parts of speech should be expressed in parallel form—in other words, verbs should be paralleled by verbs, adjectives by adjectives, nouns by nouns, and so on. Analyze the differences in these before-and-after examples.

Incorrect parallel verbs (infinitive phrase and participial phrase)

Aiming at higher profits, our programs have already begun *to increase efficiency* on the production line and *controlling costs* in purchasing.

Correct parallel verbs (two infinitive phrases)

Aiming at higher profits, our programs have already begun *to increase efficiency* on the production line and *control costs* in purchasing.

Incorrect parallel adjectives (adjective and noun)

The company's new products are *exciting* and a *sensation*.

Correct parallel adjectives

The company's new products are *exciting* and *sensational*.

Incorrect parallel nouns (noun and progressive verb)

Colleagues describe me as an advocate of *action* and *innovating*.

Correct parallel nouns

Colleagues describe me as an advocate of *action* and *innovation*.

When presenting a list of bulleted sentences, aim for parallelism by making the first word of each sentence the same type (all verbs, all nouns, and so on). This is not a hard-and-fast rule, especially when you're presenting a lengthy list of bullets (in which case, you should probably divide the list with subheadings for readability); however, you should definitely shoot for consistency in word form when presenting a short list with just three to five items. The *Before* example here is unsettling to read because each line begins with a different form of verb or noun.

Before

Contributions:

- *Charted* post-acquisition strategy for divestiture of nonperforming assets and reinvestment in high-performing assets.

- *Securing* new business with high-net-worth clients, adding multimillion-dollar properties to investment portfolio.

- *Enhancement* of asset value and revenue stream, in some cases generating as much as an eightfold increase in annual revenue.

Starting each line with the same verb form makes these contributions easier to digest.

After

Contributions:

- *Charted* post-acquisition strategy for divestiture of nonperforming assets and reinvestment in high-performing assets.

- *Secured* new business with high-net-worth clients, adding multimillion-dollar properties to investment portfolio.

- *Enhanced* asset value and revenue stream, in some cases generating as much as an eightfold increase in annual revenue.

The next *Before* and *After* set reveals another tack for correcting nonparallel sentence structure. The first Qualifications Summary begins with a smorgasbord of word forms (noun, verb, adjective).

Before

Qualifications Summary:

- Experienced *collections manager* with in-depth knowledge of consumer, real estate, credit card, and commercial credit.

- *Guide* members toward responsible action in their financial affairs as a proactive credit counselor.

- *Diligent* in researching with notable success in asset searches and skip traces.

Unlike most sentences that begin with action verbs, this new list illustrates how to start each line with a noun (modified by an adjective). The consistency in usage makes for a much smoother read than before.

After

Qualifications Summary:

- Experienced *collections manager* with in-depth knowledge of consumer, real estate, credit card, and commercial credit.

- Proactive *credit counselor* able to guide members toward responsible action in their financial affairs.

- Diligent *researcher* with notable success in asset searches and skip traces.

Parentheses

Use parentheses for subordination. When you use parentheses to enclose a complete sentence, place the period inside the parentheses, as in the second sentence of the following example.

> As a native of Minnesota, I look forward to returning to the Twin Cities and making a long-term commitment to the area. (My husband, a promotions director with Warner Brothers, accepted a promotion with the local affiliate and has already moved to Minneapolis.) If your calendar permits, I would like to meet during my next visit, scheduled for December 24 through January 12.

When you use parentheses at the end of a sentence—whether to enclose a phrase or a complete sentence—the period goes after the closing parenthesis.

> My generalist experience in human resources includes recruitment, benefits administration, and training and development (management team-building, technical skill development, and quality-improvement programs).

Parts of Speech

There are eight groupings of words that make up the parts of speech. Following is a quick primer that tells what each part does, gives examples, and advises on usage within the résumé or cover letter.

Part of Speech	Function	Examples	Advice for Use in Résumé or Cover Letter
Adjectives	Describe nouns	*exciting, challenging, outstanding, impressive, difficult, hard-hitting, excellent, top-performing, aggressive, seasoned*	Use sparingly; avoid more than two consecutive adjectives—in other words, don't say "Developed *innovative impressive, state-of-the-art* program" when one adjective would suffice. Best to substantiate adjectives with concrete proof—for instance, if you use the term *top-performing,* say "As a top-performing sales associate, led the region in product launches."

Part of Speech	Function	Examples	Advice for Use in Résumé or Cover Letter
Adverbs	Modify verbs, adjectives, or other adverbs	spoke *beautifully*, managed *assertively*, documented *meticulously*	Use sparingly; as with adjectives, best to document glowing adverbs with examples.
Conjunctions	Connect phrases or clauses	*and, but, or, nor, for, yet, so*	Punctuate properly (see colons and semicolons).
Interjections	Show emotion	*Wow!, Oh!, My!*	It's unlikely you'll use many interjections in your résumé or cover letter (more appropriate for writing to friends to describe the wonderful job offer you received).
Nouns	Name things	*computers, vendors, company, law firm, president, technician, background*	Use liberally; avoid abstract nouns (words such as *background, company,* and *technology,* which express ideas); instead, focus on tangible nouns or noun phrases (things you can touch or experience with your senses, such as *14 years in television advertising sales for ABC-affiliate KSWR*).
Prepositions	Show the relation of a noun to some other word	*at, by, in, to, near, from, with,* etc.	Avoid multiple prepositions in sentences; look for occurrences that you can turn into possessives.

(continued)

(continued)

Part of Speech	Function	Examples	Advice for Use in Résumé or Cover Letter
Pronouns	Are used in place of a noun; come in several classifications	Personal pronouns, I *you, he;* demonstrative pronouns, *this, that, these;* relative pronouns, *who, whose, whom;* interrogative pronouns, *who, which, what;* indefinite pronouns, *each, either, any, few, all*	Eliminate personal pronouns from your résumé; challenge yourself *not* to start the majority of sentences with *I* or *my* in the cover letter; use *your* to show an employer focus in the cover letter; when using a pronoun to refer to a company, use *it* rather than *they.*
Verbs	Express action	*manage, process, build, achieve, capture, deliver, assist, coordinate, design, review, approve*	Use liberally through-out résumé and cover letter; avoid helping verbs—forms of *to be* and *have* (see "Auxiliary or Helping Verbs," earlier in this chapter).

Passive Voice

You should avoid passive voice because it uses more words (and more space) and delivers less impact. The result is a weak, vague, or indirect writing style.

Passive

The report was presented by the sales manager.

Active

The sales manager presented the report.

In the preceding example, the verb *was presented* shows something being done to the subject of the sentence, *the report*. In the active example, components of the sentence are rearranged so that the subject, *the sales manager*, performs the action *presented*. Be on the lookout for tendencies toward passive voice, especially when writing your cover letter. If you have been careful to trim helping verbs and prepositional phrases from your résumé-speak, you will be less likely to fall into the passive voice.

Periods

Use a period at the end of every sentence with no space before it.

Incorrect

Our next project is on the calendar for March .

Correct

Our next project is on the calendar for March.

Omit periods after bulleted items that are not complete sentences.

Experienced in operating various business office equipment:

- multiline phones (up to 15 lines with 40 extensions)
- multitasking copiers/scanners/laser printers
- binding machinery
- computerized postage meters

Periods can be used after all entries in a bulleted list if one or more entry contains an additional separate phrase.

Contributions:

- Doubled enrollment in women's issues and anger-management groups.
- Started a new mentor program, teaming licensure candidates with veteran counselors. Analyzed the impact of this program.
- Conducted a community outreach campaign for spousal abuse that received considerable television and radio coverage.

How many spaces should you include after a period? Tradition held that a period at the end of a sentence should be followed by two spaces, but times are changing. Modern composition methods aim for close word spacing; so, in more and more business communications, the number of spaces after a sentence is being curtailed to just one. A line with narrow spacing between words is called a *close* line; a line with wide spacing is an *open* line. Too many open lines detract from readability and can lead to the phenomenon called a *river*—wide white spaces meandering vertically down the page. The reason for the change in spacing after periods is an attempt to shore up the banks of these rivers. One space after a period, rather than two, is especially helpful in avoiding excessive gaps in space caused by justified text (text with flush left and right margins).

Possessives

Possessives frequently cause trouble for those who don't get to practice their writing skills often. Formed by adding an apostrophe to a noun, the possessive form signals ownership or possession, thus the term *possessive*.

> The *company's performance* (meaning *the performance of the company*)

> *After one month's campaigning* (meaning *a campaign lasting for one month*).

> Within the *conglomerate's portfolio* (meaning *the portfolio of the conglomerate*)

Plural possessives are even more of a challenge for writers. The National Résumé Writers' Association (NRWA) publishes a Certification Study Guide for professional résumé writers who want to test for the Nationally Certified Résumé Writer credential. The grammar and punctuation section of the Certification Study Guide points out common errors with respect to plurals and possessives.

Incorrect
More than 12 years experience

Correct
More than 12 years' experience

Correct
More than 12 years of experience

In the second example, the apostrophe replaces the word *of.* The accuracy of this apostrophe is one of the most frequent questions I hear from job seekers. To understand how it works, reverse the phrase and look for a preposition. If *of* or *for* is in the picture, a possessive is required.

Original
My experience of 12 years

Plural possessive
My 12 years' experience

Substitution with other phrases reveals the same need for a possessive.

Original
The proposal from our three vice presidents was approved. [9 words]

Plural possessive

Our three vice presidents' proposal was approved. [7 words]

Possessives are popular in résumé writing because they lessen the number of words needed to express a thought. Compare how the use of a possessive shortens the preceding example from nine to seven words. When it comes to squeezing your professional life history onto a page or two, every word counts. One or two words often make the difference in saving an extra line of type.

Watch out for these common mistakes when it comes to using apostrophes.

- **Plurals:** If a word ends in "s" (such as "achievements," "responsibilities," or "qualifications"), it does not necessarily need an apostrophe. To check whether a word ending in "s" warrants an apostrophe, ask yourself this question: Is it a case of one versus two or more (one achievement versus two achievements)? If yes, an apostrophe is not necessary.

- **It's vs. its:** Use an apostrophe for the contraction *it's,* meaning "it is." Do not use an apostrophe when *its* refers to possession, such as "we are proud of its special place in history." To help you remember this rule, ask yourself this question: Does the word with an apostrophe (it's) make sense if I split it into two words (it is)? For instance, it would not make sense to say "we are proud of it is special place in history"; therefore, no apostrophe is necessary.

Prepositions

Prepositions are connective words such as *at, by, in, to, from,* and *with.* To prune your writing, watch for multiple prepositions in the same sentence. There will often be opportunities to combine or rephrase them to shorten your sentence.

Before

Trained personnel *on* the business aspects *of* the company that fell outside *of* their typical business orientation.

After

Trained personnel in cross-functional business areas.

In your quest to weed out unnecessary prepositions, watch that you don't omit essential prepositions.

Incorrect

Our campaign received attention in newspapers, periodicals, and on talk radio.

Correct

Our campaign received attention in newspapers, in periodicals, and on talk radio.

Incorrect

My commitment and track record for developing innovative campaigns are unmatched.

Correct

My commitment to, and track record for, developing innovative campaigns are unmatched.

When deciding whether the preposition *to* is needed after the word *commitment,* say the sentence aloud without the words that make up the second phrase *(and track record).* Doing so is your clue that another preposition is in order because it is clumsy to say *My commitment <u>for</u> developing innovative campaigns is unmatched.* Set off the phrase with commas (before and after) if the phrase interrupts the flow of the sentence.

Can you end a sentence with a preposition? Yes. Your writing will appear stilted if you adhere to the never-end-a-sentence-with-a-preposition myth.

Stilted

Your organization has much of which to be proud.

Acceptable

Your organization has much to be proud of.

Stilted

Your proposal for contract work is definitely something into which I will look.

Acceptable

Your proposal for contract work is definitely worth looking into.

Stilted

Your employees need tools with which to work. As your trainer, I can provide multimedia seminars that are interactive, entertaining, and educational.

Acceptable

Your employees need tools to work with. As your trainer, I can provide multimedia seminars that are interactive, entertaining, and educational.

Quotation Marks

Quotation marks indicate that you are using someone else's words exactly as spoken or written. You should place periods and commas before the closing quotation mark (this practice dates back to the days when typesetters placed the larger quotation character after the smaller period character to help prevent the period from literally dropping off the line of type). Semicolons and colons are placed after the closing quotation mark. Do not put a space between the quotation mark and words or punctuation. Use curly quotes rather than straight quotes (straight quotes are the symbol for "inches").

Straight quotes, incorrect spacing around quotation marks

A key client, the vice president of purchasing at Baxter Bros., indicated that I was " the best sales rep he had come across in 20 years of doing business. "

Curly quotes

An excerpt from a recent performance evaluation written by my supervisor indicates I am "ready, willing, and able for any and all challenges"; at the end of my three-month probationary period, I am confident you will write the same.

Quotation marks are also appropriate for coined words or business jargon not likely to be familiar to your reader.

Our R&D team pioneered "edutainment" software, providing young learners with interactive multimedia that is both educational and, in the words of my 5-year-old, "a blast to operate."

Sentence Fragments

A sentence fragment is a phrase or clause that is treated as a separate sentence when it should be incorporated with adjacent words to make up a complete sentence. Avoid fragments in résumé and cover letter writing.

Sentence fragment

Completion of inventory processing.

Fragment repaired

I forwarded materials to customers on completion of inventory processing.

Slashes

This punctuation mark is known by a number of names, such as diagonal, slant, slash, solidus, and virgule. With the advent of World Wide Web addresses, *slash* seems to have become the term of choice (using the term *solidus* in pronouncing http://www.topresume.com/ is a tongue-twister). Along with the slash's multiple names, it has multiple uses. *The Gregg Reference Manual* (McGraw-Hill/Irwin) suggests a slash for these uses:

- To express alternatives (stop/start, and/or, inside/outside)
- To indicate that a person or thing has two functions or components (partner/general manager, client/server network)
- To represent the word *per*

The Chicago Manual of Style adds four more uses:

> To signify alternative word forms or spellings (purchasing/procurement, materials/materiels); to indicate a period extending over portions of two calendar years (fiscal year 1994/95); as shorthand ($450/week, c/o); or to mean "divided by" in a fraction (1/25).

Dr. David Noble, author of *Gallery of Best Resumes* and *Gallery of Best Cover Letters,* advises writers to think twice before using *and/or,* with this rationale:

> "This stilted expression is commonly misunderstood to mean two alternatives, but it literally means three.... Example: If you don't hear from me by Friday, please phone and/or fax me the information on Monday.... The sentence really states three alternatives: just phone, just fax, or phone and fax."

You can eliminate the confusion associated with the use of *and/or* by using just one of the connectives—*and* or *or*—but not both.

When typing a slash, make sure that it is leaning forward (/) and not backward (\). Do not insert spaces on either side of the slash. There are exceptions to this rule: Use spaces on both sides of a slash in a heading to increase readability of the words, and use spaces throughout body text when the résumé will be scanned. In the latter case, there will be less likelihood the scanner will misinterpret the slash as part of the prior or subsequent characters.

Split Infinitives

Infinitives refer to a verb form. When you precede a verb with the word *to,* you have formed an infinitive *(to manage).* Splitting infinitives refers to placing an adverb between the *to* and the verb. Do your best to avoid split infinitives. First, try other placements of the adverb—after the object of the verb, immediately following the verb, or immediately before the verb.

Incorrect

Before making a decision, I want *to thoroughly tour* the facility.

Correct

Before making a decision, I want *to tour* the facility *thoroughly*.

If alternative placements are awkward or confusing, then split the infinitive.

Awkward

I was advised *to negotiate carefully* contracts for commodity exports because they would affect the company's financial stability.

Confusing

I was advised *to negotiate* contracts for commodity exports *carefully* because they would affect the company.

Correctly split infinitive

I was advised *to carefully negotiate* contracts for commodity exports because they would affect the company.

When two infinitives appear in a series, it is not necessary to write the word *to* for the second or subsequent references unless you want to do so for special emphasis.

Incorrect

With four weeks to deadline, I had to solicit, to train, and to delegate assignments to volunteers.

Correct

With four weeks to deadline, I had to solicit, train, and delegate assignments to volunteers.

Tense

Tense (not to be confused with the feeling you are inclined to have prior to walking into an interview) refers to the property of a verb that expresses time. There are 14 tenses in English, only a few of which you'll be concerned with in writing your résumé. Use them appropriately to convey when you did something (past tense), when you are in the midst of doing something (present tense), and when you are planning to do something (future tense).

Name of Tense	Example	Where to Use in Résumé/Cover Letter	Example of Usage
Present tense	I manage	Present job description	Manage shipping operations for agricultural export operation.
		Current accomplishments	Hold record for lowest cost ratio among four national facilities.
Past tense	I managed	Past job descriptions	Managed warehouse operations for 500,000-sq.-ft. distribution facility servicing five Western states.
		Past accomplishments	Improved inventory record accuracy from 72% to 97%.
Future tense	I will manage	Cover letter	I will guarantee a similar record of contributions with your firm.
Present progressive	I am managing	Description of activities currently in progress	Managing 9-month, $2.5 million construction project that will double warehouse area and allow for sophisticated atmospheric/ quality controls.
Past progressive	I was managing	Description of past activities	Implementing structured processes and procedures (cycle counting, input/output controls) for ISO compliance.

Verbs

Verbs are either active or passive (see "Active Voice" and "Passive Voice" earlier in this chapter). Résumé-speak calls for beginning sentences with action verbs. Glance at appendix C for a list of action verbs for disciplines such as administration, communications, finance, management, sales, teaching, technical, and general professions. As often as possible, use the present or past tense of the word rather than a noun or gerund.

Present: manage

Past: managed

Noun: management

Gerund: managing

Some verbs are easily confused and misused. Make sure you have these puzzling pairs straight.

adverse (noun meaning antagonistic, hostile, harmful)
averse (to oppose or have a feeling of dislike)

affect (to have an influence on, to touch or move the emotions of)
effect (to produce as a result, cause to occur, bring about; also used as a noun, as in "special effects")

appraise (to evaluate, estimate, or judge)
apprise (to inform or give notice)

assure (to inform confidently, to convince)
ensure (to make sure or certain of, to make certain that)
insure (to cover with insurance, to guarantee, to make safe or secure)

choose (to select)
chose (the past tense of choose)

complement (to add to, complete, or bring to perfection)
compliment (to express praise, admiration, or congratulation)

emerge (to come into sight, to rise up or come forth, to become evident or obvious)
immerse (to involve profoundly, to submerge or cover completely with a liquid)

imply (to involve or suggest by logical necessity, to hint, to suggest)
infer (to conclude from evidence or deduce)

lay (to put or place)
lie (to recline, rest, or stay)

raise (to lift or cause to lift)
rise (to ascend, to increase in value)

Writing in the First Person

In grammar, *person* refers to whether a person is speaking (which is referred to as *first person*) or is spoken about (which is referred to as *third person*). Preferred résumé-speak calls for writing in the first person. You can test for first person by silently inserting the personal pronoun "I" in front of the verb that starts the sentence.

Incorrect

("I") Manages plant operations.

Correct

("I") Manage plant operations.

If the pronoun *I* fits in front of the verb, you have written in first person. Alternatively, if the personal pronoun *he* or *she* fits, you have written in third person. This job description for a teacher was written in third person.

Before

Teaches two sections of EHD50, an undergraduate education course designed to introduce prospective teaching candidates to the profession. Places, supervises, and evaluates 125 students at various school sites and works closely with district staff to coordinate students' initial teaching assignments. Provides staff development at both the district and university level. Advises Multiple Subject Credentialing Committee in realigning university elementary education delivery program. Contributes to university Department of Education committees involved with multiple and single-subject curriculum and credentialing.

To shift from third to first person, remove the "s" or "es" at the end of the verbs.

After

> Teach two sections of EHD50, an undergraduate education course designed to introduce prospective teaching candidates to the profession. Place, supervise, and evaluate 125 students at various school sites and work closely with district staff to coordinate students' initial teaching assignments. Provide staff development at both the district and university level. Advise Multiple Subject Credentialing Committee in realigning university elementary education delivery program. Contribute to university Department of Education committees involved with multiple and single-subject curriculum and credentialing.

Be thorough when converting copy from third person to first person. People have a tendency to correct the first verb in the sentence and overlook those that might follow, such as in the second sentence of the preceding example. Here, the candidate has three verbs to adjust beyond the initial verb *place*.

The third-person presentation was popular in the 1980s when executive recruiters frequently prepared résumés for their candidates. The benefit of this technique is that the credibility of statements made in the résumé is elevated because a supposed objective bystander is singing your praises. There are also drawbacks:

- You distance yourself from the reader, giving the impression that an intermediary or agent is required to present and interpret your skills.

- You give the reader no clue about your writing skills because the résumé was presumably prepared by someone else.

If you are an executive exploring new challenges through the screen of an executive recruiter, you might want to consider writing your résumé in the third person. Even so, you lose the "reach-out-and-touch" feel that comes from writing in the more traditional first person.

Prune, Prune, Prune

After using the tips outlined in the preceding sections, reread your résumé for the express purpose of spotting redundancies. Your mission is to spot and correct these common errors:

- Words that repeat themselves throughout the résumé—substitute with an alternative keyword or eliminate them.

- Words that repeat themselves within the same sentence—avoid using the same word twice in a sentence.

- Concepts that repeat themselves—eliminate duplications.

- Excessive use of prepositional phrases—test whether you can rework them into a possessive (see the section on possessives earlier in this chapter).

The following are a few examples of redundancies and how to eliminate them.

Before

California State University, Fullerton, Fullerton, CA

After

California State University, Fullerton

Before

University of California, San Francisco, California

After

University of California—San Francisco

Before

Increased sales by 20%.

After

Increased sales 20%.

Before

Managed purchasing and procurement functions for supplier with more than 4,000 items in product line that was doing an average annual purchasing volume of more than $500,000. [27 words]

After

Managed procurement for supplier with 4,000+ items; annual purchasing volume exceeded $500,000. [12 words]

Before

I believe in a straightforward and honest approach to mediation for soliciting cooperation and collaboration of all environmental and business concerns in developing a "win-win" situation. [26 words]

After

Using a candid, collaborative mediation style, I have brought together opposing environmental and business interests to yield "win-win" outcomes. [19 words]

Before

Accomplished company CEO who turned a stagnant furniture company into the largest furniture dealer in the country. [17 words]

After

Accomplished CEO who turned a stagnant furniture company into the nation's largest dealer. [13 words]

For paring some commonly used but wordy phrases, use these tips from David F. Noble, Ph.D., author of *Gallery of Best Resumes* and instructor of business communication, technical writing, and professional editing.

Wordy Phrase	Pruned Phrase
at the location of	at
for the reason that	because
in a short time	soon
in a timely manner	on time
in spite of everything to the contrary	nevertheless
in the event of	if
in the proximity of	near
now and then	occasionally
on a daily basis	daily
on a regular basis	regularly
on account of	because
one day from now	tomorrow
would you be so kind as to	please

Now that you've learned to write succinctly, or, on account of the fact that, and in the event of possible typos, in the immediate future it will be necessary to read on a thorough basis at the location of the next section, so would you be so kind as to...

Proof, Proof, Proof

Last in the editing process; proof, proof, proof—and proof again. By far, the biggest pet peeve employers named in the résumé survey was typos. Your résumé is a representation of your *best work*—it must be error-free. Use your computer's spelling checker and grammar checker, but don't rely on them entirely. They are fallible, as the unknown author of this poem proves.

I have a spelling checker,
It came with my PC;
It plainly marks four MI revue,
Mistakes I dew not sea.
I've run this poem write threw it,
I'm sure your pleas too no,
Its letter perfect in it's weigh,
My checker tolled me sew.

Because you have worked diligently on your résumé, you are too close to the project to manage this all-important task on your own. Enlist the aid of a competent reader: a trusted business person who writes for a living, an English teacher, an editor, a certified résumé writer. . . someone whose eyes don't glaze over when you ask for assistance identifying split infinitives, comma splices, or passive voice. One tiny comma misplaced, one letter transposed, or one word misused can honestly make the difference between getting an invitation to interview or getting a "Dear John/Jane" letter.

Top 10 Résumé Proofreading Tips

Use this 10-step list for proofreading your résumé:

1. Print out the résumé. (It's easier to spot typos on a piece of paper than it is on a computer screen.)

2. Read it slowly, one word at a time. Give special attention to these items:

   - Dates of employment

   - Phone numbers and e-mail address (Pick up the phone and call the numbers you have listed. Send an e-mail to the e-mail address listed.)

   - Spelling of proper nouns (Check your name, employers, cities.)

   - Headings (If one category heading is boldfaced and underlined, are all boldfaced and underlined? Have you duplicated a category heading?)

   - Consistency of formatting (If one employer entry is indented half an inch, are all indented half an inch?)

3. Mark any changes on the proof with a pen. (Use ink colors like green or red to help changes stand out.)

4. Read it backwards, one word at a time. (This process forces you to look at each word, rather than each sentence, where your brain can "fill in" information because it knows what the sentence is supposed to mean. Starting at the bottom of the résumé, take a business card or similar-sized piece of paper and cover up all but the last word. Read that word. Is it spelled correctly? Uncover the next-to-last word. Is it spelled correctly? Repeat this process for every word on the page. Mark any changes on the proof with a pen.)

5. Make the changes to the document on your computer.

6. Print it again.

7. Read it again.

8. Compare the proof version with pen marks to the new proof. Check off that each correction was made, and that when you made the correction, you didn't cause another problem elsewhere on the résumé.

9. Let it sit overnight. (Looking at it with fresh eyes can make all the difference.)

10. Ask two other capable proofreaders to read it with a critical eye.

Visual Artistry: The Missing Link

"People forget how fast you did a job—but they remember how well you did it."

—Howard W. Newton, American Advertising Executive

How do you impress employers *before* they ever read your résumé? Just like the marketing wizards and advertising gurus do—with visual appeal.

Imagine that it is your sweetheart's birthday and you've just stepped into a gourmet shop to find a little gift. The display of chocolates catches your eye. Some come wrapped in rich-looking gold foil, some are cradled in heart-shaped boxes, and some are packaged to give you a glimpse of the goodies inside. On the shelf beneath these enticing temptations is a stack of plain boxes wrapped in what looks to be white butcher paper; unadorned print spells out the words "chocolate candy." The sales clerk approaches and asks whether there is anything he can help you with. You inquire about the chocolates and learn that they are all priced the same (even the generic-looking selection on the bottom shelf). The sales clerk further enlightens you that, without question, the chocolates in the white butcher paper far-and-above taste the best. But you had your heart set on the pretty ones in the gold foil! Now what? With our sweethearts none the wiser, many of us would opt for the nicely packaged gift to make a better impression.

357

Although you (and your résumé) are not a commodity, the hiring process has some parallels to the chocolate scenario. Visual appeal is critical, yet both novice and experienced writers often disregard it. This artistry is frequently the missing link in a résumé's evolution from average to outstanding.

If your experience and credentials are impressive, visual appeal will enhance them. If you have some minor flaws or even a glaring hole in your background, visual appeal can help overcome those weaknesses. Without visual appeal, you will look homogenous (at best) amid the stack of your competitors. With visual appeal, you win that all-important, never-to-have-a-second-chance-at favorable first impression. Essentially, visual appeal allows you to out-position your competition at the starting gate, an enviable position to be in because front-runners frequently win the race.

What exactly is visual appeal? Albeit somewhat intangible, visual appeal is the quality that classifies your résumé as "pretty." Visual appeal can also mean that your résumé looks easy to read. It extends an invitation and offers a measure of energy to help the reader get started reading. It gives the impression of "wow, this is impressive" *before* the reader ever scans one word. Although visual appeal is subjective, there are a few objective, tangible principles that you can rely on to improve the attractiveness of your résumé. Let's take a look at them.

Design Elements

Like your wardrobe, your résumé should *fit* you. The résumé design for an established business-law attorney applying to an old-line Boston firm will be different from that of a Generation-X Webmaster applying to an Internet service provider. There is no one-size-fits-all design. With the capabilities of word-processing and desktop-publishing software, the possibilities for design variations are endless. If your word-processing program includes résumé templates, you might want to experiment with them. They tend to work best if you have a strong, progressive work history. If you don't fall into this category (and you don't know how to customize the template to your needs), the template designs can be limiting.

There are a number of traditional and not-so-traditional résumé designs throughout this book. In reviewing the résumés, look for the following design elements, which transform good résumés into gorgeous résumés:

★ Visual pattern

★ Balance and symmetry

★ Tasteful font-work

Create a Visual Pattern

Remember those fashion no-no's your mother nagged you about? Don't wear white shoes with a dark, winter print. Don't wear horizontal stripes if you're trying to camouflage a few extra pounds. Never mix paisley print with buffalo plaid. A few fashion tips can help your résumé earn a place on the best-dressed list. In this section on visual pattern, you'll learn how to use tabs, create white space, accentuate important text with bullets, organize information into groups of threes, and other important techniques for creating a visual pattern.

Before getting into these pointers, we'll look at the critical role that consistency plays in attractive formatting. It's important that you select a pattern and stick with it. You can be creative in your design, but you must be rigid in your application of it. In other words, you can choose from a number of fonts, tab sets, and special treatments to dress up your copy; however, once you have made those choices, don't introduce new combinations somewhere else in the résumé.

Consistency Counts

Design consistency can make a résumé more visually palatable and give your reader a sense of order, logic, and purpose. Although readers are primarily looking at the content of your résumé, they also can tell certain things about you from the appearance of your résumé. Though not a sure-fire determinant, the appearance might tell the reader that you know better than mixing paisley and plaid. With that in mind, be sure to do the following:

- Use the same font and point size for each and every heading throughout the résumé.

- Use the same font for all body copy throughout the résumé (occasional use of italic within the same font family is acceptable).

- Use the same amount of line space between headings and copy for each and every entry.

- Use the same line spacing between headings and horizontal rule lines for each and every category.

- Use consistent tab sets and bullet styles for all bulleted items within a category heading.

Use Tab Stops Sparingly

To create a pleasing visual pattern, limit your use of tab stops. Depending on the design you choose, you might need only two or three (this number will increase if you use two or three columns of bulleted items under a heading). Every tab stop on the page gives the reader another invisible vertical line to visually absorb. Limited use of tab stops (two or three) minimizes these invisible yet discernible markers. Excessive use of tab stops erodes the sense of pattern.

Wise Use of Tab Stops Improved Terrence's Résumé

Magic

The next *Before* résumé (see Résumé 8.1) illustrates the vertical vertigo effect. The Qualifications Summary uses three columns for keyword items, Accomplishments start at two different tab stops, and Education uses yet another tab stop. In the *After* version (see Résumé 8.2), only three tab stops are used throughout the résumé. The left column of keywords in the boxed summary lines up with the bulleted text in the Experience section, giving the eye one less vertical line to deal with. The Education section is centered, tying the format to the beginning of the page, which also uses centered text. Full justification is also used to help visually define the right margin.

Accomplishments are indented equal amounts on both sides to complement the centering done elsewhere in the résumé. A similar style of bullet is used for the second bullet, instead of mixing squares and circles, as seen in the earlier version.

Apply White Space Liberally

White space—crucial to accentuating visual pattern—refers to any space on the page that is not covered by type. Proper positioning of white space can significantly enhance the readability and appeal of your résumé. The Professional Association of Résumé Writers concurs. In its examination for the Certified Professional Résumé Writer status, writers are graded on a number of criteria for their preparation of a fictitious résumé—white space and readability are an important component. While serving as an evaluator for PARW's and NRWA's certification boards, I repeatedly saw this visual pitfall—insufficient white space—even among experienced writers.

It is a challenge to find the balance between adequate white space and thorough content in a one-page résumé. To squeeze out maximum white space, you'll need to become friends with some of the lesser-known functions of your word-processing software. Relying solely on the default line spacing to create white space is akin to wearing a baseball glove to take a splinter out of a child's toe: It won't do the trick.

The next two *Before* résumé excerpts (on page 363) demonstrate the limitations of default settings. The first is presented with only single spacing between paragraphs; the second, with double spacing. Written for an executive, the longer, semi-narrative copy is characteristic of résumés for senior-level officers conducting their searches exclusively through retained recruiters. The large amount of text makes readability all the more important.

Résumé 8.1: Before

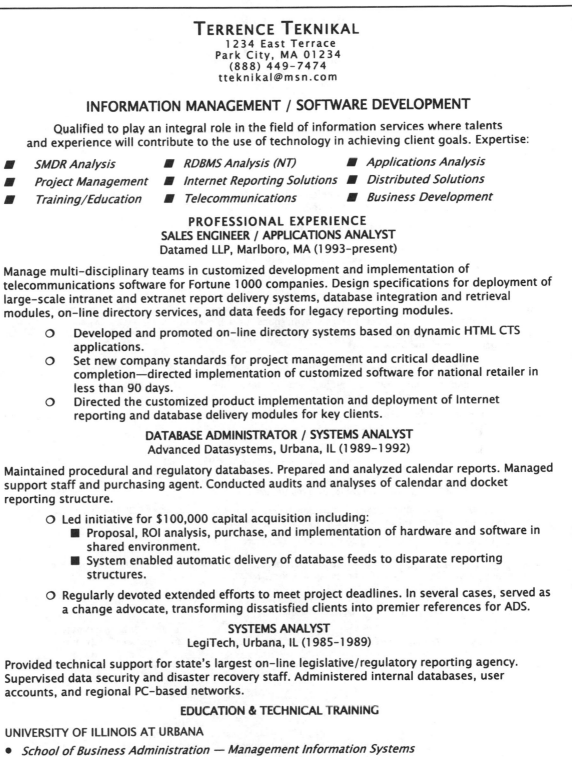

TERRENCE TEKNIKAL
1234 East Terrace
Park City, MA 01234
(888) 449-7474
tteknikal@msn.com

INFORMATION MANAGEMENT / SOFTWARE DEVELOPMENT

Qualified to play an integral role in the field of information services where talents
and experience will contribute to the use of technology in achieving client goals. Expertise:

- *SMDR Analysis*
- *Project Management*
- *Training/Education*
- *RDBMS Analysis (NT)*
- *Internet Reporting Solutions*
- *Telecommunications*
- *Applications Analysis*
- *Distributed Solutions*
- *Business Development*

PROFESSIONAL EXPERIENCE
SALES ENGINEER / APPLICATIONS ANALYST
Datamed LLP, Marlboro, MA (1993-present)

Manage multi-disciplinary teams in customized development and implementation of
telecommunications software for Fortune 1000 companies. Design specifications for deployment of
large-scale intranet and extranet report delivery systems, database integration and retrieval
modules, on-line directory services, and data feeds for legacy reporting modules.

- Developed and promoted on-line directory systems based on dynamic HTML CTS
  applications.
- Set new company standards for project management and critical deadline
  completion—directed implementation of customized software for national retailer in
  less than 90 days.
- Directed the customized product implementation and deployment of Internet
  reporting and database delivery modules for key clients.

DATABASE ADMINISTRATOR / SYSTEMS ANALYST
Advanced Datasystems, Urbana, IL (1989-1992)

Maintained procedural and regulatory databases. Prepared and analyzed calendar reports. Managed
support staff and purchasing agent. Conducted audits and analyses of calendar and docket
reporting structure.

- Led initiative for $100,000 capital acquisition including:
  - Proposal, ROI analysis, purchase, and implementation of hardware and software in
    shared environment.
  - System enabled automatic delivery of database feeds to disparate reporting
    structures.
- Regularly devoted extended efforts to meet project deadlines. In several cases, served as
  a change advocate, transforming dissatisfied clients into premier references for ADS.

SYSTEMS ANALYST
LegiTech, Urbana, IL (1985-1989)

Provided technical support for state's largest on-line legislative/regulatory reporting agency.
Supervised data security and disaster recovery staff. Administered internal databases, user
accounts, and regional PC-based networks.

EDUCATION & TECHNICAL TRAINING

UNIVERSITY OF ILLINOIS AT URBANA

- *School of Business Administration — Management Information Systems*

- *School of Computer Science and Engineering — Computer Science*

Portfolio Available

Résumé 8.2: After

TERRENCE TEKNIKAL

1234 East Terrace
Park City, MA 01234
(888) 449-7474
tteknikal@msn.com

INFORMATION MANAGEMENT / SOFTWARE DEVELOPMENT

Qualified to play an integral role in the field of information services where talents and experience will contribute to the use of technology in achieving client goals. Expertise:

☐ SMDR Analysis	☐ RDBMS Analysis (NT)	☐ Applications Analysis
☐ Project Management	☐ Internet Reporting Solutions	☐ Distributed Solutions
☐ Training/Education	☐ Telecommunications	☐ Business Development

PROFESSIONAL EXPERIENCE

SALES ENGINEER / APPLICATIONS ANALYST
Datamed LLP, Marlboro, MA (1993-Present)

Manage multidisciplinary teams in customized development, implementation, and service of telecommunications software for Fortune 1000 companies. Design specifications for deployment of large-scale intranet and extranet report delivery systems, including database integration and retrieval modules, online directory services, and data feeds for legacy reporting modules.

- Developed and promoted online directory systems based on dynamic HTML CTS applications.

- Set new company standards for project management and critical deadline completion—directed implementation of customized software for national retailer in less than 90 days.

- Directed the customized product design, implementation, and deployment of Internet reporting and database delivery modules for key clients.

DATABASE ADMINISTRATOR / SYSTEMS ANALYST
Advanced Datasystems, Urbana, IL (1989-1992)

Maintained six procedural and regulatory databases. Managed four support staff and purchasing agent. Conducted audits and analyses of calendar and docket reporting structure.

- Led initiative for $100,000 IT capital acquisition—researched vendors, analyzed ROI, purchased equipment, and implemented hardware and software in shared environment.

- Introduced automatic delivery of database feeds to disparate reporting structures.

- Regularly devoted extended efforts to meet project deadlines. In several cases, served as a change advocate, transforming dissatisfied clients into premier references for ADS.

SYSTEMS ANALYST
LegiTech, Urbana, IL (1985-1989)

Provided technical support for state's largest legislative/regulatory reporting agency. Supervised data security and disaster recovery staff. Administered three internal databases, user accounts, and regional PC networks.

EDUCATION & TECHNICAL TRAINING

UNIVERSITY OF ILLINOIS AT URBANA

School of Business Administration — Management Information Systems
School of Computer Science and Engineering — Computer Science

☐ ☐ ☐

Before

Brought on board to manage pivotal transition associated with expiration of critical patent and to correct operational issues affecting both customer satisfaction and profit. Manage bicoastal manufacturing and distribution centers; supervise 8 direct reports (managers of east coast and west coast operations, supply chain management, production, marketing, sales, distribution, and international service operations); and am accountable for 67 indirect reports. Lead virtual solution teams in reconstruction of all business applications. Supervise manufacturing group operating high-performance production lines (proprietary technology unique to industry). Direct sales and marketing for Australian subsidiary.

- *Revenue Performance and Profit Improvement:* Exceeded annual revenue plan, recapturing a 20% lag in year-to-date figures upon accepting post. Cut pricing of raw material resins for hard dollar savings of nearly $2 million.
- *Sales and Marketing:* Led marketing and sales initiative, shifting from premium pricing to competitive pricing in anticipation of patent expiration; identified broader market component as focus for new business development (a $1 billion domestic market). Led marketing initiative for start-up Australian division that boosted sales approximately 48%.
- *Operational Reengineering:* Inherited open order file approaching $8 million with 80% back orders—reduced to $2.5 million with 25% back order. Corrected inventory position from $15 million to $8.5-$10.5 million with appropriate mix. Put expandable procedures in place to sustain aggressive growth (projected for continued annual growth of 28%).
- *Technology Advances:* Initiated technology advances—in less than 5 months, put primary planning systems in place and positioned company to implement world-class ERP system (a $1 million BaaN program).
- *Team-Building:* Created concept for Business Unit Manager, a position cross-pollinated over organizational lines to facilitate rapid decision making. Transitioned workforce into diverse, highly skilled team committed to growth initiatives.

Now the same text, with corrections and double-spaced between paragraphs to add white space.

Before

Brought on board to manage pivotal transition associated with expiration of critical patent and to correct operational issues affecting both customer satisfaction and profit. Manage bicoastal manufacturing and distribution centers; supervise 8 direct reports (managers of east coast and west coast operations, supply chain management, production, marketing, sales, distribution, and international service operations); and am accountable for 67 indirect reports. Lead virtual solution teams in reconstruction of all business applications. Supervise manufacturing group operating high-performance production lines (proprietary technology unique to industry). Direct sales and marketing for Australian subsidiary.

- *Revenue Performance and Profit Improvement:* Exceeded annual revenue plan, recapturing a 20% lag in year-to-date figures upon accepting post. Cut pricing of raw material resins for hard dollar savings of nearly $2 million.

- *Sales and Marketing:* Led marketing and sales initiative, shifting from premium pricing to competitive pricing in anticipation of patent expiration; identified broader market component as focus for new business development (a $1 billion domestic market). Led marketing initiative for start-up Australian division that boosted sales approximately 48%.

- *Operational Reengineering:* Inherited open order file approaching $8 million with 80% back orders—reduced to $2.5 million with 25% back order. Corrected inventory position from $15 million to $8.5-$10.5 million with appropriate mix. Put expandable procedures in place to sustain aggressive growth (projected for continued annual growth of 28%).

- ***Technology Advances:*** Initiated technology advances—in less than 5 months, put primary planning systems in place and positioned company to implement world-class ERP system (a $1 million BaaN program).

- ***Team-Building:*** Created concept for Business Unit Manager, a position cross-pollinated over organizational lines to facilitate rapid decision making. Transitioned workforce into diverse, highly skilled team committed to growth initiatives.

Clearly, the second of these two presentations is easier to read. The catch-22 comes when you realize that the double-spaced version will push a one-page résumé over to a second page, and a two-page résumé to three or four pages. The above double-spaced example requires about 1½ inches more vertical space than its predecessor. This is a good amount of distance to sacrifice when you consider that, after subtracting top and bottom margins and your name and address, you have just 8 inches of sell-time in a one-page résumé.

The solution is to massage the between-paragraph spacing. Once again, here is the executive's excerpt, this time with adjustments between paragraphs reduced to approximately one-half of a traditional double space after responsibilities and one-third of a traditional double space between accomplishments. This solution buys back about .6 inches of space from the *Before* version immediately above and still allows readers to take a visual breath between paragraphs.

After

Brought on board to manage pivotal transition associated with expiration of critical patent and to correct operational issues affecting both customer satisfaction and profit. Manage bicoastal manufacturing and distribution centers; supervise 8 direct reports (managers of east coast and west coast operations, supply chain management, production, marketing, sales, distribution, and international service operations); and am accountable for 67 indirect reports. Lead virtual solution teams in reconstruction of all business applications. Supervise manufacturing group operating high-performance production lines (proprietary technology unique to industry). Direct sales and marketing for Australian subsidiary.

- ***Revenue Performance and Profit Improvement:*** Exceeded annual revenue plan, recapturing a 20% lag in year-to-date figures upon accepting post. Cut pricing of raw material resins for hard dollar savings of nearly $2 million.

- ***Sales and Marketing:*** Led marketing and sales initiative, shifting from premium pricing to competitive pricing in anticipation of patent expiration; identified broader market component as focus for new business development (a $1 billion domestic market). Led marketing initiative for start-up Australian division that boosted sales approximately 48%.

- ***Operational Reengineering:*** Inherited open order file approaching $8 million with 80% back orders—reduced to $2.5 million with 25% back order. Corrected inventory position from $15 million to $8.5-$10.5 million with appropriate mix. Put expandable procedures in place to sustain aggressive growth (projected for continued annual growth of 28%).

- ***Technology Advances:*** Initiated technology advances—in less than 5 months, put primary planning systems in place and positioned company to implement world-class ERP system (a $1 million BaaN program).

- ***Team-Building:*** Created concept for Business Unit Manager, a position cross-pollinated over organizational lines to facilitate rapid decision making. Transitioned workforce into diverse, highly skilled team committed to growth initiatives.

White space works wonders! You can learn the word-processing function keys and commands to manipulate this magic later in the chapter (see "Tweaking Tips").

Make Bullets Work for You

Major word-processing programs offer automatic bullets at the click of a button. Many people get carried away with the bullet feature because it is so easy (and admittedly fun!) to use. Those who do get carried away end up with what I call a "polka dot" résumé—the type where every paragraph or sentence is preceded by a bullet. Avoid the temptation to do this.

Before

PROFESSIONAL EXPERIENCE

UNICEF — NATIONAL HEADQUARTERS
Acting Division Director

Responsibilities
- Closely coordinate all activities of the division, maintaining excellent communications with both the Emergency Services and Hunger Relief management teams.
- Oversee a $4 million departmental budget and exercise positive control of expenditures.
- Update the Vice President of Emergency Services on activities of the division and make management recommendations as appropriate.
- Ensure national collaborations and strategic alliances are maintained and coordinated.
- Provide supervisory oversight and support to 42 staff.
- Ensure that timely and accurate communications with internal and external units and customers are achieved.

Achievements
- Oversaw the relocation of 40 departmental staff and supporting materials and equipment to new corporate site.
- All staff mid-year Work Performance Appraisals completed on time.

Along with an edited Responsibilities section and an elaboration on Accomplishments, the *After* version shows how bullets were used to accent the candidate's three key skill areas and draw the reader's eye to specific accomplishments that substantiate those areas. It helped the candidate land a coveted promotion in her organization.

After

QUALIFICATIONS SUMMARY

QUALIFIED FOR UNICEF'S EXECUTIVE MANAGEMENT TEAM based on my 16–year history with the organization and ardent commitment to its cause. Strengths:

- division operations management
    - integrated program and service delivery
        - emergency services and hunger relief program management

PROFESSIONAL EXPERIENCE

UNICEF — NATIONAL HEADQUARTERS

Acting Division Director

Hands-on executive with excellent performance record in strategic planning, development, and leadership at division and national levels. Supervise teams of 40+. Promote communications with internal customers, external customers, and vendors. Foster national collaborations, strategic alliances, and partnership programs. Garner senior management approval for long-range strategic plans. Well-versed in program management (conceptual design, programming, internal communications, technical/administrative support, follow-up).

- **Operations Management:** Selected for interim management assignments, influencing positive change for chapters in transition or need of operational and financial turnaround. Completed recent fiscal year $100,000 under budget.

- **Program and Service Delivery:** Increased Customer Satisfaction Survey scores to 89%, an improvement of 8%. Oversaw relocation of 42 departmental staff, materials, and equipment to new corporate site, meeting all project benchmarks.

- **Emergency Services Management:** Established support systems and supervised service delivery to accommodate three concurrent national disasters.

Bullets signal to your reader that something important and impressive follows. Overusing them only detracts from the meatier portions of your résumé. Consider reserving bullets for accomplishments or relatively short lists.

When it comes to mixing bullets on the same page, stay with a graphical theme throughout your résumé. The oversized bullet in the Qualifications section above is used as a design element; a smaller bullet with a similar style complements it in the Accomplishments section. A résumé with three different types and sizes of bullets is overly accessorized. If your content calls for three different types of bullets, start with the heaviest bullet in the Qualifications section, a lighter bullet for accomplishments, and a lighter bullet than that for a sublist under an accomplishment.

Tip The section "Establish a Logical Sizing Hierarchy" later in this chapter pertains to fonts. You can also apply this concept to bullets.

Note how the bullets on each of the following lines are similar in shape and design. In general, a combination of two bullets within the same set works nicely on the same page. You can also mix diamonds and arrows together.

Square set:	■ ▪ ❑ ◻ ◻ ◻ ◻ ◙
Circle set:	● • ○ ○ ○ ● ⊙ ◎
Diamond set:	◆ ❖ ◆ ◇ ◇ ◇ ◇ ◈ ⊿
Arrow set:	▶ ▷ ➤ ➡ ➤
Specialty set:	▨ ✳ ✦
Pointer set:	➜ ➔ ➔ ➔
Slanted pointer set:	➹ ➹ ➹
Pointing finger set:	☛ ☞
X's and check mark set:	☒ × ☑ ✓

Think in Threes

The mind likes a group of three. Whether making decisions about format, number of items to include in a list, or items in a sentence, consider using threes to group your thoughts. In the preceding résumé excerpt for the UNICEF Division Director, you will note the theme of threes. Within the Qualifications Summary are three key skill areas, completed later by the employer entry with three bulleted items to support those skill areas. Several sentences contain lists or phrases of three (see the first, third, and fourth sentences under Acting Division Director). Although not shown here, the résumé is finished off with a repeat of the graphics used in the beginning summary section (three larger boxes were centered on the last line of the résumé). The "think in threes" mantra is a loose guide and you need not apply it religiously in 100 percent of cases. Don't think that you can never again write a sentence that contains a list of two items or four items. Just be aware that groups of three often balance best.

Keep Headings to a Minimum

For a clean look with more white space, limit the number of category headings used on a page. Three to five is usually sufficient, with the lesser number preferred. When you have five or more categories and any of them contains just one or two lines under the category heading, experiment with combining the more sparsely populated sections. The following *Before* and *After* illustrations saved several line spaces for candidates using one-page résumés.

Before

AFFILIATIONS

Member, American Society for Training and Development (ASTD); Member, American Council on Exercise (ACE)

TECHNICAL SKILLS

Proficient: WordPerfect 8.0; MS Office '97 (Word, Excel, Powerpoint); MS Publisher; SPSS+; Internet navigation

Combining these two sections pares nine lines to just four.

After

AFFILIATIONS, TECHNICAL SKILLS

Member: American Society for Training and Development; American Council on Exercise
Proficient: WordPerfect 8.0; MS Office '97; MS Publisher; SPSS+; Internet search engines

The next *Before* picture includes three headings of list-driven material. By its nature, a list of short lines draws attention to itself. When the item is a major selling point and you have ample room to spare, present it in this manner. If space is an issue, and it often is, consider the *After* example as an alternative.

Before

EDUCATION

CALIFORNIA STATE UNIVERSITY, FRESNO

Degree: Bachelor of Science, Business Administration
Option: Human Resource Management

CERTIFICATION

SOCIETY OF HUMAN RESOURCE MANAGEMENT

Professional in Human Resources

CONTINUING EDUCATION

Partial list of seminars: Sexual Harassment, Discrimination, Union Prevention, Compensation, Conflict Resolution

Three separate categories totaling nearly 13 lines now become one category of 4 lines.

After

EDUCATION, CERTIFICATION, CONTINUING EDUCATION UNITS

B.S., Business Administration ▪ **Option in HR Management**—California State University, Fresno
Professional in Human Resources (PHR)—Society of Human Resource Management
CEUs—Sexual Harassment, Discrimination, Union Prevention, Compensation, Conflict Resolution

The next example reduced 16 lines to 9, enabling this risk-management specialist to keep his résumé on one page. The *After* example uses a full-width format, with Education & Credentials split into two columns as a space-saving device. Bullets under the categories provide a visual marker to help distinguish text from headings.

Before

EDUCATION

M.S., Health Administration, UCLA
B.S., Microbiology, Boston College

CREDENTIALS

Registered Environmental Assessor
Certified Occupational Health & Safety Technologist

AFFILIATIONS

American Industrial Hygiene Association
American Society of Safety Engineers
National Fire Protection Association
California Occupational Safety Engineers

After

EDUCATION & CREDENTIALS

▪ M.S., Health Administration, UCLA   ▪ Registered Environmental Assessor
▪ B.S., Microbiology, Boston College   ▪ Certified Occupational Health & Safety Technologist

AFFILIATIONS

▪ American Industrial Hygiene Association   ▪ National Fire Protection Association
▪ American Society of Safety Engineers   ▪ California Occupational Safety Engineers

The next example details how a teacher advertises her ability to assist with co-curricular activities (sports, the arts), traditionally a strong selling point in the teaching profession.

Before

COACHING EXPERIENCE

Golden Plains School District, Joaquin, Iowa

- ◆ Track Coach, 7th-8th Grade Co-Ed (1997-1999)
- ◆ Soccer Coach, 7th-8th Grade Girls' League (1995-1997)

Valley Unified School District, Exeter, Iowa

- ◆ Volleyball Coach, Girls' 9th-12th Grade, Sierra League (1992-1995)

ATHLETIC EXPERIENCE

Participated in soccer, volleyball, and competitive swimming throughout high school and college. Understand the value of using discipline, teamwork, and sportsmanship to increase students' self-esteem.

THE ARTS

Extensive experience in all aspects of drama, musical theater, and choir. Toured seven European countries as featured soloist for USC Concert Choir. Frequently incorporate drama and musical activities in the classroom.

In the following *After* example, specific grade levels are dropped for coaching experience, which broadens the impression of her coaching experience. Dates and school names were made nonspecific because teaching experience listed earlier in her résumé provided this information. Note also that each paragraph begins with a noun. In addition to saving seven or eight lines of space, this format also provides more visual uniformity than the format in the *Before* example.

After

ADDITIONAL SKILLS

Coach: Seven years' coaching experience as Track and Soccer Coach at Golden Plains and Volleyball Coach at Valley View High School.

Athlete: Participated in soccer, volleyball, and competitive swimming throughout high school and college. Understand the value of using discipline, teamwork, and sportsmanship to increase students' self-esteem.

Performer: Extensive experience in all aspects of drama, musical theater, and choir. Toured seven European countries as featured soloist for USC Concert Choir. Frequently incorporate drama and musical activities in the classroom.

Segment Paragraphs

Some situations make it difficult to avoid lengthy or thick blocks of text. For instance, individuals who have worked at the same company for most of their careers might need to devote the majority of their copy to one position. If this is the case, use the segmenting technique to break up an otherwise thick paragraph. *Segmenting* refers to grouping similar responsibilities together and presenting them in multiple paragraphs, as this investigator needed to do after spending 21 years with the same public agency.

Segmenting Made Martin's Résumé More Readable

Magic

The *Before* Career Profile (see Résumé 8.3) uses excessive white space at the expense of a dense job description. Changes in the *After* version (see Résumé 8.4) feature a single-spaced bulleted list, redeeming two extra line spaces that can then be used for the body of the job description. The job description becomes much more readable with its division into five subcategories, beginning with Accomplishments.

Résumé 8.3: Before

MARTIN GERBACH

555 East Terrace
San Diego, California 91111
(555) 555-5555

CAREER PROFILE

LICENSED INVESTIGATOR with impressive 20+ year career in law enforcement. Resolved investigations involving complex criminal charges:

◻ Insurance Fraud	◻ Sexual Assault	◻ Internal Audits
◻ Fraudulent Health Claims	◻ Child Abu	◻ Mail Fraud
◻ Staged Auto Collisions	◻ Drug Violations	◻ Burglary & Auto Theft

PROFESSIONAL EXPERIENCE

SAN DIEGO POLICE DEPARTMENT, SAN DIEGO, CALIFORNIA

Senior Investigator (1986–Present)
Investigator (1981–1986)

Experience includes a full range of felony and misdemeanor complaints. Prepare for and conduct surveillance and undercover operations. Prepare and serve search warrants. Gather, preserve, and analyze forensic evidence for use in court. Interview and interrogate witnesses and suspects. Prepare written and oral reports. Testify in court as Expert Witness. Manage approximately 550 cases on an annual basis. As Officer-in-Charge, perform management responsibilities in absence of sergeant. Supervise investigators and support personnel. Hold lead role on cases involving multiple agencies. Develop and present training for universities and police academies. Serve as Training Officer for newly assigned investigators. Provide consultation to field officers. Assist state licensing agencies with investigation of physicians, psychologists, dentists, and other professionals. Utilized current technology to access critical data for investigative purposes. Familiar with Windows and DOS-based applications. Setup and operate video and audio surveillance equipment. Have detailed knowledge of criminal and civil court procedures and depositions.

Accomplishments: Maintained a conviction rate of approx. 95% on cases filed. Frequently obtained confessions to avoid lengthy and costly jury trials. Secured convictions without physical evidence to support victims' allegations. Conducted more in-house criminal investigations than any investigator on the force. Maintained a clean record throughout career, with no litigation resulting from investigative practices. Built relationships with a comprehensive network of contacts. Prepare and deliver statements to the press.

LICENSURE, CONTINUING EDUCATION (partial list)

Licensed Private Investigator (#PI 54321) . . . Certified as Expert Witness in Sexual Assault by the Presiding Judge of the Superior Court, County of San Diego . . . Basic Peace Officer Standards and Training Certificate . . . General Education Studies, San Diego State University and California State University, Long Beach . . . Annual Continuing Education (40 hours) in Sexual Assault Training . . . Behavior Analysis Seminars . . . State Compensation Fraud Seminar sponsored by the California Association of District Attorneys.

AFFILIATIONS

California Sexual Assault Investigators Association . . . California Association of Private Investigators . . . San Diego Police Officers Association . . . American Society of Industrial Security

Résumé 8.4: After

MARTIN GERBACH

555 East Terrace
San Diego, California 91111
(555) 555-5555

CAREER PROFILE

LICENSED INVESTIGATOR with impressive 20+ year career in law enforcement. Resolved investigations involving complex criminal charges:

- Insurance Fraud
- Fraudulent Health Claims
- Staged Auto Collisions
- Sexual Assault
- Child Abuse
- Drug Violations
- Internal Audits
- Mail Fraud
- Burglary & Auto Theft

PROFESSIONAL EXPERIENCE

More than 5 years as Investigator and 16 years as Senior Investigator with the San Diego Police Department, specializing in insurance fraud and sexual assault. Accomplishments and experience:

Accomplishments: Maintained a conviction rate of approx. 95% on cases filed. Frequently obtained confessions to avoid lengthy and costly jury trials. Secured convictions without physical evidence to support victims' allegations. Conducted more in-house criminal investigations than any investigator on the force. Maintained a clean record throughout career, with no litigation resulting from investigative practices.

Scope of Investigations: Experience includes a full range of felony and misdemeanor complaints. Conduct surveillance and undercover operations. Order and serve search warrants. Gather, preserve, and analyze forensic evidence for use in court. Interview and interrogate witnesses and suspects. Prepare written and oral reports. Testify in court as Expert Witness.

Case Management/Administration: Excellent time management skills, handling approximately 550 cases annually. As Officer-in-Charge, perform management responsibilities in absence of sergeant. Supervise investigators and support personnel. Hold lead role on cases involving multiple agencies.

Communications: Develop and present training for universities and police academies. Serve as Training Officer for newly assigned investigators. Provide consultation to field officers. Assist state licensing agencies with investigation of physicians, psychologists, dentists, and other professionals. Build relationships with a comprehensive network of contacts. Prepare and deliver statements to the press.

Technical Skills: Utilized current technology to access critical data for investigative purposes. Familiar with Windows and DOS-based applications. Setup and operate video and audio surveillance equipment. Have detailed knowledge of criminal and civil court procedures and depositions.

LICENSURE, CONTINUING EDUCATION (partial list)

Licensed Private Investigator (#PI 54321) . . . Certified as Expert Witness in Sexual Assault by the Presiding Judge of the Superior Court, County of San Diego . . . Basic Peace Officer Standards and Training Certificate . . . General Education Studies, San Diego State University and California State University, Long Beach . . . Annual Continuing Education (40 hours) in Sexual Assault Training . . . Behavior Analysis Seminars . . . State Compensation Fraud Seminar sponsored by the California Association of District Attorneys.

AFFILIATIONS

California Sexual Assault Investigators Association . . . California Association of Private Investigators . . . San Diego Police Officers Association . . . American Society of Industrial Security

Balance Is Beautiful

Interior designers, artists, and others endowed with creative talents will tell you that balance plays a part in the artistic process (excluding the genre of really "out there" art, of course). Balance and symmetry also play a part in good résumé design. In résumé-speak, balance refers to the distribution of weight, or copy, on the page.

Pay Attention to Vertical Balance

Top and bottom margins and left and right margins are the first place to look for balance. Pay careful attention to make sure that left and right margins are equidistant. Top and bottom margins can vary by .1 to .2 inches, with a lesser amount of space at the bottom. Some résumé writers adhere to 1-inch margins on all sides. Others narrow these margins to as little as .5 inch and .4 inch for top and bottom margins and .75 inch for left and right margins. I prefer .8 inch and .7 inch for top and bottom margins, and .9 inch for left and right margins.

If you start your résumé at .8 inch for a top margin but have more than an inch of blank space at the bottom of the page (say the last line of your text is at position 9.2 inches), center the page vertically to keep it from looking top-heavy (in MS Word, use File, Page Setup, Layout, Vertical Alignment, Center; in Corel WordPerfect, use Format, Page, Center). The other correction you can make for a top-heavy résumé is to add small but equal amounts of line space between headings (see "Change Line Height" later in this chapter). In addition to top and bottom balancing, give thought to balancing copy on the page, as described in the next four sections.

Balancing a Two-Column Format

A common design defect is the "leaning tower of Pisa" effect that can occur when you use a traditional two-column layout. Use of the term *column* here refers to a visual block of text rather than actual use of the column function in your word-processing program. In this familiar layout, headings appear in a left column and copy in a right column. Notice the misuse and waste of white space under the category headings, which causes this résumé to be more than a bubble off-plumb.

Before

PROFESSIONAL EXPERIENCE

JOHNSON ENGINEERING, Shawnee, Michigan

Field Surveyor (1998-Present)

This is the text of the résumé. Starting this far to the right wastes valuable white space in the area immediately to the left of this paragraph. The result is imbalance. It is exacerbated if the hyphenation function is turned on, causing text to hyphenate on virtually every line.

MILLER CONTRACTING, Shawnee, Michigan

Rodman / Chainman (1993-1998)

This is the text of the résumé. The lean-to-the-right effect becomes more pronounced with more and more employment entries, especially when hyphenation is turned off. An entire page of this is distracting. Moreover, this format is a breeding ground for unsightly white space between words. Note solutions to leaning problems immediately below.

EDUCATION

UNIVERSITY OF MICHIGAN . . .

SKILLS

AutoCAD, MS Project . . .

You might have heard the old advertising saying, "The more you tell, the more you sell." In résumés, the problem is that you can't sell more if you don't have the space to tell more. In the *After* example, shifting the concentration of the body copy to the left grabs an additional 1.25 inches of horizontal space to do more telling and selling.

After

PROFESSIONAL EXPERIENCE	JOHNSON ENGINEERING Shawnee, Michigan
1998-Present	**Field Surveyor**

This is the text of the résumé. By stacking the heading "Professional Experience" (moving the second word of the heading underneath the first word at the left margin), you can reclaim an inch of valuable space. If dates are solid, position them to the left of this copy; if not, move them to the right-hand margin or after the title, as shown in the preceding example. Starting at this point gives you a wider area to write job descriptions and keeps the appearance of the résumé from "leaning" too far to the right.

	MILLER CONTRACTING Shawnee, Michigan
1993-1998	**Rodman / Chainman**

This is the text of the résumé. You have now corrected the lean-to problem and, at the same time, gained valuable white space. Now that you have more room to tell your story, you'll undoubtedly leave employers with the thought, "where have you been all my life!"

EDUCATION	UNIVERSITY OF MICHIGAN . . .
SKILLS	AutoCAD, MS Project . . .

Magic

A Two-Column Format Worked for Gail

A two-column format typically provides plenty of space for entry-level, support staff, and a number of other candidates. The next résumé (see Résumé 8.5) is a variation on the two-column format and uses a vertical line to separate the two vertical blocks of text. Dot leaders extending to the right margin help break up horizontal sections of text. Potentially "dead" space in the left column is used well with the inclusion of the candidate's goal and summary statement.

Management and professional candidates, by the nature of their experience, have extensive information to present and warrant more copy than other candidates. For this reason, I tend to use a full-width design for experienced candidates. When you apply a few formatting tricks, a full-width design can hold more copy than a two-column format.

Résumé 8.5

GAIL T. MOSS

Target:

Media Sales

Broadcast sales professional
with 6 years' experience as
account executive with Fox
affiliate and 20 years' experience
in sales support and traffic
management with
CBS affiliate

124 West Menlo
Pasadena, CA 92121

(888) 449-7474

Business Development and Revenue Growth . . . .

Contributed to station's unprecedented sales increase of more than 400% . . . through diligent cold calling and account service, developed business with major agencies and direct accounts numbering 100+, overcoming sales objections associated with a smaller/independent television station.

Solicited and secured "first time" prestigious clients and nontraditional advertisers including Filene's (obtained within 60 days of hire), Barnes & Noble, Ford, and political advertisers . . . built relationships with agencies that had never aired or not aired for several years . . . created special packages, such as the Olympics Review and Jimmy Stewart Memories Week, and sold programs at premium rates . . . sales leader in negotiating rates with local/regional/national clients and agencies.

Promotions and Value-Added Projects . . . .

Recognized for a number of "firsts" with the station . . . created cross-promotion with Home Base and Amblin Entertainment for X-Files promotion (included promotion for on-air use) . . . put together Macy's promotion with in-store appearance of Seinfeld cast member . . . assembled co-op promotion with 40-member merchant group and chamber of commerce . . . coordinated and hosted Fun Fair at Pasadena Zoo to premiere new cartoon block (obtained Toys-R-Us as event sponsor) . . . coordinated first-time station sponsorship of booth (Disney retailer).

Additional Skills . . . .

Elevated station's image through upgrade of marketing materials, sales tools, and computer technology for client proposals and agency avails . . . coached account executives in use of avails and proposals, rate negotiations, procedures for order confirmation, and follow-up (N/A's, MG's) . . . introduced higher pricing structure used by entire sales staff . . . produced commercials (concept, shoots, editing) . . . hired and coordinated talent, directors, technicians, writers, and support staff.

Sales Support . . . .

Improved productivity of account executives and sales managers by handling preemptions and assisting in selling paid programs . . . maximized avails through inventory control . . . 1st employee to receive Sales Hero of the Year Award.

Employment History . . . .

Account Executive — KSTL TV (Fox), Pasadena, CA (1992-Present)
Sales Support — KXTQ TV (CBS), Pasadena, CA (1982-1992)
Traffic Management — KXTQ TV (CBS), Pasadena, CA (1972-1982)

Education . . . .

Bachelor of Science, Business Administration — University of Southern California

Balancing a Full-Width Layout

Full-width, or full-horizontal, designs present their own challenges with respect to balance and readability. When you use coast-to-coast margins, it is easy to end up with a solid block of text that resembles the shape of an upright refrigerator.

Magic

A Full-Width Layout Worked for George

It is difficult to find where company entries start and stop in the full-width *Before* example (see Résumé 8.6). Give your readers some visual handles to locate points of interest. Compare the *Before* example with the *After* version (see Résumé 8.7). You'll see that different bullets are used for the Qualifications section, centering sets off headings, and indentations of .2 on the left and .35 on the right for accomplishments add interest and readability. At the same time, you gain enough room to add horizontal lines to help break up text and to finish off the bottom of the page with a repeat of the circular, shadowed bullet.

Although full-width layouts require an extra line space after each heading, you can usually recover this space by starting the bulk of copy at or near the left margin. The exception would be when you have more than, say, five headings on a page. For every heading you use, you'll need an additional line space. For example, four headings require 8 line spaces, five headings require 10 line spaces, and so on. (To learn tricks for limiting or combining ancillary headings, refer to "Keep Headings to a Minimum" earlier in this chapter.)

Here's a hint that will make full-width formats more readable: Keep paragraphs short, aiming for three to four lines. *The Chicago Manual of Style* recommends that text intended for continuous reading, such as a book, contain 65 to 70 characters per line (in other words, 65 or 70 individual letters and spaces per line). When working with a full-horizontal layout where text begins near the left margin of the page and continues across the full width of the page, you can accommodate 60 percent or more of these numbers (in other words, more than 100 characters per line), depending on font selection.

Even though résumés aren't considered "continuous reading," lengthy paragraphs can quickly overwhelm readers. If you load your paragraphs with five or more lines of 100-plus characters, readers will need a machete to hack their way through. (Review "Segment Paragraphs," earlier in this chapter, for tips on how to break up lengthy paragraphs.)

Résumé 8.6: Before

GEORGE KALEBSEN

444 West Carlson
Carlsbad, California 95555
(888) 449-7474

QUALIFICATIONS

Profit-oriented manager with strong record of improving:

- Financial Performance: Improved delinquency rates by as much as 45%, capturing more than $1.5 million in "lost" revenue over career.

- Employee Productivity: Identified and capitalized on team members' strengths to accommodate a three-fold increase in work volume without need for additional staff.

- Customer Relations: Advocate a customer-focused orientation; frequently negotiated pay-out plans to maintain marginal customers in salable position.

PROFESSIONAL EXPERIENCE

The Financial Group, Baltimore, Maryland (5/96-Present)

Foreclosure Department Supervisor: Recruited to equip department for aggressive growth phase (portfolio grew from approx. $1.4 billion to near $2.0 billion in 12 months). Manage collection portfolio of 1,000 accounts. Train, supervise, and evaluate 5 Loan Counselors. Point person, handling communications with outside agencies (attorneys, 1st mortgage companies, title companies, trustee services).

- Accommodated 60+% growth in collection portfolio (from 600 to 1,000) without additional staff.

- Held delinquency to 2½% (1½% below industry average) for approximate annual savings of $500,000.

- Built spreadsheets in Excel to improve integrity of, and access to, financial data.

Credit Corporation, Baltimore, Maryland (1990-1996)

Assistant Branch Manager: Selected as change agent to turnaround nonperforming branches for financial institution specializing in B&C and other high-risk loans.

- Baltimore: Increased production 47%; sourced and negotiated 3 profitable dealer contracts; reversed inordinately high turnover rate (90+%) through recruitment, training, and coaching of technical and support staff.

- Frederick: Improved branch's performance ranking for growth and profit from #10 to #5 among 28 branches; increased Smart Loan Portfolio from $400,000 to $600,000 through sales and technical training of 50+ life agents.

- Rockville and Wheaton: Cut delinquency rates 8% and 4½% for personal and real estate loans respectively (Rockville) and, in less than 6 weeks, dropped delinquency rates by 6.2% (Wheaton).

Ford Consumer Credit, Wilmington, Delaware (1989-1990)

Regional Operations Manager: Accountable for strategic planning, operations, and evaluation of 8 branches in Delaware and Maryland (staff of 25; lending portfolio of $3.0 million).

- More than doubled volume of applications while maintaining virtually unchanged operating budget.

- Eliminated 8-week backlog in loan processing through double-teaming program.

TECHNICAL STRENGTHS & LICENSURE

Technical expertise in real estate (conforming and nonconforming) and consumer lending including origination, underwriting, servicing, and troubleshooting. Well-versed in Excel, Word, Q&A, Action System, and USFN. Licensure: Property & Casualty; Life & Health Insurance Sales; Real Estate Sales; Notary Public.

Resumé 8.7: After

GEORGE KALEBSEN

444 West Carlson
Carlsbad, California 95555
(888) 449-7474

QUALIFICATIONS

Profit-oriented manager with strong record of improving:

○ **Financial Performance:** Improved delinquency rates by as much as 45%, capturing more than $1.5 million in "lost" revenue over career.

○ **Employee Productivity:** Identified and capitalized on team members' strengths to accommodate a 3-fold increase in work volume without need for additional staff.

○ **Customer Relations:** Advocate a customer-focused orientation; frequently negotiated pay-out plans to maintain marginal customers in salable position.

PROFESSIONAL EXPERIENCE

THE FINANCIAL GROUP, BALTIMORE, MARYLAND (5/96–Present)

Foreclosure Department Supervisor: Recruited to equip department for aggressive growth phase (portfolio grew from approx. $1.4 billion to near $2.0 billion in 12 months). Manage collection portfolio of 1,000 accounts. Train, supervise, and evaluate 5 Loan Counselors. Point person for communications with outside agencies (attorneys, 1st mortgage companies, title companies, trustee services).

- Accommodated 60+% growth in collection portfolio (from 600 to 1,000) without additional staff.

- Held delinquency to 2½% (1½% below industry average) for approx. annual savings of $500,000.

- Built spreadsheets in Excel to improve integrity of, and access to, financial data.

CREDIT CORPORATION, BALTIMORE, MARYLAND (1990–1996)

Assistant Branch Manager: Selected as change agent to turn around nonperforming branches for financial institution specializing in B&C and other high-risk loans. Assigned to the following branches:

- Baltimore: Increased production 47%; sourced and negotiated 3 profitable dealer contracts; reversed inordinately high turnover rate (90+%) through recruitment, training, and coaching of technical and support staff.

- Frederick: Improved branch's performance ranking for growth and profit from #10 to #5 among 28 branches; increased Smart Loan Portfolio from $400,000 to $600,000 through sales and technical training of 50+ life agents.

- Rockville, Wheaton: Cut delinquency rates 8% and 4½% for personal and real estate loans (Rockville); in less than 6 weeks, dropped delinquency rates 6.2% (Wheaton).

FORD CONSUMER CREDIT, WILMINGTON, DELAWARE (1989–1990)

Regional Operations Manager: Accountable for strategic planning, operations, and evaluation of 8 branches in Delaware and Maryland (staff of 25; lending portfolio of $3.0 million).

- More than doubled volume of applications with a virtually unchanged operating budget.

- Eliminated 8-week backlog in loan processing through double-teaming program.

TECHNICAL STRENGTHS & LICENSURE

Technical expertise in real estate (conforming and nonconforming) and consumer lending including origination, underwriting, servicing, and troubleshooting. Well-versed in Excel, Word, Q&A, Action System, and USFN. Licensure: Property & Casualty; Life & Health Insurance Sales; Real Estate Sales; Notary Public.

○ ○ ○

Balancing Unevenly Distributed Copy

Beyond horizontal and vertical balance, other factors detract from visual balance, such as unevenly distributed copy and extreme margins. Margins that are too wide or too narrow or use a combination of the two on the same page can throw off the balance of the résumé.

Magic

Patricia's Résumé Became a Good Balancing Act

The next *Before* example (see Résumé 8.8) shows this off-balance look. The first half of the page uses 2-inch margins, followed by .75-inch margins, and then back to 2-inch margins to center the Education section.

In the *After* example (see Résumé 8.9), shifting margins to a consistent 1-inch margin on the left and right helps to redistribute the weight. In addition, the original two-column keyword list is presented in a three-column format. Two-column listings can sometimes look lonely if the items listed are short words or if there is too much white space around the columns. In this case, the three-column presentation helps define a more traditional margin and is equally spaced with approximately .5 inch of white space between margins and each column.

Another revision to the following résumé is the use of a diamond-shaped bullet for the items in the Strengths section. The same type of bullet is centered at the bottom of the page to provide visual closure to the résumé. Conversely, I used an arrow-shaped bullet under both Qualifications and Employment Summary, which helps to develop a consistent pattern for the eye to follow. Because the text following the bullets in both of these sections rests at the same tab stop, I used the same style of bullet. Introducing another style of bullet along the same vertical axis would add one more design element to the résumé and cause the page to look too busy.

I also made spacing adjustments between headings and text in the following example (see "Tweaking Tips," later in this chapter, for the technical steps for doing so). Compare how in the *Before* example the candidate's associate's degree stands out rather than her bachelor's degree. This is because the bachelor's degree is pushed up against the heading. By adding line height after the heading (not an entire hard return), the bachelor's degree is now the more prominent of the two degrees.

Résumé 8.8: Before

PATRICIA T. AMES
15315 18th Street, #111
Scottsdale, AZ 85012
(802) 971-1492

STRENGTHS

▸ Operations Management   ▸ Policy Development
▸ Sales & Marketing   ▸ Advertising & Promotions
▸ Food & Beverage   ▸ Key Account Service
▸ Staff Development   ▸ Guest Services

QUALIFICATIONS

Experienced professional with strong career in profitable management of distinguished hotel properties. Strengths as strategic planner, motivational speaker, and change agent. Expertise in impacting bottom-line profit through these avenues:

▸ **Revenue Growth:** Delivered more than $1.5 million in revenue increases, setting new record for Scottsdale property. Conceived and launched ventures; salvaged non-performing assets to become financially-viable, flagship operation.

▸ **Business Process Re-engineering:** Captured $750,000 in additional gross operating profit through efficiency improvements. Process owner of Re-engineering Training & Development for The Hyatt Hotel Group.

▸ **Service Enhancements:** Earned #1 ranking in U.S. for Guest Service on Condé Nast Traveler's 1998 Gold List (scored 3rd internationally)—inclusion on list was "a first" for exclusive property.

EMPLOYMENT SUMMARY

THE HYATT HOTEL & RESTAURANT GROUP   1993-Present
General Manager, Scottsdale Inn, Scottsdale, Arizona (250-room, 4-diamond hotel/conference)   (1997-Present)
General Manager, The Vintage Inn, Prescott, Arizona (97-room, 4-diamond hotel)   (1995-1997)
Assistant Manager, Playa de Oro Resort, Santa Barbara, California (exclusive resort facility)   (1993-1995)

EDUCATION

Bachelor of Science, Food, Hotel and Tourism Management
Rochester Institute of Technology

Associate of Applied Science, Hotel and Restaurant Management
Fullerton City College

Résumé 8.9: After

PATRICIA T. AMES

15315 18th Street, #111
Scottsdale, AZ 85012
(802) 971-1492

STRENGTHS

◆ Operations Management	◆ Advertising	◆ Sales & Marketing
◆ Policy Development	◆ Promotions	◆ Key Account Service
◆ Staff Development	◆ Food & Beverage	◆ Guest Services

QUALIFICATIONS

Experienced professional with strong career in the profitable management of distinguished hotel properties. Strengths as strategic planner, motivational speaker, and change agent. Expertise in affecting bottom-line profit through these avenues:

▸ **Revenue Growth:** Delivered more than $1.5 million in revenue increases, setting record for Scottsdale property's 75-year history of operation. Conceived and launched ventures; salvaged nonperforming assets to become financially viable, flagship operation.

▸ **Business Process Reengineering:** Captured $750,000 in additional gross operating profit through efficiency improvements, purchasing directives, and employee incentive program. Process owner of Reengineering Training and Development for The Hyatt Hotel Group.

▸ **Service Enhancements:** Earned #1 ranking in the United States for Guest Service on Condé Nast Traveler's 1998 Gold List (scored 3rd internationally)—inclusion on list was "a first" for exclusive property.

EMPLOYMENT SUMMARY

THE HYATT HOTEL & RESTAURANT GROUP   1993-Present

▸ **General Manager,** Scottsdale Inn, Scottsdale, Arizona *(350-room, 4-diamond hotel/conference center)* (1997-Present)

▸ **General Manager,** The Vintage Inn, Prescott, Arizona *(97-room, 4-diamond hotel)* (1995-1997)

▸ **Assistant Manager,** Playa de Oro Resort, Santa Barbara, California *(exclusive resort facility)* (1993-1995)

EDUCATION

Bachelor of Science, Food, Hotel and Tourism Management
Rochester Institute of Technology

Associate of Applied Science, Hotel and Restaurant Management
Fullerton City College

◆ ◆ ◆

Balancing Impact Statements

Bulleted impact statements, whether sitting alone under an Accomplishments or Qualifications heading or following a job description, can be logically grouped for greater balance. For instance, in a list of five bulleted items where each contains between one to three lines, consider grouping the heavier, or longer, impact statements first, followed by the lighter, or shorter, impact statements. A longer impact statement is often a meatier accomplishment and is therefore the most logical choice for a first entry. I've written the next *Before* and *After* examples in Spanish so that you'll focus on the look rather than the words (for those fluent in the language, you might recognize bits and pieces of some children's nursery rhymes). Compare how this *Before* presentation is not as pretty as the following *After* example.

Before

Contributions:

➤ Yo tengo un cochinito guardado en mi ropero. El es un animalito que cuida mi dinero. Con diez centavos diarios lo voy a alimentar, y cuando esté muy gordo lo voy a quebrar.

➤ Cinco centavos en mi bolsa. Este es para el chicle; este es para un anillo; este es para un tambor; estos los guardaré en mi bolsa hasta que escoja otra cosa.

➤ Pin-uno, pin-dos, pin-tres, pin-cuatro, pin-cinco, pin-seis, pin-siete, pinocho, pinguino.

➤ Allá está el sol cominedo un caracol y enchando las cáscaras a un árbol. Allá está la estrella cominedo la paella, y enchando las cáscaras a una botella. Allá está la luna comiendo la tuna y enchando las cáscaras a la laguna.

➤ No quiero oro, ni quiero plata. Yo lo que quiero es romper la piñata.

Now, here is the same material reorganized according to line length.

After

Contributions:

➤ Allá está el sol cominedo un caracol y enchando las cáscaras a un árbol. Allá está la estrella cominedo la paella, y enchando las cáscaras a una botella. Allá está la luna comiendo la tuna y enchando las cáscaras a la laguna.

➤ Yo tengo un cochinito guardado en mi ropero. El es un animalito que cuida mi dinero. Con diez centavos diarios lo voy a alimentar, y cuando esté muy gordo lo voy a quebrar.

➤ Cinco centavos en mi bolsa. Este es para el chicle; este es para un anillo; este es para un tambor; estos los guardaré en mi bolsa hasta que escoja otra cosa.

➤ Pin-uno, pin-dos, pin-tres, pin-cuatro, pin-cinco, pin-seis, pin-siete, pinocho, pinguino.

➤ No quiero oro, ni quiero plata. Yo lo que quiero es romper la piñata.

This is another of those soft rules—the artistic patrol won't be after you if you break the rule, but it might win you some extra visual appeal points if you do (just make sure that you don't bury the most important accomplishment!).

Justification—Ragged Right or Full Justification?

Opinions are divided on the ragged right or full justification question. A *ragged right* margin, more formally referred to as *left justification,* means that text lines up on the left margin, creating an uneven right edge, just as the text does in the following example.

> This paragraph has a ragged right edge, meaning it is left-justified. The benefit to this presentation is that readers can more speedily read or scan information. It also avoids the unsightly spaces between words that can result from full justification.

Full justification means that space is expanded between words on a line so that both the left and right margins are straight and even.

> This paragraph has evenly balanced left and right margins, meaning it is full justified. The chief benefit to full justification is that it is often more aesthetically pleasing. Full justification can also be a space-miser: by packing a few more characters on each line, you can possibly save one or two line spaces throughout the résumé.

There are benefits to both. Studies conducted by WordPerfect early in the 1990s indicate that text formatted with a ragged right margin is faster to read. Despite these findings, most newspapers, magazines, and books use full justification. The benefit to full justification is that it is "prettier" and more balanced-looking. Some writers prefer the more aesthetically pleasing presentation full justification creates. The speed-readability of ragged-right margins doesn't come into play because résumé paragraphs are typically short. The other benefit I have found to full justification is that it packs words in such a way that more characters can fit on one line. If you have chosen left justification and find your résumé spilling over to a second page by just a line or two, try highlighting the body of the résumé and then switching to full justification.

Hang It on the Wall!

Here's an unscientific experiment to determine whether your résumé is balanced. Print two copies of your résumé. Take one and tape it to a wall as if it were a picture. Take the other one and turn it upside down; then tape it to the wall near the first. Step far enough back that you can't read the words. If the content of either looks especially lopsided, consider making some adjustments.

Use Typefaces Tastefully

Dozens of typefaces, or fonts, come as standard features in popular word-processing programs. Beyond these, you can purchase additional fonts on disk or download them from various sources.

Fonts come in two flavors: serif and sans serif. Serif fonts have fine lines that finish off the main strokes of the letters, sometimes called "feet." Serif fonts dress up documents with a more traditional, formal look. Sans (meaning *without*) serif fonts do not have feet and produce a simple, clean look. The following table shows some of the most popular serif and sans serif fonts.

Serif Fonts	Sans Serif Fonts
Arrus BT 12 point	Abadi MT Condensed Light, 12 point
BernhardMod BT 12 point	**Albertus 12 point**
Bodoni MT Ultra Bold	Antique Olive 12 point
Book Antiqua 12 point	Arial 12 point
Brush Script MT 12 point	Century Gothic 12 point
Calisto MT 12 point	CG Omega 12 point
CG Times 12 point	*Comic Sans MS 12 point*
Charter BT 12 point	EngraversGothic BT, 12 point
Chelthml TC Bk BT 12 point	Futura Bk BT, 12 point
Clarendon Condensed 12 point	Letter Gothic, 12 point
COPPERPLATE GOTHIC LT, 12 POINT	Lucida Console, 12 point
Courier, 12 point	Lucida Sans Unicode, 12 point
Footlight MT Light, 12 point	Maiandra GD, 12 point
Galliard BT, 12 point	News Gothic MT, 12 point
Garamond, 12 point	NewsGoth BT, 12 point
GeoSlab703 Lt BT, 12 point	Swis721 BlkEx BT, 12 point

Serif Fonts	Sans Serif Fonts
Goudy Old Style, 12 point	Technical, 12 point
Harrington, 12 point	Theatre Antoine, 12 point
Humanst521 Lt BT, 12 point	Univers, 12 point
Lucida Calligraphy, 12 point	ZapfHumnst BT, 12 point
Paddington, 12 point	
Rockwell, 12 point	
Thunderbird, 12 point	
Times New Roman, 12 point	

The Brush Script and Lucida Calligraphy fonts would be classified more appropriately in a separate category of script fonts, but I have included them in the serif column for the sake of simplicity.

Point size is a measurement device that refers to the height of each character. There are 72 points per inch.

This is 9 point

This is 12 point

This is 18 point

This is 24 point

The point size for fonts in your résumé can range from 9 points to 12 points. Your name can be a few point sizes larger than the rest of the text, especially if it is a "short" name (such as Lori Lee or Jay Boz) that needs help standing out.

Choosing a Font

Your choice of font is an important decision because the font plays a major role in your résumé's personality. In general, the more senior the position you seek, the more traditional the font selection should be. Font selection also goes hand in hand with layout/pattern. If you've chosen an unusual layout, you might want to pair it with a more decorative font. For instance,

Lucida Calligraphy might be appropriate for an artist whose résumé is list-oriented and light on copy. Comic Sans, which gives the appearance of a child's handwriting, might be appropriate for a kindergarten teacher's résumé.

Fonts That Buy More Space

Although each sample in the preceding table is printed in the same size, you will note that some take up less space than others. Résumés that are rich in text might benefit from a type of condensed font to maximize space. If you have difficulty making copy fit on your page, dabble with the point size, taking it down .5 to 2 points in size. If this compromises readability, revert to a skinnier font.

> This is Century Gothic 12 point font. It is considered a "fat" font and will take up a substantial amount of space. [22 words]

> This font is News Gothic BT. Although this example is also 12 point, the News Gothic font fits much more on a line than does the Century Gothic 12 point. [30 words]

When you're preparing a scannable résumé, beware of using a font that's too tightly packed, where letters touch each other, because it will distort during the scanning process. This is especially true for serif fonts. Later in this chapter are tips for expanding character spacing; also refer to chapter 9 for tips on preparing a scannable résumé.

Use Discretion in Mixing Fonts

You can avoid design bloat by limiting your selection of fonts to two. In many cases, one is plenty. If you choose to introduce a second font, save it as an accent for headings or your name instead of mixing it haphazardly within the body copy. Reserve the more decorative fonts (such as Harrington or Bodoni) or bold fonts (such as Clarendon Condensed or Albertus) for category headings. A full page of any of these is too heavy, much like dining on chocolate decadence dessert for breakfast, lunch, and dinner.

The following *Before* example displays a number of design faux pas. The overly decorated résumé uses three different fonts presented in various dress (italics, bold, point sizes ranging from 10 to 18) and produces only a siren effect: It gets attention, but only as an annoyance.

Before

SAMANTHA JONES
1255 WEST SHAW AVENUE
FONTANA, CALIFORNIA 98765
(555) 222-2222
SAMANTHAJONES@HOTMAIL.COM

SALES EXPERIENCE

PHARMACEUTICAL SALES REPRESENTATIVE

Pharmco Pharmaceuticals, Oklahoma City, Oklahoma (6/xx-Present)

Generate sales of hypertensive, respiratory, and migraine products, calling on neurologists, pulmonologists, allergists, family practitioners, internists, and Ob/Gyn physicians, as well as clinical and retail pharmacists. Demonstrated knowledge of multiple systems and disease processes.

*Exceeded sales forecast for all products, generating 118%, 116%, and 106% of quota.

*Launched new migraine product, achieving highest percent-to-goal in region.

SALES REPRESENTATIVE

American Home Care, Oklahoma City, Oklahoma (19xx–19xx)

Performed marketing and public relations functions in managing OKC sales territory. Called on physicians, hospitals, pharmacies, skilled nursing facilities, and durable medical equipment companies. Promoted company through presence at trade shows/community events and presentation of educational inservices for physicians and medical office staff. Generated statistical reports, analyzed referral patterns, and initiated appropriate marketing strategies.

*Achieved a near three-fold increase in sales units . . . favorably impacted market presence and consumer awareness.

*Gained access to previously "no see" physicians, increasing physician accounts from 200 to 480 in a three-year period.

The *After* example limits the font selection to essentially two: Bodoni Extra Bold for the name and Sales Experience category heading (14 points for the name, 12 points for the category heading) and ZapfHumanst Dm BT for address, position title, and company name (11 points, boldfaced). A sister font, ZapfHumanst BT, was used for text and accomplishments. The point size is one size smaller than the title and company names. These changes clean up and calm down the above passage.

After

SAMANTHA JONES

1255 W. Shaw Avenue
Fontana, CA 98765
(555) 222-2222
samanthajones@hotmail.com

SALES EXPERIENCE

PHARMACEUTICAL SALES REPRESENTATIVE

Pharmco Pharmaceuticals, Oklahoma City, Oklahoma (6/xx–Present)

Generate sales of hypertensive, respiratory, and migraine products, calling on neurologists, pulmonologists, allergists, family practitioners, internists, and Ob/Gyn physicians, as well as clinical and retail pharmacists. Demonstrated knowledge of multiple systems and disease processes.

* Exceeded sales forecast for all products, generating 118%, 116%, and 106% of quota.

* Launched new migraine product, achieving highest percent-to-goal in region.

SALES REPRESENTATIVE

American Home Care, Oklahoma City, Oklahoma (19xx–19xx)

Performed marketing and public relations functions in managing OKC sales territory. Called on physicians, hospitals, pharmacies, skilled nursing facilities, and durable medical equipment companies. Promoted company through presence at trade shows/community events and presentation of educational inservices for physicians and medical office staff. Generated statistical reports, analyzed referral patterns, and initiated appropriate marketing strategies.

* Achieved a near threefold increase in sales units . . . favorably affected market presence and consumer awareness.

* Gained access to previously "no see" physicians, increasing physician accounts from 200 to 480 in a three-year period.

Another visual adjustment made in the preceding example involved white space around the bullets. A comparison of the *Before* and *After* excerpts shows how the text is adjusted to the right; it also now aligns under the wording rather than under the bullet (see the "Adding or Subtracting Spacing Between Bullets and Text" sections under "Use Bullets Strategically").

Go Easy on Bold, Underline, and Italic

The admonition about not mixing too many fonts also holds true for using bold, underline, and italic. Go easy! Reserve bold treatment for your name, category headings, company names, or titles (you'll read more on this subject in the next section, "Establish a Logical Sizing Hierarchy"). Anything more screams at your reader, as does this next *Before* example.

Before

ABC MANUFACTURING COMPANY, San Diego, California (19xx–Present)
<u>**Sales Representative**</u>
Manage large west coast sales territory for international distributor of engineered performance plastics. Demonstrated versatility in selling to engineers, purchasing managers, and executives of original equipment manufacturers that service diverse markets (construction, automotive, cycling, manufacturing, food processing, agricultural, mining, computer). Provide high-tech engineering solutions in compliance with ISO standards, working closely with clients throughout a two- to three-month sales cycle. Source new suppliers. Maintain knowledge of an extensive product line of machined, molded, and injection-molded seals and rings.
Accomplishments
⇒ *More than doubled territory sales volume each of the last three years.*
⇒ *Led sales team in development of new accounts.*
⇒ *Negotiated pricing with manufacturers to ensure profitable resale on the secondary market.*
⇒ *Selected among team of nine to present sales and product training to inside sales staff.*
⇒ *Completed intensive 12-month technical and sales internship program.*

XYZ CONSULTING SERVICES, San Diego, California (19xx–19xx)
<u>**Marketing Representative**</u>
Instrumental in development of corporate business plan for start-up company, including creation of comprehensive marketing element. Marketed medical billing to physicians and medical staff. Gained new accounts through market research, telemarketing, cold calling, and networking. Presented training on medical billing software to new customers.
Accomplishments
⇒ *Built business from start-up, generating more than $25,000 in monthly revenue.*
⇒ *Developed customer training program used as model by subsequent branches.*

On occasion, it might be appropriate to add bold to highlight a few, select portions of text. The following *After* excerpt contains the same text as the preceding *Before* excerpt; however, you'll note the addition of white space between paragraphs, as well as a greater measure of self-control when it comes to using boldfacing.

After

ABC MANUFACTURING COMPANY, San Diego, California (19xx–Present)

<u>Sales Representative</u>

Manage large west coast sales territory for international distributor of engineered performance plastics. Demonstrated versatility in selling to engineers, purchasing managers, and executives of original equipment manufacturers that service diverse markets (construction, automotive, cycling, manufacturing, food processing, agricultural, mining, computer). Provide high-tech engineering solutions in compliance with ISO standards, working closely with clients throughout a two- to three-month sales cycle. Source new suppliers. Maintain knowledge of an extensive product line of machined, molded, and injection-molded seals and rings.

Accomplishments

⇒ More than **doubled territory sales volume each of the last three years.**

⇒ **Led sales team** in development of new accounts.

⇒ Negotiated pricing with manufacturers to ensure profitable resale on the secondary market.

⇒ **Selected among team of nine** to present sales and product training to inside sales staff.

⇒ Completed intensive 12-month technical and sales internship program.

XYZ CONSULTING SERVICES, San Diego, California (19xx–19xx)

<u>Marketing Representative</u>

Instrumental in development of corporate business plan for start-up company, including creation of comprehensive marketing element. Marketed medical billing to physicians and medical staff. Gained new accounts through market research, telemarketing, cold calling, and networking. Presented training on medical billing software to new customers.

Accomplishments

⇒ Built business from start-up to **generate more than $25,000 in monthly revenue.**

⇒ Developed customer training program used as model by subsequent branches.

Think twice before using underlining. Rarely will you use it for anything other than company names or position titles, and you shouldn't use it for both of those. As with boldfacing, on some occasions you might want to underline important text to help draw the reader's eyes to juicy information, just as the next example does. (Refer to chapter 2 for the full-page *After* résumé of Sean Roberts, from which the following excerpt was taken, as well as the corresponding *Before* example.)

KEY ACCOMPLISHMENTS / VALUES OFFERED

Strategic Planning:	Envisioned business initiatives to <u>earn record profits, capturing returns of 30%</u> or better for companies with historically stagnant performance. Led process to craft short- and long-range strategic plans. Comprehensive experience in marketing, finance, operations, estimating, engineering, and bonding.
Profit Performance:	Delivered approximately <u>$10 million in additional profit through value-added engineering</u>. Focused on developing alternative, like-type systems and cost-effective construction methods without compromising design intentions.
Startup Operations:	Opened several new branches in competitive markets and <u>met targets for break-even and profit performance as many as 12 months ahead of schedule</u>. Industry contacts attracted "known" talent in estimating, MIS, and field operations.
New Market Development:	Targeted, courted, and sustained private and public sector relationships that led to <u>more than $1 billion in new business over career</u>. Laid groundwork for new players to gain status as qualified bidder and land negotiated projects.
Negotiations & Troubleshooting:	Maintained <u>litigation-free claims record</u>. Paired business savvy with technical expertise to avoid costly disputes. Corporate troubleshooter for turnaround of problem projects (averted $500,000 loss on environmentally sensitive project).

An italic font is appropriate for book titles, foreign words, and quoted passages. With prudent judgment, you can also sprinkle an italic font sparingly in a portion of a sentence or perhaps a whole sentence—*but never entire segments, such as all of the impact statements.* (See the two preceding *Before* résumé excerpts for examples of overuse of italics in the accomplishments section.) Bullets and effective use of white space are better tools for setting off these items (see "Use Bullets Strategically" later in this chapter).

Establish a Logical Sizing Hierarchy

Remember the stacking boxes that little children play with? The boxes typically come in a set of 10, each box graduated in size so that a large box holds a slightly smaller box, which holds a slightly smaller box, which holds a slightly smaller box, down to a tiny box about the diameter of a golf ball. Most parents of toddlers have these stacking boxes in their arsenal of entertainment. It's fun watching little ones develop their spatial skills as they figure out that a specific order is required for things to come together and, no matter how hard they might shove, a large box just won't fit into a smaller box.

There is a logical sizing scheme to consider as well when you're using caps, bold, underlining, and other treatments for text. Think about the stacking boxes when it comes to your name, category headings, company names, position titles, and text. For greater visual appeal, they should "stack," or fit together.

The following example presents a logically ordered scheme for font-work. Use it as a guide in dressing your text with logical sizing and emphasis.

You'll want to select approximately four to six of these levels for your résumé. More will visually assault your reader with too many styles to absorb.

THIS IS YOUR FULL NAME	Level 1
<u>CATEGORY HEADINGS IN RÉSUMÉ</u>	Level 2
AN ALTERNATIVE CATEGORY HEADING STYLE	Level 3
AN ALTERNATIVE CATEGORY HEADING STYLE	Level 4
COMPANY NAMES, ALL CAPS & BOLD	Level 5
COMPANY NAMES, ALL CAPS	Level 6
COMPANY NAMES IN SMALL CAPS, BOLDED	Level 7
<u>**Position Titles—Bold, Underline, Initial Caps**</u>	Level 8
Alternative Position Title or Subcategories Below Title	Level 9
Your address and telephone number as part of the header	Level 10
Body text of résumé presented in lowercase	Level 10
Italics, use sparingly for special emphasis or for titles of publications	Level 11

This hierarchy is not all-inclusive, nor is it a rigid pecking order that you must follow in presenting your text. Rather, it is intended to provide a sense of order and to illustrate how you can control your reader's eye by adding visual importance to certain pieces of your text. Reserve the biggest look, level 1, for your name. Remember that your résumé will sit on someone's desk next to others—you want *your* name to stand out. Avoid the common mistake of giving your address and telephone number the same level of treatment as your name. The following *Before* header shows how using the same size for the entire header (level 5) can cause the reader's eye to be drawn to the city, state, and ZIP code rather than the name.

Before

ANNE ELAINE WOLTERS

1234 GARDEN GROVE AVENUE

GARDENSIDE, CALIFORNIA 99999

(888) 555-5555

ANNEWOLTERS@ATTBI.COM

Your name should stand out more prominently than your address and telephone number. The next *After* example uses level 1 to accentuate the name, level 10 to present the mailing address and e-mail address, and level

9 (one level higher than the level used for the addresses) to help the telephone number stand out a shade more than the addresses. In the *After* header, the name is now the focal point, rather than the city and state.

After

ANNE ELAINE WOLTERS

1234 Garden Grove Avenue
Gardenside, California 99999
annewolters@attbi.com
(888) 555-5555

Use levels two through four (pick just one) for your category headings; then another lower level for company names, and so on. Be cautious about jumping from a lower level to a higher level and then back to a lower level or repeating a level for different pieces of information, as in this next *Before* illustration (level 8 is inappropriately used for both the category heading and position title). The result is a busy, thick-looking presentation.

Before

Professional Experience (Level 8)

COMPANY NAME (LEVEL 2)

Position Title (Level 8)

BODY COPY (LEVEL 7)

This choice of levels is more logical.

After

PROFESSIONAL EXPERIENCE (LEVEL 4)

COMPANY NAME (LEVEL 7)

Position Title (Level 8)

Body copy (Level 10)

Underlining category headings can be overkill. When plenty of white space surrounds a category heading (such as *Professional Experience* above), your reader's eye will naturally be drawn to it. The addition of an underline in cases like this is analogous to using a sledgehammer to kill a gnat. In the above example, the fact that the heading rests on the left margin more than an inch away from the remaining text automatically gives it a more prominent level; therefore, I opted against the use of underlining. It might, however, be helpful to underline headings when you're using a layout in which category headings are centered or visually "lost" in some way.

As a substitution for underlining category headings, consider adding the subtle touch of enlarging the first letter of each word in the heading. You can do this by highlighting the first letter with your cursor and then using the Format, Font command to increase the point size by four to six points. An alternative is to use the small caps font function; then increase the overall point size of the heading by a few points so that the heading doesn't shrink too much. In the following example, the first letters in the words *Professional Experience* are increased from 12 points to 18 points.

PROFESSIONAL EXPERIENCE

COMPANY NAME

<u>Title</u>

Body copy.

Your circumstances might call for a break from the traditional levels I just outlined. For instance, if you want to de-emphasize the name of a lesser-known company and highlight an impressive title, you might choose to present the company name without bold or caps (a lower level than normal). Then jump up a level or two for the title by using bold and underline.

PROFESSIONAL EXPERIENCE

Obscure Company Name, Remoteville, California

<u>VICE PRESIDENT</u>

Manage everything under the sun. Direct chief cook and bottle washer. Wear 14 hats simultaneously.

This next alternative for showcasing titles also works and adheres more closely to the sizing sequence presented in the second example above. In this case, the title wins first-place positioning to overshadow the obscure company name.

<u>**VICE PRESIDENT**</u>

Obscure Company Name, Remoteville, California

Manage everything under the sun. Direct chief cook and bottle washer. Wear 14 hats simultaneously.

The same techniques can work with your Education section too. Have you earned a degree from a lesser-known university? Spell out the degree to give more visual emphasis to it and give it a higher level order than the school name.

Podunk University

Master of Business Administration

or

Master of Business Administration — Podunk University

For those who attended an impressive college yet did not graduate, "sell" the school name in lights (bold, caps) followed by the degree program in bold text (if it's impressive) or regular text (if the major is not related to your job target).

IVY LEAGUE SCHOOL NAME

Degree Program: **Business Administration / Emphasis in Finance**

In all of your font-work, look for elements of interest to your reader and then thoughtfully consider how to guide your reader's eye toward those selling points.

Now that you have a handle on the elements of design—pattern, symmetry, and font-work—it's time to review the technical tools that can make these elements materialize.

Tweaking Tips

To put this chapter's design elements into practice, you'll need some technical know-how. Following are easy-to-follow tips that will enable you to manipulate tables, white space, line height, character spacing, text size, bullets, and rule lines. Instructions are included on these features for the two most popular word-processing software programs: Microsoft Word and Corel WordPerfect. The screen shots illustrate the how-to's in Microsoft

Word (version 2003; the same steps generally work in earlier versions as well as in Word XP). If you are using different software, explore the Help function to find similar tools.

Technical Tools to Create Tables

Tables are an effective tool to control the look of your résumé. They can be used as a substitute for tabs (left tabs, center tabs, or right tabs) to hold text in imaginary columns. The heading in Figure 8.10 was created using a table. Although the light-gray gridlines are revealed to give you an idea of where the table cells start and stop, you will want to "hide" gridlines in your final resume (see step 8 that follows).

Follow these steps to create a table like the one in Figure 8.10.

1. Starting with a new document, set your left and right margins (the margins for this example were set at .9). If you do not set left and right margins prior to creating the table, it will adhere to default margins.

2. From the Table menu, click Insert, Table. An Insert Table box will appear. Under Table Size, enter 3 for number of columns, and 3 for number of rows. Under AutoFit Behavior, select the Fixed Column Width radio button. Click OK. You'll now have a three-column, three-row table.

3. In the second column of the first row, type your first and last name and then center the text within that cell of the table (with your cursor in the cell with your name, click Format, Paragraph, and then choose Centered from the options for Alignment).

4. In the first column of the second row, type your street address. In the first column of the third row, type your city, state and ZIP code. Make sure this text is left-justified.

5. In the second column of the third row, type your e-mail address and center the text for that table cell.

6. In the third column of the second row, type your mobile phone number. In the third column of the third row, type your alternate telephone number. To right-justify the text in these two cells, highlight both cells and then select Format, Paragraph. In the Alignment box, select Right under the drop-down arrow options.

Figure 8.10: A Heading Created Using a Table

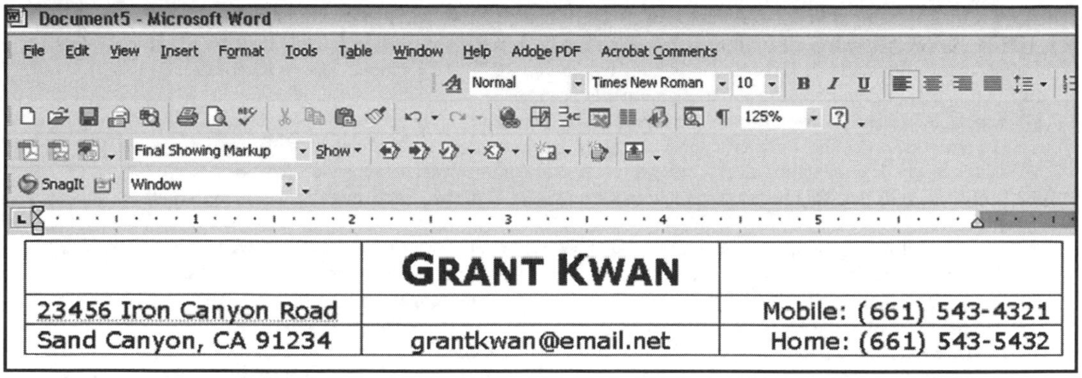

7. To remove the black border lines of the table, position your cursor anywhere within the table. From the Table menu, select Table Properties. Under the Table tab, select Borders and Shading. Under Settings, click None. Click OK to close the Borders and Shading box, and then OK once more to close the Table Properties box.

8. To hide the shaded gray gridlines before sending your resume to employers, position your cursor anywhere within the table. From the Table menu, select Hide Gridlines. If you need to view the gridlines again for table modifications, select Show Gridlines from the Table menu.

You can use tables throughout your document. Some people create their professional experience section using tables, adjusting the column gridlines by dragging them to the desired width for a left-hand column for dates and a right-hand column for experience. Tables are also useful in a three-column listing of keywords, or a two-column listing of coursework or professional associations.

Add White Space

White space is your ally—befriend it by mastering the Format menu in your word-processing program. This menu will give you much greater control (you can take the baseball gloves off!).

Note in this next *Before* example how the original writer used a bunched-up layout to try to conserve space. Not knowing how to add partial line spaces between paragraphs caused his strong position title to hide under the Professional Experience category heading and his multiple accomplishments to blur into one thick paragraph.

Before

PROFESSIONAL EXPERIENCE
Vice President, Sales & Marketing — Rainmaker Mfg. Co., Nogales, Arizona
Planned and directed sales activity for plastic and metal products in the irrigation and mining markets. Management
team member with hands-on involvement in sales, marketing, R&D, and customer service functions. Developed
distribution networks in domestic and foreign markets.

♦ Accepted relocation assignment to turnaround newly acquired drip irrigation company that, at time of purchase, was
  in a sharp sales decline. Initially, conducted comprehensive analysis with input from all employee levels and
  subsequently developed new dealer base, introduced new products, and expanded sales force.

♦ Led division to four-fold increase in sales with strong gain in market share, enabling company to sell for substantial
  profit.

♦ Member of R&D team that developed two new products, both of which earned annual honors from *Agricultural
  Engineering* (the official publication of ASAE) as among the top 50 developments in agriculture.

♦ Designed marketing and sales plan to launch new product, a concept new to the irrigation industry, now rapidly
  becoming industry standard for frost protection segment of the citrus industry.

♦ Led successful expansion into retail DIY market. Became a successful factor in national/mega-retailers such as K-
  Mart and Wal★Mart. Developed presentation and packaging, created sales/agent organization, and designed sales
  programs consistent with retail practices.

♦ Developed and implemented strategies to penetrate emerging market (mining) with existing drip irrigation product.
  Gained leading market share, with drip equipment for heap leach mining of gold and silver, now the standard
  practice within the United States.

♦ Against direct competition from major US center pivot manufacturers, sold full turnkey project supplying side roll
  equipment for 10,000-acre project.

Now compare the *Before* with the *After* example. The latter is unquestion-
ably prettier to look at and easier to read.

After

PROFESSIONAL EXPERIENCE

Vice President, Sales & Marketing — Rainmaker Mfg. Co., Nogales, Arizona

Planned and directed sales activity for plastic and metal products in the irrigation and mining markets. Management
team member with hands-on involvement in sales, marketing, R&D, and customer service functions. Developed
distribution networks in domestic and foreign markets.

♦ Accepted relocation assignment to turn around newly acquired drip irrigation company that, at time of purchase,
  was in a sharp sales decline. Initially conducted comprehensive analysis with input from all employee levels and
  subsequently developed new dealer base, introduced new products, and expanded sales force.

♦ Led division to fourfold increase in sales with strong gain in market share, enabling company to sell for substantial
  profit.

♦ Member of R&D team that developed two new products, both of which earned annual honors from *Agricultural
  Engineering* (the official publication of the ASAE) as among the top 50 developments in agriculture.

♦ Designed marketing and sales plan to launch new product, a concept new to the irrigation industry, now rapidly
  becoming industry standard for frost protection segment of the citrus industry.

♦ Led successful expansion into retail DIY market. Became a successful factor in national/megaretailers such as K-
  Mart and Wal★Mart. Developed presentation and packaging, created sales/agent organization, and designed sales
  programs consistent with retail practices.

♦ Developed and implemented strategies to penetrate emerging market (mining) with existing drip irrigation product.
  Gained leading market share, with drip equipment for heap leach mining of gold and silver, now the standard
  practice within the United States.

♦ Against direct competition from major U.S. center pivot manufacturers, sold full turnkey project supplying side roll
  equipment for 10,000-acre project.

It took me exactly 35 seconds to add the extra white space in the *After* example. To master the function keys and commands that generated this extra white space, please, sit down now at your computer and try these simple steps that follow. They will transform the appearance of your résumé from rough-around-the-edges to well-groomed.

Adding Space Between Paragraphs in MS Word

1. Position your cursor anywhere in the paragraph you want to add space after.

2. Click on Format, Paragraph and then choose Indents and Spacing.

3. In the box to the right of the words "Spacing After," change 0 points to 6 points. This will add approximately half a space after the paragraph versus an entire line space. Depending on the font, the height of one line will equal approximately 12 points.

4. Be zealous in applying the same line adjustments to like-type text—if you add 6 points of space after every accomplishment for your most recent employer, do the same for accomplishments under every subsequent employer.

Adding Space Between Paragraphs in Corel WordPerfect

Most die-hard WordPerfect fans will tell you that Corel WordPerfect software allows the user more control than does MS Word. I tend to agree, but that control comes at a price. In this case, the price is that you must be very specific about *where* the cursor is positioned when you tell the program to do something. Accordingly, to add space after a paragraph in WordPerfect, follow these steps:

1. Place your cursor at the end of the paragraph (after the final punctuation mark on the line).

2. Click on Format, Typesetting, Advance, and Down from Insertion Point.

3. In the vertical distance box, type .08; then press Enter. You can vary this number; .08 equals approximately half a line space. When I need white space but am already tight on top and bottom margins, I might add as little as .03 inches between a position title and a subsequent paragraph of responsibilities. This can squeeze out a fingernail of space, which can sometimes make a world of difference.

Change Line Height

Another method to gain white space is to shift space from one part of the résumé to another. For instance, by slightly compressing the vertical distance between lines within paragraphs, you can then add that space in the vicinity of the Accomplishments section or other important material that needs an extra dose of white space. Shrinking the line height may be all you need to keep a line or two from spilling over to a new page. The next *Before* and *After* examples show text at default and compressed settings.

Before

Provided guidance to loan officers on portfolio management. Developed credit structures that addressed key issues and reduced risk exposure to bank. Negotiated legal and enforceable strategic resolutions for commodity, water, and environmental issues; additionally dealt with grower lien laws, management capabilities, cash flows, and financial positions. Secured bank's position by working closely with legal counsel in documentation process.

After

Here's the line height reduced by just one point (from 12 to 11).

Provided guidance to loan officers on portfolio management. Developed credit structures that addressed key issues and reduced risk exposure to bank. Negotiated legal and enforceable strategic resolutions for commodity, water, and environmental issues; additionally dealt with grower lien laws, management capabilities, cash flows, and financial positions. Secured bank's position by working closely with legal counsel in documentation process.

As with all special formatting, be consistent. If you compress the line height on one job description, compress all job descriptions the same amount.

Adjusting Vertical Space Between Lines Within Paragraphs in MS Word

1. With your cursor anywhere on the paragraph you want to compress, click on Format, Paragraph, and choose Indents and Spacing.

2. Under Line Spacing, click on the drop-down arrow, select Exactly, and reduce the point size from the default to a smaller number.

3. In experimenting with reducing points, start with one point less than the default setting. The "right" amount can vary depending on the font you are using, so use good judgment in making sure text isn't too bunched up and characters don't touch between lines.

Adjusting Vertical Space Between Lines Within Paragraphs in Corel WordPerfect

1. Position your cursor above the text you want to change to affect all subsequent text or highlight a block of text to affect only that text.

2. Click on Format, Line, Height.

3. Change the setting from Automatic to Fixed.

4. Depending on the font you are using, you might opt for as few as .15 inches between lines. Again, use good judgment to determine whether lines are too crowded.

Expand Character Spacing

You might have noticed that some of the letter spacing in the category headings within various résumé examples in this book appears more spread out. This is called *expanded text,* or *kerning,* and it is a subtle method to enhance the readability of boldfaced material or to emphasize a particular title or subcategory. Expanded text is an especially helpful tool for submitting a scannable résumé because it prevents boldfaced letters from touching, which can cause a mistranslation of words in the scanning process. Note in the following lines how the second line is longer than the first, despite containing one fewer word *(NOT)*.

THIS BOLDED, ALL CAPS TEXT IS NOT EXPANDED.

THIS BOLDED, ALL CAPS TEXT IS EXPANDED.

(The second line is expanded about 2 points).

Expanding Text in MS Word

1. Highlight the string of text you want to expand, such as your name or a category heading.

2. Click on Format, Font, Character Spacing.

3. Click on the Spacing drop-down arrow and then select Expanded.

4. To the right of this box is a button that says "By"; you can either accept the default number or increase it to 1.1, 1.2, 1.3, or larger. The higher the number, the larger the space between letters.

```
Font                                                    ? X

   Font    Character Spacing    Text Effects

   Scale:        100%        ▼

   Spacing:      Expanded     ▼    By:  1.1 pt   ▲▼

   Position:     Normal       ▼    By:           ▲▼

   □ Kerning for fonts:              ▲▼  Points and above




   Preview

              ClearfaceGothicExtraBold


   This font style is imitated for display. The closest matching style will be printed.

   Default...                        OK         Cancel
```

Expanding Text in Corel WordPerfect

1. Highlight the text.

2. Click on Format, Typesetting, Word/Letter Spacing.

3. In the Letter Spacing dialog box, change Set Pitch to a lower number. You'll need to experiment with this number depending on the font you are using.

Tricks to Make Text Fit

If you find that text is spilling over by a few lines, use the handy "shrink" feature built into MS Word and Corel WordPerfect.

Shrinking Text in MS Word

1. Click on File, Print Preview.

2. Click the Shrink to Fit icon near the top below the main file menu. The Shrink to Fit icon is pictured with two pages and an arrow pointing to one page. If you get an error message that says "unable to shrink the document" return to normal view and delete any blank line spaces; then try again.

3. Click the Close Preview icon.

Shrinking Text in Corel WordPerfect

1. Click on Format, Make Text Fit.

2. Fill in the number of pages you want the résumé to be in the Desired Number of Pages to Fill box. The program automatically makes adjustments to font size, line height, or margins, depending on which boxes you check in the dialog box.

3. Click Make It Fit.

If you don't like the automatic adjustments the program makes (sometimes it reduces the font size too much), press Ctrl+Z on your keyboard and the résumé will expand to its original shape. This program works in reverse as well. To beef up a sparsely populated résumé or turn a one-and-one-half-page résumé into a two-page résumé, follow the same steps and increase the number of pages in the Desired Number of Pages to Fill box.

Use Bullets Strategically

Earlier in this chapter, I emphasized that you should reserve bullets for special material such as impact statements in a chronological format. Veering from this advice, I'll add that a functional résumé format might call for bullets before every item, as the next example shows. Regardless of when or where you use bullets, be mindful that spacing around the bullet, type of bullet, and size of bullet will affect whether the bullets are effective. Let's first review how to create bullets.

Creating Bullets in MS Word

1. Click on the paragraph you want to bullet.
2. Click the bullet icon on the button bar.

The default setting for bullets in MS Word looks like this.

Staff Education & Development

- Taught basic and advanced fetal monitoring and strip interpretation, equipping physicians and nurses with skills to improve patient outcomes. Coordinated strip review sessions with physicians at Metropolitan Hospital.

- Coordinated nursing inservices and participated in development of staff education classes for the western states region.

- Participated in the development of cesarean section clinical pathway.

- Developed and implemented tubal ligation program for labor and delivery.

- Conducted labor and delivery hospital tours for various groups, including teen pregnancy groups.

Creating Bullets in Corel WordPerfect

1. Highlight the text you want to bullet.

2. Click the bullet icon on the button bar.

The default settings for bullets in Corel WordPerfect look like this.

Staff Education & Development

- Taught basic and advanced fetal monitoring and strip interpretation, equipping physicians and nurses with skills to improve patient outcomes. Coordinated strip review sessions with physicians at Metropolitan Hospital.

- Coordinated nursing inservices and participated in development of staff education classes for the western states region.

- Participated in the development of cesarean section clinical pathway.

- Developed and implemented tubal ligation program for labor and delivery.

- Conducted labor and delivery hospital tours for various groups, including teen pregnancy groups.

The distance between bullets and text in WordPerfect adheres to the tab settings you have in place. The default tab set is a tab at every half-inch, which is usually too much distance between a bullet and regular text (a bullet before a subheading or a headline item might call for this wider spacing). Text positioned too far from a bullet draws the reader's eye to the bullet rather than to the text. See the next WordPerfect formatting section for how to fix this.

Adding or Subtracting Spacing Between Bullets and Text in MS Word

1. Place your cursor anywhere within the bulleted paragraph.

2. Click on Format, and select Bullets and Numbering.

3. Select Bulleted and then click on Customize in the bottom-right corner.

4. Change the settings on Bullet Position and Text Position until you get the effect you want.

- This is an example of text that wrapped with a hanging indent in MS Word. Note how this second line of text lines up under the first line of text rather than the bullet.

- This is an example of text that wrapped without a hanging indent. This positioning is not as visually appealing as the hanging indent shown immediately above because the text obscures the bullet, causing the reader to lose sight of preceding and subsequent bullets.

Adding or Subtracting Spacing Between Bullets and Text in Corel WordPerfect

As with most word-processing functions, several roads lead to the same result. One of the quickest is the following:

1. Position your cursor above the text you want bulleted—preferably toward the top of the page so that all bullets throughout your résumé will adhere to the same tab set and line up consistently.

2. Click View and then Ruler (if Ruler is already checked, do not click it again because that will make the ruler disappear).

3. On the ruler bar immediately above your screen, you will see a series of triangles, each representing a tab stop spaced ½ inch apart.

4. With your cursor on the ruler, click on the triangle closest to the right of where your bullet appears; drag that tab stop to the left so that it rests approximately $^3/_{16}$ to ¼ inch away from the tab stop that your bullet is lining up with.

Your bullet spacing should change from the first line below to the second.

-     Now is the time for all good men to come to the aid of the country.

- Now is the time for all good men to come to the aid of the country.

Changing the Type of Bullet in MS Word

1. Highlight the bulleted text.

2. Click on Format and select Bullets and Numbering. This will give you seven options from which to choose for the type of bullet.

3. If you want to see more options, click the Customize button, click the Bullet button (or the Character or Picture button in Word XP), and

select the font (such as Zapf Dingbats or Wingdings). From here, you can click on different-sized squares, arrows, plus signs, diamonds, check marks, hollow circles, shadowed circles, and so on.

Changing the Type of Bullet in Corel WordPerfect

In version 12, follow these steps:

1. Highlight the text you want bulleted.

2. Click on the down arrow immediately to the right of the bullet icon and choose from one of the various bullet options.

3. Or you can click More and choose from any of those options, or click More Bullets, select the Iconic Symbols set, and scroll through the options.

You might want your bullets to reflect some icon of your industry. For instance, a college piano teacher used the musical treble clef sign found at the bottom of the Typographic Symbols set to bullet her impact statements.

To change the type of bullet in earlier releases of WordPerfect, follow these steps:

1. Highlight the text you want bulleted.

2. Click on Insert, Bullets and Numbers.

3. Highlight in the dialog box one of the five options for bullets.

You can significantly expand your bullet options by circumventing the bullet function altogether and using Insert Characters followed by a hard indent. To do so, follow these steps:

1. Click Insert and then Character.

2. A dialog box will pop up with the words "Character Set" at the top left. Click on the item under the words "Character Set" to reveal 15 different sets of characters from which to choose.

You'll find that the Typographic Symbols set and Iconic Symbols set provide some of the better options for interesting bullets. Be sure to scroll down through the entire set to see all the possibilities.

Size of Bullets

One last word on bullets. Your goal in using bullets is to make the reader think "wow, look at these impressive accomplishments," not "wow, look at these big bullets." To accomplish the former, aim for a bullet that is about the size of the lowercase letters to the right of it; anything much smaller gets lost and anything much larger can be distracting.

- Too small
- Too large
- On the mark
- Too small
- Too large
- On the mark

Use Rule Lines

You should use a *rule line* under your contact information. It both sets off your name and guides your reader's eye to start reading the résumé. Note how your eye meanders in this *Before* example, yet quickly finds its way to Qualifications in the *After* example.

Before

SUSAN BRITTON WHITCOMB

12345 Easy Street
Westville, CA 95555
(559) 222-7474
coach@lovemycareer.com

QUALIFICATIONS

More than 14 years' experience ...

After

SUSAN BRITTON WHITCOMB

12345 Easy Street
Westville, CA 95555
(559) 222-7474
coach@lovemycareer.com

QUALIFICATIONS

More than 14 years' experience ...

Inserting a Rule Line in MS Word

1. Position your cursor anywhere on the last line of your contact information (in the above case, the e-mail address).

2. Click on Format, select Borders and Shading, and click the Borders tab.

3. Select Paragraph from the Apply To options.

4. In the Preview box above that, simply click your cursor below the shaded text area, and a horizontal rule will appear.

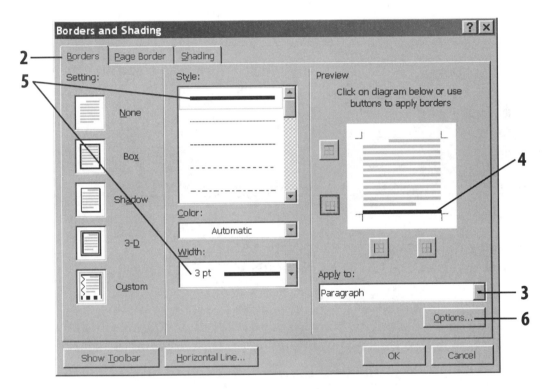

5. Next, select from among the many Style and Width options to get the desired effect.

6. To reposition the rule line (add more space above it), click on Options.

7. Change the default From Text, Bottom setting to 12 points, or simply "grab" it with your cursor and drag it down where you want it.

Border and Shading Options ? ×

From text

Top: 1 pt | Left: 4 pt

Bottom: 12 pt | Right: 4 pt

7

Preview

OK | Cancel

Inserting a Rule Line in Corel WordPerfect

In Corel WordPerfect 12, follow these steps:

1. Click Insert, Line, Custom Line.

2. Explore your many options for Line style, Line color, and Line thickness, as well as Space above line and Space below line. Click OK.

3. To change any attribute of the line in the future, select the line with a left-click of your mouse. Then right-click and select Edit Horizontal Line. The menu described in step 2 will reappear.

In earlier versions of WordPerfect, follow these steps:

1. Click on Graphics, Custom Line, and then Line Styles to reveal the same 30-plus options.

2. Click OK after deciding on the line style.

3. To add space between the line and text, position your cursor before the graphic line; then follow the steps outlined earlier under "Adding Space Between Paragraphs in Corel WordPerfect."

Other Graphic Elements

Charts, graphs, tables, text boxes, logos, watermarks, drop caps, industry icons, and spot color are among the other graphic accessories available to you. If you choose to use them, remember that they should be applied like jewelry—tastefully and sparingly. (Paper style, of course, also plays a part in visual appeal of a presentation résumé. For more information on résumé papers and envelopes, please see chapter 10.)

Typically, you will want to have one main design point on the résumé: your name. Adding a text box, table, or graphic might potentially fight with your name for attention, so exercise discretion with these add-ons. Moreover, the extra effort involved in finding the perfect industry icon or watermark might go unappreciated—human resources managers polled in the résumé preference survey (see appendix B) indicated that the use of an icon does not measurably improve a candidate's chance of being selected for an interview. This does not mean you cannot use one.

Visual Artistry Made the Difference

Magic

To give you an idea of how you can use graphic elements, review the résumé and cover letter examples (8.11 through 8.18) at the end of this chapter. Note factors such as the positioning and size of the graphic element, the distance between it and surrounding text, and appropriateness to the candidate's profession or industry.

> *Caution* Résumés with graphic elements or specialty paper should be reserved for human eyes only. Distance yourself from these treatments when preparing résumés to be included in a text-based database or submitted online. With the prevalence of résumé databases and electronic searches, you should prepare both a presentation résumé and a text-only résumé. (See the next chapter on e-résumés.)

Cover Letter 8.11: How a Cover Letter Can Complement a List-Oriented Résumé

DILLAN G. OBERG

12 High View Lane ✦ Los Angeles, CA 91212 ✦ (213) 442–1432 ✦ dillano@email.com

---

What do you look for in a copywriter? Do you need someone who:

    ✓ Understands what motivates consumers to buy?

    ✓ Can easily spot a product's features and translate them into benefits?

    ✓ Uses concepts and words that are easy for consumers to understand?

    ✓ Works well with creative and production teams?

    ✓ Produces campaigns that meet clients' goals—on time and within budget?

If so, I can deliver.

Before deciding on a career in advertising, I did my homework. I researched the training and talent needed to succeed. From account executives and creative directors like yourself, I learned that a degree is helpful (although it doesn't guarantee success!). I've since completed a Bachelor of Arts in Broadcast Communication. The other ingredient—talent—is refined with practice and guidance from seasoned creative staff.

The enclosed résumé outlines my experience since graduating from University of California, San Diego. Working on feature films and television commercials has really given me a taste of what goes into successful projects. At this stage in my career, I'm ready for a position that will put me at the heart of the creative process.

Your schedule is no doubt busy. I'd like just four minutes of telephone time to see if my skills would be a good match for your agency. I'll call within the next week. In advance, thanks for your consideration.

Sincerely,

Dillan G. Oberg

Enclosure

Résumé 8.12: Use of a Table

DILLAN G. OBERG

12 High View Lane ✦ Los Angeles, CA 91212 ✦ (213) 442–1432 ✦ dillano@email.com

Objective: **To contribute to the creative development of advertising campaigns.**

EDUCATION

UNIVERSITY OF CALIFORNIA, SAN DIEGO   [date]

Bachelor of Arts Degree: Broadcast Communications

QUALIFICATIONS

✦ **Writing:** Familiar with conceptual development and writing styles for print and television ads. Wrote and produced news programs, talk show scripts, sitcom programming, PSAs, and other styles while completing Broadcast Communications degree.

✦ **Communications:** Proven ability to interface with a wide range of disciplines within the production process.

✦ **Artist:** Bronze, steel, and ceramic sculpture; aluminum and bronze casting; pottery; and glass blowing.

PROFESSIONAL EXPERIENCE

Employer	Project	Assignment	Location	Date
Iki Productions	"Ikiban" Independent Feature Film	Production Assistant	Los Angeles, California	[mo/yr– Present]
Unicorn Productions	"Where the Wind Stops" Independent Feature Film	Production Assistant	Los Angeles, California	[mo/yr– mo/yr]
Bellemma Films	"Mascara" Independent Feature Film	Production Assistant	Los Angeles, California	[mo/yr– mo/yr]
M.B.A. Films	Sprint Wireless Communication Television Commercial	Art Department	Santa Cruz, California	[mo/yr– mo/yr]
Union Square Productions	S.O.S. Soap Sponge Television Commercial	Art Department	San Francisco, California	[mo/yr– mo/yr]
Hal Riney/Radical Media	Abs–Master Television Commercial	Art Department	Mill Valley, California	[mo/yr– mo/yr]
Genton Research Laboratories	"Recreation of Life" Machine Performance	Craft Services/ Technician	Santa Clarita, California	[mo/yr– mo/yr]
Solstice Productions	"Winter Solstice" Independent Feature Film	Production Assistant	San Francisco, California	[mo/yr– mo/yr]
McCain Erickson/Goal Line Prod.	AT&T Television Commercial	Craft Services	Los Angeles, California	[mo/yr– mo/yr]
Lifeline Productions	"Life Beyond" Independent Feature Film	Production Assistant	Los Angeles, California	[mo/yr– mo/yr]

✦ ✦ ✦

Résumé 8.13: Use of a Graph

VIRGINIA S. GANT

1234 Lake Circle ♦ Burlingame, California 94222 ♦ vgant@gte.net
(415) 222-1222

QUALIFICATIONS

PROFIT-CONSCIOUS SALES MANAGER with proven success in building and motivating high-growth sales organizations. Equally competent in direct sales, including national/key account management. Career highlights:

♦ **Sales Management** — Recruited, developed, and coached national distributor sales organization that more than doubled sales volume for six consecutive years. Led market expansion from local to national distribution, positioning company as the industry leader in recreational water treatment solutions.

♦ **Marketing** — Researched and identified target markets, selected channels of distribution, determined pricing structure, and developed packaging for new products. Successfully introduced new items that gained #1 market share in less than one year.

♦ **Technical Sales** — Strong technical background in sales of chemical products for recreational and industrial water uses. Led research and development functions for new treatment systems including label development, regulatory compliance, and market support. Excellent relationships with federal and state EPA officials.

PROFESSIONAL EXPERIENCE

CRAY COMPANY, BURLINGAME, CALIFORNIA   [date]–[date]

VICE PRESIDENT, MARKETING & SALES

Led this small, privately held company with sales in one western state through successful expansion into the national marketplace. Given complete autonomy for profit center reengineering and market alignment for the Recreational Chemical Division. Established and directed manufacturer's rep sales force. Established relationships with and serviced key national accounts. Directed advertising, merchandising, and account management strategies.

Accomplishments

▸ Recognized market opportunities and initiated expansion to build strong national market presence, achieving revenue growth of $100,000 in 1st year sales to more than $2 million in [date]:

▸ Launched new products and line extension (R&D, EPA approval, pricing, market planning, sales presentations), capturing leading market share in less than six months.

▸ Secured new business with national accounts such as Wal★Mart (10 states), Home Depot, and Orchard Supply Hardware, negotiating prime retail space and capturing maximum distribution in accounts.

▸ Built number and quality of accounts from 100 to over 1,300.

▸ Maintained lucrative profit margins (7-8% over industry average) throughout rapid growth stage.

▸ Consulted clients such as The Disney Company and Caesar's Palace regarding above-ground water treatment.

STORE MANAGER, K&M COMPANY, BURLINGAME, CALIFORNIA   [date]–[date]

EDUCATION, AFFILIATIONS

Tom Hopkins Sales Seminar ... technical seminars on water treatment chemistry sponsored by Buckman Laboratories ... ongoing self-initiated study. Member, Association of Water Treaters and community service club.

♦ ♦ ♦

Résumé 8.14: Use of a Text Box

KELLAN VICKERS

1234 Washoe Drive
Palo Alto, CA 94112
Business: (408) 333-1112
Residence: (408) 444-2222
kvickers@compuserve.com

Experienced business manager/administrator with strengths in:

▸ Strategic planning and profitable management of regional operations
▸ Supervision of licensed sales, technical, and support staff
▸ Fiscal management and internal productivity enhancements
▸ Compliance with stringent regulatory requirements
▸ Servicing and retaining high net-worth customer base

QUALIFICATIONS

More than 17 years' experience in operations and management with Fortune 500 company. Career marked by fast-track promotion through positions as client service representative, operations supervisor/manager, and administrative manager; presently executive 2nd-in-command for Silicon Valley. Delivered impressive 42% profit margin while annualized revenues grew from $12 million to $36 million. Noted for analytical skills, contingency planning, problem solving, and foresight for damage control. Especially skilled at building rapport with licensed sales professionals, support staff, and valued customers. Prior military career as Intelligence Officer in central Europe. Fluent in German, some fluency in Russian.

PROFESSIONAL EXPERIENCE

VICE PRESIDENT, ADMINISTRATIVE MANAGER—New York Securities, San Jose, CA   1981–Present

Executive team member, accountable for planning, implementation, and evaluation of business operations that support three financial planning/brokerage offices in San Jose, Saratoga, and Campbell. Collaborate with resident vice president on issues relating to market positioning, growth strategies, expense controls, technology development, and sales team development. Prepare and monitor $21 million operating budget. Approve suitability of transactions for more than 90 brokers. Direct a support staff of 25. Ensure regulatory compliance and facilitate audits (SEC, NASD, NYSE and other exchanges, California Department of Corporations, internal audits). Oversee communications and computer infrastructure (industry-specific and Windows-based systems).

- Supported a threefold growth in revenues—simultaneously decreased expense ratio 2.25%.

- Ranked among top branches in the nation for regulatory compliance.

- Reduced turnover of support staff from 50% to virtually nil.

- Controlled a primary expense category (telecom)—aggressive monitoring of New York/New Jersey home office allocations yielded more than $93,000 in income returned to San Jose and Saratoga branches in 12-month period.

- Tasked with start-up of new Campbell office and brought to profitable level 12 months ahead of goal; led expansion of San Jose and Saratoga offices, managing added expenses within improved expense ratio.

- Influenced shift in sales culture from transaction-orientation to full-service, planning-based business utilizing a broad array of products and services—efforts maximized high-return accounts and minimized high-maintenance accounts.

- Achieved manager status in 3½ years, officer status in another 2 years (typical management track takes 10+ years).

INTELLIGENCE OFFICER—United States Army   1977–1981

Stationed primarily in Germany, supporting infantry battalion deployed in the strategic area of central Europe. Awarded Meritorious Service Medal (peacetime equivalent of Bronze Star) and Army Commendation Medal.

EDUCATION

Attended UCLA's Anderson Graduate School of Management (rated among top 10 business schools by *US News and World Report*). Coursework emphasis: international management, foreign language, and business administration.

Graduated *summa cum laude* from University of California, Berkeley—double major in German and Russian. Attended University of Freiburg im Breisgau, Germany, as recipient of Kiwanis Graduate Fellowship.

■ ■ ■

Résumé 8.15: Use of a Drop Cap

HOLLY ALLADIAN

halladian@aol.com

HIGH-TECHNOLOGY SALES,
MARKETING & NEW
BUSINESS DEVELOPMENT

27 Sunset Place East
Fishkill, NY 11060
(212) 234-5678

SUMMARY

Performance-driven sales professional with proven talent for expanding customer base, cultivating strategic relationships, maximizing account sales, and servicing a notable account list. Leading-edge presentation, negotiation, and closing skills.

Complementary strengths in management with an eye for talented, committed team players. Skilled in training and developing under-performing individuals into consistent quota achievers. Intuitive in identifying weak links, anticipating market conditions, and planning for contingencies.

Technologically astute. Career history includes technical sales positions with Apple Computer and Net Avenue. Fluent in information and communications technologies. Advanced PC and Mac skills; extensive knowledge of PowerPoint, Excel, FrontPage, HTML, and in-house relational databases.

SALES EXPERIENCE

SENIOR SALES ACCOUNT EXECUTIVE—Net Avenue, New York, NY   1989–Present

Execute sales/marketing programs in high-profile NYC territory, personally generating more than $3.2 million in annual advertising revenue. Accountable for sales performance for three campaigns, including tactical plans, new product launches, and account strategies. Create a three-year marketing plan for every customer, identifying unique selling features and tailoring strategies to position businesses for success.

Representative Sales Achievements

➠ Yielded unsurpassed record for sales growth, exceeding recent campaign goals by 362%, 141%, 186%, 161%, and 124% in five geographic sectors.

➠ Captured above-average growth in revenue, increasing personal sales from $2.2 million to over $3.2 million per year.

➠ Earned #1 position for sales performance among sales teams of up to 30 in five of the past six campaigns.

➠ Earned virtually every sales honor possible for five consecutive years, including Net Avenue's exclusive Roundtable of Leaders (reserved for top 5% based on indices of professionalism, accuracy, and sales).

Leadership/Management Talents

➠ As one of three Master Sales Representatives, provided sales leadership and training in selling strategies, operations, and systems information. Coached "probationary" reps, equipping several with tools to perform above objective.

➠ Selected to pilot new technology programs: field-tested applications designed to facilitate the sales process; recommended modifications to make equipment more user-friendly; member of team that led statewide rollout.

Prior Experience/Accomplishments

➠ **Senior Sales Representative** with Nynex Yellow Pages: Set still-unsurpassed record for directory sales; Presidential Winner as top Sales Representative in New York.   1986–1989

➠ **Technical Sales Representative** with Apple Computers. Presented and closed $240,000 contract, one of first university campuses to break allegiance with IBM for Macintosh platform.   1985–1986

EDUCATION

Bachelor of Science Degree, Business Administration/Finance—State University of New York   1986
Continual professional development courses include semiannual **Sales, Technology, and Communication** seminars.

Résumé 8.16: Use of an Industry Icon

LANCE A. MATHIAS
Post Office Box 55555
Fremont, CA 55555   (555) 555-5555

SUMMARY OF QUALIFICATIONS

HIGHLY SKILLED HVAC TECHNICIAN offering 20 years of diverse experience:

- ❏ Installation, troubleshooting, overhaul, and repair of computer-regulated environmental control systems for residential, commercial, and industrial establishments (A/C units ranging from ½-ton to 250-ton chillers).

- ❏ Supervision of apprentice-level, air-conditioning and refrigeration maintenance workers and electricians.

- ❏ State certification to instruct community college classes in air-conditioning, refrigeration, and heating.

- ❏ Business background as owner and manager of a full-service, air-conditioning and heating repair company.

PROFESSIONAL EXPERIENCE

MATHIAS MAINTENANCE, Pasadena, CA   1991–Present

HVAC Technician/Principal

Built new business from start-up to sales in excess of $300,000. Provide design, installation, repair, and maintenance services for air-conditioning, refrigeration, and heating systems. Sourced and secured service contracts with major educational institutions, government agencies, regional shopping malls, and manufacturing companies.

CAL WEST TECHNICAL COLLEGE, Pasadena, CA   1987–Present

Instructor—Air-Conditioning, Refrigeration & Heating

Teach course providing basic theory and hands-on experience in installing, troubleshooting, and repairing environmental control systems.

ENVIRONMENTAL-AIR, Cambria, CA   1979–1991

Air-Conditioning/Refrigeration Maintenance Technician

Installed, repaired, and performed preventative maintenance on commercial and large, complex industrial systems. Also held position as Electrician.

EDUCATION

CAL WEST TECHNICAL COLLEGE, Pasadena, California

- ▪ **Certificate in Air-Conditioning Technology**
- ▪ **Graduated with 4.0 GPA**

❏ ❏ ❏

Cover Letter 8.17: Use of a Graphic Image

SASHA BERENTON

1420 East Rainwater • Great City, GA 23456
(313) 212-1212

September 12, xxxx

Mr. Kelly Valcom
CITY ZOOLOGICAL SOCIETY
123 West Coronado Drive
San Diego, California 90121

Dear Mr. Valcom:

As an avid and long-time supporter of the City Zoological Society, I am very interested in the Marketing Coordinator position currently available with the zoo. As a volunteer during the past several years, I have watched with pride as the zoo has matured in offering a strong combination of wildlife, conservation, and education programs.

Qualifications I can offer the City Zoological Society stem from my background in education, marketing, and business environments. More specifically, my work:

    as a **marketing consultant** would draw on my ability to create and execute comprehensive marketing, promotions, special events, and direct mail campaigns . . .

as an **educator** has provided me with both the ideas and the district contacts to involve schools throughout the valley in "interactive" support programs. I am a firm believer that tapping the resources of our youth will ensure long-term support of the zoo's mission. . .

as a **volunteer** with the Zoological Society has provided insight into the marketing and special events currently conducted by the Zoological Society. I served as Volunteer Registration Coordinator for the most recent Safari Night and Big Band Zoobilation events. I have also involved my students in zoo fund-raising and hands-on projects such as tree-planting . . .

as a **business professional** has given me strong computer skills (spreadsheet, database, word processing, graphics) and, most importantly, an understanding of the need for stretching limited operating funds while achieving bottom-line results. Moreover, I have the organizational, administrative, and technical skills to see projects through to completion.

Attached are my résumé and letters of reference, which are indicative of my professionalism, marketing skills, work ethic, pride in accomplishing goals, and commitment to quality.

There are a number of ideas on cross-promotional programs and outreach projects that I would enjoy sharing with you.

Sincerely,

Sasha Berenton

Enclosures

Résumé 8.18: Use of Spot Color

MARIA HIELO

| 4321 Wawona Lane | Santa Fe, NM 87654 | (443) 423-3215 |

Education:

Master of Art History (emphasis in Pre-Columbian Art)   1997
Bachelor of Arts (special major Art History, minor Humanities)—*summa cum laude* (4.0 GPA)   1994
New Mexico State University

Professional Experience:

Santa Fe Community College: Instructor   1997–Present

♦ Designed, developed, and taught new course: Pre-Columbian Art. Course explores Andean and Mesoamerican art, architecture, and cultural traditions.

Chucanga City College: Instructor   1/96–5/96

♦ Taught two classes of Art History 10, Ancient and Primitive Art Architecture. Course included Paleolithic through Gothic, Sub-Saharan Africa, Pre-Columbian Mesoamerica, Pre-Columbian Andes, and Native American Art.

Santa Fe Art Museum: Exhibition Cocurator   4/95–11/95
Pacha Tambo: Earth Resting Place, Janet Hughes Pre-Columbian Peruvian Collection

♦ Performed all curatorial duties including: writing and editing wall test, in-depth research, consultation with scholars, textile conservation, design and layout of show, design of mounts, and public speaking.

Santa Fe Art Museum: Education Committee Cochair   9/95–8/96

♦ Organized new Spring Lecture Series. Coordinated and wrote workbook for *Let's Talk Art*, an educational experience for grade school students. Presented docent training for Stratton Collection of Pre-Hispanic art.

Gareth Terensen Pre-Columbian Peruvian Collection: Intern   1993–1994

♦ Assisted in preparing condition reports, photography, storage, research, and classification of 650 Peruvian artifacts.

Medi-Systems Health Care: Director of Marketing   1984–1986

♦ Directed public relations, marketing, and sales for Santa Fe region.

Publications:

"Deadly Deceptions: Women as Betrayers," *Mortals, Maidens and Mothers: Re-presenting Women in Renaissance Prints* (exhibition catalog), 1996.

Let's Talk Art: Pre-Columbian Museum Adventure Workbook. Edited workbook and contributed majority of text. Published by Chucango Art Museum, in collaboration with Santa Fe School District and the Smithsonian Institution, 1995.

Wrote and edited wall text for exhibition entitled, "*Pacha Tambo:* Earth Resting Place," 1995.

Professional Organizations:

Current Memberships

Santa Fe Art Museum: Docent for Pre-Columbian collection, Council of 100; Santa Fe Metropolitan Museum; County Archaelogical Society; Archaelogical Institute of America; Women's Network; Arte Americas; Phi Kappa Phi National Honor Society; and Golden Key National Honor Society.

References Available upon Request

Although résumé 8.18 is not printed in color, a rich-looking royal blue was applied sparingly to the horizontal lines and the box that framed the name of this art history instructor. This treatment is available to anyone with access to a color printer. You can access color by highlighting the desired text you want to colorize and clicking Format, Font; then, click Color and select the color you desire.

Top 10 Visual Appeal Tips

1. **Be consistent in design treatments.** Use the same tab spacing or amount of vertical space between every category heading. If you apply bold and underline to one position title, use these treatments consistently on all other position titles throughout the résumé. The same idea holds for treatment of company name, position title, space between paragraphs, or bulleted accomplishments.

2. **Avoid starting too many consecutive lines with bullets.** This polka-dot effect doesn't allow you to control the reader's eye; fewer groupings of bullets will help guide the reader's eye to key information.

3. **Add white space.** Use the Format, Paragraph, Indents and Spacing command to add, say, 5 to 8 pts of space before or after paragraphs.

4. **Minimize the space between the bullet position and the text position.** Between .15 to .2 is ideal.

5. **Reserve bullets for accomplishments rather than responsibilities.**

6. **Limit the number of tab stops on the page.** Too many causes the résumé to look busy.

7. **Break up lengthy paragraphs.** Organize paragraphs into logical pieces of information with a subheading.

8. **Balance the résumé top-to-bottom** and **left-to-right.** Avoid the Leaning-Tower-of-Pisa look.

9. **Use one font style, possibly two.** You could reserve the second font for, say, your name or category headings.

10. **Design within the "Food Chain."** Use a logical hierarchy of font-work (bold, underline, point size of fonts) and case (all caps, small caps, upper and lower case) to provide a sense of order and to control the reader's eye toward important information.

Chapter
9

E-Résumés, E-Portfolios, and Blogs

"Technological progress is like an axe in the hands of a pathological criminal."

—Albert Einstein

A decade ago, job seekers had to ask themselves, "will I need an electronic résumé in my search?" Today, the question is not "will I…?," but "which kind…?" Ignoring the trends in technology is a bit like turning your back on the ocean—eventually you'll get blindsided by a wave that can leave you sputtering. Take the time to learn the basics.

Electronic résumés (e-résumés) come in assorted flavors—each with a specific form and function. This chapter covers two key types:

- **ASCII plain-text résumés:** Used when pasting a résumé into an e-mail message or a Web site e-form/résumé-builder.

- **Web résumés, e-portfolios, and blogs:** Web-based career marketing documents, providing you with a 24/7 online marketing presence.

You'll find the essentials of electronic résumés in this chapter. We'll also briefly cover scannable résumés later in this chapter. Note that a scannable résumé in printed format is not, technically, an e-résumé; however, it can become an e-résumé after it has been scanned and included in an employer's software program for tracking applicants and candidates. Scannable résumés are nearing extinction, as the majority of employers prefer that you e-mail rather than fax your résumé.

The following sections show the how-to's for creating and using ASCII and Web résumés or e-portfolios. There are a number of curves to watch for when preparing them. Done incorrectly, your e-résumé could be lost in an Internet "black hole"; done correctly, it can help you reach for the stars.

ASCII Text Résumés

To create a text résumé, it is helpful to have an understanding of ASCII. Pronounced "ásk-ee," it stands for American Standard Code for Information Interchange. An ASCII file is a plain-Jane presentation—no graphics, no rule lines, no bullets, and so on—but it's crucial for sharing files between various computer platforms and applications. *Platform* is the term used to describe the type of computer hardware, such as a PC, Macintosh, UNIX workstation, or mainframe terminal. *Applications* refer to the software—in this case, word-processing software—such as Microsoft Word or WordPerfect. ASCII uses a coding scheme that assigns a value to letters, numbers, punctuation marks, and certain other characters. Each character receives a seven-digit binary number (0000000 through 1111111), creating a mathematic, universal language that's readable from Azerbaijan to Zimbabwe.

After you have converted your text résumé (also known as a plain-text résumé) to ASCII format, you can paste it into an e-mail message or into e-forms at your target company's Web site or a career site (for instance, CareerBuilder.com or 6figurejobs.com). Steps to convert and paste your résumé into an e-mail or e-form are covered on pages 429–430.

There are benefits to pasting your résumé directly into an e-mail message; the reader then sees everything you are sending in one neat bundle of information. Conversely, if you send your résumé as an "attachment" to the message, you are sending an extra "envelope," requiring that the receiver open and handle an additional piece of information. In some cases, that information isn't in the same language as the computer's native tongue, which causes file-compatibility problems. Also, many employers are wary of opening a file attached to an e-mail because it might contain a virus. Many employers specify "no attachments" in their job postings, and others might simply delete your message if it has a file attached.

When e-mailing a résumé, unless requested to do otherwise, paste your résumé into the e-mail message. The recipient then has the ability to view, print, copy, or save your résumé.

> *Caution* A "message attack" is my name for an e-mail message containing an attached file that could just as easily have been included in the body of the e-mail message. Message attacks earn their name because they put readers on the defensive by stealing precious time and mental energy. When readers log on to find dozens of e-mail messages awaiting them, they might be tempted to skip the download requirement on messages from strangers. Attachments take extra time to scan for viruses and extra aspirin to manage the headache caused when files are in a format that isn't compatible with the system (or when incompatibility causes the subsequent printout to look as if you wrote your résumé in Cyrillic). Whenever possible, adhere to the motto "Paste Avoids Waste" to conserve your readers' precious time.

The Advantages and Disadvantages of ASCII Résumés

The following are **advantages** of using an ASCII résumé:

- Is universally readable by any computer system.

- Can be manipulated easily from an e-mail message into an employer's résumé database.

- Can be distributed in seconds to dozens, hundreds, or even thousands of employers, recruiters, or employment Web sites.

- Is cost-effective. The cost to use a résumé-distribution service that can send your résumé to thousands of contacts within seconds is typically very inexpensive when compared to distributing your résumé via a traditional snail-mail campaign.

- Shows employers that you have technical know-how.

The following are **disadvantages** of using an ASCII-format résumé:

- Lacks visual appeal because it is straight text and allows for virtually no formatting.

- Can be difficult to read when it is printed, especially if the conversion from a word-processing program to the ASCII-file format was done without following the correct steps.

- If distributed to hundreds of recruiter sites via a résumé-distribution service, ASCII résumés can be unwelcome to recruiters who are searching for only people in a specific industry.

- Encounters increased competition when posted at a major career site.

ASCII Résumé Do's and Don'ts

Use the following list of Do's and Don'ts as a quick guide for preparing the ASCII-text version of your résumé. If you have little or no experience converting files into ASCII, I highly recommend reading the section on "Steps for ASCII Conversion" that follows this quick guide.

Do's

* When e-mailing your résumé, use the "Plain Text (*.txt)" conversion option in Microsoft Word 2003 (after clicking "Save," you'll see a pop-up window; here you'll want to check the "Insert line breaks" button). If you're working in an older version of Microsoft Word, use the "Text Only with Line Breaks" option. In WordPerfect, use the "ANSI Windows Text" conversion option. Regardless of your word-processing program, before converting be sure to shorten the line length throughout the document by increasing the right margin from 1 inch to 2 inches. (For complete instructions, see "Converting to ASCII for E-mailing Using MS Word or Corel WordPerfect" later in this chapter.)

* When pasting your résumé into an e-form, use the "Plain Text (*.txt)" conversion in MS Word and the "ANSI (Windows) Generic Word Processor" conversion in Corel WordPerfect.

* Use only keyboard characters that are transferable to ASCII text.

* Replace any bullets with asterisks (*) or other ASCII-supported keyboard characters (if it appears on your keyboard, it's an ASCII character).

* Add white space liberally to improve the readability of the document.

* Consider using a row of characters, such as tildes (~), above or below category headings to help set them off.

* Delete header information from the second page of your traditional, printed version.

* Test your e-mailable résumé by sending it to your own e-mail address or to the e-mail address of a friend.

Don'ts

* Don't place more than 60 characters on each line (characters include spaces and punctuation marks).

* When converting a traditional/presentation résumé to an ASCII résumé, don't forget to save the new ASCII résumé under a new document name to help you keep track of your different résumé versions. For instance, you might save your résumé that you will paste

into e-mails as *resume4email.txt* or your résumé that you will paste into e-forms as *resume4eforms.txt*. If you're using an older version of MS Word or WordPerfect, it might be necessary to type the file extension ".txt" when you create the new file name.

➤ Unless you've been told that an e-mail attachment is acceptable, don't attach a Word or WordPerfect document to an e-mail message when someone requests your résumé via e-mail. Instead, paste an ASCII-text version of the document into the body of the e-mail message. (Alternatively, you could both attach an MS Word or PDF version and paste the résumé into the body of the e-mail, which gives the recipient a choice of formats.)

➤ Don't send anything other than your résumé. Check to make sure that you delete any miscellaneous information, embedded comments, track changes marking, or other notes that might have been included at the bottom of the résumé document. (I've heard of job seekers sending a résumé to a prospective employer where the résumé file also contained a cover letter addressed to another target company.)

Steps for ASCII Conversion

Your goal in creating an ASCII résumé is to strip the original résumé document of all formatting so that it is readable by any computer. There are several ways to convert a file to ASCII and several opinions on which type of conversion (with line breaks or without line breaks) is best. It depends on whether you'll need the résumé to be pasted into an e-mail or pasted into an e-form at a Web site. I recommend two different sets of steps: one for converting a résumé to ASCII for e-mailing and one for converting to ASCII for posting at Web sites. We'll look at each process separately.

Converting to ASCII for E-Mailing Using MS Word or Corel WordPerfect

1. **Change the margins.** With your word-processing software open and the résumé on screen, highlight the entire document (Ctrl + A). Click File, Page Setup. Enter 1.0 (for one inch) in the box labeled Left. Enter 2.0 (two inches) in the box labeled Right. This step shortens the length of the lines, which is important for controlling line breaks.

2. **Change the font.** Use a fixed-width font, such as Courier or Courier New. With the document still highlighted, change the font by clicking Format, Font. Scroll through the font selections in the drop-down box labeled Font or Font Face. Click on Courier. In the drop-down box for Font Size, choose 12 pt. Click OK. Use the Esc (escape) key to unhighlight the document. The 12-pt font places fewer characters on a line and helps prevent unattractive line wraps—aim for no more than 60 characters per line (a space counts as a character).

This next example shows an ASCII conversion where the *Before* ASCII version used a 10-point Times Roman font and .9 inch left and right margins. The result shows that this is how *not* to do it, as it is very laborious to read.

```
                    SENIOR MANAGEMENT TEAM
                    High-Tech Manufacturing
Performance-driven business executive with U.S. and international experience in strategic
planning, competitive market
development, operations, information technology, and marketing through distribution. More
than 15 years
of management and
P&L experience in world-class manufacturing organizations. Proven ability to turnaround
under-performing operations, drive
growth/profit, and expand global markets. Progressive experience with automated, computer-
controlled
manufacturing systems.
MBA marketing and finance skills. Knowledge of SAP R3 and BaaN. Skilled in assembling
cohesive teams, addressing morale
and skill-set issues, and linking individual motivation with organizational mission.
```

In the *After* version, the right margin was set to 2 inches, font changed to Courier, and point size increased to 12-point prior to saving the file in ASCII format. The result is a much cleaner read.

After

```
SENIOR MANAGEMENT TEAM
High-Tech Manufacturing

Performance-driven business executive with
U.S. and international experience in strategic
planning, competitive market development,
operations, information technology, and
marketing through distribution. More than 15
years of management and P&L experience in
world-class manufacturing organizations.
Proven ability to turnaround under-performing
operations, drive growth/profit, and expand
global markets. Progressive experience with
automated, computer-controlled manufacturing
systems. MBA marketing and finance skills.
Knowledge of SAP R3 and BaaN. Skilled in
assembling cohesive teams, addressing morale
and skill-set issues, and linking individual
motivation with organizational mission.
```

3. **Use Save As, choosing Plain Text (*.txt).** Click File, Save As. In the Save As Type box, scroll down and select Plain Text (*.txt); in older versions of Microsoft Word, choose Text Only with Line Breaks. For Corel WordPerfect users, scroll up in the File Type box and select ANSI (Windows) Text.

4. **Rename and save the file.** In the File Name box, type a new name for the file; for example, "resume4emailing." This will help you differentiate this résumé from other versions of the résumé you might create. Click OK.

5. **Customize the conversion options.** A popup box will appear that says, "Warning: Saving as a text file will cause all formatting, pictures, and objects in your file to be lost." In this box, place a checkmark in the "Insert line breaks" option. Then click OK.

6. **Accept the warning.** A dialog box will appear that says, "The document may contain text content which will be lost upon conversion to the chosen encoding. To preserve the content, click No to exit this dialog, then choose another encoding that supports the languages in this document. Continue with Save?" Choose "Yes."

7. **Close the file.** Click File, Close to remove the file from the screen. After doing so, follow the steps for cleaning up the conversion in the next section.

Converting to ASCII for Pasting into E-Forms

1. **Use the Save As function.** With your word-processing software open and the résumé on screen, click File, Save As.

2. **Rename the file.** In the File Name box, type a new name for the file; for instance, *resume4eforms*. This will help you differentiate this résumé from other versions of the résumé. (Do not click Save yet!)

3. **Choose Plain Text (*.txt).** Click the drop-down arrow in the Save As Type box; scroll down and select Plain Text (*.txt) if you're using MS Word. For Corel WordPerfect users, scroll up in the File Type box and select ANSI (Windows) Generic Word Processor.

4. **Accept the conversion options.** A popup box will appear that says, "Warning: Saving as a text file will cause all formatting, pictures, and objects in your file to be lost." Leave all the options in this dialog box at the default settings. Click OK.

5. **Accept the warning.** A dialog box will appear that says, "The document may contain text content which will be lost upon conversion to the chosen encoding. To preserve the content, click No to exit this dialog, then choose another encoding that supports the languages in this document. Continue with Save?" Choose "Yes."

6. **Close the file.** Click File, Close to remove the file from the screen. After doing so, follow the steps for quick cleanup of an ASCII conversion in the next section.

> *Tip* White space is your best ally in creating a visually appealing ASCII-text résumé. Use the Enter key on your keyboard to add a line space between paragraphs. This will "open up" the look of the résumé. Add a line space above and below important words or subheadings, such as job titles or "Accomplishments." Add line spaces between a bulleted list of sentences. Break long paragraphs into a series of shorter paragraphs. White space won't matter a bit to a search engine, but a real reader will eventually appreciate the readability.

Quick Cleanup of an ASCII Conversion

1. **Use a text editor for cleanup.** Use a text-editor program to tidy up your résumé for e-mail transmission. Windows operating systems contain a built-in text editor called Notepad. To start the program, click the Windows Start button; then click Programs, Accessories, Notepad. Open the file (for instance, *resume4emailing.txt*) that you saved earlier (click File, Open).

2. **Format the contact information.** If your header (name, address, telephone, e-mail) was originally formatted with anything other than centered text, you'll find that the header information is all jumbled. Reformat this data, placing everything on the left margin. Use a separate line for your name; street address; city, state, ZIP; each telephone number; e-mail address; Web résumé URL; or blog (if applicable).

3. **Fix any glitches.** Review the document, repairing any bullets that went astray. All bullets should have converted to an asterisk (*), although sometimes they morph into a question mark. Other characters that might have converted incorrectly include ellipses, em dashes (—), or any letters with diacritical markings (for instance, the accented e's in *résumé*).

Before

```
n       Designed and built 5,000-sq.-ft. corporate
offices.

n       Designed and supervised construction of two
plant additions, adding 80% in additional floor
space.

n       Wrote Field Manager's Handbook to minimize
legal liability regarding UFW union labor.

n       Led management effort to decertify union,
prevent property damage, and protect 800 nonunion
workers.

n       Created quality-control program, resulting in
a 30% decrease in rejected loads.
```

After

```
* Designed and built 5,000-sq.-ft. corporate offices.

* Designed and supervised construction of two plant
additions, adding 80% in additional floor space.

* Wrote Field Manager's Handbook to minimize legal
liability regarding UFW union labor.

* Led management effort to decertify union, prevent
property damage, and protect 800 nonunion workers.

* Created quality-control program, resulting in a 30%
decrease in rejected loads.
```

In the preceding example, the spaces after the * signs were created with the spacebar rather than the Tab key. ASCII converts tabs to spaces, so you should remove extra spaces so that there is just one space between the bullet characters and text. Also, because Westerners are more comfortable reading from left to right, be sure to remove any center alignment.

Resist the temptation to try to give your ASCII version visual appeal. For instance, bulleted items that extend to two lines lose some of their visual distinction when the second line of text does not line up under the first. To counter this, some people prefer to insert a hard return after the first line and add spaces in front of the second line until the characters line up, as in this next example.

```
*   Wrote Field Manager's Handbook to minimize legal
    liability regarding UFW union labor.

*   Led management effort to decertify union, prevent
    property damage, and protect 800 nonunion workers.

*   Created quality-control program, resulting in a 30%
    decrease in rejected loads.
```

Avoid the formatting in the preceding example. This trick might provide for a prettier read (if the recipient uses the same or a similar default font), but it also presents potential problems with keyword searches involving compound keywords. Note where the words "legal liability" fall in the preceding example. If recruiters search for the keywords "legal liability," your résumé might not be found despite having included the phrase. This is because "legal" appears on one line and "liability" appears on the second. The computer would not read it as one continuous phrase; instead, it would see the word "legal," followed by a series of spaces, and then the word "liability." Other noun phrases, such as "contract negotiations," "10 years' experience," or "intellectual property" could also be missed.

4. **Add white space.** To improve readability, separate each paragraph with two line spaces. Always place two line spaces before category sections to set them off clearly.

5. **Set off category headings.** Format résumé category headings (Qualifications, Education, Experience, and so on) in ALL CAPS. Consider accenting category headings by adding a series of tildes (~~~) or equal signs (===). Use the same treatment for each résumé category. When choosing the character you'll use to set off category headings, select only from the characters seen on your keyboard (as opposed to any special symbols you can insert from your word-processing program).

Note how the following category headings were set off with different keyboard characters, each of which is readable by all types of computer systems.

```
PROFESSIONAL EXPERIENCE
~~~~~~~~~~~~~~~~~~~~~~~~~~~~~~~~~~~~~~~~

PROFESSIONAL EXPERIENCE
======================================

PROFESSIONAL EXPERIENCE
oooooooooooooooooooooooooooooooooooooooo
```

PROFESSIONAL EXPERIENCE
I-I-I-I-I-I-I-I-I-I-I-I-I

PROFESSIONAL EXPERIENCE
****

PROFESSIONAL EXPERIENCE
....

When extending a series of characters to set off category headings as in the preceding examples, limit the total number of characters on the line to 40 or 50. (I prefer 40, which prevents the appearance of line breaks if someone is viewing the file in a minimized screen such as MS Outlook's mail.) You can check the character count per line by copying the line in question from your Notepad program into a blank MS Word document and then clicking Tools, Word Count. The line "Characters (with spaces)" tells you how many characters are in the line.

In addition to setting off category headings, I advise that you quickly escort readers to your accomplishments. You can overcome the loss of design tools in the ASCII version by setting off the word "Accomplishments" or "Contributions" with a line space above and below. (Often this word is omitted in presentation résumés because the design itself clues readers that certain items are indeed accomplishments.) You can further accentuate accomplishments by adding keyboard characters before or after the heading, as these do:

*** Contributions ***

Accomplishments

Impacts
~~~~~~

This sort of window dressing will help readers differentiate sections of the résumé and quickly see information that *you* deem important. Just as in a presentation résumé, be careful to avoid design bloat. Choose only one style from the preceding suggestions for all of your category headings and use the same treatment each time you present your contributions.

Caution   You can add visual accents to an ASCII-text version by using standard keyboard characters, such as an asterisk (*), a plus sign (+), a hyphen (-), a tilde (~), or the lowercase letter "o." Any of these characters will convert without distortion. Avoid special characters such as "smart quotes" ("curly quotes" as opposed to "straight quotes") or mathematical symbols such as the plus-or-minus sign (±). Although it's a standard keyboard character, the greater-than sign (>) can cause conversion confusion in an e-mail message, so avoid this character as a replacement for bullets.

6. **Delete unnecessary information.** If your original presentation résumé is two pages, it should contain your name and possibly a page number or contact number at the top of page two. Remove this header information from page two of your ASCII version because it is unlikely that it will appear at the top of a page when printed from an e-mail message. Leaving in the header for page 2 tattles to the reader that you originally had a two-page or longer résumé, which can be a psychological weight that you don't want to add.

Caution When sending e-mail communications to prospective employers, don't let the informal nature of e-mail be your undoing. Despite the casualness associated with e-mail, you must still pay close attention to spell-checking and correctly punctuating messages. If you forego what you know to be good grammar, syntax, capitalization, or punctuation in an e-mail message, your reader might assume that you really don't know any better.

---

7. **Save your changes.** After cleaning up your ASCII résumé, you will need to resave it to keep the changes. With the document still in the Notepad text editor, click File, Save. The file will remain on your Notepad screen.

Caution Are you sending more than you intended? When saving your résumé as an ASCII file, make sure it is only the résumé that you are saving. If you have included correspondence to other target companies or miscellaneous notes on your job search within the same file as your résumé, "cut" this information from the document and save it under a separate file name. You don't want to accidentally e-mail your résumé along with cover letters written to other companies!

---

8. **Do a test run.** To see what your ASCII version might look like to an e-mail recipient, test it by sending an e-mail message to yourself and to a friend who has a different e-mail program than yours. With the file named *resume4emailing.txt* open in the Notepad text editor, click Edit, Select All; then click Edit, Copy (or click the right button on your mouse, touch "a" on your keyboard; right-click the mouse again, then touch "c" for copy). Open your e-mail program (such as MS Outlook or Mozilla Thunderbird) to prepare an e-mail. Address the e-mail to your own e-mail address. In the Subject or Regarding box, type *ASCII résumé test* or some other title you prefer. (When applying to employers, you will reference the position title or a brief summary of your skills, such as "Resume: Award-winning Web designer, 6 years' exp").

In the message area, type yourself a brief cover letter (just as you would with a real employer); then, one or two lines below your cover letter message, press Ctrl + V (or Shift + Insert) to paste your ASCII-text version into the body of the message. Send the e-mail. Once you open it, you can print the message and get a feel for what your readers will receive when you e-mail your résumé to them. It's also wise to find a friend with a different e-mail program and run the same test.

> *Tip* E-mail spam filters may keep your résumé from arriving at your intended location. To reduce this risk, avoid common words associated with spam, such as "free," "expand," "trial," and "mortgage."

After following the preceding conversion and cleanup formulas, you should have an e-mail-ready résumé that you can use over and over again for e-mailing and posting to e-forms. Résumé 9.1 illustrates a presentation résumé (*Before* version) that has been converted to an ASCII text-only version (*After* version).

Résumé 9.1: Before

AMY RICCIUTTI

776 Whiting Lane • Greenville, ME 00247
(203) 433-3322
aricciut@compuserve.com

PROFESSIONAL EXPERIENCE

ROCKWOOD INSURANCE, Augusta, ME   10/95–Present
Independent agency specializing in commercial coverage for transportation and lumber industries

Underwriting Manager: Recruited by partner/sales manager to manage underwriting in support of aggressive expansion/business development campaign. Liaison to five agents and some 50 companies. Underwrite $6 million in renewal coverage and $200,000 in new business on a priority basis (commercial and personal lines). Collaborate with agents to protect loss ratios. Maintain knowledge of company submission standards and acceptability of accounts. Aggressively process submissions to meet critical deadlines and offer better premium to customers.

- Developed focus and structure for newly-created position — established underwriting and customer service infrastructure to support a projected $500,000 increase in annual revenue.

- Achieved new agency record for retaining renewal accounts.

- Earned accolades from insurance companies for having "most complete submissions."

- Trained 2 Customer Representatives, equipping them with technical knowledge to service complex accounts.

- Designed and introduced Quote Worksheet and Agent Checklist to standardize and streamline underwriting.

- Diplomatically mitigated circumstances involving premium increases and non-coverage of claims.

COAST INSURANCE SERVICES, Brunswick, ME   1990–1995

Senior Customer Service Representative: Accountable for policy maintenance, renewal retention, new business submissions, claims, CSR training, and liaison work for independent agency with $7 million in premium.

- Assisted with AMS Novell network upgrade (resident expert for software installation, troubleshooting).

- Took on several new books of business during tenure without need for additional support staff.

BURRELL INSURANCE, Oklahoma City, OK   1987–1989

Customer Service Representative (Commercial Lines) for primarily oil-field related clients (equipment maintenance, drilling, oil field contracting, welding, wrought iron erection, construction).

EDUCATION, LICENSURE

INS 21 (Principles of Insurance); INS 23 (Commercial Principles of Insurance); Personal Lines (Property and Auto); Commercial Lines (Property); E&O Coverage; Employee Practices Liability; Property & Casualty Agent (#760923)

Résumé 9.2: After

```
AMY RICCIUTTI
Greenville, ME
(203) 433-3322
aricciut@compuserve.com

PROFESSIONAL EXPERIENCE
=========================================================

ROCKWOOD INSURANCE, Augusta, ME
10/95-Present

Independent agency specializing in commercial coverage for
transportation and lumber industries.

Underwriting Manager...

Recruited by partner/sales manager to manage underwriting in
support of aggressive expansion/business development
campaign. Liaison to five agents and some 50 companies.
Underwrite $6 million in renewal coverage and $200,000 in
new business on a priority basis (commercial and personal
lines). Collaborate with agents to protect loss ratios.
Aggressively process submissions to meet critical deadlines
and offer better premium to customers.

*** Contributions ***

+ Developed focus and structure for newly created position;
established underwriting and customer service infrastructure
to support a projected $500,000 increase in annual revenue.

+ Achieved new agency record for retaining renewal accounts.

+ Earned accolades from insurance companies for having "most
complete submissions."

+ Trained 2 Customer Representatives, equipping them with
technical knowledge to service complex accounts.

+ Designed and introduced Quote Worksheet and Agent
Checklist to standardize and streamline underwriting.

+ Diplomatically mitigated circumstances involving premium
increases and noncoverage of claims.


COAST INSURANCE SERVICES, Brunswick, ME
1990-1995

Senior Customer Service Representative...

Accountable for policy maintenance, renewal retention, new
business submissions, claims, CSR training, and liaison work
for independent agency with $7 million in premium.
```

(continued)

(continued)

```
*** Contributions ***

+  Assisted with AMS Novell network upgrade (resident expert
for software installation, troubleshooting).

+  Took on several new books of business during tenure
without need for additional support staff.



SUPPORTING SKILLS, INFORMATION
=============================================================

*** Education *** INS 21 (Principles of Insurance). INS 23
(Commercial Principles of Insurance). Personal Lines
(Property and Auto). Commercial Lines (Property). E&O
Coverage. Employee Practices Liability. Property & Casualty
Agent (# 760923)

*** Computer *** Windows 3.1. Windows 95. MS Works. MS
Office. WordPerfect. AMS Novell. DOS and UNIX-based
programs. Redshaw. OIS and FSC Rating Systems. PS4 Proposal
System.

*** Affiliations *** National Association of Insurance
Women. National Association of Female Executives. Volunteer,
Marine Mammal Center.


=============================================================
```

How to Post an ASCII Résumé to a Web Site

Use your *resume4eforms.txt* file to post your résumé to a career Web site or submit to a company's Web site. Submitting your résumé to a Web site is very easy, much like sending an e-mail. Some sites require you to work through a series of fill-in-the-boxes (e-forms) for your vital information, as well as establish a username and password. Make it easy on yourself by using the same username and password for each Web site you post to—choose something unique in hopes that no one else will have the same username and password at the next Web site you visit.

For an active online search, consider posting your résumé to some of the top career sites, such as these, which are listed according to their traffic ranking from Alexa.com, an Amazon.com company that continually crawls the Web to gather information on some 16 million sites:

1. **CareerBuilder:** www.careerbuilder.com

2. **Monster:** www.monster.com (you'll find that posting your résumé here takes a bit longer because Monster has a unique system for compiling your career information)

3. **Yahoo! HotJobs:** hotjobs.yahoo.com

4. **America's Job Bank:** www.ajb.dni.us (as this book went to press, the government announced that this site would be phased out and cease to operate by June 30, 2007).

5. **Net-Temps:** www.net-temps.com

6. **Vault:** www.vault.com

7. **Job.com:** www.job.com

8. **4jobs.com:** www.4jobs.com

9. **Employment 911:** www.employment911.com

You can find one of the most comprehensive listings of career sites at The Riley Guide (www.rileyguide.com). Margaret Dikel (formerly Riley) has compiled a list that will help you navigate the resu-maze of databases on the Web.

Tip There's a new solution when it comes to maintaining confidentiality while conducting an online job search. Look for sites that offer "push technology." Instead of having you post your résumé on the Internet, this technology calls for you to enter an e-mail address along with basic information on your desired job title, location preference, salary requirements, and so forth. New job postings that match your criteria are then "pushed" to you by e-mail. You can review a detailed job description and decide whether you want to apply. No more fretting that your boss will find you floating around the Internet and think you've lost your company loyalty.

Web Résumés, E-Portfolios, and Blogs

Easy-to-use Web-site-development software has helped inspire exponential growth in the number of Web sites out there. Much as using a calculator skips the mathematical steps required to calculate square roots and cosines, applications such as Macromedia Dreamweaver and Microsoft FrontPage allow you to skip the painstaking exactitudes of Web programming languages such as HTML. Microsoft Office and Corel WordPerfect also offer advanced conversion capabilities that convert text and graphics into HTML, although there are drawbacks to using this simplified method.

Should you create an online presence? It depends. If your search requires you to display technological talents, artistic abilities, or simply the impression of a top-notch professional, it might be entirely appropriate to offer employers a sampling of your wares in an online format. Virtually any profession can use a Web résumé, which gives you the appearance of being an Internet-savvy, "A" candidate and the benefit of a 24/7 Web presence.

If you use a Web résumé, e-portfolio, or blog, don't forgo submitting an ASCII résumé (that references your Web résumé URL) to recruiters or employers because recruiters often look first to résumé databases for their applicant pool. Once the employer or recruiter has established an interest in you via the ASCII résumé, he or she can visit your amplified material online. With this two-pronged format strategy (ASCII and Web-based), you can cover all your bases.

Company Web Sites Outhire the Big Job Boards

According to Internet recruiting consultants Gerry Crispin and Mark Mehler, these sources accounted for Internet hires:

- 67.9 percent from company Web sites
- 17.6 percent from niche job sites
- 8.7 percent from Monster
- 4.1 percent from CareerBuilder
- 1.8 percent from Yahoo! HotJobs

Although networking is critical (never attempt a job search without face-to-face or voice-to-voice interaction), reinforce it by applying online to your target company's Web site.

A well-designed Web résumé delivers information in a smorgasbord fashion, so that viewers can choose quickly material that is of the greatest interest (for instance, full-text letters of recommendation from references or e-mail links to references). At the same time, viewers who want a full-course rundown of your professional history can do so by clicking through Web pages that compartmentalize your experience, education, affiliations, and other pertinent information.

The Advantages and Disadvantages of Web Résumés

The advantages of a Web résumé, e-portfolio, or blog are as follows:

- Can make a more impressive impact than a traditional résumé through use of visuals, color, links, video, or audio files.

- Provides a wealth of material without overwhelming the viewer; subordinate documents, such as letters of recommendation and examples of work, can be included as additional Web pages, without loading down the reader with the physical weight of printed matter.

- Indicates technical know-how on the part of the candidate, or, at the very least, an appreciation for technology's role in job search protocol.

- Provides you with a 24/7 Web presence, silently networking for you and giving employers instant access to your qualifications any time of the day or night.

- Provides employers with audible evidence of your communication skills through use of audio files.

- Provides employers with visual evidence of your interpersonal skills or important "soft" skills through use of video files.

- Provides employers with a good sense of your thought processes and personality when it comes to a blog.

- Helps employers identify with an applicant through the use of "common" images, such as logos from professional affiliations and universities.

- Enables employers to see samples of your work. For instance, graphic artists can display designs, analysts can submit sample reports, and executive chefs can feature food art.

- Can link viewers to other Web sites; for instance, the site of your professional affiliation or an organization that honored you with an award.

- May include actual audio testimonials from your references.

Consider these disadvantages of an online presence:

- Takes a considerable investment of time to develop the concept, layout, and content for a well-designed Web résumé.

- Has hidden costs that can add up quickly, such as Dreamweaver Web-page-development software, online service provider and hosting fees, InterNIC registration fees (if you are obtaining your own URL), search engine optimization (for instance, Web Position Gold), miscellaneous costs of promoting the Web site, and so on.

- Requires a learning curve to master the intricacies of the Web-page-development software or HTML coding.

- Takes extra time for employers to view graphics or video files or listen to audio files.

- Reaches only employers that are recruiting online (if you are relying solely on an electronic résumé instead of teaming it with a traditional, presentation version).

The Technical How-Tos of Web Résumés

There are three basic options for creating a Web résumé:

- Use an online résumé-builder.

⚹ Do it yourself using Web-page-development software.

⚹ Hire a Web designer or an e-portfolio/résumé service that specializes in Web résumés to custom-design your Web résumé or Web portfolio.

Online Résumé-Builder Services

The fast and easy way to create an attractive Web résumé is to use an online résumé builder. There are free services at sites such as America Online (included with your monthly subscription fee) or Yahoo!, although you have limited customization and confidentiality features with the latter. There are also low-cost sites (approximately $39 to $99) that provide greater control of confidentiality, as well as design options.

For a simple, one-page online résumé, my favorite résumé-builder site is CareerFolios.com. You choose your design and color theme, enter the content of your résumé, and, *voila*, a Web résumé is created. The only technical requirement is that you know how to copy and paste sections of your résumé into e-forms. The system then takes your information and combines it with predesigned templates to give you a professional Web page. Cost is $39 and includes six months of hosting.

The next *Before* example shows a résumé in ASCII format viewed in the Notepad text editor that comes with Microsoft Windows; the *After* screen capture shows a portion of the résumé in the CareerFolios.com Web résumé format.

Before

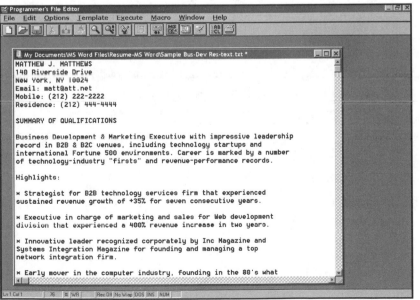

After

Do-It-Yourself Web Résumés

Creating a very basic Web résumé is easier than you think, provided that you own the right software *and* have a place to "hang" it on the Web (for instance, some Internet service providers allot a certain amount of space for you to post your Web pages if you have an e-mail account with them). Recall that earlier in this chapter, I listed a number of steps to strip the codes from your presentation résumé to convert it to an ASCII version. In its very simplest form, it takes only one step to convert your presentation résumé into an HTML format if you have MS Word (version 7 or higher) or Corel WordPerfect (version 8 or higher).

To do so, follow these steps:

1. With your word-processing program running, open the file that contains your presentation résumé (the one that uses attractive fonts, formatting, graphic accents, industry icons, and so on).

2. Once your résumé is on the screen, check that there is no tag-along information included, such as cover letters, miscellaneous notes, or any other personal information you don't want included on your Web page.

3. Then use this series of clicks: File, Save As, Save As Type, Web Page, Save. You now have a Web résumé in HTML format.

If you're in a hurry, this is a fast and simple formula. However, as with most things in life, the more you put into it, the better it will be. In this case, that means you'll need to tweak, tweak, tweak. Follow these steps:

1. Open your browser program (in Windows 95 or higher, click Start, Programs, and then choose your browser program). You don't need to be connected to your Internet service provider at this point.

2. Once in your browser, click File, Open.

3. Then type the full path name of where you saved your HTML version. For instance, in MS Word it might be c:\My Documents\yourname.html, with "yourname" being whatever you typed when you saved it).

4. Click Open to see your future Web page. If you love what you see, great.

5. If you want to make some changes, print the document so that you can remember exactly what you want to change; then minimize the browser file you're working on (you don't need to exit the browser program).

6. Go back to your word-processing or editing program and tweak any glitches as necessary.

To create a Web résumé with some design distinction, you can use Web-page-development software, such as Dreamweaver or FrontPage. This will make it easier to add graphics, photographs, or sound files. The addition of these types of files accomplishes two things:

- First, these files engage the viewer beyond the level of a basic text-only presentation because they cater to a viewer's preferred learning style (visual, auditory, or kinesthetic).

- Second, and most important, the addition of graphics, video, or sound files gives tangible evidence of your talents as a designer, presenter, communicator, and so on. For instance, a fashion designer could display graphic images of his designs, a key accounts manager could include video of an important sales presentation she recently conducted, and a manager could provide an audio clip that contained highlights from a meeting where he led a planning or problem-solving session.

> *Tip* For an online gallery of photographs and images that you can incorporate into your Web résumé, visit http://creative.gettyimages.com/. This site features the work of professional photographers and offers beautiful stock photos for approximately $20 per image. Using these images guarantees that you will be in compliance with copyright laws, whereas copying images from other sources could be an infringement of copyright law.

Another option for creating a Web résumé is to tackle learning HTML programming. To do so, log on to the Internet, go to your favorite search engine, and type in something like "how to write HTML" or "HTML tutorial." You'll get hundreds of resources from which to choose. If your foray into HTML is for this one-time shot at a multimedia résumé, you might want to try this shortcut: Use an existing résumé from the Web to create a template for your HTML résumé.

To do so, follow these steps:

1. Go to a career Web site that allows public access to its résumés and find one that appeals to you in terms of layout and design.

2. Save the résumé, using File, Save As.

3. From here, open Windows Notepad (Start, Programs, Accessories, Notepad).

4. Open the file and, *voilà,* you have instant HTML programming at your disposal.

Don't be overwhelmed at all the <> signs. This coding simply instructs how the text should look on-screen. If you've worked with WordPerfect's Reveal Codes, you'll have a feel for the code on/code off principle. Your task is to delete the original writing and replace it with your own information; do be mindful not to delete the coding.

To put your Web résumé on the Web, you will need Internet service. Inquire with your Internet service provider about free Web space for subscribers and online tutorials for uploading a Web page. If you do not have an Internet service provider, sites such as Yahoo! GeoCities (http://geocities.yahoo.com) offer free Web page space. If the site you choose requires you to have special software known as ftp (**f**ile **t**ransfer **p**rotocol) to upload Web pages to its server space, you can obtain free ftp software. Go to www.download.com, then type the phrase "ftp" to find and download a free or trial version of ftp software. Your new Web space provider will be glad to give you instructions on how to upload a document.

Hire a Pro

For those who lack the time or desire to master the creative and technical aspects of developing an online presence, I recommend that you hire a pro. The following providers can create an impressive online presence for you:

- **www.brandego.com:** Founded by Kirsten Dixson, a leader in using technology in career management, Brandego provides a comprehensive career-management solution that combines the best of personal branding, career e-portfolios, Web design, and direct marketing.

- **www.blueskyportfolios.com:** The creation of Phil and Louise Fletcher, BlueSkyPortfolios allows job seekers to take control of their online image and personal branding. The team designs, writes, and hosts online portfolios for job seekers across a wide range of industries.

- **www.powertalent.net:** Career expert Laura DeCarlo offers a complete set of enabling technology solutions and will help you design, build, and market an e-portfolio.

- **www.corporatewarriors.com:** Don Straits, president of Corporate Warriors, offers a suite of services for executives, including e-portfolios.

- **www.acorncreative.com:** The branding and Web development experts at this award-winning site were pioneers of e-portfolios.

- You can also use a blog platform to build an e-portfolio yourself (check the resources in the section on blogs later in the chapter).

Web Résumé Do's and Don'ts

Regardless of what means you use to produce a Web or multimedia résumé, keep these do's and don'ts in mind:

Do's

- Use a Web résumé to augment and support, not replace, the ASCII version of your résumé.

- Choose a quiet background color, one that neither competes for the reader's attention nor conceals colored hyperlinks. (Just as you'd pass over hot-pink or sunshine-yellow paper stock for a presentation résumé, also forgo loud background colors on your Web résumé.)

- Use a Web-friendly font, such as Arial, Verdana, or Times Roman.

- Make sure your e-mail address is an active "mailto" link so that when viewers click it, they'll be transported directly to their mail program to write you an e-mail message. (If you're creating the Web résumé using an HTML editor, the HTML tag should read <a href="mailto:johndoe@email.com">johndoe@email.com</a>. Of course, be sure to substitute your own e-mail address for the address of "johndoe@email.com" in both locations.)

- Provide a navigation system that will take the viewer immediately to the categories of your résumé, such as Experience, Education, Computer Skills, and so on.

- Make hyperlinked text or graphics look clickable. Viewers shouldn't have to guess which images are hyperlinks and which are not.

If you're creating a single-page Web résumé that is quite long, intersperse "click-the-ruby-slipper" hyperlinks every 25 lines or so that say "return to home" or "top of page." Viewers appreciate the ability to get back quickly to the top of your document with just one click. (You don't want them chanting Dorothy's mantra, "There's no place like home.")

Alter the colors of visited and unvisited links to help viewers keep track of where they've been.

Don'ts

Don't go overboard with hyperlinks. As noted earlier, your e-mail address near the top of the document should always be active. (See "Hyperlinks or Hyperjinx?" later in this chapter for more thoughts on links.)

Avoid "heavy" artwork (such as 500K GIF or JPEG files that take minutes to download). Stick to files that are in the 20 to 30K range). Also avoid cartoons that might cast a less-than-professional shadow on your candidacy. Again, be extremely careful to use artwork that is in the public domain. Using the latest résumé cartoon from Dilbert or B.C. could land you in hot water with copyright laws.

Avoid italic text because it can be very hard to read, especially in smaller font sizes. If you do use italics, add **_boldfacing to the italics_** to improve legibility.

> *Tip* It is illegal for an employer to ask for photos from applicants, with the exception of professions such as acting and modeling. It is not illegal, however, for you to provide a photo in your Web résumé or e-portfolio. Employers have been sensitivity-trained and legislatively mandated to look beyond your physiognomy. If you include your photo when applying for a job in the business world, you risk being disqualified as a candidate by a fastidious human resource representative. On the other hand, employers do eventually see you once the interview process begins and will judge you partially on your appearance, especially when considering you for positions that require interaction with customers. Providing prospective employers with a clue about your appearance and professionalism in the form of a video or graphic file can, in many cases, be to your advantage.

What to Include in an E-Portfolio

Pages in an e-portfolio might include a project history, leadership profile, biography, executive summary, branding statement, philosophy statement, press clippings, technical skills, course work or professional-development workshops and seminars, research work, volunteer or pro bono work, publications, patents, awards, charts and tables, work-related pictures, testimonials, and success stories. Each category is typically given a separate page and identified with tabs that are indexed and linked to the home page of your e-portfolio.

E-portfolios can also include streaming audio and video clips. For example, an audio file might contain your networking introduction and a few of your main career highlights. Video might include clips of presentations that you have given. If you need help with developing streaming audio and video, www.audiogenerator.com or hipcast's www.audioblog.com can manage the process for you.

Within your e-portfolio, include your résumé in several downloadable file formats, such as .doc, .rtf, PDF, and ASCII plain-text formats. And, if you publish a blog, you will want to add a link to your blog as well (as long as the content is professional rather than personal).

The sample in figure 9.3, created by Kirsten Dixson of Brandego.com, illustrates how an e-portfolio can capture interest and convey qualifications.

Figure 9.3: A Sample E-Portfolio

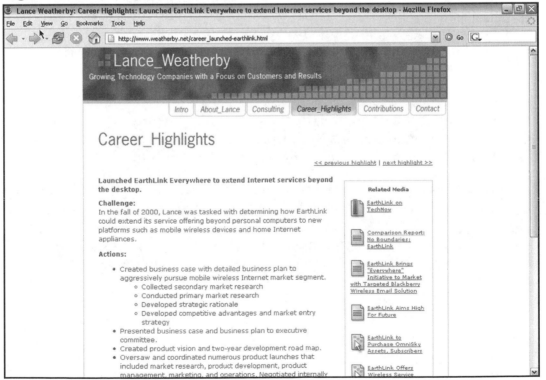

The candidate, Lance Weatherby, emphasizes his brand with the tagline "Growing Technology Companies with a Focus on Customers and Results." Note how the navigation system across the top of the page provides links to an Intro, About_Lance, Consulting, Career_Highlights, Contributions, and a Contact page. The Career Highlights page featured here offers links to a variety of video, audio, and graphic illustrations that prove the candidate's ability to deliver results.

Hyperlinks or Hyperjinx?

As I alluded to in the list of do's and don'ts, hyperlinks in a Web résumé can easily backfire. Recall that hyperlinks are images or words that usually appear in a different color; when you click on them, they take you to another file without you having to exit a document and type the full URL.

Be certain that links to another site (as opposed to somewhere within your Web site) support your candidacy rather than detract or divert attention from it. For instance, when listing the companies for which you worked, you might use a link to take the reader to that company's Web site. If Dell Computers happened to be a former employer, you could easily lose your viewer among the plethora of pages that the Dell Web site contains. Let's consider another example. You might be considering a link to your alma mater. If so, think twice. Some universities and colleges include the résumés of other graduates—no sense adding to your competition. Hyperlinks to organizations that broadcast your alliance with a political party or controversial social issue can be either a "bonding" experience or a death knell.

Beyond your e-mail address, safe links to consider include publications that display articles you have authored, affiliations that include your name as an officeholder, or organizations from which you received an award. Other than these, keep hyperlinks to other sites to a bare minimum.

You can, however, include links within your Web site that will take the viewer immediately to categories on your résumé, such as Experience, Education, Computer Skills, and so on. (The underlined words in the preceding sentence are hyperlinks and will appear in a color different from that of the text when viewed on a computer screen.) Under Experience, you might link to a progressive list of positions that you have held. The candidate in résumé 9.4 provided links to category headings, along with another set of links under Experience that take the reader directly to specific skills: Leadership, Revenue Performance & Profit Improvement, Sales & Sales Staff Development, Manufacturing Operations, QC, QA, Product Development, Human Resources. In keeping with the first rule of Web résumés—to augment and support, not replace, an ASCII résumé—this accomplishment-based résumé provides much more detail than does his e-mail résumé.

Résumé 9.4

GERALD F. SCOPP

123 Front Street
East Brunswick, NJ 08816

(732) 334-1114
gscopp@aol.com

CLICK TO VIEW MY
QUALIFICATIONS, EXPERIENCE, EDUCATION, AFFILIATIONS

QUALIFICATIONS

Performance-driven business executive with significant record for driving aggressive growth/profit, turning around under-performing operations, and expanding into national/international markets. *Increased annual revenues for manufacturer from $200,000 to $9 million.*

More than 10 years' P&L accountability with verifiable record of conceptualizing innovative, profitable new ventures / business alliances — especially skilled in assembling key players, finances, and resources to ensure their success. Broad skill-set encompasses:

general management	product development & launch	QC, QA, operations
marketing & sales	R&D, regulatory affairs, compliance	manufacturing, distribution
finance & accounting	purchasing, inventory management	engineering (plant, pharmaceuticals)

EXPERIENCE

PHARMACEUTICAL LABORATORIES
East Bay, New Jersey

Transitioned an established, old-line pharmaceutical company from vulnerable position
with limited product mix and regional audience to a diversified manufacturer with international reach.

Joined closely-held corporation as Director of Sales in 1982, advancing to Vice President of Sales &
Marketing in 1985, Senior Vice President in 1992, and President/CEO in 1999.

Leadership, Revenue Performance & Profit Improvement:

- *Business Impacts:* Captured an overall 3,500% sales increase over management tenure; boosted profits to run consistently above industry average; expanded market from two states to international scope; diversified products, expanding number 18-fold.

- *Diversification:* Led market diversification to eliminate seasonal fluctuations. Entered negotiations with national beverage companies to augment summer sales, formed new subsidiary, and established infrastructure (legal, financing, facility purchase/retrofit, staffing, distribution channels, etc.) — accomplished entire start-up in just 90 days . . . subsidiary now generates $5 million in annual sales.

- *Contract Negotiations:* Negotiated competitor's request to purchase registered product from their initial offer of $10,000 to more than $.5 million.

- *Growth:* Authored strategy for $3 million capital infusion to support R&D investment.

- *Export:* Researched and brought to fruition export business in Asia and Europe that represented $2 million in initial sales.

- *Expense Reductions:* Formed alliance with Swiss importer of raw materials that slashed supply costs more than 40%.

[GO TO TOP / HOME]

Sales & Sales Staff Development:

- Converted in-house sales force to national broker network — move lowered sales costs dramatically, while attracting and retaining many of the best-connected, most productive pharmaceutics brokers in the U.S.

(continued)

(continued)

- Delivered unprecedented growth in the company's 60-year history.

- Sourced new national and regional accounts, gaining full and maximum multi-store distribution — frequently came away from first-time account meetings with orders in excess of $1 million.

- Delivered ten-fold growth in sales of liquid pharmaceutics to $12 million per annum.

- Targeted and secured government contracts valued at $3 million in sales.

Manufacturing Operations, QC, QA:

- Recruited key personnel — regulatory affairs director, chemists, manufacturing manager — who provided the industry knowledge and technical depth to support aggressive expansion of product line.

- Earned flawless audit record with federal and state regulators throughout growth phase.

- Expanded combined plant capacity to 100,000-sq.ft. including the construction of a 25,000-sq.ft., state-of-the-art facility — directed construction management, served as liaison to city agencies (planning, licensing, permitting). Moved project along to meet ambitious construction schedule.

- Indirectly supervised three manufacturing facilities and a distribution center with total staff of 170.

Product Development:

- Researched patent expirations for potential new generic products — initiated 2-year planning process for R&D, FDA-approval, and new product launch to coincide with patent expirations. Expanded number of liquid products from 5 to 90.

- Revitalized product with stagnant sales in limited geographic area to gain dominant national market share among chain drug stores, wholesalers, distributors, and HMO's.

- Approached German pharmaceutical company rumored to plan divestiture of a generic division; managed negotiations to acquire 20 liquid formulas and countered opposition from the multinational company's board of directors — structured deal that yielded an additional $7 million in subsequent sales at literally no cost to company.

[GO TO TOP / HOME]

Human Resources:

- Promoted a management-labor doctrine that valued an open-door philosophy, internal promotions, employee performance incentives, and profit sharing.

- Held plant personnel turnover to a minimal 2% — workforce reflected a diversity of Filipino, Vietnamese, Spanish, and African-American ethnicity.

- Instituted English classes to promote literacy among second language learners.

EDUCATION

University of Massachusetts, Amherst
Bachelor of Science Degree, Business Administration — Emphasis in International Marketing

Army and Navy Academy Graduate
(subsequent military service in Intelligence/Special Communications)

AFFILIATIONS

National Association of Pharmaceutical Manufacturers (NAPM)
Drug Information Association (DIA)
American Educational Research Association (AERA)

[GO TO TOP / HOME]

> *Tip* Integrate your paper and electronic résumés by cross-referencing each of them. In other words, list the full URL of your e-portfolio on your presentation résumé so that readers can look you up on the Internet. Reference the full URL of your e-portfolio in your e-mail version so that readers can link directly to it from their e-mail program. Provide employers who are viewing your e-portfolio with the opportunity to download an ASCII plain-text version of your résumé, which can then be added to a résumé database or forwarded to networking contacts.

You can also link your e-portfolio to a PDF presentation version of your traditional résumé. The PDF file allows viewers to print an exact replica of your presentation version, with all its attractive formatting and font-work, and avoids the unattractive look associated with printed ASCII or e-mail résumés.

> *Tip* If your computer doesn't have the ability to create a PDF, you can convert your MS Word résumé by using the handy online tool at www.pdfonline.com/convert_pdf.asp.

Using Your Web Résumé

Kevin Skarritt, award-winning Web site designer at Acorn Creative (www.acorncreative.com), offers these recommendations for using your Web résumé or e-portfolio. "Motivate readers to view your Web résumé with the prospect of learning something more about you," he says. Instead of adding only the URL (www.myresume.com) near your address and telephone number at the top of your presentation résumé, also plant an enticing statement within the body of the résumé or at the bottom of the résumé.

You can use a variation on one of the following example statements to offer employers the prospect of seeing more than a duplicate of your presentation résumé in electronic form:

> To view award-winning logos designed for manufacturing and education clients, visit my Web résumé at www.myresume.com.

> Excellent communication skills can be verified by listening to my audio responses to interview questions at my Web site: www.myresume.com.

> Video clips of training presented at a recent corporate sales meeting can be viewed at my Web site, www.myresume.com.

Entire books are devoted to developing handsome Web pages, as well as myriad resources on the World Wide Web. Your Internet service provider might offer tips under its member services, or you can use your favorite search engine to look up free tips on adding video and sound, or using Java or Flash scripts to jazz things up. Searching for **"how to develop web page" + free** at Google.com yields more than 2 million resources.

Technical tweaking aside, make sure that the Web résumé delivers more than a straight-text, e-mailable version; and, even more important, make sure that it is professional. On the last note, I interviewed a recruiter who indicated that, on more than one occasion, links from an e-mail résumé to the candidate's Web résumé required negotiating homey Web sites, replete with family pictures and the kid's refrigerator artwork. Then, after making the recruiter feel much like a captive audience after miles of home movies from a complete stranger, the elusive Web résumé either didn't load properly, wasn't there, or was the same information originally viewed in the e-mail. To make sure you don't add to the frustrations of already-harried human resource professionals, either place your résumé front-and-center at your Web site; or, even better, separate it entirely from the family chronicles with its own URL.

Marketing Your Web Résumé

Now that you have your Web résumé, how do you plan to make people aware of it?

I recommend avoiding the fee-based "announcement blast" services, as they succeed only in overflowing your e-mail inbox with spam. Instead, register it at these free sites:

- **Google:** www.google.com/addurl.html
- **Yahoo!:** http://submit.search.yahoo.com/free/request (you will be required to create a Yahoo! ID before you can add your site)
- **Open Directory:** http://dmoz.org/add.html

Beyond search engine registration, include your URL in all these locations:

- Your e-mail signature line
- ASCII plain-text and presentation résumés
- Letterhead, business cards, networking cards, exteriors of envelopes, and so on

Getting on the Blog Bandwagon

With 40,000 new blogs launched every day, blogs are rapidly becoming mainstream online publishing tools. Just what is a blog? Short for Web log, a blog is a Web page of thoughts, ideas, and commentary reflecting the personality of the writer. Typically updated daily or at least weekly, a blog also allows for public interaction and comment on the blog author's postings. Blogger.com (owned by Google), which helps people create blogs, describes a blog as "a personal diary. A daily pulpit. A collaborative space. A political soapbox. A breaking-news outlet. A collection of links. Your own private thoughts. Memos to the world."

Corporate recruiters and executive search firms are now using blogs as a prescreening tool. To stay on the radar screen and build a personal online brand, create a blog focused on your area of expertise. (At the very least, you can post your comments to blogs of recruiters or high-profile contacts in your industry.)

What to Include in a Blog

A blog gives you a chance to demonstrate your skills and expertise in your field, build a community, and create an interactive forum. You can write about projects you are working on, industry events, ongoing research, current trends, new products, and evaluations. You can also include articles or papers you have written, a bio, project histories, a downloadable résumé, an audio presentation, links to your Web site, your Web résumé, or links to other relevant Web sites. The content can also include a blogroll, which is a list of links to your favorite blogs. This allows you and your readers to connect with others who share similar interests.

Creating a Blog

Creating a blog is fairly easy and does not require knowledge of complex coding. There are several services that will host your blog—some are free, whereas some charge a small licensing fee. Two free sites include the following:

- www.blogger.com/start
- http://spaces.msn.com

For a small fee, you can create a blog hosted by either of these sites:

- www.typepad.com
- www.blogharbor.com

Each site has a wizard to step you through the setup process. If you would like to host your blog on your own server, you can purchase Web log publishing software from www.movabletype.org.

You will need to publish regular posts and respond to questions from people posting to your blog. The goal is to create an ongoing dialog with your visitors. Posts require a journalistic writing style. Remember, this is being published on the Internet and anyone can access your blog, so think carefully before posting any personal information. Your online content may be available for many years to come!

Using RSS (Really Simple Syndication) Technology

If you create a blog or post to others' blogs, you'll need to proactively add information and review recent posts. However, if you prefer that blog posts be sent directly to your e-mail inbox, you can use RSS technology—this will help you track your favorite blogs and alert you when new posts are published. An RSS news aggregator can download information into your blog and is an easy way to produce content-rich information for your blog while reducing the amount of research and writing involved. You can find examples of RSS news aggregators at the following sites:

- **Feed Reader:** www.feedreader.com
- **Feedburner:** www.feedburner.com/fb/a/home
- **Bloglines:** www.bloglines.com
- **Pluck:** www.pluck.com
- **Newsgator:** www.newsgator.com/home.aspx

You can also use Google's alerts as a source of information for content (www.google.com/alerts).

Advanced bloggers syndicate their blog content using RSS, giving them an especially high profile.

Marketing Your Blog

To market your blog on the Internet, list it with these blog search engines:

- **Technorati:** www.technorati.com
- **Daypop:** www.daypop.com
- **Blogarama:** www.blogarama.com
- **BlogTree:** www.blogtree.com

Another way to market your blog is to post to other blogs and embed a link to your source/blog. In addition, cross-linking on your blog role to other blogs will increase your blog's presence and ranking in the search engines.

Monitor recruiter blogs: The Electronic Recruiter Exchange blog at www.erexchange.com/blogs will keep you up on trends used by recruiters and executive search firms.

Scannable Résumés

Where do scannable résumés fit into the e-résumé equation? Technically, a printed résumé suitable for scanning by an optical character reader (OCR) is not an e-résumé. It can become an e-résumé, but only after being processed by an OCR and saved in a format (such as ASCII) that can be saved and searched. In the 1990s, scannable résumés were popular, with employers requesting that applicants submit their résumés by mail or fax. More than a decade later, scannable résumés are much less common, with employers opting for the faster route of an ASCII or MS Word résumé submitted by e-mail. Should you encounter an employer's request for a scannable résumé, read on. If not, skip to the next section.

> *Tip* Resist the temptation to fax your résumé from your present employer's office, as it will include a header with your employer's information on it. In addition to the courtesy of not conducting personal business on the employer's clock, you also risk a mis-dial, which can result in the recipient's faxing back to inform the sender that the résumé didn't arrive at the right destination!

Scannable Résumé Do's and Don'ts

When sending a scannable résumé, you should be cognizant of two components: format and content. The first has to do with initial readability by the scanner; the second requires that your information be loaded with keywords and worthy of being read.

Content and keywords were covered in chapter 5, so I'll assume that, figuratively speaking, you've zipped a zillion or so keywords into your résumé and you're confidently waiting for some researcher to find your goldmine of qualifications. However, you still won't be found if the scanner had difficulty with the initial readability of your scannable résumé. The primary key to readability is this: Choose a font that allows no letters to touch or bleed together. Poor paper quality can also lead to bleeding, as can ink-jet printers. (And if by any chance you still have a dot-matrix printer hanging around, do not use it to print your résumé.)

> *Tip* When faxing a résumé to be scanned, set the fax to "fine mode"—the recipient will receive a better-quality copy.

Review this laundry list for maximum computer readability of your scannable résumé.

Do's

Follow the company's directions for creating a scannable résumé, if provided; if none are provided, play it safe by adhering to the following more-rigid specifications.

- Use a clean typeface that ensures that letters do not touch one another. Sans-serif fonts such as Arial, Helvetica, Univers, and Lucida are good choices, as are the serif fonts Times New Roman and Courier (see the list of fonts in chapter 8 for more examples). Use a minimum of 10-point type for a sans-serif font and 11-point type for a serif font such as Times New Roman.

- Consider expanding the character spacing of the entire document by .3 to .5 pts to prevent characters from touching.

- Use crisp white (or very light-colored) paper, 8½ by 11 inches.

- Send an original.

- Use a laser printer.

- List your name on the top line and use separate lines for address, each phone number, fax, and e-mail. If your résumé goes to two pages, put your name and telephone number (on separate lines) at the top of the second page as well.

- Keep text left-justified with a ragged right margin.

- Use a traditional layout (avoid columns).

- Use hard carriage returns (by pressing the Enter key on your keyboard) only at the end of a paragraph.

- Be detailed (but concise) about your job experience; avoid abstract nouns and focus instead on tangible, concrete nouns. (In other words, don't say "computer skills" when you could say "Linux, Windows, PowerBuilder, Oracle.")

- Use common headings such as Objective, Summary, Summary of Qualifications, Accomplishments, Experience, Strengths, Education, Professional Affiliations, Publications, Certifications, Honors, Personal, Miscellaneous, and so on.

Clearly indicate your job target (for scanning systems that are dependent on an operator to input your skills classification). For instance, if you are interested in a variety of administrative positions, list the possibilities and separate them with slashes:

Administrative Manager / Administrator / Business Administrator / Business Manager

Some companies have less-definitive titles, such as "Administrative Support Partners." Look through a company Web site or try calling the human resources department for a list of titles. In most cases (if you can get past a voice-mail system), an employee will be happy to assist.

Don'ts

Don't use fancy paper or the popular recycled papers (a speck in the paper can turn an "O" into an "8" or an "i" into an "l").

Avoid graphics, industry icons, borders, columns, or a landscape (paper turned sideways) presentation.

Don't use fancy bullets (some scanners can read only a solid bullet, a square, and an asterisk).

Eliminate tabs.

Don't condense spacing between letters.

Don't hyphenate words at the end of a line in the body of the résumé.

Don't use a hard carriage return at the end of a line (unless it's the end of a paragraph).

Don't print on both sides of the paper.

Don't staple together multiple pages or cover letters.

> *Tip* Special characters such as ampersands (&), percent signs (%), pound signs (#), and slashes (/) can wreak havoc with scannability. When possible, avoid these characters by spelling them out. Place a space before and after a slash (Education / Training) so that the slash doesn't lean against another letter and cause it to be misinterpreted. For example, the characters /n might be mistakenly conjoined and interpreted as an *m*.

The following résumé example contains enhanced formatting and expanded character spacing to ensure scannability. The header, category headings, and boldfaced subheadings are expanded 1.5 points and the body text is expanded .3 points (see "Expand Character Spacing" in chapter 8 for details). Although this résumé was reduced in size to accommodate the book format, the original font size when printed on 8½-by-11 paper is 11 points.

Résumé 9.5

TERRY F. HEEBERGER

555 Washoe Avenue   Mobile: 555-555-5555
Pirie, OH 55555   heeberger@home.com

OBJECTIVE & QUALIFICATIONS

Qualified for supervisory / management positions in production, manufacturing, or distribution. Highlights:

➢ **Team leader / department supervisor:** More than six years of supervisory experience in shipping, receiving, and warehousing, with record of exceeding goals for productivity, cost-containment, and quality.

➢ **Company-minded and self-directed:** Noted by management for initiative, analytical skills, and ability to develop and motivate team members in union environment.

➢ **Training:** Degree included courses in business, computer literacy (MS Excel, Word, PowerPoint), marketing, and communications. Selected for company-sponsored management training.

EXPERIENCE

WALGREEN'S DISTRIBUTION CENTER

11/96-Present

(1.8-million-sq.ft. center ships 36 million cartons annually, supplying 300 stores in a 4-state area)

Distribution Supervisor

Cross-trained in and supervised various departments, including Repack, Quality Assurance, JIT, Put Away, Accelerated Flow-Through, and Case Pack. Currently perform responsibilities of an Operations Manager on second shift, ensuring key department (Case Pack) runs productively, safely, and cost efficiently. Direct a crew of 21-26 warehouse laborers, with responsibility for employee development, evaluations, discipline, and dismissals. Control $38 million labor and operating budget. Monitor manhours-to-volume ratios.

Team Contributions

➢ Increased productivity from 22 to 28.5 cartons per manhour (#1 among 14 centers nationwide).

➢ Exceeded cubilization goal 10% (from 80% to 90% cubic feet per shipment).

➢ Increased order fill rate from 98.5% to 99.5%.

➢ Saved $3.2 million in labor expenses in prior fiscal year; virtually eliminated overtime.

➢ Improved productivity from 12 to 15 pallets per hour in Put Away Department.

➢ Helped implement inventory control system, improving turnaround on unloading-storage-reshipment of merchandise from one week to 24 hours.

Other Achievements

➢ Promoted from Laborer to Supervisor in 18 months (normal advancement track is 3-4 years).

➢ Frequently assigned by management to turn around problem areas.

➢ Selected to troubleshoot and operate key equipment for optimum merchandise flow.

EDUCATION

BALL STATE UNIVERSITY

Bachelor of Science Degree in Business Administration (1996)

Applicant-Tracking Systems: What Happens After You E-Mail or Post Your Résumé?

If you have delivered your résumé to a recruiter by e-mail or posted it to a Web site, it will most likely encounter an applicant-tracking system. The use of electronic applicant-tracking systems—the technology that stores résumés and manages applicant data—is increasing steadily. This technology allows companies to deal with hundreds or thousands of applicants using a fraction of the time and manpower a manual system would demand.

Positive Aspects of Applicant-Tracking Technology

There are both positives and negatives to applicant-tracking technology for job seekers. On the plus side, you can find yourself eligible for positions you did not apply for or would not have initially considered. Some software has an "automatch" function, allowing you to be considered for any open position for which you are minimally qualified. Another benefit is that once your résumé is scanned, you will stay "in the system" from six months to several years (depending on the company's protocol or a state's legal requirements) and possibly be called on for that dream job at a point when your job search has cycled into hibernation mode. Those hired by a company with sophisticated tracking technology have a greater opportunity to be promoted from within because their résumé is on file. Perhaps most critical, tracking systems help level the playing field for job seekers. Your résumé is not selected based on how visually attractive it is; instead, it's selection is based on the value of its content, much as relationships ought to be.

Negative Aspects of Applicant-Tracking Technology

Now for the liabilities. Major corporations can receive more than 1,000 résumés each week during peak recruiting periods. When those résumés are received by surface mail, human hands must process and scan them. Although not the norm, there is potential for résumés to get lost, crumpled, or separated from a cover letter (which is a good reason to put your name and telephone number on all pages to be scanned). Perhaps the biggest hurdle is that it is tough to have a voice-to-voice, let alone face-to-face, contact with someone in HR. As far as HR staff is concerned, once your résumé has been received, you are in the system. If your qualifications match a job order, the company will contact you. In other words, "Don't call us, we'll call you."

Sometimes when applying for a job, you'll encounter a sophisticated voice-mail system that can lead you through a prescreening query of 10 or so questions. If you meet the criteria, you're awarded an applicant-tracking number. Once awarded a number, you place the number on your résumé and then fax it to an 800 number, only to wonder where it went, whether it got there, who sees it next, and when you might get a response.

Tip Credit goes to a client of mine who came up with a strategy for outsmarting the computer screener. Faced with defeat after repeatedly trying to break into a leading international company, my client (whom I'll refer to as Eleanor) saw an ad for a sales position with this same target company. A call to the 800 screening number told her, "If you have applied within the past month, you will not be eligible for a new applicant number." (Translate: You are already in the system and did not match our requirements for the new job, so don't try again!)

Indeed, she had applied within the last month. One might question her method's ethicality, but it was certainly efficacious: Eleanor circumvented the telephone screening by using her maiden name, which she at times used for business. Despite her earlier résumé being in the system, this time she prevailed and earned an applicant-tracking number to post on her résumé (which was identical to the previous résumé other than the last name). It appeared that the hiring team was simply looking for "fresh" candidates because within days, Eleanor got a call from a sales manager who was conducting telephone prescreening!

There is one more job-seeker liability when it comes to applicant-tracking technology. Human resource professionals have frequently been referred to as gatekeepers, closely guarding the great wall that surrounds Career City, USA. With the addition of applicant-tracking technology, those gates can be even more impenetrable unless you have the right keys—*keywords*. Refer to chapter 5 for a discussion of keywords.

Conflicting Advice

If you've done any reading on the subject of preparing your résumé for an applicant-tracking system, you'll probably note conflicting advice. The reason is that some technology is more sophisticated than others. The more advanced systems can solve a number of résumé riddles with near humanesque reasoning powers to do the following:

- **Do simple math.** They can add up how many years of experience you have.

- **Unscramble initialed degrees.** They know that a BS is a Bachelor of Science—you don't have to write it both ways. They can interpret whether an MS means a Master of Science degree, multiple sclerosis, or Microsoft.

- **Extract skills** from many styles of résumés, such as chronological (up to six jobs in order by date), achievement, functional, and combination résumés.

- **Convert search requests to match synonyms,** such as converting "well spoken" to "communication skills."

Résumés of the Future

Savvy job seekers will pay attention to what, as well as who, is reading their résumés in the months and years to come. As technology advances (which is as certain as the sun rising tomorrow), look for a move toward paperless recruiting and the development of a profile system that captures vital candidate information in a format most usable to the individual company.

With regard to résumé databases, it's possible we'll see an increase in standardization of résumé data (in other words, little variation in category headings, order of categories, and so on), making it possible to submit your résumé to one site and then have that service submit the résumé to thousands of employers.

ASCII-text versions could fall by the wayside if e-mail systems ever become completely standardized (for instance, if America Online's e-mail program were to be perfectly compatible with MS Outlook or other popular systems). With Web-site-development software becoming more common and easy to use, e-résumés will continue to evolve into three-dimensional, multipage portfolios with much greater depth and breadth. Although keywords will continue to play a role in evaluating candidates, it could be that your e-mail address is the most important keyword you'll ever use, especially if corporate recruiting continues to shift from sorting through résumés to shooting out e-mail announcements to notify candidates of hot new openings. Tomorrow will tell.

Meantime, as long as Hewlett Packard continues to make printers and people prefer to hold reading material in their hands, the traditional, printed presentation résumé will be with us. Likewise, as long as technology bulldozes its irreversible course and paves the way to access information by palm devices, mobile phones, and television screens, the e-résumé will also be with us. Future-thinking careerists will be armed and ready with both.

Top 10 Technology Tips for E-Résumés, E-Portfolios, and Blogs

1. Be prepared with multiple formats of your résumé.

2. Create an ASCII plain-text résumé for pasting into online résumé builders (such as those found at www.careerbuilder.com and www.monster.com) and e-forms at employer Web sites.

3. You'll also use an ASCII résumé for e-mail when the employer has requested a plain-text or unformatted résumé. When e-mailing an ASCII résumé, paste it into the body of the e-mail message.

4. Remember to create two different ASCII résumés for e-forms and e-mail. An ASCII résumé without line breaks works best for e-forms and an ASCII résumé with line breaks works best for e-mail. See "Converting to ASCII for E-mailing" and "Converting to ASCII for Pasting into E-forms" earlier in this chapter.

5. After converting your résumé into ASCII format, always take a few minutes to clean up the unavoidable formatting hiccups and glitches that occur. See "Quick Cleanup of an ASCII Conversion" earlier in this chapter.

6. If an employer accepts e-mail attachments (some don't), ask about the preferred format. Employers are most accustomed to receiving MS Word files in either the traditional .doc format or Rich Text Format (RTF). The RTF format is created using the "File, Save As" function in MS Word.

7. Adobe Acrobat's Portable Document Format (PDF) is another increasingly common option for e-mail attachments. If your computer system doesn't have the ability to create a PDF, go to www.pdfonline.com/convert_pdf.asp, where you can upload your résumé file for conversion. The system will then send you an e-mail with a file attachment containing the PDF résumé.

8. Consider creating a Web résumé, e-portfolio, or blog to give you tech-savvy, 24/7 marketing visibility.

(continued)

(continued)

9. Remember that professionalism is key to a successful online presence. Snarky blogs won't create a positive impression with recruiters, and photos of the kids and pets shouldn't be a part of your career e-portfolio.

10. When in doubt on the technical how-to's or short on time, enlist the help of competent professionals to create your e-résumé, e-portfolio, or blog. See the resources in this chapter for e-portfolios and blogs, or go to www.cminstitute.com/mrw.html to find a Master Résumé Writer. The investment in you and your career is worth it.

Cover Letters and Other Parts of the Puzzle

"I have made this letter longer than usual, because I lack the time to make it short."

—Pascal
Lettres Provinciales

Cover letters are a critical component of your job search arsenal and a necessary companion to your résumé. A good cover letter complements your résumé and encourages the recipient to read everything you have presented. A great cover letter is on-brand, reveals your understanding of the employer's needs, and hints at your professionalism and style. A magical cover letter does all of the above and more, propelling you "far 'above' the madding crowd."

Magical cover letters scream—ever so politely—that you have the intelligence, experience, and soft skills to be the answer to an employer's staffing problem. Marginal cover letters can also scream—unfortunately, the message might not be a positive one. An under-par cover letter might appear to be "another canned letter" from an applicant going through the motions of looking for work, or "another self-centered, self-aggrandizing applicant" who hasn't once indicated an interest in the company's needs.

In the course of aiding candidates in the job search process, I have discovered that their attitudes toward cover letters are divided into two camps: those whose dread of writing letters is akin to tackling inorganic chemistry, and those who think that there's nothing to it—"don't you just slap a few paragraphs together and say you want the position?" The former sometime need only a word of encouragement and a few writing tips (they often do quite well, thank you); the latter often need a crash course in business etiquette and marketing, along with a reality check on how very competitive it is on planet job-search. A poorly written cover letter can knock you out of contention for career opportunities—positions you are qualified for—and leave you wondering why your search is taking so long.

Writing good copy is enormously difficult. Experienced copywriters skilled in their craft earn handsome six-figure incomes. They write, rewrite, edit, seek critiques, and edit some more. You should too. Don't tackle writing your letter in one sitting. Write; then come back to it later. Few of us have the gift of Stephen King, who is rumored to write his best-sellers longhand one time through; more of us can align ourselves with Hemingway—he supposedly rewrote the last chapter of *For Whom the Bell Tolls* more than 20 times.

To help your cover letters mature from marginal to magical, I'll focus on two elements: first, a discourse on strategy and style; second, the segments of a cover letter. Later in the chapter are tactics for dealing with "sticky wickets" such as missed filing deadlines, blind box ads, relocation, and job termination. You'll also learn about other job search communications, such as developing a letter for mass mailing, writing to a "headhunter," creating career summary sheets, and crafting interview thank-you notes that really sell. Finally, I'll cover the anatomical mechanics of a cover letter. I encourage you to read completely the first two sections on strategy and segments before putting pen to paper (or your fingertips to the keyboard). You can apply the proper mechanics applied later.

Strategy and Style

With respect to strategy and style, there are three points to remember:

- Value, value, value
- Talk, don't tell
- Reveal a secret

The Value Mantra

Your mantra in cover letter writing should be "value, value, value." Value means that you offer something of worth. To help you focus on value, ask yourself these questions:

- What problems does the employer need solved?
- How can I prove I can be of help to the employer?
- Is what I am saying relevant to this particular employer's concerns?
- Am I putting the employer's needs above my needs?

You probably noticed a common thread in each of these questions. It's the *employer's* perspective. Are you writing to the employer's needs or to your own? One method to gauge where the emphasis lies is to do some math. Count the number of "I's," "my's," and "me's" in your letter. Too many of these point to a me-focus rather than an employer-focus.

In the *Before* example (see Cover Letter 10.1), "I" is used five times; "my," three; and "me," just once, for a total of nine personal pronouns. This imbalance shifts the letter's focus toward the candidate's concerns rather than the employer's interests.

Now weigh the value the second optician offers to prospective employers in the *After* example (see Cover Letter 10.2). The count on this letter still includes some personal pronouns (I = 2; my = 1; me = 0), but they are couched in phrases that focus on the employer's needs, as evidenced by the five-time occurrence of the pronoun "your." (The material in the second paragraph is based on industry research.)

Cover Letter 10.1: Before

Selva Senterd-Kandadate
4321 Lane Drive
Sunnyside, CA 93456
(408) 432-1234
ssk@email.com

[date]

Robert Sneed, Human Resources Director
OPHTHALMOLOGY DOCS UNLIMITED
1234 E. Zee Street
Sunnyside, CA 93456

Dear Mr. Sneed:

I am writing to inquire about employment opportunities as an optician with your eyecare group. I require a position that will grow into an opportunity that will allow me to utilize my management and training abilities.

My optician skills and experience are noted on the enclosed résumé. I am certain that with my abilities I can make an immediate and valuable contribution to your organization.

I would appreciate an opportunity to meet to discuss my qualifications. Thank you.

Sincerely,

Selva Senterd-Kandadate

Enclosure

Cover Letter 10.2: After

Val U. Kandadate

1234 Shady Drive
Sunnyside, CA 93456
(408) 321-4567
value@email.com

[date]

Robert Sneed, Human Resources Director
OPHTHALMOLOGY DOCS UNLIMITED
1234 E. Zee Street
Sunnyside, CA 93456

Dear Mr. Sneed:

As an experienced optician, I am writing to inquire of your need for licensed staff with strong technical and interpersonal skills.

Practitioners are particularly challenged by the changes healthcare has encountered with the advent of managed care. Beyond providing quality care, medical groups must operate efficiently and profitably. You will note on the enclosed résumé an award for Manager of the Year—this award was based on overall unit profitability and performance. Despite ranking as the lowest volume store in the district, our sales performance was among the highest in the nation, as well as the district—

- ◆ sales increased an average of 26%;

- ◆ refunds were reduced 50% to a record low of .6%; and

- ◆ patient satisfaction scores soared as a result of personalized service, frame selection, and visual merchandising.

I love my profession—the satisfaction that comes from helping people see better is, of course, rewarding. Beyond that, many patients approach me with the mind-set that glasses are a "necessary evil." I pride myself on bringing the right measure of enthusiasm and fashion into the equation so that by the time patients render payment, they feel they not only *see* better, but also *look* better.

Given my six years' experience, licensure as a Registered Dispensing Optician and National Contact Lens Examiner, and commitment to quality patient care, there is a strong likelihood I would quickly become a valued member of your optical services team. At the convenience of your schedule, may we meet to discuss your practice's needs?

In advance, thank you for your time.

Sincerely,

Val U. Kandadate

Enclosure

Val's letter pushes all the right buttons for Mr. Sneed. She is technically skilled with dual licensure, she can sell and make people feel good about spending money on eyewear, and she has an understanding of what it takes to make a practice profitable. Her message sings value, value, value. There is no question that Val U. Kandadate will be classified as an "A" candidate. "A" candidates are accorded "WOW" status—Winners, Outstanding, and Wanted. Poor Selva is relegated to "C" status: just another job applicant going through the motions.

Sell, Don't Tell

When was the last time you asked your spouse or significant other to go to an event—something you love to do, but something the other wouldn't necessarily choose for entertainment? If the following monologue has played at your house, it may be evidence that you are "telling" rather than "selling."

Before

"Honey, the musical *Les Miserables* will be in town next weekend. I've already got the tickets, and we'll be going with Jean and Bob. We'll leave the house around 5:00 and have dinner at Le Bistro first. This is the most wonderful musical. I'm so excited about seeing it. I know you'll love it." [Husband translates: I hate the traffic in the city, and there go my plans to spend the weekend camping in the mountains.]

Now the same request, presented as if hubby has some option in the matter, or will at least benefit from the whole affair.

After

"Honey, Le Bistro is having its early-bird special next Saturday night. I know how you love their rack of lamb, and it's such a great deal at half price. What would you say to asking Bob and Jean to join us? You always comment on how much fun we have with them. And remember, my mom gave us that coupon for free baby-sitting so we could have a night out. How about making a night of it and seeing *Les Miserables?* It's such a moving story, full of drama and adventure, and set in early 19th-century France." [Husband now gets something out of the deal: favorite food at half the price, favorite friends, free baby-sitting, promise of a classic story full of favorite interests—history, action-adventure, man's triumph against the odds. He now gladly accommodates wife's wishes.... Wife also promises to go wilderness camping with hubby the following weekend!]

"Selling" works much better than "telling." It's a principle of human nature and good relationships. I recognize that it's difficult to sell in a letter. It is by nature a one-way conversation because the recipient has no opportunity to answer you directly or interject thoughts or questions. You can, however, make it more of a conversation by painting a picture of appeal, instead of making demands or simply stating the facts, as this next *Before* example (see Cover Letter 10.3) does.

Cover Letter 10.3: Before

ROLAND HILLS
9090 West Augusta
Fenton, Georgia 30303
(877) 432-4321
roland@geo.com

[date]

Dear Mr. Employer:

I am writing about your advertisement for a Store Manager. Please review my enclosed résumé for details of my qualifications.

My background includes three years of experience at HomeLife USA. My responsibilities include store management, sales, and merchandising. I am also responsible for training retail sales associates. I hold a degree in marketing from San Jose State University.

I would appreciate an opportunity to interview for this position. Thank you for your consideration.

Sincerely,

Roland Hills

Enclosure

Following is Roland's letter, reworked from "telling" into a more conversational "selling" style.

Cover Letter 10.4: After

ROLAND HILLS

9090 West Augusta
Fenton, Georgia 30303
(877) 432-4321
roland@geo.com

[date]

Dear Mr. Employer:

You are advertising for a Store Manager. As a retail management professional with three years' experience, a cross-industry background that includes sales of consumer furnishings and appliances, and a degree in marketing, my credentials should meet your requirements.

During my time as store manager with HomeLife, I consistently met the challenge of promoting high-margin sales in an industry known for competitive pricing. To accomplish this, I focus on equipping my 12-member sales team with solution-based sales tools and product-oriented sales incentives. In doing so, the branch has earned a number of accolades (detailed on the enclosed résumé), as well as these awards:

- Most Improved Sales Volume (region-wide)

- Best Profit Margin Increase (district-wide)

- Top Store for Display & Visual Merchandising (district-wide)

Although corporate is pleased with my performance, the parent company's restructuring on a national scale necessitates that I explore other options. Your opportunity appears to be a situation that would benefit from my talents and experience. If so, I will touch base with your assistant this Friday to learn when we might meet.

Sincerely,

Roland Hill

Enclosure

Roland has succeeded in painting a picture of an educated professional who is knowledgeable about the employer's products and experienced in delivering sales and profit increases. He, too, merits "A" status.

Reveal a Secret

Employers hire humans, not machines. They want to know what makes you tick. They want to know that your soft skills—those less tangible but all-important interpersonal skills and work habits—will be a good fit with the corporate culture. Provide them with a peek inside; lower your shield just a hair and let them know, indeed, what makes you tick. I don't suggest that you spill your deepest, innermost thoughts (save that for confession). I do, however, suggest that you weave in some tidbit that reflects your personality, philosophy, or character. The type of position you are applying for will dictate what, if anything, you reveal—in some cases, it won't be appropriate; in other cases, it will. Use your discretion; then test-market it on a trusted colleague. The optician's cover letter (Val U. Kandadate) printed earlier in this chapter is an example of revealing a peek into personality—her third paragraph is reprinted here.

> I love my profession—the satisfaction that comes from helping people see better is, of course, rewarding. Beyond that, many patients approach me with the mind-set that glasses are a "necessary evil." I pride myself on bringing the right measure of enthusiasm and fashion into the equation so that by the time patients render payment, they feel they not only *see* better, but also *look* better.

These next two examples are excerpts from letters that were written for a candidate whose broad skill base enabled him to target very different disciplines. The first excerpt addresses his environmental engineering background; the second, his interest in human resources and staff development. Both give employers an indication of what sparks his energy.

Engineering

> Issues relating to the environment, safety/health, and technology generate an enthusiasm in me like no other. Some of my most rewarding work centered on hazardous-waste research for the Department of Energy and the Environmental Protection Agency while I served as a technical project manager for an environmental engineering firm (my "Q" security clearance can be readily reactivated). More recently, I have put my science background to work as a town selectman, where I serve on the board of directors of a regional landfill and waste-recycling facility.

Human Resources

> My most rewarding work has centered on authoring human resource–related publications and articles, as well as presenting seminars on the same. My training topics often cut across industry boundaries and equip professionals from all disciplines with the personal-development skills to make a difference in an organization. Complementing this background is my present academic focus—I am pursuing a second master's in Organizational Behavior from the University of Massachusetts-Amherst.

This next full-text cover letter (see Cover Letter 10.5) gives a "real" glimpse of the candidate's personality and philosophy. Claire's letter reveals her passion for the arts and education, along with her broad credentials and experience.

Cover Letter 10.5

Claire O'Shaughnessy

1234 East Sunnyside   cos2000@aol.com
Allentown, PA 44444   (888) 449-7474

[date]

Adelle Starell, Department Chair
Department of Theatre
State Center Community College District
1234 Fulton Mall
San Francisco, CA 95432

Re: Opportunities as Assistant Professor, Department of Theatre

Dear Ms. Starell:

Thank you for your time on the telephone yesterday. As you indicated, it appears my background may be the perfect fit for your new opening. The enclosed résumé will help you make that decision. From it you will note extensive work as a teacher, director, and actor, both in the United States and abroad.

For the past 15 years, theatre has been the outlet for my first love, which is teaching. Depending on your needs, I am qualified to teach a full complement of drama/theatre courses—Acting, Movement, Voice, Playwriting, Public Speaking, and Drama as an ESL tool. Other content areas, such as English and History, can also be covered.

I am passionate about using the arts as a medium for education. Dovetailing on England's success for drawing youth to the arts, my desire is to bring new, student-authored play material to the stage. I sense that, for theatre to revive and thrive in America, it must be in touch with the local community and have a positive societal impact. Our youth, especially at the secondary and postsecondary levels, can find a productive outlet for their voice as they deal with significant cultural, economic, and social challenges through drama.

Given my international professional background, teaching experience, and extensive conservatory training, I am confident I would make an excellent addition to your faculty. Though living abroad for the past few years and finishing my degree in the Northeast, I have long regarded California as my home (I spent the majority of my youth there) and look forward to returning come June of next year.

My plans include a trip to the Bay Area over the winter break. Perhaps we can sit down together at that time.

Best regards,

Claire O'Shaughnessy

Enclosure

The Segments of a Cover Letter

In the old days, there were three straightforward parts to a cover letter:

- **The introduction:** Typically a perfunctory statement that mentioned the position you were applying for and how you learned of it.
- **The body:** One or two paragraphs that summarized your experience and career goals.
- **A final paragraph:** Often an invitation to review your résumé and request that the screener call if interested.

Today, those three parts have taken on new functions:

- **The carrot:** An introduction that is fresh, interesting, and relevant.
- **The corroboration:** Content that communicates your brand, shows an intelligent understanding of the employer's needs, and confirms your ability to fill those needs.
- **The close:** A confident finish that might suggest a meeting or invite the reader to take further action.

Let's look at each of these elements individually.

The Carrot

The name Cecil B. DeMille was virtually synonymous with Hollywood film-making during the first half of the 20th century. His films, known for their creativity and grand scale, were built on a model that starts with an H-bomb and builds to a climax. You can apply this philosophy, tempered with a heavy dose of professionalism, to the introduction of your cover letter. While I'm on the subject of filmmaking, let me take this opportunity to replay the soundtrack from chapter 2—it's the AIDA theme again (attention, interest, desire, action). Your goal in the first paragraph is to earn the reader's attention. You can do so with a "carrot."

The carrot metaphor has its origins from dangling a carrot in front of a workhorse to encourage the animal to keep plodding through the fields. At the end of the day, Old Betsy did get her carrot and probably some nice oats, too. Your carrot should be tasty enough to entice the staffing professionals to go on, enjoy the work of plowing through your qualifications, and be rewarded at project's end when a mutually beneficial employment relationship ensues.

Consider presenting your carrot in the form of intrigue, an inspirational quotation, an interesting fact, or a strong appeal. The goal is not to be outlandish but to coax the recipient to read on, as these examples do.

Example of Intrigue [New Graduate]

Little did I know that leaving my native France to work for the summer as an *au pair* would lead to a career in international business.

Example of Inspirational Quotation

Employment is nature's physician, and is essential to human happiness. Galen made this observation in the second century, and it is still true in the 21st century. It is this philosophy, along with seven years' experience in job development with public and private agencies, that I bring to the position of career guidance specialist for the Welfare-to-Work program.

Example of an Interesting Fact

Labor statistics indicate that people change careers an average of three times during their working life. I am pursuing one of those changes! As a career secretary, I wish to continue this work; however, my goal is to transition from government service and apply my skills in a more creative setting. Your advertising agency is among my top choices.

Example of Appeal

Could your company benefit from a "work-smart" salesman who built his client list from zero to 275 and transitioned the company's focus on high-margin sales from 36% to 75%?

Tip Before leading off with an interesting carrot, provide the reader with a frame of reference by using a subject line under the inside (company) address, as shown here.

Charlene Capovilla
ABC, Inc.
123 Easy Street
Sunnyland, CA 98765

Re: Career opportunities as Guidance Specialist

In homage to Mr. DeMille, don't be afraid to drop your bomb. The first sentence of your cover letter sets the stage and can make the difference between "B" movie or blockbuster status. Note how a standard opening (see Cover Letter 10.6) is improved in the *After* example (see Cover Letter 10.7).

Cover Letter 10.6: Before

NENG YANG
333 North Vassar
Los Angeles, CA 90240
(213) 222-3333
nyang@excite.com

[date]

Li Kun Xie, Placement Specialist
Inner-City School District
1234 S.W. 42nd Avenue
Los Angeles, CA 90242

Re: School Counselor, Southeast Asian At-Risk Populations

Dear Ms. Xie:

I am writing to inquire about opportunities in secondary school counseling with Inner-City School District.

Cover Letter 10.7: After

NENG YANG
333 North Vassar
Los Angeles, CA 90240
(213) 222-3333
nyang@excite.com

[date]

Li Kun Xie, Placement Specialist
Inner-City School District
1234 S.W. 42nd Avenue
Los Angeles, CA 90242

Re: School Counselor, Southeast Asian At-Risk Populations

Dear Ms. Xie:

A school counselor made the difference in my life.

Although limited in my ability to read or write English when I graduated from high school, my minority counselor encouraged me to go to college. A native of Laos, I had been in the United States for only a few short years. The prospect of college was appealing but daunting—no one in my family had ever gone beyond high school. Since that time, I have sharpened my literacy skills and gone on to earn a Master of Arts in Educational Counseling and Student Services. Working with special needs and underrepresented populations, such as those your district serves, is my primary goal.

From the enclosed résumé, you will note experiences in both academic/student services and psychological counseling roles. I am also active in the Hmong community—my reputation as a workshop presenter has earned invitations to speak at community groups and school districts throughout California. Literacy, family systems, and higher education for the Southeast Asian community are typically my themes.

Your School Counselor position would make use of these rich academic, cultural, and personal experiences. Moreover, your students have the promise of both a trained academic counselor and successful role model who understands the culture and the challenges facing youth.

In advance, thank you for your consideration. I look forward to meeting with your interview panel.

Sincerely,

Neng Yang

Enclosure

In this applicant's situation, it was appropriate to reveal his "secret," because it implies that he can relate to the student population at Inner-City School District. Neng uses a powerful form of persuasion: personal identification. We experience an immediate bond when we can personally relate to another's circumstances. Apply this psychological truth in your writing, and it will bring you closer to your reader.

Following are a few more strong introductions that capture attention and position the applicant above the crowd.

Sales Professional

Eight years ago, I started my career in sales while still a "green" college kid, selling vacuums door-to-door (and wore out two pairs of soles over the course of one year). Today, I sell high-margin technology solutions to Fortune 2000 companies (and rack up more than 6,000 sky miles each month). My sales manager has elevated me to "gold" status based on performance as the #1 sales producer on an 8-member team of experienced sales engineers.

Management Professional

As a business executive, I believe an organization's success is predicated on several factors, one of which is a talented management team.

Plant Manager

Delivering solid productivity increases has been the norm throughout my 12-year career in plant operations. My commitment to you would be the same: simplify processes, develop workforce competencies, and boost output.

Name-dropping is another effective strategy for beginning a cover letter. When a common colleague enters the equation, your status in the reader's eyes is elevated from "don't know you from Adam" to "must be a decent guy if so-and-so recommended him."

Dear Mr. Smithers:

Tyler Bradford suggested I contact you about openings in the Engineering Department of International Avionics. Tyler, whom I worked with recently at ABC Avionics, can speak to my project-management and electrical engineering skills.

or

Dear Mrs. Michaels:

I am pleased that Linda Weller thought highly enough of me to recommend that I contact you. Linda is aware of my interest in mid-level accounting positions in the entertainment industry....

This next example mentions a member of the board of directors of the organization, implying the board member's silent endorsement of the candidate.

It is my understanding from Marlene Sterling that John Britton is retiring from the helm after a long tenure with your organization. His excellent reputation in the construction industry is well deserved, and your committee will have a formidable task in selecting his successor.

With virtually 20 years' experience in construction lending, I believe I have much to offer as Resource Lender's new President/Chief Executive Officer. My management career track with Nation's Bank and Bank of America encompasses significant leadership experience in organizational management, business development, and credit management and policy formation. [etc.]

When "name dropping," always ask permission to use the contact's name before committing it to print.

The Corroboration

corroborate 1 to strengthen or support. **2** to attest the truth or accuracy of. **3** to confirm.

This section of your cover letter should strengthen or support, not restate, information from your résumé. To attest the truth or accuracy of your résumé, you might offer a skills summary with specific number-based accomplishments. Don't lean too heavily on cataloging your soft skills (such as effective communication skills, analytical problem-solving skills, and team-oriented skills). At this point, they might be considered unsubstantiated and self-serving. Note how these next four examples offer evidence to back up their claims of specific skills.

Individual with sales and management experience in the building materials industry, applying for sales position with roofing supplier

Qualifications I can bring to Weyerhaeuser are outlined on the enclosed résumé. You'll note that I've spent nearly a decade in building materials sales, highlights of which are these:

- Captured more than $8 million in sales volume while launching a new central California territory.

- Gained 35% share of the commercial building materials market through expansion of ready-mix business.

- Boosted profit margin to 6% above industry average through management of time, resources, and systems.

- Hired, trained, and supervised an aggressive sales team who were well versed in competitive building materials.

What is not mentioned on the résumé is that I virtually grew up in the roofing business. My father owned Cal-Valley Roofing, so I had an early exposure to the industry and the people associated with it.

Library Acquisitions Specialist applying for Financial Analyst position with school district

In reviewing Rocklin Unified's position announcement, I notice that my background and skills closely match your requirements. Briefly, my qualifications are these:

⇒ Recent experience in **Rocklin Unified School District** with responsibility for managing in excess of $1 million in State textbook and library funding . . . implemented conversion from manual to computer system that cut in half the time required to process acquisitions.

⇒ Prior experience as **bookstore coordinator** in a postsecondary educational setting, where my responsibilities included training, supervising, and evaluating a staff of five, in addition to monthly financial analysis of accounting, inventory, and sales data . . . revenue unit generated a 12% increase over prior year's figures.

⇒ Solid understanding of generally accepted accounting principles, in addition to regulations unique to **school district accounting** in compliance with the Accounting Manual for California State School Districts . . . earned unqualified marks on recent state audit.

⇒ Additional experience as **accountant** for private industry, with responsibility for financial statements, profit flow/cash flow analysis, and general ledger reconciliation.

⇒ **Bachelor's degree** with applied coursework in Managerial Accounting and Financial Accounting.

Accounting professional applying for work with CPA firm; letter rationalized a "meandering" career history and overcame no experience with public accounting firms

With the close of the tax season, your firm is likely looking forward to next year's demands and evaluating the need for new staff accountants. If so, please consider the enclosed résumé. Qualifications I bring to your organization:

■ **Experience as revenue agent with the IRS:** Four years' experience as a revenue agent with the Internal Revenue Service. Training included intensive coursework in individual, sole proprietorship, partnership, and corporate tax law, as well as training in the Tax Reform Act, fraud awareness and bribery, TEFRA, audits of tax shelters, and a variety of quality management seminars.

My performance merited above-average scores on evaluations and resulted in assignment to the more difficult and technically complex cases. Supervisors characterized me as "very cooperative" and "willing to participate in other assignments," as evidenced by my volunteer service at taxpayer assistance programs and selection as an Automated Exam System Coordinator for my 10-member examination group.

■ **Broad range of financial experiences:** Prior experience as a tax consultant and financial planner with IDS/American Express Financial Advisors. In addition to preparing tax returns for business clients, my financial planning responsibilities extended to retirement planning, estate planning, college planning, debt management, tax minimization, survivor protection, and income/asset protection.

More recently, I served as finance manager for a high-volume dealership where my responsibilities involved negotiating customer transactions, securing financing, and managing flooring contracts. Since September, I have focused on completing my degree and servicing my accounting and tax clients (the majority are individuals and small businesses that I have worked with part-time since 1990).

■ **Academic Preparation:** Currently enrolled in Master's in Taxation Program at Valley College of Law. Completed graduate studies in taxation at San Jose State University and a baccalaureate degree in Business Administration/Economics from St. Mary's College. Also, presently studying for the Enrolled Agent exam next month and the CPA exam in approximately six months.

Insurance professional applying for position in another state

My 12 years in the insurance industry encompass comprehensive experience in corporate audit/reinspection and multibranch claims management assignments. While managing southern California's 7-branch district, *our business retention rates escalated to a record 93%.* This fact should substantiate my ability to develop, implement, and monitor business retention systems on a regional scale.

The position also calls for strong technical skills. During my tenure with Nation's Insurance, I taught continuing education courses in property damage, bodily injury, auto estimatics, subrogation, salvage, litigation management, and industry computer applications (ADP, Mitchell, CCC). The training system developed was used as a model by other districts throughout the western region.

Tip Find your voice. Your writing needs to reflect your vocabulary and speech patterns, as well as your thinking. Although reading books like this one can be helpful, I caution you not to copy ideas word for word. Instead, study the style and the strategy underlying each sentence. Substitute your industry terminology and your typical vocabulary until it flows with your "voice." Letter writing becomes easier with practice.

All of the preceding cover letters work because they offer value: They address employer needs and substantiate statements whenever possible. Your prospective employer will appreciate receiving meaty information, backed by documented accomplishments.

The Close

A strong closing summarizes your qualifications and suggests that a next step be taken, such as a telephone call or personal meeting. The summary can be brief, taking the form of just a few words.

Given my technical skills, familiarity with the product line, and understanding of your clients' needs, I could step into the position and be of immediate assistance.

Sincerely,

Joy Toworkwith

Enclosure

This executive candidate warrants a longer closing.

> It appears that Agribusiness Bank is well positioned for growth. To bring this growth to fruition, you will need a leader who understands agriculture, is well connected in the local ag community, ensures that wise credit decisions are made, balances the financial resources of the institution, and has the ability to adapt to a changing environment. I offer my expertise.
>
> Sincerely,
>
> A. G. Rate-Aplikint
>
> Enclosure

Sales professionals will tell you that one of the biggest factors in losing a sale is not asking for the order. Opinions vary on follow-up strategy when it comes to closing your cover letter. Should you mention that you will call to follow up, or should you ask the recipient to call you? It depends. In large organizations, a follow-up call will often be thwarted by barbed-wire voice-mail systems. There may be a greater likelihood of contact in smaller organizations. Some interpret a "follow-up" statement as strong-armed effrontery; some think it courteous that you'll do the work of making a call instead of giving the hiring manager one more thing to do. If you are in sales, my vote is to ask for the order—offer a follow-up call on a specific date. In other cases, weigh each situation individually. You can always phone later even if you have not mentioned that you will call.

Your closing should be confident, but not pushy. If you're the shy type, bolster yourself to go beyond this Milquetoast closing.

> Would you be kind enough to review my résumé? Thank you, and I hope to hear from you.

If your personality leans toward sanguinity—you assume everybody loves and admires you—watch that your closing doesn't border on brazenness.

> There's no doubt in my mind that I would be an asset to your company. I will be in your area on Friday and will drop by to discuss my candidacy.

The following close strikes a balance between being assertively confident and considerately respectful.

Given my international experience, production record, and graduate training, I feel confident we may have some mutual interests. Your assistant mentioned an urgent need to fill the position. Business travel will take me out of state for the next week; if your calendar permits a meeting sometime before Friday, the 27th, I would appreciate any accommodation you can provide. You can reach me by 24-hour pager, 888-449-7474.

Best regards,

John Q. Candidate

Enclosure

Tip Got writer's block? If you're having trouble putting your thoughts down on paper, try this secret. Turn on a tape recorder and verbally compose the letter, without fear of making it a perfect presentation worthy of a Toastmasters award. Transcribe the tape. Often you'll find that many of the phrases and expressions you needed were already inside you.

The Anatomy of the Cover Letter

The anatomical terms for the parts of your cover letter include the following:

- **Header:** This is your name and contact information, including personal e-mail address (avoid using an e-mail address that's associated with your employer). The header should match exactly the header from your résumé. An exception would be when you've used a two-column vertical format for your résumé with your name appearing in the left column. If this is the case, center your header information for the cover letter.

- **Date:** According to *The Gregg Reference Manual,* the date should be the day you typed the letter. If there is more than a couple of days discrepancy between the date it is typed and the date you're mailing it, redate the letter.

    Here's a trick I learned from Ken Cole, an executive recruiter based in Florida. When doing a targeted mailing, drop your letters in the Sunday post. In cases where you anticipate a two-day mail delivery, this will put your correspondence on the recruiter's desk on Tuesday, typically the lightest mail day of the business week.

✦ **Inside address:** This includes the contact name, title, company name, street address or box number, city, state, and ZIP. If you have both a street address and a post office box, list the post office box below the street address. Postal sorting machinery reads from the bottom up and will deliver to the lowest line when given both a street and box number. Make certain that the ZIP code identifies the box number and not the street address.

Your Name
Address
City, State Zip
(888) 888-8888
youremail@isp.com

Header

date — *Date*

Contact Person's Name, Title
FULL COMPANY NAME
Street Address
City, State Zip

Inside address

Re: Title of position applying for — *Subject line*

Dear Ms. [Last Name of Contact Person]: — *Salutation*

Body of letter begins here. This is your three-second opportunity to earn the reader's unwavering attention. [see The Carrot]

Continue with body of letter. Provide succinct, hard-hitting corroboration of your qualifications. [see The Corroboration]

Close your letter on a positive and upbeat note. [see The Close].

Sincerely, — *Complimentary closing*

Body

Writer's Identification (your full name to match your letterhead) — *Writer's identification*

Enclosure — *Enclosure notation*

P.S. May or may not be used. [see P.S.] — *Post script*

Subject line: Typically the title of the position for which you are applying. Staffing professionals track where their best hires come from so that they can spend their advertising dollars wisely. For this reason, it's courteous to mention where you learned of the position. Adding this reference to the subject line can save you the perfunctory mention of it in the body of the letter.

Subject: Sales Engineer, Sept. 6 issue of *San Jose Mercury News*

Salutation: The formal word for *Dear so-and-so*. The inside address and salutation together make up the opening of the letter. When addressing a woman, use the courtesy title Ms., unless you know that the individual has a preference for Miss or Mrs.

Body: The text, or copy, of your letter (the carrot, the corroboration, the close).

Complimentary closing: "Sincerely" is the most common complimentary closing for first-time correspondence. When you're on friendly terms with the reader, you might try one of these: "Best regards," "Regards," "Fondly," or "Best wishes." If you go with "Very truly yours," make sure you avoid the common pitfall of spelling truly with an "e."

Writer's identification: This is your name, which should match the name you have used at the top of your résumé. If you have a stately, formal name, such as William Everett Cantrell III, but everyone on the planet calls you Bill (and you want your prospective employer to do so as well), you can type and sign the name Bill Cantrell.

Tip On business correspondence, you often see two sets of initials below the signature line to signify who dictated and who typed the letter. For instance, SBW/jg might indicate that Susan Britton Whitcomb dictated the letter and Jean Gatewood typed it. Even though you might be both author and typist, it is not necessary to include your initials on job search correspondence.

Enclosure notation: When including your résumé with a letter, type the word "Enclosure" two lines below your name. This clues the reader that there is something more to review. If you include information beyond the résumé, make it plural and type how many pieces you are including in parentheses.

Enclosures (2)

Post script: A great place to present a final idea or afterthought. Use it to make your letter more conversational, personal, and memorable, as these examples illustrate.

P.S. I just opened the morning paper and saw the article on your company on the front page of the Business section. Kudos!

P.S. I've been doing some research on unified messaging. This might be the solution for the communications problem you mentioned with your field technicians.

P.S. I learned from a reliable source that Best-Tech will be opening a regional distribution center here in the fall. You might want to pass this information along to your friend who specializes in relocation services for new executives. Jorge Gonzalez is the contact at Best-Tech (feel free to mention my name).

Sticky Wickets

The following sections look at a few of the common questions and problems that arise with cover letters.

To Whom It May Concern?

Every book or article written on cover letters tells you to write to a specific person, not "Dear Human Resources." Of course, we know that contacting a specific person is the best method, but let's be realistic. There might be times when you won't know who that person is, and there might be times when the person wishes to remain anonymous. Consider this print ad, known as a blind box ad.

Inventory Manager

7+ yrs' exp., wholesale distribution, computer-literate. Send res., cover letter, and salary history c/o:

Sacramento Bee
Box M172
Sacramento, CA 95825

Blind boxes can create angst in job seekers. "Am I writing to a direct competitor? Will I unknowingly apply to my present employer?"

There are a couple of ways to circumvent a blind box ad. The easiest is to call the newspaper running the ad and ask whether the ad was placed by Company X (your employer). The other tactic is to have a sponsor respond—preferably someone of superior rank to you who can write under the guise of "knowing someone" who would be perfect for the job, together with a brief description of your qualifications. If confidentiality is not a concern, accept that the company wants to remain anonymous. In these cases, it is acceptable to omit the salutation (Dear Ms. Recruiter) and use a subject line (re:) instead.

> Date
>
> *Sacramento Bee*
> Box M172
> Sacramento, CA 95825
>
> Attention: Human Resources
>
> Re: Inventory Manager, advertised in Sunday edition of *Sacramento Bee*
>
> As an APICS-certified inventory control specialist, my management and technical skills have resulted in tangible contributions to production output, inventory accuracy, technology advances, and quality improvements.
>
> [etc.]

When classified ads provide only a street address, use a reverse business directory to track down the company name. From there, a telephone call can often yield a contact name. Don't be embarrassed to ask for the spelling—there are hundreds of creative names out there these days (Csilla, Metheesa, Zay, Xia), unisex names (Mr. Pat Long? or Ms. Pat Long?), along with the variations on many of the traditional names (John/Jon, Jane/Jayne, Kelly/Kellie, Karla/Carla, Anne/Ann).

Missed a Filing Deadline?

Acknowledge it.

> I apologize for applying beyond the closing date. I only recently became aware of the opening and am hopeful that your search has not yet turned up the "perfect" match.

Sometimes stating the reason for your delay is appropriate.

> Business travel called me to the East Coast for the past two weeks, so I learned of your opening only today.

or

> I recognize your filing deadline was last week. Jane Dean, whom you know through AMA, brought the position to my attention just today and thought I might be an excellent addition to your staff.

Terminated from a Job?

Silence is golden. Give no explanation in your cover letter. You can deal with this can of worms more adroitly in person than you can in writing. An anonymous and insightful source once expressed words to this effect: We are slaves to our written word, servants to our spoken words, and captive to our thoughts. Rehearse how you will handle tough situations, such as a termination, and save your approach for a face-to-face meeting (see the companion book *Interview Magic,* also published by JIST, to ace your interview). We recall as little as 14 percent of what we hear; possibly, your interviewer will lump your termination explanation in with the 86 percent that is forgotten.

Relocating?

Some people advise not mentioning in your cover letter that you are "available for relocation," with the argument that you would obviously be available for relocation or you would not be applying for a job in another area. Most people will have a basic curiosity about why you are moving, so you might as well answer the unvoiced question. It can lend credibility to your move and allay employer fears that you might not stick around for long.

> My wife (a native of the area) and I will be relocating as a result of her promotion to the Warner Brothers affiliate in Detroit.

This next solution kills two birds with one stone: It addresses the relocation issue and legitimizes an informal stint as a consultant.

> [description of most impressive accomplishments with significant employer, followed by...]

> Since that time, I have helped a number of organizations (national and regional companies primarily based in the East and Midwest) with significant challenges—from complete startup of new manufacturing ventures to management and operational restructuring that turned around negative balance sheets. Several of these consulting engagements resulted in attractive offers for permanent employment... but my roots are on the West Coast (my wife and I are committed to the Los Angeles area, recently making our home in the South Bay). Thus, the impetus for my inquiry.

Dealing with Salary

Print ads often ask that you send a résumé, cover letter, and salary history. Avoid providing a salary history when responding to an ad for these two reasons: If your salary is higher than the position is paying, you may be screened out; if your salary is lower, you may lock yourself into a lower salary than the company might have offered. There are a couple schools of thought on how to manage salary requests. One is to acknowledge the employer's request for salary, but to sidestep any mention of past earnings with this sort of verbiage.

> My recent earnings have been reflective of contributions made to my employer. I am confident your compensation plan is market-competitive, and I would be open to discussing this matter during the course of an interview.

This strategy could cause you to be screened out, never to be called for an interview. It's a chance you might want to take if you want to hold your salary close to the vest. For those who do, there's a ray of hope. Conversations of recruiters and human resources professionals reveal that a candidate who looked very strong on paper yet averted the salary history request would still be called in for an interview.

The other thought is to acknowledge the employer's request and provide a salary range.

> Regarding salary, my earnings as Program Manager ranged from $55,000–70,000 dependent on team-performance bonuses. Salary is not my primary motivation. Being part of a collaborative policy-making team that can favorably affect the company and its customers is my greatest concern.

or

> Past compensation has been in the mid-$40,000 range. My current requirements would be in line with industry standards.

Avoid supplying a formal Salary History on a separate sheet of paper with details of earnings history at each employer. One or two sentences knitted into the cover letter will usually suffice.

Other Types of Letters

Job search communications can also take the form of a targeted mailing, recruiter letter, networking letter, thank-you letter, follow-up letter, or acceptance letter. You might even find yourself challenged with situations such as how to gracefully bow out after accepting an offer or cover a major faux pas you made in an interview. Following are strategies and examples for some of the more common communications.

Direct-Mail Campaigns

If you have preconceived notions that direct mail is only for Publishers Clearing House and credit-card companies, think again. Direct mail remains an incredibly effective form of advertising and selling (the steady flow of "junk" mail in your mailbox should confirm your suspicions that someone is profiting). Direct-mail sellers can do well with a response rate of just 1 or 2 percent; the secret is that they cast a broad net to ensure a good catch. You must too. A list of several hundred (minimum) will increase the odds of a favorable response rate. Conversely, direct mail to a limited list of 20 or 30 companies may yield disappointing results, but that isn't to say it shouldn't be done. All you need is one or two good bites. If you would like to employ a professional to help with your direct-mail campaign, here are two services that I can recommend:

* Job Bait (www.jobbait.com)

* Pro/File Research (www.profileresearch.com)

Your goal in employing this medium is to prepare a highly focused direct-mail piece that targets a specific size of company, industry, or placement firm specializing in that industry. This letter was written for a recent law school graduate targeting firms that specialize in international law.

Cover Letter 10.8

GERRY COLDWELL
4876 Yosemite Lane
Oakhurst, CA 93621
gerry@attbi.com
(559) 222-7474

[date]

[contact name, title]
[name of law firm]
[street address]
[city, state zip]

Dear _____:

Having obtained my J.D. from Boalt School of Law in May, I am presently seeking interviews with firms that are recruiting recent graduates who demonstrate strong potential to become valued members of your legal staff. Although acquiring broad experience is my immediate goal, I am especially interested in firms that devote a portion of their practice to international law and/or "white collar" criminal law, areas in which I would like to specialize in the years to come.

Among the experiences and qualities I bring to your firm are these: practical experience developed while a Legal Intern with a criminal/civil litigation practice; leadership skills demonstrated while founding the Legal History Club at Boalt and serving in a number of community and fraternal organizations; and international experience gained while living in Germany and traveling extensively throughout Western Europe.

Given the combination of these experiences, I am confident I have developed a professional resourcefulness and personal diversity that will enable me to significantly contribute to your firm. I would appreciate the opportunity to personally convey what I might contribute as an associate attorney.

Thank you for your time and consideration.

Sincerely,

Gerry Coldwell

Enclosure

Writing to a Recruiting Firm

Make certain you understand an executive recruiter's role. It is not so much to find you a position as it is to fill a company's specific request for management talent. Whether contingency or retained, executive placement firms work for the client company. When approaching a recruiting firm, use the traditional cover letter strategy but make sure it's clear that you can be of assistance to one of their clients, not the firm itself, as the next cover letter illustrates (see Cover Letter 10.9).

Cover Letter 10.9

Jason Senong
EXECUTIVE RECRUITERS INTERNATIONAL
12122 W. 49th Street, Suite 123
Los Angeles, CA 90012

Dear Mr. Senong:

Conversations with John Bradford and Douglas Sterling indicate that your firm is a key player in the ag chemical industry when it comes to executive placement.

As you may have heard, Interchem International was recently acquired by Major Conglomerate, Inc. My division appears to not fit with MCI's long-term vision for growth. Accordingly, the timing is right to explore new opportunities. Could one of your clients benefit from my track record in domestic and international sales?

- As VP, Sales & Marketing for Interchem International, I was challenged with strategy plans and program execution to build domestic sales for the company's bio-tech subsidiary, one of the world's largest producers of synthetic technical pheromones. Over my six-year tenure, we were successful in growing business from start-up to near $40 million in annual sales.

- For the past two years, I have been charged with opening new markets in Europe, Asia, the Eastern Bloc, and Latin America as VP, International Sales. Our team's successes are significant, with more than $12 million in new business credited to the revenue line.

Given the right opportunity, I can duplicate these accomplishments. I would imagine medium-to-large ag chemical manufacturers would be most interested in my skills. There are tremendous market opportunities for specialty ag biopesticides in the Far East. From my perspective, these opportunities lie dormant for lack of proper distribution channels--something my contacts could quickly remedy.

May we talk?

Sincerely,

James Bradford

Enclosure

For executive searches, consider using monarch-size stationery ($7\frac{1}{4}$ by $10\frac{1}{2}$ inches) to elevate your status.

Thank-You Letters—A Chance to Resell Yourself

Time for a pop quiz. What is your letter-writing mantra? If you missed it, go back and read the beginning of this chapter because you'll need to know the chant for your thank-you letters as well. The interview is over, and it's time to send a thank-you. You did everything "right" in the interview:

You listened carefully and thought before answering; you addressed the employer's specific concerns with vivid vignettes from your experience; you took notes about those concerns to refresh your memory when it came time to pen your thank-you letter. Now, at all costs, avoid the "canned" thank-you letter that could be used for any job, from underwriting to undertaking. (I hate to confess that this next letter—10.10—was part of my word-processing boilerplate forms in the mid-1980s.)

Thank-You Letter 10.10: Before

Dear Jeanine:

Thank you for your time recently to discuss employment opportunities with ABC Company. Your comments were informative and helpful and served to confirm my interest in the position.

Given my qualifications, I believe my skills would be a strong match for the position's requirements and help to contribute to your goals for the organization.

Should you have additional questions, please do not hesitate to contact me. I look forward to hearing from you.

Sincerely,

Read the next follow-up letter and tell me whom you think Jeanine would rather have working for her (see Thank-You Letter 10.11).

Thank-You Letter 10.11: After

Dear Jeanine:

You were extremely generous with your time today. I hope our two-hour meeting didn't throw off the rest of the day's calendar! I trust you will agree that it was time well spent, as I sensed we connected on every major point discussed.

Your insights on Internet marketing were particularly intriguing. My background in international marketing and technology solutions seems made to order. As I mentioned, at M&M Company, I helped design the marketing stratagems that opened our markets to Mexico and Canada. What I failed to mention is that I was instrumental in introducing advertising within podcasts, a concept well ahead of the curve at that time.

I remain very interested in the position and would like to touch base with you on Friday to see where we stand.

Enthusiastically,

> *Tip* When it comes to writing, throw away the stilted forms and speak—really talk—to the person. Visualize a busy professional opening and reading your letter. How would she react? How would you react if the same information were written to you? If it's a follow-up or thank-you letter, remember pieces of your conversation. Speak those words onto your paper. Imagine a dialogue, flowing and comfortable. If necessary, review some of the editing techniques in chapter 7 to smooth any rough edges.

Other Pieces of the Puzzle

This section covers some other important parts of your job search correspondence.

References

How many references do you need and who should you use? Depends. Recent graduates should include a minimum of three references consisting of college instructors, as well as former and present employers who can attest to your ability to juggle a full course schedule and manage that part-time job with maturity and professionalism.

Senior executives usually use the "my life is an open book" approach and provide broad access to former bosses, subordinates, peers, clients, and vendors. John Lucht, in his career guide, *Rites of Passage at $100,000 to $1 Million+: Your Insider's Lifetime Guide to Executive Job-Changing and Faster Career Progress* offers this advice to the upper-echelon job seeker: "With a 'safety-in-numbers' long list of references, even if the worst occurs... your nemesis is called *and* treats you unfairly... your potential employer has right at his or her fingertips the names and numbers of additional people who will balance the bad words with a far more fair and favorable account."

Professionals typically supply five or more individuals who fall within the "former bosses, subordinates, peers, clients, and vendors" category. If you're involved in industry associations or community not-for-profit groups, you can augment your list to include individuals from these groups (for example, the Executive Director of the local chapter of the American Heart Association, who will rave about your ability to raise funds or orchestrate large-scale events—any activity that boosts your candidacy). Avoid character references from your rabbi, priest, or minister, as well as friends or relatives—all might provide stellar comments about you but might be taken with a grain of salt given their potential bias. There is just no substitute for a business reference who confirms that you always showed up on time, always could be counted on to do your job, and always went the extra mile.

When to Send References

Save your references for a later round in talks with employers. Sending a list of references initially with the résumé gives employers more paperwork to sift through and your reference sources more interruptions to deal with. Your supporters will be more inclined to spend time discussing your candidacy once or twice with serious buyers than they will over and over again with undecided window shoppers. You may choose to bring your reference list to the interview or mail it as part of your interview follow-up correspondence.

When and How to Ask for References

When your job is eliminated because of company initiatives (rightsizing, reengineering, consolidation, closures, and so on), the time to ask for a written letter of recommendation is before you leave. Your supervisor's empathy quotient runs highest at this point and your strengths and contributions to the company will be fresh in his or her memory. Even when your leaving is not under the best of circumstances, approach your supervisor about a letter of recommendation. If you can agree on the content, you can use the letter as a substitute for a telephone reference check. Calls to disgruntled supervisors months or years later are not often handled with the patience and grace you would hope. Another benefit to a written letter of recommendation is that it saves you from having to track down your former supervisor, whose career may have taken him or her to new opportunities in different companies or a new geographic area.

When requesting letters of recommendation from former associates, approach them with a phone call. Always give your full name and some frame of reference: Remember, "Joe" might not have thought of you in some time, and you don't want him stumbling around his memory banks thinking "Jerry who?" This script may be of assistance:

> Joe, hi, this is Jerry VanSteele. It's been a few years since we worked together at City Engineering. How are things with you?

Once Joe responds, follow with,

> Joe, I've always admired your ability to navigate the corporate waters, as well as your engineering skills. I'm exploring some new career opportunities, and I'd like to enlist your counsel. What suggestions do you have that would help me improve my marketability?

Joe may think of something, but more than likely he'll mention what your strengths and skills are. You follow with

> Well, thank you, Joe. Listen, I'll take your advice about _____ "

(Echo whatever Joe mentioned—going to B-school, earning additional licenses, brushing up on public speaking skills... whatever.) Then add,

> Which of my strengths would you feel comfortable emphasizing in a reference letter? When you mention that strength, could you bring it to life by using some specific numbers, such as the 20 percent savings in...

If the conversation doesn't go as well as you would have hoped and Joe can't think of anything nice to say, you have tested the waters before your prospective employer gets a chance and saved yourself from a lukewarm reference.

Rethinking the "Reference Page" with Some Creative Persuasion

Reference lists are typically an index of names, addresses, and phone numbers. The *Before* picture (see Reference List 10.12) illustrates the traditional, generally accepted format. In my book, it's a bit ho-hum.

Reference List 10.12: Before

ELAINE WELLER

elaineweller@msn.com
222 East Fruitlands ◆ Concord, MA 01642
(978) 444-2222

REFERENCES

Preston Whitehead, District Manager
ASTRA MERCK PHARMACEUTICALS
432 North Wilson Avenue
Lexington, MA 01565
(978) 444-3333
email@abc.com

Purvis Ellingham, Product Manager
ASTRA MERCK PHARMACEUTICALS
432 Route 2A
New Brunswick, NJ 02345
(888) 212-2121
email@abc.com

Marlene Sterling, District Manager
ABBOTT, DIAGNOSTICS DIVISION
432 North Wilson Avenue
Lexington, MA 01565
(978) 444-3333
email@abc.com

W. D. Steinberg, M.D., Chief of Pediatrics
CHILDREN'S HOSPITAL
2121 North Minarettes
Waltham, MA 01442
(503) 222-1122
email@abc.com

William Metters, Ph.D., Executive Director
NORTHEASTERN MEDICAL SOCIETY
925 East Welton
Boston, MA 01223
(503) 222-1111
email@abc.com

Candace Fourche, Executive Director
AMERICAN HEART ASSOCIATION
1234 E. Bountiful
Concord, MA 01452
(978) 444-3333
email@abc.com

Now look at the *After* reference list (see Reference List 10.13). Let me share with you a trade secret that can really make your reference list "sing your praises." Add a sentence or two after (or to the side of) each contact that describes your relationship to the reference and what you accomplished while working with the person.

Reference List 10.13: After

ELAINE WELLER

elaineweller@msn.com
222 East Fruitlands ◆ Concord, MA 01642
(978) 444-2222

REFERENCES

Individual	Relationship and Range of Knowledge
Preston Whitehead, District Manager ASTRA MERCK PHARMACEUTICALS 432 North Wilson Avenue Lexington, MA 01565 (978) 444-3333 email@msn.com	Immediate supervisor at Astra Merck. Will verify three-fold sales increases in new hypertensive, respiratory, and migraine products. Can speak to my tenacity in courting "no see" physicians and turning them into loyal, major accounts.
Purvis Ellingham, Product Manager ASTRA MERCK PHARMACEUTICALS 432 Route 2A New Brunswick, NJ 02345 (888) 212-2121 email@msn.com	While I was employed with Astra Merck, Mr. Ellingham selected me and two other key sales professionals to collaborate on launch strategies for a new antiherpetic product. Northeast region met target goals ahead of schedule and gained top market share by close of first-year sales.
Marlene Sterling, District Manager ABBOTT, DIAGNOSTICS DIVISION 432 North Wilson Avenue Lexington, MA 01565 (978) 444-3333 email@msn.com	Immediate supervisor at Abbott Diagnostics. Can confirm consistent #1 ranking in a district with eight sales representatives, in addition to record incremental increases over goal, market share, and prescriptions sold. Will also elaborate on my ability to orient and train new sales representatives.
W. D. Steinberg, M.D., Chief of Pediatrics CHILDREN'S HOSPITAL 2121 North Minarettes Waltham, MA 01442 (503) 222-1122 email@msn.com	Dr. Steinberg served on the committee that granted hospital formulary status for new IV antibiotic. Can document my presentation skills, understanding of systems/disease processes, and ability to interface with medical team and hospital administrators. Children's Hospital was key to phenomenal territory sales growth.
William Metters, Ph.D., Executive Director NORTHEASTERN MEDICAL SOCIETY 925 East Welton Boston, MA 01223 (503) 222-1111 email@msn.com	Chief executive of a 2,000-member physicians group. Dr. Metters can speak to my planning and public relations skills as he has observed me plan and publicize major educational events for NMS physicians that featured nationally recognized leaders in healthcare.
Candace Fourche, Executive Director AMERICAN HEART ASSOCIATION 1234 E. Bountiful Concord, MA 01452 (978) 444-3333 email@msn.com	Community leader. Solicited my assistance with several fund-raising events, the most significant of which was Heart's annual gala, a formal dinner-dance and auction that netted more than 35% over prior year. Ms. Fourche will confirm my event planning and media relations skills, as well as my ability to motivate a tireless volunteer corps.

◆ ◆ ◆

This format can guide your prospective employer toward discussing the traits that you would like to emphasize about your personality. In the preceding example, Mr. Employer can pick up the telephone and call one of six individuals who together will paint a composite of your sales, presentation, event planning, training, and community-relation skills.

Networking Cards

A small card, either business-card size or a 3 by 5, is a useful tool in networking situations, especially when it isn't convenient to carry around full-page résumés that can so easily be crinkled, smudged, or otherwise defaced. Michael Farr pioneered this idea back in the 1970s and dubbed it the JIST Card, an acronym for his Job Information Seeking and Training program. In his book *The Quick Resume & Cover Letter Book,* Farr itemizes these six benefits to a JIST Card:

- Creates a positive first impression
- Provides specific details related to what a job seeker can do
- Presents performance-related information in a memorable way
- Provides both an effective tool for generating job leads and for presenting information
- Predisposes most readers to consider giving the job seeker an interview
- Provides information that can be presented or read in under 30 seconds

Networking cards should contain your name, contact information, job target, skills summary, and a major accomplishment. In some cases, it might be a snapshot of the first one-third of your résumé. You can use these next two examples as a template.

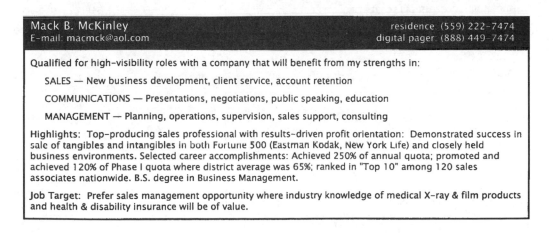

Mack B. McKinley
E-mail: macmck@aol.com

residence: (559) 222-7474
digital pager: (888) 449-7474

Qualified for high-visibility roles with a company that will benefit from my strengths in:

SALES — New business development, client service, account retention

COMMUNICATIONS — Presentations, negotiations, public speaking, education

MANAGEMENT — Planning, operations, supervision, sales support, consulting

Highlights: Top-producing sales professional with results-driven profit orientation. Demonstrated success in sale of tangibles and intangibles in both Fortune 500 (Eastman Kodak, New York Life) and closely held business environments. Selected career accomplishments: Achieved 250% of annual quota; promoted and achieved 120% of Phase I quota where district average was 65%; ranked in "Top 10" among 120 sales associates nationwide. B.S. degree in Business Management.

Job Target: Prefer sales management opportunity where industry knowledge of medical X-ray & film products and health & disability insurance will be of value.

Jose Mercardo

jmercado@iquest.net
(317) 333-4444

Recent graduate with Associate degree in Applied Science & Technology. Ten years' prior experience as Electrician's Assistant (commercial, residential) and Automotive Repair Technician (fuel-injection engines).

Hands-on training includes:

- Electronic Technology: Direct current principles, alternating current principles, semiconductor devices, solid state amplifiers, digital electronics.

- Advanced Digital Technology: Digital counters, multiplexers and demultiplexers, digital-to-analog and analog-to-digital converters, memory circuits, arithmetic logic unit and numerical systems.

- Electronic Communication: Vacuum tubes, amplifiers, power supplies, transmitters, receivers, antennas and wave propagation.

Earned President's List and Dean's List honors while carrying full course load and working 25 hrs/wk (perfect attendance record over last three years with Builders Supply, Inc.).

Motivated, reliable, own full set of tools, available for travel and out-of-town assignments.

 Tip You can also turn the preceding networking cards into a snazzy e-mail signature at www.plaxo.com/signature.

If you prefer a traditional business-card size, virtually any printer or large office-supply store can assist you. Space constraints will limit you to just the basics, or you can print your cards double-sided, as in the next example.

[front of card]

Jennifer Black-DeBeau, R.N.

(559) 222-7474

12 years' experience as managed care nurse reviewer and registered nurse in acute care environments.

Degrees/Certification:

BSN, University of San Francisco
Registered Nurse (CA #RN433443)
ACLS/BLS/PLS Certification
Case Management Certification

[back of card]

Special Skills: Nurse Reviewer for retrospective review of ER bills, ER admits, home IV infusion, home health, chemotherapy, chiropractic, surgical, outpatient, and other services. Technical resource to CSRs, Medical Director, providers, and members. Case manager for large out-of-network claims and services.

Accomplishments/Contributions: Achieved annual percentage of savings goal of under 45% when contract pricing applied for payment. Realized corporate cost-containment goals for COB and subrogation. Met 24-hour turnaround time for Customer Service Specialist and Claims Processor.

Never send your business card from a current employer with your cover letter, résumé, or other job search correspondence. It is akin to writing your cover letters on company letterhead. You can have personal business cards printed for as little as $10—a nominal investment to boost your professionalism while networking.

> *Tip* For the price of putting up with an ad, you can get free business cards at www.vistaprint.com. (The back of the card contains a small logo advertising VistaPrint.)

Addenda

Addenda items are becoming more common for management candidates. The supplementary material may take the form of these ideas:

- One-page summary of a multi-page résumé

- Projects page

- Brand statement

- Leadership profile highlighting several key skills with examples of challenges met and results delivered

- Endorsements page (an expanded full-page version of the endorsements idea shown in Résumé 1.11 in chapter 1)

For a wealth of ideas on material for your career marketing portfolio, see *Executive's Pocket Guide to ROI Resumes and Job Search* by Louise Kursmark and Jan Melnik (JIST, 2007). This leadership profile, developed by executive résumé writer and career coach Deborah Wile Dib, is included in the book.

Leadership Profile 10.14

Thad Von Braun

LEADERSHIP PROFILE   CMO
GROWTH MANAGEMENT & CULTURE CHANGE _____ AdFocus

Challenge   To ensure future growth, improve market presence/share, and optimize long-term profitability, company needed to refocus its marketing activities. Determined two priorities: 1) reduce reliance on cable television for lead generation, and 2) shift business model to improve existing customer acquisition and cultivate new platform/culture focused on remarketing.

Actions   Developed and executed (phased in to control costs and mitigate risk) PRM & CRM strategies and leveraged related solutions, campaigns, and partners for teleservices, database administration, and lettershop fulfillment. Expanded TV broadcasting buying into hybrid-DRTV, syndication, network, spot, and PI. Helped restructure marketing organization into online advertising and online customer-service delivery systems.

Results   ➡ Cut reliance on cable TV to 30% from 55% and began process of reducing costs (in an environment of three-year, near-100% increase in TV advertising costs). Increased customer acquisition from Internet by 200%.

➡ Created marketing campaigns to turn "prospects" into "purchases" in nine customer segments. Reduced lost calls and improved throughput rates to sales agents as much as 75% by enhancing telephony IVR messaging and logic.

➡ Doubled lead generation from Yellow Pages at 40% better cost-efficiency than cable TV.

➡ Maintained on-air presence during periods of low inventory and generated an abundance of leads through hybrid-DRTV and syndication.

Analysis   Changed a "can't-do" culture to a "can-do" culture. Strategies and actions—against seemingly "impossible" odds—salvaged the business, retained its market share lead, established effective PRM-CRM model for new-product launches, and created a pathway for future growth.

LEADERSHIP PROFILE   Transglobal Marketing
CLIENT FEE REVENUE GROWTH _____ Account Director

Challenge   Increase client fee revenues and protect company's standing as industry's thought leader.

Actions   Differentiated company from competition by marketing core competencies and service offerings that were difficult to replicate. Targeted acquisition efforts to start-up companies (high-potential segment during peak in the IPO and dot-com market) seeking and willing to pay premiums for total marketing outsourcing solutions vs. investing in marketing internal infrastructures.

Results   *Delivered 530% growth—to $4+ million from $750,000—in client fee revenue over three years.*

Analysis   Valuable to clients for ability to create needs-specific programs. Valuable to agencies as a consistently top-ranking contributor to business development, customer acquisition, and revenue generation.

LEADERSHIP PROFILE   Brand Manager—Good Reads for Kids
BRAND DEVELOPMENT & POSITIONING _____ Simon & Schuster

Challenge   Launch and grow a current-member marketing brand in an extremely mature sector.

Actions   Part of core team that set out to understand evangelical Christian market—the heartland of America (virtually a world away from New York City), then tapped into nontraditional communications outlets in home schooling, pastoral newsletters, and PR, and aggressively marketed to niches as they were identified.

Results   *Delivered what was touted as most successful launch of a new bookclub category in 25+ years. The Good Reads for Kids brand generated $35 million in new revenue (1996) to company. Contributed to 66% growth in membership (1995) and effected 13% improvement in sales-per-catalog.*

Analysis   Undaunted by facing an unfamiliar market and unaffected by a general air of pessimism (most said this market was opportunity-barren). Researched, learned, then applied creative energy, marketing knowledge, and branding expertise to help make project a success.

2224 Central Park West #10B, New York, NY 10020 ▪ 212-949-5555 (home) ▪ 914-505-7915 (mobile) ▪ tvbraun@aol.com

Thad Von Braun page 2 of 2

LEADERSHIP PROFILE — CMO AdFocus
LEAD GENERATION & CUSTOMER ACQUISITION

Challenge Improve effectiveness of the online channel for lead generation and customer acquisition.

Actions Represented marketing as senior member on cross-functional management team tasked with building better online "mousetrap." Allocated internal IT resources and participated in sourcing, hiring, and directing activities of external consultants and channel experts.

Results *Achieved 30% signup and purchase rates from online channel—up 300% from previous years—and created 25% offline spillover from online-generated advertising, without additional offline marketing spending.*

Analysis Strong IT orientation. Adept at leveraging technology to achieve both marketing and business objectives. By reducing the artificial barriers to interaction and enabling the customer to choose how they wished to buy, we changed our business paradigm. Being vigilant about removing barriers to purchase earns money.

LEADERSHIP PROFILE — Account Director Transglobal Marketing
CLIENT/CAMPAIGN CYCLE IMPROVEMENT

Challenge Accelerate time-to-market and improve quality, efficiency, and cost effectiveness of development and production life cycle.

Actions Rallied and led seasoned, cross-functional team of professionals that shared entrepreneurial orientation and sense of urgency. Conceived, developed, and managed deployment of sweeping campaign, including television, radio, direct mail, fulfillment collateral, and infrastructure.

Results *Exceeded client's expectations for hitting a category in-market sweet spot by deploying full-scale, integrated marketing and advertising campaign in six weeks.*

Analysis Never object to taking on the "impossible," regardless of complexities. Senses and skills are fueled when the pressure is on. Consistently able to lead a team and "make it happen."

LEADERSHIP PROFILE — CMO AdFocus
PUBLIC RELATIONS

Challenge Utilize public relations to drive lead generation volume at cost comparable to traditional cable television advertising rates.

Actions Initiated aggressive courtship of high-volume media outlets and high-profile personalities, developed an infrastructure to handle peak call volume, and retained a public relations agency.

Results Secured four-minute spot on NBC's *Today Show*, generating most leads from any television placement in company's history. Online visits increased 20% during that same period.

Analysis Proficient in linking public relations strategies and events with traditional marketing and advertising campaigns to optimize lead generation, brand recognition, and, ultimately, sales revenues.

LEADERSHIP PROFILE — CMO AdFocus
MARKETING & ADVERTISING COLLATERALS

Challenge Create targeted high-impact collaterals more swiftly and at less cost than a traditional full-service agency.

Actions Utilized contact network (highly competent freelance creative and strategic talent) to design and produce all required creative advertising materials from TV to inserts to sales collateral.

Results Exceeded creative needs for all AscendOne brands at 50% of cost of using full-service agency.

Analysis Over 10+-year career, have assembled, and continue to maintain, a Rolodex of readily available contacts and relationships. Such a list keeps costs down and generates creative, high-quality work.

2224 Central Park West #10B, New York, NY 10020 ▪ 212-949-5555 (home) ▪ 914-505-7915 (mobile) ▪ tvbraun@aol.com

(continued)

(continued)

Thad Von Braun

LEADERSHIP TESTIMONIALS

MARKETING · BRANDING · ADVERTISING · PUBLIC RELATIONS

"You are one of the most creative, smart, hardworking and passionate people I've ever worked with. You made significant contributions while you were here. Most notable was your willingness to be bold, creative, and tenacious…. Any success we have with remarketing around here is because of your recognition and pursuit of the approach."

President & CEO, AdFocus

"Your greatest accomplishment at Transglobal was the P&G business that you won and built. They are tough customers; they were looking for something new and innovative in channel and in marketing. One piece of business was parlayed into a portfolio that was a showpiece for the agency, for the creative department, and for our industry… Those accounts were the foundation for Transglobal, the hot shop, the place to be, the one clients had to see in their reviews. You did it; no one else could, and I really believe that."

EVP, Transglobal Marketing

"I thought the prospecting and remarketing system and creative that went with it was outstanding because you developed it from idea to full implementation at a VERY LOW COST. I also thought your work on IVR and call flow was top-notch."

COO, AdFocus

"When you decide something must be done…you work harder than everyone else to achieve the goal. You have vision and creativity, and you have a strong network of external resources. My hope is that you taught us well enough and left a network [for us] to draw on so everything will get done."

Managing Partner, KMG Group

"In my opinion, your greatest accomplishment is how you've influenced the organization to move beyond the status quo, make changes, and strive to grow into a highly functional company—the energy and passion you brought to AdFocus will definitely be missed. No one else has the breadth of knowledge on various topics."

Marketing Manager, AdFocus

"The partnership and team building you created—for a difficult account such as Beck's—that brought together diverse individuals from two continents [was a major accomplishment], and you are good at keeping the team involved and informed. You have an amazing understanding of data."

Director of Production, Transglobal Marketing

"Thad is a very intelligent and driven manager. He identifies with the projects he manages and invests a great amount of energy in them. He is goal-oriented and measures his success by the results, not the effort."

Managing Director, Canada, Simon & Schuster

"You modeled how to be a strong team player (for all levels); very supportive of the company vision (even if you had questions/concerns)… [You] created an infrastructure for marketing unparalleled by predecessors (and challenged our old ways of doing things)… You know what is the right thing to do…[are] extremely bright, able to think strategically and see well 'down the road'…and design a game plan to get there."

Senior Director, Waterman Corporation

"[You are] extremely innovative. Able to find solutions to very difficult company issues… A master at dissecting data and presenting it… Able to take a small amount of data and in a very short time (minutes or seconds, it seems to me) and tell the story the data represents…and use technology to the company's advantage… You know how to think it out and then…convey matters in words that people can understand."

President, Grisham Consulting Group

2224 Central Park West #10B, New York, NY 10020 ▪ 212-949-5555 (home) ▪ 914-505-7915 (mobile) ▪ tvbraun@aol.com

Paper

Paper should be conservative and distinctive, especially for supervisory, management, and executive candidates. The tried-and-true colors—eggshell and white—still rate, even though some might call them boring. Color selection for nonmanagement candidates is less restrictive and can include a gamut of muted colors. Look for a high rag content for a weightier paper; 70-pound text weight gives just enough starch without going to a cover-stock weight, which is too heavy for résumés.

Specialty papers are very popular. The range is limitless, from simple paper with a marble-looking top or side strip to fancy paper with gold-foil embossing. (I've seen one that has the appearance of soft clouds with a small seagull stamped in gold at the top right—great for a motivational speaker.)

One of my favorite papers is a style appropriate for people who teach or work with children. Appearing in the bottom-left corner is a small, black chalkboard and a bright red apple; the chalkboard reads "100 years from now it will not matter what my bank account was, the sort of house I lived in, or the car I drove, but the world may be a different place because I was important in the life of a child." (See chapter 3 for the full-text version of educator Randy Bez's résumé, 3.15.)

PaperDirect has quite a selection of papers (call for its catalog, 1-800-A-PAPERS, or see the Web site at www.paperdirect.com). Most of PaperDirect's styles are intended for business use (letterhead, brochures), but many can be converted for résumé use as well. Your local FedEx Kinko's or other copy shop will sometimes have stock suitable for résumés.

Perhaps the best place to look for paper is a résumé service, which often carries these types of papers:

- **Border-embossed papers.** A subtle double-line border is embossed ¼-inch from the edge of the paper.

- **Panel papers.** These come in different color combinations of white and silver, cream and gold, white and gold, dove gray and gray—the first color listed in these pairs is a ¼-inch strip at the outer edge of the page and the second color takes up the remaining space on the page, giving the appearance of a picture frame.

- **Gold-foil embossed papers.** The paper is a light gray with tiny flecks of blue and maroon with a ¼-inch maroon strip at the top edge. Within the strip is a gold-stamped word indicating an industry or profession, such as Education, Hospitality, Management, or Sales.

One of the few résumé books to showcase actual paper styles is JIST's *Gallery of Best Resumes* by Dr. David Noble. In it, you'll get an idea of how you can use more than a dozen paper styles to debut your résumé.

Sending Your Cover Letter and Résumé

Next I discuss the options you have for mailing your job-search package.

By Surface Mail

Resist the temptation to fold your résumé into thirds and stuff it into a #10 business-size envelope. Always use a full-page envelope (9 by 12 or 10 by 13) when surface mailing your résumé. It simply looks nicer when it arrives on the recruiter's desk. Most office-supply stores carry white catalog envelopes, a nice change from the standard wheat or manila color. Catalog envelopes seal along the long end of the envelope and add a touch of class to your mailing. Many paper suppliers and résumé services stock full-page envelopes to match linen or specialty résumé papers.

A commemorative stamp is also a nice touch. Be sure to include two ounces worth of postage even when your 9 by 12 envelope weighs just one ounce. The postal service requires the second stamp to handle larger pieces of mail.

By Fax

Most fax software shrinks text by a point size or more. With this in mind, you should increase the size of your font by one point when faxing your cover letter or résumé. If you use a fax machine (as opposed to computer software), remember to choose bright white paper for your hard copy. Be sure to review chapter 9's list of do's and don'ts for preparing scannable résumés.

By E-Mail

If you know your recipient's preference for receiving e-mailed résumés, respond accordingly. Recruiters typically request cover letters and résumés via one of two methods:

1. **Résumé attachment:** Here, the cover letter is pasted into the body of the e-mail message and the résumé is included as an attachment in MS Word or PDF format.

2. **Résumé in body of e-mail:** The second option is to paste both the cover letter and résumé into the e-mail message. This can be a formatted version (with boldfacing, underlining, special fonts, and so on) or an ASCII-text version. Position the résumé a few lines below the letter. If you're unsure of the recipient's preference for résumé delivery, you can also include a copy of your résumé as an attachment. Conciseness is key, so look for ways to pare down the text of your traditional, surface-mail cover letter. The following example (10.15) shows how the Library Acquisitions Specialist abbreviated her cover letter (see pages 509–510) and then added her ASCII-text résumé to the body of the e-mail.

> *Tip* Avoid composing a cover letter from scratch in your e-mail program. Instead, compose it in your word-processing program, where you have aids such as the thesaurus and spell-checking functions. This method also allows you to save each letter in your documents folder with a unique filename; for example, "Ltr-Levi-Strauss-Merchandise-Mgr.doc," which is helpful in locating job search correspondence at a later date and using prior letters as templates for new correspondence.

E-Mail Cover Letter and Résumé 10.15

```
Thank you for considering my application for the position of
Financial Analyst. A text version of my résumé follows,
highlights of which include:

Textbook and Library Funding—Managed in excess of $1 million
in State funding…implemented computer conversion that cut in
half the time required to process acquisitions.

Bookstore Management—Trained, supervised, and evaluated
staff of five; provided monthly financial analysis of
accounting, inventory, and sales data…revenue unit generated
a 12% increase over prior year's figures.

Technical Skills—Solid understanding of generally accepted
accounting principles, regulations unique to school district
accounting, AMCSSD compliance…earned unqualified marks on
recent state audit.

I look forward to the interview process.

Dale Forth

Résumé:

Dale Forth
(805) 222-2345
dforth@aol.com

CAREER GOAL===============================================

Management opportunity in the field of Education where
experience and skills will positively affect operational
performance, financial operations, and student services.

EDUCATION=================================================

Bachelor of Business Administration, American University

COMPUTER==================================================

Extensive background with IBM-compatible and Macintosh
platforms; Excel, Quattro, Quicken, Microsoft Word,
WordPerfect 8.0, PowerPoint.
```

(continued)

(continued)

```
EXPERIENCE===================================================

ROCKLIN SCHOOL DISTRICT, Rocklin, California, 7/97-Present

Library Acquisitions Specialist: Manage $1.068 million in
State textbook and library funding. Supervise and train
support staff. Project and update ADA, determine
allocations, and order instructional materials and library
books for 30 district school sites. Work closely with
director of curriculum development and business services.

Approve and code all payables. Perform beyond scope of
position description:

+ Initiated use of Excel software that enhanced financial
reporting/financial analysis capabilities, improved access
to funds, and expedited acquisitions process.

+ Designed spreadsheets to track four different funding
sources at each of 30 school sites.

+ Trained and evaluated support staff.

AMERICAN UNIVERSITY, San Diego, California, 1/92-6/97

Bookstore Coordinator (Manager): Managed total range of
bookstore operations including staff supervision and
training, accounting functions, pricing, merchandising,
inventory control, display, and promotions. Selected student
textbooks, instructor textbooks, and supplemental materials
to serve a month-to-month format. Planned, organized, and
supervised seasonal activities such as monthly book buy-
backs and used book sales. Maintained excellent working
relationships with administrators, faculty, and students.

+ Forecasted inventory requirements for 20 courses monthly,
making purchases of more than $300,000 annually.

+ Determined retail pricing for all books, achieving double-
digit gain over prior-year margins.

+ Introduced monthly statistical and narrative
reconciliation of accounting, inventory, and sales.


# # #
```

Futurist Career Management

With this book, my desire has been to provide you with more than just the
"how to's" of writing a résumé. Knitted throughout has been my philosophy
behind career management: Manage your career as if you were running

your own business. You must have a long-range strategic plan, a mission statement that you are passionate about, marketing materials, and meaningful data to measure your progress. Regardless of your role in an organization, focus on contributing to profits and quantifying a return-on-investment (ROI) to your employer/customer—cultivate new business, cut costs, increase productivity, improve quality, and retain loyal and satisfied customers. This perspective will position you head-and-shoulders above your competition in the job search process.

Your job search does *not* end when you find a new job. More than likely, you will be presented with this challenge again. Maintaining an employer perspective can be the impetus to build your network of invaluable contacts, grow in industry knowledge, mature your soft skills, and augment your technical talents. The natural outgrowth is that you will have automatically positioned yourself to advance as new challenges present themselves.

Tip Are you looking for definitive answers to questions such as, "How many references? Should I use a one-page or two-page résumé? Do I include my last employment that lasted only six weeks? Should I tell people the real reason I left my last job?" There *is* one right answer to all of your job search questions. The answer is, "It depends." It depends on your unique set of circumstances and the job market in your area. Unfortunately, there are rarely "one-size-fits-all" solutions to tough issues.

Be wary of falling into the "fear and blame mode." It is easy to do with the stress caused by interrupted paychecks and disrupted routine. There's a tendency to think, "If I just follow these seven steps to the letter, I'll find a job. Then if the magic formula doesn't work, I can blame the person who told me to follow those seven steps." Shift the accountability squarely on your shoulders; then throw those shoulders back and hold your head high. You will survive this transition!

Seek out solid job search resources, evaluate the advice as it relates to your own circumstances, develop a plan, and attack it aggressively. Beyond that, be proactive in dealing with the emotional ups-and-downs of job search. Take care of yourself: Exercise, eat well, seek out your true friends, attend religious services, and give your time to an organization that really needs volunteers. The healthier you are—emotionally, physically, and spiritually—the greater the likelihood that you'll land on your feet in an opportunity better than your prior situation.

To manage your next career move with confidence and success, you will need to attend to these three elements *while* you are gainfully employed:

- Continually educate yourself and update your skills, especially those involving technology.

⚹ Regularly network with colleagues and collaborate with coworkers.

⚹ Challenge yourself to always deliver value that impacts the organization's bottom line and builds your brand, and be sure to update your Career Management File monthly with tangible evidence of your return on investment (see chapter 6).

In doing so, you'll find it a breeze when it comes time to write the sequel to your résumé. May it be a tremendous success story!

Top 10 Cover Letter Tips

1. Mention a referral source whenever possible. For example, "John Doe mentioned you were looking for new talent for your new procurement project."

2. After mentioning your referral source, mention a benefit: "My 10-year background as a procurement supervisor has enabled me to cut costs at least 20% without sacrificing quality."

3. Briefly summarize the breadth of your experience, whether number of years' experience, relevant titles you have held, or range of qualifications in a certain area.

4. Include accomplishments—always!

5. Set off accomplishments with bullets.

6. Don't restate verbatim information from the résumé.

7. Avoid obligatory language, such as "Enclosed please find a copy of my résumé." Instead, you might say, "You'll note on my résumé a track record for exceeding goals by more than 25 percent...."

8. Avoid lofty language. Read the letter out loud—if you stumble over polysyllabic words that are unnatural to your way of speaking, rewrite with simpler language.

9. When pasting a letter into an e-mail, make the letter as short as possible and use bullets to set off accomplishments. Recruiters get tired of scrolling through lengthy e-mails.

10. If you're unsure of your recipient's preference for receiving cover letters and resumes by e-mail, double up! For instance, if you're sending your résumé in the body of an e-mail message, also attach it as an e-mail attachment and mention "For convenience, I have included a duplicate copy of my resume in MS Word format." If you're sending your résumé as an attachment, paste an ASCII text version into the e-mail two to three lines below your signature. Add a P.S. that says, "Although my résumé is attached in PDF format, I've also pasted it below should you prefer an ASCII plain-text format."

Appendix

A

Worksheets to Catalog Professional History

U se the worksheets in this appendix to catalog your professional history, including the information in the following list. This information will help you write your résumé.

- Qualifications
- Professional experience
- Education
- Computer skills
- Professional organizations
- Community involvement
- Awards and honors
- Publications
- Presentations
- Patents
- Personal information
- Endorsements

WORKSHEETS TO CATALOG PROFESSIONAL HISTORY

QUALIFICATIONS

Refer to chapter 5 and table 5-4 for instructions on using and writing a qualifications summary. Choose from these suggested items:

Title/functional area: _____

_____

Subcategories of functional area or core competencies: _____

_____

_____

Industry: _____

_____

Number of years of experience: _____

Expertise, strengths, specialization: _____

_____

"Combination" accomplishment or highlights of accomplishments: _____

_____

Advanced degree, certification, licensure: _____

_____

Language skills, international business skills: _____

_____

Technical/computer skills: _____

_____

Personal profile/management style: _____

_____

Affiliations: _____

_____

Employers, schools with name recognition: _____

_____

PROFESSIONAL EXPERIENCE

A.   Your most recent employer

Company name: _____

Company's location: City _____ State _____

Month/Year you were hired: _____ / _____

Month/Year you left: _____ / _____ (list "Present" if still employed)

Your most recent title: _____

List any prior positions with the company (if applicable): _____

_____

Company annual sales (if public): $_____

Indicate whether company is regional, national, or international: _____

Distinguishing characteristics of company (such as "the nation's leading   manufacturer of widgets," "the world's 2nd largest distributor of high-tech components," "the region's dominant real estate brokerage," etc.):

_____

_____

Briefly describe your scope of accountability, listing items in order of importance. Refer to chapter 5 for complete instructions on writing job descriptions.

1. _____

_____

2. _____

_____

3. _____

_____

4. _____

_____

5. _____

_____

6. _____

_____

Contributions / Impact Statements: What did you do to help the company become more profitable, operate more efficiently, or solve specific problems? Be specific about how you did it and what the "before" and "after" facts are. Refer to chapter 6 for ideas on developing impact statements.

1. _____
_____

2. _____
_____

3. _____
_____

4. _____
_____

5. _____
_____

6. _____
_____

7. _____
_____

B. **The employer prior to your current (or most recent) employer**

Company name: _____

Company's location: City _____ State _____

Month/Year you were hired: __ / __

Month/Year you left: __ / __

Your title: _____

List any prior positions with the company (if applicable): _____
_____

Company annual sales (if public): $_____

Indicate whether company is regional, national, or international: _____

Distinguishing characteristics of company:
_____

Briefly describe your scope of accountability, listing items in order of importance. Refer to chapter 5 for complete instructions on writing job descriptions.

1. _____
_____

2. _____
_____

3. _____
_____

4. _____
_____

5. _____
_____

6. _____
_____

Contributions / Impact Statements: What did you do to help the company become more profitable, operate more efficiently, or solve specific problems? Refer to chapter 6 for ideas on developing impact statements.

1. _____
_____

2. _____
_____

3. _____
_____

4. _____
_____

5. _____
_____

6. _____
_____

C. **The employer prior to company listed under "B."**

Company name: _____

Company's location: City _____ State _____

Month/Year you were hired: _____ / _____

Month/Year you left: _____ / _____

Your title: _____

List any prior positions with the company (if applicable): _____
_____

Company annual sales (if public): $_____

Indicate whether company is regional, national, or international: _____

Distinguishing characteristics of company:
_____

Briefly describe your scope of accountability, listing items in order of importance. Refer to chapter 5 for complete instructions on writing job descriptions.

1. _____
_____

2. _____
_____

3. _____
_____

4. _____
_____

Contributions / Impact Statements: Refer to chapter 6 for ideas on developing impact statements.

1. _____
_____

2. _____
_____

3. _____

D. The employer prior to company listed under "C."

Company name: _____

Company's location: City _____ State _____

Month/Year you were hired: _____ / _____

Month/Year you left: _____ / _____

Your title: _____

List any prior positions with the company (if applicable): _____

_____

Company annual sales (if public): $_____

Indicate whether company is regional, national, or international: _____

Distinguishing characteristics of company:

_____

Briefly describe your scope of accountability, listing items in order of importance. Refer to chapter 5 for complete instructions on writing job descriptions.

1. _____

_____

2. _____

_____

3. _____

_____

4. _____

_____

Contributions / Impact Statements: Refer to chapter 6 for ideas on developing impact statements.

1. _____

_____

2. _____

_____

3. _____

_____

E. **The employer prior to company listed under "D."**

Company name: _____

Company's location: City _____ State _____

Month/Year you were hired: _____ / _____

Month/Year you left: _____ / _____

Your title: _____

List any prior positions with the company (if applicable): _____
_____

Company annual sales (if public): $_____

Indicate whether company is regional, national, or international: _____

Distinguishing characteristics of company:
_____

Briefly describe your scope of accountability, listing items in order of importance. Refer to chapter 5 for complete instructions on writing job descriptions.

1. _____
   _____

2. _____
   _____

3. _____
   _____

4. _____
   _____

Contributions / Impact Statements: Refer to chapter 6 for ideas on developing impact statements.

1. _____
   _____

2. _____
   _____

3. _____
   _____

EDUCATION

Education can include university, community college, vocational trade school, or night classes. Refer to chapter 5 for complete instructions on presenting education.

A.   Name of institution: _____

Location (city and state): _____

Dates (year started to year completed): _____ to _____

Your major: _____

Did you complete a degree? Yes _____   No _____

If yes, what degree? (For example, "Master of Arts in Education Administration")
_____
_____

If you are a recent graduate, consider including a list of important or relevant coursework:
_____
_____

Second school (if applicable)

Name of institution: _____

Location (city and state): _____

Dates (year started to year completed): _____ to _____

Your major: _____

Did you receive a degree? Yes _____   No _____

If yes, what degree? (For example, "Bachelor of Arts in Communications")
_____
_____

B.   Seminars or conferences relevant to your career (seminar title, date, location, sponsoring organization): _____
_____
_____
_____

C.   Credentials and licenses: _____
_____
_____

COMPUTER SKILLS

List software, hardware, operating systems, or programming languages with which you are familiar. Examples might include standard office-computing programs (such as MS Office with Word, Excel, PowerPoint, and Access), contact management software, Web design and development tools, graphics programs, programming languages, or industry-specific programs. _____

_____

_____

_____

_____

_____

PROFESSIONAL ORGANIZATIONS, COMMUNITY INVOLVEMENT

Be sure to mention any leadership positions, such as president, treasurer, or committee chairperson, as well as the names of your professional affiliations and community organizations. Refer to chapter 5 for more information on describing affiliations. _____

_____

_____

_____

_____

_____

AWARDS, HONORS

This section can include awards from college (if recent), work, or community service. Refer to chapter 5 for more information on listing awards or honors. _____

_____

_____

_____

_____

PUBLICATIONS, PRESENTATIONS, PATENTS

Include publications, professional writing, formal presentations, and patents. Refer to chapter 5 for information on bibliographic form. _____

_____

_____

_____

_____

BIO BITES, PERSONAL INFORMATION, ADDITIONAL DATA

Refer to table 5-8 in chapter 5 for comprehensive ideas on developing this section.

Do **NOT** include your birth date, height, weight, marital status, religion, or political affiliation. Do consider including items such as the following.

Interests/Hobbies—Concentrate on those related to your profession or of general interest (for instance, if you coach a Babe Ruth baseball team and are looking for a position in sporting good sales, say so; or, if you are a jogger and clock 20 miles a week or compete in races, say so!): _____

_____

_____

Special Abilities—These skills should relate to your target position (for instance, if you are in sales, special abilities might include public speaking, making formal client presentations, serving as a television or radio spokesperson, networking, negotiating contracts, and so on): _____

_____

_____

_____

Language(s)—Fluent, business vocabulary, or conversational skills: _____

_____

Professional Profile—Think in terms of the employer's point of view and what is needed in an employee (for instance, if you describe yourself as "dependable," provide evidence of the characteristic, such as "Dependable—perfect work attendance record for past 5 years"): _____

_____

_____

_____

_____

ENDORSEMENTS

Refer to chapter 5 for ideas on when and how to use this strategy to your advantage. _____

_____

_____

_____

_____

Appendix B

Survey: What Employers Really Want in a Résumé and Cover Letter

What do employers want to see in a résumé and cover letter? The following statistics reflect feedback from companies that responded to a survey sent to employers listed in the book *The 100 Best Companies to Work For* (Plume/Penguin Books).

Although not statistically significant, responses are generally consistent with and support accepted job search protocol. This information is intended as a guide for résumé preparation; I encourage you to use common sense and good judgment in applying survey results to your situation.

Résumés

1. Applicants with 15 to 30 years of experience should list only the last 10 to 15 years on their résumés.

   35% agree   65% disagree

2. If salary history is requested in a job announcement and an applicant does NOT include it, but is otherwise qualified, the applicant would still be called for an interview.

   85% agree   15% disagree

3. If a bachelor's degree is requested in a job announcement and an applicant does not have a degree, but is otherwise qualified, the applicant would still be called for an interview.

39% agree   61% disagree

4. If an applicant has valid reasons for gaps between employers or "job-hopping" (for example, downsized, spouse relocated, career on hold to raise children), the applicant should briefly list these reasons on the résumé.

74% agree   26% disagree

5. When listing personal strengths on the résumé, the applicant should *also* include a statement that shows evidence of the trait (for instance, the trait "committed" should be followed with a statement such as "frequently volunteered extended hours to meet critical project deadlines").

72% agree   28% disagree

6. Thorough descriptions of past job responsibilities should always be included.

48% agree   52% disagree

7. Verifiable accomplishments should always be included.

88% agree   12% disagree

8. Military service and honors should always be included.

79% agree   21% disagree

9. A separate list of references should also be included with the initial application materials.

19% agree   81% disagree

10. A résumé that is poorly organized or has typos will eliminate an otherwise qualified applicant.

82% agree   18% disagree

11. Tasteful use of spot color or a small graphic related to the industry can enhance the applicant's résumé.

39% agree   61% disagree

12. A résumé should always contain evidence that the applicant can make your company stronger (in other words, more competitive, more profitable, smoother functioning).

    75% agree   25% disagree

13. If an applicant started a new job in the past 2 months, but found the job was not what it was represented to be and is therefore looking for another position, the applicant should include this recent job on the résumé.

    85% agree   15% disagree

14. Paper color should always be white or off-white.

    70% agree   30% disagree

15. The length of a résumé should be

    12%—1-page, never longer

    67%—kept to 1 or 2 pages

    21%—as long as needed to convey the applicant's qualifications

16. What are your greatest pet peeves in résumés? (See the following table.)

17. What are the most common mistakes you've seen applicants make in applying to your company? (See the following table.)

25 Pet Peeves and Common Résumé Mistakes Noted by Some of America's Top Employers

Type of Offense	Comments from Staffing Professionals from Top U.S. Companies
Content	1. Leaving out dates
	2. No chronological listing of work
	3. Overstatement of responsibility
	4. Too much detail, usually around job descriptions
	5. Summary of work history by type instead of listing the exact company and job performed
	6. Baseless description of personal strengths
	7. Entitlement mentality ("I have my degree; I'm sharp; what can you do for me")
Accomplishments	8. No accomplishments listed, only job duties
	9. Statements of accomplishments without a clear indication of where or when they were made
	10. Pumped up to look as if the candidate has qualifications that he or she does not possess
	11. Accomplishments separated from work history so that it's not clear what was done where
Visual	12. Fancy fonts
	13. Photo included
	14. Graphics
Grammar, Technical	15. Typos
	16. Misspellings
	17. Fluff wording
	18. Poor grammar
	19. Incomplete sentences
Organization	20. Disorganized
	21. Too long
	22. Two pages from beginners
	23. Poor organization
	24. Lack of clear direction, focus
	25. Covering up or lying about gaps in employment or lack of degree

18. What are the most important elements you look for in an applicant?

    1. Directly related experience

    2. Accomplishments

    3. Evidence of leadership skills

    4. Communication skills (clear, concise)

    5. Work ethic (hard worker, loyalty, good attitude)

    6. Education

    7. Initiative

    8. Team-orientation

    9. Good fit with the company

    10. Job stability

Cover Letters

19. A well-written cover letter can improve the odds of a less-qualified applicant obtaining an interview.

    75% agree   25% disagree

20. An applicant who has done research on your company or the position they're applying for will receive greater consideration than those who send a generic cover letter.

    91% agree   9% disagree

21. Addressing a letter to the appropriate individual will improve an applicant's chance of getting an interview.

    70% agree   30% disagree

22. A cover letter with résumé is welcomed even when no job openings are available.

    88% agree   12% disagree

23. Applicants should ask for an interview in the cover letter.

    53% agree   47% disagree

24. Applicants who follow up with a phone call will improve their chances of getting an interview.

    37% agree   63% disagree

25. Sending a duplicate copy of the résumé to the departmental manager will help the applicant's chances of getting an interview.

29% agree   71% disagree

26. Résumés with cover letters receive preference over résumés without cover letters.

53% agree   47% disagree

27. The tone of a cover letter should be (check any that apply):

18%—bold and creative

82%—assertive yet polite

0%—passive and understated

Appendix
C

Action Verbs with Sample Phrases

ction verbs, especially when introducing an accomplishment or statement that conveys your value, can bring life to your résumé. Refer to the charts in this appendix when writing all your job search materials.

Administration, Operations

Action Verb	Sample Phrase
abbreviated	Abbreviated time to complete process by 20 percent without sacrificing quality of service.
abolished	Abolished burdensome reporting requirements.
accepted	Accepted additional responsibility for implementing new system.
accommodated	Accommodated a 25 percent increase in workload without need for additional staff.
accomplished	Accomplished project ahead of schedule.
acted	Acted as manager's representative in matters relating to policy administration.
adapted	Adapted national program to better meet local demographic needs.
adhered	Adhered to strict clinical protocols.
adjusted	Adjusted staffing schedule to meet fluctuating seasonal demands.
administered	Administered operations for contract compliance.

(continued)

(continued)

Action Verb	Sample Phrase
admitted	Admitted patients and served as primary contact for new "meet-a-customer, keep-a-customer" program.
advised	Advised team of performance expectations and measurement standards.
aided	Aided in office reorganization that boosted productivity 10 percent.
alerted	Alerted employees to changes in project priorities.
altered	Altered work-flow processes to reduce "holdovers."
amended	Amended text of contracts to clarify buyer and seller responsibilities.
appointed	Appointed to cross-functional task force to solve specific problem.
approved	Approved and expedited requests for material.
arranged	Arranged details for speaker programs (facilities, registration, food and beverages, publicity, volunteers).
arrived	Arrived at conclusions based on thorough research and analysis.
attacked	Attacked "difficult" projects that had been abandoned by former incumbents.
authorized	Authorized purchase requests for all 14 branch departments and two satellite offices.
bid	Bid on new projects that were lucrative to the company.
bored	Bored through slow-moving approval process with county, obtaining project permits in half the normal time.
calmed	Calmed employee concerns about proposed reorganization and maintained productivity throughout change.
carried	Carried the bulk of responsibility, generating 40 percent of workload among five-member team.

Action Verb	Sample Phrase
caused	Caused long-standing issues to be resolved through open dialogue and conflict-resolution exercises.
chaired	Chaired committee that explored new compensation structure and incentive program.
changed	Changed operation from outmoded paper system to electronic system.
checked	Checked paperwork for accuracy and completeness.
chose	Chose interiors and furnishings for new office.
circumvented	Circumvented red tape to move project forward.
classified	Classified material by date and category.
cleaned	Cleaned up filing backlog.
cleared	Cleared personnel for assignments.
commenced	Commenced work on complex, two-year project.
complied	Complied with federal and state regulations.
confirmed	Confirmed and expedited orders.
consolidated	Consolidated four operations in Vermont and Colorado into a centralized unit.
continued	Continued department's ranking as most productive among 12 branches, generating average billable rate of 92.9 percent.
coordinated	Coordinated multidisciplinary team in meeting all project benchmarks.
corrected	Corrected processes to eliminate downtime.
counseled	Counseled probationary employees on methods to improve work performance.
delegated	Delegated assignments to technical and administrative teams.
designated	Designated team leaders for new reengineering effort.
detailed	Detailed performance expectations to subordinates.

(continued)

(continued)

Action Verb	Sample Phrase
dispatched	Dispatched drivers to expedite deliveries and maximize backhauls.
disseminated	Disseminated directives from corporate office and interpreted policy to employees.
divided	Divided departmental responsibilities to better distribute workload.
documented	Documented baseline measurements to provide historical data.
enforced	Enforced corporate policy to improve productivity.
enhanced	Enhanced systems already in place to boost efficiency.
enlisted	Enlisted the aid of marketing and sales to better understand customer needs.
enrolled	Enrolled new customers in program.
ensured	Ensured compliance with federal and state regulations.
entered	Entered data on computer system and generated reports.
examined	Examined summary data and made recommendations.
extended	Extended life of equipment through proper maintenance and service.
fabricated	Fabricated models using CNC equipment.
facilitated	Facilitated weekly employee meetings.
fashioned	Fashioned new model to support paperless work environment.
filed	Filed documents with state and regulatory agencies.
followed	Followed clinical protocols.
formed	Formed alliance with key vendor and provided onsite office space for vendor partnership program.
forwarded	Forwarded orders to order processing.
fulfilled	Fulfilled contract requirements.

Action Verb	Sample Phrase
gathered	Gathered, assembled, and analyzed monthly production data.
grouped work	Grouped employees into cross-disciplinary teams.
handled	Handled 20-percent increase in work volume.
held	Held expenses below budget.
hurried	Hurried key-account orders through manufacturing and distribution.
implemented	Implemented program to improve productivity.
imported	Imported raw materials from European supplier at roughly half the cost.
incorporated	Incorporated customer-driven focus into all levels of organization.
integrated	Integrated information systems unit with sales and production functions, focusing technical team on meeting needs of field sales staff and customers.
interpreted	Interpreted raw data into meaningful material for program planning.
invented	Invented device to speed file processing.
inventoried	Inventoried 10,000 SKUs using new computer software.
learned	Learned new software through independent study; served as resource to train other users.
maintained	Maintained commercial and industrial properties.
marked	Marked materials for shipment.
measured	Measured and analyzed productivity.
modified	Modified program to meet needs of regional users.
molded	Molded inexperienced workers into competent professionals through intensive mentoring and staff-development initiative.
monitored	Monitored progress, analyzed variances, and took corrective action.
moved	Moved proposal through committee to meet peak seasonal demands.

(continued)

(continued)

Action Verb	Sample Phrase
multiplied	Multiplied productivity as a result of technology and training initiatives.
notified	Notified customers of changes in pricing and delivery schedules.
obtained	Obtained authorization from headquarters for new program.
omitted	Omitted duplicative steps to improve departmental productivity.
operated	Operated full range of business-office equipment.
ordered	Ordered business-office supplies.
organized	Organized office and warehouse space to accommodate 25-percent increase in volume.
outlined	Outlined proposal for new system.
oversaw	Oversaw diverse, multilingual staff.
packaged	Packaged products using computer-controlled machinery.
packed	Packed shipments for export.
pared	Pared reporting process to virtually half the original time.
perceived	Perceived need for improved customer communications and helped design new program.
pioneered	Pioneered use of just-in-time purchasing program, a concept new to the medical industry.
placed	Placed candidates in job-appropriate summer internships.
prepared	Prepared statistical and narrative reports for presentation to board of directors.
printed	Printed and distributed weekly reports to satellite offices.
prioritized	Prioritized projects and established timelines.
procured	Procured raw materials from domestic and overseas vendors.
produced	Produced full line of widget products.

Action Verb	Sample Phrase
proposed	Proposed reorganization of department that was accepted by corporate and subsequently adopted nationwide.
provided	Provided management with weekly analysis of administration and operations.
received	Received praise for leadership in chairing new quality-improvement committee.
recommended	Recommended revisions to contracts based on statistical analysis.
recorded	Recorded data for future use.
registered	Registered R&D products with patent office.
released	Released new products.
relieved	Relieved manager of administrative duties.
remained	Remained available for 24-hour, on-call status.
remodeled	Remodeled offices, including space plans, color and design theme, and furnishings.
reorganized	Reorganized office layout to maximize use of limited space—space planning accommodated a 20-percent increase in staff.
requested	Requested input from employees on issues.
retooled	Retooled operations to equip frontline employees with greater information access.
revamped	Revamped processes to meet fluctuating sales demands.
reviewed	Reviewed contracts and forms for accuracy and completeness.
revised	Revised policy and procedure manual, bringing it into compliance with current labor laws.
rotated	Rotated stock on regular basis to eliminate perishable loss.
scanned	Scanned documents and loaded information into database.
scheduled	Scheduled meetings using e-mail and calendaring programs.
screened	Screened applicant résumés for required skills and experience.

(continued)

(continued)

Action Verb	Sample Phrase
sequenced	Sequenced work flow to better fit with layout of production machinery.
set	Set new standards for safety and accident prevention.
shipped	Shipped goods via air and ground transportation.
shortened	Shortened production cycle by more than 20 percent.
sourced	Sourced new suppliers that provided quality raw materials at one-third the cost.
specified	Specified requirements for newly created position.
speeded	Speeded processing of important documents.
studied	Studied plant productivity and identified areas for improvement.
submitted	Submitted reports to management and corporate office.
supplied	Supplied raw materials to production line.
supported	Supported management in the marketing function.
surveyed	Surveyed competitors and made note of each operation's strengths and weaknesses.
tended	Tended daily administrative operations, freeing manager to concentrate on leadership responsibilities.
totaled	Totaled daily sales by SKU for seven sales clerks.
tracked	Tracked product movement through production, packaging, warehousing, and distribution.
typed	Typed correspondence, memos, reports, and proposals.
used	Used advanced features of Microsoft Word to prepare lengthy reports.
validated	Validated continuing-education units for renewal of licenses and credentials.
verified	Verified pricing and extended invoices.

Communications

Action Verb	Sample Phrase
acknowledged	Acknowledged tireless volunteer corps with a "Bless the Angels" recognition campaign.
acquainted	Acquainted with key contacts in business and government.
addressed	Addressed groups of 20–30 on a regular basis.
advertised	Advertised in new print vehicles, generating a 10:1 ratio on marketing funds.
aimed	Aimed marketing campaign to reach untapped demographic segment.
answered	Answered customer inquiries regarding products, delivery, and billing cycle.
appealed	Appealed to target market by addressing primary concerns.
arbitrated	Arbitrated long-standing disputes, bringing divergent interests to agreement.
aroused	Aroused public interest in new program.
asked	Asked by sales manager to present "closing" strategies at national sales meeting.
assessed	Assessed potential impacts to organization and advised executive team on management of critical issues.
associated	Associated with community groups and paraprofessional organizations to expand networking contacts.
avoided	Avoided potential customer-relations issues through proactive print and broadcast campaign.
blended	Blended needs of internal customers (engineering, sales) and brought groups to consensus.
briefed	Briefed cross-functional team leaders on progress.
broadened	Broadened company's reach to Hispanic customers.
called	Called on network of contacts to help build new business.

(continued)

(continued)

Action Verb	Sample Phrase
chronicled	Chronicled history of company for 50-year celebration.
circulated	Circulated memos that reduced miscommunications with employees.
clarified	Clarified discrepancies in documents.
communicated	Communicated news and progress to satellite offices.
composed	Composed copy for collateral marketing materials.
conveyed	Conveyed procedural changes in a timely manner.
corresponded	Corresponded with Internet customers and catalogued standard responses for common questions.
critiqued	Critiqued copy for new marketing materials.
defined	Defined position responsibilities and performance standards.
delineated	Delineated program goals and implementation phases.
demonstrated	Demonstrated products at sales presentations.
described	Described complex, technical data in laymen's terms.
diffused	Diffused volatile situation through "flash fax" communication with prime supporters.
discussed	Discussed methods to solve problems.
disseminated	Disseminated newsworthy information to key customers.
drafted	Drafted legal documents.
edited	Edited and proofed copy.
elaborated	Elaborated on product benefits.
elicited	Elicited favorable coverage from broadcast and print media.
engaged	Engaged customers in open-ended questions.
explained	Explained confusing legalese to second-language learners.

Action Verb	Sample Phrase
expressed	Expressed appreciation to medical center's volunteer staff by hosting a well-received masquerade ball.
fielded	Fielded questions from audience.
focused	Focused company newsletter on issues of greatest interest to customers.
garnered	Garnered support of government officials for new construction project.
greeted	Greeted customers and remembered unique personal facts, such as birth of a child or a special career achievement.
heightened	Heightened consumers' awareness of product through aggressive telemarketing campaign.
hosted	Hosted informal luncheons for ancillary medical staff.
indicated	Indicated unique features that differentiated product.
influenced	Influenced decision makers.
informed	Informed the public of upcoming events.
interpreted	Interpreted documents and conversations for Spanish-speaking customers.
introduced	Introduced new personnel policies to staff.
kept	Kept employees informed of industry advancements.
mediated	Mediated conflicts between staff and administration.
moderated	Moderated monthly Internet chats for industry association.
negotiated	Negotiated contracts to benefit of company.
persuaded	Persuaded customers to buy products, over-coming various stalls and objections.
praised	Praised support staff for contributions.
presented	Presented workshops for licensed and technical staff.
produced	Produced series of television advertisements.
profiled	Profiled customers for inclusion in contact database.

(continued)

(continued)

Action Verb	Sample Phrase
proofread	Proofread memos, correspondence, reports, print advertisements, and various collateral marketing materials.
publicized	Publicized all new product releases, staff advancements, company awards, and community service.
published	Published annual reports, newsletters, and other communiqués.
queried	Queried database for relevant information.
reached	Reached target market through a combination of print advertising vehicles.
recognized	Recognized employee contributions with new employee-appreciation program.
replied	Replied to customer inquiries about product warranties.
reported	Reported to board of directors.
represented	Represented company in a variety of public-speaking engagements.
resumed	Resumed negotiations with key customer after resolving several roadblocks.
routed	Routed requests for information to appropriate department.
settled	Settled liability issues out of court.
spoke	Spoke to groups of 50 or more to promote company's commitment to the community.
spruced	Spruced up image of company's marketing materials with three-dimensional logo and new photography.
strengthened	Strengthened relationships with customers through monthly newsletter communications.
suggested	Suggested methods to improve performance.
translated	Translated conversations and documents from English to Spanish.
voiced	Voiced concerns about industry changes with potential negative impact to operation.
wrote	Wrote correspondence, memos, reports, and proposals.

Finance, Accounting

Action Verb	Sample Phrase
absorbed	Absorbed increased costs while maintaining gross margins on par.
accrued	Accrued additional profits through investment of pension funds.
accumulated	Accumulated record number of gifts through long-term fund-raising efforts.
adjusted	Adjusted general ledger codes to comply with new tax-reporting requirements.
allocated	Allocated funds for new construction.
allotted	Allotted financial and technical resources to augment staff training.
analyzed	Analyzed cost variances and recommended appropriate action.
audited	Audited construction, agribusiness, manufacturing, general business, service sector, and governmental entities.
averted	Averted potential tax liability.
balanced	Balanced bank statements for seven entities.
boosted	Boosted profit margins more than 12 percent.
bought	Bought materials and supplies using competitive bid process.
bridled	Bridled out-of-line expenses through new purchase-order request system.
brought	Brought previously outsourced accounting functions in-house, saving some $25,000 in annual CPA fees.
budgeted	Budgeted seasonal workforce requirements.
calculated	Calculated return on investment.
captured	Captured 12-percent gain in net profit.
closed	Closed books monthly.
collected	Collected on accounts 180 days past due.
compared	Compared five-year statistical history with current data.

(continued)

(continued)

Action Verb	Sample Phrase
computed	Computed depreciation schedules.
controlled	Controlled labor and operating expenses within budget.
corrected	Corrected history of nonexistent budget planning, establishing detailed budgeting and cash-flow reporting process.
counteracted	Counteracted increase in rental expenses with decrease in communications expenses.
cut	Cut costs in primary expense category by 45 percent.
decreased	Decreased operating budget five percent annually, despite rising raw-materials costs.
defrayed	Defrayed costs by implementing new rental program.
disbursed	Disbursed construction funds to subcontractors.
disposed	Disposed of assets associated with closure of Acton office.
dissolved	Dissolved partnership and restructured organization as limited liability corporation.
distributed	Distributed grant money to 12 school sites.
divested	Divested nonperforming assets.
doubled	Doubled returns on pension fund investments.
earned	Earned "gold star" on audit package from Big 6 firm, a first for the company.
economized	Economized on use of contract labor without sacrificing quality or integrity of financial data.
eliminated	Eliminated variances in financial data through redesign of accounting system.
estimated	Estimated return-on-investment for proposed equipment purchases.
exceeded	Exceeded projections for cost reductions, finishing year at 11 percent under budget.
executed	Executed lending documents.
factored	Factored soft costs into equations.

Action Verb	Sample Phrase
financed	Financed aggressive expansion, providing financial savvy and tax expertise to position company for profitable mergers and acquisitions activity.
forecast	Forecast line items for annual budget.
formulated	Formulated financial models.
funded	Funded loans, generating an average of $885,000 per month against a goal of $750,000 per month.
gained	Gained significant ground in cleaning up two-year records-maintenance backlog.
generated	Generated highest billable production in a seven-member public accounting firm and attracted 20-plus new clients to firm.
increased	Increased average audit realization by 50 percent.
invested	Invested reserve funds to perform above industry average, representing an additional four percent in profits.
liquidated	Liquidated outdated stock.
locked	Locked in interest rates at record low.
made	Made monthly journal entries.
managed	Managed finance and accounting functions, including budgeting, cost accounting, managerial accounting, financial reporting, banking relationships, and purchasing.
minimized	Minimized risk and exposure.
originated	Originated qualified, complete, and accurate loan packages.
planned	Planned business process reengineering that led to an 11-percent rise in gross margins.
prepared	Prepared comprehensive operating and capital budgets.
projected	Projected returns based on various scenarios.
purchased	Purchased raw materials from overseas sources.
reconciled	Reconciled discrepancies in accounting records.

(continued)

(continued)

Action Verb	Sample Phrase
recovered	Recovered losses associated with flooding disaster.
reduced	Reduced primary expense category by 25 percent.
reimbursed	Reimbursed employees for attendance at conferences.
renegotiated	Renegotiated equipment service contracts, capturing a hard-dollar savings of $75,000 in first year.
reported	Reported financial position and made investment recommendations at monthly board meetings.
represented	Represented clients before IRS and lending institutions, as well as local and state regulatory agencies.
researched	Researched incongruities in financial data.
sold	Sold obsolete equipment at prices above market value.
sourced	Sourced venture-capital funding.
spent	Spent marketing funds wisely, generating a 12:1 return on advertising dollars.
stretched	Stretched limited operating funds.
trimmed	Trimmed more than 17 percent from next fiscal year's budget.
underwrote	Underwrote new venture using creative financing plan.

General Professions

Action Verb	Sample Phrase
accomplished	Accomplished goals, meeting or exceeding standards for all performance areas.
achieved	Achieved production standards above company average.
advanced	Advanced company's mission for developing innovative software solutions for home and business use.

Action Verb	Sample Phrase
ascended	Ascended quickly through the ranks, from junior account executive to division manager in less than six years.
attained	Attained designation as certified widget maker.
augmented	Augmented skills through self-study and annual attendance of professional conferences.
awarded	Awarded "Employee of the Year" for contributions to morale and productivity.
balanced	Balanced college, work, and family responsibilities while completing degree.
began	Began new program that affected productivity and was subsequently implemented in other branches.
benefited	Benefited from company-sponsored training.
branded	Branded by management as trainee with "great potential."
brought	Brought creative new vision to position.
caught	Caught on quickly, completing six-week training program in less than four weeks.
challenged	Challenged with new assignment that required notable analytical and problem-solving skills.
cited	Cited for exemplary performance.
collaborated	Collaborated with interdepartmental team of accounting, engineering, operations, sales, and distribution.
committed	Committed time, talents, and resources to community and industry associations.
communicated	Communicated regularly with home office, department leaders, vendors, and customers.
completed	Completed tasks within time and budget constraints.
conserved	Conserved limited operating funds for startup company.
contributed	Contributed to company's mission of providing affordable staffing solutions.
cooperated	Cooperated with members from all six departments to accomplish special projects.

(continued)

(continued)

Action Verb	Sample Phrase
created	Created new programs and systems to meet demands.
elected	Elected by peers as department representative for new task force.
exceeded	Exceeded performance criteria, earning top marks on recent evaluation.
facilitated	Facilitated change environment during reengineering process.
finished	Finished tasks in a timely manner to meet critical deadlines.
functioned	Functioned efficiently in a self-directed position.
furthered	Furthered the department's goals for customer service.
graduated	Graduated with solid general management skills from prestigious training program.
improved	Improved productivity ratings by 12 percent.
increased	Increased billable hours by 15 percent.
initiated	Initiated systems that eliminated variances in inventory data.
led	Led team that designed operationally sound infrastructure to support aggressive growth phase.
mastered	Mastered new concepts quickly, qualifying for promotion to next level six weeks ahead of schedule.
named	Named "Employee of the Year," an honor voted on by both management and employees.
nominated	Nominated "Teacher of the Year," one of five in a district with 200 teachers.
offered	Offered assistance on special projects.
optimized	Optimized use of time and resources.
organized	Organized work to meet project benchmarks.
overhauled	Overhauled position, transforming it from a process-only function to information-based service with significant customer interaction.
participated	Participated on multidisciplinary task force that planned new technology upgrade.

Action Verb	Sample Phrase
partnered	Partnered with customers, helping them attain their goals for retail sales.
performed	Performed the following management-support functions: represented chief executive before various employee groups, task forces, and community organizations; orchestrated internal administrative affairs; supervised nine-member office staff; and coordinated executive's site visitation for 70 district locations.
processed	Processed sales orders for international customers.
progressed	Progressed with company's growth, beginning as secretary for startup operation and advancing to administrative manager for a six-branch district.
promoted	Promoted through a variety of operations and customer-service positions.
proposed	Proposed new vision for customer service—assembled materials that responded to issues and simultaneously promoted new products or future purchases.
read	Read as many as 15 industry journals, business newspapers, and financial magazines monthly.
selected	Selected for prestigious training team charged with updating skills of company's sales force nationwide.
sent	Sent to specialized training in Frankfurt, Germany.
sharpened	Sharpened skills through hands-on college course work and simulation exercises.
solved	Solved problem of speeding expedited shipments without increasing costs.
started	Started new employee-appreciation program.
stimulated	Stimulated discussion among accounting and shipping department leaders to resolve recurring problems.
streamlined	Streamlined department work flow through implementation of local area network and integrated software.

(continued)

(continued)

Action Verb	Sample Phrase
strengthened	Strengthened reputation of customer-service department by providing timely, accurate responses and post-sale follow-up to customers.
succeeded	Succeeded in turning around operation's tendency to miss important client deadlines.
surpassed	Surpassed annual quota requirement in just nine months.
tackled	Tackled projects that had been abandoned for more than a year.
thrived	Thrived in fast-paced, technology-driven business environment.
upgraded	Upgraded quality of marketing materials through computer-aided design skills.
volunteered	Volunteered in the community as representative of company.
won	Won confidence of managers, resulting in early promotion to senior administrative technician.
worked	Worked in tandem with engineering team to understand the product-development cycle.

Human Services, Health Care

Action Verb	Sample Phrase
advocated	Advocated for underserved populations.
cared	Cared for patients with complex, multisymptom diseases.
comforted	Comforted victims as member of first-response team.
consoled	Consoled victims and family members.
counseled	Counseled client caseload with a variety of affective and schizophrenic disorders.
dedicated	Dedicated to serving women recovering from domestic abuse.
devoted	Devoted more than a decade of professional service to underserved migrant populations.

Action Verb	Sample Phrase
eased	Eased tensions in multiracial, inner-city neighborhood.
embraced	Embraced the uniqueness and worth of all cultures.
encouraged	Encouraged clients recovering from substance abuse.
enriched	Enriched the lives of at-risk children through linkages with a mentor program.
fostered	Fostered relationships with geriatric clients.
healed	Healed volatile, blended-family relationships.
helped	Helped clients access no-cost or low-cost community resources.
interceded	Interceded on behalf of non-English-speaking clients.
intervened	Intervened on behalf of minors.
kindled	Kindled hope for family members of children suffering from leukemia.
lifted	Lifted the spirits of geriatric patients through movement and music-therapy sessions.
nursed	Nursed outpatient HIV patients, administering antibiotic, antiviral, chemotherapy, and investigational agents.
nurtured	Nurtured relationships between disassociated family members.
prescribed	Prescribed therapeutic activities to facilitate restoration of movement.
reconciled	Reconciled victims and offenders through court-ordered reconciliation program.
referred	Referred clients to community resources that provided financial aid, health care services, and work-skills training.
rehabilitated	Rehabilitated patients suffering from CNS trauma.
touched	Touched the lives of at-risk youth, several of whom turned from involvement in gangs to return to school and complete their GEDs.

Management

Action Verb	Sample Phrase
abandoned	Abandoned "preferred" products that yielded negligible returns in favor of innovative items that yielded three times the margin.
abated	Abated onerous regulatory fees by addressing situations before they escalated to injunctions and fines.
accelerated	Accelerated pilot study time, enabling company to bring new product to market before competitor.
allayed	Allayed employee concerns about pending merger.
alleviated	Alleviated pressures caused by temporary staffing shortages by implementing a comprehensive cross-training program.
amassed	Amassed a formidable team that represented some of the industry's top talent.
anticipated	Anticipated industry trends through analysis of economic and business data.
appraised	Appraised situation, considering enterprise-wide impacts on operations and customer satisfaction.
approached	Approached by company to rectify underperforming operation.
appropriated	Appropriated resources for a much-needed employee-appreciation program.
assembled	Assembled a cohesive team of licensed professional staff and technicians.
blocked	Blocked an attempt by major competitor to court company's key accounts.
bundled	Bundled services to gain greater returns.
charged	Charged with reversing downward spiral in sales.
charted	Charted new course for company.
commanded	Commanded highly skilled technical team of Ph.D. scientists engaged in biogenetic research.

Action Verb	Sample Phrase
commended	Commended team efforts and individual contributions in company newsletter.
commissioned	Commissioned with task of launching new digital PCS operation.
complemented	Complemented sales of ABC product with creation of unique add-on service.
conceived	Conceived idea for marketing partnership with popular radio station and regional shopping mall.
conducted	Conducted financial, legal, and business affairs of organization.
conferred	Conferred with industry analysts.
considered	Considered and encouraged input from all levels of the organization.
consolidated	Consolidated production lines from three locations.
constructed	Constructed new production facility, business offices, and showroom.
consulted	Consulted with purchasing managers and decision makers throughout sales cycle to ensure purchases would solve specific customer needs.
contracted	Contracted with raw materials suppliers at savings of 20 percent.
converted	Converted company from manual operation to paperless system.
dealt	Dealt with complex issues affecting sales and customer satisfaction.
delivered	Delivered above-average returns.
designed	Designed an innovative and well-received employee review system.
determined	Determined pricing structure based on market research and economic projections.
developed	Developed inexperienced employees into solid performers.
devised	Devised "boutique customer-service" program to counter megaretailer's entry into market.

(continued)

(continued)

Action Verb	Sample Phrase
directed	Directed 17-member staff in finance, information systems, customer service, and sales functions.
empowered	Empowered employees through information access and shared decision-making protocol.
ended	Ended a four-year term of negative earnings.
established	Established infrastructure for new organization, developing human resources, accounting, information systems, and service departments in four weeks.
evaluated	Evaluated staff performance and provided development plans to promote employee career growth.
exchanged	Exchanged ideas, challenges, and encouragement in a group of select business leaders from various disciplines.
expanded	Expanded operation to maximum capacity.
experienced	Experienced in full range of project management, from concept through completion.
experimented	Experimented with alternative distribution sources, one of which enabled product to reach market two weeks faster than normal.
found	Found new vendors through Internet searches.
framed	Framed plans for spin-off subsidiary to stabilize sales in slow winter months.
headed	Headed task force that reengineered warehousing and distribution functions.
included	Included personnel in planning and decision-making process.
influenced	Influenced decision makers to fund pilot tests for experimental products.
initiated	Initiated company's entry into the public-works sector, a volatile yet highly lucrative market.
inspired	Inspired employees by modeling leadership and responsibility in work and community commitments.

Action Verb	Sample Phrase
instilled	Instilled new sense of direction to old-line company with floundering sales.
instituted	Instituted program to reward employees for suggesting ideas that were accepted for companywide implementation.
invited	Invited employee participation in reengineering process.
issued	Issued corporate directives for aggressive business-development initiative.
joined	Joined forces with allied agencies for unique private-public sector partnership.
knitted	Knitted together a unique team representing broad government, media, business, and education segments of community.
led	Led small, private company through volatile period associated with competition from well-financed national rival.
lessened	Lessened impact of critical patent expiration by issuing competitive pricing initiative and exploring broader market component as focus for new business development.
listened	Listened to employee suggestions for improving systems; implemented several proposals that improved productivity and earned handsome bonuses for employees.
looked	Looked for new methods to boost productivity.
managed	Managed full scope of operations.
mandated	Mandated intensive employee development and advancement program.
maneuvered	Maneuvered organization through cumbersome regulatory changes.
merged	Merged disparate operational systems into cohesive program.
merited	Merited the attention of corporate headquarters for improvements in all performance areas.
mobilized	Mobilized cross-functional work teams to service new customer that virtually doubled revenue for company.

(continued)

(continued)

Action Verb	Sample Phrase
modeled	Modeled leadership through hands-on involvement in business operations and promotion of new open-door policy.
motivated	Motivated distributor network to promote company product line as priority product.
mounted	Mounted aggressive campaign to counter competition from megaretailer.
narrowed	Narrowed gap between dominant market-share leader.
navigated	Navigated course to enable company to comply with complex set of new environmental restrictions.
overcame	Overcame inherited problem associated with open order file approaching $8 million with 80 percent back orders—within nine weeks, reduced file to $2.5 million with 25 percent back orders.
paced	Paced implementation phases to sustain aggressive growth, projected to continue at an annual rate of 28 percent for the next five years.
pepped	Pepped up the production of an experienced workforce by providing innovative time-off-for-performance and pension-plan incentives.
piloted	Piloted program that enabled new products to clear research and development phase in nearly half the time.
planned	Planned six-month, one-year, and five-year goals for operation.
pointed	Pointed mailroom department in new direction, transitioning it from a process orientation to an internal customer-service focus.
presided	Presided over monthly unit meetings.
profited	Profited from new export program that generated a 40-percent return.
pruned	Pruned several middle-management layers from old-line company on verge of bankruptcy.

Action Verb	Sample Phrase
pushed	Pushed company toward Internet marketing while electronic commerce was in its infancy— early entry positioned company as a primary resource for information, as well as products and services.
raised	Raised expectations for all levels of employees and provided aggressive staff-development program that equipped employees with tools to excel.
rallied	Rallied employees after unexpected death of company's respected founder and chief executive officer.
recruited	Recruited talented team of engineers, researchers, and technical staff.
rectified	Rectified organizational issues affecting order turnaround.
redirected	Redirected efforts of sales team to focus on high-net, repeat sales.
reengineered	Reengineered business units enterprise-wide.
replaced	Replaced disparate data systems with relational databases.
retained	Retained talented, committed employees who helped boost productivity more than 25 percent.
returned	Returned operation to profitable status in just six months.
reversed	Reversed downward spiral for sales and market share.
revitalized	Revitalized stagnant operation with total quality improvement program.
rewarded	Rewarded employee contributions with point system that applied toward salary bonus.
seized	Seized market opportunity available with growing Pacific Rim demand for California agricultural products.
shaped	Shaped new lending policy that reduced financial institution's risk exposure.

(continued)

(continued)

Action Verb	Sample Phrase
sponsored	Sponsored nonprofit event to increase community name recognition.
steered	Steered management team through six months of negotiations, ultimately landing competitive contract with major manufacturer.
stimulated	Stimulated sales of XYZ line, a lucrative but difficult-to-sell product that had been virtually ignored in past years.
supervised	Supervised business managers in inventory, sales, and service units.
tagged	Tagged by president to cross disciplinary lines and tackle IT/IS issues that had been handicapping business-support systems.
tied	Tied employee compensation and advancement to definable performance standards.
took	Took reins of six-month-old company foundering for lack of management expertise and marketing savvy.
transformed	Transformed facility from production line operation to "cross-pollinated" work groups, boosting employee productivity, collaboration, and creativity.
turned	Turned negative newspaper article about the industry into an opportunity to communicate with customers; countered press report with "success stories" and offered discount coupon that boosted monthly sales, as well as customer goodwill.
undertook	Undertook an employee-driven cleanup program that dealt with a recurring graffiti problem.
unified	Unified employee commitment and loyalty to company through a comprehensive employee-assistance program.
united	United newly acquired branches with divergent systems and cultures into a cohesive regional operation.
upheld	Upheld workplace values and promoted mission statement of benefiting both investors and customers.

Action Verb	Sample Phrase
valued	Valued input from all levels of organization.
viewed	Viewed challenges as opportunities.
weathered	Weathered challenging economic and industry conditions, earning company ranking among top three widget companies in the state for the past 15 years.
withstood	Withstood onslaught of competition by well-financed, multinational companies.
wove	Wove societal and environmental values into management philosophy.
yoked	Yoked with talented management team, collaborating on a variety of successful planning, technical, and operations projects.

Sales, Sales Support, Customer Service

Action Verb	Sample Phrase
accentuated	Accentuated unique selling features to differentiate and position products.
achieved	Achieved quota for 10 consecutive months.
acquired	Acquired 200 new accounts in less than six months.
added	Added new services to boost average ticket sale.
adopted	Adopted a "client first" mentality to promote repeat business.
advised	Advised customers on sales, maintaining a view of long-term business relationships.
annihilated	Annihilated prime competitor's market position.
appeased	Appeased customers who were upset over rate increases and persuaded them to remain with company.
aspired	Aspired to generating record sales for company—set new performance benchmarks for sales growth, market penetration, and customer retention.
bettered	Bettered prior year's performance by 20 percent.

(continued)

(continued)

Action Verb	Sample Phrase
blotted	Blotted out company's three-year record of declining sales.
boasted	Boasted the region's highest customer-satisfaction ratings.
broke	Broke company's 20-year record for new business development.
built	Built relationships with potential new customers.
catered	Catered to exclusive clientele.
cemented	Cemented relationships with customers.
closed	Closed sales for junior account executives, securing business from 95 percent of customers closed.
consummated	Consummated complex transactions involving cooperation between multiple entities.
convinced	Convinced customers to shift loyalties from competitors and try XYZ products.
cultivated	Cultivated relationships with key referral contacts in the OEM market.
displayed	Displayed equipment and fielded questions regarding operation, maintenance, and warranty.
doubled	Doubled sales volume during first year in territory, a record for the company.
drove	Drove sales increases by focusing on high-net-profit items.
enlarged	Enlarged territory, tapping under-serviced outlying areas.
enticed	Enticed new customers through attractive displays and creative promotions.
established	Established company as a significant player in the home health care market.
exercised	Exercised discretion in negotiating financing terms on sales of up to $10,000.
familiarized	Familiarized customers with company features and benefits.

Action Verb	Sample Phrase
forged	Forged alliance with respected service company, providing customers with value-added service for future maintenance and repair needs.
fought	Fought competitor entry into market with aggressive promotional campaign.
gained	Gained significant strides with previously "no see" accounts, earning audiences with influential decision makers in the XYZ industry.
gave	Gave presentations in a variety of community, school, and business forums.
generated	Generated 175 new accounts that each averaged an opening order of $7,000.
grew	Grew territory sales, channeling efforts away from small physician practices to major health care organizations.
hoisted	Hoisted branch sales volume from bottom quartile to top five percent in a region of 35 branches.
ignited	Ignited stagnant sales operation, showing a 14-percent gain after four prior years of "flat" sales.
incited	Incited sales team to record performance through motivational training and product incentives.
infused	Infused sales team with confidence to win top region sales honor, outproducing regions in major metropolitan areas.
interested	Interested prospective customers in product through free trial subscription; converted 80 percent of subscribers to long-term contracts.
involved	Involved in industry, community, and nonprofit organizations as part of networking efforts.
jacked up	Jacked up lagging sales to finish year on budget.
launched	Launched new product, gaining full and maximum distribution with all key customers.
leveraged	Leveraged position with new customers, offering impressive record for service and reliability.

(continued)

(continued)

Action Verb	Sample Phrase
linked	Linked customers with informational resources as value-added service.
made	Made inroads and headway with previously inaccessible clients.
marketed	Marketed full line of products and services.
mended	Mended relationships with clients who had not received personal sales calls in more than a year.
monopolized	Monopolized high-tech widget market, capturing approximately 65 percent of total market sales in geographic area.
negotiated	Negotiated financing terms, delivery costs, and quantity discounts.
nurtured	Nurtured relationships with key accounts, increasing frequency of call cycle from six to four weeks.
opened	Opened new territory and attained projected goals.
outdistanced	Outdistanced competitors by providing impressive multimedia sales presentations, preferred customer pricing, and free user training.
penetrated	Penetrated Hispanic market, generating an additional 35 percent in sales.
pursued	Pursued high-net-margin accounts, bringing in six new large insurance agency contracts.
quadrupled	Quadrupled sales during tenure with firm.
ranked	Ranked as top producer among sales team of 10.
rebuilt	Rebuilt territory that had suffered from merger restructuring.
related	Related product benefits to customer's needs.
renewed	Renewed relationships with neglected customers.
secured	Secured new business in the electronic commerce sector.

Action Verb	Sample Phrase
set	Set sales team goals for yearly, quarterly, and monthly sales production for three product lines.
snagged	Snagged prestigious account, a longtime customer of company's chief competitor.
sold	Sold full line of widget products.
solicited	Solicited first-time business with national accounts.
spurred	Spurred sales team to finish year over budget.
swayed	Swayed customers "on the fence" to commit to purchasing products.
swept	Swept the region in all performance indicators: sales volume, new accounts, and average ticket order.
tapped	Tapped new niche market, estimated to yield more than $1 million in revenue in the next fiscal year.
topped	Topped prior year's stellar performance, earning national recognition for new product sales.
traveled	Traveled regularly throughout four-state Western region.
tripled	Tripled sales volume in an established territory.
urged	Urged customers to purchase warranty contracts.
vaulted	Vaulted territory sales production from number 15 to number 2 in district.
won	Won large sale contract with a long-sought institutional account.
yielded	Yielded record sales for the company's 10-year history.

Teaching, Staff Development

Action Verb	Sample Phrase
adapted	Adapted corporate training materials to meet the needs of multicultural staff.

(continued)

(continued)

Action Verb	Sample Phrase
addressed	Addressed the needs of students with varied learning modalities.
affirmed	Affirmed the uniqueness and capabilities of every student.
cautioned	Cautioned students of consequences associated with drugs and invited ex-gang member as guest speaker on the subject.
celebrated	Celebrated major cultural holidays for more than 10 countries as third-grade classroom teacher.
charted	Charted and provided feedback on students' progress.
clarified	Clarified textbook material.
coached	Coached new hires throughout three-month orientation period.
collaborated	Collaborated with special-education instructors and resource teachers to develop individualized educational plans for students with special needs.
communicated	Communicated complex theories in easily understood, relational concepts.
conducted	Conducted interactive training sessions.
demonstrated	Demonstrated principles through laboratory experiments.
designed	Designed engaging, entertaining lessons for adult students.
educated	Educated students in an open classroom setting.
empowered	Empowered at-risk students by exposing them to college and career opportunities.
enabled	Enabled students with learning disabilities to grasp new concepts.
equipped	Equipped developmentally delayed adolescents with daily living skills (shopping, banking, arranging transportation, and so on).

Action Verb	Sample Phrase
grouped	Grouped diverse students—those from various academic levels and cultural backgrounds—to implement a cooperative-learning pilot program.
guided	Guided students through the maze of accessing financial aid.
implemented	Implemented new curriculum that focused on science and technology in the primary grades.
influenced	Influenced change in the lives of at-risk young people, several of whom turned from gang involvement and finished high school.
informed	Informed seminar attendees of regulatory changes and compliance issues.
inserviced	Inserviced staff on techniques to recognize signs of substance abuse.
instructed	Instructed classes in American history.
lectured	Lectured on material and provided follow-up, hands-on learning opportunities.
mentored	Mentored new teachers, providing guidance on classroom management, discipline, and lesson plans.
quizzed	Quizzed students on course material.
reinforced	Reinforced learning through integrated curriculum lessons.
reiterated	Reiterated important concepts while addressing a variety of learning modalities.
taught	Taught alternative-education students vocational skills.
trained	Trained certificated staff on new state reading standards.

Technical

Action Verb	Sample Phrase
analyzed	Analyzed department's future IT needs and drafted plan to ensure strategic alignment with overall business plan.

(continued)

(continued)

Action Verb	Sample Phrase
certified	Certified weights and balances of precision equipment.
conceptualized	Conceptualized and developed scripts to support infrastructure security—scripts were subsequently used as models for current monitoring tools.
connected	Connected satellite users with main office through networking devices.
created	Created reference materials, quickly bringing technicians and system operators to high levels of competency.
decoded	Decoded encrypted data.
designed	Designed software solutions for widget-processing industry.
detected	Detected faulty components.
equipped	Equipped district with videoconferencing capabilities.
evaluated	Evaluated system failures and pinpointed errors.
expanded	Expanded system capabilities.
fabricated	Fabricated components per customer specifications.
facilitated	Facilitated complex migration to updated operating system.
fixed	Fixed recurring problems that had eluded prior technicians.
gauged	Gauged user needs and system capabilities and recommended appropriate hardware upgrade.
grasped	Grasped quickly concepts and procedures for new operating system and selected from staff of 12 to train other technologists (training is normally outsourced).
honed	Honed troubleshooting skills through advanced IBM component-level troubleshooting course.
identified	Identified user needs and modified system accordingly.

Action Verb	Sample Phrase
installed	Installed new system, providing users with uninterrupted service during project.
integrated	Integrated accounting functions with sales, warehousing, and shipping.
investigated	Investigated recurring computer crashes; traced glitch to vendor software and served as liaison in problem resolution.
isolated	Isolated technical malfunctions at the component level.
mastered	Mastered intricacies of new software and was called on as resident expert to explain advanced functions.
planned	Planned move of mission-critical business systems to alternative computing platform, including all international business support, publications, regulatory, and distribution systems.
preserved	Preserved integrity of data.
prevented	Prevented system failures that had plagued previous system administrators.
programmed	Programmed in ASP.net, XML, C#.net, CSS, IIS, SQL Server, and Oracle PL/SQL.
reconstructed	Reconstructed corrupted data using various software tools.
reengineered	Reengineered data-management foundation on IBM mainframe platform from VSAM flat-file environment to SQL-based DB.
relied	Relied on crack technical team to program and test new software release.
repaired	Repaired and maintained 200-user network.
restored	Restored 100 percent of data after earthquake disaster.
retrieved	Retrieved and manipulated data.
revolutionized	Revolutionized use of software, engineering an innovative data-acquisition and analysis platform to gather and analyze flight-test data for experimental aircraft.

(continued)

(continued)

Action Verb	Sample Phrase
safeguarded	Safeguarded data through disaster-recovery protocol.
salvaged	Salvaged mismanaged IT conversion (a $300,000 capital investment)—directed installation project for world-class computer system to support 24-hour, seven-day operation.
searched	Searched Internet using a variety of sophisticated search commands.
showed	Showed nontechnical staff how to conduct advanced Boolean searches.
systematized	Systematized protocols to improve procedure-execution accuracy from 85 percent to 99 percent.
tested	Tested new Windows-based release of software.
trained	Trained users, converting computer-phobics to technically competent operators.
troubleshot	Troubleshot puzzling hardware problems at board and component levels.
turned	Turned technicians into business professionals who understand multidimensional corporate needs and bottom-line profit.
upgraded	Upgraded hardware and software, implementing five major software upgrades over tenure.
wrote	Wrote and installed aliases that reduced input errors 50 percent and increased efficiency of routines 30 percent.

Index

F

G

X–Z

The Magic Continues!

Now that you've transformed your résumé into a winner, you won't want to miss out on equally magical advice on cover letters, interviewing, and finding a job!

416 pages
$16.95
ISBN: 978-1-59357-364-5
Order Code: LP-J3645

448 pages
$16.95
ISBN: 978-1-59357-016-3
Order Code: LP-J0163

544 pages
$18.95
ISBN: 978-1-59357-150-4
Order Code: LP-J150X